Critical issues

Point 9

Make sure you have a peaceful room where you can revise. You cannot revise properly in noisy or uncomfortable surroundings. You need to sit comfortably, but slouching in an armchair is not the right approach to your revision.

Point 10

Stick to your revision times. Do not switch on the television, begin a long conversation, or make a drink when you should be starting your revision.

All about music

Point 11

Do not play background music if it distracts you or lessens your concentration.

Point 12

Television does not rest your mind. So do not watch much television during your revision weeks.

Point 13

Revision leading to exams is usually a time of stress and anxiety. Overcome this by:

- being aware of tension and worry; do not pretend it does not affect you
- explaining to your parents, brothers or sisters how important the exams are for you. They will have some sympathy and will want to help you
- planning your revision and following a timetable that you can manage
- doing some exercises or leisure activity during the exam period
- having a calm sleep each night

HOW TO LEARN EFFECTIVELY

Many students make the mistake of thinking that reading is the same as learning.

When you are preparing for an exam don't assume that you have learned something simply because you have read it.

Learning information and ideas does not come easily to most people: it requires effort as well as self-discipline.

Point 1

There is a limit to the time for which your mind can work effectively. Do not spend more than 30 minutes at a time on memory work because after this you will not learn much more. Take a break for 15–30 minutes so that your mind is fresh when you start again.

Point 2

Find a quiet place. Make sure you are calm and not stressed. You will not learn well if TV, radio or music is distracting you.

Point 3

Divide what you have to learn into small units. You will learn the whole much more quickly this way.

Point 4

Read the section slowly and carefully about four or five times.

Point 5

You may find it helpful to record material onto a tape and then listen to it four or five times rather than say it four or five times.

Point 6

Read aloud. There is convincing evidence that this halves the time you need to learn.

Read aloud

Point 7

See if you can summarize a topic in a simple visual form such as a diagram or key points linked by arrows.

Point 8

When you have learned the topic, check that you still know it 24 hours later. This will help fix it in your memory.

Point 9

Last thing at night and first thing in the morning are often the best times for learning. But it is important to be rested and not tense when you sleep, so the time before going to bed should be a relaxation period. Saying a prayer for others may help prevent you worrying about your own interests.

Good design
for effective revision

Syllabus analysis
Ensures you do only the topics you need – no more, no less

Full coverage
Christianity, Catholic Christianity, Interfaith studies – useful for all styles of syllabus

Detailed paper by paper breakdown for each board: vital for focused revision

Brief, easy to digest chapters
Pace your revision in session-sized chunks

Half GCSE courses
If you are doing a half course you must pinpoint precisely what you need to study

Full courses: Part A
This chart tells you the chapters to study. Find your exam board.
Then highlight your syllabuses (or syllabus).
Study the chapters that are ticked.

Exam Board	Syllabuses		Chapter 1 Eucharist	Chapter 2 Collective worship	Chapter 3 The Lord's Prayer	Chapter 4 Private worship	Chapter 5 The Bible and worship	Chapter 6 Church buildings	Chapter 7 Church buildings – furnishings	Chapter 8 Church buildings – plans	Chapter 9 Cathedrals
NEAB	Syllabus A	Christianity	✓	✓	✓	✓	✓				
	Syllabus B	Christian tradition	✓	✓	✓	✓	✓	✓	✓	✓	✓
		Catholic Christian tradition	✓	✓	✓	✓	✓	✓	✓	✓	✓
		Christian life and Mark's gospel	✓	✓	✓	✓					
		Christian behaviour, attitudes and lifestyle									
		Catholic Christian behaviour, attitudes and lifestyle	✓								
	Syllabus C	Christian beliefs and practice (modular)	✓	✓	✓	✓					
MEG		Christianity through Luke's gospel and Acts	✓	✓							
		Christian perspectives on personal, social issues	✓	✓							
		Christianity	✓	✓	✓	✓	✓	✓	✓	✓	✓
London (ULEAC)		Christianity	✓	✓	✓	✓	✓	✓	✓	✓	✓
		Catholic Christianity	✓	✓		✓	✓				
		Contemporary issues and Mark's gospel									
SEG	Syllabus A	Christian Church	✓		✓	✓	✓	✓	✓	✓	✓
		Contemporary issues		✓							
		Life of Jesus: synoptic gospels									
	Syllabus B	Inter-faith studies: Christianity	✓	✓	✓	✓	✓	✓	✓	✓	✓
	Syllabus C	Catholic Christian tradition	✓								

Short courses: Part A
This chart tells you the chapters to study. Find your exam board.
Then highlight your syllabus.
Study the chapters that are ticked.

Exam Board	Syllabuses	Chapter 1 Eucharist	Chapter 2 Collective worship	Chapter 3 The Lord's Prayer	Chapter 4 Private worship	Chapter 5 The Bible and worship	Chapter 6 Church buildings	Chapter 7 Church buildings – furnishings	Chapter 8 Church buildings – plans	Chapter 9 Cathedrals	Chapter 10 Pilgrimage	Chapter 11 Advent, Christmas and Epiphany	Chapter 12 Lent, fasting	Chapter 13 Holy Week	Chapter 14 Easter	Chapter 15 Other festivals	Chapter 16 Sacraments	Chapter 17 Reconciliation	Chapter 18 Anointing of the sick
NEAB	Christianity	✓	✓	✓	✓	✓						✓	✓	✓	✓		✓		✓
	Thinking about God and morality	✓	✓	✓	✓						✓						✓		✓
SEG	Religious education	✓	✓														✓		✓
London Syllabus A	Religion and life	✓																	
Syllabus B	Christianity	✓	✓		✓	✓						✓	✓	✓	✓			✓	
	Christianity: Catholicism	✓	✓	✓	✓					✓							✓	✓	
	Christianity: Mark's gospel	✓	✓	✓	✓												✓		
MEG Syllabus A	Christianity through Luke and Acts		✓	✓								✓	✓	✓	✓	✓			
	Christian perspectives on personal, social and world issues																	✓	✓
	Christianity		✓																
Syllabus B		✓	✓	✓	✓	✓	✓	✓	✓	✓	✓						✓	✓	✓

PLAN YOUR REVISION

Preparing the way

Most people find it difficult to prepare carefully for their GCSEs, partly because this is the first time they have had to prepare so much for so many exams. It takes effort and discipline to follow a revision plan.

Point 1

Before you can start you must have the syllabus for the exam. You can obtain a copy from your teacher or your exam board. Like this book, it tells you what you need to know and do for your exam.

Point 2

Make sure you have seen at least one previous exam paper. Be familiar with the structure of the paper:

- number and type of questions you will have to answer
- how long you will be given to answer
- your choice of questions.

Point 3

From the syllabus and the paper you can decide what to revise in this book. Where there is no choice of questions you must learn as much of the syllabus as you can. If there is a choice, you may not need all the syllabus: consult your teacher or parent about what is best to revise.

Planning your revision

Point 4

Start your final revision about 10 weeks before the exam.

Point 5

Divide the sections of the book you need into 10 groups so that you set topics you will revise each week. Fix the list to the wall in your room and tick the topics off as you revise them.

Point 6

Write a weekly timetable for all your subjects. Some people prefer to revise just one subject each day. Others like to study more than one subject each day. Do what suits you.

Remember:

- 30–40 minutes at a time is enough when you are learning or memorizing. Then take a break and let your mind rest.
- Set the length of your rest periods; then you won't relax for the rest of the day instead of for just half an hour.
- Be realistic about your timetable. Don't think you can work for 12 hours a day. However, if you plan only one hour's work each day you won't do enough.

Point 7

If you start revising and find you can't keep to your timetable because it is too difficult or awkward, do not abandon it. Alter it so that you have a timetable that works for you.

Point 8

Don't be surprised if you do not always follow your timetable. That is normal. But do keep an eye on your progress to make sure you are keeping up overall.

Point 1

Do not panic. A little nervousness helps to sharpen concentration, but too much dulls the mind; it prevents you from thinking clearly and inhibits your memory.

Take 10 or 20 quick breaths to calm your nerves and relax your stressed mind.

An alternative is to take three or four deep breaths, but you may find that this also slows down your rate of thinking and impedes your ability to recall all that information you carefully learned.

Don't panic

Point 2

The exam is usually divided into parts. Be careful to spend the right amount of time on each part. If you spend too much time on the first part of the paper, you will not have enough time to write satisfactory answers to the other questions.

Point 3

Your answers to some questions will be in essay form.

You must write as much as you can for each of the questions. The amount of information you write is as important as the quality of what you write. The 'scope' and 'development' (the terms used by the Chief Examiner) of your answers will influence the mark you obtain.

Point 4

Pace yourself

Do not put all your energy into the first half hour.

Make sure you answer the last of the essay questions as well as the first of the essay questions. Do not spend half an hour on the first essay question and then find you have no time left for the last essay question.

Point 5

Answer the actual question: read the question carefully so that you understand exactly what you have to do. For example:

- If the question asks what Christians believe about abortion, you will obtain no marks for writing down what *you* think about abortion.
- If the question asks what Catholics believe about the value and importance of the sacrament of baptism, you will obtain no marks if you simply write what happens in the ceremony of baptism.
- If the question asks what can be learned about forgiveness from the parable of the forgiving father, you will obtain no marks for simply writing out the parable.

Point 6

Do not waffle.

Point 7

Some questions ask you what you think.

You must write more than one reason to support your opinion. You should explain each reason in some detail.

You must also say something about the opposite point of view (for example, any reasons that support it). You will not obtain full marks unless you do this.

Point 8

Make sure you are familiar with the syllabus. You should have a copy of it.

Point 9

Remember that there are three main groups of Christians – Catholics, Protestants, Orthodox. Do not think that Catholics or Protestants are the only Christians. Do not describe Protestants or Orthodox or Catholics as non-Christians!

Point 10

Do not say that Jesus taught 10 commandments.

He taught 2 commandments – do you know what they were?

Point 11

Make sure you leave 5 minutes at the end of the paper to quickly re-read your answers.

Exam Board Addresses

For syllabuses and past papers contact the Publications office at the following addresses:

Midland Examining Group (MEG)
c/o University of Cambridge Local
Examinations Syndicate
1 Hills Road
CAMBRIDGE
CB1 2 EU
Tel. 01223 553311

Southern Examining Group (SEG)
Publications Department
Stag Hill House
GUILDFORD
Surrey
GU2 5XJ
Tel. 014843 302302 (Direct line)

Northern Examinations and Assessment Board
(NEAB)
Devas Street
MANCHESTER
M15 6EX
Tel. 0161 953 1180

EdExcel (London)
Stewart House
32 Russell Square
LONDON
WC1B 5DN
Tel. 0171 331 4000

Northern Ireland Council for the Curriculum,
Examinations and Assessment (NICCEA)
29 Clarendon Road
BELFAST
BT1 3BG
Tel. 01232 261200

Welsh Joint Education Committee (WJEC)
245 Western Avenue
Llandaff
CARDIFF
CF5 2YX

Scottish Examination Board (SEB) for full
syllabuses
Ironmills Road
Dalkeith
Midlothian EH22 1LE
Tel. 0131 636 6601

or recent papers from the SEB's agent
Robert Gibson & Sons Ltd
17 Fitzroy Place
Glasgow G3 7SF
Tel. 0141 248 5674

Remember to check your syllabus
number with your teacher!

CONTENTS

Continued

Michael Foley & Gordon Geddes

Religious Studies: Christianity GCSE

MACMILLAN

Acknowledgements

The authors and publishers wish to thank the following for permission to use copyright material:

Associated Press p. 89; Ateliers et Presses de Taizé, France p. 12; The Bible Reading Fellowship p. 17; David Bonsor for artwork on pp. iii, iv, v, 304; CAFOD pp. 255, 261, 262; The Central Board of Finance of the Church of England for extracts from *The Alternative Service Book 1980*, pp. 243, 245, 247, 248, 255–6, 287, 288, 290, 292, 334, 335; The Dean and Chapter of Chester Cathedral p. 139; The Dean and Chapter of Lincoln pp. 29, 32; Michael Foley pp. 54, 57, 80, 212, 307; Gordon Geddes pp. 21 (right), 22, 41, 91, 111, 194, 217, 219, 269, 290; Father Hardy at St Edward the Confessor, Milton Keynes p. 192; Hodder & Stoughton Ltd and Zondervan Publishing House for scripture quotations taken from the New International Version of the Holy Bible; International Consultation on English Texts for the English translation of the Apostle's Creed and Nicene Creed; John Murray Ltd pp. 69, 70 from Clegg & Mackean *Advanced Biology* (1994); John Rylands University Library of Manchester p. 129; Merseyside & Cheshire Alcohol Services p. 274; The Metropolitan Cathedral of Christ the King Liverpool pp. 30, 31; Misereor Medienproduktion und Vertriebsgellschaft mbH, Aachen, Germany p. 266; Mount Saint Bernard Abbey, Leicester p. 199; News Team International Ltd p. 47; Father Noonan at Our Lady of Lourdes Church, Milton Keynes p. 189; The Northern Examinations and Assessment Board for questions from past examination papers; Ed O'Connell p. 184; The Society for the Protection of Unborn Children p. 232; Sarah Thorley pp. 9, 18. 21 (left), 45, 168, 173; Steven Turnbull for artwork on pp. 18, 23, 24, 25, 26, 27, 38, 42, 115, 120, 136, 137, 140, 142, 153, 170, 180, 182, 251, 280, 291; Walsingham National Shrine of Our Lady p. 34; The White Fathers, Sutton Coldfield p. 63.

Every effort has been made to trace all the copyright holders but if any have been inadvertently overlooked the publishers will be pleased to make the necessary arrangement at the first opportunity.

First published 1997 by
MACMILLAN PRESS LTD
Houndmills, Basingstoke, Hampshire RG21 6XS
and London
Companies and representatives
throughout the world

ISBN 0–333–64737–8

A catalogue record for this book is available from the British Library.

This book is printed on paper suitable for recycling and made from fully managed and sustained forest sources.

10   9   8   7   6   5   4   3
06   05   04   03   02   01   00

Printed in Hong Kong

This is a practical book. It is written to help GCSE candidates to prepare for exams. It is not meant to be a book about the whole Bible or the whole of modern Christianity.

For that reason the only subjects and the only Bible passages covered are those in one or other of the Religious Studies GCSE syllabuses that are examined for the first time in 1996. There is, for instance, no reference to the Old Testament background to themes such as *Kingdom of God* and *Son of Man*.

The subjects are presented at the level of a strong GCSE candidate.

You will not need everything in this book. The authors have covered the subject matter of all the Christianity syllabuses of EdExcel, MEG, NEAB and SEG. The chart at the beginning of each part shows you which chapters of the book are relevant to your course.

Care has been taken to cover the special Catholic syllabuses. Where necessary, there is special coverage of a topic for the Catholic syllabuses.

Make sure you have a copy of the syllabuses you are studying.

Each syllabus contains a number of passages from the Bible. Most passages are covered here. Use the index at the back of the book to find the passages you need. Quotations are taken from the NIV (*New International Version*).

If you normally use the *Good News Bible*, understand that it is different from other versions. Other versions set out to translate what the original writer *said*. The Good News Bible instead often has what the original writer *meant*.

As an example, take a verse from the Sermon on the Mount, Matthew 6³:

NIV: When you give to the needy, do not let your left hand know what your right hand is doing.
GNB: When you help a needy person, do it in such a way that even your closest friend will not know about it.

Christians disagree in their use of the word 'Church'. We have sidestepped these differences by using the word 'Church' to describe a group of people. We use the word 'church' to refer to a building in which Christians meet and worship.

The syllabuses state that candidates should know and understand common Christian beliefs and practices. Candidates should also know that there are three main Christian traditions: Catholic – Orthodox – Protestant. Each tradition has particular beliefs and practices. We mention them where they are important.

We have followed the principle of naming each Christian tradition by the name used by the members. Thus we use the term Catholic, not Roman Catholic. This is not to deny that many Christians – Anglicans for example – regard themselves as part of the universal Catholic Church. In the Apostles' Creed Christians state their belief in the One Holy Catholic and Apostolic Church. Also, much of what is said about Catholics applies to those belonging to the Catholic tradition in the Anglican church.

Examination practice or guidance is given for each section or group of sections. A number of specimen questions and answers are provided. Many of the answers are examples of the type of response often made by candidates. With them are given the marks that would be awarded and the reasons for the marks. You should study the comments carefully, as they are designed to point out some common errors.

PART A

Worship and festivals

Full courses: Part A

This chart tells you the chapters to study. Find your exam board.
Then highlight your syllabuses (or syllabus).
Study the chapters that are ticked.

Exam Board	Syllabus	Syllabuses	Ch 1 Eucharist	Ch 2 Collective worship	Ch 3 The Lord's Prayer	Ch 4 Private worship	Ch 5 The Bible and worship	Ch 6 Church buildings	Ch 7 Church buildings – furnishings	Ch 8 Church buildings – plans	Ch 9 Cathedrals
NEAB	Syllabus A	Christianity	✓	✓	✓	✓	✓	✓	✓	✓	✓
	Syllabus B	Christian tradition	✓	✓	✓	✓	✓	✓	✓	✓	✓
		Catholic Christian tradition	✓	✓	✓	✓	✓				
		Christian life and Mark's gospel	✓	✓	✓	✓					
		Christian behaviour, attitudes and lifestyle									
		Catholic Christian behaviour, attitudes and lifestyle	✓								
	Syllabus C	Christian beliefs and practice (modular)	✓	✓	✓	✓					✓
MEG		Christianity through Luke's gospel and Acts	✓	✓							
		Christian perspectives on personal, social issues	✓	✓							
		Christianity	✓	✓		✓	✓	✓	✓	✓	✓
EdExcel (London)		Christianity	✓	✓	✓	✓	✓				
		Catholic Christianity	✓	✓	✓	✓	✓	✓	✓	✓	✓
		Contemporary issues and Mark's gospel									
SEG	Syllabus A	Christian Church	✓	✓	✓	✓	✓	✓	✓	✓	✓
		Contemporary issues		✓							
		Life of Jesus: synoptic gospels									
	Syllabus B	Inter-faith studies: Christianity	✓	✓	✓	✓	✓	✓	✓	✓	✓
	Syllabus C	Catholic Christian tradition	✓								

Full courses: Part A

This chart tells you the chapters to study. Find your exam board.
Then highlight your syllabuses (or syllabus).
Study the chapters that are ticked.

Exam Board	Syllabus	Syllabus name	Ch 10 Pilgrimage	Ch 11 Advent, Christmas and Epiphany	Ch 12 Lent; fasting	Ch 13 Holy Week	Ch 14 Easter	Ch 15 Other festivals	Ch 16 Sacraments	Ch 17 Reconciliation	Ch 18 Anointing of the sick
NEAB	Syllabus A	Christianity		✓	✓	✓	✓		✓		✓
NEAB	Syllabus B	Christian tradition		✓	✓	✓	✓	✓	✓		
NEAB		Catholic Christian tradition	✓	✓	✓	✓	✓	✓	✓	✓	✓
NEAB		Christian life and Mark's gospel									
NEAB		Christian behaviour, attitudes and lifestyle									
NEAB		Catholic Christian behaviour, attitudes and lifestyle		✓					✓	✓	✓
MEG	Syllabus C	Christian beliefs and practice (modular)	✓	✓		✓	✓	✓	✓	✓	✓
MEG		Christianity through Luke's gospel and Acts		✓	✓	✓	✓	✓			✓
MEG		Christian perspectives on personal, social issues							✓		
MEG		Christianity	✓	✓	✓	✓	✓	✓	✓	✓	✓
EdExcel (London)		Christianity		✓	✓	✓	✓	✓	✓	✓	✓
EdExcel (London)		Catholic Christianity	✓	✓	✓	✓	✓	✓	✓	✓	
EdExcel (London)		Contemporary issues and Mark's gospel	✓	✓	✓	✓	✓	✓	✓	✓	✓
SEG	Syllabus A	Christian Church	✓	✓	✓	✓	✓	✓	✓		✓
SEG		Contemporary issues			✓	✓	✓			✓	
SEG		Life of Jesus: synoptic gospels	✓	✓	✓	✓	✓	✓	✓		
SEG	Syllabus B	Inter-faith studies: Christianity		✓	✓	✓	✓	✓	✓		✓
SEG	Syllabus C	Catholic Christian tradition			✓				✓	✓	✓

Short courses: Part A

This chart tells you the chapters to study. Find your exam board.
Then highlight your syllabus.
Study the chapters that are ticked.

Chapter	NEAB: Christianity	Thinking about God and morality	SEG: Religious education	EdExcel Syllabus A: Religion and life	EdExcel Syllabus B: Christianity	Christianity: Catholicism	Christianity: Mark's gospel	MEG Syllabus A: Christianity through Luke and Acts	Christian perspectives on personal, social and world issues	Christianity	Syllabus B: Christianity
Chapter 1 Eucharist	✓	✓	✓	✓	✓	✓	✓				✓
Chapter 2 Collective worship	✓	✓	✓		✓	✓	✓	✓		✓	✓
Chapter 3 The Lord's Prayer	✓	✓				✓	✓	✓			✓
Chapter 4 Private worship	✓	✓			✓	✓	✓				✓
Chapter 5 The Bible and worship	✓				✓						✓
Chapter 6 Church buildings											✓
Chapter 7 Church buildings – furnishings											✓
Chapter 8 Church buildings – plans											✓
Chapter 9 Cathedrals		✓									✓
Chapter 10 Pilgrimage						✓					
Chapter 11 Advent, Christmas and Epiphany	✓					✓		✓			
Chapter 12 Lent; fasting	✓					✓		✓			
Chapter 13 Holy Week	✓					✓		✓			
Chapter 14 Easter	✓					✓		✓			
Chapter 15 Other festivals								✓			
Chapter 16 Sacraments	✓	✓	✓			✓	✓				✓
Chapter 17 Reconciliation						✓	✓			✓	✓
Chapter 18 Anointing of the sick	✓		✓	✓		✓		✓	✓	✓	✓

Eucharist

There are other names by which this service is known:

- Holy Communion
- Mass
- The Liturgy
- Lord's Supper
- Breaking of the Bread.

These words have slightly different meanings, each reminding us of a different way of thinking of the service:

Eucharist	thanksgiving and praise
Communion	being close to God
Liturgy	public service. The word 'service' is used here in the sense of 'offering a service', doing something for someone. The liturgy is the worshipper's offering to God.
Lord's Supper	the meal to which Jesus invites his followers.
Breaking of the Bread	sharing the meal in fellowship.

The word 'mass' probably comes from the concluding words in the Latin rite, *Ite, missa est,* meaning 'Go, you are sent on a mission'. The modern version is 'Go in peace, to love and serve the Lord'.

Most Christians would say that most, if not all, of these ideas are true.

- They offer thanks and praise as they remember Jesus' sacrifice.
- Just as the Passover meal Jesus shared with his disciples was an expression of God's covenant with his people, so the eucharist is a covenant meal.
- It is a meal shared with God and one's fellow-Christians.
- The worship is an offering to God.

The Passover meal

Passover is a Jewish festival. It celebrates the time when God saved the Israelites from Egypt. God made an agreement with them, a **covenant**: if they would be his people, he would be their God.

When the Israelites were in Egypt, they were slaves to Pharaoh, the King of Egypt. Moses told Pharaoh that he had to let the people go. If he did not, Egypt would suffer a series of plagues. In the last of these, an angel of death would come. He would kill the eldest son of every Egyptian family, but would pass over every Israelite home. So that

the angel would recognize the Israelite houses, each family sacrificed a lamb and sprinkled the blood on the doorpost. God freed them from slavery in Egypt. He led them through the desert for 40 years. He looked after them, so that they arrived safely in Israel (Palestine).

The new covenant

The Passover is for Christians the sign of the covenant that God made with his chosen people, the Jews. With the death and resurrection of Jesus a new covenant is made with God. Christians believe that there is no longer any need for Passover lambs to be offered year by year. Jesus is the true Passover lamb, offered once for all for the sins of the world.

> Christ, our Passover lamb, has been sacrificed.
> 1 Corinthians 5[7]
>
> [Jesus] entered the Most Holy Place once for all by his own blood.
>   Christ is the mediator of a new covenant, that those who are called may receive the promised eternal inheritance.
> Hebrews 9[12,15]

The importance of the eucharist

- Among Orthodox, Catholics and Anglicans the eucharist is the main act of worship. It is celebrated at least once a week, every Sunday.
- Among Methodists, Baptists and United Reformed Church congregations the main Sunday worship is usually pulpit-centred. The eucharist is celebrated only once or twice a month.
- Quakers and the Salvation Army do not celebrate the eucharist. They believe that outward symbols are unimportant and unnecessary. What matters is the relationship with God, within the heart.

The eucharist is held in such high honour by most Christians because:

1. Jesus told them to remember him in this way. He said, when he gave the disciples the bread and wine, 'Do this in remembrance of me' (Luke 22[19]).
2. The meal at which he said these words, the Last Supper, took place the night before he died on the cross.
3. Catholics, Orthodox and many Anglicans believe that

at the eucharist the body and blood of Jesus are present. Jesus' sacrifice on the cross can never be repeated, but the body he offered on the cross is present on the altar.

4. Many Christians believe that when they receive the bread and wine, Jesus is with them in a special way. The different ways in which they think of Jesus being present are explained below in the section 'What happens to the bread and wine at the eucharist?'.

The Last Supper

On the night before Jesus was crucified he ate a Passover meal with the disciples. At the meal he took bread, blessed and broke it, and gave it to the disciples, saying, 'This is my body'. Then he took a cup of wine, blessed it, then passed it to the disciples with the words, 'This is my blood of the new covenant, which is poured out for many' (Mark 14$^{22, 24}$).

What happens to the bread and wine at the eucharist?

There are two ways in which Christians understand what happens when the priest or minister uses the words of Jesus himself – 'This is my body', 'This is my blood'.

1. Jesus is really present in the bread and the wine. It is the risen Jesus who is present. Although he is in a different form, not the form of his earthly body, when the communicants (the people receiving communion) receive the bread and wine, they receive him personally to themselves. This is the generally accepted belief among Catholics, Anglicans and Orthodox.

2. Jesus is present with his people throughout the whole eucharist. They experience his presence when the scriptures are read, in their fellowship together and in receiving the bread and wine. However, the bread and wine do not change in any way; they are symbols of his presence in every part of the service. This is the usual belief among Methodists, Baptists and members of the United Reformed Church.

The bread used for the communion may be ordinary bread. This is the custom among Methodists, Baptists and others. The use of ordinary bread can be taken to show that Jesus takes something ordinary and transforms it into something divine. In the same way he can take a human life and transform it if it is offered to him.

Among Anglicans and Catholics it is more usual for wafer bread to be used. Wafer bread is **unleavened**: made without yeast. At the Passover meal Jews eat unleavened bread. So those who use wafer bread believe that in this way they are following the example of Jesus.

At Anglican, Catholic and Orthodox eucharists alcoholic wine is used, as would have been used at the Last Supper. Among Methodists, Baptists and others, some of whose members do not drink alcohol on principle, unfermented grape juice is used at the communion.

The eucharist (Catholic)

The service has a number of parts.

Introduction and penitential rite

- Everyone makes the sign of the cross. There is an introductory prayer or hymn.
- Each member of the congregation reflects on what they have done wrong.
- The priest then says: 'May almighty God have mercy on us, forgive us for our sins, and bring us to everlasting life'.
- The priest says: 'Lord have mercy. Christ have mercy. Lord have mercy'. The congregation repeats each phrase after him.
- Then everyone says the Gloria prayer, unless it is Advent or Lent. It is a prayer of praise. The prayer starts with the words: 'Glory to God in the highest, and peace to his people on earth'.

Liturgy of the Word

On Sundays there are three readings from the Bible. Between each reading, there is a prayer from the Bible.

- A first reading, usually from the Old Testament. It has a connection with the third reading.
- A psalm.
- A reading from the New Testament, usually one of Paul's letters.
- An alleluia verse, to welcome the Gospel.
- Finally, a reading from the Gospel. This is the most important reading. The priest reads it.
- The priest's homily. It should be an explanation of God, based on the readings from the Bible.
- Then everyone stands and says the Nicene Creed, to demonstrate their common beliefs. (See Chapter C1, *Apostles' Creed and Nicene Creed*.)
- Finally, there are prayers, usually called the bidding prayers or prayers of the faithful. These are prayers asking God for help – for the people at the eucharist, those who are sick, and anyone else in need.

Liturgy of the eucharist

- The gifts are brought to the priest: bread and wine, and money.
- The priest says prayers over the bread and wine, including: 'Blessed are you Lord, God of all creation. Through your goodness, we have this bread to offer, which earth has given and human hands have made. It will become for us the bread of life.'
- The priest starts the eucharistic prayer. Everyone praises God: 'Holy, holy, holy Lord, God of power and might, heaven and earth are full of your glory . . .'
- Then the priest invokes the Holy Spirit: 'Let your Holy Spirit come upon these gifts to make them holy, so that

they may become for us the body and blood of our Lord, Jesus Christ.'

- Next comes a most important point in the eucharist. The priest says the words of Jesus at his last supper. Catholics believe that the bread and wine become the risen Jesus – the body and blood of Jesus. The priest says: 'Take this, all of you, and eat it: this is my body which will be given up for you. Take this, all of you, and drink from it: this is the cup of my blood, the blood of the new and everlasting covenant. It will be shed for you and for all so that sins may be forgiven. Do this in memory of me.'
- There are more prayers, said by the priest, before everyone says the Lord's Prayer.
- Then everyone shakes hands with the people around them, a sign of peace. They say: 'Peace be with you.'
- There are some more prayers, including a prayer for forgiveness. Everyone says: 'Lamb of God, you take away the sins of the world, have mercy on us . . . Grant us peace.'
- The climax of the eucharist is when people receive communion. Members of the congregation go to the priest (or minister of communion). The priest holds up one of the consecrated breads (also called the host) and says: 'the Body of Christ'. The communicant says: 'Amen', takes the consecrated bread and eats it.
- There is usually some silent prayer, before the eucharist ends. The priest may say: 'Go in peace to love and serve the Lord.'

It is essential to Catholics that the person leading the worship at the eucharist, the celebrant, is a bishop or priest.

In the Catholic Church children first receive Holy Communion from about the age of seven.

The bread used at a Catholic eucharist is unleavened wafer bread.

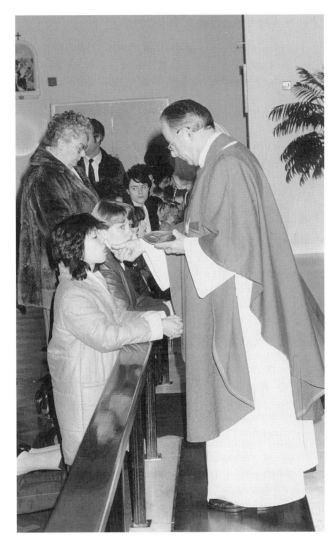

The eucharist (Anglican)

The service has a number of parts.

- Praising God. Hymns are sung and prayers of praise are said.
- The worshippers confess their sins and ask for forgiveness.
- Hearing the Word of God. There are readings from the Bible, the last of which is the Gospel. A sermon is usually preached, often explaining the readings of the day. The Creed is said, as all join in stating their faith.
- Prayers are offered for the Church, the national and international community, the local Church and community, those in special need, the sick and those who care for them and for those who have died, especially those who have died recently or whose anniversaries fall about that date.
- Sharing fellowship with other Christians. One way in which this fellowship is expressed is through **exchanging the Peace**. Worshippers shake hands or embrace. They greet each other with words such as 'Peace be with you'.

- The offertory. As well as meaning the money offered by the people, the offertory includes the offering to God of the bread and wine that will be used at the consecration. The gifts are brought in procession to the altar to stress that they are the offerings of the faithful.
- The bread and wine are consecrated with the words of Jesus – 'This is my body', 'This is my blood' – and received by the communicants.
- The eucharist is outward-looking. At the end the people go out into the world to be the Church, serving the world in the spirit of Jesus Christ.

It is essential to Anglicans that the person leading the worship at the eucharist, the celebrant, is a bishop or priest.

In the Anglican Church it is normal for young people to wait until the time of confirmation, from the age of 11 upwards, before receiving Holy Communion.

The bread used at the eucharist in the great majority of Anglican churches is unleavened wafer bread. In some, ordinary household bread is used.

The Orthodox liturgy

- The first part of the service is the **Liturgy of the Word** or the **Liturgy of the Catechumens**. (A catechumen is someone preparing for baptism.) Psalms and prayers are sung, as is a reading from the Bible. Then comes the Lesser Entrance: the priest brings the book of the gospels from behind the iconostasis and sings the gospel for the day. (See Chapter A8, *Church buildings – plans*, for a description of an Orthodox church.) A sermon may follow.
- The second part is the **Liturgy of the Faithful**. The bread and wine are brought in procession – the Greater Entrance. They are taken through the Royal Doors, and there, out of sight of the people, the priest offers prayers to God. He recalls the goodness of God in creation and in sending his Son to save the world. He recalls the Last Supper, and he consecrates the bread and wine to be the body and blood of Christ. The bread is broken into pieces and placed in the chalice that contains the wine. A spoon is used to administer the sacrament to the communicants.
- Some of the bread is not consecrated. What is not consecrated is broken into small pieces. At the end of the liturgy the priest stands in front of the Royal Doors, and worshippers take some of the unconsecrated bread, the *antidoron*.

The Orthodox liturgy is always led by a priest.
Children may receive communion from the time when they are baptized as infants.
Ordinary bread and wine are used.

Methodist communion

In the United Reformed Church and among Baptists the order of service is similar to the Methodist rite.

- The communion is usually held once or twice a month. Sometimes it is held during or after the regular morning or evening worship. This means that at the communion service, or during the service that precedes it, there is reading and preaching of the scriptures and prayer for the needs of the world. In Methodist churches the Sunday on which there is a communion service is called 'Sacrament Sunday'. The full order of the communion service is used, with reading and preaching and with prayers for those in need.
- The words of Jesus – 'This is my body. This is my blood' – are spoken over the bread and the wine in a prayer that recalls the Last Supper.
- The people receive the bread and wine. After a prayer of thanksgiving they go out from the church into the everyday world.

'Go in peace in the power of the Spirit
to live and work to God's praise and glory.
Thanks be to God.'
(Final prayers of the service in the *Methodist Service Book*)

Communion is usually led by a minister, though sometimes a lay person will preside.
Communion is usually open to those who wish to receive. For instance, among Baptists there is usually an open invitation to those who know and love the Lord Jesus as their personal Saviour and who are in a right relationship with their fellow-Christians.
Ordinary bread is used. Unfermented wine or grape juice is used rather than ordinary wine since many members do not drink anything alcoholic.

Why do some Christians not celebrate Holy Communion?

The Salvation Army and the Quakers do not have Holy Communion services. They believe that outward signs are not important. They believe there is a danger that Christians may be more devoted to the sacrament than to the Saviour symbolized in the bread and wine. What matters is the way Christians accept Jesus Christ in their hearts.

In teaching that outward signs are not important, the founder of the Salvation Army, William Booth, included the routines of the Army itself – such as the wearing of uniform or the dedication of children. He said: 'Neither water, sacraments, church service, nor Salvation Army methods will save you without a living change of heart.'

Examination practice

1. Describe a communion service in **either** a Methodist **or** a Baptist church. On what event in the life of Jesus is it based? (10 marks)
   Write up to one side of A4, giving a full account of both the Communion service and the Last Supper.
2. In what ways would **either** the Catholic mass **or** the Orthodox liturgy be different from the communion service you have already described? (6 marks)
   Write around half a side of A4. Make your points clearly, mentioning not only obvious differences in the worship but also differences in the underlying beliefs.
3. Why is it important to many Christians to receive Holy Communion regularly? (4 marks)
   Half a side of A4 should be plenty this time. Make sure the reasons you give are carefully and relevantly presented.

Liturgical and non-liturgical worship

Worship can be either liturgical or non-liturgical.

- Liturgical worship follows a set ritual with a pattern of words and actions. It is used regularly and is familiar to the worshippers.

    Some Christians appreciate the regular, familiar pattern of liturgical worship. Others find it boring, with the same form of service, the same prayers week by week.
- Non-liturgical worship is much more flexible in its form.
    - It may follow a simple regular pattern. In the Methodist or United Reformed Church, for instance, the service (if it is not a communion service) may not be taken from a set prayer book but may, week by week, follow the same pattern of hymns, Bible readings, prayers and preaching.
    - The worship may have no set pattern at all but may be free and spontaneous. Examples would be the silent meeting of the Quakers or the exuberance of Pentecostal worship.

Christians of the different Churches do not necessarily believe that one form of worship is better than another. All are different ways of approaching God. If different people feel closer to God through different types of worship, then let all worship in the ways which suit them best.

This chapter is mainly concerned with descriptions of non-liturgical worship.

Traditional Methodist worship

What follows is a pattern that might well be used during a typical Methodist act of worship. It is not a rigid form that must always be followed.

- The service will probably begin with a hymn – traditionally Methodists sing hymns with great feeling. The words of the hymn are all-important. For that reason the person announcing a hymn reads the whole of the first verse very expressively, so that the congregation may concentrate on the words and their message. A number of hymns will be sung during the service.
- The opening hymn is followed by prayer. Very often the leader prays **extempore**: that means, he or she does not use a set form from a book but relies on the Holy Spirit to guide the words. The words of the prayer may cover a number of matters. There may be praise to God, followed by intercession for the needs of the world and

for particular individuals. The prayer may be followed by the Lord's Prayer, said or sung.
- Bible reading is an important part of the worship. Usually there will be two readings, one from each Testament. They are often chosen by the preacher.
- The preaching of the sermon is an important part of the worship. The congregation have come expecting to hear the word of God read in the lessons and proclaimed by the preacher.
- The service ends with further prayer and hymn-singing and the pronouncing of the Benediction (blessing).

Taizé

In 1940, Brother Roger came from Switzerland to Taizé, a semi-abandoned village in Burgundy, France. He was 25 years old, and he had come there to offer shelter to political refugees, notably Jews fleeing the Nazi persecution, and to work out a call to follow Christ in a community that would attempt to live the Gospel call to reconciliation day after day. A few years later he was joined by his first brothers, and in 1949 several of them committed themselves for life to celibacy and to material and spiritual sharing. Taizé thus took its place as part of the great monastic family.

Young people have been coming to Taizé in ever greater numbers since 1957–8. From all over the world, they take part in week meetings. Some weeks their number goes up to as many as 6 000. Three times a day, everyone gathers with the brothers for prayer in the Church of Reconciliation. It is a very meditative form of prayer in which singing and silence have always played a large part.

This then is the context in which the 'songs of Taizé' have been developed. When the number of visitors to Taizé began to increase, and more and more young people from different countries and languages started arriving, the brothers felt the need to find a way for everyone to join in the prayer and not simply be observers. At the same time they felt it was essential to maintain the meditative quality of the prayer, to let it be an authentic encounter with the mystery of God revealed in Jesus Christ. Finally, it was found that music whose core was a simple refrain sung over and over again made possible a prayer that was both meditative and yet accessible to all.

Charismatic worship

Charismatic worship is based on the belief that individual Christians are filled with the Holy Spirit and that the Spirit moves different people to join in the worship in different

Wait for the Lord

One of the chants sung at Taizé (music: Jacques Berthier)

ways. It is not limited to a few branches of Christianity. There are charismatics among members of all the Christian denominations.

> In the last days, God says,
>   I will pour out my Spirit on all people.
> Your sons and daughters will prophesy,
>   your young men will see visions,
>   your old men will dream dreams.
> Even on my servants, both men and women,
>   I will pour out my Spirit in those days,
>   and they will prophesy.
>   Acts 2$^{17-18}$ quoting Joel 2$^{28-29}$
>   From the account of the Day of Pentecost

> If anyone speaks in a tongue, two – or at the most three – should speak, one at a time, and someone must interpret. If there is no interpreter, the speaker should keep quiet in the church and speak to himself and God.
>   1 Corinthians 14$^{27-28}$

Charismatic worship is seen as a great outpouring of the Spirit.

- People sing, dance, embrace, clap, as they feel the Spirit move them.
- They may raise their arms in the air: 'I want men everywhere to lift up holy hands in prayer' (1 Timothy 2^8)
- When they pray, they pray extempore – as explained earlier, that means they pray using words as they come into their heads, inspired by the Spirit.
- Some may speak in tongues or sing in tongues – what they say is not a recognizable language, but they themselves know what it means and others gather from the sound and from their body language what they are saying.
- The worshippers may become ecstatic, filled with excited joy at their experience of God.
- Some may prophesy, with a word from God. Someone may be moved to say something like 'I feel the Lord would have me say, "Do not be ashamed, do not be afraid to speak boldly because I have empowered you to be my witnesses. Go forth in the name of the Lord of Hosts and I will indeed be with you, says the Lord".'
- Some may come forward for healing. Others will pray over them, that they may be healed, sometimes anointing them with oil.

Quakers

Quakers speak of a meeting rather than a service. They meet in a room that has chairs in a circle, and sit waiting for the inspiration of the Holy Spirit. There is no leader.

If one of those present feels moved by the Spirit to speak, or to read from the Bible, he or she will do so as a ministry to those present. When the reading or the ministry is over, silence returns. All return to their waiting on the Holy Spirit.

At the end of the appointed time the worshippers shake hands in fellowship.

Hymn-singing

Hymns can be part of either liturgical or non-liturgical worship.

Hundreds of thousands of hymns have been written. Most are used very little and are eventually forgotten. Some hymns remain popular for years.

- Some hymns are closely based on the Bible: see the examples in Chapter A5, *The Bible and worship*.

Compare the hymn 'While shepherds watched their flocks by night' with Luke 2^{8-14}.

- Some are written for a particular time in the Christian year. Examples are Christmas carols or hymns written about the events of Holy Week ('When I survey the wondrous cross', 'The old rugged cross') or Easter ('Jesus Christ is risen today'). Some are written as, say, evening hymns, such as 'The day thou gavest, Lord, is ended'.

- Most hymns are general hymns, which can be used at any time. Examples are 'Lord of the dance' and 'Shine, Jesus, shine'.

An important factor in the popularity of a hymn is its tune. The hymn 'O Jesus, I have promised to serve thee to the end' was a popular hymn with a number of well-known tunes. Because the hymn was popular a new tune was written for it in 1960 – and that new tune also has become well known.

Hymn-singing is an important part of worship because:

- People enjoy singing hymns – and enjoyment is an important part of worship.

- The words of hymns often express very well what people feel about God and what they want to say to him. Hymns are prayers that are sung.

- Through hymns everyone can actively join in the worship. They feel that they themselves are offering praise to God.

Examination practice

1. What is charismatic worship? (10 marks)
   Write at least half a side of A4, giving as lively as possible an account of the worship.

2. Describe a Quaker meeting. Why do Quakers worship in this way? (4 marks)
   Write 6–10 lines, being sure you answer both parts of the question.

3. Why are hymns important in Christian worship?
   (6 marks)
   Write about half a side of A4. Take a selection of hymns you know and explain the meaning for the examiners.

THE LORD'S PRAYER

Introduction

'I can't pray.'

Some of us find it difficult to pray because we do not know what to say when we pray; or we lose concentration quickly when we pray. Other people are uncertain about the best way to pray: is it all right to ask God to do favours for us? Or should we ask God to do favours for people who need help, such as those who suffer or those who starve?

Christians believe that Jesus knew God. So they value any advice he gave about how to pray. He taught a prayer to his disciples. (Christians call Jesus 'Lord', so they refer to this prayer as the Lord's Prayer.) There is an account of this prayer in Luke's and Matthew's gospels (see next page), but not in the gospels of Mark or John. Paul does not mention the Lord's Prayer in any of his letters.

Early Christians said this prayer three times a day.

> The self-sufficient do not pray,
> the self-satisfied will not pray,
> the self-righteous cannot pray.
>
> Leonard Ravenhill

Meaning

Notice three significant features of this prayer:

- The person who says this prayer does not use the word 'I' or 'me'. Instead, the words 'we' and 'us' are used. This implies that nobody should pray solely for him or herself.

- Each part of the prayer is not a request to God; it is a demand. For example, it is not 'please forgive us our sins', but 'forgive us our sins'. This shocks some Christians, never mind non-Christians, as they firmly

Two versions of the Lord's Prayer

Matthew 6 [7–13]	Luke 11 [2–4]
(Jesus was teaching his disciples.) 'And when you pray, do not keep on babbling like pagans, for they think they will be heard because of their many words. Do not be like them, for your Father knows what you need before you ask him. This, then, is how you should pray:	One day Jesus was praying in a certain place. When he had finished, one of his disciples said to him, 'Lord, teach us to pray, just as John taught his disciples.' He said to them, 'When you pray, say:
Our Father in heaven, hallowed be your name, your kingdom come, your will be done on earth as it is in heaven. Give us today our daily bread. Forgive us our debts, as we also have forgiven our debtors.	Father, hallowed be your name, your kingdom come. Give us each day our daily bread. Forgive us our sins, for we also forgive everyone who sins against us. And lead us not into temptation.'
And lead us not into temptation, but deliver us from the evil one.'	

believe that we cannot demand anything from God. They believe we can only ask God to do things.

• It is short.

Our Father in heaven

Jesus advised his followers to talk to God as a child speaks with a father. He could have recommended approaching God as though he was a judge, or a king, or a master. These are popular images of God in the Old Testament. But Jesus called God *abba*, which means 'dad', and advised others to do the same.

Unfortunately, not all children have a happy or comfortable relationship with their fathers. Jesus must have had in mind an exemplary child–father relationship. What does that involve? Perhaps, trust that a father will give protection; confidence that a father will provide food, clothing and other basic needs; belief that a father offers sound advice to his child; acceptance of the greater power and authority of a father; conviction that a father will listen to his child; conviction that a father will grant a child's request, if the father thinks it is in the best interest of his child; assurance that a father will give comfort and consolation in time of trouble; and so on.

Christians believe that, when they were baptized, they were joined to Jesus Christ. Because they also believe that Jesus is the 'Son' of God, they conclude that baptism has made them members of God's family. Thus they follow the example of their 'brother' Jesus and talk to God as their 'father'.

Some people think of God as living in the heavens or stars; this is a symbolic way of saying that God is greater than we can imagine, too great for us to be able to meet him

in the way we meet other people on earth. In addition, religious believers do not use the word 'father' literally when they describe God as father. The word 'father' is used literally only of a natural father. So to distinguish God from a natural father, he is the the 'heavenly father'.

> 'My words fly up, my thoughts remain below;
> Words without thoughts never to heaven go.'
> Shakespeare

hallowed be your name

'Hallowed' is an old English word that we do not use any more; instead we use the word 'holy'. When we describe God as holy, we mean that he is quite different from any other person; he is mysterious; he is great beyond all description; he is more important, powerful and attractive than anything else we have known or can imagine.

For a Jew, a person's name *was* that person. So when they said that a person's name should be hallowed, they meant that the person should be hallowed.

Translated into simple English, this statement could be: **may we respect you, recognize how great you are, and give you reverence and worship.**

Your kingdom come;
your will be done on earth as it is in heaven.

These two statements mean the same. The second line is a description of the phrase 'God's kingdom', in the first line. It assumes that in heaven – where we imagine God to live – everybody does what God wants. By contrast, people on earth do not act in the way that God wants: we are sometimes selfish, greedy, vindictive, unforgiving and indifferent to the sufferings of other people. 'Your will be done on earth as it is in heaven' is a prayer that this may change.

Christians take Jesus as their example of how to behave, to bring God's kingdom on earth. They believe that Jesus always pleased God. He was the perfect person.

'Your kingdom come' can also be a prayer for Christ to come on earth a second time. The first Christians believed that Christ would come to earth a second time, before they died, to establish perfectly the kingdom of God on earth. He did not. And so subsequent Christians modified this belief. They still believed that Christ would come to earth a second time, not in their lifetime, but before the end of the world. Some Christians today continue to believe that Christ will come on earth a second time, to establish perfectly the kingdom of God. They pray for it to happen soon: **Your kingdom come**.

Give us today our daily bread

There are different interpretations of this statement. One interpretation starts with an important event in Jewish history. The Jews believed that God sent Moses to free them from working as slaves in Egypt. After they came out of Egypt, they were wandering in desert land with nothing to eat. They believe that God sent them a special bread every morning to stop them from starving. They called this bread *manna*. This daily bread showed that God looked after them, that he cared for them, and that he had a special affection for them.

So this statement may mean that we want God to provide the food that we need to survive. This is not an important prayer for most of us who live in Western Europe, where there is much luxury food and no prospect of hunger. But this statement has considerable meaning for people who are starving; and for people who have some food, but only for today, not tomorrow.

This statement can also mean that we want God's help, to guide and to strengthen us, especially when we find it difficult to act in the way God wants. We need spiritual strength. We find it difficult to to be patient, to be forgiving, to be considerate, and so on. Christians believe that one way God gives this help is through the 'bread' of the eucharist. It is the daily bread.

But this statement is not only about **daily bread**, it is also about **today**. So though this statement means that we should ask God to strengthen and guide us, it also means we should seek his help just for today. We should ask God to help us cope with each day as it comes.

> Lord, I shall be very busy this day.
> I may forget you, but do not forget me.
> Jacob Astley before the battle of Edgehill

Forgive us our debts,
as we also have forgiven our debtors.

The word 'debt' can be translated as 'sin'. This statement is

quite clear. We all do wrong. We need God to forgive us. But if we want God to forgive us, we must also forgive others, and forget the resentments and grudges that we hold on to.

Jesus taught that we must be as perfect as God. God forgives. And so he expects us to forgive our enemies. That's easy to say. But perhaps impossible to do? Or difficult, but possible?

And lead us not into temptation,
but deliver us from the evil one.

This statement implies that life on earth cannot be like life in heaven. In life on earth, we cannot avoid temptation to do wrong. Yet we can be aware of this difficulty and seek God's assistance when we are tempted to do wrong.

Evil thoughts and evil intentions come from our own feelings and ideas. There is a natural inclination to want to behave in an evil way. Christians call this 'original sin'. Yet there is also a natural inclination to do good. These two contrasting inclinations often lead to a struggle within the soul or mind of a person.

There is a paradox here. Unless we are tempted, we do not grow as people: we do not learn to understand ourselves or other people. On the other hand, when we continuously give in to temptation, we become unpleasant, even evil; we make other people miserable; we become unhappy ourselves; and there is little evidence that God is present in our lives or actions.

Christians are confident that they can rely on the power of God's Spirit to cope with temptation. They believe that none of us, by our own effort, can cope adequately with temptation.

Some Christians believe there is a devil (Satan, the Evil One); he continually causes evil thoughts and temptations in our minds. Other Christians think that talk of the devil is an imaginative way of describing just how powerful our evil thoughts can be – this is particularly the case when we want to do a good act, but we are persistently pestered by the desire to do the opposite, evil act.

The words 'Lead us not into temptation' suggest to some people that we are sometimes tempted by God. Christians certainly do not think of God as a tempter in the usual sense of someone trying to make us sin. In modern English, a better expression would be, **Do not put us to the test**.

> Pray as if everything depended on God.
> Act as if everything depended on you.
> Ignatius Loyola

For yours are the kingdom, the power and the glory,

This prayer was added to the end of the Lord's Prayer. It was added soon after the gospels were written. The prayer repeats what is in the first part of the Lord's Prayer, though it is no longer a prayer demanding something. Instead, it is a prayer worshipping God and thanking him. We thank him for the coming of his kingdom on earth, and for the powerful help he gives us; and we worship him because he is so great.

Amen.

Many Christians add this word at the end of the prayer. It means 'so be it', or 'I agree with all that has been said'.

Other prayers of Jesus

The following are examples of Jesus' prayers:

- In the garden of Gethsemane, Jesus prayed:

  > '*Abba*, Father, everything is possible for you. Take this cup from me. Yet not what I will, but what you will.'
  >
  > Mark 14[36]

- On the cross, Jesus prayed:

  > 'My God, my God, why have you forsaken me?'
  >
  > Mark 15[34]

- On the cross, Jesus also prayed:

  > 'Father, forgive them, for they do not know what they are doing.'
  >
  > Luke 23[34]

- As he was dying, Jesus prayed:

  > 'Father, into your hands I commit my spirit.'
  >
  > Luke 23[46]

Jesus' parables about prayer

- Friend asking for help at midnight (Luke 11[5–8])
- Widow and judge (Luke 18[1–8])
- Pharisee and tax collector (Luke 18[9–14])

See Chapter C19, *Luke's Gospel – Parables*, for information on these parables.

Examination practice

1. Select any **two** phrases from the Lord's Prayer. State the meaning of each one. (3 marks)
   Write about six lines.

2. How might prayer help a Christian to be considerate to other people? (8 marks)
   Write about three-quarters of a side of A4.

3. Explain why the Lord's Prayer is important to Christians. (6 marks)
   Write about half a side of A4.

4. 'Prayer is a waste of time. People are only talking to themselves.'
   Do you agree? Give reasons for your answer. Show that you have considered the opposite point of view. (8 marks)
   Write about three-quarters of a side of A4.

PRIVATE WORSHIP AND DEVOTIONS

4

What is prayer?

Prayer is conversation with God. The conversation involves prayer of different kinds:

- Adoring and praising God.
- Confessing sin. This sort of confession is not to be confused with the sacrament of reconciliation (see Chapter A17, *Reconciliation (penance, confession)*). The person praying thinks back over the last day or week, remembers any sins, and asks God's forgiveness.
- Thanksgiving to God for particular blessings and pleasures, not only for oneself but for others as well.
- Asking for God's blessing and support for other people. There may be general prayers for people in need, such as those who are starving, or the prayer may be for someone whom the person praying knows and loves.
- Asking for things they themselves need – not just for possessions but, more importantly, for help in living a good Christian life, for the grace to love and serve God.
- Listening to God. Christians do not expect a voice thundering from heaven, but a sense that God is guiding them and leading them in this or that way.

Why do Christians pray?

- Jesus taught Christians to pray. He taught them to pray to God, who is a loving, heavenly Father.

- Prayer is an offering to God. They pray to express their love of God.
- It is a basic Christian belief that God is always ready to hear the prayer of every individual. Personal, individual prayer is important as well as public worship.
- Prayer is an opportunity to experience the presence of God.
- They receive spiritual strength in prayer.
- They may receive guidance from God which will support them in their everyday lives.

Meditation

Meditation is a form of prayer in which people first clear their minds of any thoughts that may make it difficult to concentrate on God. Then they simply think of God. They may concentrate on some aspect of God's nature, such as the love shown by Jesus in dying on the cross, or the idea of God as Father. They are, in a sense, spending time in God's company.

One way to think of meditation is to imagine yourself sitting in the company of someone you love very greatly. Even when neither of you is saying anything, your minds may be full of thoughts about each other. Those thoughts come naturally, springing from your love. In the same way, a person who loves God may concentrate on him simply out of a deep love for him.

The Jesus Prayer

The Jesus Prayer is a favourite prayer for many Christians, especially Orthodox Christians. It is a short prayer, of four phrases.

Lord Jesus Christ,
Son of God,
have mercy on me,
a sinner.

It is repeated, perhaps a hundred or even a thousand times. It is said slowly. It is a meditative prayer – the person praying concentrates on Jesus while saying the prayer. Sometimes the person praying coordinates breathing with the words of the prayer – breathing in while saying the first phrase (Lord Jesus Christ), breathing out while saying the second phrase (Son of God), breathing in while saying the third phrase (have mercy on me), and breathing out while saying the fourth phrase (a sinner).

The Jesus Prayer is a way of praying rather than just a prayer. Those praying aspire to bring Christ into their lives and to follow Christ's way of thinking about the world, about people and about God.

Bible reading

For Christians of all denominations, Bible reading is an important part of the spiritual life.

The usual practice is to have a list of readings for each day, which will cover different books of the Bible in turn,

SUNDAY 11 AUGUST

Philippians 1:3–6 (NRSV)

I've started, so I'll finish

I thank my God every time I remember you, constantly praying with joy in every one of my prayers for all of you, because of your sharing in the gospel from the first day until now. I am confident of this, that the one who began a good work among you will bring it to completion by the day of Jesus Christ.

Magnus Magnusson, of *Mastermind* fame, has made a very odd statement into a catch-phrase: 'I've started, so I'll finish.' But it's not a bad motto for life. There is something very sad about incomplete things, and something very satisfying about finishing a job properly. Jesus could say to his Father at the end of his life, 'I have finished the work you gave me to do.' It had been hard and painful, and ended on a cross, but he had done it.

Here Paul is assuring the young church at Philippi that God—not the apostle—would complete the good work he had begun among them, in his own time ('by the day of Jesus Christ').

What was true for Philippi is true for St Philip's, if you see what I mean! We may feel that many tasks are incomplete. Our Sunday school class doesn't seem to respond. Confirmation candidates drop away. Numbers aren't what they were. But what God has started he will finish. It is his work, not ours.

And what is true of churches is true of individuals. We may have children who were baptized and brought up in the faith, but now seem far from it. But if God began a work, if even a 'mustard seed' of faith was planted, then God will complete what he began. What he has begun he will bring to 'completion', to his own satisfaction, like a master craftsman. There are no loose ends with God!

A reflection
Help us, Lord, to trust that what you have begun you will complete in your own good time: in the Church, in those we pray for, and in ourselves. Amen.
DW

Some Christians use notes like these to help them with their daily Bible reading

Reprinted with permission from *New Daylight* January–April 1996, published by the Bible Reading Fellowship

picking out the passages most likely to be of help to the reader. However, there is no hard and fast rule as to what should be read and when. Some may choose a book of the Bible and work through it, a few verses at a time. It is better not to start at the beginning of Genesis and wade right through the Bible, a chapter at a time. That way people come across some very difficult chapters in the early books of the Bible and are put off reading altogether.

Some people have books to help them in their Bible reading. For instance, the Bible Reading Fellowship publishes booklets that give a reading for each day and a short comment or explanation of the chosen passage.

Before beginning to read the passage for the day, the reader will pause to remember the purpose of reading. The Bible is the Word of God. So they pray that there may be a special insight or message for them in those verses. They read, praying that they may find something new about God and his will for them.

Rosary

A rosary is used, mainly by Catholics, to help them concentrate on their prayer.

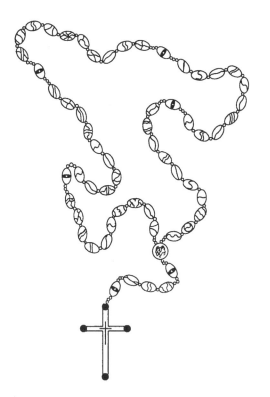

A rosary

As they hold each bead in turn they say a prayer, such as the Gloria, the Lord's Prayer or the Hail Mary, then move on to the next bead. The rosary has five sets of beads called *decades*. Each decade contains ten beads; for each bead the person praying says a Hail Mary. As each decade is used, the person praying will concentrate on a particular event in the life of Jesus or Mary.

When Catholics meditate on the joyful mysteries, during the five decades they will think in turn of the Annunciation (Mary being told by the angel that she is to bear a child), Mary's visit to Elizabeth when she was pregnant, the birth of Jesus, the presentation of Jesus in the temple when he was a baby, and the finding of Jesus in the temple when he was twelve years old. See Chapter A11, *Advent, Christmas and Epiphany*.

When Catholics meditate on the sorrowful mysteries, they will think in turn of Jesus in his agony in the Garden of Gethsemane, his being scourged (whipped), the crown of thorns, Jesus carrying the cross to Calvary, and the crucifixion.

When Catholics meditate on the glorious mysteries, they will think of the resurrection, the ascension (see Chapter A15, *Other festivals*), the descent of the Holy Spirit (see Chapter C22, *The Acts of the Apostles*), the assumption of Mary (see Chapter D15, *Mary, mother of Christ*) and the crowning of Mary.

What is the point of using the same words over and over again? It is a way of concentrating, helping the person praying to focus attention on God and keep out distracting thoughts.

Stations of the Cross

In Catholic and in many Anglican churches there are around the walls a series of pictures called the Stations of the Cross. They represent different points along the way that Jesus went from his trial by Pilate to his crucifixion and burial. Sometimes there is a fifteenth station for the resurrection. The original stations are of course in Jerusalem, on the Via Dolorosa – the road along which Jesus carried the cross – and at the place of the crucifixion. People go from one station to the next, pausing at each to think and to pray.

Prayers to the saints

Catholics believe that the saints are with God in heaven. There they offer their prayers – their intercessions – for those who have not yet come into the presence of God. First among the saints is the Blessed Virgin Mary.

When they pray, Catholics ask the saints to pray to God for them. In no sense do they pray to the saints as they pray to the Father, Son or Spirit.

Icons

Icons are an essential feature of the spiritual life of the Orthodox Church.

Icons are more than pictures. They are statements about God. They contain something of the nature of the person portrayed on them.

Orthodox Christians kiss the icon as they enter church

On entering the church each Orthodox Christian buys a candle, lights it and places it in front of an icon. They kiss the icon and sign themselves three times with the sign of the cross. During the liturgy they may use the icons on the iconostasis to focus their minds on God as they pray.

The lighting of candles

Sometimes when Christians pray they light candles to symbolize the prayers they offer. Orthodox Christians light candles as they kiss the icon on entering the church. When they pray in a church, Catholics often place lighted candles on a stand by a statue of, say, the Virgin Mary or the Sacred Heart.

Examination practice

1. Why do Christians pray? (10 marks)
   Write about a side of A4.

2. Explain why some Christians use (a) rosaries (b) icons in their prayer. (6 marks)
   Write about half a side of A4.

3. Do you think that it is important to Christians that their prayers are answered? Give reasons for your answer.
   (4 marks)

   Write about half a side of A4.

THE BIBLE AND WORSHIP 5

Introduction

As Christians believe that the Bible is the Word of God, it is used a great deal in worship.

Reading from the Bible

Passages from the Bible are read at virtually all services of all churches.

- In some churches (such as Methodist or United Reformed Church) the worship is frequently **pulpit-centred.** The pulpit is the place from which the Bible is read and the sermon is preached. The pulpit is situated in the most prominent place in the building so that everyone may see and hear. The very fact that the pulpit is given so central a position shows how important the Bible is to the worshippers.

  Normally the Bible reading is chosen by the preacher. The choice will depend on the theme of the service and, particularly, the sermon.
- In churches in which the worship is **liturgical** (such as Catholic, Anglican or Orthodox) the Word of God is an important part of the liturgy. The readings at the eucharist follow a given pattern – a two- or three-year cycle, related to the Christian year. At other services – baptisms, confirmations, marriages, ordinations and funerals – there are Bible readings relevant to the rite. The same applies to the sacraments of reconciliation and anointing of the sick. (See Chapter A17, *Reconciliation*

(penance, confession), and Chapter A18, *Anointing of the sick.*)
- In Quaker meetings, Friends may well feel moved to read from the scriptures.

The Book of Psalms

In Anglican churches psalms are said or sung during the services of Morning and Evening Prayer.

In Catholic churches parts of the psalms are said or sung during Mass. Psalms figure prominently in the monastic community prayer, seven times a day.

Hymns

Many hymns are based on the Psalms and other passages of scripture. Note the two examples overleaf.

Eucharist

Some of the actual words used at the eucharist are taken from the Bible. For instance, in a number of denominations, just before the bread and wine are taken by the priest or minister, the people recall that they are joining with those in heaven in praising God. They use the words of the angels (Isaiah 6[3] and Revelation 4[8]):

Holy, holy, holy Lord,
God of power and might,
Heaven and earth are full of your glory.

The words that Jesus spoke at the Last Supper are used as the bread and wine are taken during the Thanksgiving:

> We praise you, Lord God, King of the universe,
> through our Lord Jesus Christ,
> who on the night in which he was betrayed,
> took bread, gave thanks, broke it, and gave it to his disciples, saying,
> 'Take this and eat it. This is my body given for you.
> Do this in remembrance of me.'
>
> *Methodist Service Book*

Examination guidance

If you are asked a question about the way in which the Bible is used in worship, read the question carefully.

- Does the question refer to one particular denomination? Or one style of worship – pulpit-centred worship for example? Or does it ask for a contrast between different denominations?

Concentrate first on the reading of scripture, as described in the first part of this section. If the question requires a more wide-ranging approach, use other examples.

Psalm 23¹⁻³:

The Lord is my shepherd: therefore can I
lack nothing.
   He shall feed me in a green pasture: and
lead me forth beside the waters of comfort.
   He shall convert my soul: and bring me
forth in the paths of righteousness, for his
Name's sake.

The Lord's my shepherd; I'll not want.
   He makes me down to lie
In pastures green. He leadeth me
   The quiet waters by.
My soul he doth restore again,
   And me to walk doth make
Within the paths of righteousness
   E'en for his own name's sake.

Philippians 2¹⁰⁻¹¹:

At the name of Jesus every knee should bow,
in heaven and on earth and under the earth,
and every tongue confess that Jesus Christ is Lord,
to the glory of God the Father.

At the name of Jesus
   Every knee shall bow,
Every tongue confess him
   King of Glory now.
'Tis the Father's pleasure
   We should call him Lord,
Who from the beginning
   Was the mighty Word.

CHURCH BUILDINGS 6

Introduction

An architect planning a building has to ask, 'What is this building for?' This is true of any building, whatever it is. It is true of a house, a theatre, a school, a supermarket, a station – and a church.

What are church buildings for?

A church building is a place for the worship of God. The design of the building must be suitable for the worship of that particular congregation.

   Christians believe that God is everywhere, at all times. They can pray to him at any time, wherever they happen to be. None the less, church buildings are often regarded with great reverence and affection. Some are places where people have worshipped for centuries. They may have been built in particular holy places. Others are very modern buildings; the worshippers may have raised the money for them and watched them being built.

A church is often called a house of God. It is a place where a person can share with others the experience of worship. At other times it is a quiet place to pray and to be alone with God.

How does the purpose of the building affect the design?

- All church buildings have to provide enough room for the worshippers. Usually, people sit for at least part of the service, so there must be comfortable seating. Some churches use long benches called **pews**, firmly fixed to the floor. Others prefer **chairs**, which can easily be rearranged. If some people are to stand – and usually in an Orthodox church the congregation stand – there must be plenty of room for them as well.

  In some churches the congregation kneel to pray. For them, there must be comfortable **kneelers** or hassocks. Also, the chairs or pews will have to be a little further apart to allow each person sufficient space.
- Every church must have at least one focal point. A focal point is a place in the building to which the eye is naturally drawn. In a Catholic or Church of England building the focal point is the **altar**; in a United Reformed church it is the **pulpit** or **lectern**; in an Orthodox church it is the **iconostasis** and the **Royal Doors**. Everybody, in every corner of the church, must be able to see the focal points. They must also be able to hear the minister, the preacher and anyone else taking a leading part in the service.
- A church building is used for other services as well as the main Sunday worship. There may be smaller, weekday services. The building may be used for personal prayer or for the sacrament of reconciliation. There will be baptisms, marriages and funerals. The church must be designed with these things in mind.
- The atmosphere of the building is important. Some

churches will be bright and cheerful while others will have very little direct light. Some will be very plain while others will have colourful windows, statues, icons or other decorations.
- Of course, every church must be warm in winter and cool in summer. No one wants to worship in a place that is uncomfortably hot or cold! Keeping a steady temperature can be a problem – and not only in ancient buildings.

By looking at the way the furniture in a church is arranged you can tell what happens at the services.

Look at the two pictures below.

In the picture on the left, the central feature is the altar. The main Sunday service in this church is the eucharist.

In the picture on the right, the main emphasis is on reading the scriptures and on preaching. That is why the pulpit is the central feature.

The outside of a church building

How can you recognize a church from the outside?

Many traditional churches have towers that can be seen from a distance. They are landmarks and also, for the local community, constant reminders of their Christian faith. Some have spires or steeples, pointing symbolically towards heaven. Other churches have large crosses on their outer walls. Some are built with a ground plan that is in the shape of a cross. Many face to the east, towards the rising sun – as the rising sun is a symbol of resurrection.

Some churches have bells to call people to worship. The bells can weigh anything from 250 kg to 1000 kg.

Why have special buildings?

The church in the picture overleaf was once a cheese warehouse. A group of Christians in Crewe were planning to build a new place of worship. They decided instead to buy the old warehouse.

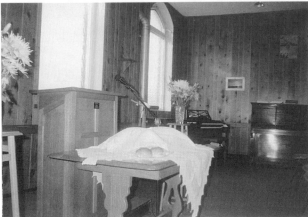

The second picture shows the building arranged for Sunday worship. During the week the same part of the building is used for clubs and meetings. Before and after the Sunday services the furniture has to be rearranged. Young people play table tennis and snooker in the room they use for worship.

Words from the Bible

[God said:] 'My house will be called a house of prayer for all nations.'

Isaiah 56[7]

Stephen said: 'The Most High does not live in houses made for men. As the prophet says:
  Heaven is my throne
    and the earth is my footstool.
  What kind of house will you build for me?
    says the Lord,
    Or where will my resting place be?
  Has not my hand made all these things?'

Acts 7[48–50]

Examination practice

1. Look at the picture of the church building that was once a cheese warehouse.
   (a) What does the word 'holy' mean?   (3 marks)
       Write four to five lines.
   (b) Would you say that a church like the one in the picture is a holy place? Give reasons for your answer.   (8 marks)
       Write about three-quarters of a side of A4.

2. Imagine this building with table tennis and pool tables. Would it feel right to have a youth club in this building? Give reasons for your answer.   (5 marks)
   Write about three-quarters of a side of A4.

Introduction

Some of the furnishings found in churches are common to a number of denominations. They are illustrated and described here. Features that are characteristic of one denomination in particular are described in Chapter A8, *Church buildings – plans*.

Altar or communion table

The altar or table is the place at which the eucharist (by whatever name it is known in that particular denomination) is celebrated.

At one time, in Catholic and Anglican churches, it was usual for the altar to be against the end wall of the church. The priest would stand by the altar with his back to the people, as if praying to God 'out there'. Now it is much more usual for the priest to face the people, as though they were a family gathered round a table with God among them.

The word *altar* reminds Christians of the sacrifice of Jesus Christ on the cross. (In the Old Testament an altar was a place where sacrifice was offered.) The word *table* reminds them of the eucharist as a meal shared with Jesus and with the Church, his followers.

If the worshippers receive communion kneeling there will probably be a communion rail in front of or round the altar/table.

There are usually candles on the altar in Catholic and Anglican churches, symbolizing Jesus as the Light of the World. There is usually a crucifix or a cross on, above or behind the altar. Often the altar is decorated with flowers.

Note that in a Quaker meeting house the table serves a different purpose. The Bible and other Quaker books are placed on it, to be used if someone feels moved to read to the meeting.

Pulpit

The pulpit is the place for preaching. It is usually raised so that the preacher can be seen and heard. In some churches the Bible readings are read and even the whole service led from the pulpit.

Lectern

The lectern is the place for reading the scriptures. In some churches the preacher may preach from the lectern.

Font

The font is the place for baptism in most churches where people (usually infants) are baptized by sprinkling or pouring water on the forehead. Often, especially in older buildings, it is near the door of the church, as by baptism

Christians enter the Church. In other churches, especially modern buildings or ones that have been redesigned, the font is in full view of the congregation. The whole church can see the new member being admitted and can join in the welcome together.

Baptistry

The baptistry is a sunken pool in which people (adults or young people old enough to understand and choose to be baptized) are baptized by total immersion.

CHURCH BUILDINGS – PLANS 8

Introduction

Different denominations worship in different ways. Their buildings will show those differences. In this section you will find pictures and plans of churches of different denominations.

A Catholic church

- **Altar**. The focal point of the building is the altar. The main act of worship is the Mass (eucharist). The priest stands behind the altar to lead the worship.
- **Crucifix**. A crucifix is always prominent in a Catholic church, usually behind or above the altar.
- **Lectern**, from which the scriptures are read and the homily preached.
- **Font**, placed where the whole congregation can witness the baptism.
- **Tabernacle**. The tabernacle is like a safe built into the sanctuary wall. In the tabernacle is kept the consecrated bread and wine, the body and blood of Jesus Christ. When the sacrament is in the tabernacle there is a red light nearby. When the sacrament is taken to sick people it is taken from the tabernacle. Catholics reverence the sacrament by genuflecting (going down on one knee) or bowing.
- **Confessionals** – small rooms where a priest can in

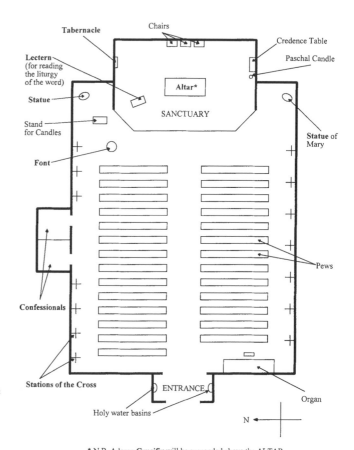

* N.B. A large **Crucifix** will be suspended above the ALTAR, or placed on the wall behind the ALTAR

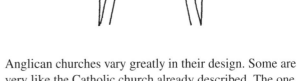

private give a person the sacrament of reconciliation.

- **Statues** are used to help Catholics concentrate in their prayer. In front of some statues, especially those of the Sacred Heart and the Virgin Mary, there is a stand for candles. A Catholic will light a candle, spend some time in prayer and go away; the candle will symbolize the prayer.
- **Stations of the Cross**. A series of 14 pictures illustrating the path of Jesus from the point when he was sentenced by Pilate to his burial. They are used for a service of meditation on the passion and death of Jesus. (See Chapter A12, *Lent; fasting*.)

An Anglican church

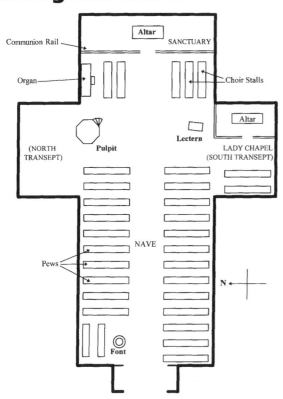

Anglican churches vary greatly in their design. Some are very like the Catholic church already described. The one shown here is typical of many.

- **Altar**. The focal point of the building is the altar. The main act of worship is the eucharist. The priest stands behind the altar to lead the worship.
- **Lectern**, from which the scriptures are read.
- **Pulpit**, from which the sermon is preached.
- **Font**, placed near the main door, symbolizing baptism as admission to the Christian Church.

A Methodist church

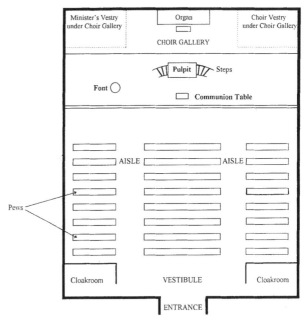

- **Pulpit** – the focal point of the church. The minister may lead the whole service from the pulpit, including the Bible readings and the sermon.
- **Communion table**. Smaller and less central than the altar in a Catholic or Anglican church.
- **Font**, near the front so that all may see.

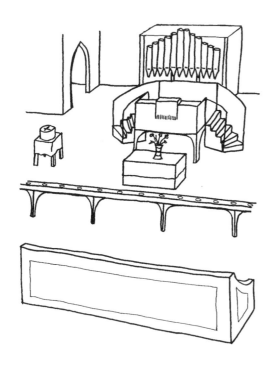

A Baptist church

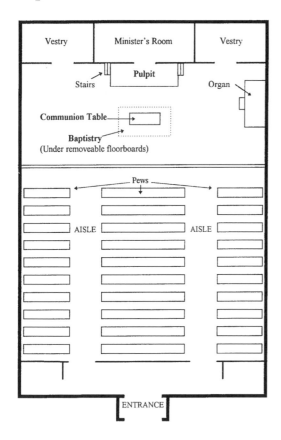

- **Baptistry**. As baptism is believers' baptism by total immersion, the pool for baptism is in a central place, under floorboards that can easily be moved when necessary. The congregation not only wish to see the baptism but also hear the persons to be baptized give their testimony or make their statement of faith.

An Orthodox church

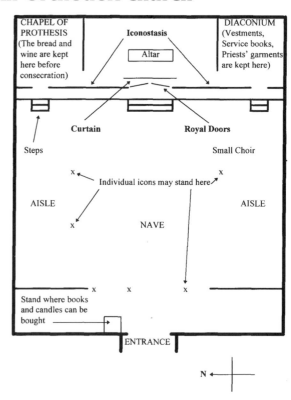

- **Pulpit** – the focal point of the church. The minister may lead the whole service from the pulpit, including the Bible readings and the sermon.
- **Communion table**. Smaller and less central than the altar in a Catholic or Anglican church.

The church is in two parts. The big screen, which is covered with icons, is called the **iconostasis**. The screen symbolizes the divide between earth (the main part of the church, where the congregation sit or stand) and heaven (the sanctuary).

In the centre of the iconostasis are the **Royal Doors**, behind which there is a curtain. The opening of the Royal Doors and the drawing back of the curtain symbolize God opening the way for man to approach and be united with him.

The priest comes through the doors at the Lesser Entrance, when the book of the gospel is brought through and the gospel is read. The doors are shut and the curtain drawn during the consecration. Then, at the Greater Entrance, the bread and wine are taken to the altar for the consecration. Later the doors are opened again and the consecrated bread and wine, the body and blood of Christ, are brought through to the people.

A Quaker meeting house

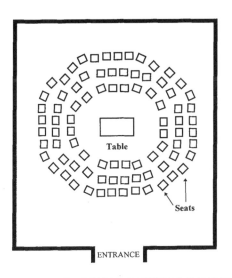

Quakers speak of their meeting house. They do not describe it as a church. It is a very simple place, without signs or symbols. There is a table in the middle with a Bible on it. Chairs are arranged all round so that the Quakers may sit in silence together.

Examination guidance

It is an advantage if you know two or more church buildings of different denominations. They can be local churches. The examiner will be able to judge whether or not you understand the way in which the building is arranged and how it is used for worship.

Visit each church and ask yourself:

- To which denomination does this building belong?
- What is the focal point of this church?
- Why is it the focal point? What is the main act of worship?
- Can the focal point be seen from all parts of the church?
- What other furnishings are there in the church? Why are they there?

- Is the church well designed for a baptism? a marriage? a funeral?
- What symbols are there in the church? Why are they there? If there are none, is there a reason for their absence?
- Is the atmosphere of the church right?
- Is the church a place to which people can come and pray quietly?

Make sure you can draw a simple ground plan of the building. Use a drawing to illustrate an answer if you think it improves the answer. You will receive credit not for your skill as an artist but for showing knowledge and understanding of the building chosen.

1. Choose any Church building or other place of Christian worship known to you.
    (a) Say which denomination it belongs to. (1 mark)
    (b) Describe the main features inside the building and explain how they are used in worship. (10 marks)

2. Choose another place of Christian worship, belonging to a different denomination. Describe **two** differences between it and the building you have already described. Explain why there are these differences. (8 marks)

3 Sometimes appeals are made to raise very large sums of money to repair ancient church buildings. Giving your reasons, say whether you think it is right for Christians to spend so much on places of worship. (5 marks)

1. I have chosen a Catholic church.

    The church is large and over a hundred years old. It is called Saint Mary's.

    The altar is at the front of the church, near the back wall. It has been brought forward so that the priest can face the people during the service. It is raised up a bit so that everyone can see it. It is important because the Mass happens at the altar.

    Near the altar there is a reading stand. That is where the readings and the prayers are said. The priest gives his talk from the reading stand.

    The font is on wheels. They bring it out and put it in front of everyone when there is a christening. It is important for everyone to see what is happening because the baby is joining the church and all the members want to welcome the child.

    There are some statues around the walls. People pray in front of them and light candles for their prayers. There are pictures of the stations of the cross showing what happened when Jesus was crucified. There are rooms where people go to confess their sins. The organ is in the gallery at the back.

(a) The candidate has correctly named and identified a Catholic church. It is clear from what follows that the church described is Catholic.
(Score: 1 mark)

(b) The examiner will not know St Mary's but that does not matter. The marking will be done on the basis of what could be true of a Catholic church.

The description makes a number of good general points. The altar is described as being the focal point of the building. The reasons for its position – away from the wall and raised above the floor level of the main part of the church – are given. Other important furnishings are described and the purpose explained.

Some of the words used are not the most appropriate. For instance, 'lectern' would be a better word to use than 'reading stand' and 'homily' or 'sermon' rather than 'talk'. Some detail is omitted; for example, what do the statues represent? The language is rather clumsy in places – 'The altar is at the *front* of the church, near the *back* wall'.

No drawing. The candidate could have scored an extra mark or two with a clear plan with explanatory comments.

The marking of this description might be a shade more generous than the marking of a description of a Quaker meeting house. The meeting house would be just as good a choice, gaining full marks for a full answer, but less difficult to describe. The examiner would not wish to penalize you for choosing a difficult example and might make some allowance for the difficulty when marking.
(Score: 7 marks out of 10)

2. The second church building I have chosen is a Baptist church.

    The first difference is there are no statues. This is because Baptists don't pray to saints. Also, they like their churches to be plain, without statues and pictures.

    The other difference is that they have a baptistry instead of a font. This is because they have believers' baptism. They say that a person should be old enough to choose to be baptized.

The two differences are correctly chosen. The first, that there are no statues, is explained correctly and simply. The second, the use of a baptistry, is not correctly explained. Adults are baptized at a font in many denominations, if they were not baptized when they were infants. The reason for the baptistry is that the adults are baptized by total immersion.
(Score: 4 marks out of 8)

3. No I don't think people should spend a lot of money on churches because I don't believe in God. If there was a God why is there so much suffering in the world? I don't believe a loving God would allow people to suffer. If the money was spent on supplying people with clean water it would do far more good.

    Some churches are very beautiful and attract lots of visitors. Places like Canterbury would not have a tourist trade if the cathedral was not there. The cathedral helps the local economy and supports jobs. So in a place like that it is necessary to spend money keeping the church in order.

This is not the sort of response the examiner would be expecting! None the less, it is a fair answer and would be given full credit if it were good enough. Certainly candidates would not be penalized for saying they do not believe in God.

The first point is obviously sound – if there is no God, there is no need for the buildings anyway. The idea that the money could be better spent is a fair point and would be credited. The question 'why is there so much suffering in the world?' would not gain any marks because the question is not about whether or nor there is a God. The point about tourism is, again, legitimate and would gain some credit. However, the response fails to evaluate the concept that there is a need for a place set aside for worship.
(Score: 2 marks out of 5)

Examination practice

1. What are the main features of an Orthodox church? Why are they important in Orthodox worship? (12 marks)
   Write at least a side of A4. Make sure you explain the importance of each feature you describe.
2. Describe **three** ways in which you would expect a Baptist church to be different from an Orthodox church. Why are there these differences? (9 marks)
   Write enough to describe and explain each difference fully.
3. Why do Christians think it is important to have places specially set aside for worship?
   (4 marks)
   Write half to three-quarters of a side of A4.

CATHEDRALS

Anglicans, Orthodox and Roman Catholics have cathedrals as well as the smaller local places of worship.

The Anglican and the Catholic Churches are organized in **dioceses**. Some dioceses are huge, especially in countries where there are few Christians. The leader in each diocese is the bishop. Each diocese is divided into **parishes**. A cathedral is the central place of worship, the mother church of a diocese. So the headquarters of each diocese is not an office or a hall but a place of worship, a cathedral.

The word 'cathedral' comes from the Latin word *cathedra*, which means a seat or throne. In each cathedral there is a *cathedra* – a throne for the bishop of that diocese. The bishop does not have the responsibility of the daily worship at the cathedral; his ministry is to the whole

Lincoln Catheral (Anglican) towers majestically over the city

The altar, pulpit and lectern can be seen in the vast nave of the cathedral. Behind the altar is the organ screen.

diocese. The regular worship is the responsibility of a group of clergy based at the cathedral, the chief of whom may be known as the **dean** or **provost**.

A cathedral has all the basic features of a church of the same denomination. For instance, an Anglican cathedral has a main altar, a lectern, a pulpit and a font. It is much larger than an ordinary church, as it is sometimes used for services attended by thousands of people. Everything is on a larger, grander scale. Each cathedral is different from others in a distinctive way. See the pictures and ground plans of the two cathedrals below.

Thousands of people visit cathedrals every year.

- Some come as regular worshippers; every cathedral has its own regular congregation of local people who use the cathedral for worship as others use a parish church.
- Others come to visit the cathedral because it is a great and beautiful house of God.
- Some come as pilgrims to worship at the cathedral, perhaps as part of a large number of worshippers coming together for some special celebration.
- Many people come, of course, as tourists. They may come as Christians or simply as people who enjoy fine buildings.

The staff of the cathedral have a ministry to all these people. They will try to help them see the cathedral in such a way as to show the Christian beliefs and values that the building represents. There will almost always be someone in the cathedral, usually a priest, to whom people can speak, privately if they wish, about any spiritual matter that interests or concerns them.

At set times during the day, services are held or prayers are said. For instance, daily prayers have been said in Chester Cathedral every single day for over 900 years, since 1092.

This modern cathedral has a central altar. The congregation gather round the altar for the Mass. Even those at the back are not far from the altar. Round the walls are the emblems of the various dioceses in the Archdiocese of Liverpool, which covers the north of England.

Liverpool's modern Metropolitan Cathedral (Catholic). The lantern on top of the cathedral is in the shape of a crown, representing Christ the King, to whom the cathedral is dedicated. The design therefore has a message to those who see it from outside.

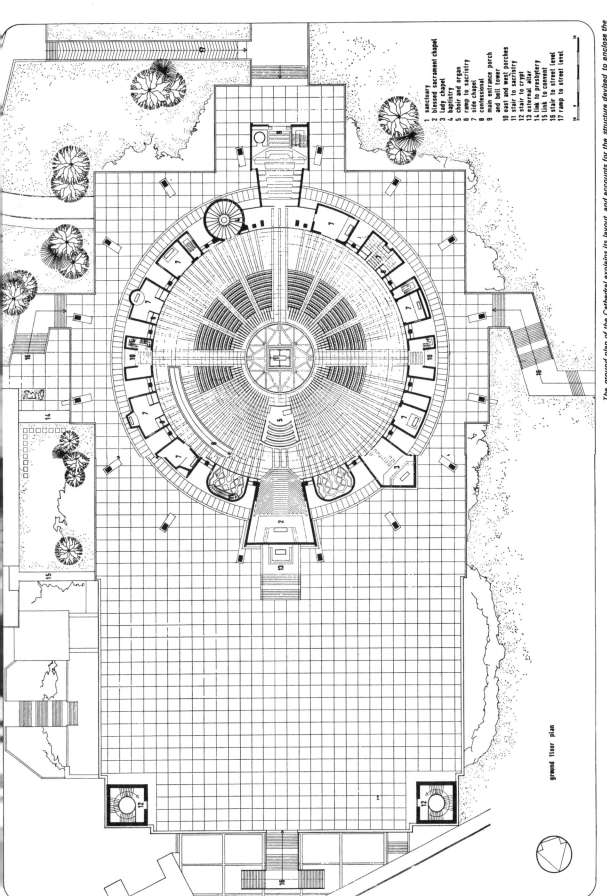

1 sanctuary
2 blessed sacrament chapel
3 lady chapel
4 baptistry
5 choir and organ
6 ramp to sacristy
7 side chapel
8 confessional
9 main entrance porch and bell tower
10 east and west porches
11 stair to sacristy
12 stair to crypt
13 external altar
14 link to presbytery
15 link to convent
16 stair to street level
17 ramp to street level

The ground plan of the Cathedral explains its layout, and accounts for the structure devised to enclose the great liturgical space grouped round the central altar. Despite the position of the sanctuary one sees, from the arrangement of the seating, that the lay worshippers will not gather all round the celebrants. The main chapels, the Baptistry, and the other surrounding spaces which are used as porches, for confessionals, and as chapels yet to be furnished, are also shown. Small black squares and rectangles denote the bases of the building's concrete supports, while on the left is the plaza laid out over the Lutyens crypt.

ground floor plan

PLAN OF LIVERPOOL METROPOLITAN CATHEDRAL

The usual features of a Catholic church are to be found here: the altar, the tabernacle, the crucifix, the font, the confessionals, the statues, the side chapels – on a grander scale.

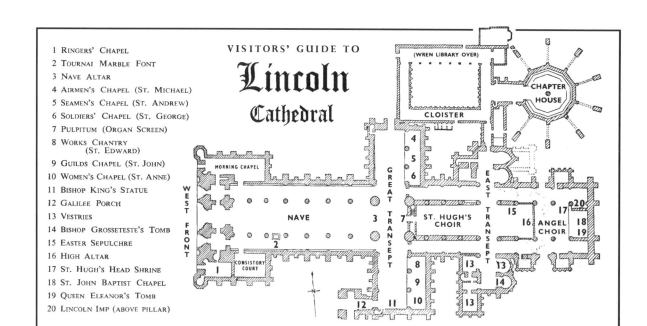

VISITORS' GUIDE TO
Lincoln
Cathedral

1 RINGERS' CHAPEL
2 TOURNAI MARBLE FONT
3 NAVE ALTAR
4 AIRMEN'S CHAPEL (ST. MICHAEL)
5 SEAMEN'S CHAPEL (ST. ANDREW)
6 SOLDIERS' CHAPEL (ST. GEORGE)
7 PULPITUM (ORGAN SCREEN)
8 WORKS CHANTRY (ST. EDWARD)
9 GUILDS CHAPEL (ST. JOHN)
10 WOMEN'S CHAPEL (ST. ANNE)
11 BISHOP KING'S STATUE
12 GALILEE PORCH
13 VESTRIES
14 BISHOP GROSSETESTE'S TOMB
15 EASTER SEPULCHRE
16 HIGH ALTAR
17 ST. HUGH'S HEAD SHRINE
18 ST. JOHN BAPTIST CHAPEL
19 QUEEN ELEANOR'S TOMB
20 LINCOLN IMP (ABOVE PILLAR)

As well as the nave and altar, note some of the other features of the cathedral: 1) The various small chapels used for services that do not need the large area of the nave. Some have special links with the community, such as the Works Chapel and the Women's Chapel; 2) The smaller choir areas, used for the regular daily worship; 3) The cloisters (covered walkways); 4) The chapterhouse. The chapter is the group of priests responsible for the life and worship of the cathedral.

Examination practice

1. What is a cathedral? Describe the main features of a typical Catholic or Anglican cathedral. (You may, if you wish, describe a cathedral known to you.)

   (10 marks)

   Write about one side of A4.

2. What place do cathedrals have in the life of the Church? (5 marks)

   Write about half a side of A4.

3. Smoking is not allowed in the restaurant of a certain cathedral. When asked, one of the clergy said, 'We put ashtrays out, but it didn't feel right, so we took them away again.'

   Why do you think he said that? Giving your reasons, say whether you agree with him. (5 marks)

   Write about half a side of A4.

PILGRIMAGE

Introduction

To find God and to get his help: this is a central aim of all pilgrims.

Since the time of Christ, Christians have visited the place of his birth, activity and death. They wanted to feel closer to God, to obtain forgiveness, and so on. The Catholic Church has always accepted pilgrimage as one way that we can get closer to God.

> Lamb of God, you take away the sins of the world: have mercy on us.
> Lamb of God, you take away the sins of the world: grant us peace.
>
> Catholic ceremony of eucharist

The Protestant Churches have generally rejected the practice of pilgrimage. They say it gives a false understanding of God. It encourages people:

- to believe that they can find God in a particular place, instead of believing that God is everywhere;
- to think they can obtain from God what they want – this is magic, not religion;
- to think that if they go to a certain place, then God is more likely to answer their prayers – this is superstition, not religion;
- to worship places, relics, statues, and special objects. This is idolatry. One of the Ten Commandments forbids this, as God is a spirit. It says:

> You shall not make for yourself an idol in the form of anything in heaven above or on the earth beneath, or in the waters below. You shall not bow down to them or worship them.
>
> Exodus 20[4]

Why people go on pilgrimage

There are several reasons why Christians go on pilgrimage:

- To visit the places where Jesus lived and taught, to experience the atmosphere, so they can deepen their understanding of Jesus' teaching and obtain a deeper understanding of God.
- To obtain a favour for themselves: to be cured of an illness or a disability; to achieve success in their job; to become more affluent; to overcome a difficulty such as shyness; and so on.
- To seek special help for someone else, perhaps one of their children, who faces a difficult situation: for example, mental illness, a bad relationship with husband or wife, childlessness, and so on.
- To atone and do penance for a particular sin that haunts them, such as ruthless treatment of people to make money, or adultery, or abuse of their spouse, and so on.
- To thank God for a blessing they believe he has given them.
- To fulfil a promise. Some pilgrims are there because they had promised to undertake the pilgrimage if God gave them what they wanted. They believe he answered their prayers.
- To experience God or become more aware of him. They feel that this is more likely in a holy place.
- To have a relaxing time and a good holiday.

> [Elijah] travelled for forty days and forty nights until he reached Horeb, the mountain of God. There he went into a cave and spent the night.
>
> 1 Kings 19[8]

particular, they have visited the place where he died and then rose from the dead.

Pilgrims go to many places in the Holy Land. They go to Cana, the place where Jesus performed his first miracle, turning water into wine. They visit Capernaum, where Jesus preached in the synagogue. They go to the hillside where Jesus preached the Sermon on the Mount, overlooking the beautiful Sea of Galilee. They pray in churches built on sites associated with events in the life of Jesus, such as the feeding of the 5000. They go down to the Jordan; many fill bottles of water, to be used at the baptism of a member of the family when they return home. They travel the road from Jericho to Jerusalem and, when the coach struggles to cope with the steep gradient, they marvel that people could make the climb to the Holy City.

Some of the sites they visit have an importance that does not relate to the ministry of Jesus. Pilgrims visit Qumran, where they see the place where the Dead Sea Scrolls were found. They take the cable car to the fortress of Masada, where about 1000 Jews resisted the might of the Roman army and, finally, committed suicide together rather than fall into the hands of their attackers. They swim in the Dead Sea and experience the strange effect of floating on its salty surface.

The most important sites to which they go are:

- **Bethlehem**, where they enter the grotto. A star on the ground marks the spot where, it is said, Jesus was born. Above it is an ancient church, the Church of the Nativity. It is bedecked with treasures, the gifts of pilgrims rich and poor, presented for over 1000 years.
- **Jerusalem**, where there are countless places associated with Jesus and his ministry. Pilgrims walk down the Mount of Olives, down the steep Palm Sunday road, wondering as they go just how the people, let alone the donkey, kept their feet without falling. They follow the Via Dolorosa, the route along which Jesus carried the cross; they stop to pray at the Stations of the Cross, places at which different moments in that journey are remembered. (For more on the Stations of the Cross see Chapter A4, *Private worship and devotions*.) Inside the Church of the Holy Sepulchre are the traditional sites of the crucifixion and of the tomb in which Jesus was buried, and which is therefore the place where he rose from the dead.

A pilgrimage to the Holy Land is an unforgettable experience. The beauty of a eucharist at an altar on the edge of the Sea of Galilee, or the sight of the spot where Jesus died on the cross, is something pilgrims have for the rest of their lives. Whenever they hear the familiar Bible stories, they see in the mind's eye the places where these things actually happened.

Palestine

The Holy Land is where Jesus walked on earth. For centuries pilgrims have longed to see the places where Jesus was born, lived, taught and performed miracles. In

Lourdes

This is a town in the south of France. It is in the Pyrenees mountains. In 1858, a teenage girl named **Marie** (who later changed her name to **Bernadette**) believed she had several visions of Mary, the mother of Jesus. Bernadette's parents were poor farmers, and she was uneducated. During one of the visions, the lady told Bernadette to dig nearby and to drink the water she would discover. Bernadette dug, and uncovered a spring, whose waters were found to have healing powers.

It was not long before people came to Lourdes, to see for themselves what was happening. Some were simply curious. Others were hoping for a miracle. Some visitors had disabilities, such as lameness, that doctors could not cure. They drank from Bernadette's stream and some were cured. Lourdes quickly became a famous pilgrimage centre.

Nowadays, millions of pilgrims, including many who are sick or disabled, visit Lourdes every year. There are special hotels for the sick and disabled. The town is full of hotels and souvenir shops.

Pilgrims visit the grotto where Bernadette had her visions. There is a statue of Mary in the grotto where Bernadette says she saw the lady. The statue is a replica of what Bernadette saw in her vision. There are many large candles burning, lit by pilgrims hoping that God will answer their prayers. There are crutches hanging in the grotto, left by those who were cured there.

People pray at the grotto, either individually or in groups. As one of their favourite prayers is the rosary, many pilgrims have rosary beads in their hands (See Chapter A4, *Private worship and devotions*, for details of the rosary.)

Pilgrims visit the place where Bernadette uncovered a stream. Some bathe in a special pool of water fed from the stream, perhaps hoping to be cured of an illness, or because they believe that Mary told Bernadette to encourage people to bathe in this water. Others drink from taps fed by the stream; and they take home bottles of stream water for friends who are ill, hoping the water might heal them.

Pilgrims pray at one of the several churches on the site. Or they make the Stations of the Cross. Or they join the many processions around the site. People sing and pray together, as they process round the site. There is one particularly impressive procession; it is candle-lit and takes place in the late evening when it is dark.

There is a peaceful and prayerful atmosphere at the pilgrimage site at Lourdes, in spite of the large number of people there.

Walsingham

This place of pilgrimage is dedicated to **Mary**, the mother of Jesus. In 1061, the lady who owned much of the land in Walsingham had a dream: in her dream she went to Nazareth and saw the home that Jesus and his parents lived in; she heard someone tell her to build a similar house in Walsingham.

Walsingham soon became the most popular pilgrimage centre in England. It was particularly popular with those who wanted to travel to Palestine, the birthplace of Christ, but could not afford it.

This all ended abruptly in the sixteenth century. Henry VIII declared himself head of the Church in England. He ordered the destruction of the buildings at Walsingham. Thus Walsingham ceased to be a place of pilgrimage.

Walsingham is now restored. The Catholic shrine was restored just before the end of the nineteenth century. The Anglican shrine was restored in 1931. Thus there are two centres of pilgrimage, one Catholic and the other Anglican. There is also an Orthodox church. The directors of the shrines think that ecumenism is important, and so they particularly aim to unite Anglican, Orthodox and Catholic Christians in their worship at their shrines. They welcome Christians from all denominations.

Today, Walsingham is a place of pilgrimage for those who seek help, peace, forgiveness, quiet, or comfort. They may find what they are looking for; they may not. The shrine is a quiet place. It is an opportunity to find tranquillity, leading to prayer and, possibly, rest.

About 250 000 people visit the shrine every year. They pray before the statue of Mary. They pray the eucharist in the main church or in the open air. They receive the sacrament of reconciliation. They spend time in quiet prayer and thought. They have discussions with other people. They pray the Stations of the Cross.

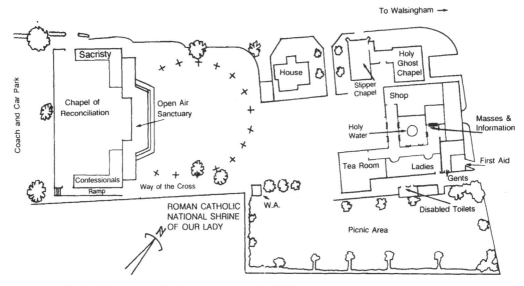

Walsingham, in eastern England, became a pilgrimage centre nearly 1000 years ago

When there are hundreds of pilgrims, there is an atmosphere of great activity and joy.

Many pilgrims walk the 'holy mile'. They take their shoes off to walk a mile from one shrine to another, just as Moses took his shoes off when he saw the burning bush, and realized he was in the presence of God. All pilgrims hope they can have a deeper sense of God. They want his help.

Effects of pilgrimage

People who go on pilgrimage may benefit in one of the following ways:

- They have a greater respect for God. They seem to be more aware of his presence – unseen, but real.
- They are less agitated and angry; they are not so selfish and frustrated if they do not get their own way. They seem to have acquired some of the gifts of the Spirit of God: gentleness, peace, kindness, patience, and so on.
- They see things differently. Before they went on pilgrimage, they may have been preoccupied with their problems. After the pilgrimage, they may understand the people who cause them aggravation; they may understand that things cannot be perfect in this world; they may understand that other people are weaker than themselves.
- They may be cured of an illness, physical or mental.
- They spend some of their time helping other people.

A pilgrim's view

If there is one place on this earth that I would wish to visit, it is Palestine or the Holy Land, because of the important role it has played in world history. It is the land of the three monotheistic faiths: Christianity, Judaism and Islam. For Christians, it is the land where Jesus Christ was born, lived, suffered and died; for the Jews it is the land of the Torah and Abraham; and for the Muslims, the land where their prophet ascended into heaven. Sad to say, for this very reason, it is and has been a land of war, strife and much suffering as Christians, Jews and Muslims struggled and fought for possession of the scenes and places sacred to them. It seems incongruous that all three who believe in one God cannot agree to allow each other to worship in the places sacred to them. On the other hand, it looks as if power and domination become more important than the holy places.

I plan to visit Palestine soon. My time there will not be more than five or six days, so I must plan my itinerary carefully. There is so much to be seen and absorbed, from Abraham to Jesus. I would wish to have much longer, but I feel if I could get a general picture of certain places then I am sure that, from the many books

on the subject, the whole history would become more alive for me.

I realize that after 2000 years it is difficult to pinpoint some of the scenes and places mentioned in the gospels. Churches, temples and mosques have been built, destroyed and rebuilt many times. For this reason the architecture would not interest me as much as the scenes from the Bible. Maybe one or two exceptions – for example, the church of the Pater Noster where the Lord's Prayer is printed on the walls in 62 languages; also, what is said to be the oldest church in the world, built by Constantine, over the cave of Bethlehem.

I would hope that my first place of pilgrimage would be Bethlehem. As the crow flies, the next place would be the Via Dolorosa, where I would follow as closely as possible the road travelled by Jesus on his way to Calvary.

Gethsemane, of course, will be a must. It is at the foot of the Mount of Olives. I understand from historians that olive trees still there are off-shoots of those under which Jesus prayed. A healthy olive tree would last for seven or eight hundred years. Here I would want to spend time in prayer and contemplation seeing in imagination Jesus praying, being arrested and being hustled out of the garden to be brought before Caiaphas.

I hope to spend at least one whole day around the Lake of Galilee in the area where Jesus began his preaching, spent most of his public life and worked most of his miracles. Sitting or walking by the lake with the synoptic gospels in hand could be an enjoyable and fruitful way of spending a few hours.

Nazareth, if time permitted, would also be a place to visit. And as we travel I know we will pass, and perhaps stop for a short look, many more places of interest both in the Old and New Testaments.

Sister Mary Clune
(a member of the Society of Saint Columban)

Examination practice

1. Give **two** reasons why some people go on pilgrimage.
   (3 marks)
   Write about six lines.

2. Select **two** places of pilgrimage. Explain what pilgrims do at these places. (10 marks)
   Write about one side of A4.

3. Pilgrims believe they benefit from their journey. In what ways might they benefit? (8 marks)
   Write about three-quarters of a side of A4.

4. 'People go on pilgrimage just for a holiday.'
   Do you agree? Give reasons for your view. Show that you have considered the opposite view. (8 marks)
   Write about three-quarters of a side of A4.

Introduction

Christmas is the time when Christians celebrate the birth of Jesus. It is celebrated by most Christians on 25 December. Orthodox Christians have Christmas on 6 January.

Bible passages relating to the birth of Jesus

Luke Chapter 1

Verses 26–38

The angel Gabriel told Mary that she would be the mother of the Son of God. Mary was afraid when she heard the angel's greeting. He told her not to fear, as God had favoured her. Her child, whom she was to call Jesus, would be the Messiah and the Son of God. When Mary asked how this could be, as she was a virgin, the angel told her that the Holy Spirit would cause her to conceive the child. Gabriel told her that her cousin Elizabeth was also pregnant (Elizabeth's child was John the Baptist). Mary's answer was, 'I am the Lord's servant. May it be to me as you have said.'

Matthew Chapter 1

Verses 18–25

Matthew describes the events from Joseph's position. When Joseph found that Mary was pregnant, his natural reaction was to end the betrothal quietly. In a vision Gabriel told him that Mary had conceived through the action of the Holy Spirit. The child was to be named Jesus (meaning, 'The Lord saves'). Thus the prophecy would be fulfilled that a virgin would bear a child who would be known as Emmanuel (meaning 'God with us'). Joseph and Mary did not have intercourse before Jesus was born.

Luke Chapter 2

Verses 1–7

A census was ordered by Caesar Augustus, the Roman Emperor. Joseph and Mary went to Bethlehem because Joseph was descended from King David, who was from Bethlehem. While they were there, Mary gave birth to Jesus. He was put in a manger because there was no room in the inn.

Verses 8–20

An angel appeared to some shepherds to tell them 'A saviour has been born to you; he is Christ, the Lord.' They would recognize the baby as one in a manger. A company of angels appeared praising God: 'Glory to God in the highest and on earth peace to men on whom his favour rests.' The shepherds went to see the child. They spread the word about what they had seen.

Verse 21

According to Jewish law, Jesus was circumcised on the eighth day after his birth.

Verses 22–39

Again according to the law, Jesus was taken to the temple at Jerusalem to be consecrated to the Lord, because he was a firstborn male. An old priest called Simeon was there. God had promised Simeon that he would live to see the Messiah. (*Messiah* and *Christ* mean the same thing; see Chapter C6, *Jesus – his identity*.) When Jesus was brought in Simeon immediately recognized him as the Messiah. He took the child in his arms and said that now he was ready to die because he had seen the Saviour. He said that Jesus would be 'a light for revelation to the Gentiles and the glory of Israel'. By this he meant that Jesus had come to show the light – to make God known – to people of every race. Simeon warned Mary that Jesus would challenge many people in Israel – and, he told her, 'a sword will pierce your own soul too'. An old prophetess, Anna, who was there at the time, also praised God for the birth of Jesus.

Verses 40–52

Luke moves on in time to when Jesus was 12. Joseph and Mary took him to Jerusalem for the Passover festival. After the festival, the whole party set off back home. After a time, Joseph and Mary realized that Jesus was not in the group and turned back to look for him. After three days they found him in the temple. He was among some learned men, who were amazed by his understanding and the things he said. Mary told him, 'Your father and I have been anxiously searching for you.' Jesus replied, 'Didn't you know that I had to be in my Father's house?' The words must have hit Mary. Though she knew he was the Son of God, she and everyone else would naturally have spoken of Joseph as his father. When Jesus said 'Father' he clearly meant God. For all that, he went back to Nazareth with them and obeyed them as a human child should.

Matthew Chapter 2

Matthew describes a totally different series of events.

Verses 1–12

Some wise men (note that Matthew does not say there were three of them, nor that they were kings) came from the east to Herod's palace in Jerusalem. These wise men were *magi*, astrologers, men who were reckoned to be able to read messages from God in the stars. They asked to see the newborn king of the Jews, whose star they had seen in the east. Herod was worried – he obviously saw this child as a threat to his throne. His own scholars told him that the scriptures said that the Messiah would be born in Bethlehem. So Herod told the wise men to find the Messiah and then to tell him where the child was, so that he too could worship him. The wise men followed the star to Bethlehem, where they worshipped Jesus. They presented gifts – gold, frankincense and myrrh. They were warned by God not to return to Herod.

Verses 13–25

In a vision Joseph was warned to escape to Egypt with Mary and the child. Herod was so desperate to kill the new king that he sent his soldiers to kill every boy in Bethlehem aged two and under. After Herod's death, Joseph and Mary brought Jesus to Nazareth, where he grew up.

Why is the birth of Jesus Christ so important to Christians?

The birth of Jesus Christ is important to Christians because they believe he is God the Son. He has always existed. His birth at Bethlehem was different from every other human birth. The baby in the manger was not a completely new being: he was God the Son taking a human nature. (The word 'incarnation' means 'in flesh' – God come in flesh.)

Christians believe that Mary gave birth to Jesus without having intercourse with Joseph. The Holy Spirit caused Mary to be pregnant. Her child was not an ordinary human child but God the Son becoming human. As the Apostles' Creed states, 'He was conceived by the power of the Holy Spirit and born of the Virgin Mary'.

An angel told Joseph that Mary had conceived a child by the Holy Spirit. The angel said to him: 'You are to give him the name Jesus, because he will save his people from their sins.' The angel said this because the name Jesus means 'The Lord saves'. Christians speak of Jesus as Saviour, the one who by his death and resurrection saves them from the power of sin.

Christians see the birth of Jesus as a wonderful expression of God's love for the human race. That is why Christmas is celebrated with such great joy.

In John's gospel the writer stresses the meaning of the birth of Jesus:

In the beginning was the Word, and the Word was with God, and the Word was God. He was with God in the beginning.

Through him all things were made; without him nothing was made that has been made . . .

The Word became flesh and made his dwelling among us. We have seen his glory, the glory of the One and Only, who came from the Father, full of grace and truth.

John 1[1–3, 14]

God so loved the world that he gave his one and only Son, that whoever believes in him shall not perish but have eternal life.

John 3[16]

Advent

- Advent is the time leading up to Christmas, a time of preparation for Christmas. It begins on the fourth Sunday before Christmas – the Sunday between 27 November and 3 December.
- 'Advent' means **approach** or **coming**. It is a time of eager looking forward. Some of the Advent customs reflect the way in which Christians look forward to the celebration of the birth of Jesus.
- Advent is also a time for thinking about his **Second Coming**. Jesus said that one day he would return to the world. When he comes again, it will be as a judge. Sometimes a preacher will give a series of sermons on the subjects of death, judgement, hell and heaven.
- Christians do not think of the Second Coming as something to be feared. They believe that it will be a glorious time for those who believe in Jesus. They will be with Jesus for ever.
- Advent is a time for thoughtful preparation and prayer. For Catholics the sacrament of reconciliation is an important part of the observance of Advent.

Epiphany

- Epiphany is the time following the 12 days of Christmas. The Feast of Epiphany itself is 6 January.
- 'Epiphany' means 'showing, revealing'. During Epiphany Christians remember times when Jesus was shown to the world as Saviour and Messiah.
- On the day itself, Christians remember the visit of the wise men (magi) to the baby Jesus. They were the first people who were not Jews to see Jesus. Their visit symbolizes the fact that Jesus was more than a Messiah for the Jewish nation; he is the Saviour of the whole world.
- The wise men would have been greatly respected. It is

significant for Christians that these great men actually **worshipped this baby**.

- The gifts are taken to have symbolic meanings. Gold is because Jesus is King; frankincense because he is God; myrrh because his death was a sacrifice.
- During the Epiphany period that follows, Christians remember how Jesus was made known to the world in many ways. For instance, they remember his baptism, with the voice from heaven saying 'This is my beloved Son'. The liturgy invites people to remember his miracles as signs of a unique power, the power of God.

Customs associated with Advent and Christmas

Advent wreath

An Advent wreath is a ring of greenery with five candles. The centre candle is white and large. The others are usually purple, the colour of penitence, for Advent. On the first Sunday in Advent and during the following week one purple candle is lit. On the second Sunday and during that week two candles are lit, three in the third week and four in the fourth. During the 12 days of Christmas all five candles are lit.

The lighted candles stand for Jesus, Light of the World. The wreath is another way of building up the excitement as Christmas draws near. 'The Lord is coming!'

Sometimes one of the candles is pink. It represents the third Sunday in Advent, the half-way point in the season.

The leaves used in the wreath are evergreen, representing the eternal life brought by Jesus.

Advent calendar

An Advent calendar is made of card, with 24 numbered windows. It is placed in a prominent position in the home. One window is opened each day.

Advent calendars are not always used to sell chocolates! They traditionally are a way of thinking about the Christmas message day by day. There may be, behind each window, a picture or a text related to the message of Christmas.

Advent candle

The Advent candle is a candle marked with the numbers 1 to 24. One number is burned away every day. The candle is another way of representing Jesus as the Light of the World.

Christingle

A Christingle is an orange with a candle set in the top. It has a red ribbon round it. Four sticks are pushed into the orange. Each has on it small sweets or raisins or something similar.

The orange represents the world. The candle stands for Jesus, the Light of the World. The ribbon is the blood of Jesus, shed for the sins of the world. The sweets and raisins stand for the fruits of the earth. The four sticks can mean the four corners of the earth. Some people say the four sticks are the four seasons of the year – spring, summer, autumn and winter.

Christingle services take place during Advent. Children come, often bringing with them envelopes of money for a particular charity – a popular one is the Children's Society. As the children present the envelopes they are each given a Christingle. The Christingles are lighted and the lights in the church are switched off. By candlelight everyone may sing a carol.

Christmas crib

A crib, a model of the stable at Bethlehem in which Jesus was born, is placed in many homes and churches at Christmas. In it are figures of Joseph and Mary, the shepherds (and perhaps a sheep), an ox and an ass. The figure of Jesus in a manger may be there when the crib is first put in place, or it may be placed in the crib during the Midnight Mass on Christmas Eve. When the 12 days of Christmas are over, at Epiphany, the figures of the shepherds may be removed and those of the wise men placed there instead.

Carol singing

Carol singing has long been a part of Christmas. Some children start singing their carols from house to house long before Christmas! More acceptable is organized singing by groups of people raising money for a church or charity.

Carol services

Carol services are very popular. Carols are sung and lessons relating to the Christmas message are read. Some congregations insist that Christmas carol services must take place during the 12 days of Christmas, after Christmas Day itself, because they say that Advent is a solemn season. Usually, however, the services are held before Christmas as people look forward to the celebration and think about the meaning of the birth of Jesus Christ.

Midnight Mass

Midnight Mass is very popular in Anglican and Catholic churches. It celebrates the birth of Jesus at the very beginning of Christmas Day. The service may begin before midnight – about 11.30 p.m. on Christmas Eve – but the Communion will not be reached until midnight has passed.

The church is fully decorated, with the crib in place. The hymns, readings and prayers all relate to the birth of Jesus Christ, the Son of God.

There are many services on the morning of Christmas Day. Those services will be for people of all ages. Carols and Christmas hymns will be sung and the account of the birth of Jesus remembered in many different ways.

Christians feel it is most important to worship on Christmas Day itself.

Christmas cards

This is not an ancient custom – the first Christmas cards in Britain date from about 150 years ago. Nowadays they come in all sorts and sizes, with many different mottoes and messages. To many Christians it is important that their Christmas cards have a Christian message for their friends.

Christmas presents

People give presents to family and friends at Christmas. Many make a point of making gifts to charities or to poor people.

As Christians give presents they may well think of the wise men bearing their gifts to the infant Jesus. But most of all they will think of Jesus himself, God's gift to the human race.

Examination guidance

1. Choose **either** Advent **or** Christmas. For the festival you have chosen, describe **two** customs used by Christians to celebrate the festival.
   Explain the reason for each custom you have chosen. (10 marks)

2. The Apostles' Creed says that Jesus was 'conceived by the power of the Holy Spirit and born of the Virgin Mary'. Why are these words from the creed important to Christians? (6 marks)

1. *I have chosen mistletoe for my first answer. Mistletoe was used by the Druids in pagan times. Nowadays it is put in houses and people kiss underneath it. It symbolizes the idea that God is love.*

   My second example is the Christmas Crib. St Francis invented the crib to help him teach people about the birth of Jesus. It is a model of the place where Jesus was born. There is Joseph and Mary, the ox and ass, the shepherds and the Wise Men. In some churches the baby is put there during the Midnight Mass. It is left in place for 12 days.

   The first answer scores nothing. As the candidate says, mistletoe was a pagan observance. If you are asked for the Christian meaning of a custom you will get not credit for anything pagan, however accurate and interesting the information may be.

   The second answer is relevant. The candidate knows what the crib is; the information about St Francis is correct. The custom of placing the Wise Men in the crib at Epiphany is not mentioned. No attempt is made to explain the custom. In part the meaning is obvious – the crib is there to help people to visualize the scene when Jesus was born. It also serves as a focus for prayer and devotion.
   (Score: 0 marks for the first example, 3 marks for the second)

2. *Christians think these words are important because Joseph was not the real father of Jesus. Mary conceived him without having sex with Joseph. That makes Jesus different from other people and special.*

   The candidate has failed to make the point that Christians believe Jesus to be the Son of God. To say that Joseph was not his natural father is not enough. It needs to be stated positively that Christians believe that Mary conceived through the power of the Holy Spirit because Jesus was God's Son.

   Better candidates would use the words 'Virgin birth' (*not* 'immaculate conception', which is something different!) They would also write about the pre-existence of Jesus – perhaps even referring to John Chapter 1. They might explain the meaning of the name of Jesus – Saviour.

   The candidate does have the basic idea of what the words mean and why they are significant.
   (Score: 2 marks out of 6)

Examination practice

1. Describe a church service that takes place at Christmas. Name a denomination in which the service would be likely to take place. (7 marks)
Write about three-quarters of a side of A4.

2. Why is Christmas an important festival for Christians? (7 marks)
Write about three-quarters of a side of A4.

3. Christmas has become very commercialized. Do you think Christians should welcome this commercialization? Give reasons for your answer, showing that you have considered more than one point of view. (6 marks)
Write about half a side of A4.

LENT; FASTING

Introduction

Lent is a period of 40 days leading up to Easter. (The 40 days are from Ash Wednesday to Holy Saturday, not counting Sundays.)

The 40 days represent the 40 days that Jesus spent fasting in the desert.

The Temptation of Jesus (Matthew 4$^{1-11}$, Luke 4$^{1-13}$)

The two accounts of the temptation of Jesus are very similar. (There is also a brief account in Mark 1$^{12-13}$.) These notes are based on Luke.

Jesus had just been baptized by John. Filled with the Holy Spirit he went into the desert. There he stayed for 40 days. Three times he was tempted by the Devil. Each time he resisted the temptation, answering the Devil with words of scripture.

- Jesus did not eat during that time and, at the end, was hungry. The Devil tempted him to turn stones into bread. Jesus answered, 'Man does not live on bread alone'. (Matthew adds the words 'but on every word that comes from the mouth of God'.)

If Jesus had done what the Devil said, he would have made life much easier for himself, in a way that an ordinary human being could not. He had come to offer his own perfect human life as a sacrifice for sin. If he used his divine power to make life easier, he would not be leading a normal human life.

When Jesus said, 'Man does not live on bread alone' he didn't just mean 'survive'. He meant 'live life to the full'.

- The Devil took Jesus to the top of a high mountain and showed him all the kingdoms of the world. He offered them all to Jesus if he would worship him. Jesus replied, 'Worship only God'.

Whether Jesus was actually transported to a mountain or whether all this was in the imagination, we cannot tell. Again, Jesus answered with words of scripture. Again, the temptation was about something vital to Jesus' ministry. He had come not just to draw people to him but to lead them to God.

- The Devil took him (again, perhaps in imagination) to the highest point of the temple in Jerusalem. 'Throw yourself down,' he says, adding words of scripture himself this time:

> 'He will command his angels concerning you to guard you carefully; they will lift you up in their hands, so that you will not strike your foot against a stone.'

Jesus answered with a firm, 'Do not put the Lord your God to the test'.

If Jesus had descended safely from the temple no doubt people would have flocked to him as a great wonder-worker. Yet again, the temptation hit at something central to his mission. There were times during his ministry when people were attracted to him because they wanted to see miracles and wonders. Jesus did not want to be admired as a wonder-worker. He wanted to be accepted as Saviour and Lord.

(Note that Matthew has the second and third temptations in reverse order.)

Some Christians do not believe that the Devil physically

appeared to Jesus. They believe that the Devil is a symbol of temptation.

The way Christians keep Lent

Although the 40 days of Lent relate to the 40 days Jesus spent in the desert, the season of Lent is above all a time of preparation for Easter. Lent began as a time when adults preparing for admission to the Church disciplined themselves strictly before being baptized during the Easter liturgy.

In time it was seen as good for all Christians to prepare for Easter in this way.

Lent is a time for

- **repentance**. Catholics prepare for Lent by means of the sacrament of reconciliation. The day before Lent begins is called **Shrove Tuesday**. It gets its name from the word 'shrive', an old English word that means 'to hear confession and grant absolution'.
- **simple worship**. In many churches there are no flowers or other decorations during Lent. The hymns are more subdued. In this way the contrast between the solemn time of preparation and the joy of Easter is the more striking.
- **self-discipline**. Many Christians make and keep a Lent rule, which has one or more of the following:
  - Giving up a pleasure, harmless in itself, as a discipline. For instance, a person may give up sugar in tea, or biscuits. Any money saved is given to a charity.
  - Giving up a sin, such as swearing or losing one's temper. Of course, when at the end of Lent a person starts eating biscuits again, he or she doesn't feel free to swear as much as he likes! The aim is to get rid of the sin once and for all. The fact that a pleasure is given up for Lent is a constant reminder to try to get rid of the sin. Every time a person wants a biscuit, it is a reminder that he or she must try not to swear.
  - Taking on an extra spiritual task. A Christian might decide to spend more time in worship, prayer or Bible reading during Lent. Some churches have weekly discussion groups or prayer meetings. One Lenten service is the Stations of the Cross. (See Chapter A4, *Private worship and devotions*.)
  - Taking on some kind, neighbourly act for the six weeks of Lent. For instance, Lent comes at the right time of year for helping an elderly neighbour get his or her garden ready for the summer.

Ash Wednesday

Lent begins with repentance for sin and a resolve to turn to a better way of life.

On Ash Wednesday in Catholic and some Anglican churches the sign of the cross is made in ash on the foreheads of the worshippers. In the Bible we are told of people 'repenting in sackcloth and ashes'. The ash is placed on each person's forehead with words such as

> 'Remember that you are dust, and to dust you shall return. Turn away from evil and follow Christ.'

Examination practice

1. Give an account of the temptations of Jesus.

   (10 marks)

   Write about one side of A4, making sure that you give a clear account of each temptation and the way in which Jesus replied to the Devil.

2. Describe **two** ways in which some Christians keep Lent. Explain why they do so. (8 marks)

   Write about three-quarters of a side of A4.

Introduction

Holy Week is the last week in Lent. It ends at Easter.

During Holy Week Christians remember the events leading up to the death and burial of Jesus. The main days in Holy Week are:

- Palm Sunday
- Maundy Thursday (Holy Thursday)
- Good Friday
- Holy Saturday.

The ceremonies of Holy Saturday are described in Chapter A14, *Easter*.

Palm Sunday

Palm Sunday marks the day when Jesus rode into Jerusalem on a donkey. Crowds of people greeted him. They threw branches from the nearby palm trees on the road and laid their clothes on the ground for him to ride over them. They shouted 'Hosanna!', which means 'save now!'

- In the Old Testament a prophet, Zechariah, foretold that the Messiah would come, riding on a donkey. Jesus knew that prophecy and so did the people.
- A Roman emperor or general might ride in triumph into a city. Flowers and garlands might be thrown in his path. The people were welcoming Jesus in triumph, as a mighty leader.

On Palm Sunday in many Catholic and Anglican churches there is a procession. The procession may begin a short distance away and go to the church. Palm branches or crosses may be carried; palm leaves folded in the shape of a cross may be distributed to the congregation. The service is an act of praise and welcome to Christ the King.

Jesus rode into Jerusalem knowing that he was going to his death. The Palm Sunday service also reminds the worshippers of the cross of Jesus. The kingship of Jesus is seen in the power of his love, shown in his death on the cross. His kingship is also shown in his victory over the power of sin and death. Palm Sunday points forward to Good Friday and Easter Day.

Maundy Thursday (Holy Thursday)

Maundy Thursday marks the day of the Last Supper.

The word 'Maundy' comes from the first word of the traditional Latin anthem for the day, *Mandatum novum do vobis*, which means 'A new commandment I give you'. The new commandment that Jesus gave to his disciples at the Last Supper was 'Love one another as I have loved you'.

At the Last Supper Jesus washed the feet of the disciples. This would normally have been a task for a servant, a slave. Peter protested that Jesus should not be washing his feet, but Jesus insisted. When Jesus had finished he said:

> Do you understand what I have done for you? You call me 'Master' and 'Lord', and rightly so, for that is what I am. Then if I, your Lord and Master, have washed your feet, you ought also to wash one another's feet. I have set you an example: you are to do as I have done for you.
>
> John 13[12–15]

At the Maundy Thursday eucharist in Catholic and some Anglican churches the priest washes the feet of 12 members of the congregation. He does this to remind them that they should be ready to serve others, as Jesus did.

At the Last Supper Jesus took bread, blessed it, broke it and gave it to the disciples, saying 'This is my body'. Later he took a cup of wine, blessed it and gave it to them saying, 'This is my blood'. Christians remember the Last Supper at every eucharist. They remember the Last Supper especially strongly on Maundy Thursday because it was on the Thursday, the day before he was crucified, that Jesus first spoke these words.

After the Last Supper Jesus took his disciples into the Garden of Gethsemane. There he spent three hours in prayer. Judas brought the soldiers to arrest Jesus. His disciples left him and ran away. In some churches the Maundy Thursday eucharist ends abruptly, without a blessing, to represent the disciples running away. In other churches there is a Watch by the Cross. People stay after the eucharist and pray silently, as if watching with Jesus. The Watch may continue until midnight or even until the time for the Good Friday service. If the Watch is to last so long, different people will volunteer to be there at certain times, so the Watch is never broken; others will join them as and when they can.

Good Friday

Good Friday is the most solemn day in the Christian Year. It is the day when Christians remember the crucifixion of Jesus. They think of the way in which he was tried, beaten, crucified and buried.

Christians do not remember the crucifixion as a humiliating defeat. Jesus could have avoided his fate, either by using his divine power or simply by proving how false were the accusations against him. He could have avoided death if he had not challenged the religious leaders by riding into Jerusalem on the Sunday and by his teaching in the temple during that week. Instead, Jesus went to his death, knowingly and deliberately. By his death he paid the penalty for all the sins of the human race. He showed the love of God by his sacrifice of himself on the cross.

So Christians think of Jesus' crucifixion as a victory over the power of sin and a self-sacrifice for all who believe in him.

Good Friday is observed in different ways by different denominations.

- In many churches all decorations, statues and pictures are removed to show that Good Friday is a most holy, solemn day.
- In many places the denominations join together for an act of witness. For instance, Christians from all denominations may meet at a given place near a town centre and walk together to a central place in the town. At the front there is often someone carrying a huge cross, just as Jesus carried his own cross. When they reach their destination there is an act of worship in which Christians of all denominations join.
- In Catholic and some Anglican churches there is a special liturgy for Good Friday. It includes readings from scripture, especially an account of the passion and crucifixion of Jesus from John's gospel. This gospel is sometimes read or even acted in a dramatized form. Then a wooden cross is placed in front of the

congregation. People may come individually to kiss the cross. While the cross is in place there are prayers of adoration and intercession – showing that Christians can pray only because Jesus sacrificed himself on the cross.
- Many churches have a service on Good Friday to remember the crucifixion. The service is designed to help the worshippers think deeply about the meaning of the crucifixion through hymns, readings, preaching and prayer. In some churches, mainly Anglican, there will be a service lasting three hours, from midday to 3 p.m. The three hours may be spent mainly in readings and preaching; there may also be part of the Good Friday liturgy.
- In the Orthodox Church there is a liturgy for Good Friday evening. It concentrates on the burial of Jesus. An icon of Christ wrapped in burial clothes is brought into the church. The worshippers each come and kiss the figure as an act of reverence.

Examination guidance

The first important point about answering a question on Holy Week is to be sure that whatever you write about is indeed in Holy Week. No credit would be given for a response describing the liturgy for Ash Wednesday. Holy Saturday should be accepted, though of course the liturgy runs over into Easter Day. Responses covering Palm Sunday, Maundy Thursday and Good Friday are completely acceptable.

Candidates should know the events that are remembered on each day. They should be able to give examples of special liturgies or other ceremonies and the reasons for them.

Examination practice

1. Describe what happened when Jesus rode into Jerusalem on a donkey. Why did the people welcome him so excitedly? (11 marks)
   Write about three-quarters of a side of A4. Make sure you answer the second part of the question properly.

2. Why is Good Friday so important to Christians? Describe **one** way in which the worship on that day might be different from other days. (9 marks)
   Write about three-quarters of a side of A4. At least 6 of the marks will be for the first part of the question.

Introduction

Easter Day celebrates the resurrection of Jesus. It is the greatest festival of the Christian year. So central is the resurrection to Christianity that Christians keep Sunday as their weekly holy day. (See Chapter E29, *The Ten Commandments*.)

Most Christians believe that Jesus really died and really rose again. The Apostles' Creed stresses that he 'was crucified, dead and buried'. As evidence they refer to the following:

- The tomb (grave) was empty. The body had gone from the place of burial.
- The dead body was never produced.
- There were many eye-witnesses who insisted that Jesus was alive. Each of the gospels names people who had seen him. Luke and John in particular give long accounts of what happened when Jesus did appear.
- His followers did not believe he had risen until they had seen him for themselves. Once they had seen him, nothing could shake their belief that he had risen. Many of them were put to death because they refused to say that he had not risen. They would not have been prepared to die for something they knew to be a lie.

A few Christians do not think it is necessary to believe that Jesus did physically rise. They think of the accounts of the resurrection as symbols of Jesus' being always present with those who believe in him. Death was not the end of Jesus. The resurrection was a spiritual event, not a physical one.

The resurrection of Jesus is so important to Christians because:

- By dying and rising again Jesus proved that there is something after death. If he was dead on the Friday and alive on the Sunday he must have existed on the Saturday.
- Jesus himself told his followers that he would go and then return.
- Jesus came to overcome sin and death. The resurrection is the sign that the power of Jesus was stronger than the power of death.

Christians see the resurrection as relevant to them because

- Jesus died and rose again to take away human sin. Therefore their sins can be forgiven.
- Jesus said that those who believe in him could have eternal life. He was going to prepare a place for them. Therefore Christians believe that their own loved ones

who have died will be with God, if they accepted Jesus as Saviour and Lord. They also believe that when they die they too will be with him.

Celebrating Easter

Easter is a celebration of new life.

- The worship of Easter Day is joyful, with hymns, prayers and readings to mark the resurrection. Churches are decorated with flowers and fresh greenery. Often there is an Easter garden, a model of the tomb in which Jesus was buried.
- In some places there is a dawn service on Easter Day, remembering how the women came at first light and found the empty tomb.
- Eggs are symbols of new life. As a chick breaks out of an egg, so Jesus came out of the tomb. After the Easter liturgy Orthodox Christians break their decorated hardboiled eggs by knocking them against each other – symbolizing Jesus Christ breaking out of the tomb.

Easter liturgies

The Easter liturgies celebrate the resurrection of Jesus from the dead. The Catholic, Anglican and Orthodox liturgies make much of the idea of Jesus as the Light of the World.

In many **Catholic** and **Anglican** churches the Easter Vigil liturgy is celebrated during the hours of darkness – sometimes during the evening of Holy Saturday, often at midnight, sometimes just before dawn. The service begins in darkness, symbolizing the darkness of the tomb. Sometimes the worshippers are outside the church as the ceremony begins. A light is struck, representing the moment of resurrection.

The priest takes the Easter candle (sometimes called the paschal candle). It is a large candle, with a number of special features:

- a cross, the sign of Christ;
- the letters alpha and omega, the first and last letters of the Greek alphabet, representing Jesus as the beginning and the end of all things;
- the date, for Jesus, Lord of all time;
- five small brass knobs, representing the five wounds in the body of Jesus.

The candle symbolizes the risen Christ. It is lit throughout the Easter season, and often at all baptisms and funerals as well. Baptism is the beginning of the Christian life; at a

funeral Christians pray that the person departed has begun a new life with Jesus.

The Easter candle is lit with the newly struck light. It is carried into the church. Three times the priest stops and says 'Christ our Light' (Catholic) or 'The Light of Christ' (Anglican). Each time the congregation reply 'Thanks be to God'. The candle is taken to a prominent place in the church. As it is carried through the church, light from it is passed around as each worshipper lights his or her candle. The passing of the light represents the light of the gospel, the news of the resurrection, being taken to all parts of the world.

The *Exultet* anthem is said or sung, calling Christians to rejoice and to proclaim the resurrection of Jesus. A series of lessons are read, recalling the great acts of God as told in the Old Testament.

During the liturgy the congregation renew the vows made at their baptisms. It is a reminder that baptism vows are made for life. In the early church, baptisms always took place at Easter. Christians believe that they are baptized into the death of Jesus. When they are baptized they are born again; they begin a new life in Jesus. That is why they remember their baptisms at Easter.

The liturgy ends with the eucharist of Easter.

The **Orthodox** liturgy is very similar to that used by Catholics and Anglicans. As the women came to the darkened tomb, so the worshippers gather outside the darkened church. The priest carries a lighted candle, from which everyone lights their smaller candles. The church is left in darkness while the candlelit procession makes its way round the church. At midnight the priest throws open the church door with the words 'Christ is risen'. The people give the joyful reply, 'He is risen indeed'. They go together into the church for the liturgy celebrating the resurrection. The liturgy for Easter is full of joy. The first Bible readings recall God's great acts throughout the centuries before the coming of Jesus Christ. The readings from the New Testament proclaim the great news of the resurrection of Jesus. The liturgy reaches its climax when the congregation receive in Communion the body and blood of the risen Lord.

Alleluia

Alleluia means 'Praise the Lord'. The word is often used in Christian worship as an outburst of praise and joy. An Alleluia chant is used before the gospel at a Catholic Mass (except during Lent). The word 'Alleluia' is particularly used in celebrating the resurrection of Jesus.

Examination guidance

1. What do Christians celebrate at Easter? Why is Easter so important to them? (7 marks)

2. Describe how Easter is celebrated by **either** Catholics **or** Orthodox. (8 marks)

3. In many countries Easter is a holiday time. Do you think it is good that many holidays are religious festivals? (5 marks)

1. At Easter Christians celebrate the resurrection of Jesus. The resurrection is important to them because they see it as a proof that Jesus did come back to life after he was crucified. His coming back proves that he has broken the power that sin and death had over people. Christians believe that when they die there is another life for them, with Jesus in heaven.

Some Christians find it hard to believe the resurrection, in the sense that Jesus' body actually came to life again. They believe that even though he was crucified he is still alive and he is with Christians in the world today.

The candidate has taken into account the fact that different Christians have different opinions about the resurrection. In fact, what he says about those with doubts – ' They believe that even though he was crucified he is still alive and he is with Christians in the world today' – would also be true of those who take the Bible literally. A number of points are raised in a sensible way.

(Score: 5 marks out of 7)

2. I have chosen the Catholic celebration. They come to the church in the dark. This is because the tomb was dark when Jesus was buried there. The priest strikes a light; this is for when Jesus came back to life. The priest takes the Easter Candle. The candle represents the risen Jesus. It has on it a cross, the letters Alpha and Omega (for Jesus the beginning and end of everything like the letters are the beginning and end of the Greek alphabet), brass studs for the five wounds of Jesus and the date (year). He blesses the candle and lights it from the light he has struck.

    He carries the candle into the church. All the people have little candles and light theirs from his. As he goes he calls out 'Christ our Light' and people answer each time 'Thanks be to God'.

    The candle is placed in a large candlestand. The priest sings a long anthem about Jesus rising from the dead. There are some readings from the Old Testament.

    Next, the people are asked to renew their baptismal vows. That means they say again the promises their parents and godparents made when they were baptized.

    Then there is the eucharist for Easter. It is like any other eucharist but the hymns and prayers are for Easter. A lot of them have 'Alleluia' in. Alleluia means 'Praise the Lord.' It is said a lot at Easter.

The candidate has given a full response. A large range of points are clearly made. The writer shows understanding of the reasons behind many of the ceremonies. There are small points which could be improved: for instance, no reason is given for the Old Testament readings. Even then, it would be a harsh examiner who did not give full marks.
(Score: 8 marks out of 8)

3. Yes, I think it is a good thing that Easter is a holiday. It means people can go to church if they want to. Also, it means that everyone remembers Easter. It's the same with Christmas. If Easter wasn't a holiday I would forget when it was.

    I know some people are not Christians and aren't interested in Easter. Even then, it is usually a good time to have a holiday. It is spring and the sun sometimes shines. It doesn't always shine at Easter! Anyway, it is as good a time as any for people who are not Christians. Having a holiday reminds everyone of Jesus and how he died and rose again.

    Holidays are for celebrating special things. Jesus rising from being dead is more special than anything else to Christians.

Once again, a good effort by this candidate. A number of points are made sensibly. The last point, which shows that the candidate knows that the resurrection is important to Christians, is a very good one.
(Score: 4 marks out of 5)

Examination practice

1. Describe **one** religious ceremony associated with Easter and explain its meaning.   (8 marks)
    Write about three-quarters of a side of A4.

2. Some Christians do not think it is necessary to believe that Jesus actually did rise bodily from the grave. Why do they hold this opinion? Do you think they can still be counted as Christians?   (8 marks)
    Write about three-quarters of a side of A4.

Ascension

This is the day when Christians remember the Ascension of Jesus – when he left the disciples for the last time. (See the notes on Acts 1^{9-11} in Chapter C22, *The Acts of the Apostles – main themes*.)

Reasons why the event is important to Christians are:

* Jesus returns to heaven.
* Jesus returns to be in glory with God the Father.
* Jesus, Son of God, having taken human nature, does not leave it behind; he returns to heaven as man as well as God – so a human person is seen to be in heaven.

It was important to people living in the first century that Jesus went up until they could not see him any longer. They believed in heaven above the earth and hell beneath.

In the twentieth century we know that the world is round. Christians no longer think of heaven as 'up there' and hell as 'down there'. They do not think of heaven and hell as set places somewhere in the universe, however distant. They think of heaven as being with God, hell as being cut off from God.

Catholics are expected to mark the day by celebrating the eucharist. The readings and prayers are specially chosen for Ascension Day.

Pentecost (also known as Whitsun)

Pentecost celebrates the coming of the Holy Spirit to the disciples. The festival also celebrates the presence of the Holy Spirit in the Church ever since. The hymns, prayers and readings used at the eucharist and at other services are chosen because they relate to the coming of the Holy Spirit to the apostles and, even more, his presence in the Church today.

(For a description of the coming of the Spirit at Pentecost see the notes on Acts 2 in Chapter C22, *The Acts of the Apostles – main themes*. On the Spirit in the Church today see Chapter C5, *God – the Holy Spirit*.)

Christians believe that the Holy Spirit is with them, to give them strength and guidance for their everyday lives and for their Christian witness and mission. It is vital to them that the Holy Spirit is with them.

The Apostles told everyone about their faith and did everything in their power to bring others to Christ. Christians today believe they should let the world know about the gospel of Jesus Christ.

One custom associated with Whitsun is the **Whit Walks**,

a tradition in the north of England. Thousands of Christians, of all ages, meet together and march through the town or city. Sunday Schools and organizations such as the Scouts or Guides carry their banners and standards. Whatever the weather, the Whit Walk goes on. Thousands more people line the streets to watch the walk. The procession is an act of witness, letting everyone know that they are followers of Jesus Christ and members of the Church.

Christians taking part in a Whit Walk in Manchester

When Whit Week was a holiday the processions took place during that week, especially on the bank holiday, Whit Monday. Nowadays many of the processions are on the Spring Bank Holiday Monday, though some take place on Saturdays two or three weeks later.

Harvest thanksgiving

In every society the bringing in of the harvest is something to celebrate. Everyone needs food, so everyone needs a good harvest. Christians thank God for the harvest.

Crops grow because of the way God created the world. He arranged the seasons. Farmers plan confidently because they know they can rely on nature. There may be good years and not such good years, but they know there will be a harvest.

> As long as the earth endures,
> seedtime and harvest,
> cold and heat,
> summer and winter,
> day and night
> will never cease.
>
> Genesis 8^{22}
>
> All good gifts around us,
>   Are sent from heaven above,
> Then thank the Lord, O thank the Lord,
>   For all his love.
>
> From the Harvest hymn
> 'We plough the fields and scatter', M. Claudius

At a harvest thanksgiving Christians bring gifts of food and flowers to decorate the church. The gifts are a sign of their gratitude to God. These gifts are later given to people in need. That need may be:

- **a need for food**. The gifts from an area where people have all they need may be taken to an area where there is great poverty.
- **a need to be loved**. The fact that someone has thought of them to bring them a gift can be very moving to an elderly or sick person.

Christians in wealthy countries realize that people in some other countries – especially in the Third World – suffer from lack of food and other essentials. At a harvest thanksgiving prayers are said for the starving and the hungry. Gifts of money may be sent to Christian Aid, Cafod or some other agency that works to relieve suffering in the poorest communities.

While Christians thank God for the harvest, they think also of another harvest – the harvest of souls that will come at the end of the world. The idea comes from the words of Jesus himself, as shown in the way he explained the meanings of two of his parables.

- The harvest symbolizes a harvest of souls, people brought into the kingdom by the witness and teaching of those who follow Jesus. Thus Christians often think of the mission of the Church at Harvest.

> Others, like seed sown on good soil, hear the word, accept it, and produce a crop – thirty, sixty or even a hundred times what was sown.
>
> The parable of the sower (Mark 4^{20})

- The harvest symbolizes the final harvest of souls, which will come at the Last Judgement.

> The one who sowed the good seed is the Son of Man. The field is the world and the good seed stands for the sons of the kingdom. The weeds are the sons of the

evil one. . . The Son of Man will send out his angels and they will weed out of his kingdom everything that causes sin and all that do evil.
>
> The parable of the weeds (Matthew 13$^{36-43}$)

Three festivals included in the EdExcel Catholic syllabus

Good Shepherd Sunday (the fourth Sunday of Easter)

The readings and special prayers for the day focus on the theme of Jesus the Good Shepherd. The idea of Jesus as a shepherd is one that gives great comfort and reassurance to many believers.

> The Lord's my shepherd; I'll not want.
>   He makes me down to lie
> In pastures green. He leadeth me
>   The quiet waters by.
>
> Psalm 23, adapted by
> W. Whittingham and others
>
> Jesus said, 'I am the good shepherd; I know my sheep and my sheep know me – just as the Father knows me and I know the Father – and I lay down my life for the sheep'.
>
> John 10$^{14-15}$

Corpus Christi (the Thursday that falls 11 days after Pentecost)

The words *Corpus Christi* mean 'The Body of Christ'. The festival celebrates the giving to the human race of the sacrament of the eucharist, the Holy Communion.

The sacrament of the eucharist is the main act of worship for Catholics. In the eucharist they receive the body and blood of the risen Jesus. On Corpus Christi they focus their thoughts on the sacrament itself and its meaning, and thank God for the blessings they receive when they receive the body and blood of Christ. (See Chapter A1, *Eucharist (Holy Communion, Mass)*.)

The night on which the Last Supper took place was the night before the crucifixion. The Last Supper, when the first eucharist took place, is therefore celebrated every Holy Thursday. However, there are other ceremonies on Holy Thursday, as on the other days in Holy Week. So that Catholics can turn their thoughts and prayers to the wonder of the sacrament without being distracted by other ceremonies, they observe Corpus Christi as a separate festival.

Christ the King (Sunday before Advent Sunday, the last Sunday of the Christian Year)

This Sunday celebrates the kingship of Jesus Christ. It is a joyful, triumphant festival.

There are many places in the Bible where the kingship of God is stressed. In particular, note Jesus' teaching about the Kingdom of God.

Young people are given a special place in many churches on the festival of Christ the King. Young people may well take some part in the liturgy. There may be a special collection for youth work.

Examination practice

1. Give an account of the ascension of Jesus. Why is the ascension important to Christians?

    (8 marks)

    Write about three-quarters of a side of A4.

2. Describe a way in which some Christians celebrate Pentecost (Whitsun). Why do they celebrate in this way? (7 marks)
    Write about half a side of A4.

3. Harvest festivals are very popular occasions. Why do you think this is so? (5 marks)
    Write about half a side of A4.

SACRAMENTS: LITURGICAL WORSHIP 16

How many sacraments?

Catholic and Orthodox Christians have seven sacraments:

- baptism
- confirmation
- eucharist (mass)
- penance (reconciliation)
- marriage
- orders
- anointing of the sick.

Most Protestant Churches (for example, Baptists, Presbyterians, Methodists, United Reformed Church) have two sacraments. These Churches say that, according to the gospels, Jesus started two sacraments, and only two sacraments:

- baptism
- eucharist (Lord's Supper).

However, some Christian groups do not believe in any sacraments. For instance, the Salvation Army believes that outward symbols are unimportant and unnecessary – what matters is our relationship with God, within the heart. And the Society of Friends (Quakers) believes that all of life is a sacrament, so anything can be a symbol of God.

What are sacraments?

When Christians celebrate the sacraments they believe, and they may feel, that Christ and God are present. Thus we can describe the sacraments as 'doors to the sacred'. They are symbols of something that is sacred and mysterious. The word used by Orthodox Christians is not sacraments, but 'mysteries'. The word 'mysteries' was translated into Latin as *sacramenta*, and then into English as 'sacraments'.

> The eucharist is called a mystery because what we believe is not the same as what we see. We see one thing and believe another.
>
> John Chrysostom

The primary Christian belief is that there is a God, whom we cannot see or hear – at least, not directly or literally. Yet Christians say they experience God in this life. One way they can do this is through the sacraments.

Celebrating the sacraments is the main form of worship in the Catholic, Orthodox and Anglican Churches.

Many Protestant Christians (such as Presbyterians, Baptists and the United Reformed Church) put a greater emphasis on worship without sacraments. They have readings from the Bible, sermons, hymns and prayers – without sacramental signs. They follow the teaching of Calvin (one of the leaders of the Protestant Reformation), who said that worship should be centred on the word of God.

Liturgy

The word 'liturgy' refers to the formal worship of Christians. When they meet together to pray to God, they may use words and actions that their leaders have fixed. This is called **liturgy**. The priest leading the worship does not decide what the prayers and actions will be. These have already been decided by the Church leaders, the bishops.

Liturgy is important in the Catholic, Orthodox and Anglican Churches. Their main liturgical acts are the sacraments. In each sacrament Christians celebrate the death and resurrection of Christ, as they believe it is through the death and resurrection of Christ that they get to God.

For a summary of the prayers and actions in each sacrament, see the individual chapters on the seven sacraments: D1, *Baptism*; D2, *Infant baptism*; D4, *Confirmation*; A1, *Eucharist (Holy Communion, Mass)*; A17, *Reconciliation (penance, confession)*; E5, *Marriage ceremony*; D12, *Bishops, priests, deacons: Orders*; A18, *Anointing of the sick*.)

The Catholic bishops at the Second Vatican Council (which took place in the 1960s) said:

> the liturgy is the summit towards which the activity of the Church is directed . . . all who are made sons of God by faith and baptism should come together to praise God in the midst of his Church, to take part in the sacrifice and to eat the Lord's Supper.

So the Catholic bishops said that the eucharist is the central act of liturgical worship. Anglican and Orthodox Christians have the same view. Indeed, Orthodox Christians usually use the word 'liturgy' to describe the celebration of just the eucharist.

Yet not all Christians have liturgy. Some prefer not to have fixed prayers or actions when they meet to pray. The minister leading the worship decides what the prayers and actions will be, though there is usually the same pattern for the service each week. (For information about such non-liturgical worship, see Chapter A2, *Collective worship, non-liturgical*.)

Private worship

Christians pray collectively, but they also pray privately. Private worship is not liturgical worship, as the Church leaders have not fixed what happens. In private worship each individual decides what to do and say:

- whether to stand, sit, kneel or lie down;
- how long the prayer will last;
- whether to speak with God in a formal or in a familiar way;
- what words to use, if any (some Christians prefer to enjoy the company of God without talking to him).

(For further information, see Chapter A4, *Private worship and devotions*.)

Signs and symbols

In each sacrament there is a sign (or symbol) indicating that Christ and God are present. A sign or symbol is something that we can see or hear: it indicates that God – whom we cannot see or hear – is present. There are many signs in each of the sacraments. Catholics believe that each sacrament has some signs that are more important than the other signs; it is these signs that make Christ and God present. They are called 'effective signs' in the following table.

Sacrament	Effective sign, which is seen	Effective sign, which is heard
Baptism	Water that is poured over the head of the baptized person	The words of baptism: 'I baptize you in the name of the Father, the Son and the Holy Spirit.'
Confirmation	When the bishop (a) stretches his hands over the head of the candidate (b) puts chrism oil on the forehead of the candidate (optional in the Anglican rite)	The words of confirmation: 'Be sealed with the gift of the Spirit'
Eucharist (Holy Communion, Mass)	Bread and wine	The words of consecration: 'This is my body given for you . . . This is the cup of my blood . . .'
Penance (Reconciliation Forgiveness)		(a) the penitent: – expresses regret for having sinned – confesses sins – intends to make up for sins committed;

(b) the priest's words of absolution: e.g. 'May the God who forgave Peter when he wept bitterly, who forgave the prostitute when she washed his feet with her tears, forgive you . . .'

Anointing of the sick	Anointing of the sick person's forehead and hands	The words of anointing: 'May the Lord in his love and mercy help you with the grace of the Holy Spirit' (while anointing forehead) and 'May the Lord who frees you from sin save you and raise you up' (while anointing hands).
Orders	When the bishop stretches out his hands over the person to be ordained	A special prayer, for example: '. . . Almighty Father, grant to this servant of yours the dignity of the priesthood. Renew within him the spirit of holiness . . . '
Marriage		The consenting words of the husband and wife; e.g. 'I . . . do take you to be my lawful wedded husband/wife, to have and to hold from this day forward ...'

Sacraments of initiation

The first three sacraments (baptism, eucharist, confirmation) are sacraments of initiation. They are the foundation of Christian living. These sacraments enable someone to:

- receive the risen life of Christ;
- become part of God;
- become a full member of the Church;
- become strengthened to follow Christ's example to care for other people;
- receive the Spirit of God;
- make the journey through this life to God in the next life.

In the sacraments of initiation, Christians believe they receive Christ, so they can become like him. He was a priest, a prophet and a king.

Christ was a priest. In his life on earth he offered himself to God, a sort of sacrifice: he always did what God wanted him to do. Christians should follow his example.

Christ was a prophet. As he knew God, he could speak about God with authority. And he had the courage to speak about God, even though this displeased the religious leaders. This cost him his life. Christians should be able to follow his example.

Christ was a king. He started the kingdom of God. He told his disciples to baptize others to bring them into the kingdom of God. Thus Christians should bring others into the kingdom of God.

Importance of the sacraments

The sacraments usually come at critical moments in our life – birth, growing up, failure, success, marriage, illness, death. It is at such times that we often turn to God. We ask him to help us, to comfort us, to guide us, to give us hope, to explain things to us, and so on.

The sacraments of baptism and the eucharist are more important than the other five sacraments. Baptism is important because it is the start of Christian life and the first of the sacraments. The eucharist is important because it is Christians' main way of worshipping God; and it is their chief way of celebrating the presence of the risen Christ in their lives. Most Christians receive this sacrament frequently.

The sacraments of reconciliation and anointing of the sick are sacraments of healing. They aim to forgive, to mend broken relationships, to restore health of body and mind, and to bring peace where there is stress and conflict.

The sacrament of marriage and the sacrament of ordination are sacraments of mission in the Church. They enable us to help others, and they encourage us to contribute to the growth of the Church.

Baptism is the first sacrament; we cannot receive any other sacrament until we are baptized. Why? Because the sacraments are for members of the Church, and by baptism we become members of the Church.

Christians can receive some sacraments only once: baptism, confirmation, and orders. They can receive the other sacraments more than once.

The eucharist is the sacrament most often received by Christians. Catholics call it the sacrament of sacraments.

Thus we can see that Christians believe the sacraments are important, for several reasons – they

- make God and Christ present;
- unite people in the Church;
- bring believers together to celebrate the sacraments;
- were started by Jesus;
- strengthen a Christian to become a better person;
- help a Christian to understand life better;
- bring comfort, reassurance, healing and forgiveness;
- foster a sense of purpose and direction in life.

> He who was visible as our redeemer has now passed into the sacraments.
>
> Pope Leo the Great

Definitions of a sacrament

We should have understood by now that there is more than one definition of the word 'sacrament'. Here are some examples. All of them are correct. The first three are short.

- Sacraments are signs of the sacred.
- Sacraments are signs that God is present; they give God's help.

- 'Sacraments are signs and instruments by which the Holy Spirit spreads the grace of Christ the head throughout the Church, which is his Body.' (Catholic Catechism)
- Sacraments are for all to see; they are public. Yet they are also about what is unseen. They bring God closer to us, and they bring us closer to God. They make us members of God's family: for instance, baptism, eucharist and confirmation. They help us along in life: for instance, marriage and ordination. They help us in times of trouble: anointing of the sick. They bring God's forgiveness for our sins: reconciliation.
- 'The purpose of the sacraments is to sanctify [people], to build up the Body of Christ, and, finally, to give worship to God. Because they are signs they also instruct. They not only presuppose faith, but by words and objects they also nourish, strengthen and express it. That is why they are called sacraments of faith.' (Catholic bishops at Second Vatican Council)
- 'Sacraments were instituted by Christ. As actions of Christ and of the Church, they are signs and means by which faith is expressed, worship is offered to God, and our sanctification is brought about. Thus they contribute in the most effective manner to establishing, strengthening and manifesting ecclesiastical communion.' (Catholic code of Canon Law)

Which of these definitions makes most sense to you? Learn one short definition and one long definition. Make sure you understand them.

Examination guidance

State the meaning of the term 'sacrament' for a Catholic.   (3 marks)

First answer
because you have to sacrifice yourself to these if you are a catholic

There is nothing relevant in this answer.
(Score: 0 marks out of 3)

Second answer
It brings us closer to God and the kingdom of God.

This candidate has made a relevant point. However, there are three marks for this answer, so there should be a fuller explanation to gain more than one mark.
(Score: 1 mark out of 3)

Third answer
A sacrament is like a stage that we go through in life, each one strengthens us as a person. We can behave more like Christ.

A good answer. But there are some important aspects of a sacrament not mentioned: the presence of God; the presence of Christ; and so on. There has to be a fuller answer for three marks.
(Score: 2 marks out of 3)

Fourth answer
It is a gift from God through which we receive strength and love and grace from God. It is a way for us to renew our relationship with God and keep close to him, and follow his ways.

This is a very good answer. The candidate has made several relevant points, quite enough to merit three marks.

This question was given five lines for the answer. Although this answer would not use the five lines, it has made important points succinctly. It is quality that counts.
(Score: 3 marks out of 3)

Fifth answer

They are signs of grace, started by Jesus, through which we receive the strength and courage to allow us to witness to Christ. They are a sign of our love for God and his for us. They bring us closer to God and help us to understand both God's work and our vocation.

This is an excellent answer. You can't get much better than this. It has to merit full marks.
(Score: 3 marks out of 3)

Examination practice

1. What is the connection between baptism, confirmation and the eucharist? (3 marks)
    Write about six lines.

2. Explain the meaning of the main symbols in each of the seven sacraments. (8 marks)
    Write about three-quarters of a side of A4.

3. 'The sacraments strengthen a Catholic for the difficulties of daily life.'
    Explain what this statement means. (10 marks)
    Write about one side of A4.

4. 'It is possible to experience God in this life.'
    Do you agree? Give reasons for your view. Show that you have considered the opposite point of view.
    (8 marks)
    Write about three-quarters of a side of A4.

RECONCILIATION (PENANCE, CONFESSION) 17

Introduction

There are several names for this sacrament:

*   sacrament of reconciliation
*   sacrament of conversion
*   sacrament of penance
*   sacrament of confession
*   sacrament of forgiveness.

> 'There will be more rejoicing in heaven over one sinner who repents than over ninety-nine righteous persons who do not need to repent.'
>
> Jesus (Luke 15[7])

Sin and forgiveness

In Luke's gospel, Jesus' last act before he died was to forgive those who killed him. It is as though he had to do this before he could enter God's kingdom. He set the pattern.

Christians believe that we all have to forgive and receive forgiveness. But we do not naturally or easily forgive, especially when someone has deeply offended us. Revenge and retaliation are instinctive reactions. People find it

difficult to let go of a grudge, even when they want to let go.

So, why do Christians insist on the importance of forgiving? They say that God is forgiving. He expects humans to follow his example. Jesus said:

> 'Love your enemies and pray for those who persecute you, that you may be sons of your Father in heaven. He causes his sun to rise on the evil and the good, and sends rain on the righteous and the unrighteous. If you love those who love you, what reward will you get? Are not even the tax collectors doing that? And if you greet only your brothers, what are you doing more than others? Do not even pagans do that? Be perfect, therefore, as your heavenly Father is perfect.'
>
> Matthew 5[44–48]

Ceremony of reconciliation

A person who goes to this sacrament is a 'penitent'.

There are three ways of celebrating this sacrament in the Catholic Church. The most frequent way is the individual rite of reconciliation.

*   Penitents pray to God for courage to be honest and to face their 'real selves'.

The moment of forgiveness in the sacrament of reconciliation, as the priest raises his right hand and says: '. . . I absolve you from your sins'

- Penitents then prepare for this sacrament by thinking carefully about their faults. They can concentrate on remembering as many of their sins as possible, or they can concentrate on something in their life that they want to change (for instance, if they are constantly greedy; or if they are frequently ill-tempered and bad mannered; or if they continually criticize other people; and so on).
- A penitent then goes into the room where the priest is. The penitent may either sit opposite the priest so they see each other, or kneel behind a grill so that the priest does not see the penitent, but can hear what the penitent says.
- The priest should welcome the penitent. The priest says a suitable prayer, such as 'May God help you to know your sins and trust in his mercy'.
- There should be a reading from the Bible – such as the parable of the lost sheep; or part of the account of Jesus' death, when he forgave those who crucified him. The purpose of the reading is to remind the penitent that God forgives.
- The penitent tells his or her sins to the priest.
- The priest may say some words of encouragement. Or the priest may discuss with the penitent how best to overcome a frequent sin or temptation.
- The priest allots a penance. The priest may make the penance fit the sin (for instance, a priest may tell someone to give money to an organization such as Cafod if that person confesses to being miserly with their money). But the penance is more likely to be a prayer that the penitent has to say.
- The penitent expresses regret for his or her sins. The penitent might pray, 'Father, I have sinned against you. Be merciful to me.'

- The priest says the words of absolution. He raises his right hand, or places it on the penitent's head, and says a prayer of forgiveness: 'God, the Father of mercies, through the death and resurrection of his Son, has reconciled the world to himself . . . May God give you pardon and peace, and I absolve you from your sins.'
- There is a final prayer, of thanksgiving. The priest blesses the penitent.

Other ceremonies

There is a second and a third way to celebrate this sacrament in the Catholic Church. Both are similar to the ceremony outlined above.

In the second, there is a group ceremony with individual confession. People come together in church. They prepare, as a group, for the sacrament: they say prayers; they listen to Bible readings; they listen to the priest's homily; they may sing a hymn. There is then silence as, individually and quietly, each considers their own sins. After this, each person tells their sins to a priest. This is done privately. Each person also says a prayer, in front of the priest, about how sorry they are for their sins. The priest gives absolution to each individual. After people have individually confessed their sins to a priest, everyone joins together again: they say some final prayers.

In the third, there is a group ceremony without individual confession. People come together in church. They prepare, as a group, for the sacrament: they say prayers, they listen to Bible readings; they listen to the priest's homily; they may sing a hymn. There is then silence as, individually and quietly, each considers their own sins. After this, each person confesses silently and individually to God – but there is no individual confession to a priest. Together, people say a prayer about how sorry they are for their sins. The priest gives absolution to everyone at the same time, not to each one individually. Then there are some final prayers.

Effects of sacrament of reconciliation

- The most important effect is that a person is reconciled with God.
- Equally important, the penitents should resolve to be reconciled with people they have harmed; or to be reconciled with people who have harmed them.
- There is a sense of relief at receiving forgiveness.
- There is determination to improve a particular attitude or behaviour, and to avoid certain sins.
- The penitent should be more understanding and forgiving to others.

Importance of this sacrament

The Catholic bishops encourage Catholic lay people to go frequently to the sacrament of reconciliation. Yet lay people do not often go to this sacrament. Many Catholics go regularly to the sacrament of the eucharist, but go rarely to the sacrament of reconciliation. They have different reasons for this.

- The introduction to the eucharist is similar to the third way of celebrating the sacrament of reconciliation; and so every time Catholics celebrate the eucharist, they celebrate reconciliation as well. Thus they do not think it is important to go to the individual celebration of the sacrament of reconciliation.

- They find it is embarrassing and discomforting to confess to someone their defects and sins. Thus they are reluctant to go to the individual celebration of the sacrament of reconciliation.

- They can tell God, privately, their sins and he will forgive.

Examination guidance

Why do Catholics believe that the sacrament of Penance is important? (2 marks)

First answer
because you can go and sin again

There is nothing relevant in this answer.
(Score: 0 marks out of 2)

Second answer
because they get forgiven by God

This candidate has made a relevant point. But there are two marks for this question. So there should be more than a terse explanation to gain the two marks.
(Score: 1 mark out of 2)

Third answer
They believe that penance is important because it means you want your sins to get forgiven to get you closer to God.

A good answer; it elaborates on the initial point.
(Score: 2 marks out of 2)

Fourth answer
Because as we sin regularly we need this to be taken away from us. By saying we are sorry God forgives our wrongdoings and helps us to do better.

Another good answer. There is sufficient detail in it to merit the two marks.
(Score: 2 marks out of 2)

Examination practice

1. 'Catholics only go to the sacrament of reconciliation so they can sin again.'
   What might a Catholic reply to this comment?
   (3 marks)
   Write about six lines.

2. State what happens and is said in the ceremony of reconciliation. (10 marks)
   Write about one side of A4.

3. Christians believe that God forgives. How might this belief affect their lives? (6 marks)
   Write about half a side of A4.

4. 'You cannot really forgive other people if they have hurt you badly. Nor should you.'
   Do you agree? Give reasons for your view. Show that you have considered the opposite point of view.
   (8 marks)

   Write about three-quarters of a side of A4.

Sickness and death

We all dread a serious illness. If we are seriously ill, we may feel helpless, powerless, frustrated, and acutely angry. We may become totally wrapped up in our difficulty, quite uninterested in anybody or anything else. We may glimpse death. We can easily lose faith in God. We may find life meaningless.

On the other hand, the experience may assist us to become more mature. It may make us less self-centred. It can help us to see what is important in life. It can help us to change our ambitions. It may lead us to change our behaviour. It can encourage us to look for God.

Jesus and the sick

According to Mark's gospel, Jesus spent most of his first day's ministry in curing people. First, he cured a man with an evil spirit. Next, he cured Simon's mother-in-law, who had a fever. Then:

> That evening after sunset the people brought to Jesus all the sick and demon-possessed. The whole town gathered at the door, and Jesus healed many who had various diseases. He also drove out many demons, but he would not let the demons speak because they knew who he was.
>
> Mark 1$^{32-34}$

Soon after this, some men brought a paralysed friend to Jesus. They could not get near Jesus because people were crowded round him. So they made a hole in the roof and lowered their friend. Jesus told the man his sins were forgiven. He then told the man to pick up his mat and go home, which he did. (Mark 2$^{1-12}$).

On one occasion, Jesus helped a woman who had been ill for twelve years. She suffered from a haemorrhage, an escape of blood from the blood vessels.

> She had suffered a great deal under the care of many doctors and had spent all she had, yet instead of getting better she grew worse. When she heard about Jesus, she came up behind him in the crowd and touched his cloak, because she thought, 'If I just touch his clothes, I will be healed.' Immediately her bleeding stopped and she felt in her body that she was freed from her suffering.
>
> (Mark 5$^{26-29}$)

On another occasion, a man came to Jesus' disciples and asked them to cure his son. A spirit possessed the boy – it robbed him of speech and made him go into convulsions.

The disciples could not cure the boy. Jesus told the spirit to leave the boy. The spirit shrieked, sent the boy into a convulsion, and left him. The boy looked like a corpse. Jesus took the boy by hand and lifted him to his feet. He explained that only prayer could overcome this kind of spirit. (Mark 9$^{14-29}$).

Near the end of his life, Jesus went to Jerusalem. He passed through Jericho. A blind man, Bartimaeus, who was a beggar, shouted out:

> 'Jesus, son of David, have mercy on me!'
> Many rebuked him and told him to be quiet, but he shouted all the more, 'Son of David, have mercy on me!'
> Jesus stopped and said, 'Call him.'
> So they called to the blind man, 'Cheer up! On your feet! He's calling you.' Throwing his cloak aside, he jumped to his feet and came to Jesus.
> 'What do you want me to do for you?' Jesus asked him.
> The blind man said, 'Rabbi, I want to see.'
> 'Go,' said Jesus, 'your faith has healed you.'
> Immediately he received his sight and followed Jesus along the road.
>
> (Mark 10$^{46-52}$)

Jesus sent out his disciples to follow his example. They went out and told people to repent. They drove out many demons. They anointed many sick people with oil and they healed them (Mark 6$^{12-13}$).

Jesus told the parable of the sheep and the goats, to illustrate how important it was to help people in need. In this parable, Jesus explained how he would judge people when he returned. He would welcome into God's kingdom those who fed the hungry and visited the sick. He would reject those who did not feed the hungry and did not visit the sick (Matthew 25$^{31-46}$).

> Heal the sick!
> The Church has received this charge from the Lord and strives to carry it out.
>
> Catholic Catechism

Purpose of this sacrament

Christians can receive this sacrament when they are seriously ill, or when they are old and frail.

The main purpose of this sacrament is to assure a sick person – who may be anxious, fearful, uncertain and despondent – of God's concern and love. This sacrament can bring a sick person closer to Christ.

The sacrament may also encourage healthy people to

follow Christ's example, and to care for sick people.

Oil is used in baptism, which is the start of Jesus' life in a Christian; in confirmation, which strengthens Jesus' power in a Christian; and in the sacrament of the sick, which conforms a Christian to the death and resurrection of Jesus. So it is not surprising that this sacrament is frequently given to a person who is dying. It helps a Christian to pass from this world to the next one.

Anointing of the sick is more likely to take place at home, or in a hospital. The six other sacraments are usually administered in a church.

The sacraments of communion and penance are often given with the sacrament of anointing of the sick.

Ceremony

This is the Catholic ceremony.

- When the priest arrives, he greets the people and then sprinkles holy water. He may say: 'Let this water call to mind our baptism into Christ, who by his death and resurrection has redeemed us'.
- The priest gives a short talk about Jesus and his concern for sick people (see above).
- Those present say the penitential rite: they say sorry to God for the times they have hurt him and hurt other people. The priest may hear the sick person's confession and give absolution. (See Chapter A17, *Reconciliation*.)
- There are readings from the Bible (for example, an occasion when Jesus healed a sick person. Perhaps the passage in James' letter, where he says: 'Is anyone of you sick? He should call the elders of the church to pray over him and anoint him with oil in the name of the

Lord. And the prayer offered in faith will make the sick person well . . .' James 5[13–15]).
- Then there is a litany of prayers for the sick person. The priest says several, different, short prayers (such as, 'Relieve the sufferings of all the sick'). After each short prayer, the people say, 'Lord have mercy'.
- The priest lays his hands on the sick person, in silence. Everything is still.
- Then comes the anointing. The priest anoints the sick person's forehead and says: 'Through this holy anointing may the Lord in his love and mercy help you with the grace of the Holy Spirit'. Everyone says: 'Amen'. Then the priest anoints the hands of the sick person and says: 'May the Lord who frees you from sin save you and raise you up'. Everyone says: 'Amen'.
- Then the priest says another prayer. The prayer will depend on whether the sick person is elderly, or is about to have an operation, or is a child, or is dying, and so on. In the case of someone about to have surgery, he may say: 'God of compassion, our human weakness lays claim to your strength. We pray that through the skills of surgeons and nurses your healing gifts may be granted to this person.'
- Everyone joins in saying the Lord's Prayer.
- There is Communion (see Chapter A1, *Eucharist* for details of this.)
- The ceremony finishes with a final blessing (for example, 'May the Lord guide you and give you strength').

> The wounded person needs, above all, someone who will listen, because in all suffering we seek first a friend who welcomes us, who appreciates us, who finds what we have to say important.
>
> Jean Vanier

In the sacrament of the anointing of the sick the priest prays as he anoints first the head and then the hands of the person that is ill

Signs

There are two important signs seen in this sacrament.

First, the laying of hands on the sick person's head. This is a sign of the coming of the Holy Spirit. The Spirit brings strength and courage to fight the illness, or to accept the illness.

Second, the anointing of the sick person's head and hands. Anointing has many meanings. Here, it probably means: healing, soothing, comfort, relaxation, peace, and consecration to Christ.

There is one important sign heard in this sacrament: the words the priest says when he anoints a sick person.

Effects

The main effect of this sacrament is that people feel the power of God to cope with their illness. Thus, this sacrament often brings effects such as:

- **physical healing**. The sick person recovers from the illness.
- **spiritual healing**. The sick person learns to forget old hatreds and grudges, to forget the times when people have hurt them, to live at peace with themself.
- **forgiveness of sin**. The sick person decides to forgive others who have caused them hurt and bitterness, or learns to accept God's forgiveness for an awful deed committed by themself.
- **uniting with the suffering of Christ**. The sick person recognizes the similarities between their life and Christ's life. They become more united with Christ. They understand him better. They feel closer to him; they may feel he is closer to them.
- **facing difficulties**, rather than running away from them. The sick person recognizes the difficulties of the illness, rather than ignoring them or pretending they did not exist.
- **reduction of anxiety**. The sick person becomes less stressful and worried.
- **courage**. The sick person can face unpleasant and stressful news about their health.
- **peace**: with others, with oneself, with God.
- **preparation for the final journey**, if they are dying. The dying person gains strength to face the unknown and to step out into the dark, in spite of fear.

Examination guidance

One of the sacraments is the anointing of the sick. How might this sacrament help a Catholic? (3 marks)

First answer

because in their life they will have to help someone who is ill, like nurse them better and get things for them.

There is nothing relevant in this answer.
(Score: 0 marks out of 3)

Second answer

It might help a Catholic because it will show you must have faith, you must pray and that if you do pray you will be healed, and if you go to church it will also help.

There is a glimmer of understanding here. There are some important ideas, like faith, prayer and healing; but the candidate does not clearly or coherently explain these points. The statement about going to church is not relevant to the question.
(Score: 1 mark out of 3)

Third answer

This sacrament can help a Catholic who is sick by giving them hope and courage to face their illness. The people are forgiven so their relationship with God is rebuilt in case they die. Fear and anxiousness are lifted from the person and they may often recover.

An excellent answer. The candidate has made several relevant points. These points are expressed clearly and tersely. This is better than a flowery or emotive answer that may appear eloquent, but makes few substantive points.
(Score: 3 marks out of 3)

Examination practice

1. Many seriously ill Catholics welcome the sacrament of the anointing of the sick.
   Explain why. (3 marks)
   Write about five lines of A4.

2. What happens and what is said in the sacrament of the anointing of the sick? (10 marks)
   Write about one side of A4.

3. Jesus helped many sick people. How might this influence a Christian's outlook and actions? (8 marks)
   Write about three-quarters of a side of A4.

4. 'Christ healed people who were incurably ill. Why can't priests today do similar miracles?'
   What would you say? Show that you have considered more than one answer. (8 marks)
   Write about three-quarters of a side of A4.

Short courses: Part B

This chart tells you the chapters to study. Find your exam board.
Then highlight your syllabus.
Study the chapters that are ticked.

Chapter	NEAB – Christianity	Thinking about God and morality	SEG – Religious education	EdExcel (London) Syllabus A – Religion and life	EdExcel Syllabus B – Christianity	Christianity: Catholicism	Christianity: Mark's gospel	MEG Syllabus A – Christianity through Luke and Acts	Christian perspectives on personal, social and world issues	MEG Christianity	MEG Syllabus B – Christianity
Chapter 1 How do we get to know God?	✓	✓	✓	✓	✓	✓	✓	✓		✓	✓
Chapter 2 Religious experience		✓	✓	✓		✓					✓
Chapter 3 Arguments for the existence of God – I		✓	✓	✓							✓
Chapter 4 Arguments for the existence of God – II		✓	✓	✓							✓
Chapter 5 Arguments against the existence of God – I		✓	✓	✓							✓
Chapter 6 Arguments against the existence of God – II		✓	✓	✓							✓
Chapter 7 The Nature of God – I	✓	✓	✓	✓	✓	✓	✓	✓		✓	✓
Chapter 8 The Nature of God – II	✓	✓	✓	✓	✓	✓	✓	✓		✓	✓
Chapter 9 Creation; evolution	✓	✓	✓	✓	✓	✓	✓	✓	✓		✓
Chapter 10 Suffering and evil – I	✓	✓	✓	✓	✓	✓	✓	✓		✓	✓
Chapter 11 Suffering and evil – II	✓	✓	✓	✓	✓	✓	✓	✓		✓	✓
Chapter 12 Can we describe God? – some difficulties	✓	✓	✓	✓	✓	✓	✓	✓		✓	✓
Chapter 13 Can we describe God? – some solutions	✓	✓	✓	✓	✓	✓	✓	✓		✓	✓

Full courses: Part B

This chart tells you the chapters to study. Find your exam board. Then highlight your syllabuses (or syllabus). Study the chapters that are ticked.

Exam Board Syllabuses

- **NEAB** — Syllabus A: Christianity; Syllabus B: Christian tradition; Syllabus C: Catholic Christian tradition; Christian life and Mark's gospel; Christian behaviour, attitudes and lifestyle; Catholic Christian behaviour, attitudes and lifestyle; Christian beliefs and practice (modular)
- **MEG** — Syllabus C: Christian beliefs and practice (modular); Christianity through Luke's gospel and Acts; Christianity; Christian perspectives on personal, social issues
- **EdExcel (London)** — Christianity; Catholic Christianity; Contemporary issues and Mark's gospel
- **SEG** — Syllabus A: Christian Church; Contemporary issues; Life of Jesus: synoptic gospels; Syllabus B: Inter-faith studies: Christianity; Syllabus C: Catholic Christian tradition

Chapter	Christianity (NEAB A)	Christian tradition (NEAB B)	Catholic Christian tradition (NEAB C)	Christian life and Mark's gospel	Christian behaviour, attitudes and lifestyle	Catholic Christian behaviour, attitudes and lifestyle	Christian beliefs and practice (modular)	Christianity through Luke's gospel and Acts (MEG)	Christianity (MEG)	Christian perspectives on personal, social issues (MEG)	Christianity (EdExcel)	Catholic Christianity (EdExcel)	Contemporary issues and Mark's gospel (EdExcel)	Christian Church (SEG A)	Contemporary issues (SEG A)	Life of Jesus: synoptic gospels (SEG A)	Inter-faith studies: Christianity (SEG B)	Catholic Christian tradition (SEG C)
Chapter 1 How do we get to know God?	✓	✓	✓	✓			✓	✓	✓	✓	✓	✓		✓	✓		✓	✓
Chapter 2 Religious experience			✓				✓				✓	✓						
Chapter 3 Arguments for the existence of God – I											✓							
Chapter 4 Arguments for the existence of God – II											✓							
Chapter 5 Arguments against the existence of God – I																		
Chapter 6 Arguments against the existence of God – II																		
Chapter 7 The Nature of God – I	✓	✓	✓				✓	✓			✓	✓						
Chapter 8 The Nature of God – II	✓	✓	✓				✓	✓			✓	✓			✓			
Chapter 9 Creation; evolution	✓					✓	✓	✓			✓	✓	✓		✓			
Chapter 10 Suffering and evil – I	✓				✓			✓			✓	✓		✓				✓
Chapter 11 Suffering and evil – II	✓				✓			✓			✓		✓					
Chapter 12 Can we describe God? – some difficulties	✓	✓	✓	✓			✓	✓		✓	✓	✓		✓			✓	
Chapter 13 Can we describe God? – some solutions	✓	✓	✓	✓			✓	✓		✓	✓	✓		✓			✓	

HOW DO WE GET TO KNOW GOD?

Introduction

There is a difference between getting to know about God and getting to know God, just as there is a difference between a tourist and a pilgrim. This is an important distinction to remember as we go through this chapter.

There are several ways to discover God. Yet any of us may find one or two ways more useful than the other ways.

We have to be careful about describing God as acting in human ways. In this chapter we may describe God as though he was human. But do read Chapters B12 and B13 to appreciate the limits of any description we make about God.

Imagination at work?

Some people believe there is no God. And they believe that people who feel they are getting closer to God are either deceiving themselves or are deceived by other people – they may think they are getting closer to God, but it is mere wish-fulfilment. (For more details see the appropriate section in Chapter B5, *Arguments against the existence of God – I.*)

Nature

This is the most frequent reason why people think about God.

People are reminded of God by natural things such as the stars, the sea, the mountains, the clouds, and so on. Not all the time. But occasionally some people have an indescribable experience when contemplating, for instance, the sea or a mountain. It makes them think of God.

The desert is a particularly curious place. Most religious leaders have spent some time in the desert. It was there that they learned about God – in emptiness and loneliness, in barrenness and nothingness, in silence. The desert is both fearsome and fascinating, like God.

Moses had an experience of God in the desert. It influenced the rest of his life, and it influenced all Jewish people, all Christian people, and all Muslim people. Quite an influence!

> Moses . . . led the flock of sheep to the far side of the desert and came to Horeb, the mountain of God. There the angel of the Lord appeared to him in flames of fire from within a bush. Moses saw that though the bush was on fire it did not burn up. So Moses thought 'I will go over and see this strange sight – why the bush does not burn up.'

> When the Lord saw that he had gone over to look, God called to him from within the bush, 'Moses, Moses!'
>
> And Moses said 'here I am.'
>
> 'Do not come any closer,' God said. 'Take off your sandals, for the place where you are standing is holy ground.' Then he said 'I am the God of your father, Abraham . . .'
>
> At this Moses hid his face, because he was afraid to look at God.
>
> The Lord said 'I have indeed seen the misery of my people in Egypt. . . . So I have come down to rescue them . . .'
>
> Exodus 3^1–4^{16}

The prophet **Elijah** had an experience of God in the desert. It profoundly altered his understanding of God. It contrasts with Moses' experience of God.

> Elijah was afraid [because Queen Jezebel was going to kill him] and ran for his life . . . he travelled for forty nights until he reached Horeb, the mountain of God. There he went into a cave and spent the night. . . .
>
> Then a great and powerful wind tore the mountains apart and shattered the rocks before the Lord, but the Lord was not in the wind.
>
> After the wind there was an earthquake, but the Lord was not in the earthquake.
>
> After the earthquake came a fire, but the Lord was not in the fire.
>
> And after the fire came a gentle whisper. When Elijah heard it, he pulled his cloak over his face and went out and stood at the mouth of the cave . . .
>
> 1 Kings 19$^{1-13}$

Jesus was driven by the Spirit of God into the desert. It entirely altered the rest of his life.

> At once [after Jesus' baptism] the Spirit sent him out into the desert, and he was in the desert for forty days, being tempted by Satan. He was with the wild animals, and angels attended him.
>
> Mark 1$^{12-13}$

(See Chapter B3, *Arguments for the existence of God – I*, for further information on getting to know God from the natural world.)

Religious experience

Some people feel they have an experience of God himself. See Chapter B2, *Religious experience*.

Worship

For Christians, worship is a traditional way to develop their understanding of God. Today, some Christians find church worship helpful because it deepens their understanding of God. Yet many Christians find church worship boring and tedious: it does not deepen their understanding of God.

There are different styles of worship in different Christian churches. Some are more formal and sober (liturgical worship). Others are more flexible and emotive (non-liturgical worship).

(For details on liturgical worship, see the chapters on each of the seven sacraments. In particular, look at the chapters on baptism (D1, D2) and eucharist (A1). For non-liturgical worship, see Chapter A2, *Collective worship, non-liturgical*.)

Music

For most of us music is a way of expressing and understanding our feelings and sensibilities. It enables us to explore what goes on in our spirit (soul, or mind). It seems to take us to deeper parts of our spirit than our thoughts normally do. So, for some people, music is a useful way of tuning in to God.

God incarnate

All Christians believe that Jesus Christ is the most important religious leader: that he is the best way to get to know God. There is no hesitation or dispute about this. Christians believe that Jesus was God made man, so he taught with authority about God. His way of life shows us what God is like, and his death and resurrection have important consequences for us. See the two chapters on Jesus (C6 and C7) for details.

Religious writings

For Christians, the Bible, especially the New Testament (because it is about Jesus), is a primary source for finding out about God. They believe it is a special book because God had a hand in writing it. Thus they think it is a reliable way to find out what God is like.

See Chapter C11, *The Bible*, for details. Also have a look at the chapters on Mark's gospel (C12–C17) and Luke's gospel (C18–C21).

Church leaders

Christians have divergent beliefs about the importance of Church leaders in helping us to get to know God.

For some Christians, such as Orthodox, Catholic and Anglican, the bishops are the successors of the apostles of Jesus, through the laying on of hands at ordination. They are the ones to whom Jesus entrusted his teaching, so they can reliably tell us what Jesus said about getting to God. Hence the teachings of the councils of bishops are

important. Read Chapter C1, *Apostles' Creed and Nicene Creed*. See also Chapter D12, *Bishops, priests, deacons: Orders*.

Thus, for Catholics, Orthodox and Anglicans, there are two very important sources for understanding Jesus and God: the teachings of the bishops (often called the *magisterium* of the Church), and the Bible. Other Christians, such as Baptists and Presbyterians, emphasize the importance of the Bible alone as a source for understanding Jesus and God.

Other people

People who are outstandingly good make us stop and think, possibly about God: for example, Mother Teresa. She causes most of us to wonder about the source of her goodness.

A modern carving of the crucifixion of Jesus. Christians believe the death and resurrection of Jesus have enabled us to know God.

Thus people who demonstrate self-sacrifice point us to the selfless love of God. And what about people who never complain and never criticize? Perhaps they point us to the understanding and indulgence of God. And what about people who assist those who suffer or who are miserable? Perhaps they point us to the compassion of God. And people who do not deliberately hurt others? Perhaps they point us to the love of God.

Our own lives

The way we live our own lives can block or assist our understanding of God.

Suppose we are continuously selfish. Perhaps we shall not understand how generous God is. What if we are unforgiving and keen to bear grudges? Perhaps we shall not understand how forgiving God is. And if we are intolerant of other people? Then we shall not understand how patient, open-minded and considerate God is. And if we frequently lie, cheat and deceive? Perhaps we can never understand how straightforward and honest God is.

We are self-interested. This is healthy, because it helps us to learn about ourselves, to take an interest in other people, to be curious about the natural world, and to wonder about God. Unfortunately, we have an instinct to be too interested in ourselves. We can become preoccupied with our ambitions – even with reliving ways we have been hurt. And if we become wrapped up in ourselves, we learn little about God, because we ignore anyone or anything that might curtail our self-absorption. See Chapter C9, *Human nature*.

On the other hand, if we are loyal to other people, we may begin to understand how self-sacrificing God is. If we try to accept that other people cannot be perfect, then we begin to attune our mind to God's. And if we can learn to forgive, then we start to become like God.

Special places

Some people find that a pilgrimage has made a considerable difference to their knowledge and understanding of God. See Chapter A10, *Pilgrimage*.

Quiet reflection

> Speak through the earthquake, wind and fire,
> O still small voice of calm!
> O still small voice of calm!
>
> From the hymn 'Dear Lord and Father of mankind'
> by John Greenleaf Whittier

It is often said that we cannot find God in a noisy, busy world. We can find God only in silence, quietness and emptiness. But this is difficult for most of us, as we do not like silence. We are used to persistent background noise: perhaps the television, or music, or traffic, or people talking. We feel uncomfortable when there is silence; we become restless and want to do something to break the silence.

Yet we have to learn to be silent to find God.

If God is within us (**immanent**) as well as outside us (**transcendent**), then we have to learn to be still and to become aware of our spirit (some people prefer to call it mind or soul). It is in our spirit that we are close to God. So the more we are aware of our spirit, the closer we come to God. That is why many people find that quiet, private prayer or meditation is a good way to discover God within ourselves.

See Chapter A4, *Private worship and devotions*. See also Chapter D14, *Nuns, monks, sisters, brothers: religious institutes*.

Sad experiences

It is easy to ignore God in happy times. We just enjoy ourselves.

Because of this, Christians deliberately remember God at happy times. They have special celebrations for birth and marriage. See Chapters D1–D3 on baptism and Chapter E5 on the marriage ceremony.

For most of us it is at times of sadness that we start to think of God: for example, the death of someone we loved; or a serious accident or a serious illness; or when we have been humiliated; or when we have done something badly wrong and we cannot forget it.

In such situations we may blame God for what has happened, and we may feel either that he does not exist or that he cannot be good. Alternatively, we may feel that God has come closer to us, and that he understands our suffering. Perhaps we may have contradictory feelings.

Whatever the precise consequences, we tend to think of God when we suffer.

See Chapters B10 and B11, *Suffering and evil*, for more information.

Alternatively . . .

It is possible to ignore God as well as get to know him. It is also possible to avoid God – even hide from him – perhaps because we are:

- too interested in enjoying ourselves;
- too interested in making money;
- absorbed in our studies, jobs or careers;
- disgusted by the evil things in this world;
- apprehensive that God may ruin our lives and demand too much of us;
- very independent and self-sufficient, and unwilling to accept that someone else can be greater than us;
- too busy to have time to stop and think;
- afraid of what we may find;
- fascinated by the improvements we can make to this world;
- keen to make a better world, one made by humans;
- put off by people who are religious and who go to church.

Concluding comment

Some of us think we are looking for God. Christians believe the opposite is true: God is looking for us. An illustration of this view is the story of the forgiving father, or the story of the lost coin, or the story of the lost sheep. See Chapter C19, *Luke's gospel – parables*, for a summary of these stories.

Examination practice

1. Suggest why some people are afraid of God or avoid him. (3 marks)
   Write about six lines.

2. Name **four** ways in which people feel they get to know God.
   What might they learn about God? (10 marks)
   Write about one side of A4.

3. Atheists believe there is no God. How might this affect the way they look at birth, serious illness and death? Christians believe there is a God. How might this affect they way they look at birth, serious illness and death?
   (8 marks)
   Write about three-quarters of a side of A4.

4. Do you think that prayer, worship and the sacraments are useful ways of getting to know God?
   Give reasons for your view. Show you have understood more than one point of view.
   (8 marks)
   Write about three-quarters of a side of A4.

RELIGIOUS EXPERIENCE

2

Introduction

Religion is about God.

Some people say religion is about getting to know God.

Others say religion is about doing what God wants. They argue that it is not possible to know God, because God and humans are quite different. He is infinite and humans are finite. What is finite cannot meet what is infinite. To say that humans can meet God is like saying that a human can get to know a stone, which is absurd, because the two are quite different. Thus religion is not about getting to know God, but about doing what God wants. To do what God wants, we have to know what God wants, so we need prophets. God communicates with prophets, without meeting them directly. Prophets then have the task of telling us what God wants.

Most Christians think that religion is both doing what God wants and getting to know him, the first leading to the second.

Most Christians also believe it is important to have a personal relationship with Jesus, and through him, with God.

A religious experience can be a direct experience of God. A religious experience can also be an awareness or feeling about God, which is not a direct experience of him.

Christians disagree about how well a person can get to know God in this life. Some (called mystics, such as John of the Cross and Teresa of Avila) say they have had a direct experience of God in this life. Most Christians think a direct experience of God is possible only after death – in this life we can experience God, but only indirectly.

Examples from the Bible
Old Testament

The first Jew was **Abram**. In one account, God tells him he will be the father of a great nation. Abram asks for a sign. (In Old Testament times the dividing of animals as described here was a traditional ritual that bound two parties together.)

> So the Lord said to him, 'Bring me a heifer, a goat, and a ram, each three years old . . . Abram brought all these to him, cut them in two and arranged the halves opposite each other . . .
>
> As the sun was setting, Abram fell into a deep sleep, and a thick and dreadful darkness came over him . . . When the sun had set and darkness had fallen, a smoking firepot with a blazing torch appeared and passed between the pieces. On that day the Lord made a covenant with Abram.
>
> Genesis 15$^{9-18}$

The great leader of the Jews was **Moses**. In his time the Jews were slaves to the Egyptians. Moses, under God's guidance, led them to freedom. On their journey, the Jews camped every night.

> Now Moses used to take a tent and pitch it outside the camp some distance away, calling it the 'tent of meeting'. . . As Moses went into the tent, the pillar of cloud would come down and stay at the entrance, while the Lord spoke with Moses. Whenever the people saw

the pillar of cloud standing at the entrance to the tent, they all stood and worshipped, each at the entrance to his tent. The Lord would speak to Moses face to face, as a man speaks with his friend.

Exodus 3[7–11]

In contrast, **Elijah**, a prophet, had an experience that had a quite different tone. Queen Jezebel intended to kill Elijah, so Elijah fled to a cave on Mount Horeb. He was told,

'Go out and stand on the mountain in the presence of the Lord, for the Lord is about to pass by.' Then a great and powerful wind tore the mountain apart and shattered the rocks before the Lord, but the Lord was not in the wind. After the wind there was an earthquake, but the Lord was not in the earthquake. After the earthquake came a fire, but the Lord was not in the fire. And after the fire came a gentle whisper. When Elijah heard it, he pulled his cloak over his face and went out and stood at the mouth of the cave.

1 Kings 19[11–13]

New Testament

Jesus – just before he started to teach, to heal and to defeat evil spirits – was baptized by John the Baptist in the river Jordan.

As Jesus was coming up out of the water, he saw heaven being torn open and the Spirit descending on him like a dove. And a voice came from heaven: 'You are my Son, whom I love; with you I am well pleased.'

Mark 1[10–11]

Saul, who later changed his name to Paul, was travelling to Damascus to capture some Christians and take them back to Jerusalem.

As he neared Damascus on his journey, suddenly a light from heaven flashed around him. He fell to the ground and heard a voice say to him, 'Saul, Saul, why do you persecute me?'
'Who are you, Lord?' Saul asked. 'I am Jesus, whom you are persecuting,' he replied. 'Now get up and go into the city, and you will be told what you must do.'

Acts 9[3–6]

About 40 days after the crucifixion of Jesus, the first **disciples** were having one of their regular meetings.

Suddenly, a sound like the blowing of a violent wind came from heaven and filled the whole house where they were sitting. They saw what seemed to be tongues of fire that separated and came to rest on each of them. All of them were filled with the Holy Spirit and began to speak in other tongues [languages] as the Spirit enabled them . . . [Jews from different countries heard them] Utterly amazed, they asked: 'Are not all these men who are speaking Galileans? Then how is it that each of us hears them in his own native language?'

Acts 2[2–8]

Examples from mystics

The sixteenth-century Spanish mystic, **Teresa of Avila**, had countless visions. This is just one of them.

Being in prayer on the feast day of the glorious St Peter, I saw or, to put it better, I felt Christ beside me; [she says she did not actually see something outside her, nor did she see something in her imagination], but it seemed to me that Christ was at my side . . .

Later, she comments that:

It is incorrect to think that the vision is like that experience of someone blind or in the dark who doesn't see the other at his side. There is some likeness in this comparison but not a great deal, because in such a case the person experiences with his senses: either he hears the other person speak or stir, or touches him. In the vision there is nothing of this, nor do you see darkness; but the vision is represented through knowledge given to the soul [mind] that is clearer than sunlight.

Autobiography of Teresa of Avila

John of the Cross, who also lived in the sixteenth century, preferred to write about his experiences in poetry. This is an extract from one of his poems.

I entered into unknowing
Yet when I saw myself there
Without knowing where I was
I understood great things;
I shall not say what I felt
For I remained in unknowing
Transcending all knowledge.

This knowledge in unknowing
Is so overwhelming
That wise men disputing
Can never overthrow it,
For their knowledge does not reach
To the understanding of not-understanding,
Transcending all knowledge.

And if you should want to hear:
This highest knowledge lies
In the loftiest sense
Of the essence of God;
This is a work of His mercy,
To leave one without understanding,
Transcending all knowledge.

Collected Works of John of the Cross

Other examples

John Wesley, the leading person in the first years of the Methodist movement, gave the following description of a turning point in his life.

In the evening I went very unwillingly to a society in Aldersgate Street, where one was reading Luther's preface to the epistle to the Romans. About a quarter to nine, while he was describing the change which God works in the heart through faith in Christ, I felt my heart strangely warmed. I felt I did trust in Christ, Christ alone for salvation: and an assurance was given me that he had taken away *my* sins, even *mine*, and saved *me* from the law of sin and death.

The Journal of John Wesley

The following experience took place in 1985 at **Melleray** in Ireland. A group of people were praying in front of a statue of Mary, the mother of Jesus.

Shortly after prayer, Our Blessed Lady appeared as usual – first the cloak of the statue blowing in the wind, with flowing golden hair, then as she spoke the apparition became the very clear head and shoulders vision – a young tanned face, with blue eyes, but this time wearing a veil.

Turning towards the people on the road, Our Blessed Lady said, 'Sorry' and turning back she said, 'I want prayers . . . The world must improve and the world must believe. If the world does not improve the devil will take over the Church.' . . .

Then Satan appeared on Our Blessed Lady's left, laughing and jeering at her. She was weeping . . .

The vision disturbed many people who could not understand how Satan could appear with Our Blessed Lady.

Melleray Grotto committee

The following is an account of a baptism in the Spirit. **Charles Finney** comes into his room.

. . . [As I] was about to take a seat by the fire, I received a mighty baptism of the Holy Ghost. Without any expectation of it, . . . the Holy Spirit descended upon me in a manner that seemed to go through me, body and soul. I could feel the impression, like a wave of electricity, going through and through me. Indeed it seemed to come in waves and waves of liquid love . . . I wept aloud with joy and love . . . How long I continued in this state . . . I do not know. [Someone came to see him and asked if he was in pain]) I gathered myself up as best I could, and replied, 'No, but so happy that I cannot live.'

William James,
The Varieties of Religious Experience

Types of religious experience

We can see from these examples that religious experiences vary considerably.

We can also see that some find it difficult to express what happened in their experience. They do not say clearly what actually took place. Instead, they use symbols and images to try to explain what happened.

Some people claim to have had a religious experience that is not as direct and powerful as some of the ones we have quoted above. They say that they felt God was present, or they felt his help. Yet, they do not claim to have experienced God directly. They may have had this experience when they were in trouble, or when they received a sacrament, or when they prayed, or were listening to music, or when they saw something beautiful, especially a natural beauty.

Genuine religious experiences

Teresa of Avila knew that some people reported religious experiences that were fraudulent; they deliberately made them up to get attention.

Yet Teresa believed that she, and others, had genuinely experienced God himself. But she also knew that if someone genuinely feels they have had an experience of God, this is not a guarantee that they did experience God. Teresa suggested three possible explanations for a religious experience:

- God caused it.
- The Devil caused it.
- The person's own imagination caused it.

Teresa believed it was possible to tell whether God had caused a religious experience. She used two criteria:

- Does the content of the experience agree with what the Church teaches?
- Does the experience leave a person joyful, peaceful, calm and willing to do God's will, and not restless, angry, unhappy, disturbed?

If the answer to both questions is yes, then she thought it was likely that God had caused the experience of himself. If the answer is no, then she thought it was likely that the devil had caused the experience of God; or it was likely that the person had simply imagined it themself.

Healthy and sick experiences

William James, a philosopher with a keen interest in religion, described some religious experiences as healthy and others as sick.

Those who had **healthy** experiences were optimistic that good things would happen. They were not happy when they suffered. They repented their sins and believed that God had forgiven them. They had confidence in God. And they were joyous people, not moody and despondent people.

Those who had **sick** experiences were gloomy and sad people. They were excessively engrossed with suffering. They were too absorbed in themselves. They were exceedingly preoccupied with their sins. They saw evil and failure everywhere. And they saw nothing admirable or attractive about other people or the world.

Objections to religious experience

Some people believe that all religious experience is false. Anyone who claims to have a religious experience is either mistaken or has lied. There are several arguments to support this view, such as:

- If religious experiences are genuine, then we should all be able to have such an experience. But most of us do not have a religious experience.
- If we knew God directly, we would inevitably like him: he is so good, we would find it impossible not to like him. But God wants us to decide freely to like him. So, God does not allow us to have a direct experience of him in this life. This means that religious life on earth is based on faith.
- It is too easy for someone who is lonely, or who is depressed, or who is afraid, to imagine that they have had a religious experience.
- God does not exist. There is no spiritual reality outside ourselves. Therefore, a religious experience is not possible.
- People experience only what they believe. A Hindu would have a vision of Krishna, not Jesus. A Christian would have a vision of Jesus, not Krishna. So it is our religious beliefs that make us have religious experiences.
- Some people are hyper-suggestible. They are too quick to imagine things, and they do not critically question what they imagine. These are the people who have religious experiences.
- People from different religions have different religious experiences. A Catholic sees Mary; a Protestant feels the Holy Spirit; a Hindu meets Krishna; a Buddhist experiences the Buddha. So each of them gives a different description of a religious experience. But, if these were genuine religious experiences, wouldn't the descriptions be the same, or similar?
- God is totally different from human beings. It is not possible to have a direct experience of him.

Arguments for genuineness of religious experience

- If we see a bus in front of us, we do not doubt it, unless we have a good reason to doubt it. If we experience God, we should not doubt it, unless we have a good reason to. We should always assume that our experience is correct, until we have a good reason to doubt it.
- We accept what someone tells us, unless we have good reason not to believe them. If we always doubted what someone told us, our life would be stifled. We could not lead a normal life. We would also have twisted personalities. Consequently, if someone tells us that they have had a religious experience, then we should believe them – unless we have a good reason to doubt them. If we know someone who is honest, and that person tells us they have had a religious experience, then we have a good reason to believe them – they are honest.
- If someone claims a religious experience, and they change their way of life for the better, then this substantiates their claim.

Examination practice

1. Some people say they have had an experience of God. Give an example. (3 marks)
   Write not more than six lines.

2. Some people say they have had a religious experience. Explain the arguments for and against believing them. (10 marks)
   Write about one side of A4.

3. Suppose someone has an experience of God. What might be the effect on that person? (8 marks)
   Write about three-quarters of a side of A4.

4. Quote an example of a religious experience. Do you believe it? Give reasons for your view. Show that you have considered the opposite view. (8 marks)
   Write about three-quarters of a side of A4.

Introduction

Does God exist? We may already have a definite view. And perhaps no argument will alter our point of view. Still, that does not stop us from taking a keen interest in arguments for or against the existence of God. But will we consider them with an unbiased mind?

Some useful words

theist: someone who believes there is a God.
atheist: someone who believes there is no God.
agnostic: someone who is not sure if there is a God. There may be a God, but there is not convincing evidence for or against the existence of God.

Argument from experience

Some people say they have experienced God. Consequently, they have no doubt that God is real. See Chapter B2, *Religious experience*, for more ideas on this.

Argument from tradition

Most people in all other ages have believed in God.

In our materialistic age fewer people have believed in God. This may be because newspapers and television encourage us to want sexual pleasures, or to gain money, or to get a prestigious job, or to get power over other people. Such opportunities attract us, as we are not instinctively interested in the welfare of other people. Consequently, we ignore God. We refuse to accept that we are finite. We forget that we are mortal; and we forget that we have to face God when we die. Unhappily, we may also neglect our responsibilities to other people.

Despite all these temptations, most people in our generation dimly perceive that there is a God.

In all other times people have been more aware of these matters. Most of them have acknowledged that there is a superior power – God. They have realized that they must face this power when they die. Can they all be wrong?

Argument from the design of the world

This has always been the most appealing argument for the existence of God. One famous form of this argument was

written by **William Paley**, an English Christian who lived in the eighteenth century.

He suggested that if we look at a watch, we notice that all the parts fit together: all the wheels, cogs, springs and other parts depend on each other. And they fit together for a purpose, so we cannot explain the operation of the watch by chance. We have to infer that the watch has a maker.

Now, said Paley, the same argument applies to the world. All the parts of nature fit together in a purposeful way. And the world is far more complicated than a watch, so we cannot explain the world by chance. There has to be a maker.

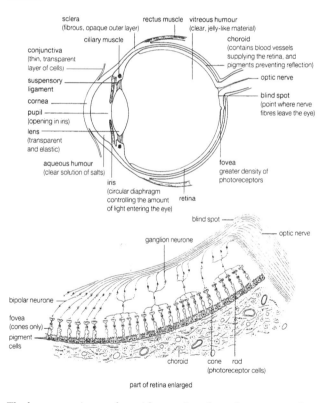

The human eye is complex, with many interdependent parts, and an obvious purpose – to enable us to see. Can the parts of an eye come together by chance? Most unlikely. So doesn't an eye imply a Designer and Maker?

Argument from the beauty of the world

If we gaze at the stars and imagine how vast the universe is; or if we consider how extraordinary and complex the human body is; or if we are amazed by a flower, a cloudy sky, or mountains; or if we marvel at a calm sea – then we

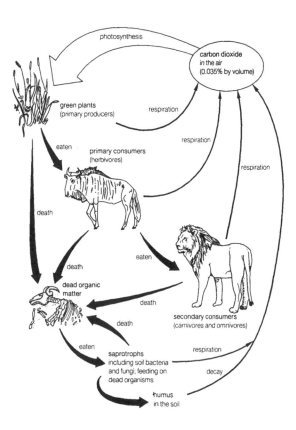

There is a cycle in nature. The life and death of animals and plants fit together with a purpose – to enable the world to survive. Can this happen by chance? Does it not imply a Designer and Maker? Source: Adapted from Clegg & Mackean, Advanced Biology (1994), John Murray Ltd

may feel that there has to be some power behind everything.

Augustine was a North African Christian who lived in the fourth and fifth centuries. He wrote:

> Question the beauty of the earth, question the beauty of the sea, question the beauty of the air . . ., question the beauty of the sky. . . . These beauties are subject to change. Who made them if not the Beautiful One who is not subject to change?

Argument from the existence of the world

This is a common argument for the existence of God. Many people think that we cannot give a convincing reasoned argument to prove that God exists. They think that many of the arguments for and against the existence of God are clever, yet confusing. They think that we can either get deflected into showing how clever our argument is, or we may think that because there are so many conflicting ideas, we must presume there is no God. In both cases, we forget that we are trying to make sense of the world.

Yet most of us feel there has to be a Something, simply because the world exists. We feel that there has to be some explanation for the world. We suspect that there has to be some power greater than ourselves – greater than the world. Otherwise the world would not make sense. We do not have

any clear understanding of this power. We may be faintly aware that it has to exist. Or we may be definite that it does exist.

Argument from causes to a First Cause

There are different versions of this argument. The following version comes from **Thomas Aquinas**, a Christian theologian who lived in Italy in the thirteenth century.

If something happens, it is caused by something else, which is caused by something else, and so on. We do not observe anything that causes itself. Nor can something cause itself, for it would then precede itself, which is impossible.

For example, there is a cause why I am reading this book. And that cause also has a cause. And so on. But a series of causes cannot go back for ever. It has to stop somewhere, otherwise there would be no effects, and I would not be reading this book.

So there has to be a first cause, to which everyone gives the name 'God'.

Some people call this the **cosmological argument**. But this name is also used for other arguments: for example, for the argument from contingency; or for the argument from the existence of the world; or the argument from the beauty of the world. So be careful when examiners mention the 'cosmological argument'. They might mean any argument that starts with the world (cosmos) and concludes that God must exist.

Argument because the world is contingent

This is a precise argument by **Aquinas**. The word 'contingent' is not a word we use much. If something is contingent, it requires another thing for it to exist. A contingent thing does not necessarily have to exist.

Aquinas said this argument is:

> based on what need not be and what must be . . .
>
> Some things we come across can be but need not be, for we find them springing up and dying away, thus sometimes in being and sometimes not.
>
> Now everything cannot be like this, for a thing that need not be, once was not; and if everything need not be, once upon a time there was nothing.
>
> But if that were true there would be nothing even now, because something that does not exist can only be brought into being by something already existing.
>
> So that if nothing was in being, nothing could be brought into being; and nothing would be in being now, which contradicts observation.
>
> Not everything therefore is the sort of thing that need not be; there has to be something that must be . . .
>
> One is forced therefore to suppose something that must be, and owes this to no other thing than itself . . .

This is a remarkable argument for the existence of God. It is perhaps the critical argument for the existence of God. Most of us struggle to understand it, even after reading it ten times.

Aquinas is suggesting:

- that everything we know is contingent: it does not have to exist.
- But if this was the only kind of thing that existed, then nothing could ever have come into existence, since something contingent cannot explain the universe, as it is dependent on something else.
- So, to explain the existence of contingent things, there has to be a necessary thing.

Argument from the idea of God

Anselm was a Christian who lived in the eleventh century. He was born in Italy, moved to France, and then to England, where he became archbishop of Canterbury.

He thought that we could prove that God exists simply by looking carefully at the idea of God. His argument is short. We call it the **ontological argument**. It goes like this:

- What do we mean by God?
- Something perfect in all ways. We could not think of anything more perfect.
- But suppose God does not exist.
- Then he is not the most perfect thing we can think of.
- So, if God is the most perfect thing we can think of, then he must exist.

Argument from successful prayer

Some Christians claim that God has answered their prayers. They may have asked God to help their parents to sort out their arguments. They may have asked God to heal a grandparent who was seriously ill. They may have asked God to help them to pass an exam. And they got what they asked for. Consequently they have evidence that God exists.

Argument from moral behaviour

Most of us know that we have a conscience. Perhaps we cannot describe it clearly; yet we do not doubt that we have a conscience. Some Christians believe that as we have a conscience, there must be a God.

There are different versions of this argument. One version was put forward by the Catholic bishops at the **Second Vatican Council** (which met in the 1960s). They said:

> Deep within his conscience man discovers a law that he has not laid upon himself but which he must obey. Its voice, ever calling him to love and to do what is good

> and to avoid evil, tells him inwardly at the right moment: do this; shun that. For man has in his heart a law inscribed by God. . . . There he is alone with God whose voice echoes in his depths.

A second version of the argument is by **John Newman**, an English theologian who lived in the nineteenth century. He said that if we do something wrong then we feel bad about it. We may have enjoyed doing wrong, but our conscience makes us feel guilty about it, and we feel ashamed at what we have done, as we feel responsible for what we have done. On the other hand, if we do good, we feel pleased. Our conscience makes us feel proud because we feel we have acted responsibly.

Now, argued Newman, if we feel responsible, proud and guilty about our behaviour, this implies that there must be someone to whom we are responsible – not to any human person, but to someone greater: a power beyond this world.

A third version of the argument from moral behaviour is by **Immanuel Kant**, a German philosopher who lived in the eighteenth century. He said that we know what is right and we know what is wrong. We also know that we should do right and avoid wrong, whatever the consequences – that is our duty. And each of us decides whether we do right or wrong. Nobody else decides for us.

Now, argued Kant, if we do our duty and we do what is right, it should lead to the perfect society. And in this perfect society good people should be rewarded with a happy life. But we know that we do not have the perfect society on earth, and that good people do not always have the reward of happiness in this life. So Kant inferred from this that there must be a life after death, where good people are rewarded with happiness. And only a God could do this. So there must be a God.

Argument from miracles

Suppose we know someone who is seriously ill with cancer. The doctor says that she will not recover. A second doctor says the same. And suppose everyone at the local church prays for that person to recover, and she does recover. The doctors tell us they have no explanation for the cure. Is that a miracle? Does it prove that there is a God?

You may have heard about a person who had badly shattered legs from a car accident. The doctors tried to mend them, but were unsuccessful. They regretfully told the patient he would have to use a wheelchair, as he would not be able to use his legs again. He went to Lourdes, a pilgrimage centre in France (see Chapter A10, *Pilgrimage*, for details of Lourdes). On the third day there, he got out of his wheelchair and walked. He never used his wheelchair again. Is that a miracle? Does it prove there is a God?

Suppose we were with Jesus when he fed a crowd of 5000 people with five loaves and two fish. There were 12 baskets of leftovers (Mark 6^{30-44}). Would we have thought this was a miracle? And does it prove there is a God?

Suppose someone we knew came back from the dead. Would that be a miracle? And does it prove there is a God?

Examination practice

1. What is the difference between a theist, an atheist and an agnostic? (3 marks)
   Write about six lines.

2. Select **four** arguments for the existence of God.
   Explain each one. (10 marks)
   Write about a side of A4

3. Christians believe there is a God.
   How might this influence their attitude to the world, to themselves and to others? (8 marks)
   Write about three-quarters of a side of A4.

4. Select **one** argument for the existence of God.
   Do you agree with it? Give reasons for your view.
   Show that you have understood more than one point of view. (8 marks)
   Write about three-quarters of a side of A4.

ARGUMENTS FOR THE EXISTENCE OF GOD – II

Pascal's curious argument

Blaise Pascal, a Frenchman who lived in the seventeenth century, said there was no convincing argument for or against the existence of God. Yet, he said, none of us can ignore this matter. We all have to decide how to live our lives. We have to decide either to behave as God wants us to, or to behave as we want to.

Thus we have to decide whether to believe there is a God or to believe there is no God. And as there is no convincing evidence, we have to choose.

Well, which should we choose to believe? Which one will we bet on?

If we choose to believe that there is no God, and we lead selfish lives, what might we gain? Punishment in hell! What might we lose? Heaven!

If we choose to believe in God, and we lead our lives the way God wants us to, what might we gain? Heaven! What might we lose if there is no God? Nothing, because we will not exist!

Thus Pascal thought it was obvious that we should choose to believe in God.

Can we prove God exists?

Do Christians believe we can prove that God exists? They disagree.

Some Christians say that there are valid arguments to show that God exists. For instance, the Catholic bishops at the **First Vatican Council** (1869–70) said:

> . . . God, the origin and end of all things, can be known with certainty by . . . reason from the things that he created; for (as Paul says in Romans 1[20]) 'since the

> creation of the world his invisible attributes are clearly seen, being understood through the things that are made'.

Other Christians agree with **Karl Barth**, a prominent Protestant theologian who lived in the twentieth century. They believe that human reasoning is inaccurate and untrustworthy because of original sin. (See Chapter C9, *Human nature*, for information on original sin.) They say that some of the arguments for the existence of God may sound fine; yet they are unconvincing, as original sin has deformed human reasoning and made it unreliable. Thus we cannot prove God exists. Instead, they believe that we have to rely solely on God revealing himself to us. Now all Christians believe that God revealed himself to us when he became the man Jesus. So these Christians stress that the only way we can find out about God is through what Jesus said and did.

Yet others emphasize the importance of faith in God. They say that if we can prove the existence of God, then we cannot have faith in him. **Hick**, a twentieth century philosopher, says that God wants us to choose to believe in him, and God wants us to choose to love him. Yet if it was obvious that God existed, and if it was obvious that he was a good and lovable person, we would have no choice but to believe in him and to love him. Consequently, so that we can choose to believe in him, God decides to remain hidden: he gives us enough evidence to think there may be a God, but not enough evidence to convince us that there must be a God. The evidence is ambiguous. Therefore, the arguments for God's existence are tantalising, but not sufficiently persuasive.

Objections

Suppose there is an easy question on the exam paper: it tells us to write any argument for the existence of God. But then it tells us to mention any objection to this argument. Some of us may have clear ideas of what to write, but some of us may be uncertain. So here are some suggestions.

Argument from experience

See Chapter B5, *Arguments against the existence of God – I*, and Chapter B2, *Religious experience*.

Argument from tradition

Perhaps many people in the past did believe in God. Yet we can argue that they were uneducated and superstitious, so it is not surprising that they believed in God. Nowadays, aren't we better educated and more rational? So it is not surprising that more people today do not believe in God. The view of an educated, rational person must be more convincing than that of an uneducated, superstitious person.

Argument from the design of the world

Animals compete with each other and are aggressive to each other. Animals hunt and kill other animals for food and territory. Only the fittest survive – that is, those that have strength and cunning, rather than those that cooperate and help each other. How can we call this a well-designed world? It seems a badly designed world.

Humans are like animals. See Chapters B10 and B11, *Suffering and evil*, for details.

Thus the argument from design ignores all the cruelty and suffering in the world. For how can hatred, misery, mutilation, torture, hunger, death, and so on fit into a world that is supposedly well designed? These things indicate a disorganized, or even a purposeless world. So, instead of saying that the world is badly designed, perhaps a better explanation is to say that the world is not designed – that things happen by chance (randomly), rather as the winner of the National Lottery is chosen by chance (randomly).

Evolution also indicates that the world is not designed. There are changes in the environment that happen by chance. For instance, a volcano may make a new island. At the same time there are chance mutations in birds and animals. For instance, a bird with a short, fat beak may by chance give birth to a bird with a long, thin beak. And this freak offspring is better adapted to the changed environment, so it survives instead of the bird with the short, fat beak. (See Chapter B9, *Creation; evolution* for more information.) Evolution is not planned; it happens by chance. So there is no Designer.

Argument from the beauty of the world

Such perceptions of the world are ephemeral and occasional. They are not typical, as there is much ugliness and cruelty in the world. What about children who are born deformed? And insects on a hot day? And partners who commit adultery? And neighbours who are selfish? And people who murder, rape and terrorize other people in their own country? These things are not part of a beautiful world. Perhaps the Ugly One (the Devil) made them. If so, the Beautiful One does not have much control over this world – he is not much of a God.

Argument from the existence of the world

The world does not need any explanation. It just is. It has no purpose. Some people cannot accept this, and want to invent a God to explain the world, but that is simply their inability to accept that the world has no explanation.

Argument from causes to a First Cause

There could be an infinite series of causes. In which case, there is no first cause.

Argument because the world is contingent

It is unintelligible to talk of something that must be, as we are not aware from our experience of any such thing. So the idea of a necessary being is nonsense.

Argument from the idea of God

We may think something *should* exist, but this does not mean that it *does* exist.

Argument from successful prayer

What about those people whose prayer was not successful? We cannot answer that God was punishing them, because we would then make God into a nasty, vindictive person. Nobody can believe in that kind of God.

Argument from moral behaviour

This argument starts with the assumption that we have a common sense of right and wrong. Yet we do not discover any laws within us that tell us what we should do and what we should not do. Instead, we decide what is right and wrong. Consequently, we have different views on what is right and what is wrong, and there are no objective moral laws that bind us, and for which we feel a sense of responsibility.

Alternatively, we can agree that we all have a common sense of right and wrong. But instead of saying that we get this sense of right and wrong from God, we can say that we get a sense of right and wrong by seeing what benefits other people. We have a sense of right and wrong because we want to do the best for society, not because God has put the thoughts into our minds.

Argument from miracles

If God exists, why doesn't he help all those who need help, rather than the occasional person? And if he is so good, why is there so much suffering and evil in the world? See Chapters B10 and B11, *Suffering and evil*, for more information.

Pascal's curious argument

Suppose we choose to believe in God and there is no God – we shall have lived a life of self-denial and unhappiness on earth, with no happiness after death. A pointless sacrifice!

Suppose we choose not to believe in God, and there is a God – won't he have mercy on us?

So we have everything to gain if we do not believe in God. We lose nothing if we do not believe in God.

Examination practice

1. Pascal's argument for belief in God is a curious argument. Explain why. (3 marks)
   Write about six lines.

2. Select **five** arguments for the existence of God. Explain the objections to each of them.
   (10 marks)
   Write about one side of A4.

3. Atheists believe there is no God.
   How might this influence their attitude to the world, to themselves and to others? (8 marks)
   Write about three-quarters of a side of A4.

4. Select **one** argument for the existence of God.
   Do you disagree with it? Give reasons for your view. Show that you have understood more than one point of view. (8 marks)
   Write about three-quarters of a side of A4.

ARGUMENTS AGAINST THE EXISTENCE OF GOD – I

Introduction

It is not easy to prove that the Loch Ness monster or Father Christmas do not exist. We can say that there is no evidence that they exist, but this does not necessarily mean they do not exist. Some people think it is the same with God. We can only say there is no evidence that he exists; but this does not mean he does not exist.

However, we shall see from the following sections that there are some arguments that aim to prove that God does not exist.

Some useful words

theist: someone who believes there is a God.
atheist: someone who believes there is no God.
agnostic: someone who is not sure if there is a God. There may be a God, but there is not convincing evidence for or against the existence of God.

Atheism

There have been more atheists in the last 150 years than at any other time in human history. We can explain this in two contrasting ways.

- Perhaps it is because we have learned to free ourselves from the fear of hell, and to free ourselves from the desire for heaven. We have learned to accept that there is no reason why we exist; and to accept that we do not exist after death. We have learned not to let religious leaders intimidate us. We have learned that we can improve life on earth without God. And we have learned that reason and science, not religious faith, tell us what is true.

- Or perhaps the technological successes of the last 200 years have made us over-confident about our ability to solve all problems and to answer all questions. So we think we can manage without God. We think we can sort out all wars and conflicts, without God's help; and we think we can establish the perfect society on earth, without God's help. And perhaps the opportunities to earn money, to have sex, and to get a good job have encouraged us to concentrate on money, sex and work, and to ignore things like God and death.

And perhaps we have been educated, at school, by the newspapers, and by television, to be excessively critical of everything. Consequently, we doubt all things, including God.

Atheists are convinced that we can prove that God does not exist. Here are some of the arguments.

Argument from miracles

This argument presumes that religious people use miracles to prove that there is a God. The argument points out that miracles are not possible. Consequently, there is no proof that God exists.

David Hume proposed several arguments to show why we cannot believe in miracles. He was a Scottish philosopher who lived in the eighteenth century. His most important arguments are the first one and the final one.

- Examples of miracles would be: if a person rises from the dead; if lead is suspended in air; if wood burns without being consumed; or if water does not put out fire.

  We can see from these examples that a miracle is something that goes against the laws of nature. A law of nature is something that we have always observed to have happened, in any age or in any country. So, for example, no one has ever seen a person come back from the dead. Thus it is a law of nature that people do not come back from the dead. Consequently, people cannot come back from the dead. It is not possible. Therefore, miracles are self-contradictory.
- There have been no miracles witnessed by enough educated people: that is, people (according to Hume) who are intelligent, accurate and trustworthy witnesses.
- Some people think they have seen a miracle. This is simply because they are 'greedy' for miracles. They are desperate to see wondrous things. The same reason explains why some people are keen to believe in miracles.
- Only people in barbarous nations believe in miracles. Once a nation becomes civilized, its people no longer believe in miracles.
- Every religion uses miracles to claim it is the true religion. This makes us suspicious of any claim for any miracle.
- In the case of any reported miracle (for instance, that someone has come back from the dead), we should ask this question: What is more likely – that the person reporting the miracle was mistaken; or that the miracle happened? In every case, we would go for the first answer. Therefore, we cannot believe in miracles.

Argument because the idea of God is contradictory

Theists say that God is spiritual: that he has no body. Yet they also say that God loves, that God forgives, that God judges, and so on.

However, someone who loves, forgives or judges has to act. We can only know if someone loves, forgives or judges by what they do or say. And people can act or speak only if they have a body. Someone without a body cannot act or speak.

Consequently, it is contradictory to say that God is a spirit and that he loves, judges and forgives. And so the idea of God must be meaningless.

Argument from suffering and evil

This is the most impressive argument against the existence of God. It goes like this:

- Christians believe that God is wholly good; they also believe God can do anything (he is omnipotent – i.e. all-powerful).
- However, there is considerable suffering and evil in the world.
- This means: either God cannot be wholly good, or God cannot be omnipotent.
- If he was wholly good, he would want to stop the evil and suffering. And if he was omnipotent, he could stop the evil and suffering.
- So the Christian God does not exist.

See Chapters B10 and B11, *Suffering and evil*, for more ideas.

Argument from unanswered prayer

Some people claim that God has not answered their prayers. They may have asked God to help their parents to sort out their arguments. They may have asked God to heal a grandparent who was seriously ill. They may have asked God to help them to pass an exam. And they did not get what they asked for. Consequently they have evidence that God does not exist.

Argument from experience

We have never seen a flying saucer, so we do not believe in flying saucers. Nor have we seen the Loch Ness monster, so we do not believe it exists. Nor have we seen Father Christmas, so we do not believe that he exists.

Most of us have not experienced God, so we do not believe that there is a God.

Some people claim to have experienced God, but they are mistaken.

Perhaps they were desperate for help, and so they imagined that they experienced God. We cannot blame them; yet we are not convinced by their experience, as it is unhealthy.

Perhaps they are just odd. They are often loners who find it difficult to mix with the rest of us. They are sensitive and vulnerable. Hence they withdraw from our company as soon as they are hurt, and in their loneliness they seek some other kind of companionship. So they easily imagine there is a God that can console them. We cannot blame them, but we are not convinced by their experience, as it is the result of a disordered mind.

Arguments from wish fulfilment

These are impressive explanations why some people believe in God.

We do not get everything we want. We also find that other people are stronger than us, and that other people quite often hurt us.

Now most of us can manage to cope with this. For instance, we change things so that we get what we want, or we assert ourselves so that we are as strong as other people, or we prevent others from hurting us, or we avoid situations where we will be frustrated, or we accept situations that we cannot change.

Unfortunately, some people cannot cope, so they invent God. There are two famous versions of this argument.

Freud

Freud was an Austrian psychologist who lived in the nineteenth and twentieth centuries.

He said that our fathers protected us when we were children. Whenever we were in danger, they shielded us. Whenever we felt insecure, they comforted us. Whenever we needed help we could go to them and ask for it. And so on.

Now that we are grown up we have to look after ourselves, but we find that the natural world and the social world are hostile.

Left to ourselves, particularly if we live in an undeveloped country, it is difficult to cope with changes in the weather. The freezing winter can kill us if we do not have warm clothing and secure shelter. The sun can be too hot, there can be too much rain, or there can be insufficient rain – all these can destroy crops, and leave us without food. There are insects that can cause serious diseases and that devastate crops. And so on.

Left to ourselves, we find it difficult to cope with insecurity, sickness and death. We dread such things.

Left to ourselves, we also find it difficult to cope with other people, as they compete with us in many ways. They want to show that they are superior to us, so they try to make us look small. They want more power than us. They want to be more popular than us. They may physically intimidate us.

Now those of us who are educated and mature can face these difficulties, accept the real world, and be brave.

But other people cannot cope, so they invent a new

Father, one who has superior powers. They imagine there is a Father up in the sky who will look after them, just as their natural father did when they were younger. They believe that this Father will welcome them into his kingdom when they die. But all this is simply wish fulfilment, rather like some of our dreams.

Marx

Karl Marx was a German philosopher who lived in the nineteenth century.

Marx said that there have always been two opposing classes in society: the smaller class (the wealthy people), who exploit; and the larger class (the poor people), who are exploited. This leads to conflict between the two classes. The exploiting class want to hold on to their privileged and domineering position, and so they refuse to allow the exploited class to share their wealth. However, the exploited class want to change things, so that they can have a fairer share of wealth. In the end, the exploited class will have to revolt violently against the dominant class, to get a fairer share of wealth. But the exploited are reluctant to do this.

Now, suggested Marx, the exploiting class invented God to help them maintain their domineering position. If they could claim that God gave them the right to be wealthy, then the poor might remain poor. And this ruse of the wealthy was successful. The exploited class were willing to believe in God and his love. This belief helped them. They could put up with misery and exploitation in this life if they believed that, after death, they would enjoy happiness in heaven, and the exploiters would go to hell and suffer. Marx thought the poor should have challenged the rich people: that the poor should have tried to get a better life now on earth. Instead, the poor willingly believed in God, and they accepted the help of priests to worship God. They thought that God wanted them to suffer in this life. So God was a consolation to them in their misery. He was their 'opium'.

Examination practice

1. Suggest why there are more atheists today than at any previous time.   (3 marks)
   Write about six lines.

2. Select **four** arguments against the existence of God. Explain them.   (10 marks)
   Write about one side of A4.

3. Atheists believe there is no life after death.
   How might this influence their attitude to the world, to themselves and to others?   (8 marks)
   Write about three-quarters of a side of A4.

4. Select **one** argument against the existence of God.
   Do you agree with it? Give reasons for your view.
   Show that you have understood more than one point of view.   (8 marks)
   Write about three-quarters of a side of A4.

Argument from materialism

This is the most popular argument to prove that there is no God.

Material things are things we can touch, see, or hear; or sometimes taste or smell – for instance, a table, a chair, or a book. We all agree that such things are real.

Spiritual things are things we cannot touch, see or hear; and we cannot taste or smell them – for instance, our minds. We cannot touch our minds, nor can we see them, nor can we hear them, and we certainly cannot taste or smell them.

Materialists believe that the only real things are material things. They believe that there is only one true test for whether something is real: can we touch it, see it, hear it, taste it or smell it? If we can, then it is real. If we cannot, then it is not real. This test is called the **empiricist's test**.

Materialists also note that scientists have increased our knowledge of the world. We all agree that scientists have given us information about both the stars and the atom that was not even imagined 50 years ago. Did you know that astronomers have detected stars ten billion light years away? It would take ten thousand million years, travelling at the speed of light (approx 300 000 km per second, or 186 282 miles per second), to reach these stars. Almost incredible!

Scientists have also been very successful. Their ideas have led to enormous advances in our technology: for instance, to the nuclear bomb, flights to the moon, space shuttles, control of diseases, computers, better and cheaper food, sophisticated cars, marvellous sound quality on CDs, and so on. Consequently, materialists argue that the scientific way of looking at things must be the only true way of looking at things. And as materialists believe that scientists use nothing but the empiricist's test, they conclude that the empiricist's test is the only way to find out if something is real or useful.

Now, we cannot see, touch or hear God. We cannot point to him and say: 'There he is'. We certainly cannot smell or taste him, as he is a spiritual thing. So, we cannot empirically discover God. We cannot identify him in any way. Thus we must conclude that God cannot exist.

Argument because statements about God have no meaning

For any statement is to be meaningful, we must know what might prove it false. This is a **falsification test**.

For example, if I say, 'I have a book in my hand', we could accept this as a meaningful statement only if we knew what might prove this statement false.

In this case, we can propose this test: if we do not see the book in my hand, then my statement is false. Thus, as I have a falsification test, I can say my statement is meaningful.

Now theists say that God exists. If we ask them what might prove their statement false, they tell us that there is nothing that might prove it false. But there has to be something that might prove their statement false, if we are going to accept their statement as having meaning. So we have to conclude that their statement is meaningless: too vague to mean anything. Thus we cannot even consider whether it is true or false. It is simply meaningless.

Objections

Suppose there is an easy question on the exam paper: it tells us to write any argument against the existence of God. But then it tells us to mention any objection to this argument. Some of us may have clear ideas of what to write, but some of us may be uncertain. So here are some suggestions.

Before we start, we have to understand the **empiricist fallacy**.

A **fallacy** is an argument that seems to be true, but is mistaken.

An **empiricist** is someone who believes that the only way to find out if something is true or real is to test it using one of our senses. As we have seen above, this is called the empiricist's test. Can we see it? Can we touch it? Can we hear it? Can we taste it? Can we smell it? If we can, it is real or true. If we can't, it is not real or true. And most of us agree that this is a sensible test.

However, there is a contradiction in the empiricist's test. We cannot prove this test by seeing it, touching it, and so on. So, by its own test, it is not true. The empiricist's test is a fallacy. The empiricist's test may be one way to discover if something is true or real, but it can't be the *only* way to discover if something is true or real.

We often find the empiricist fallacy in arguments against the existence of God.

Argument from miracles

The first of Hume's arguments is illogical. He says that someone cannot come back from the dead because no one has ever seen someone come back from the dead. This is a classic example of a **circular argument**: to prove that a miracle cannot happen, Hume assumes that a miracle has never happened. But we cannot assume what we have to prove.

In the last of his six arguments Hume says that anyone

who reports a miracle must be mistaken. But this is not true. For example, if one of our friends tells us that she has seen a dead person alive and well, do we believe her? We shall certainly start by doubting her. Yet suppose that we really trust her, that we think she is convinced of what she believes, and that we notice her way of life has improved because of her experience. We might then think she was right rather than mistaken.

Argument because the idea of God is contradictory

This is an example of the empiricist fallacy, which we often meet in arguments against the existence of God. It assumes that something is real only if it can be seen, touched, felt, tasted or smelled.

Now we know that we humans show our spiritual activities through our bodies. Thus we show we have thoughts by speaking. We show we love someone by what we do – by being attentive, courteous, kind, self-sacrificing, and so on.

We also know that thinking and loving are not things we can see, hear or touch. Yet we do not doubt that they are real. So there is no reason, in principle, why these activities cannot take place without a body, if there is a being without a body.

Argument from suffering and evil

See Chapters B10 and B11, *Suffering and evil*.

Argument from unanswered prayer

If God does not answer prayers, this does not prove he does not exist.

If someone does not answer my letters, does it prove that person does not exist? Possibly, but there are other explanations: she may be ill; she may be on holiday; she may not want to answer my letters; and so on.

Similarly, if God does not answer prayers, this may be because he does not exist. But there are other explanations: he has answered them, but not in the way I want; he has not yet answered them; he has some reason for not answering them; he has answered 'no'; he is not like a genie that I can summon up to do what I want whenever I want; and so on.

Argument from experience

See Chapter B2, *Religious experience*.

Argument from wish fulfilment

Suppose Freud or Marx is right: that people imagine there is a God because this is the only way they can fulfil their wishes. This does not prove there is no God. The argument only explains why people believe in God, and we cannot conclude from this that there is no God.

It is possible that Freud and Marx are right, and it is also possible that there is a God. Both may be true. They are compatible, not contradictory.

Argument from materialism

This is another example of the empiricist fallacy. We explained at the start of this section why the empiricist test is self-contradictory. The argument from materialism uses the empiricist's test. It assumes that if we cannot see, hear or touch something, then it cannot be real. So the argument from materialism is flawed.

We might also consider, for example, our thoughts or our feelings. We do not see, hear or touch them, but we are convinced they are real. We do not believe that our thoughts are nothing but electric impulses – we know that they are more than that. And we do not believe that our feelings are nothing but chemical changes in our bodies – we are aware that they are more than that. So it is wrong to think that only material things are real.

Argument because statements about God have no meaning

The falsification test is another instance, though more subtle, of the empiricist fallacy. It assumes that something is meaningless if we cannot see it, touch it, and so on. But we have seen that the empiricist test is contradictory and false, so we cannot conclude that statements about God have no meaning.

In any case, there is a simpler test to see if a statement is meaningful. We ask if we understand the statement. If we do, it is meaningful. If we don't, it is meaningless. This is a more useful test than the falsification test.

Conclusion

Some people have open minds when they listen to arguments for or against the existence of God.

But many of us find it difficult to be open minded on this matter. We are like the judge who wanted to reduce crime, and so tended to reach decisions before he had heard all the evidence. On one occasion this judge was trying a man accused of stealing cattle. The judge listened carefully to the prosecution lawyer, who argued that the man was guilty. However, when the defence lawyer stood up to argue that the man was innocent, the judge told him not to bother, as this would only confuse the jury!

See Chapter C9, *Human nature*, for more ideas about the characteristics of humans.

Examination practice

1. Explain the empiricist fallacy. (3 marks)
   Write about six lines.

2. Select **five** arguments against the existence of God. Explain the objections to each of them.   (10 marks)
   Write about one side of A4.

3. Christians believe there is a life after death. How might this influence their attitude to the world, to themselves, and to others?   (8 marks)
   Write about three-quarters of a side of A4.

4. Select **one** argument against the existence of God. Do you disagree with it? Give reasons for your view. Show that you have understood more than one point of view.   (8 marks)
   Write about three-quarters of a side of A4.

THE NATURE OF GOD – I

Introduction

Which of these statements is true?

- God is odd.
- God listens to me.
- Only God knows what God is like.
- God became a man.
- Any description of God must be inaccurate.
- God is in everything.
- God is unimaginable.
- God loves me.

Most Christians believe that all these statements are accurate, even though some of them seem to contradict each other. This assortment of statements illustrates how difficult it is to have a nice, tidy picture of God.

Is God elusive?

Some Christians do have a neat, clear view of God. But most Christians believe that God is elusive. As soon as they think they have understood God, he surprises them by showing them that they have misunderstood him. They then realize how easy it is to make God in their own image: to think of him as though he was human, albeit an extraordinary human. So they become less confident about how well they know him. They begin to appreciate that God is odd – quite different from humans. And they may even wonder if statements about God have any meaning.

See Chapter B12, *Can we describe God? – some difficulties*, for further details.

Despite these difficulties, Christians claim that we can know something about God. Even more important, Christians claim that we can get to know God. In this chapter we consider the typical Christian answers to the more philosophical questions about God.

Is God material or spiritual?

Material things are things we can touch, see, or hear; or sometimes taste or smell – for instance, a table, a chair, a book, or the person next to us. We all agree that such things are real.

We are material. We can see, touch and hear ourselves and others, so we accept that we are real.

Spiritual things are things we cannot touch, see or hear; and we cannot taste or smell them – for instance, our ideas. We cannot touch our ideas. Nor can we see them. Nor can we hear them. And we certainly cannot taste or smell them. Yet most of us know they are real.

It is the same with our feelings, such as anger, annoyance, joy, or triumph. We cannot touch them. Nor can we see them. Nor can we hear them. Nor can we taste or smell them. But most of us discern that they are real, not imaginary.

Thus humans are a mixture of material and spiritual.

God is quite different from us. We cannot see, touch or hear God. We certainly cannot smell or taste him. He is not material, just spiritual. We find this hard to understand.

The Catholic Catechism says:

> In no way is God in man's image. He is neither man nor woman. God is pure spirit in which there is no place for the difference between the sexes. But the respective 'perfections' of man and woman reflect something of the infinite perfection of God: those of a mother and those of a father and husband.

So God is not in man's image. Yet many people think God is a man, and so they misunderstand the Christian description of God. Christians describe God as Father, Son and Spirit. Many people, including Christians, understand these words literally. They do not realize that these words cannot be used literally, as God the Father, Son and Spirit are not human persons. See Chapters B12 and B13, *Can we describe God?*, for more information about the way we may use words to describe God.

Is God personal or impersonal?

Christians use the words 'Father', 'Son' and 'Spirit' to describe God. The words 'Father' and 'Son' denote persons. The word 'Spirit' denotes something impersonal.

Thus Christians believe we can imagine God as either personal or impersonal.

However, Christians prefer to think of God as a person, though many of them are aware that it is a mistake to imagine God as a human person. (See Chapter B13, *Can we describe God? – some solutions*, for a more precise explanation.) Christians prefer to think of God as a person because they believe that God made us to share in his life, to have a relationship with him, to receive his love, and to love him. And, in our experience, only persons can have a loving relationship. Impersonal things, such as rocks, do not love each other.

For details on the Christian understanding of God, read these chapters: C2, *God: Trinity*; C3, *God – the Father*; C4, *God – the Son*; C5, *God – the Holy Spirit*; C6, *Jesus – his identity*; C7, *Jesus – his mission; sin and salvation.*

Since God is a spirit, there is no accurate picture of him. Consequently, we can imagine God in different ways. Here are some examples, all done by young people.

Is God transcendent?

The Christian answer is 'yes'.

To say that God is transcendent means that he is different from everything else. God is much greater than anything else.

Orthodox Christians stress the transcendence of God in two ways. First, they place great importance on negative statements about God (which they call **apophatic statements**). Thus it is important to say what God is not:

- he is not male or female;
- he is not a human;
- he is not made;
- he is not touchable;
- he is not visible;
- he is not comprehensible;
- he is not mortal; and so on.

Second, they distinguish between God's essence and his energies. God's **essence** is that aspect of him that we can never know or approach. God's **energies** are that aspect of him that we get to know through creation and through Jesus Christ.

Orthodox Christians believe that their distinction between God's essence and his energies shows:

- first, that God is unapproachable, as he is so different from us; and
- second, that people can approach God, through creation and through Jesus.

Thus, by distinguishing God's essence and his energies, Orthodox Christians maintain that God is transcendent, even though they also believe that people can get to know him.

Warning

If one idea about God dominates the way we understand him, or if one idea controls the way we talk with him, then Christians believe we distort what God is like. Thus if we excessively emphasize that he is transcendent (or immanent), or that he is personal (or impersonal) then we are likely to make God what we want him to be, rather than what he is.

There are advantages and dangers in emphasizing that God is transcendent.

If Christians emphasize that God is transcendent, they are conscious how mysterious he is. They realize it is impossible to compare God with things that they know. They are in awe of God, and they do not make the mistake of thinking that God is a super-human. They understand that there is an unbridgeable difference between God and humans.

In their prayers and services, they will favour set prayers. And in their prayers they will concentrate on worshipping God, on appreciating his greatness and wonder. Their prayers will not say much about their ordinary, daily lives; about their loves and hates for each other; about poor people and rich people.

Christians may overemphasize that God is transcendent.

Then they may become reluctant to think of God as a person. They may make him remote, unapproachable, too unknowable. They may think that religion has little to do with daily matters: prejudice and discrimination; poverty and wealth; abortion and euthanasia; peace and war; marriage and divorce; sickness and failure; love and hatred; work and leisure; and so on.

Instead, Christians may think that religion is about telling God how important he is, about going to church once a week to tell him this, about making sure that they repair their churches so people can worship there, about punishing people who swear or blaspheme, and so on.

Examination practice

1. Many religious people think that God is elusive.
   Explain what they mean. (3 marks)
   Write about six lines.

2. 'God is spiritual, not material.'
   Explain the difference. (6 marks)
   Write about half a side of A4.

3. Some Christians emphasize that God is transcendent.
   What differences might this make to their worship, and to their interest in this world? (8 marks)
   Write about three-quarters of a side of A4.

4. Do you think God is personal or impersonal?
   Give reasons for your view. Show that you have understood more than one point of view. (8 marks)
   Write about three-quarters of a side of A4.

Is God immanent?

Christians believe that God is **immanent**. This means that God is with us; he is in us.

Christians have much to say about God's immanence. They believe that God made us to know him and to love him. They believe that God became a man to show his love for us. They believe that God is with us in many different ways, including sacraments.

For details on the Christian understanding of God's immanence, read these chapters: C4, *God – the Son*; C5, *God – the Holy Spirit*; C6, *Jesus – his identity*; C7, *Jesus – his mission; sin and salvation*; A16, *Sacraments: liturgical worship*.

When Christians emphasize that God is immanent, they see him as a person with whom they can have an easy relationship, as he always welcomes people with a kind word. They are certain that God is interested in whatever daily problems worry them, so they ask him to sort out any difficulties they face. They are confident that God believes in the just causes they support, and they have no doubt that God is always on their side. Consequently they may prefer to use their own words when they pray. Their prayers are usually chatty rather than formal. Their services are warm and lively. And they express openly their emotions, often through song and music.

Warning

There is a danger in overemphasizing the immanence of God.

Christians may be unaware that there is an infinite gulf between people and God. They may think they are so familiar with God that they can pray to him informally, while people less advanced than themselves have to use formal prayers. Thus they become haughty and over-confident. Perhaps they forget that God will one day judge them – he will judge them on how they treated other people and how generously they used their wealth. Perhaps they only remember God when they feel like it, or when they want to. Perhaps they, rather than God, become the focus of their religious services. And perhaps their emotions mould the way they see God.

Thus they may make God in their own image and likeness, rather than overcome their feelings and try to see God as he is.

Is God infinite?

We are **finite**. That means we are limited. For example:

- We are mortal: one day we shall die.
  We do not know everything: what we do know is only a little of what there is to know.
- We are not all-powerful: we may be more intelligent and capable than animals, but we cannot fly, nor can we prevent accidents, nor can we be in two places at once, and so on.
- We often do wrong, even though we know what is right.

God is **infinite**. God is not limited in any way. For example:

- God is immortal: God can never die.
- God knows everything, present and past. Perhaps God even knows what will happen in the future.
- God is all-powerful: he made the world and everything in it; God can do anything (though this does not mean that God can do logically impossible things, such as make a round square).
- God is totally good: God never does anything wrong; God never thinks anything evil.

Is God evil?

Definitely not, is the Christian answer. He is not evil. He has not created anything evil. And he has never done anything evil. See Chapter C3, *God – the Father*, for more information.

In that case, where does evil come from?

- Mainly from people, is the Christian answer. See Chapter C9, *Human nature*.
- Also from the devil, is a traditional Christian answer. The devil is usually called Satan. According to one tradition, Satan was one of the angels that God created. Angels are spiritual beings that have minds, thoughts and feelings, but no body. God created them good. But Satan and some other angels rebelled against God, preferring to do evil rather to do good.

Satan hates God and causes as much evil as he can in this world, stirring feelings of hatred and vengeance in people, so they turn against each other and against God. Satan tries to mislead people, so he is often called the 'father of lies'. Thus humans are a sort of battleground, where God and Satan are fighting. God wants us to do good, and Satan wants us to do evil.

Many contemporary Christians discard this explanation of evil. They realize that people can feel an extraordinary desire to do something evil, which they may try to resist. Yet people can find the desire overwhelming. And so some Christians imagine the desire comes from Satan, a power outside themselves, who pressures them to do an evil action that they do not want to do. They prefer to believe Satan causes the evil desires in them, rather than to believe that they themselves can desire to do something evil.

For other Christian explanations of evil, see Chapters B10 and B11, *Suffering and evil.*

> I tried to find out where evil comes from, and there was no answer.
>
> Augustine of Hippo

One God or many gods?

Christians reject the belief that there is more than one God. They believe there is only one God. Nothing can equal God. He is unique.

However, we should be cautious about saying there is only one God, as God is a spirit. We do not usually count spiritual things. Indeed, it is difficult to count spiritual things. When we count, it is usually things that we can see or touch: for instance, books, or tables, or people. We do not generally count ideas or feelings. They are spiritual. Yet

ideas are distinct and different, so we distinguish them. So we can tentatively count them – we can say that we have one or several ideas. Similarly, we can say there is only one God, rather than many gods.

Read Chapters B12 and B13, *Can we describe God?* They explain why our words about God are partial.

Though Christians maintain there is only one God, they believe there are three forms of God. But they do not use the word 'form'. They use the words 'person' or 'dimension'. They say there are three persons or dimensions in God: Father, Son and Spirit. Each of these persons is distinct. Yet there is only one God.

For further details see Chapter C2, *God: Trinity.*

Conclusion

We only discover what God is like if we are open-minded.

It is easy for Christians to become close-minded. They may think their religion has ready-made answers about the nature of God, so they close their minds to finding out about him. To illustrate this, an Indian Christian, de Mello, told about a sinner who was excommunicated by the Church. The sinner complained to God that other Christians had barred him from going to church. God replied: 'What are you complaining about? They won't let me in either!'

Examination guidance

Do you think that people today can experience the help of Jesus and God today?
Give reasons for your answer. Show that you have thought of more than one point of view. (5 marks)

First answer

I think that people can experience the help of God, because someone might be very ill and which there is no help for, but they might go somewhere such as Lourdes in France, and be cured, which many people have been. The people which have been there and been helped have been very ill for a long period of time, and have been to many doctors and had many operations and still not been cured but then they are better, which I feel is God helping them.

This candidate has made a relevant point: that very ill people can experience the help of God at Lourdes. Still, this is the only relevant point the candidate has made.

To obtain 3 or 4 marks, one point is not enough. To obtain 3 marks, several different points are required.

The candidate has written many words. Despite this, the answer gets a score of only 2 marks. This is because the candidate has given a flimsy development of the one point. The candidate could have developed this point more substantively and thus attained 3 marks.

The candidate has not written anything about the opposite point of view. Yet the question expressly asks the candidate to do this.

The candidate could have given a reason why some people hold the opposite point of view. Or the candidate could have said why the opposite point of view is unconvincing. Either is an acceptable way of considering the opposite point of view.

(Score: 2 marks out of 5)

Second answer

Yes I do think that you can experience the help of Jesus or God today. You might not experience it at close hand and directly, but there are many other ways.

For instance, God is always present in good people. These people allow God to work through them as they help others.

This is an exceptional answer.

- The candidate has made relevant points; and expressed each point clearly.
- There are diverse points. Each is distinctive yet appropriate to the topic.
- The candidate has also analysed, examined and

When Christians go to Mass it brings them closer to God. It is a time for prayer and remembrance. We can ask God for help in our family lives, at work, at school. In some ways this helps us. We feel that God is with us and that gives us strength and courage to face life and our problems.

We can also receive God's love and help through other sacraments, especially the sacrament of the sick. In this sacrament sick people may feel that God gives them courage to get better, or not to be anxious about death.

In some parts of the world, for example Lourdes, people can feel God's help physically as well as emotionally and spiritually. It can help them to get well. They have such a strong faith. They can experience God's love and power; this helps them to get better.

If you have faith in God, he can help you anywhere.

Third answer

I am not sure. Indeed, I doubt it.

I know people think they can receive the help of Jesus and God today through sacraments such as the anointing of the sick. They feel they are given faith and courage from God; this helps them to accept their illness, or even to make a complete recovery.

People also think they receive help from Jesus by reading the Bible and listening to his teaching. They are convinced they receive courage to help them live their lives.

Yet I find it hard to accept that we can receive help from Jesus and God because we neither see them nor hear them. We have no solid proof that they help us. People have only faith.

If God and Jesus do help, then surely we would all experience it, not just a few.

And how can people believe that God and Jesus help when there is so much awful suffering in the world?

I believe we can receive help from family, friends, doctors and such like, because we have all experienced such help.

developed some of the points, at times in a sophisticated way.

These are the principal characteristics of an excellent answer.

Thus this is an excellent answer. So why has the candidate received only 4 of the 5 marks? Because the candidate has not referred to the opposite point of view.

Beware! When you have to give your personal opinion, you can become engrossed in your answer. You may then forget to say something about the opposite point of view. And you will lose marks.

(Score: 4 marks out of 5)

Another excellent answer.

- The candidate has made relevant points; and expressed each point clearly.
- There are varied points. Each is distinctive yet appropriate to the topic.
- The candidate has also analysed, examined and developed some of the points, at times in a refined way.
- The candidate has also considered carefully, even sympathetically, the opposite point of view.

So, this is an answer that clearly deserves all five marks.

(Score: 5 marks out of 5)

Examination practice

1. 'God is infinite.'
   What does this mean? (3 marks)
   Write about six lines.

2. Most religious people think that God is not evil. So how do they explain where evil comes from? (6 marks)
   Write about half a side of A4.

3. Some Christians stress that God is immanent.
   What differences might this make to their worship, and to their interest in this world? (8 marks)
   Write about three-quarters of a side of A4.

4. What is the best way to describe God?
   Give reasons for your view. Show that you have understood more than one point of view. (8 marks)
   Write about three-quarters of a side of A4.

CREATION; EVOLUTION

Introduction

The book of Genesis begins with an account of God creating the heaven and the earth. Throughout the Bible God is described as the creator. His power and his wisdom as shown in creation are cause for wonder and for worship.

> When I consider your heavens,
>   the work of your fingers,
> the moon and the stars,
>   which you have set in place,
> what is man that you are mindful of him?
>
> Psalm 8$^{3-4}$

> He set the earth on its foundations;
>   it can never be moved.
> You covered it with the deep as with a garment . . .
> He makes springs pour water into the ravines;
>   it flows between the mountains.
> They give water to all the beasts of the field;
>   the wild donkeys quench their thirst . . .
> How many are your works O Lord!
>   In wisdom you made them all.
>
> Psalm 104

Scientists have discovered much evidence about the origin of the universe. They suggest theories to explain the process by which, over millions of years, the universe evolved until it reached its present state. Their theories are based on sound evidence.

To some people it seems that the more scientists discover, the less we need to use belief in God to explain the universe. Also, because the ideas of scientists are so different from what is written in Genesis, they feel the Bible is discredited.

Others believe that scientists are discovering more and more about the wonderful way in which God created the universe.

The creation narratives in Genesis

There are two creation narratives in the book of Genesis. They are quite different. In some points they contradict each other.

In the first account (Genesis 1^{1}–2^{3}) God clearly has a plan. His power is shown in the way he creates. He speaks the word and things happen as he has planned. All that he does is good.

> And God said, 'Let there be light,' and there was light. God saw that the light was good.
>
> Genesis 1^{3}

Each day for six days a further part of God's plan is put into effect. Heaven and earth are made separate. Dry land is raised above the waters of the seas. Vegetation is created, with seed to make possible the process of reproduction. Sun, moon and stars are created. The animal kingdom is created, living creatures of all kinds. Last of all the human race is created in God's image, male and female.

> So God created man
>   in his own image,
> in the image of God
>   he created him;
> male and female
>   he created them.
>
> God blessed them and said to them, 'Be fruitful and increase in number; fill the earth and subdue it. Rule over the fish of the sea and the birds of the air and over every living thing that moves on the ground.'
> God saw all that he had made, and it was very good.
>
> Genesis 1$^{27-28, 31}$

The second account (Genesis 2$^{4-25}$) begins:

> When the Lord God made the earth and the heavens – and no shrub of the field had yet appeared on the earth and no plant of the field had yet sprung up, for the Lord God had not sent rain on the earth and there was no man to work the ground, but streams came up from the earth and watered the whole surface of the ground – the Lord God formed the man from the dust of the ground and breathed into his nostrils the breath of life, and man became a living being.
>
> Genesis 2$^{4-7}$

So this version assumes that at the time of the creation of the first man neither the vegetable kingdom nor any other part of the animal kingdom existed. Vegetation is created after man, when God plants the Garden of Eden for man's benefit.

In this account, God does not seem to have the clear overall plan that the writer of the first account describes. God realizes he has not got it right. God feels the man should not be alone. So God creates the animal kingdom and brings them to man, who gives them names. Still God has not got it right. Man still needs a companion. So the man is made to sleep. God takes one of his ribs and from it forms woman. Man now has a suitable companion.

> The man said,
> 'This is now bone of my bones
>   and flesh of my flesh;
> she shall be called "woman",
>   for she was taken out of man.'
>
> Genesis 2^{23}

Note that these two accounts are different:

- Events take place in a different order.
- God is described in a quite different way.

In the first account, he is all-powerful. No mention is made of anything, any material, he used in creating. It appears that he created everything from nothing. He creates simply by saying the word, and everything at every stage is very good.

In the second account, he creates man and woman by moulding material that is already there; he takes a number of attempts to get everything right and to his satisfaction.

Fundamentalist Christians accept the accounts of the creation given in the book of Genesis. They believe that the apparent contradictions can be reconciled.

Other Christians see the two accounts as simply being what the writers believed to be true. There is evidence that similar versions of the creation were believed by people of other nations. The big difference between the accounts of other nations and those in Genesis is that in the other versions other gods are named: in one version from Babylon, very similar in some ways to the version in Genesis 1, the creation follows a conflict between two of the gods. Both versions in Genesis describe creation as the work of the one true God.

Christians believe that God has always existed – he did not have a beginning but everything else exists because of God's power in creation. Everything owes its existence to him. Therefore he is said to be the 'first cause' of all things.

(See Chapter C3, *God – the Father*, and Chapters B3 and B4, *Arguments for the existence of God*.)

Evolution

'Evolution' means a gradual working out – a development. In particular, the word is used to describe the way in which, over a period of thousands of millions of years, the universe reached the stage it has reached today – and will continue to develop. It includes the idea that higher forms of life have gradually come from lower forms.

There are two basic theories of the origin of the universe:

- The **big bang** theory. According to this the universe began some thousands of millions of years ago with an explosion, as a result of which, in the first millionth of a second, a fireball thousands of kilometres in diameter was formed. It has been expanding ever since. Over a vast length of time part of the fireball cooled so that first atoms and then molecules were formed and so, by a long process, the universe came into being.
- The **steady-state** theory. According to this theory the universe is infinitely old. It is a steady state – the density of matter is the same at all times and at all points. The universe is seen to become larger all the time, with new matter being created as the universe expands.

Christian belief would not be greatly affected whichever of the two theories was found to be true. Christians would still believe that everything began, and has evolved since that beginning, because of the way in which God created the universe.

Scientists have developed the theory of evolution using evidence, especially from fossil remains of dead creatures and the relationship of species to each other. The evidence can be seen, examined and checked. True, the picture is not complete. In particular, there is no clear evidence to show a transition from apes to humans. None the less, while scientists may differ over some of the detail of what happened and how, the general principle of evolution is accepted.

One thing that cannot be proved, of course, is that evolution occurred because of God. While some people see his power and his plan in each stage of evolution, others believe that each stage has been either random or the result of natural selection.

Evolution and Christian belief

Fundamentalist Christians see that there is a contradiction between Genesis and the idea of evolution. Therefore Genesis, being part of God's word, must be right and the theories of scientists are wrong where they go against Genesis. Some fundamentalists point out that the order of events in the first creation narrative in Genesis is really the same as in the pattern of evolution, and that one explanation may be that where Genesis speaks about six days, each day might be equivalent to thousands, if not millions, of years.

Many Christians do not see a conflict between the theories of scientists and their own beliefs. They do not take Genesis as a literal account. They accept that ideas about the origin of the universe have changed in the last 2500 years. Indeed, scientists do not pretend that they never make mistakes. Any theory may be changed as more knowledge, more evidence comes to light.

Christians who think in this way do not feel threatened by the idea of evolution. Science is telling them more about God and his creation. The more that science reveals about the universe, the more they marvel at the greatness of God who created it.

Evolution does affect their belief in one important way. Creation is not something that happened and was completed at some point in the distant past. It is a continuing, unending process. They should not say 'God created the universe'. They should say, 'God is creating the universe'.

Charles Darwin put forward the idea of evolution in his book *The Origin of Species* in 1859. In his book he argued that over a long period of time the more advanced species had developed from simpler life forms. Species had adapted to their environments. Stronger species had survived, weaker species had died out – the **survival of the fittest**.

His theory went directly against the idea that each species had been created in its present form, as described in Genesis Chapter 1. He was seen as challenging the authority of the Bible and the Church. (His book was unwelcome to many scientists as well, as it went against much of what they had been teaching.) He remained a believer in God himself. On his deathbed a visitor found him with an open Bible in his hand. He was reading the Letter to the Hebrews, which he called the Royal Book.

Father Pierre Teilhard de Chardin, who lived in the first half of the twentieth century, was a priest and a scientist. He was greatly respected for his knowledge of physics, geology and palaeontology (the study of ancient things, especially the earliest history and development of everything living). He was greatly excited by advances in scientific knowledge, and spent much time and energy in research. He believed that his studies gave him a deeper understanding of God as creator. He said, 'Research is adoration'.

Teilhard de Chardin saw evolution as a continuous process, through the working of natural laws. That process is the creative work of God. So God is, and always will be, active in the universe.

Teilhard de Chardin also made statements about the nature of matter:

- As evolution progresses, matter becomes ever more complex.
- As matter becomes more complex, there is a rise in the consciousness of the matter.

If Teilhard de Chardin is right in what he says about matter, then matter is something quite different from what it appears. It has in it the creative power of God.

Teilhard de Chardin saw his scientific study as a way of coming nearer to God.

Then is it really true, Lord? By helping on the spread of science and freedom I can increase the density of the divine atmosphere, in itself as well as for me, that atmosphere in which it is always my one desire to be immersed. By laying hold on the earth I enable myself to cling closely to you …

I must search and I must find.

What is at stake, Lord, is the element wherein you will to dwell here on earth.

What is at stake is your existence among us.

Teilhard de Chardin, *Hymn of the Universe*

Just before Christmas 1968 the USA lauched *Apollo 8*, the first manned flight to orbit the Moon. People all over the world were fascinated; reports on the flight dominated TV that Christmas. The flight captured the imagination of the millions of viewers who followed the progress of the three astronauts Borman, Lovell and Anders, with amazement.

On Christmas Eve the three announced that they had a Christmas message to the world. They read Genesis Chapter 1. Each astronaut in turn read part of the account of the universe being created in six days.

Extraordinary. Of all passages they might have chosen, these standard-bearers of scientific progress chose Genesis 1. They did not mean to tell the world that they believed the universe was created in six days. They chose the chapter because of what it said to them about God, creation, and the human race.

Examination guidance

Do you think that the idea of evolution is a threat to a Christian's faith? (10 marks)

I think it depends on what the Christian believes. If a Christian is a fundamentalist, it is difficult to accept the idea of evolution. How can the world have been made in six days when all the evidence is that it took millions of years? How can God have made each of the different plants and animals when fossil remains show that they developed from each other over thousands of years? I suppose they would say that God created the fossils, to make it look as though things had evolved from each other. If God did that, he would have invented a lie since he would have made things look as though something had happened which did not really happen.

I would say that the evidence for evolution is very strong. It is based on evidence that can be checked and it makes sense. It is a real threat to a fundamentalist's faith.

For Christians who are not fundamentalists the problem is not so great. They can simply say that Genesis is a part of the Bible they don't believe in. They can accept what scientists discover and prove.

Some well-known scientists are Christians. Some of the astronauts who went to the moon read the Creation story from Genesis while they were in space. They did not believe

The candidate has met the basic requirements of the answer. A distinction has been made between the fundamentalist view and that which approaches modern discoveries more open-mindedly.

Each view is presented, and the candidate's own opinions are given, with reasons. The question, about evolution being a threat to a Christian's faith, is kept properly in mind.

One aspect that is missing is the idea that through evolution the work of creation is ongoing.

Overall, the response is too superficial, not looking closely enough at some issues. For instance, Christians who do not accept Genesis 1 and 2 as literally true have their reasons. The chapters are about things that no human being could have seen (except, in places, Adam and Eve). The chapters are seen as attempts to present, accurately, what was believed at the time the chapters were written. They are seen as giving a true picture of the majesty and power of God and of the special place the human race has within creation. The candidate shows no awareness of these arguments.

When writing about those scientists who are Christians

the world was made in six days but they did believe God created it.

These Christians believe that what scientists are doing is finding out just how God did create the earth and everything on it. The more they learn, the more wonderful it shows creation to be.

Personally I think that is being a bit dishonest. Either Christians believe in the Bible or they do not. It seems a bit strange choosing which parts to believe and which to miss out. You can believe anything that way.

Evolution may not seem to trouble these Christians. They still believe that God created the universe. I think it is a little of a threat to their faith, because it makes them not believe part of the Bible.

the candidate should give names and fuller examples. *(Score: 7 marks out of 10)*

Examination practice

'I believe in God, the Father almighty, creator of heaven and earth.'
(a) Explain the different ways in which Christians might understand those words. (10 marks)
Write about one side of A4.

(b) Do you think a person can be a Christian without believing those words from the Apostles' Creed?
(5 marks)

Write about half a side of A4.

SUFFERING AND EVIL – 1

10

Introduction

It is difficult to explain suffering.

We all experience pain and suffering: physical, emotional or mental.

We also inflict pain and suffering on other people. We enjoy inflicting pain on other people: either for no reason, or because someone has hurt us. We keep such desires to ourselves. We do not want others to know that we have evil thoughts and feelings. Perhaps we are ashamed of such thoughts and feelings, as they are repellent.

> 'Let not light see my black and deep desires.'
> Shakespeare

Examples of suffering

- A headache.
- Parents arguing.

- Our best friend leaves us, or deceives us.
- Loneliness.
- Someone we love dies.
- Cancer.
- Abuse: physical, sexual or mental.
- We are made to look small.

Reactions to suffering

Christians have always found it difficult to explain suffering and cruelty.

> The world we live in often seems very far from the one promised us by faith.
> Our experiences of evil and suffering, injustice and death, seem to contradict the Good News; they can shake our faith and become a temptation against it.
>
> (Catholic bishops at the Second Vatican Council)

We can react to suffering in different ways.

- **Refusal**. I pretend it is not happening to me. I try and blot it out of my mind, or hope it will go away promptly.

- **Self-pity**. I spend my time feeling sorry for myself. I get wrapped up in my suffering. I think of nothing else but how badly I have been treated.
- **Resignation**. I passively accept the suffering. I say nothing and do nothing. I think it is inevitable.
- **Anger**. I react aggressively and vigorously against the situation causing the suffering. I fight it.
- **Facing it**. I can look carefully at my suffering and its causes. I can consider what might be the best way of coping and dealing with it.
- **Prayer**. There are as many ways of praying about suffering as there are ways of reacting to suffering. Here are some examples from the book of Psalms.

> My God, my God, why have you forsaken me?
> Why are you so far from saving me,
> So far from the words of my groaning?
> O my God, I cry out by day, but you do not answer.
>
> Psalm 22$^{1-2}$

> How long, O Lord? Will you forget me for ever?
>   How long will you hide your face from me?
> How long must I wrestle with my thoughts
> and every day have sorrow in my heart?
>
> Psalm 13$^{1-2}$

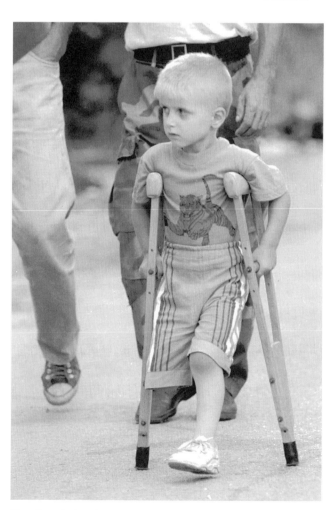

Here is a victim of war in Bosnia, which makes most of us wonder if war is worthwhile

> Let death take my enemies by surprise;
> let them go down alive to the grave.
>
> Psalm 55^{15}

> May [my enemy's] days be few;
>   may another take his place of leadership.
> May his children be fatherless
> and his wife a widow.
> May his children be wandering beggars;
> may they be driven from their ruined homes.
>
> Psalm 109$^{8-10}$

> The Lord is my shepherd, I shall not be in want . . .
> Even though I walk through the valley of the shadow of death,
> I will fear no evil,
>   for you are with me.
>
> Psalm 23$^{1-4}$

Causes of suffering and evil

The causes of suffering are often divided into two groups: natural and human.

- **Natural** causes of suffering are floods, famine, earthquakes, diseases, illnesses, and so on.
- **Human** causes of suffering are when we deliberately or accidentally hurt another person – perhaps by saying something; perhaps by hitting someone; perhaps by leaving someone.

Benefits of suffering?

Ironically, suffering can benefit us.

- Suppose I have a broken ankle. If I did not feel pain, I would not know it was broken. I would walk without realizing that I was doing irreparable damage to my leg. Pain forces me to rest and it prevents me from walking. When the ankle is repaired and I can safely walk again, the pain will disappear.
- Some doctors believe that stress causes 80 per cent of illnesses. If I have a bad case of 'flu or a bad back, it may have been caused by stress. The pain of the illness forces me to rest; it probably forces me to withdraw from the situation that is causing me too much stress. I am likely to recover from the illness when I can cope better with the situation that is causing the stress.
- Many, but not all, people who have experienced suffering acquire important personal qualities: patience in coping with frustration; consideration for other people; self-control. Without the painful experience, they would still be impatient when frustrated, inconsiderate towards others, and lacking self-control.
- Some people find that serious suffering causes them to rethink their lives. They realize they could do better things with their life. So they change their style of life.
- Christians believe that, through his suffering and death, Jesus redeemed us. His suffering benefited us. See

Chapter C7, *Jesus – his mission; sin and salvation.* Christians believe that, like Jesus, we might benefit other people through our suffering.

There is a danger in suggesting that there can be benefits from pain and suffering. It can lead people to believe that we should *want* pain and suffering. Some famous Christians were noted for the pain they deliberately inflicted on themselves. Francis of Assisi was an example. He earnestly wanted to follow the life of Christ and to be like Christ. He deprived himself, excessively, of food, sleep and rest. Consequently he damaged his body severely. In the last years of his life, he had the **stigmata** – the hand wounds and the feet wounds caused by the nails when a person is crucified.

Most Christians think that inflicting pain on ourselves is unnatural. We instinctively avoid pain and suffering. This is the way God has made us. Thus it is wrong to damage our bodies or deliberately cause pain to ourselves.

Jesus did not want pain. When he was in the garden of Gethsemane, shortly before his death, he prayed to God that he would not have to suffer. In the garden of Gethsemane, he also felt lonely. He tried to avoid the pain of loneliness by going to his three closest disciples for comfort. But they were too tired to stay awake with him. They kept falling asleep.

Suffering and the rejection of God

Fyodor Dostoevsky, the nineteenth-century Russian novelist, suggested that a good person should have nothing to do with God. As the creator of the world, God must be responsible for the evil and suffering in it. Yet, no good person would make a world with pointless evil and suffering in it. So, there must be something twisted about God.

Dostoevsky told a story to illustrate his point. Ivan went to visit his brother Aloysha, a monk. Ivan described instances of evil and cruelty: how a drunken man kept whipping a worn-out horse, simply for the pleasure of doing it; how a soldier blew out the brains of a baby in front of the mother; how a child accidentally injured the hound of an army general – so the general had the child

stripped and made to run like a chased animal, while a pack of hounds was sent after him, and tore him to pieces.

Ivan told Aloysha that we can explain any of these incidents by suggesting that God gave people free will and that they chose to do evil. Or we can explain these incidents by suggesting that those who suffered will be happy in heaven when they die.

But, said Ivan, this is too high a price to pay for heaven – I do not want anything to do with a God who can tolerate evil actions, or who can forgive terribly evil people. Such a God may exist, but I want nothing to do with him.

Other people think that, because there is evil and suffering, God cannot exist. They point to notorious incidents of suffering; they then point out that Christians believe God is both almighty and good. Well, say atheists, that proves that God does not exist, since if God was good, he would want to stop suffering; and if he was almighty, he would be able to stop the suffering.

Now it is obvious that there is unnecessary suffering in the world. We may have experienced it ourselves. We certainly read about it in the newspapers. We see it on television. If there is a God, he does not stop it. Either he cannot stop it – in which case he is not almighty. Or he will not stop it – in which case, he is not good. But a God who is not almighty, and who is not good, is not the God that Christians believe in.

Examination practice

1. Give some examples of suffering.   (3 marks)
    Write about six lines of A4.

2. Discuss the different ways in which people react to suffering.   (10 marks)
    Write about one side of A4.

3. 'Suffering can benefit people.'
    Explain this statement.   (8 marks)
    Write about three-quarters of a side of A4.

4. Do you think that suffering proves that God does not exist?
    Give reasons for your view. Show that you have considered other views.   (8 marks)
    Write about three-quarters of a side of A4.

Suffering without explanation?

Auschwitz, in Poland, where the German Nazis used gas to kill two million people (mainly Jews) and then burnt the bodies

An incident at Auschwitz

One day when we came back from work, we saw three gallows rearing up in the assembly place . . . Roll call. SS all around us, machine guns trained: the traditional ceremony. Three victims in chains – one of them . . . a child. He was livid pale, almost calm, biting his lips. The gallows threw its shadow over him . . . The three victims mounted together on to the chairs. The three necks were placed at the same moment within the nooses.

'Long live liberty!' cried the two adults.

But the child was silent.

'Where is God? Where is He?' someone behind me asked.

At a sign from the head of the camp, the three chairs tipped over.

Total silence throughout the camp. On the horizon the sun was setting.

'Bare your heads!' yelled the head of camp. His voice was raucous. We were weeping.

'Cover your heads!'

Then the march past began. The two adults were no longer alive . . . But the third rope was still moving; being so light, the child was still alive . . .

For more than half an hour he stayed there, struggling between life and death, dying in slow agony under our eyes ... He was still alive when I passed in front of him. His tongue was still red, his eyes were not yet glazed.

Behind me, I heard the same man asking: 'Where is God now?'

And I heard a voice within me answer him: 'Where is he? Here he is – he is hanging here on this gallows . . .'

Soelle

Explanations of suffering and evil

All attempts to explain evil end in explaining it away.

E. Brunner

In spite of Brunner's judgement, people have always wanted to understand and to explain evil and suffering. Here are some of the explanations.

Free will

It is humans that cause most suffering. **Augustine** was a North African Christian who lived in the fourth and fifth centuries. He said that God made everything in the world good, including the angels and humans. God gave all his creatures free will: the ability to choose to do good and the ability to choose to do evil. An angel chose to do evil; he turned against God. He became known as the devil. The devil persuaded the first humans, Adam and Eve, to disobey God. They did. See Chapter C3, *God – the Father*, for some details.

Ever since then, humans have constantly chosen to do evil as well as good. We have been under the influence of original sin; and we have been under the influence of the devil. According to Augustine, God foresaw that we would misuse our free will, but he still created angels and humans with free will. He thought it was better to bring good out of evil. So he sent his Son, Jesus, to reconcile us to himself. Jesus died on the cross to save us from original sin.

Children to adults

Children inevitably make mistakes. **Irenaeus** was a missionary bishop who lived in the second century. He thought that human development was like a child growing up. He said that the first humans, Adam and Eve, were the infancy of the human race. God made humans imperfect, so it is not surprising we make mistakes, such as disobeying God, and hurting other people. Adults have to learn, just as a child does. As the human race grows up, it will make fewer mistakes. It will eventually become perfect, as God intended. There will then be no more suffering.

Condition for human development

Hick, a twentieth-century philosopher, argued that if we are to develop God-like qualities, such as compassion, we can only do so in a world that is imperfect – a world in which there is evil and suffering. If we are to learn sacrificial love, there have to be situations where other people suffer. It is only when people suffer that we can show compassion, devotion and self-sacrifice.

God's punishment

Some people feel that all suffering is a punishment from God for something they have done wrong. They usually feel guilty for something particularly nasty they have done. They feel they deserve to be punished by God.

A similar explanation is sometimes applied in the case of those who suffer, yet who believe they have done nothing seriously wrong. It is suggested that these people must have forgotten that they have done wrong.

Finite world

'Finite' means having limits. **Aquinas** argued that the world had to be finite, because only God is infinite (without limits). If the world is finite, then accident, death and decay are natural. They have to happen. They cause suffering.

Test

Some people believe that suffering and pain are tests from God. They point out that it is easy to pray to God and to be good to others when things go well for us. But what happens when we suffer? Will we remain faithful to him? And be good to others? God tests us with suffering to see what we are really like.

A very famous example of this was **Abraham**. It is said that God ordered him to take his son Isaac up a mountain. Abraham had to kill his son and burn him on a wood fire as a sacrifice to God. Abraham was about to kill his son when God stopped him. Abraham had passed the test. There was no need to kill his son.

God and suffering – Jesus

Christians believe that God became a man, Jesus, who lived in Palestine 2000 years ago.

Jesus relieved pain and he removed suffering. He spent more time doing this than anything else. See Chapter C13, *Mark's gospel – miracles* for examples.

Jesus forgave sin, the main cause of much suffering. He forgave the sins of a paralysed man who was let down through a roof by his friends; he forgave a woman who was caught in an act of adultery; he forgave those who crucified him.

Jesus taught people to follow the example of God, who never does evil. He taught people to love their enemies, as

God does. He taught that people should always be good, as God is always good.

Jesus experienced pain: both emotional and physical pain: the latter, for example, when he was tortured and killed.

> The soldiers led Jesus away . . . they struck him on the head with a staff and spat on him . . . Then they led him out to crucify him.
>
> It was the third hour when they crucified him . . . Those who passed by hurled insults at him . . .
>
> The chief priests and the teachers of the law mocked him . . . Those crucified with him also heaped insults on him.
>
> At the ninth hour Jesus cried out in a loud voice . . . 'My God, my God, why have you forsaken me?'
>
> With a loud cry, Jesus breathed his last.
>
> Mark 15[16–37]

Jesus experienced emotional pain when he was in the Garden of Gethsemane. He was devastated by the thought of his trial and death. He could not sleep. He asked his friends to say awake with him – but they were tired, and they fell asleep.

Explanation of Jesus' suffering and death

Christians believe that Jesus suffered and died for our sins. See Chapter C7, *Jesus – his mission; sin and salvation* for a more detailed explanation.

Paul said (1 Corinthians 1[18–25]) that the doctrine of the cross was sheer folly to some; but to others it was the power of God.

> Where is the wise man? . . . Has not God made foolish the wisdom of the world? . . . Jews demand miraculous signs and Greeks look for wisdom, but we preach Christ crucified . . . For the foolishness of God is wiser than man's wisdom, and the weakness of God is stronger than man's strength.

Self-sacrifice

Jesus said he had to suffer and die. He said that God had sent him on a mission of self-sacrifice. So he had not come to lord it over other people. Rather, he had come to serve people; and he had come to sacrifice his life – a sort of ransom – to benefit people (Mark 10[41–45]).

Jesus told his followers that they also had to have a spirit of self-sacrifice. They had to follow his example.

> If anyone would come after me, he must deny himself and take up his cross and follow me. For whoever wants to save his life will lose it, but whoever loses his life for me and the gospel will save it.
>
> Mark 8[34–35]

See Chapter E18, *Liberation theology and the developing world*, which has something about poverty and suffering.

Coping with suffering and evil

One person's view of suffering

I was interned by the Japanese . . . I suffered many weary hours of beatings and torture.

I remember Archbishop Temple, in one of his books, writing that if you pray for any particular virtue, whether it be patience, or courage, or love, one of the answers that God gives to us is an opportunity for exercising that virtue. After my first beating I was almost afraid to pray for courage lest I should have another opportunity for exercising it . . . Long hours of ignoble torture were a severe test. In the middle of torture they asked me if I still believed in God. When, by God's help, I said, 'I do,' they asked me why God did not save me. By the help of his Spirit I said, 'God does save me. He does not save me by freeing me from pain or punishment, but he saves me by giving me the Spirit to bear it.'

When I muttered 'Forgive them,' I wondered how far I was being dramatic, and if I really meant it; because I looked at their faces as they stood round, taking it in turn to flog me, and their faces were hard and cruel, and some of them were evidently enjoying their cruelty. But, by the grace of God, I saw those men not as they were, but as they had been. Once they were little children with their brothers and sisters – happy in their parents' love, in those far-off days before they had been conditioned by their false nationalist ideals. And it is hard to hate little children.

It is true that there were many dreary moments, especially in the early morning, in a crowded, filthy cell with hardly any power to move because of one's wounds: but here again I was tremendously helped by God. There was a tiny window at the back of the cell, and through the bars I could hear the song of the Golden Oriole. I could see the glorious red of the flame of the forest tree; and something of God, something of God's indestructible beauty, was conveyed to my tortured mind.

After eight months I was released, and for the first time got into the sunlight. I have never known such joy. It seemed like a foretaste of the resurrection.

Leonard Wilson

Examination practice

1. What do you think about the incident at Auschwitz?
   (3 marks)

   Write about six lines of A4.

2. Do you think there can be a satisfactory explanation of suffering?
   Give reasons for your view. Show that you have considered different explanations. (10 marks)
   Write about one side of A4.

3. 'Christians believe that suffering is at the heart of religion.'
   Explain this statement. (8 marks)
   Write about three-quarters of a side of A4.

4. How might a Christian cope with suffering?
   (8 marks)

   Write about three-quarters of a side of A4.

CAN WE DESCRIBE GOD? – SOME DIFFICULTIES 12

What's the problem?

'Our Father in heaven'. These are the opening words of the most important Christian prayer.

Should we understand the word 'father' literally? That is, should we understand the word 'father' in the way that we normally use the word 'father'? If so, we should like to know who God's wife is; and how many other children God has; and how we can have two fathers; and so on.

Having seen these difficulties, we may conclude that we do not apply the word 'father' to God in a literal way.

And what about 'in heaven'? Do we understand this literally? If so, where in the sky shall we find God? Is he on this side of the universe, or on the other side of the universe? And why haven't the astronauts found him?

Having seen these difficulties, we may conclude that we do not use the words 'in heaven' literally.

Fundamentalists

Fundamentalists believe that descriptions of God are straightforward. They see no difficulty in descriptions of God because they think that descriptions of God are not more complex than descriptions of a dog, a house, or a person. They assume that all descriptions of God are literal. They also assume that statements about God cannot be metaphorical. So they infer that every statement in the Bible is literal.

Mystics

Mystics are people who claim to have experienced God directly. See Chapter B2, *Religious experience*, for some examples.

They know they cannot explain their experience of God adequately, and they feel that any description will be inexact and perhaps misleading.

So some of them conclude that it is wise to say nothing, and they remain silent. However, other mystics try to describe their experience of God. Yet their descriptions are vague, hesitant and allusive.

The silence of the mystics: Dionysius

Dionysius was a Christian mystic who lived in the sixth century, possibly in Syria. He has considerably influenced Christian thinking about how to describe God. He felt that the more we know God, the less we say about God. And when we really get into God, we say nothing. We do not even think anything about him. It is like darkness or nothingness. This is because a direct experience of God happens outside our normal thoughts. This experience of God cannot be translated into human thoughts. God is inexpressible.

The eloquence of the mystics: John of the Cross

Dionysius compares meeting God to darkness. A later mystic, John of the Cross, gives a more precise explanation of this comparison.

John was a monk who lived in Spain in the sixteenth century. He wrote about his experience of God. John said that we have to empty ourselves of all that is not God, including our ideas of God, if we want to meet God. First, we have to purge our sensual desires until we are disinterested in things of the flesh. John called this the dark night of the senses. Then we have to purge our ideas of God until we have no clear idea of God – just a thin thread of faith. John called this the **dark night of the soul**. When we reach the depths of the dark night of the soul, we have emptied ourselves of all that is not God. We have lost self-interest, which includes our ideas of God. We are then ready to meet God.

And having met God, our thoughts and words are unable to describe him, because no thought can adequately explain how marvellous or fantastic the experience is. So John used poetry, rather than statements, to express his experience of God. You will find one example of his poetry in Chapter B2, *Religious experience*. Here is another example: some verses from his poem 'The dark night'. He wrote this when he was in a monastery prison, jailed by fellow monks.

> One dark night,
> Fired by love's urgent longings
> – ah the sheer grace! –
> I went out unseen,
> My house being all stilled;
>
> On that glad night,
> In secret, for no one saw me,
> Nor did I look at anything,
> With no other light or guide
> Than the one that burned in my heart;
>
> O guiding night!
> O night more lovely than the dawn!
> O night that has united
> The lover with His beloved,
> Transforming the beloved in her Lover.
>
> I abandoned and forgot myself,
> Laying my face on my Beloved;
> All things ceased; I went out from myself,
> Leaving my cares
> Forgotten among the lilies.

Can we describe God adequately?

We cannot describe God adequately. There are three reasons for this.

1. Few of us have a clear knowledge and understanding of God. He is mysterious and elusive. So anything we say about him is tentative.
2. More importantly, God is completely different from anything else that we know. God is **transcendent**. That is, we do not see, hear or touch God in the way that we see, hear or touch anything else. Yet our words are about ordinary things. So they cannot adequately describe something transcendent.

   Another way to explain this is to say that God is **infinite** – he has no limits. Yet our words are based on things that are finite. So they cannot describe adequately something infinite.
3. If we do meet God, it is in the depths of our spirit, which is beyond our thinking mind. It is at a level of awareness that our thoughts do not reach. So our thoughts and words cannot grasp God.

Thus no statement about God is adequate. All statements

about God must be suggestive or symbolic. According to the Catholic Catechism:

> God transcends all creatures. We must therefore continually purify our language of everything in it that is limited, imagebound or imperfect, if we are not to confuse our image of God (who is the inexpressible, the incomprehensible, the invisible, the ungraspable) with our human representations. Our human words always fall short of the mystery of God.

Negative descriptions of God

As positive statements about God are inadequate, Dionysius argued that we cannot make statements such as God is good, God is kind, God is loving, and so on. However, according to Dionysius, some positive statements are not as inaccurate as others. Thus to say that that God exists or that he is good is not as inaccurate as saying that God is air or that he is a stone.

Dionysius argued that although we cannot use positive statements to describe God, we can still describe God. We can describe God using negative statements about him. For example, we can say that God has no body, God does not speak, God does not get angry, God does not laugh, God cannot die, and so on. Negative descriptions are accurate, as they say what God is not, rather than what God is.

Positive descriptions of God

Despite what Dionysius said, most Christians want to make positive statements about God, because they think that negative statements do not tell us what God is like. Christians want to make statements such as God created us; God is good; God is a shepherd; God will judge us when we die; and so on.

However, many Christians realize that positive statements about God cannot be straightforward.

So if Christians use positive statements about God, and these statements are not straightforward, how are we to understand them? There are several suggestions about how to understand them: for instance, as symbols; as signs; as models; as maps; as pictures; as allegories; as myths.

The authors of this book judge that we gain little insight when we explain descriptions of God in these ways. There are better ways to explain descriptions of God.

We consider four ways we may use words to describe God:

- as a story;
- as metaphors;
- as literal, but analogical;
- as literal, and straightforward.

Examination practice

1. 'God is a father.'
    What is unusual about this statement, or is it a straightforward statement? (3 marks)
    Write about six lines.

2. What do mystics say about God? (6 marks)
    Write about half a side of A4.

3. 'We cannot explain adequately what God is like.'
    Explain this statement. (8 marks)
    Write about three-quarters of a side of A4.

4. 'Negative statements about God are more useful than positive statements about God.'
    Do you agree? Give reasons for your view. Show that you have understood more than one point of view.
    (8 marks)
    Write about three-quarters of a side of A4.

CAN WE DESCRIBE GOD? – SOME SOLUTIONS 13

Stories

According to the first three gospels, Jesus used stories to teach people. Some of these stories are about God's attitude towards us.

Jesus could have said: 'God forgives us'. Instead, Jesus told the story of the forgiving father, the story of the lost sheep, and the story of the lost coin (Luke 15). See Chapter

C19 *Luke's gospel – parables* for a summary of these stories.

Jesus could have said: 'God will judge us when we die'. Instead, he told the story of the sheep and the goats, the story of the three servants, and the story of the ten girls (Matthew 25). See Chapter E24, *Christian discipleship – special texts*, for a summary of the first two stories.

It is sometimes suggested that Jesus taught in stories

because they were an effectual way to teach about God. But perhaps Jesus also believed that stories, rather than statements, were a more accurate way to describe God.

If we take a story such as the forgiving father, we can explain it using literal statements. Thus we might say that the story teaches that God tolerates us when we do wrong; that God does not punish us when we do wrong; that God wants to forgive us; that God waits patiently until we are ready to go to him; that God is overjoyed when we go to him; and so on.

Notice four important differences between the story and our literal statements.

1. We get a better understanding of God from the story than from the statements.
2. We cannot satisfactorily translate the story into statements without losing some of its meaning. We could make 20 statements, yet we would not explain completely the meaning of the story.
3. The story gives an allusive, suggestive description of God. The statements give a more precise and limiting description of God.
4. The story is evocative, and gives us a greater feeling for God. The statements are more matter of fact, as they simply give information.

Metaphors

Suppose I find it difficult to concentrate, and I say I have a butterfly mind. This is a metaphor. I am describing one thing (my mind) as something else (a butterfly). Likewise, when I describe a person as something else, my description is metaphorical.

The Bible writers frequently used metaphors to describe God. They said God is a maker, a father, a husband, a shepherd, a king, a judge, a good listener, a cloud, a fire, a wind, a potter, a rock, a saviour, a redeemer.

Why did they prefer metaphors? Did they think that metaphors explain God more satisfactorily than literal words?

A contemporary English philosopher, **Janet Soskice**, thinks this is so.

She points out that when we use a metaphor, we speak of one thing as though it was something else. So when we say God is a shepherd, we are speaking of God as though he were something else. But we do not mean he is really a shepherd. So what do we mean?

We mean, for instance, that God looks after us; he knows each of us individually; he protects us from evil people as a shepherd protects his sheep from wolves; he worries about us; and so on. These are literal statements. But they do not entirely explain how God is a shepherd.

Thus Soskice argues that we can explain a metaphor with literal statements, but we cannot reduce a metaphor to literal statements without losing some of its meaning. She believes that a metaphor has an irreducible meaning.

Soskice also suggests that metaphorical statements about God have a distinctive value – they stretch our imagination, so that we see things in a quite different way. Literal words

cannot do this. Therefore metaphors are invaluable in trying to understand God, who eludes our imagination.

Soskice also suggests that if we use different metaphors to understand God, we shall not think that any one metaphor is too accurate.

Anthropomorphisms

Some people use this word frequently. It means we describe God as if he were human.

So we say he is a king, or a judge, or a father, and so on.

Or we say he fights, he is patient, he speaks, he punishes, he is jealous, he is sorry, he is generous, and so on.

All anthropomorphic statements about God are metaphors. We describe God as something that God is not – a human person.

Literal statements

We often use words that literally describe God.

We say, for example, he is wise, he exists, he is good, he is kind, he forgives, he is just, he is merciful, he helps, he is generous, he is tolerant, he is perfect, he is intelligent, he is changeless, and so. All these statements seem to be literal.

Besides simple literal statements about God, we also make more complex literal statements about God. For example: God knows everything. God can do anything. God is beyond time. God is self-existent. God is without limits.

Metaphorical or literal?

We may find it difficult to distinguish between a metaphor and a literal statement. For instance, when we say that God is a shepherd, are we using the word 'shepherd' metaphorically or literally?

Here is a simple test to decide whether a word is used metaphorically or literally.

If I can both affirm and deny a word used to describe God, then I am using the word metaphorically. If I can affirm but not deny a word used to describe God, then I am using the word literally.

Let us apply this test to the word 'shepherd'. I can say that God is a shepherd, but I can also say that God is not a shepherd. So I am using the word metaphorically.

What about the statement 'God is wise'? I can say that God is wise, but I cannot say that God is not wise. So I am using the word 'wise' literally.

Literal, but analogical words

Thomas Aquinas was an Italian theologian who lived in the thirteenth century. He was one of the most impressive Christian theologians.

Aquinas agreed with Dionysius – we can reliably say what God is not, but we cannot reliably say what he is like. However, Aquinas thought that if we use only negative statements about God, then we do not know much about God.

So Aquinas argued that we have to make positive statements about God, even though they are imprecise, if we want to have some idea of what God is like. And Aquinas suggested five reasons why positive statements about God can have some meaning.

1. Aquinas suggested that we look at the two types of positive statement about God: metaphorical and literal statements. Which more satisfactorily describes God? He thought that literal statements do, because, if we make a metaphorical statement such as 'God is our shepherd', we ask what it means. And we expect an answer in literal words, such as 'he looks after us; he knows each of us individually; he protects us from evil people as a shepherd protects his sheep from wolves'; and so on. So literal statements are more precise, and thus superior to metaphors.

2. Aquinas defended the use of literal statements about God by pointing out that God created humans. As God has created us, some of his qualities must be found in us, however dimly. And so we can apply to God the good qualities we find in ourselves.

3. Aquinas pointed out that literal statements about God are odd. As God is infinite, and as the words we use about God refer primarily to finite things, the words we use of God are inadequate to describe him. So, although we use words literally of God, we do not use them in a straightforward way.

4. Aquinas said that our literal descriptions of God are analogical.

    If we use a word analogically we use it on two different occasions. On each occasion we use it partly differently, yet partly the same.

    For example, we say humans are intelligent and dogs are intelligent; and we are using the word 'intelligent' literally, but analogically – we are using it partly the same and partly differently.

    Thus if we say God is wise, we are using the word 'wise' literally but analogically. We mean that God is wise partly in the way that we are, but partly differently.

5. Aquinas said that any quality we apply to God has to be refined from the limited ways in which humans possess that quality. Take the quality 'good' for instance. When we do good to someone, we often have mixed motives for doing so. We may do it because we want to help someone. But we may also do it because we want other people to admire us, or because we want someone to do us a favour in return. So Aquinas says that if we describe God as good, we must first remove from the idea of good any limited or defective ways in which we humans are good. We can attribute this refined quality of 'good' to God, though we have to attribute it supremely to God: that is, we have to think of God's goodness as greater than anything we can imagine.

    Likewise, when we say God is wise, we must first remove the limited ways in which humans are wise; we then attribute the residue to God, though supremely.

Despite justifying analogical statements about God, Aquinas said that we cannot really grasp what God is like. We can say he exists; we can say what he is not; and we can say something about how we relate to God. Yet we reach the summit of our knowledge about God when we realize that we do not know him.

Literal and straightforward words

John Duns Scotus was a Scottish theologian who lived in the thirteenth century, just after Aquinas. He believed that we can use words literally of God, and that we use these words in a straightforward way rather than in an analogical way.

For example, we say God has a mind, or we say he has a will, or we say he is wise. Scotus says we attribute these qualities literally to God. But we do not include any imperfect way in which these qualities are found in humans. And we attribute these qualities to God in the highest possible degree.

However, according to Scotus, there is a better way to describe God. We can describe God using words in unique combinations, to make new ideas.

Scotus illustrates this with the words 'gold' and 'mountain'. We can use these two words separately. Yet if we combine them, we have a new idea, a 'gold mountain', which is more than just the addition of the two ideas.

In a similar way we can combine ideas to describe God. For instance: God knows everything. God can do anything. God is beyond time. God is self-existent. God is without limits.

Notice, in each case, that:

*   We are using the individual words literally.
*   The combination of words is applied uniquely to God. The combination is not used of anybody else.
*   The combination of ideas gives us a special understanding of God. For example, when we say God is the highest good, we unite the words 'highest' and 'good' to obtain an understanding of God that is more than the addition of highest and good. The combination of the two ideas gives us a new idea.

Caveat

Although descriptions of God are inadequate, most Christians still want to describe God. And they believe their descriptions have some meaning.

In this chapter, we have outlined different ways in which we use words to describe God. We have also explained why descriptions of God may make sense.

There is always the danger of thinking that our descriptions of God are adequate. This is like the drunk who is standing on a bridge, leaning over the railings, looking at the moon's reflection in the water. He thinks he is looking at the moon. Nobody can change his mind.

Examination practice

1. Explain what is meant by 'anthropomorphism'.

   (3 marks)

   Write about six lines.

2. 'Stories are a helpful way to describe God.'
   Using examples, explain why.   (8 marks)
   Write about three-quarters of a side of A4.

3. Some descriptions of God seem to use words literally. Give some examples. Aquinas and Scotus said that literal descriptions of God are acceptable. What explanation did each of them give?   (10 marks)
   Write about one side of A4.

4. 'Metaphors give more useful and accurate descriptions of God than literal statements do.'
   Do you agree? Give reasons for your view. Show that you have understood more than one point of view.

   (8 marks)

   Write about three-quarters of a side of A4.

PART C

Belief

Full courses: Part C

This chart tells you the chapters to study. Find your exam board. Then highlight your syllabus (or syllabuses). Study the chapters that are ticked.

Exam Board Syllabuses	Chapter 1 Apostles' Creed and Nicene Creed	Chapter 2 God: Trinity	Chapter 3 God – the Father	Chapter 4 God – the Son	Chapter 5 God – the Holy Spirit	Chapter 6 Jesus – his identity	Chapter 7 Jesus – his mission	Chapter 8 The Kingdom of God	Chapter 9 Human nature	Chapter 10 Funerals; death and resurrection	Chapter 11 The Bible
NEAB Syllabus A – Christianity	✓	✓	✓	✓	✓	✓	✓		✓	✓	✓
Syllabus B – Christian tradition	✓	✓	✓	✓	✓	✓	✓			✓	✓
Catholic Christian tradition	✓	✓	✓	✓	✓	✓	✓	✓		✓	✓
Christian life and Mark's gospel		✓								✓	✓
Christian behaviour, attitudes and lifestyle										✓	
Catholic Christian behaviour, attitudes and lifestyle											
MEG Syllabus C – Christian beliefs and practice (modular)	✓	✓	✓	✓	✓	✓	✓		✓	✓	✓
Christianity through Luke's gospel and Acts		✓	✓	✓	✓	✓	✓	✓		✓	✓
Christian perspectives on personal, social issues	✓	✓	✓	✓	✓	✓	✓			✓	
Christianity	✓	✓	✓	✓	✓	✓	✓		✓	✓	✓
EdExcel (London) Christianity		✓	✓	✓	✓	✓	✓		✓	✓	✓
Christianity	✓	✓	✓	✓	✓	✓	✓		✓	✓	✓
Catholic Christianity	✓	✓	✓	✓	✓	✓	✓		✓	✓	✓
Contemporary issues and Mark's gospel	✓	✓	✓	✓	✓			✓	✓	✓	✓
SEG Syllabus A – Christian Church	✓	✓	✓	✓	✓		✓			✓	✓
Contemporary issues		✓	✓	✓	✓					✓	✓
Life of Jesus: synoptic gospels								✓			
Syllabus B – Inter-faith studies: Christianity	✓	✓	✓	✓		✓	✓			✓	✓
Syllabus C – Catholic Christian tradition	✓	✓		✓		✓	✓		✓		

This chart tells you the chapters to study. Find your exam board. Then highlight your syllabuses (or syllabus). Study the chapters that are ticked.

Exam Board	Syllabuses	Ch 12 Mark's gospel – parables	Ch 13 Mark's gospel – miracles	Ch 14 Mark's gospel – passion & resurrection	Ch 15 Mark's gospel – special emphases – I	Ch 16 Mark's gospel – special emphases – II	Ch 17 Mark's gospel – special emphases – III	Ch 18 Luke's gospel – ministry of Jesus	Ch 19 Luke's gospel – parables	Ch 20 Luke's gospel – passion & resurrection	Ch 21 Luke's gospel – special emphases	Ch 22 Acts of the Apostles
NEAB	Syllabus A – Christianity	✓	✓	✓	✓	✓	✓	✓		✓		
	Syllabus B – Christian tradition	✓		✓	✓	✓				✓		
	Catholic Christian tradition		✓	✓	✓	✓				✓		
	Christian life and Mark's gospel	✓		✓	✓	✓	✓					
	Christian behaviour, attitudes and lifestyle	✓	✓			✓						✓
	Catholic Christian behaviour, attitudes and lifestyle	✓		✓	✓	✓						
MEG	Syllabus C – Christian beliefs and practice (modular)	✓		✓	✓	✓		✓	✓			✓
	Christianity through Luke's gospel and Acts	✓	✓			✓		✓	✓	✓	✓	✓
	Christian perspectives on personal, social issues			✓	✓							
	Christianity	✓	✓	✓	✓	✓	✓			✓		
EdExcel (London)	Christianity	✓		✓	✓	✓	✓			✓		
	Catholic Christianity	✓		✓	✓	✓	✓			✓		
	Contemporary issues and Mark's gospel	✓	✓	✓	✓	✓	✓			✓		
SEG	Syllabus A – Christian Church	✓	✓	✓	✓	✓	✓	✓	✓	✓		
	Contemporary issues			✓		✓						
	Life of Jesus: synoptic gospels		✓	✓	✓	✓	✓	✓	✓	✓	✓	
	Syllabus B – Inter-faith studies: Christianity	✓		✓	✓	✓	✓	✓	✓	✓		
	Syllabus C – Catholic Christian tradition		✓	✓		✓	✓	✓	✓	✓	✓	✓

Short courses: Part C

This chart tells you the chapters to study. Find your exam board. Then highlight your syllabus. Study the chapters that are ticked.

Chapter	NEAB: Christianity	SEG: Thinking about God and morality	SEG: Religious education	EdExcel (London) Syllabus A: Religion and life	EdExcel Syllabus B: Christianity	Christianity: Catholicism	Christianity: Mark's gospel	MEG Syllabus A: Christianity through Luke and Acts	Christian perspectives on personal, social and world issues	Christianity	MEG Syllabus B: Christianity
Chapter 1 Apostles Creed and Nicene Creed	✓	✓	✓		✓	✓		✓		✓	✓
Chapter 2 God: Trinity	✓	✓	✓		✓	✓		✓		✓	✓
Chapter 3 God – the Father	✓	✓	✓		✓	✓		✓		✓	✓
Chapter 4 God – the Son	✓	✓	✓		✓	✓	✓	✓		✓	✓
Chapter 5 God – the Holy Spirit	✓	✓	✓		✓	✓		✓		✓	✓
Chapter 6 Jesus – his identity	✓	✓	✓	✓	✓	✓	✓	✓		✓	✓
Chapter 7 Jesus – his mission	✓	✓	✓	✓	✓	✓	✓	✓		✓	✓
Chapter 8 the Kingdom of God		✓					✓	✓		✓	
Chapter 9 Human nature	✓		✓	✓	✓			✓	✓	✓	✓
Chapter 10 Funerals; death and resurrection	✓		✓	✓				✓	✓	✓	✓
Chapter 11 The Bible	✓	✓		✓		✓	✓	✓	✓	✓	✓
Chapter 12 Mark's gospel – parables	✓										
Chapter 13 Mark's gospel – miracles	✓				✓	✓					
Chapter 14 Mark's gospel – passion & resurrection	✓	✓	✓	✓	✓	✓					
Chapter 15 Mark's gospel – special emphases – I	✓	✓	✓	✓		✓					✓
Chapter 16 Mark's gospel – special emphases – II	✓					✓			✓	✓	✓
Chapter 17 Mark's gospel – special emphases – III	✓					✓					
Chapter 18 Luke's gospel – ministry of Jesus	✓	✓				✓		✓			✓
Chapter 19 Luke's gospel – parables	✓	✓	✓	✓	✓			✓			✓
Chapter 20 Luke's gospel – passion & resurrection	✓	✓	✓	✓	✓	✓		✓	✓	✓	
Chapter 21 Luke's gospel – special emphases	✓	✓	✓	✓	✓			✓			✓
Chapter 22 Acts of the Apostles	✓				✓			✓			✓

Introduction

'Creed' comes from the Latin word *credo*. Credo means 'I believe'.

There are several creeds. In the Orthodox tradition, the Nicene Creed is the most important. In the Catholic and Anglican tradition, the Apostles' Creed and Nicene Creed have become more important than the rest. Each of these creeds is divided into parts.

- The first is about God the Father.
- The second is about God the Son.
- The third is about God the Holy Spirit.
- The fourth is about other essential Christian beliefs.

Most Christians, including Catholics, Orthodox and Anglicans, accept the creeds as authoritative statements of belief.

Some Christian groups, such as Baptists, do not accept the creeds as a source of belief. They accept only the Bible as a reference for what a Christian should believe.

Why creeds?

Christians want to be clear about what they believe. And they need to say it briefly. They call this a profession of faith (or a symbol of faith). Most of us use the word 'creed' to describe a profession of belief.

In its early days the Church needed a creed for those who asked for baptism, to inform them about the Christian faith.

In later years the Church wanted a creed for a different reason. Christians were discussing and arguing about God and about Christ. There were several disagreements. So the Church wrote creeds to make it clear what it thought were acceptable statements about God and his creation. It hoped this would stop Christians making statements, particularly about God and Jesus, that it thought were wrong.

For instance, many Christians agreed with a priest named Arius, who believed that Christ was not really God. Arius lived in the fourth century. He taught that Jesus, the Son of God, could not possibly be equal with the God the Father. Arius said that the Father created Jesus, just as the Father created every other human person. God the Father then adopted Jesus as his Son. The principal difference between Jesus and the rest of us is that he was the first and most important person that God the Father created. But this does not make Jesus equal to the Father.

The bishops decided that this was wrong. They said that God did become a man, Jesus. Jesus was really God, not just a pretence of God. The bishops emphasized that Jesus was really God as well as really a man. They made this clear in the Nicene Creed.

The importance of creeds

- Christians believe in God. Words cannot adequately describe him. Yet some words describe him better than others. So it is wise to use the better words, rather than to say nothing.
- Christians sometimes disagree about God and about Jesus. They need some way of settling these differences of opinion. They can use the creeds to do this.
- Jesus gave the apostles authority to teach about him. (See Chapter C12, *Mark's gospel – parables* for some details.) Most Christians believe that the successors of the apostles are the bishops. The bishops therefore have authority to teach about God and Jesus. The bishops have written or approved most of the creeds, including the Nicene Creed.
- Catholics believe that the bishops of Rome, as the successors of the apostle Peter, have more authority than the other bishops. The bishops of Rome have approved some creeds, such as the Apostles' Creed.
- Saying a creed reminds Christians of the principal beliefs of their religion. This is important when some Christians emphasize particular beliefs, neglecting other beliefs.
- A creed also helps Christians to increase their understanding of God. By thinking and meditating on a creed, Christians may discern God more clearly in life, and they may learn to penetrate the mystery of God.

Faith is believing what you do not yet understand. The reward for this belief is to understand what you believe.

Augustine

Apostles' Creed

This is a summary of Christian beliefs taught since the days of the apostles. We do not know when this creed was first written, nor who wrote it. The title was first used in a letter written by a council of bishops. The letter was written in AD 390 to Pope Siricus at Rome.

The Apostles' Creed was accepted by the bishops of Rome as an important guide to Christian beliefs. Because of the importance and the authority of every bishop of Rome, other Christians in western Europe also accepted the Apostles' Creed as an important guide to Christian beliefs.

However, Christians in eastern Europe (Orthodox Christians) did not believe the bishops of Rome were so important. These Christians respected the bishop of Rome as the senior bishop. Yet they did not believe the bishop of

Rome had more authority than any other bishop. It was only all the bishops, together, who had authority in the Church. As a council of bishops has never formally approved the Apostles' Creed, Christians in eastern Europe do not believe this creed is as important as the Nicene Creed.

	Apostles' Creed	Chapter in this book
I believe in	God,	C2 *God: Trinity*
	the Father almighty, creator of heaven and earth.	C3 *God – the Father*
I believe in	Jesus Christ, his only Son, our Lord.	C4 *God – the Son*
	He was conceived by the power of the Holy Spirit,	C6 *Jesus – his identity*
		C7 *Jesus – his mission; sin and salvation*
	and born of the virgin Mary.	D15 *Mary, mother of Christ*
	He suffered under Pontius Pilate, was crucified, died, and was buried.	C14 *Mark's gospel – passion and resurrection*
		C15, C16, C17 *Mark's gospel – special emphases*
		C20 *Luke's gospel – passion and resurrection*
		C21 *Luke's gospel – special emphases*
	He descended to the dead. On the third day he rose again.	C14 *Mark's gospel – passion and resurrection*
		C15, C16, C17 *Mark's gospel – special emphases*
		C20 *Luke's gospel – passion and resurrection*
		C10 *Funerals; death and resurrection*
	He ascended into heaven, and is seated at the right hand of the Father. He will come again to judge the living and the dead.	C10 *Funerals; death and resurrection*
		A14 *Easter*
I believe in	the Holy Spirit,	C5 *God – the Holy Spirit*
	the holy catholic Church, the communion of saints,	D6 *The Church – images to explain it*
		D7 *The Church – authority and structures*
		D8 *The Church – missionary work*
		D5 *The Church: Catholic, Orthodox, Protestant*
		C22 *The Acts of the Apostles – main themes*
		C8 *The kingdom of God*
		D10 *Ecumenism*
	the forgiveness of sins,	C7 *Jesus – his mission; sin and salvation*
		A17 *Reconciliation (penance, confession)*
	the resurrection of the body, and the life everlasting.	C10 *Funerals; death and resurrection*
	Amen.	

Nicene Creed

This creed was written by bishops. They wrote it at the two important councils (meeting of bishops) of the Church. The first of these, which met in AD 325, was the Council of Nicea. The second, which met in AD 381, was the Council of Constantinople. Some people think that the bishops at two subsequent councils – at Ephesus and Chalcedon – also wrote some of the Nicene Creed.

There are three words that the Catholic Church added later. The Orthodox Church does not accept this addition to the creed. These three words are about the Holy Spirit.

They are '. . . and the Son'. They come near the beginning of the third part of the Nicene Creed.

The original wording of the creed reads:

'We believe in the Holy Spirit, the Lord, the giver of life, who proceeds from the Father . . .'

The Catholic Church later changed this to:

'We believe in the Holy Spirit, the Lord, the giver of life, who proceeds from the Father and the Son . . .'

The Nicene Creed is more explicit and detailed than the Apostles' Creed, especially about the three 'persons' of the Trinity.

Nicene Creed

We believe in	one God, the Father, the almighty, maker of heaven and earth, of all that is, seen and unseen.
We believe in	one Lord, Jesus Christ, the only Son of God, eternally begotten of the Father, God from God, Light from Light, true God from true God, begotten, not made, of one Being with the Father. Through him all things were made. For us men and for our salvation he came down from heaven; by the power of the Holy Spirit he became incarnate of the virgin Mary, and was made man. For our sake he was crucified under Pontius Pilate; he suffered death and was buried. One the third day he rose again in accordance with the Scriptures; he ascended into heaven and is seated at the right hand of the Father. He will come again in glory to judge the living and the dead, and his kingdom will have no end.
We believe in	the Holy Spirit, the Lord, the giver of life, who proceeds from the Father and the Son. With the Father and the Son he is worshipped and glorified. He has spoken through the Prophets
We believe in	one holy catholic and apostolic Church.
We acknowledge	one baptism for the forgiveness of sins.
We look for	the resurrection of the dead, and the life of the world to come.

Amen

Use of creeds in worship

- A creed is used in many acts of worship. A Christian first professes his or her faith at baptism. In a Catholic or Anglican baptism, the priest asks the baptized person to say that they reject Satan and evil; that they believe in God the Father, and in God the Son who became man and died for us, and in the Holy Spirit. In the Catholic ceremony the priest also asks the baptized person to say that they believe in the holy Catholic Church, the forgiveness of sin, the resurrection of the body and life everlasting. If a child is baptized, the parents speak for the child.
- Some Christians, such as Baptists, do not use a creed when they baptize. Instead, the people to be baptized have to make their own statements of faith. They talk about their experience of Jesus and why they want to be baptized.
- In the ceremony of confirmation, those confirmed say the baptismal creed. Their parents spoke for them at baptism. Now they speak for themselves.
- At the celebration of the eucharist on a Sunday, the Nicene Creed is said.

Examination practice

1. The creeds are important to most Christians.
   Explain why they are important. (3 marks)
   Write about six lines.

2. Choose **two** of the following 'persons':
   The Father
   The Son
   The Holy Spirit
   Say what Christians believe about your chosen 'persons'. Use the Nicene Creed in your explanation.
   (10 marks)
   Write about one side of A4.

3. Choose **three** beliefs from the Apostles' or Nicene Creed.
   Explain how each one might influence the way a Christian behaves. (8 marks)
   Write about three-quarters of a side of A4.

4. 'You can be a good Christian without believing everything in the creed.'
   Do you agree? Give reasons for your view. Show that you have considered the opposite point of view.
   (8 marks)
   Write about three-quarters of a side of A4.

Sign of the cross

✝In the name of the Father, and of the Son, and of the Holy Spirit. Amen.

We find these words and the symbol of the cross used at the beginning of most Catholic prayers, including the eucharist. The cross and the words of this prayer show two central Christian beliefs:

• that the death and resurrection of Jesus were an important part of God's work for us;
• that there is only one God – though God is Father, Son and Holy Spirit.

God is mysterious

God is mysterious: we find it difficult to understand him. God can also be elusive: we may find it difficult to get hold of him. We do not meet God as we meet other people. We are not aware of God as we are aware of clothes, houses, cars, trees, the sun or rain. We cannot see, hear or touch God. God is not something physical. God is very different from anything else we know: God transcends everything (meaning that God is quite different from anything else that exists).

> God is a spirit whom we cannot see, touch or hear. We wish to communicate with God and so we make use of symbols.
> Catholic bishops at the Second Vatican Council

It is difficult to imagine God. We usually call God 'he', but this is not literally correct – God does not have a body and so cannot be male or female.

Christians believe that we can know something about God even though he is mysterious. One very important belief that they have about God is that he is Father, Son and Spirit.

New Testament teaching about the the Trinity

The New Testament writers do not use the word 'Trinity'; nor do they describe God as three equal persons in one God. But there are passages that describe God as Father, other passages that describe Jesus as God, and other passages that describe the Spirit of God as something different from the Father and Jesus.

One New Testament passage that describes God as Father is in John's gospel, where Jesus says:

> 'Now I am going to him who sent me . . . Unless I go away, the Counsellor [Spirit] will not come to you . . . I am going to the Father, where you can see me no longer.'
> John 16⁵⁻¹⁰

In this passage, Jesus clearly speaks of the Father and the Spirit as existing separately from himself. Yet, in all the gospels, Jesus never deviates from the firm Jewish belief that there is only one God.

Many New Testament passages present Jesus as God. The gospel writers say that Jesus does things that only God can do. He raises people from the dead (for example, Jairus' daughter); he forgives sins (for example, the sins of the paralysed man); he controls nature – he feeds 5000 people with a few loaves and fishes; he calms a storm; and he walks on water.

> When evening came, the boat was in the middle of the lake, and he was alone on land. He saw the disciples straining at the oars, because the wind was against them. About the fourth watch of the night [between three and six in the morning] he went out to them, walking on the lake. He was about to pass by them, but when they saw him walking on the lake, they thought he was a ghost. They cried out, because they all saw him and were terrified.
>
> Immediately, he spoke to them and said, 'Take courage! It is I. Don't be afraid.' Then he climbed into the boat with them, and the wind died down. They were completely amazed.
> Mark 6⁴⁷⁻⁵¹

One New Testament passage that describes the Spirit of God as different from the Father and from Jesus, is in the Acts of the Apostles. In this passage, God sent his Spirit to the disciples, after the risen Jesus had left them. The disciples heard a noise like a strong wind and saw what looked like tongues of fire. They felt the power of God's Spirit (Acts 2¹⁻⁴).

Meaning of Trinity

Christians believe that God is one and God is three. They profess this belief on important occasions.

For instance, when a Christian is baptized, it is in the 'name of the Father, and of the Son, and of the Holy Spirit', showing that Christians believe that they share in the life of the Trinity.

Before confirmation a Christian must confess faith in the Father, the Son and the Spirit.

In one Christian service for a dying person, there is the following prayer:

> Go forth, Christian soul, from this world
> in the name of God the almighty Father,
> who created you,
> in the name of Jesus Christ, the Son of the living God,
> who suffered for you,
> in the name of the Holy Spirit,
> who was poured out upon you.
> Go forth, faithful Christian!

Christians are conscious of the Father as creator. They are conscious of Jesus – God the Son, who became human and died to save us. They experience the power of the Holy Spirit. The doctrine of the Trinity is an attempt to grasp and explain how this can be.

'Trinity' means three in one. Christians believe that there is one God. They also believe that this God is Father, Son and Spirit. Each of these three 'persons' is God, whole and entire, as each has the same substance. Each of these 'persons' is also distinct and different from the other two. Yet there is only one God.

This understanding of God was first clearly stated by the bishops who met at Constantinople in the year 381 after the death of Jesus. They used the word *hypostasis* to describe the Father, the Son and the Spirit. This is translated as 'person'. But for us today this word means separate individuals, which is not what the bishops at Constantinople meant. Perhaps the word 'dimension' is a better translation of the word *hypostasis*. There are three 'dimensions' in God: Father, Son and Spirit. Each is God; but each is distinct.

The Athanasian creed, probably written in the fifth century, says this about the Trinity:

> We worship one God in the Trinity and the Trinity in unity.
>   We distinguish among the persons, but we do not divide the substance. For the Father is a distinct person; the Son is a distinct person; and the Holy Spirit is a distinct person. Still, the Father and the Son and the Holy Spirit have one divinity, equal glory, and coeternal majesty.
>   What the Father is, the Son is, and the Holy Spirit is. The Father is uncreated, the Son is uncreated, and the Holy Spirit is uncreated. The Father has immensity, the Son has immensity, and the Holy Spirit has immensity. The Father is eternal, the Son is eternal, and the Holy Spirit is eternal.
>   Nevertheless, there are not three eternal beings, but one eternal being. There are not three uncreated beings, nor three beings having immensity, but one uncreated being and one being that has immensity.

Is Trinity contradictory?

Some people suggest that the idea of three in one is absurd and contradictory. They argue that some things are impossible. For example, it is not possible for a shape to be both a triangle and a circle at the same time. Neither is it possible for me to be a baby and a pensioner at the same time. Nor is it possible for us to see something that is invisible. So how can three 'persons' be equally God, yet only one God?

It is not convincing to say that God can do anything; therefore he can make three equal to one. This is unconvincing, because God cannot do absurd or contradictory things. He cannot make an object that is simultaneously an orange and a wheelbarrow. Nor can he be something that is both three and one at the same time.

Trying to understand the Trinity

For Christians the Trinity is an essential way of understanding something about God. But for many it is a mysterious way of trying to understand a mysterious God. So theologians have suggested ways to understand the Trinity.

- **St Patrick** reputedly used a shamrock to help understand the Trinity. There are three distinct parts to the shamrock; but a shamrock is one thing, not three things.
- **Gregory of Nyasa** suggested that the Trinity is like a person who is learning three subjects. Someone may be learning geography, RE and science. They are three distinct subjects, yet they are together in the mind of one person.
- **Augustine** suggested several ways of understanding the Trinity. His best-known illustration is love. He said that in the Trinity the Father loves the Son, and the Spirit is the bond of love between them – three in one.
- But Augustine thinks there is an even better way to understand the Trinity. Suppose I am thinking about myself thinking. I can distinguish three things: what I am thinking, an awareness that I am thinking, and my decision to become aware that I am thinking. Yet these three activities are inseparable, and take place in one mind.
- An easier way to think of the Trinity is to use the sun. There is the sun itself (the Father), the rays that travel out from the sun (the Son), and the warmth and light that we experience (the Holy Spirit).
- A simple way of trying to picture the Trinity is an equal-sided triangle. There are three sides, yet one triangle. Each of the sides is equal, but not identical.

Examination practice

1. 'God is mysterious.' What does this mean? (3 marks)
   Write about six lines.

2. Explain fully the Christian belief in the Trinity.
                                                    (10 marks)
   Write about one side of A4.

3. Christians believe that love is the bond between the three 'persons' of the Trinity.
How might this affect a Christian's attitude to other people? (8 marks)
Write about three-quarters of a side of A4.

4. 'It is nonsense to divide God into three parts.'
Do you agree? Give reasons to support your view. Show that you have considered different views.
(8 marks)
Write about three-quarters of a side of A4.

GOD – THE FATHER (CREATOR)

The origin

Christians believe in God the Father. He is the first 'person' in the Trinity.

The Father has always existed. No one created him. He is uncreated.

The Father is **almighty** – he can do anything, provided it is not contradictory or absurd.

The Father is present in the world; but he is not part of it: he **transcends** the world.

Because Christians believe that God is not part of the world (he transcends it), they believe the Father is quite different from the rest of us. Not only is he almighty, he is perfect – he does not do anything wrong; indeed, he *cannot* do anything wrong.

Creator

The Nicene Creed states:

> We believe in one God, the Almighty, maker of heaven and earth, of all that is, seen and unseen.

So, Christians believe the Father is the creator who made the world and all that is in it. He made the world from nothing. And he keeps it going. He did not make it from himself.

God the Father created a good, beautiful world. He did not create any evil in the world. Therefore, if there is evil in the world, it is not his fault.

However, anything that is not perfect has limitations. Hence, as created things are not perfect, it is natural that they should wither and die. God's world may be a good, beautiful world, but this does not make it a trouble-free world.

The most important part of the Father's creation is human beings – male and female. He made them in his image. They are special. He told them to be his representatives in this world.

Male or female?

God is a spiritual being. This means that God is not a material being. God has no body. So God does not have a sex. One consequence of this is that it is inaccurate to think of God as either male or female. Another consequence of this is that we cannot believe God has a wife or husband.

However, we do not easily understand what a spiritual being is. Yet we have to imagine God, using our experience and things that we do understand.

Christians could refer to God the Father as 'it', rather than 'he' or 'she', as they do not believe the Father has any sex. Yet Christians have traditionally used the word 'father' to describe God. A father is a 'he', not an 'it'.

Christians have inherited the Jewish image of God. He is a father who cares for and guides his children. He suffers with and for them. He wants the best for them. He protects them. He is willing to sacrifice many things for them. He is even willing to sacrifice himself for them.

In addition, Christians take particular note of the image of God that Jesus used. He called God 'father'.

Christians use the word 'father' metaphorically. It is not a literal description of God. Yet Christians do think of the Father as a person, rather than an object – 'he' or 'she' is a more suitable word than 'it' for the Father.

The description of God as father comes from an age when men were dominant and women were subservient. There is an occasional reference in the Old Testament to God as a mother. But it is just an occasional reference. In our time, when there is greater equality between men and women, it may be suitable to think of God as a mother, as well as thinking of God as a father – to think of God as she as well as he. If men and women have distinctive qualities, and if God created men and women, then both men and women reflect what God is like.

Creation stories

Genesis is the name of the first book in the Bible. It has two narratives about the creation of the world.

Some Christians interpret these narratives literally. They think that this is the only style of writing used in the Bible.

Most Christians, however, interpret these narratives figuratively. They think of these narrative as stories – as religious mythology. They support this view by pointing to obvious contradictions in the stories. For instance, in the first story, God makes light on the first day and the sun on the fourth day. There are also obvious contradictions between the first and second stories. For example, in the first story, God makes people last – after he has made the natural elements, the plants and the animals. Yet in the second story, God makes man first, before he makes anything else.

Christians believe these stories teach important truths, such as:

- Without God, there would be no world.
- People are the most important part of creation.
- The world is good.
- God is not responsible for anything evil in the world.
- Men and women are equal.

First story in Genesis

The world was empty, formless and dark.
The Spirit of God hovered over it.
On the first day, God made light, night and day.
On the second day, God made the sky.
On the third day, God made dry land. He also made plants and trees.
On the fourth day, God made the sun, the moon and the stars.
On the fifth day, God made the fish and the birds.
On the sixth day, God made animals. He then made humans – man and woman – in his image and likeness, to rule over the all other creatures.
On the seventh, God rested.

Second story in Genesis

God made a man (the Hebrew word for man is 'Adam') from the dust of the ground. God breathed into his nostrils the breath of life.
God put the man into a pleasant garden, in Eden.
The man could eat the fruit from any tree, except the fruit from the tree of knowledge of good and evil. If he ate from this tree, he would die.
God decided to make a companion for the man.
God made the animals, but they were not suitable companions for the man.
Then God took a rib from the man while he was asleep, and he used it to make a woman. She was equal to the man.
A serpent persuaded the woman to persuade the man to eat from the tree of knowledge of good and evil. They both did. They suddenly realized they were naked.
God cursed the serpent.
God banished Adam and Eve from the garden, in case they ate from the other tree – the tree of life – and became like God.

The man would have to earn a living by painfully cultivating the land. The woman would have to bear children through painful childbirth.

Father of the Son and the Spirit

The Christian belief in the Trinity has been explained in the previous chapter.

The Father is the first 'person' (dimension) of the Trinity. He is the source of the Godhead. The Son and the Spirit trace their origin to the Father. The Son is 'born' of the Father, from all eternity.

The Spirit 'proceeds' from the Father from all eternity. Some Christians, such as Catholics and Anglicans, add that the Spirit 'proceeds' from the Son as well as from the Father.

The Father sent his Son to redeem us. (See Chapter C4, *God – the Son*.)

The Father sends his Spirit to sanctify us: to help us to be like God. (See Chapter C5, *God – the Holy Spirit*.)

> 'As the Father has loved me, so I have loved you.'
> Jesus (John 15[9])

Father of Christians

He is the Father, primarily, of Jesus, who had a special relationship with him. Jesus reveals the Father to his followers.

He is the Father, secondarily, of all Christians, who are baptized into Jesus.

The Catholic bishops at the Second Vatican Council said:

> It pleased God, in his goodness and wisdom, to reveal himself and to make known the mystery of his will. His will was that men should have access to the Father, through Christ, the Word made flesh, in the Holy Spirit, and thus become sharers in the divine nature. By this revelation, then, the invisible God, from the fullness of his love, addresses men as his friends and moves among them, to invite and receive them into his own company.

Jesus advised his followers to talk to God as a child speaks with a father. He could have recommended approaching God as though he was a judge, or a king, or a master. These are popular images of God in the Old Testament. But, in his own prayer, Jesus called God *abba*, which means 'dad'; and he advised the rest of us to talk to God in the same way.

Unfortunately, not all children have a happy or comfortable relationship with their fathers. Jesus must have had in mind an exemplary child–father relationship. What does that involve? Perhaps, trust that a father will give protection; confidence that a father will provide food, clothing and other basic needs; belief that a father offers sound advice to his child; acceptance of the greater power and authority of a father; conviction that a father will listen to his child; conviction that a father will grant a child's request, if the father thinks it is in the best interest of his child; assurance that a father will give comfort and consolation in time of trouble; and so on.

When people are baptized, they become Christians. Christians believe that baptism makes them members of the family of God; thus they can follow the example of their 'brother' Jesus and talk to God as their 'father'.

Some Christians picture God as living in the heavens or stars: we say 'our Father in heaven'. This is a symbolic way of saying that God is great. He is greater than we can imagine – too great for us to be able to meet him in the way we meet other people on earth. He transcends all earthly things, meaning he is quite different from anything on earth. So we say God is **transcendent**.

Christians do not use the word 'father' literally when they describe God as father. The word 'father' is used literally of a human father: we know the meaning of the word 'father' because we use it of our human fathers. To distinguish God from a human father, we describe him as the 'heavenly father'. Thus we use the word 'father' primarily of human fathers, and only secondarily of God.

Yet Christians believe that God is the perfect father. The way he loves, cares, protects, and listens to his 'children' is the example that all human fathers should follow.

Examination practice

1. State what Christians believe about the Father as creator. (3 marks)
   Write about six lines.

2. Write an account of the **two** creation narratives. What do they teach about God and his creation? (10 marks)

   Write about one side of A4.

3. Christians believe God created the world. How might this influence their attitude to the natural world?
   Christians also believe God is Father. How might this influence their attitude to other people? (8 marks)
   Write about three-quarters of a side of A4.

4. Is it better to call God father or mother? What do you think? Give reasons for your view. Show that you have understood more than one point of view. (8 marks)

   Write about three-quarters of a side of A4.

GOD – THE SON

One with the Father

Christians say that the Son is equal with the Father. Both have the same substance or nature. Both are God. Yet the Son is distinct from the Father.

The Christian belief in the Trinity is explained in the two previous chapters and in the next chapter. This chapter gives more detail about the Christian belief in the Son – the second 'person' (or dimension) in the Trinity.

The Son was 'born' or 'begotten', eternally, from the Father. The words 'Son' and 'born' are used metaphorically, not literally: the Son did not have a mother, nor did he have a beginning. He is uncreated and has always existed. Christians use the word 'Son' to try and express something about his relation to the Father. They use the word 'Son' because this is the word used by Jesus to explain his relation to the Father. For instance, he told his disciples:

'As the Father has loved me, so have I loved you'.
John 15[9]

Sent by the Father

Christians believe that the Father sent his Son to redeem us. The Son became a human person, born of the virgin Mary, as Jesus, a Jew, in Palestine 2000 years ago. This was through the power of the Holy Spirit.

The writer of the letter to the Hebrews, a book in the New Testament, says:

In the past God spoke to our forefathers through the prophets at many times and in various ways, but in these last days he has spoken to us by his Son, whom he appointed heir of all things, and through whom he made the universe. The Son is the radiance of God's glory and the exact representation of his being, sustaining all things by his powerful word.

Hebrews 1[1–3]

Jesus revealed that God is Father, Son and Spirit. There was no other way we could have known this about God. It

An icon of Jesus with Mary

is not something that we could have discovered about God, simply by thinking about him.

Jesus completed the tasks his Father gave him. He spent his life doing what the Father wanted. And he died to save us from our sins. (The complications really start now.) The Son is God, so he cannot die, yet Jesus died. The Father raised the whole Jesus, not just the human dimension of Jesus, back to life. Thus the Son returned to the Father, having completed the task that the Father gave him.

Because of the Son's work on earth, we can see and understand God's love for us. We can also get to know him and to love him.

> 'I came from the Father and entered the world; now I am leaving the world and going back to the Father.'
>
> Jesus (John 16²⁸)

Jesus, God incarnate

Christians believe that God became a human person. They say God became incarnate.

For details of this belief, read Chapters C6, *Jesus – his identity*, and C7, *Jesus, his mission; sin and salvation*.

> Jesus Christ was sent into the world as the true mediator between God and men. Since he is God, all the fullness of the divine nature dwells in him bodily.
>
> Catholic bishops at Second Vatican Council

Sends the Spirit

Before he left his disciples, Jesus promised to send them the Spirit of God, his Spirit, so they would not be alone. He said:

> '. . . I will ask the Father, and he will give you another Counsellor to be with you for ever – the Spirit of truth . . . I will not leave you orphans.'
>
> John 14¹⁵⁻¹⁸

The Catholic, Anglican and Methodist Churches teach that both the Father and the Son sent the Spirit; the Spirit 'proceeds' from both the Father and the Son.

According to the Orthodox Church, the Spirit 'proceeds' from the Father alone. The Orthodox believe that the Father is the unique source of the Godhead.

Examination practice

1. Christians believe that Jesus is the Son of God. Explain what this means. (8 marks)
   Write about three-quarters of a side of A4.

2. Christians believe that God became a man, Jesus, to show his love for all people. How might this influence their attitude to God and to other people? (8 marks)
   Write about three-quarters of a side of A4.

3. 'A man cannot become a cat. Nor can God become a man.'
   Do you agree? Give reasons for your view. Show that you have understood the opposite view. (8 marks)
   Write about three-quarters of a side of A4.

One with the Father and the Son

Christians say that the Spirit is the equal of the Father and the Son. All three have the same substance or nature. Each one of them is God. Yet the Spirit is distinct from both the Father and the Son, just as each one of them is distinct from the other two.

The Christian belief in the Trinity was explained in the three previous chapters. This chapter gives more detail about the Christian belief in the Spirit, the third 'person' (or dimension) in the Trinity.

In the fourth century, when the bishops wrote the Nicene Creed, they said that the Spirit 'proceeds' from the Father. The Orthodox Church still accepts this wording, without any additions to it. The Catholic Church added to it. They said that the Spirit 'proceeds' from the Father and from the Son.

Sent

Christians believe that, after he completed his work on earth, Jesus had to return to his Father. But God did not intend to leave his followers as 'orphans', so Jesus promised he would send the Spirit of God. The disciples experienced the Spirit of God soon after Jesus' death and resurrection. This happened at the feast of Pentecost.

> Suddenly a sound like the blowing of a violent wind came from heaven and filled the whole house where they were sitting. They saw what seemed to be tongues of fire that separated and came to rest on each of them. All of them were filled with the Holy Spirit.
>
> Acts 2²⁻⁴

The Church believes that, just as the Spirit helped the first disciples, so he helps all other Christians to follow the example of Jesus.

Some Christians are particularly keen to experience the Spirit of God in an overpowering way, like the first disciples. They are Pentecostalists or charismatics. They often clap hands when they sing, and they may dance. They pray together. They become very excited at their meetings. Sometimes people faint; others speak in strange languages; some prophesy. They feel the Spirit of God agitates and thrills them.

However, most Christians experience the Spirit of God in a quieter way, rather like the Old Testament prophet Elijah. He stood on the top of mountain and experienced first a mighty wind, then an earthquake, then a fire. But God was not in any of these. Then there was a gentle whisper, and Elijah realized that the Spirit of God was with him. Likewise, Christians experience the Spirit of God when

they are joyful and patient, when they are gentle and self-controlled, when they are peaceful and kind. They feel the Spirit of God is absent or ignored when there is sexual immorality, hatred, jealousy, witchcraft, selfish ambition, anger, drunkenness, conflict, and so on.

Most Christians also experience the Spirit of God in their worship, though more sedately than charismatics. They feel that the Spirit of God encourages them to approach God with confidence and to talk to him as to a father. They remain 'sober'. They think that the Spirit of God helps them to understand the passages from the Bible that they hear at the eucharist and other acts of worship. They believe that the Spirit guides them to realize the truth – about themselves, and about other people. They pray to the Spirit for courage to be willing to listen to the truth, even though the truth may not please or comfort them. They rely on the Spirit of God to give them the strength to be like Christ, particularly when they have no desire to follow his example. They seek the comfort of the Spirit when things are falling apart and there is no human support or understanding.

> 'I will ask the Father, and he will give you another Counsellor to be with you for ever – the Spirit of truth.'
>
> Jesus (John 14¹⁶)

Thus there are two distinctive ways in which Christians experience the Holy Spirit: the exuberant way of charismatic Christians, and the quieter way of other Christians. Many Christians feel that these two ways of experiencing the Spirit of God are compatible, and so they use both in their religious services and ceremonies.

Inspirer of the Bible

Christians believe that the Spirit of God inspired the writers of the Bible. For instance, the Catholic bishops at the Second Vatican said:

> The divinely revealed realities, which are contained in the text of sacred Scripture, have been written down under the inspiration of the Holy Spirit . . . written under the inspiration of the Holy Spirit, they have God as their author . . .
>
> To compose the sacred books, God chose certain men who, all the while he employed them in this task, made full use of their powers and faculties so that, though he acted in them and by them, it was as true authors that they consigned to writing whatever he wanted written, and no more.

Symbols of the Holy Spirit

We cannot see or touch the Spirit of God; but we can know the Spirit is present by his effects. There are many symbols to describe the presence and power of the Spirit of God. However, one symbol never used for the Spirit of God is the human form: the Spirit is never imagined or drawn as a human person. The following images are used to represent the Holy Spirit.

- **Water**: this is a symbol for life. There is no life without water. A baby comes into life after spending nine months in the water of his or her mother's womb. So water symbolizes the life of God that the Spirit brings. Water is an important symbol in baptism; it signifies a new life – the Spirit of God coming into the life of a Christian.
- **Oil**: a symbol used in four of the sacraments. It is not a symbol that we use much today. Anointing with oil was a symbol in the Old Testament to show that the Spirit of God had seized a person. So oil symbolizes the strength, the courage and the healing the Spirit brings.
- **Fire**: a symbol that we easily understand. One important feature of fire is its power. When the Spirit of God comes to anyone, then there is power – to do God's work, to forget one's own interests, to stand up for the rights of the poor, and so on.
- **Cloud and light**: these metaphors occur together in the Bible, indicating that the Spirit both hides and reveals God. These are important metaphors for us today, as we alternate between believing and not believing in God. These metaphors show that it is the Spirit of God that both hides and reveals God.
- **Hand or finger**: this is an important symbol in the sacraments, though it is not a symbol in common use today. When a bishop or priest holds his hands over someone, this symbolizes that they are giving God's Spirit.
- **Dove**: this has no obvious meaning, even though it is frequently used as a symbol of the Holy Spirit. We can take the dove as a symbol of peace, tenderness, and gentleness. The Spirit of God has these qualities. Christians believe that the Spirit of God treats us peacefully, gently and tenderly. They also believe that the Spirit of God helps us to treat others peacefully, gently and tenderly.

> The Spirit helps us in our weakness. We do not know what we ought to pray for, but the Spirit himself intercedes for us.
>
> Paul (Romans 8[26])

Christian differences

There is a significant difference between the Orthodox Church and other churches (such as the Catholic and Anglican churches) about how the Spirit originates. The Catholic and Orthodox Churches had agreed that the Spirit 'proceeds' from the Father. The Nicene Creed originally had:

> We believe in the Holy Spirit, the Lord, the giver of life, who proceeds from the Father. With the Father and Son he is worshipped and glorified.

Then the Catholic Church added that the Spirit 'proceeds' from the Son as well as from the Father. (This is called the **filioque clause** – in Latin *filioque* means 'and from the Son'). The Catholic version of the Nicene Creed now had:

> We believe in the Holy Spirit, the Lord, the giver of life, who proceeds from the Father and the Son. With the Father and Son he is worshipped and glorified.

The Catholic Church argued that the Holy Spirit is the Spirit of the Father and the Spirit of the Son. The Spirit must therefore 'proceed' from the Son as well as from the Father.

The Orthodox Church has always vehemently rejected this change. We may think this is an insignificant change and a trivial disagreement. But Orthodox Christians argue that it has unacceptable consequences, such as the conclusion that there must be two Gods: the Father and the Son. The Orthodox insist that there is only one principle or source in the Trinity – the Father.

Examination practice

1. Name **two** symbols used for the Holy Spirit. Say what each one means. (3 marks)
   Write about six lines.

2. Christians believe that the Holy Spirit is important in the work of the Church. Explain what they believe. (10 marks)
   Write about one side of A4.

3. 'People do not experience God. Some just imagine they do.'
   Do you agree? Give reasons for your view. Show that you have thought of the opposite view. (8 marks)
   Write about three-quarters of a side of A4.

Introduction

Christians think that there is no word that describes Jesus adequately, so they describe him in different ways, using a variety of terms.

Messiah/Christ

Messiah is a Hebrew word meaning 'anointed one'. 'Anointed one' is a phrase that the Jews used to describe their kings, who had to be anointed with oil as a sign that God had chosen them.

Christ means the same thing – it is the Greek word for Messiah.

At the time of Jesus' ministry many Jews thought of the Messiah as a king. They expected the Messiah to be a national leader. So, when people began to think of Jesus as Messiah, it was natural that they should think of him as a king.

- Jesus' disciples thought he was going to be the king of the Jews.
- The Romans crucified Jesus because they thought he claimed to be the king of the Jews.

Jesus was persistently reluctant to accept the title of king. He talked about the kingdom of God, but he meant a spiritual, not an earthly, kingdom. And God was the king, not Jesus.

After Jesus' death the disciples had to rethink their view of Jesus. He had not become the glorious, earthly ruler they had enthusiastically anticipated. His death had shattered this expectation of him. When the disciples experienced him as resurrected, they began to think of him as Lord.

However, Christ was the most popular title that the first Christians used for Jesus. It was so popular, it became constantly used with his name. So he was called Jesus the Christ, or Jesus Christ. The word Messiah (Christ) was in ordinary use in the time of Jesus as a title. Many people today do not realize that Christ was a title. They think it is a name. So they think Jesus was his first name and Christ his second name.

> This is the good news about Jesus Christ, the Son of God.
>
> Mark 1[1] (*Good News Bible*)

Teacher/prophet

Prophets are people who have had an unusual experience of God. They usually tell people what God thinks and expects of them.

Christians think that 'prophet' is a useful description of Jesus, but also a limiting description of him.

'Prophet' is a useful description of Jesus, because one of his important tasks was teaching about God. Christians place great emphasis on the teachings of Jesus. Since they think that Jesus knew God better than anyone else, they believe his account of God is more accurate than anyone else's.

Christians believe that Jesus was the most important prophet. They accept other prophets, especially the Jewish prophets such as Elijah, Elisha, Isaiah, and Jeremiah. But they think that Jesus was the most reliable and credible prophet.

'Prophet' is a limiting description of Jesus, for two reasons:

1. Christians believe that Jesus is much more than a prophet. They believe he is God. But prophets are no more than men, even though they have a special experience of God. So to describe Jesus as a prophet may hide more important aspects of his identity.
2. Christians believe that Jesus showed us what God is like, by what he did as well as by what he said. A prophet simply speaks about God. Jesus' actions are as important as his speeches. So Jesus showed what God is like, when he healed a leper; when he forgave those who crucified him; when he forgave the sins of the paralysed man; when he cast out an evil spirit from a demented man who lived in burial caves.

> 'Only in his home town, among his relatives and in his own house is a prophet without honour.'
>
> Jesus (Mark 6[4])

Son of Man

Son of Man is an important title, because:

- it is a title that Jesus used to describe himself;
- it is the only title that Jesus used to describe himself;
- no one else in the time of Jesus used it to describe Jesus.

It is therefore a very important title in finding out what Jesus thought about himself.

Unfortunately, there are different views on what Jesus meant by Son of Man. Here is one view.

If we compare the passages in the gospels where Jesus calls himself Son of Man, we find that these passages are usually about suffering, death and resurrection.

For instance, on one occasion Jesus taught his disciples that he must suffer many things and be rejected by the elders, chief priests and teachers of the law, and that he must be killed and after three days rise again.

Mark 8[31]

On another occasion, Jesus told his disciples,

'We are going to Jerusalem . . . and the Son of Man will be betrayed to the chief priests and teachers of the Law. They will condemn him to death and will hand him over to the Gentiles, who will mock him and spit on him, flog him and kill him. Three days later he will rise.'

Mark 10[33–34]

On a third occasion, Jesus told the high priest,

'You will see the Son of Man sitting at the right hand of the Mighty One and coming on the clouds of heaven.'

Mark 14[62]

If we study the passages where Jesus calls himself Son of Man, he seems to mean the following about himself:

- He would be the opposite of a mighty king; he would be an ordinary person.
- Yet his suffering and death would help us.
- He would overcome death, because God would raise him to life again.
- In his life after death, he would be God's judge of how well we have behaved.

Suffering servant/slave

The disciples were bitterly disappointed when Jesus was killed. They had expected him to be the king who would free them from the Romans' rule. However, after his death and resurrection, they began to think about his identity in a different way. Describing Jesus as a suffering servant or slave seemed to fit his life better than describing him as a king. The idea of servant or slave also fits much better with Jesus' own description of himself as the Son of Man. Two illustrations of this are as follows.

Many years ago slaves or servants washed their master's feet before a meal. At the last meal Jesus had with his disciples, he washed their feet.

At the Last Supper that Jesus had with his disciples, he washed their feet – something that a servant or slave would do for the master. A master would not do this for a servant. So Jesus showed that he treated others as though he was their servant, even though he was entitled to behave like a master.

On one occasion before the Last Supper, James and John wanted a special favour from Jesus. They wanted to be the most important people, after him, when he became king. The other disciples were furious when they heard this, for they were just as eager to be the most important people in Jesus' kingdom. Jesus told his disciples that he did not come to be served, but to serve. He came to give his life as a ransom for many (Mark 10[45]).

God/Lord

The first three gospel writers were generally reluctant to say, explicitly, that Jesus was God. So, they described him doing things that only God could do. For example, the gospel writers say:

- Jesus walked on water, and calmed a storm (Mark 6[45–52], Mark 4[35–41]).
- Jesus fed 5000 people with a few loaves and fishes (Mark 6[30–44]).
- Jesus forgave a person's sins (Mark 2[1–12]).

Other writers in the New Testament quite confidently call Jesus either God, or God's son. For example, John's gospel reports Jesus, just before his trial and death, in conversation with God. Jesus says,

'Father, though the world does not know you, I know you, and they [my followers] know that you have sent me.'

John 17[25]

Paul, in his letter to the Christians at Philippi, says Jesus,

being in very nature God,
    did not consider equality with God something to be grasped,
but made himself nothing,
    taking the very nature of a servant,
    being made in human likeness.

Philippians 2[6–7]

Son of God/Son of the Father

'Son of God' and 'Son of the Father' are used to distinguish the second person in the Trinity from the other two (see Chapter C2, *God: Trinity*).

Jesus talked to God as a son talks to his father. Jesus' language was Aramaic (not Hebrew) and the Aramaic word he used when he spoke with God was *abba*. The usual translation for this is 'father', but it really means 'dad'. It shows that Jesus had a special relationship with God. Jesus invites Christians to use the same term; he taught them to say 'Our Father' when they talk with God.

> 'Abba, Father, . . . everything is possible for you. Take this cup from me. Yet not what I will, but what you will.'
>
> Jesus (Mark 14[36])

A special term: incarnation

Christians believe that Jesus is:

- **God**. They believe that he is really God, not some kind of half-god.
- **human**. They believe he was a real man (not the pretence of a man) – a man who had to die as all humans have to. God raised him from death, so Jesus is still a human person. Only, he is a changed human person after his resurrection. (See Chapter C10, *Funerals; death and resurrection*.)

This belief in Jesus as God and man was clearly stated by bishops at two important Councils they had: one was at a town named Nicea in AD 325; the other was at a town named Chalcedon in AD 451. Subsequent Councils, such as the Second Vatican Council, have re-stated it.

So, Christians believe that God became man. This is what the word 'incarnation' means. God became man for a purpose, so that we might get to God. A famous phrase (attributed to Irenaeus) suggests: 'God became what we are, that he might make us what he is.'

Though Christians believe that Jesus was a real man, they believe he was a man with a difference. He never did anything wrong. We know that is not possible for us to be perfect. And we find it surprising to think that any human could be perfect. Yet Christians believe that Jesus was perfect. They believe that he was tempted to do wrong, just as we are. But he never did anything wrong. He is the model of what every one of us should be.

Christian belief in the incarnation seems contradictory. How can something be both God and man? The two are quite different. It is like saying that something can be both a banana and a brick. This is absurd.

There are three possible replies to this difficulty:

- God can do anything. What seems impossible to us is not impossible for God. It is just that we cannot understand that it is possible.
- God is mysterious and elusive. In the end, we have to say that we do not understand him. Our descriptions of God can only be approximate; they cannot be precisely accurate.
- There is definite evidence from the New Testament to believe in the incarnation. The Church accepts the New Testament as the reliable word of God. (See Chapter C11, *The Bible*.)

> 'Now Christ took a complete human nature just as it is found in us poor unfortunates, but one that was without sin.'
>
> Catholic bishops at Second Vatican Council

Examination practice

1. What did Jesus mean by the phrase 'Son of Man'?

   (3 marks)

   Write about six lines.

2. Explain what Christians believe about Jesus. (10 marks)
   Write about one side of A4.

3. Christians believe that Jesus redeemed them.
   How might this influence what they say and do?

   (6 marks)

   Write about half a side of A4.

4. 'Jesus cannot be God and man. The two are totally different.'
   Do you agree? Give reasons for your view. Show that you have considered the opposite point of view.

   (8 marks)

   Write about three-quarters of a side of A4.

 # JESUS – HIS MISSION; SIN AND SALVATION  **7**

Introduction

Christians emphasize that anyone who wants to understand Jesus needs to consider two things:

- what he did;
- what he said.

> In his unbounded love, God became what we are, that he might make us what he is.
>
> Irenaeus

Kingdom of God

Although we live in a country with a democratic government, we know what a kingdom is – the king decides the rules and what is allowed. Christians believe that Jesus started God's kingdom. This means that we do God's will on earth. It also means that God does his will on earth.

Jesus introduced God's kingdom by what he did and by what he said. So:

- He **healed** people: for example, a woman who had a haemorrhage for 12 years (Mark 5^{25-34}); and a blind man named Bartimaeus (Mark 10^{46-52}).
- He **forgave** people: for example, a paralysed man (Mark 2^{1-12}); the people who crucified Jesus (Luke 23^{34}).
- He **defeated** evil, as when he cast evil spirits out of people: for example, the daughter of a foreign woman (Mark 7^{24-30}); a boy who had epilepsy and a father who was not sure he had faith (Mark 9^{14-29}).
- He **influenced** people to change their behaviour and way of life: for example, a tax collector named Zacchaeus (Luke 19^{1-9}).
- He **raised** people to life: for example, the daughter of Jairus (Mark 5^{21-43}); Lazarus (John 11^{1-44}).

There is a paradox in the Christian belief about God's kingdom. Christians believe it has come, but they believe it is yet to come. It has come because Jesus started it. It has yet to come because it is obviously not perfect – there is still much illness, hard-heartedness, evil, and selfishness here on earth. God's kingdom will be perfect only after death in the next world.

See Chapter C8, *The kingdom of God*, for further details.

Teaching

Christians believe that Jesus was a prophet and the Son of God. He knew God and what God wanted for us. So he could speak with authority about these matters. He taught that:

- God wants to forgive (Luke 15^{1-7}).
- We should love God (Mark 12^{29-30}).
- We should love everyone else, including our enemies (Luke 10^{25-37}).
- We should not think too highly of ourselves (Luke 18^{9-14}).
- There is life after death (Mark 12^{18-27}).
- We can be reconciled and united with God (Luke 15^{11-32}).
- God will judge us after our death, on whether we have helped the sick, starving, dying, imprisoned, etc (Matthew 25^{31-46}).
- God will always help us if we ask him (Luke 11^{5-13}).
- Those who concentrate on making money will not get into God's kingdom (Luke 12^{16-21}).

Show God's concern and tender hand

No one can see God. Christians believe that Jesus showed us what God is like. God would like to influence us to be like him, to be good to others. Jesus' meeting with Zacchaeus is an example of this. Zacchaeus was rich. He wanted to see Jesus. He had to climb a tree, as there was a crowd, and he could not see over their heads, because he was small. When Jesus saw him up the tree, he told Zacchaeus to come down. Jesus wanted to go to his house for a meal (a sign of friendship). The crowd grumbled because Zacchaeus was a tax collector for the Romans (and therefore disloyal to his people, as well as greedy and grasping, deceitful, unscrupulous, hard-hearted – not a likeable man). Zacchaeus said he would give half his belongings to the poor. He also said he would repay four times anyone he had cheated (Luke 19^{1-10}).

Jesus described himself as a shepherd. He showed God's concern for us, just as a good shepherd looks after his sheep. He had pity on people because they were like sheep without a shepherd (Mark 6^{34}), and so he taught them. He said he was the good shepherd who was willing to die for his sheep (John 10^{11}).

> Christ is risen from the dead!
> Dying, he conquered death;
> To the dead, he has given life.
>
> Byzantine liturgy

Resurrection

Christians believe that Jesus did more by his death and resurrection than by anything else he did (see the next section for explanations).

Christians believe that God raised Jesus from the dead. This is their number one belief. They believe some of his disciples 'met' him after his death. They believe that Jesus was the first person to rise from the dead. He now lives with God. Through rising from the dead he has made it possible for us to rise from the dead. This was the task that God gave him to do.

The gospels say that Jesus raised some individuals from the dead – the daughter of Jairus; the son of the widow at Nain; Lazarus. Jesus raised them to re-start their life on earth, just as it had been before they died.

But Jesus' own resurrection was quite different. He rose to a new life in which he cannot die. In his new life,

- he does not have a human body;
- he knows God face to face;
- he cannot suffer any more.

Christians think that the resurrection of the rest of us will be like this.

Sin and the need for help, or salvation

Christians believe that we are all inadequate – we are sinners. We know what is right and wrong, yet we frequently do what is wrong. We often have a strong, even overwhelming, desire to do what is wrong, and we give in to that desire. We hurt other people, and we hurt God. We do this quite deliberately, sometimes with an intense, but controlled, passion; sometimes with an uncontrolled passion.

Christians call this defect **original sin**. All of us experience it.

When we realize, and feel humiliated, by our original sin, we also realize that we need to be helped, or – to use a phrase in the Bible – we realize that we need to be saved.

We need to be forgiven, because we have hurt other people.

We also have to forgive those who have hurt us, but we do not want to do this. We prefer, with persistent resentment, to recall the hurt, and refuse to forgive. It is difficult to relinquish this resentment. We need help.

And we need help to do what is right, because we are incapable of continuously doing good to other people by our own efforts. We can manage to be good sometimes, but not continuously. Even if we resolve to be patient, or kind, or considerate, or forgiving, we find that it is impossible to behave in these ways all the time. We need help.

Christians believe that Jesus, through his death and resurrection, gives such help.

Special terms

The following words are often used to explain the meaning of the death and resurrection of Jesus.

Salvation

'Jesus' ('Joshua' in Hebrew) means 'God saves'. For Jews, it was important to have a name that indicated what you were like.

Christians say that Jesus saved us by his crucifixion and death. He is our saviour. The word 'save' is not used in the sense of keeping money instead of spending it. The word is used in the sense of rescuing someone in a difficult or dangerous situation. So if we knew someone who was dying because they could not afford medicine, and we bought the medicine, we would have saved that person.

Now, Christians believe that only Jesus can 'save' us. Christians believe that we are defective in some ways: we are selfish, we harm other people, we are easily frustrated, we worry too readily, and so on. Christians believe that Jesus is our saviour. Through his crucifixion and resurrection, he saves us from being inadequate.

- Jesus gives us God's forgiveness for anything we have done wrong. Now, this is comforting for most of us, because we realize that we have been mean, vindictive,

selfish, inconsiderate, and so on. And we are grateful to be forgiven. However, most of us do not want to forgive those who have committed child murder, or those who have molested children, or those who have committed any other repulsive acts. Most of us feel that such acts cry out to heaven for vengeance. They are unforgiveable. Yet, Christians believe that God forgives anybody, anything – if they are sorry for what they have done.

- Jesus gives us God's help. We know that even when we try to be patient or forgiving, we often fail. Christians believe that Jesus saves us, because he gives us the strength to be patient or forgiving, if we have the humility to want it – not necessarily all at once, but gradually.

Redemption

Christians say that, by his crucifixion and death, Jesus redeemed us. We do not use the word 'redeem' much. It means to buy something back or to get something back. So, if some terrorists captured a friend of yours and you paid a ransom to free that friend, you would have redeemed your friend.

Jesus said about himself:

the Son of Man did not come to be served, but to serve, and to give his life as a ransom for many.

Christians believe that Jesus freed us from sin and death. He did this by his death and resurrection.

- Jesus redeems us from sin in two ways. First, he is the means by which God forgives; second, he helps us to improve our behaviour, so that we do good to others rather than harm them.
- Jesus redeems us from death – he has enabled us to live with God, permanently, after our bodies have stopped working.

The bishops at the Second Vatican Council said:

The Son came . . . sent by the Father who . . . chose us and predestined us in him for adoptive sonship . . .
To carry out the will of the Father Christ inaugurated the kingdom of heaven on earth and revealed to us his mystery; by his obedience he brought about our redemption.

Reconciliation

To reconcile with someone is to make friends after falling out. There is no shortage of occasions at home or school when people argue violently, or hurt someone deeply through selfish behaviour: we then refuse to have anything to do with each other. We find it difficult to reconcile and let go of grudges. We are resentful that the other person has offended us; we find it painful or awkward to re-make the friendship; we want to hurt the other person back; we find it hard to forget. One of the best stories in the world is the 'lost son' or 'forgiving father'. It is about reconciliation. It is in Luke's gospel (15^{11-32}).

Christians believe that, through Jesus' death and resurrection, God reconciled us to himself.

The bishops at the Second Vatican Council said:

> God decided to enter into the history of mankind in a new and definitive manner, by sending his Son in human flesh, so that through him he might snatch men from the power of darkness and of Satan and in him reconcile the world to himself.

Atonement

This can mean the same as reconciliation. 'Atonement' is sometimes spelt At-one-ment to emphasize this meaning.

But atonement can mean something quite different. It concentrates on the death rather than the resurrection of Jesus. It argues that we have sinned against God. And, in justice, God should punish these sins. The punishment was the crucifixion of Jesus.

One famous version of the atonement is by **Anselm**, a Christian who lived in the eleventh century. He suggested:

- It is humans who have sinned and offended God. So it had to be a human who was punished for the sins against God.
- God is infinite; so sins have infinitely offended him. No human can offer infinite recompense. Only God could do that.
- Therefore, the ideal person to do the punishment was Jesus. He was both a man and God. The punishment for human sins was his death.

Liberation

This is a rather smart word for freedom. Christians believe that we are all inadequate. They say that some people are arrogant enough to think that they know it all and that they have no faults. But most of us realize that we make bad mistakes, that we are inconsiderate, self-centred, greedy, ignorant, weak, and so on.

Christians believe that the death and resurrection of Jesus freed us from the consequences of original sin. Jesus' death and resurrection also freed us from behaving selfishly. If we have the assistance of the risen Jesus, then we have a greater-than-human strength to cope with the desire to behave selfishly.

See Chapter E18, *Liberation theology and the developing world* for more information.

Examination practice

1. Christians believe that Jesus started God's kingdom. What does this mean? (3 marks)
   Write about six lines.

2. Explain what Christians believe about Jesus' mission. (10 marks)
   Write about one side of A4.

3. Christians believe that Jesus rose from the dead. How might this influence Christians in their attitude to death? (6 marks)
   Write about half a side of A4.

4. Redeemer, saviour, liberator, reconciler, deluded, insane, fool.
   Which of these words best describe Jesus? Give reasons for your view. Show that you have considered other views. (8 marks)
   Write about three-quarters of a side of A4.

 **THE KINGDOM OF GOD**

Introduction

The kingdom of God is a key part of Jesus' teaching. From the very start he used the words to introduce his mission.

For instance, in Mark's gospel, at the very beginning of his teaching:

> After John was put in prison, Jesus went into Galilee, proclaiming the good news of God. 'The time has come,' he said. 'The kingdom of God is near. Repent and believe the good news!'
>
> Mark 1^{14-15}

What does 'the kingdom of God' mean?

The kingdom of God is where God is accepted as king. (Matthew usually uses the phrase 'the kingdom of Heaven', but the meaning is the same.)

When Jesus began his ministry, the kingdom of God came on earth in a special way. The words of Mark 1[14-15] quoted above show that the coming of Jesus was firmly linked to the coming of the kingdom of God.

In Luke 11[14-20] Jesus was challenged by people who said that he cast out devils through the power of Beelzebub, prince of devils. He replied that if Satan was casting out devils, if he himself had the power of the devil in him, then the devil was simply destroying himself – a ridiculous suggestion. But if he was casting out devils by the finger of God, that was a sign that the kingdom of God had come to them.

The kingdom is in the hearts of human beings. In Luke 17[20-21] Jesus was asked by some Pharisees when the kingdom of God would come. Jesus said that the kingdom of God was already within them.

Once in the world, the kingdom of God may grow. The growth of the kingdom is the theme of some parables. See below.

When the final judgement comes, all those who accept God as king will be in the kingdom. Those who have not accepted the kingship of God will be outside the kingdom. Note the parables below, especially those in Matthew 25.

In Luke 17[20-37], after Jesus had said that the kingdom of God was already within them, he went on to say that the coming of the kingdom would be sudden and would catch many people unawares.

Entering the kingdom

To enter the kingdom, a person must accept it as a child (Mark 10[13-16]). By this, Jesus could have meant that Christians should still have a sense of trust and wonder.

A rich man asked Jesus what he had to do to inherit eternal life (Mark 10[17-31]). When Jesus told him he had to obey the commandments, he replied that he had done so from his childhood. But when Jesus told him that the one thing he still needed to do was to sell his property and give everything away and then follow him, the man went away sadly: that he could not do. Jesus did not say that a rich man could not enter the kingdom of God – but he did say that it was harder than a camel going through the eye of a needle.

Parables of the kingdom

A number of these parables are covered in Chapter C12, *Mark's gospel – parables.*

Matthew 13 contains a series of parables of the kingdom, some of which are also found in Mark 4. Note also the parables of Matthew 25.

Some fell along the path . . . some fell on rocky places . . . other seed fell among the thorns . . . other seed fell on good soil

The servant with five talents made five talents more . . .

The servant with two talents made two talents more . . .

The servant with one talent hid it in the ground

The parable of the sower (Matthew 13$^{1-9, 16-23}$; Mark 4 $^{1-9, 13-20}$)

A farmer went out to sow seed.

- Some fell by the path and was eaten by birds.
- Some fell on rock. It grew up quickly but, because the soil was shallow, there was little root and so it soon withered.
- Some fell among thorns and was choked.
- Some fell on good ground and produced plenty of fruit.

Jesus said that the seed in the parable represents different ways in which people receive the message of the kingdom.

- The seed on the path represents people who hear the message of the kingdom and dismiss it without a thought.
- The seed on the rock represents people who are full of enthusiasm for the kingdom at first, but then lose interest when other things crop up.
- The seed among the thorns represents people for whom other things seem more important and get in the way.
- The seed on good ground represents people who hear the news of the kingdom and respond. By the way they live they spread the news of the kingdom.

This parable is about where the kingdom is to be found, and how it spreads and grows.

The parable of the weeds (Matthew 13$^{24-30}$)

A man sowed good seed in his field. During the night his enemy came and sowed weeds among the wheat. When the wheat and weeds appeared, the farmer told his servants to leave everything until the time of harvest. Then the weeds would be burnt and the wheat stored.

This parable is about the kingdom on earth, where those who accept the kingdom live among those who do not. It is also about the final judgement.

Jesus gave an explanation of this parable. He said:

'The one who sowed the good seed is the Son of Man. The field is the world, and the good seed stands for the sons of the kingdom. The weeds are the son of the evil one, and the enemy who sows them is the devil. The harvest is the end of the age, and the harvesters are angels.

'As the weeds are pulled up and burned in the fire, so it will be at the end of the age. The Son of Man will send out his angels, and they will weed out of his kingdom everything that causes sin and all who do evil. They will throw them into the fiery furnace, where there will be weeping and gnashing of teeth. Then the righteous will shine like the sun in the kingdom of their Father.'

Matthew 13$^{37-43}$

The parable of the mustard seed (Matthew 13$^{31-32}$; Mark 4$^{30-32}$; Luke 13$^{18-19}$)

The tiny mustard seed grows to be a huge tree on which birds may perch.

This parable is about the way the kingdom grows, from its small beginning. Some people think the birds represent the people of all nations who may come to the kingdom.

The parable of the yeast (Matthew 13^{33}; Luke 13^{20})

A woman puts a lump of yeast in some dough. It grows and works through the whole mixture.

This parable is about the way the kingdom grows through the influence of Christians, those who have accepted the kingdom.

The parables of the hidden treasure and the pearl (Matthew 13$^{44-46}$)

When a person realizes that the treasure is there in the field or that the pearl is so precious, he sells everything he has to be able to buy what he wants.

Both these parables stress that once a person realizes just how precious the kingdom is, no sacrifice is too great.

The parable of the net (Matthew 13$^{47-50}$)

Fishermen haul in their catch, good and bad fish together. The bad are thrown away, the good are kept.

This parable is about the last judgement.

The parable of the householder (Matthew 13^{52})

This is almost too short to be counted as a parable! Yet it *is* a parable, as it is an example to teach about the kingdom. It is about a householder who brings out from the storeroom treasures new as well as old.

This parable is about the blessings for those who accept God's kingdom.

The parable of the seed growing secretly (Mark 4$^{26-29}$)

A man sows seed and leaves it. He does not watch it but it grows, slowly, stage by stage, until the harvest.

The kingdom of God may grow unnoticed, but it will grow, and will reach its full form when the judgement comes.

The parable of the ten virgins (Matthew 25$^{1-13}$)

Of the ten bridesmaids who were waiting for the bridegroom, five were wise and had extra oil ready while five were foolish and did not have a reserve supply. When the bridegroom came, at midnight, those who were ready went with him. The others went to get oil, and, when they reached the marriage feast, found the door shut against them.

The last judgement can come at any time. Everyone must be prepared.

The parable of the talents (Matthew 25$^{14-30}$; see also Luke 19$^{11-27}$)

A man goes on a long journey, leaving his servants with sums of money to use and increase. (A talent was a large sum of money, worth several hundred pounds. Because of this parable, it has come to mean a special skill or ability.) He gave five talents to one servant, two to a second and one to a third. The first two servants each doubled the money; the third buried his talent for safety. When the master returned, he praised the first two servants. The third was sent away and rejected.

All people have gifts of one sort or another. The gifts may be skills; they may be wealth and opportunities. All will be judged on the use they make of those talents, for good or bad.

The parable of the sheep and the goats (Matthew 25$^{31-46}$)

When the Son of Man comes at the last judgement, he will divide the whole human race into two groups, as a shepherd separates sheep from goats. Those on his right will be welcomed into eternal happiness; those on his left to eternal fire. In each case they will have been judged on how they treated Jesus when he was hungry, thirsty, a stranger, naked, sick or in prison. When they ask when they did help him, or not help him, he will reply that whatever they did, or did not do, for any other person, they were doing it for him.

It is unbelievable that a shepherd could mistake a sheep for a goat. Jesus will distinguish between those who are welcomed into the kingdom of God and those who are not just as certainly. Those who are accepted and those who are rejected may not realize why. Jesus will tell them that they have been judged on the way they treated him. When they ask when they did help him, he will say they have been judged by the way they treated those in need. In saying that, Jesus is showing how closely he identifies with those in need.

Then the King will say to those on his right, 'Come, you who are blessed by my Father; take your inheritance, the kingdom prepared for you since the creation of the world. For I was hungry and you gave me something to eat, I was thirsty and you gave me something to drink, I was a stranger and you invited me in, I needed clothes and you clothed me, I was sick and you looked after me, I was in prison and you came to visit me.'

Then the righteous will answer him, 'Lord, when did we see you hungry and feed you, or thirsty and give you something to drink? When did we see you a stranger and invite you in, or needing clothes and clothe you? When did we see you sick or in prison and go to visit you?'

The King will reply, 'I tell you the truth, whatever you did for one of the least of these brothers of mine, you did for me.'

Matthew 25$^{34-40}$

Examination guidance

The kingdom of God is central to the ministry of Jesus. So, when you answer questions on the kingdom, you may find it good to use things that are not in this chapter. Some of the syllabuses clearly expect you to do so.

NEAB Syllabus B Section 1C includes the Two Great Commandments (Mark 12$^{28-34}$) under the heading 'The kingdom of God'.

EdExcel unit 5 includes 'The kingdom of God as expressed in the teaching and actions of Jesus; present and future aspects of the kingdom of God'. Such a heading tells you to use any event or teaching that seems to fit the special emphasis of the question. Do not be limited by what is in this chapter and do not stick just to passages that have the words 'The kingdom of God' in them.

Examination practice

1. (a) Give an account of a parable that Jesus used to show that the kingdom of God would grow.
     (5 marks)
   (b) Give an account of a parable in which Jesus taught about the kingdom of God at the last judgement.
     (5 marks)
   In each case, explain what the parable means.
   The length of your answer may depend on your choice of parable. Make sure you give a full account – especially if you choose a shorter parable! Above all, make sure your choices fit the question. The explanations must be as clear as you can make them.

2. In what way did Jesus show his followers that his coming was linked with the kingdom of God?
     (5 marks)
   Write about half a side of A4. The question asks 'In what way. . .' In any question worded like this, if you

think Jesus did this in more than one way then say so. The examiner should be impressed. In this case, refer to what Jesus said about casting out devils in the name of Beelzebub, and go on from there to other relevant material.

3. How far do you think Christians today are influenced by the idea that they will one day be judged? (5 marks)
Write about three-quarters of a side of A4. You can

choose all sorts of subjects here. Does a funeral service show a belief in judgement? Do Christians show a fear of being judged? By all means, use particular people as examples. It does not matter if the examiner has never heard of the person. If you know a person who says, 'I know I shall be with God when I die' or 'I've done some dreadful things in my life', it would be perfectly all right to let them be examples.

HUMAN NATURE

In God's image

Christians believe that God made all of us in his image and likeness. Christians inherited this belief from the Jewish religion. In the first book of the Bible, Genesis, there are two stories about the origins of the world. The first story explains that humans, but not animals, have a special likeness to God.

In what way are we similar to God? Christians do not have a unanimous answer. The following have all been suggested.

- We are responsible for looking after the created world. We are accountable to God for what we do. God made the world, but he has given us the responsibility of dominating, developing and caring for it.
- We can think in a way that no other creature can. To think, to reason and to reflect are spiritual activities. These are superior to material things. God is a spirit. He is not material in any way. That part of us that is spirit – our mind (sometimes called soul) – is more like God than that part of us that is material – our body. Thus we resemble God because we have the gift of mind.
- Humans are free to behave as they decide. God is free. Animals behave instinctively. We can decide to cooperate with God, because he does not force us to do so. We have the freedom to choose between good and evil, and, unfortunately, this is the cause of so much that is bad in the world. We choose to do evil rather than to do good.

The people of our time prize freedom very highly ... In this they are right. Yet they often cherish it improperly, as if it gave them leave to do anything they like, even when it is evil.
Catholic bishops at Second Vatican Council

- Humans can develop deep relationships. But we can also make superficial relationships. We can love and hate. We can be understanding and sympathetic, or disinterested and cool towards other people. (A side effect of this is that we can accept God or ignore him, just as we can be open to his love or run away from it.)
- Humans are aware that they are aware. This is a philosopher's way of looking at humans! Nonetheless, if you think about it, you will appreciate it. We have this ability to be aware that we are thinking, judging, enjoying, hating, and so on. We can stand apart from ourselves and be aware of what we are doing and thinking. It makes us superior to any other creature. It makes us like God.

According to the bishops at the Second Vatican Council, this is a very important aspect of our lives. They said this about man (by which the bishops meant people):

For by his power to know himself in the depths of his being, he rises above the whole universe of mere objects. When he is drawn to think about his real self, he turns to those deep recesses of his being where God who probes the heart awaits him.

Above the animals

The Christian tradition is that humans are superior to animals. Though some Christians feel that they would like to meet their pets in heaven, it is the traditional Christian belief that only humans can get to heaven. Here are some reasons for thinking that we are superior to animals:

- **Intelligence**. Animals are intelligent, but they cannot match the quality of human intelligence. Human intelligence is infinitely superior to animal intelligence.

It is a different sort of intelligence. We can have intentions as well as reactions, but animals have reactions. We can plan, but animals react. We can be aware that we are aware, but animals are simply aware.

- **Relations**. Only humans can accept love from God, and love him. A real loving relationship involves give and take. It includes self-sacrifice – but you cannot have self-sacrifice that is not deliberate and accepted. An animal cannot do this.

- **Language**. Only humans can communicate their thoughts in language, showing that our mind is superior to that of animals. We can learn a human language that is not our native language. If animals were as intelligent, they would learn a human language so they could communicate their feelings. They can't.

- **Revelation**. It is the biblical view that God made humans, but not animals, in his image and likeness. In the Old Testament there are two creation stories. In both stories, humans are God's most important creation. In the first story, God told the man and woman:

> Rule over the fish of the sea and the birds of the air and over every living creature that moves on the ground.
>
> Genesis 1^{28}

Original sin

> Man is divided in himself. As a result, the whole life of men, both individual and social, shows itself to be a struggle, and a dramatic one, between good and evil, between light and dark.
>
> Catholic bishops at Second Vatican Council

Christians believe that we are all capable of doing good. Unfortunately, none of us behaves in a loving, kind, peaceful, considerate way all the time. We are often jealous, inconsiderate, self-centred, feel inadequate, hate those who hurt us, behave spitefully, resent those who are more talented than us, and so on. Christians believe it is normal that we should behave and react like this.

Christians call this **original sin**. It is what is wrong with us. We should not be like this, but we cannot help it, because we were born this way. It is an inherent part of human nature.

Made for God

Christians believe that God made each one of us to be happy. They say we can be happy only when we love and meet God. They believe that none of us will find lasting happiness in sex, money, ambition, material goods, a comfortable home, or anything else to do with this world. There is some happiness and satisfaction in any of these things, but it does not last. We shall only find permanent happiness in God.

But God hides himself: he can be elusive and he is not obvious in this life. However, we shall not be happy until we rest permanently in God, though we cannot do this in this life. We can only know God 'face to face' after death. So Christians believe that we can achieve permanent happiness – but only in the life after death. Nevertheless, our search for happiness and for God starts in this life.

> You have made us to know You, God, and we are restless, until we know You.
>
> Augustine

Changing human nature

Christians believe that there is something inadequate about all of us. Yet Christians believe that God provided the solution: he sent his Son to become a man, Jesus, to change things. Jesus was killed. God resurrected him. Through the death and resurrection of Jesus, God made it possible for us to change. Jesus **redeemed** or **saved** us. (See Chapter C7 *Jesus – his mission; sin and salvation*.)

Christians believe that baptism is the start of their Christian life. They are baptized into the death of Christ, so they die to their selfish, aggressive, bad-tempered nature. They are baptized into the resurrection of Christ, so they receive the power of the Spirit of Jesus to behave like God, in a gentle, kind, joyful, self-controlled, peaceful way.

However, we constantly have to struggle to treat others with dignity and to respect God. We cannot do it easily. We often fail. Christians need to renew the power of the Spirit of Jesus in their lives. They do this especially in the eucharist, where they receive the risen Jesus through the symbols of bread and wine. The other sacraments are also means of renewing the power of God in them. So is private prayer. So is reading and listening to the Bible, as this is the Word of God in the words of men.

Examination practice

1. What do Christians mean by the term 'original sin'?
   (3 marks)
   Write about six lines of A4.

2. Christians believe that humans are God's most important creation.
   Explain this belief. (8 marks)
   Write about three-quarters of a side of A4.

3. Christians believe that Jesus died for them.
   How might this influence what they do and think?
   (6 marks)
   Write about half a side of A4.

4. 'Humans are not different from animals.'
   Do you agree? Give reasons for your view. Show that you have considered the opposite view. (8 marks)
   Write about three-quarters of a side of A4.

10

The resurrection of Jesus

Easter celebrates Jesus rising from the dead. That is why Easter is the chief of the Christian festivals.

Christians believe that the resurrection of Jesus is relevant to them. Human beings sin. Because of sin they deserve as punishment to go to hell.

Jesus broke the power of sin and hell. He took on himself the punishment for sin. He was not only crucified; as the Apostles' Creed states, 'he descended to the dead.' His power and goodness were such that death could not hold him. He broke the power of sin and death.

Life after death

To Christians the resurrection is not just something that happened to someone a long time ago. It is a sign of the power of Jesus, even over death.

Christians believe that Jesus has made it possible for them to have life after death, in heaven. He has made it possible through his death and resurrection.

Jesus said, 'I am the resurrection and the life. He who believes in me will live, even though he dies; and whoever lives and believes in me will never die' (John 11^{25-26}).

Heaven, hell and purgatory

Christians believe that when people die their souls do not cease to exist. They move on to another life. They may move on to heaven, hell or purgatory.

Heaven, hell and purgatory are not thought of as places, however distant.

- **Heaven** is the state of being with God. It is eternal; there will be no more tears, sorrow, or sadness. Those in heaven are in a state of perfect happiness, as God made people in such a way that they could find complete happiness in the joys of heaven. Those in heaven are in the **Communion of Saints.** (See Chapter D6, *The Church – images to explain it.*) They are able to pray for those on earth. In spirit they are united with Christians on earth (and in purgatory, according to Catholics).
- **Hell** is the state of being separated from God.
- **Purgatory** is the state of preparation for heaven; people may pass from earth to purgatory and then, after being made ready to be with God, proceed to heaven.

Those who die are judged. On the outcome of that judgement depends whether they proceed to heaven, purgatory or hell. Jesus taught that the judgement is based on:

- a person's response to his teaching. 'Not everyone who says to me, "Lord, Lord," will enter the kingdom of heaven, but only he who does the will of my Father who is in heaven' (Matthew 7^{21}).
- the way a person responds to those in need. Note the parable of the sheep and the goats (Matthew 25^{31-46}).

Biblical teaching

Jesus gave some indications of what heaven is like.

- Mark $9^{43,\,45}$: Here and elsewhere Jesus spoke about entering eternal life. In these verses he contrasted entering life with going to hell.
- Luke 14^{15-24}: The parable of the great banquet. Here and elsewhere Jesus seemed to speak of heaven in terms of a great feast. At the Last Supper he said, 'I tell you the truth, I will not drink again of the fruit of the vine until that day when I drink it anew in the kingdom of God' (Mark 14^{25}).
- Luke 16^{19-31}: The parable of the rich man and Lazarus. There is a hell and there is a heaven. Lazarus is with Abraham, free from torment and suffering.
- Luke 23^{43}: Jesus said to the dying criminal, 'Today you will be with me in paradise'.
- John 14^{1-7}: Jesus said he was going to the Father, to prepare for his followers a place in his Father's house.

Paul wrote about life after death in 1 Corinthians 15:

- Jesus really did rise from the dead. Paul lists people who saw him after the crucifixion and resurrection. They were witnesses that the resurrection really happened.
- If Jesus really did rise from the dead, then there is a resurrection – something continues to exist when the body has died. Death is not the end.
- Even if Jesus did rise again, his resurrection is relevant only if it affects other people when they die.
- Jesus is the first to rise from the dead – and because of his resurrection others can rise in their turn.
- When people rise to new life they will no longer have physical bodies but what Paul calls spiritual bodies.
- The resurrection of Jesus and of those who rise to this new life is a victory over sin and death.

EdExcel (Unit 1, Christianity) candidates should note in particular 1 Corinthians 15^{12-22}. Paul writes:

- If Christ has been raised from the dead, how can anyone say there is no such thing as resurrection?
- On the other hand, if there is no resurrection, then Christ did not rise. That would make Paul's preaching worse than useless – a lie against God.

- If there were no resurrection, then the faith of Christians would be wasted. Those Christians who had died would be lost. Christians would have to be pitied because they were so mistaken.
- However, because there were so many people who saw Jesus after he had risen, the resurrection is a fact.
- Since Christ has risen, through him resurrection to a life after death is a reality.

A funeral service

Hope is important to Christians. By 'hope' they do not mean wishful thinking. They mean thinking positively about life with God in heaven when life on earth is over.

A funeral service includes readings, prayers and hymns. They all contain the note of hope.

In part, a funeral service is a celebration of the life of the person who has died. A tribute to the person is often paid. The preacher points the listeners to the hope of eternal life.

Sadness is inevitable when someone has died. There are prayers for those who mourn, and people express sympathy with the bereaved. Yet the tone of a funeral service is of trust in God. The service reflects the belief in life after death.

It does not matter whether the person is buried or cremated. The belief is that after death, in the life with God, each person has a spiritual body, not the old physical one.

Verses of scripture used at funeral services

- God so loved the world that he gave his only Son, that whoever believes in him should not perish, but have eternal life.

John 3[16]

- Neither death, nor life, nor angels, nor principalities, nor powers, nor things present, nor things to come, nor height, nor depth, nor anything else in all creation, will be able to separate us from the love of God in Christ Jesus our Lord.

Romans 8[38-39]

- Eye has not seen, nor ear heard, nor the heart of man conceived, what God has prepared for those who love him.

1 Corinthians 2[9]

Prayers from funeral services

Eternal God, the Lord of life, the conqueror of death, our help in every time of trouble, comfort us who mourn, and give us grace, in the presence of death, to worship you, that we may have sure hope of eternal life and be enabled to put our whole trust in your goodness and mercy, through Jesus Christ our Lord. Amen.

Methodist Service Book

Praise and honour, glory and thanks be given to you, almighty God our Father, because in your great love for the world you gave your Son to be our Saviour, to live our life, to bear our griefs, and to die our death upon the Cross.

We praise you because you have brought him back from death with great power and glory, and given him all authority in heaven and on earth.

We praise you because he has conquered sin and death for us, and opened the kingdom of heaven to all believers.

Methodist Service Book

Remember, O Lord, this your servant, who has gone before us with the sign of faith and now rests in the sleep of peace. According to your promises, grant to *him* and to all who rest in Christ, refreshment, light and peace; through the same Christ our Lord. Amen

Anglican Alternative Service Book

Almight God, Father of all mercies and giver of all comfort: deal graciously, we pray, with those who mourn, that casting all their care on you, they may know the consolation of your love; through Jesus Christ our Lord. Amen.

Anglican Alternative Service Book

Christians do not believe that everyone goes to heaven when they die. There is a judgement, and some may go to hell. Those who have accepted Jesus as Saviour, who have loved him and whose lives show that love, can look forward to being in his presence after death. This belief can affect a funeral service in one of two ways.

1. Some Christians believe that a person who has true faith in Jesus Christ will be in heaven after death. They thank God at a funeral because the person who has died is now at rest in heaven.
2. Others, including Catholics, believe it is necessary to pray for a dead person. However good that person's life, there is still a need for God's mercy and forgiveness. They believe that someone with true faith, who has shown that faith in good works, does go straight to heaven at death. Some go to purgatory. So they pray for the dead, that they may rest in peace. But they do not forget their belief in God as a loving, heavenly father. They pray with confidence, remembering the promises made by Jesus. They believe that those for whom they pray will in time enter heaven.

In Catholic churches it is usual to have a requiem mass, to pray for the soul of the person who has died. The requiem is a service of positive hope. The coffin is often covered with a white cloth (the pall), and the priests's vestments are white, whereas in the past the more sombre purple or black might be worn. At the beginning of the rite:

- The coffin is sprinkled with holy water and the priest says words such as 'In the waters of baptism N died with Christ and rose with him to new life. May he/she now share with him eternal glory.'

- A symbol of the Christian life, such as a book of the gospels or a cross, may be placed on the coffin. 'In life N cherished the gospel of Christ. May Christ now greet him/her with these words of eternal life: Come, blessed of my Father!'

The Mass continues with the Liturgy of the Word, with readings and the homily, and with the intercessions, which may include the following:

> In baptism N received the light of Christ. Scatter the darkness now and lead him/her over the waters of death. Lord, in your mercy, hear our prayer.
>
> Our brother/sister was nourished at the table of the Saviour. Welcome him/her into the halls of the heavenly banquet. Lord, in your mercy, hear our prayer.
>
> Many friends and members of our families have gone before us and await the kingdom. Grant them an everlasting home with your Son. Lord, in your mercy, hear our prayer.
>
> Many people die by violence, war and famine every day. Show your mercy to those who suffer so unjustly these sins against your love, and gather them to the eternal kingdom of peace. Lord, in your mercy, hear our prayer.
>
> Funeral Rites

The Mass continues to the communion in the usual way, and ends with further prayers, in which the dead person's soul is commended to God.

The coffin is sprinkled with holy water and incensed. A song of farewell is sung and the coffin is taken to the place of burial or cremation.

> Here is the last verse of a hymn very often sung at funerals. Note how the words speak of
>
> - the cross of Jesus, through whose sacrifice Christians hope for life after death;
> - being in heaven;
> - God being with a Christian, in life and death.
>
> Hold thou thy cross before my closing eyes;
> Shine through the gloom, and point me to the skies;
> Heaven's morning breaks, and earth's vain shadows flee;
> In life, in death, O Lord, abide with me.

Catholics believe in a state called **purgatory**.

The word 'purgatory' comes from the Latin word *purgare*, which means 'cleanse'. Another word from the same Latin word is 'purge'. Purgatory is not a place of punishment but of purification. It is less where the departed pay for sin through suffering than where they are prepared to enter the visible presence of God and the saints.

Purgatory is a state, rather than a physical place. People who have died in a state of grace, but still with imperfections, are in purgatory after they die until they are ready to move on to be with God.

At the requiem mass and at other funeral ceremonies prayers are offered for the dead. Catholics frequently pray for the departed, that they may rest with Jesus.

The tradition of praying for the dead is the main reason for the Catholic belief in purgatory, a belief that was formally declared by bishops of the Catholic Church at the Council of Florence (1439) and at the Council of Trent (1563). Orthodox Christians have a tradition of praying for the dead, though they do not use the word 'purgatory' to describe those waiting to get into heaven. Most Protestant Christians do not believe in purgatory. The reason for this is that it is not mentioned in the Bible, and most Protestants believe that the Bible is the only source for Christian beliefs.

Examination practice

1. Choose and name **one** Christian denomination. Describe a funeral service of that denomination.
   (6 marks)
   Write about half a side of A4.

2. Memorials for the dead often have a cross on them. Why is this so? (4 marks)
   Write about half a side of A4.

3. 'A Christian funeral should not be too sad an occasion.' Do you agree? Give reasons for your answer.
   (6 marks)
   Write about three-quarters of a side of A4. Your answer should make it clear that you understand what Christians believe about life after death.

Introduction

Christians believe that the Bible is the Word of God. The books of the Bible are their scriptures. Christians believe that the Bible is inspired – and that it is true. They believe that God speaks through the Bible – to people today, as much as at any other time in history.

The words 'bible' and 'scripture' have very basic meanings. The word 'bible' comes from a Greek word meaning 'book', and 'scripture' from a Latin word meaning 'something written'. In time both words have been given a religious meaning. All holy books, of whatever religion, are called scriptures. The books that make up the Christian scriptures have been collected into a single volume, which is called the Bible.

The Bible is in two parts

- The **Old Testament** was written before the birth of Jesus Christ. In the Bible used in the Protestant and Anglican traditions all the books were written in Hebrew. There are some extra books in the Catholic and Orthodox Old Testaments, which were originally written in Greek. These books are treated as a separate group by Protestants, who know them as the Apocrypha and regard them as having less authority than the others.
- The **New Testament** was written after the ministry of Jesus Christ, in Greek.

The various books were written by different people at different times. Other similar books were also in existence. There had to be some way by which people could know what was supposed to be the word of God and what was not. Eventually agreement was reached on what is known as the **canon** – the accepted collection of writings that make up each of the Testaments, Old and New.

The Hebrew books of the Old Testament were eventually accepted as scripture by Jews about the year AD 90. Some of the books were chosen because they described great events in the history of the Jewish nation. Others were chosen above all for their spiritual message. A group of rabbis made the final choice, and their decision was accepted by their fellow Jews. Christians included some books written in Greek as well, and these are counted among the books of the Old Testament by the Catholic and Orthodox Churches. Those in the Anglican and Protestant traditions accept those written in Hebrew as having higher authority than those of the Apocrypha.

The decision about which books, apart from the Old Testament, should make up the Christian scriptures took a long time to make. By about AD 200 the selection was just about complete, though one or two books were still considered doubtful. The first list of the books of the New Testament that is exactly the same as the one used today dates from the fourth century.

The word 'testament' means a binding promise. Another word with the same meaning is 'covenant'.

Old Testament

The Old Testament traces God's plan from the creation of the world to the time when God's people (the Jews) were waiting for the coming of the Messiah.

The first book, Genesis, begins with 11 chapters that are widely regarded as myth. To say that the chapters are myth means that most Christians accept that they may not be literally accurate in that, for instance, Adam did not live for 930 years. Christians believe that what these chapters (and the rest of the Bible) say about God *is* true – and that is what matters. (Fundamentalists, of course, regard the chapters as literally true.) This section ends with an account of the Tower of Babel, by which the human race was divided into different nations.

From Genesis 12 onwards we have the Old Covenant. God made a covenant with just one man, Abraham. That covenant passed to Abraham's descendants. In the time of Moses the covenant took a new form. God made his people into a nation for the first time. He gave them a law (Exodus to Deuteronomy contain the law). He led them to the promised land. He made a covenant – an agreement with them. If they served him, he would give them all they needed.

Often the people turned away from God. The rest of the Old Testament describes the relationship between God and his people. The relationship is shown in **histories** (books from Joshua to Nehemiah). It is shown in the books of the **prophets** (Isaiah to Malachi), who spoke God's messages to them, sometimes with threats, sometimes with encouragement – especially when telling of the coming of the Messiah.

The Old Testament also contains the beautiful devotion of the Book of Psalms and the deeply thoughtful books of Proverbs, Ecclesiastes and Job.

> Do not defraud your neighbour or rob him.
> Do not hold back the wages of a hired man overnight.
> Do not curse the deaf or put a stumbling-block in front of the blind, but fear your God. I am the Lord.
> Leviticus 19[13–14]
>
> *An example of simple justice and morality from the Old Testament Law.*

When Solomon had finished building the temple of
the Lord and the royal palace, and had achieved all he
had desired to do, the Lord appeared to him a second
time.

1Kings 9$^{1-2}$.

A verse from one of the historical books. Note how,
unlike an ordinary history, God is introduced into the
account.

You trample on the poor
    and force him to give you grain.
Therefore, though you have built stone
    mansions,
    you will not live in them;
Though you have planted lush vineyards,
    you will not drink their wine.
For I know how many are your offences
    and how great your sins.

Amos 5$^{11-12}$

Amos the prophet saw the injustice that was common
in his time. The rich were oppressing the poor. In the
name of God Amos condemned what he saw. He told
them they would not benefit from their fine
possessions, their houses and vineyards.

There are six things the Lord hates,
    seven that are detestable to him:
        haughty eyes,
        a lying tongue,
        hands that shed innocent blood,
        a heart that devises wicked schemes,
        feet that are quick to rush into evil,
        a false witness who pours out lies,
        and a man who stirs up dissension among
    brothers.

Proverbs 6$^{16-19}$

Words of wisdom from the book of Proverbs.

New Testament

The New Testament is the Christian completion of the Old
Testament. The word 'Messiah', Hebrew for 'Anointed
One', becomes the Greek word with the same meaning,
Christ. Jesus is the Messiah, the Christ.

The four key books of the New Testament are the four
gospels, written by the four evangelists: Matthew, Mark,
Luke and John. These books describe the life and teaching
of Jesus himself. Note that during a eucharist worshippers
sit for other Bible readings, but stand for those that are
taken from one of the gospels.

Matthew, Mark and Luke all describe events in much the
same way. John's gospel is different, almost a meditation,
describing events and then, in long chapters, Jesus'
teaching arising from those events.

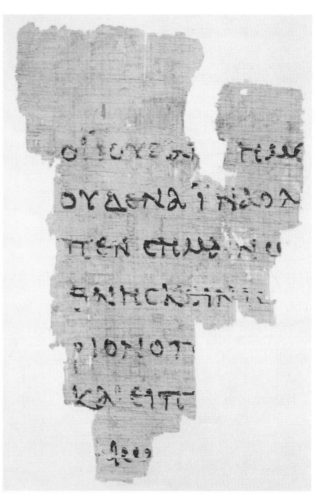

This small piece of papyrus has on it words from John 18$^{31-33}$, and
on the other side words from what must have been the next page,
John 18$^{37-38}$. The papyrus is from the first half of the second
century AD. It can be seen in the John Rylands Library,
Manchester University.

Reproduced by courtesy of the Director and University Librarian,
the John Rylands University Library of Manchester

Most of the other books of the New Testament are letters
from Church leaders (such as Paul, John, Peter and James)
to various Christians. There is one book that tells how the
Church spread (Acts of the Apostles) and one that is a
vision of heaven (Revelation).

What do Christians mean when they say that the Bible is the Word of God?

When Christians say that the Bible is the true, inspired
Word of God, they may mean it in different ways:

- Some mean that every word is **literally true**. God so
  inspired the writers that they could not possibly make
  any error. The Bible is his word just as if he dictated it
  himself. It is true in every sense of the term. People who
  hold this belief are often called **fundamentalists**.
- Some mean that the people who wrote the books of the
  Bible were **inspired** people. That means, they were
  people who were close to God through prayer and

worship and through living by his laws. This did not make them free from all error – but what they wrote came from a genuine experience of God himself. These people knew God. Because they knew God, they were able to write books that give a true picture of God. The Bible is true because it contains a true picture of God and of his will for the world.

- The Bible is about **God's activity** in the world. It is not an ordinary history book. It describes things that actually happened – and then says they happened because of what God did. In particular, the gospels present Jesus as God the Son. They describe his life as being the way in which, above all, God has made himself known, and does make himself known still. Remember that in his gospel John calls Jesus the Word of God.

- Sometimes, Christians believe, God actually **speaks** through the words of the Bible today. A person may read a passage and understand it in a way quite different from the original meaning. That does not mean he is wrong. God may be speaking to him.

Joel 2^{25}: 'I will repay you for the years the locusts have eaten.'

What does that verse mean?

Scholars would have little trouble answering. Locusts were a terrible scourge in ancient Israel. Joel wrote at a time when there was a great plague of them. Joel said the plague of locusts was a punishment from God. In time, when the people turned back to God, the plague would end. God said that then 'I will repay you for the years the locusts have eaten.'

That's what scholars say. Those same words had a different meaning for **John Dodd**.

John Dodd was a prisoner of war in Singapore during the Second World War. He came back home to freedom at the end of the war feeling that five good years of his life had been wasted.

John was not really interested in religion, but would go to church with his mother from time to time, to please her. Once, when he was with her in church, this passage from Joel was read.

'I will repay you for the years the locusts have eaten.' Those words hit John Dodd. God was going to make up for those lost years. God had a mission for him.

John had suffered imprisonment. He knew the helplessness of being a prisoner. He also knew the difficulty of finding a way of life after being released. His thoughts turned to those in HM prisons, especially the problems they faced when they came out of prison. He set up a home to which they could come. From this grew the Langley House Trust. The Trust runs homes that serve a number of purposes. Some are places where ex-convicts can begin to sort out their lives, not needing to go into the hostile world. Others are bases from which they can go into that hostile world to work, eventually easing themselves into normal everyday life.

That is how the Bible was the Word of God to John Dodd. That meaning of the verse in Joel might not ever have had that meaning for any other person. To John the verse was a true message from God. The verse was the Word of God.

Examination guidance

1. What is the difference between the Old Testament and the New Testament? (8 marks)

2. Why do many Christians read the New Testament regularly? (6 marks)

3. Do you think that, if the Bible had not been written, there would be any Christians in the world today? Give reasons for your answer. (6 marks)

---

1. *The Old Testament is about the time before Jesus, and the New Testament is about Jesus and his teaching.*

The candidate may think this is a complete answer. The fact that 8 marks are given should be a clue that a fuller reply is needed. The response should make clear that the Old Testament is about the people of Israel, their development as a nation and, above all, their relationship with their God. As the question is about the contrast between the Old and New Testaments, the candidate should say that the Old Testament looks forward to the coming of the Messiah.

By contrast, the New Testament tells of Jesus Christ, the Messiah, as having come. Time and again we read that the scriptures have been fulfilled. The gospels describe his life and his teaching – and especially his crucifixion and resurrection. Most of the books are letters written by Paul and other Christians, telling others about Jesus and also telling them how they should live their lives as Christians. *(Score: 2 marks out of 8, for saying something about each of the Testaments)*

2. Many Christians read the New Testament regularly to see what Jesus did in situations. A Christian may be in a dilemma and turn to the Bible for help. Jesus was a person who solved problems and made people care for each other. The New Testament is all about Jesus and other people who followed Jesus and his teaching. It gives them help and encouragement when they are in trouble.

Christians may find reading the Bible enjoyable as it gives them a basis of their religion and faith.

The candidate is being tested here for understanding – but there must be accurate background knowledge as well. If the question is about the New Testament, the response must clearly relate to the New Testament rather than to the Old or to the Bible as a whole.

The candidate does say 'The New Testament is all about Jesus and other people who followed Jesus and his teaching'. The knowledge shown goes little further than that. The candidate implies – but does not say clearly – that Christians look to Jesus' life and teaching for example and inspiration.

The candidate says that Bible reading gives Christians a basis of their religion and faith. For this reason, he says, they find Bible reading 'enjoyable' – a strange word to choose. A word such as 'inspiring' or 'uplifting' would have been better.

The candidate says that 'Jesus was a person who solved problems and made people care for each other'. To Christians the New Testament describes Jesus as much more than that. Christians believe in Jesus as the Messiah, the Son of God, the Word of God.

The candidate refers to 'other people who followed Jesus' without saying anything about them or what they did, taught and wrote.
(Score: 2 marks out of 6)

3. I think that if the Bible had not been written there would not be any Christians today. People would not know about Jesus and what he did. They would not know about his teaching or about his followers. Christians might have told each other stories about Jesus but by now, nearly 2000 years later, they might have got changed if they hadn't actually been written down. After all, Jesus must have said and done lots of things that have not been written in the Bible, but who remembers them now?

Lots of people come to know about God through reading their Bibles. When priests teach about Jesus they read from the Bible. They would not be able to teach like that if there were not any Bibles. When priests take the Eucharist they know they are doing what Jesus said they should do. People wouldn't be able to read the Bible for themselves and use it in their prayers. It is important for them to have the exact words of Jesus so that they can be sure of what he said about himself and the Father.

The candidate has made a number of relevant points here. Two areas are covered sensibly. The first part of the answer gets beyond the obvious 'people would not know about Jesus' to stress that things written down are more reliable than those depending on word of mouth. Then the candidate goes on to talk about the importance of the Bible in the spiritual lives of Christians, in terms of what they believe and how they pray and worship. Many candidates would not even think of these points. This answer is well above the average.
(Score: 6 marks out of 6)

Examination practice

1. What do Christians mean when they say that the Bible is the Word of God? (6 marks)
Write about half a side of A4.

2. Describe any **one** event from the Old Testament. Why do Christians read the Old Testament?
(8 marks)

Write about three-quarters of a side of A4, depending on the event chosen.

3. Would you expect that reading the Bible would have any effect on the way a person behaved? Give reasons for your answers. (6 marks)
Write about three-quarters of a side of A4.

Introduction

There are not many parables in Mark's gospel. You will find most of Jesus' parables in the gospels of Matthew and Luke. See the last section in this chapter to find what Mark thought about parables.

A parable is a story, usually quite short. The story has a meaning about God or his kingdom.

Some writers make a distinction between a parable and an allegory. What we call a parable, they call a story – it can be either a parable or an allegory. How do they decide whether a story is a parable or allegory? Take the story of the sower: if it has a simple meaning (for example, that most people take no notice of Jesus, yet some do), then it is a parable; if it has a detailed meaning (for example, the sower is Jesus, the seed is his teaching, the different types of ground are distinctive and different ways in which people respond to his teaching), then the story is an allegory.

> [Jesus said to his disciples] 'The secret of the kingdom of God has been given to you. But to those on the outside everything is said in parables.'
>
> Mark 4[11]

The parables

The sower (Mark 4[3–20])

- A farmer sowed his corn seed.
- Some fell on a path, and the birds came and ate it.
- Some fell on rocky ground; it started to grow, but soon died because there was not enough soil.
- Some fell on ground that had thorn bushes; the seed started to grow, but the thorn bushes soon choked it.
- Some fell in good soil. It grew: some of the plants had thirty grains, others sixty, others one hundred.

Jesus did not at first explain this parable. The disciples came to him and asked him to explain it. He told them he had given them the secret of the kingdom of God. He also explained why he taught in parables (see the last section in this chapter). He then said that the meaning of this parable is as follows:

- The farmer stands for the person who teaches God's message (himself).
- Some people are like the path where the seed falls: as soon as they hear the teaching, Satan comes and takes it away.
- Some people are like the rocky ground: they receive the teaching gladly, but they soon stop believing, when trouble or persecution comes.
- Some people are like the thorny ground: they believe, but they soon stop believing, because of worries, or the wish to become rich, or the desire for other things.
- Some people are like the good soil: they believe, and put it into practice, but some more than others, just as some corn plants had thirty grains, while other corn plants had one hundred grains.

Lamp on a stand / Lamp under a bowl (Mark 4[21–25])

- Does anyone bring in a lamp, and put it under a bowl or under the bed?
- Surely, he puts it on the lamp stand!

Jesus said that whatever was hidden would be brought out into the open. This is an enigmatic comment. We are not sure what it means. It may mean that the kingdom of God has been hidden, but henceforward it will be obvious to everyone. Or it may mean that Jesus came to show everyone what the kingdom of God is like. Or it may mean that the disciples should show everyone, by their lifestyle, what the kingdom of God is like. There are other guesses about the meaning of this parable and Jesus' comment on it.

The growing seed (Mark 4[26–29])

Jesus introduced this parable, saying that the kingdom of God is like this:

- A man scatters corn seed in his field.
- Over the next few months the seed grows steadily, while the farmer waits.
- When the corn is grown, he cuts it because it is ripe.

Jesus gave no explanation of this parable. So we can only guess the meaning. It may mean that the kingdom of God has started, and it will grow quietly and steadily. Or the parable may mean the kingdom of God will come some time in the future. No one can be definite about the correct meaning.

> [Jesus] did not say anything to [the people] without using a parable. But when he was alone with his own disciples, he explained everything.
>
> Mark 4[34]

The mustard seed (Mark 4$^{30-32}$)

Jesus introduced this parable, saying that the kingdom of God is like this:

* A man plants a mustard seed, the smallest seed in the world, in his garden.
* After a time, it grows to be the biggest of plants.
* The birds come and make their nests in its shade.

Jesus gave no explanation of this parable. So, again, we can only guess the meaning. It may mean that the kingdom of God is insignificant when it starts, but it will grow gradually. Or it may mean that the kingdom of God will eventually include everyone. But these are guesses. Nobody can be definite about the correct meaning.

Cursing of the fig tree (Mark 11$^{12-14, 20-21}$)

* Jesus and his disciples were leaving Bethany.
* Jesus was hungry.
* He saw a fig tree and went to see if there was any fruit on it.
* But there was none, as it was not the season for figs.
* Jesus said: 'May no-one ever eat fruit from you again.'
* The next morning, as they passed the fig tree,
* they noticed it was withered from the roots.
* The disciples said: 'the fig tree you cursed has withered.'

This seems to be a miracle, and a strange one. Jesus seems to have behaved like a bad-tempered person.

The incident is probably an acted parable. Jesus acted the story instead of telling it. There is a similar account of a fig tree in Luke's gospel, where it is a story Jesus told rather than a story he acted.

Jesus did not explain the parable.

According to Mark, Jesus goes on to talk about the importance of faith and trust in God. So the meaning could be: whatever we ask for in prayer, believe we will receive it, and it will be ours. But it could mean something quite different; possibly that, as the Jews (represented by the fig tree) did not believe in Jesus, he rejected them in favour of the Gentiles. But these are guesses.

Tenants / tenants in the vineyard (Mark 12$^{1-12}$)

* A man planted a vineyard; then he put a fence round it, dug a hole for a winepress and built a watchtower.
* He let the vineyard to tenants and he went on a journey.
* When the grape harvest came, he sent a servant to collect his share. The tenants beat the servant and sent him back with nothing.
* The owner sent another servant, but the same happened to him.
* The owner sent a third servant, but the tenants killed him.

* And this went on.
* In the end, the owner sent his son, whom he loved – the owner thought the tenants would respect him.
* But the tenants said: This is the owner's son. Let's kill him, and the vineyard will be ours.
* So they killed him and threw his body out of the vineyard.

Jesus commented that the owner will kill those men and hand the vineyard to other tenants. The Jewish leaders knew that Jesus had told this parable against them. From this, we can infer the meaning of the parable:

* The owner is God.
* The tenants are the Jewish priests and people.
* The servants are the prophets that God sent to the Jews.
* The son whom the owner loved is Jesus.
* The murder, and throwing of the body outside the vineyard, is the crucifixion of Jesus outside Jerusalem.
* The owner handing the vineyard to other tenants is God giving his message to Gentiles (non-Jews), because the Jews would not listen to Him.

> He had one left to send, a son, whom he loved. He sent him last of all, saying, 'They will respect my son.'
>
> Mark 12^6

The fig tree (Mark 13$^{28-31}$)

* When the fig tree turns green and it grows leaves, we know that summer is coming.

Jesus observed that the things he had previously spoken about – such as the sun growing dark and the stars falling from heaven – would happen before the world ended and he returned.

The day and hour unknown / No one knows the day or hour (Mark 13$^{32-37}$)

After telling the parable of the fig tree, Jesus said that no one knows when the end of the world will happen. So, be alert. It will be like:

* a man who goes on a journey, and gives each of his servants a specific task to do.
* They should be wary, because they do not know when the master will return:
* it could be at any moment!

Why Jesus taught in parables

Most of us think that Jesus taught in parables to make his teaching more interesting and understandable. Perhaps to make it memorable, as well.

Mark has a quite different opinion. He says that Jesus taught in parables so that people would not understand. Mark says that Jesus' listeners did not understand the parable of the sower; so the disciples and some others came to Jesus and asked him to explain it. Jesus explained the parable to his disciples, but not to the crowd. Jesus also told his disciples that he gave them the secret of the kingdom of God. And that he spoke in parables so that others might hear, but never understand.

> 'The secret of the kingdom of God has been given to you. But to those on the outside everything is said in parables so that,
> "they may be ever seeing but never perceiving, and ever hearing but never understanding; otherwise they may turn and be forgiven!" '
>
> Mark 4^{12}

Later, Mark re-emphasizes this point: he says that Jesus spoke to people in parables, yet explained the parables only when he was alone with his disciples.

Thus Mark is adamant that we cannot understand the teaching of Jesus, unless the disciples explain it. Mark demonstrates this by giving no meaning to the parable of the growing seed and no meaning to the parable of the mustard seed; and it is not evident what these parables mean. This highlights Mark's view that no one can understand Jesus' teaching, if it is not explained. Only the disciples understood Jesus' teaching. They are the only people who can explain the teaching of Jesus.

Mark's presentation of Jesus parables puzzles many people. They think that Jesus taught in parables to help us understand his message, not to hide it.

Examination practice

1. In Mark's gospel, Jesus told some parables that he did not explain. Summarize **two** of them.   (3 marks)
   Write about six lines.

2. What explanation did Jesus give to the parable of the sower?   (10 marks)
   Write about three-quarters of a side of A4.

3. The parable of the tenants implies that Jesus was rejected by the religious leaders.
   What might a Christian learn from this ?
   (6 marks)
   Write about half a side of A4.

4. 'You cannot learn much about God from any of Jesus' parables.'
   Do you agree? Give reasons for your view. Show that you have considered the opposite view.   (8 marks)
   Write about three-quarters of a side of A4.

MARK'S GOSPEL – MIRACLES   13

Introduction

Mark presents Jesus as a man of action. Although Mark says that Jesus taught the people, Mark does not give much of Jesus' teaching. Instead, Mark emphasizes what Jesus did: he performed miracles, he helped people, he fought with evil spirits.

Exorcisms

Jesus exorcised some people – that is, he expelled evil spirits from them.

The man with an evil spirit, at the synagogue in Capernaum (Mark 1$^{21–28}$)

This is the first miracle in Mark's gospel.

- Jesus went to the synagogue, on the Sabbath, and preached.
- The people were amazed, because he taught with authority, not like the teachers of the law.
- A man, possessed by an evil spirit, shouted: 'Have you come to destroy us? I know who you are – the holy one of God!'
- Jesus told the evil spirit to be quiet and come out of the man – it did, violently and with a shriek.
- People were amazed at this new teaching and this great authority over evil spirits.

The madman with an evil spirit at Gerasa, country of the Gerasenes (Mark 5$^{1-20}$)

Gerasa is not Jewish territory.

- Jesus went across the lake to Gerasa; a violent madman, who lived in the graveyard, met him.
- The madman knelt before Jesus and shouted: 'What do you want with me, Jesus, Son of the Most High God? Swear to God that you won't torture me!'
- Jesus asked him his name. He said, 'Legion' (meaning, 'many').
- The demons asked Jesus to send them into a herd of pigs on a nearby hill. Jesus agreed.
- The herd, about 2000, rushed over the cliff's edge into the lake and drowned.
- The pig herders went and told everybody in the nearby areas.
- People came running, and saw the madman in his right mind.
- The people asked Jesus to leave.
- As Jesus was leaving, the cured man said he wanted to go with Jesus.
- But Jesus told him to stay and tell people what God had done for him.

The foreigner who asked Jesus to cure her daughter (Mark 7$^{24-30}$)

- Jesus went to Tyre (which was not a Jewish town), in secret. But a local woman heard about him, and asked him to cure her daughter, who was possessed by an evil spirit.
- Jesus said the children should feed first: their food should not be given to dogs.
- 'Lord', she said, 'even the dogs under the table eat the children's crumbs.'
- Her answer impressed Jesus, and he told her the evil spirit had left her daughter.
- She went home, and found her daughter well.

By children, Jesus meant Jews, who called themselves children of God. By dogs, Jesus meant foreigners, non-Jews. Thus he is telling the woman that his mission is to help Jews, not non-Jews. Still, he does not deter the woman. She suggests that after he has helped the Jews, he might have a little help left over for non-Jews.

The man, with doubting faith, who asked Jesus to cure his son (Mark 9$^{14-29}$)

- Jesus (with Peter, James and John) rejoined his other disciples and found them arguing.
- A man told Jesus that the disciples could not cure his son; an evil spirit possessed the boy.

- They brought the boy to Jesus.
- The evil spirit threw the boy into a convulsion, foaming at the mouth and rolling on the ground.
- The father asked Jesus: 'If you can do anything, take pity on us and help us.'
- Jesus told the father that everything was possible for a person who believes.
- The father claimed that he did believe, but then asked Jesus for help to overcome his disbelief.
- Jesus commanded the evil spirit to leave the boy, and the boy shook violently.
- People thought he was dead, but Jesus took the boy by the hand and raised him up.
- Jesus told his disciples, privately, that only prayer could drive out this type of evil spirit.

Healing miracles

Simon's mother-in-law (Mark 1$^{29-31}$)

This is Jesus' first healing miracle.

- Simon's mother-in-law was in bed with a fever.
- Jesus took her by the hand and raised her up, cured.

That evening, Jesus healed many who had various diseases, and he drove out many demons.

A leper (Mark 1$^{40-44}$)

- A leper begged Jesus for a cure. 'If you are willing, you can make me clean.'
- Jesus had compassion, and healed him.
- Jesus told him to go and show himself to the priest and make the appropriate sacrifice.
- But, instead, the man went and talked everywhere about his cure.

Jesus became so popular, he had to stay outside the towns in lonely places.

A paralysed man (Mark 2$^{1-12}$)

- A large crowd gathered outside the house in Capernaum where Jesus was.
- Four men came, bringing a paralysed friend, but they could not get to Jesus.
- They dug a hole in the roof and lowered the paralysed man to Jesus.
- Jesus saw their faith, and told the paralysed man his sins were forgiven.
- The teachers of the law thought he was blaspheming, because only God can forgive sins.
- Jesus asked them whether it was easier to forgive sins or cure the paralysed man.
- Jesus, to prove that the Son of Man (himself) had authority to forgive sins, told the paralysed man to pick up his mat and go home. He did.
- Everyone was amazed by this.

When Jesus saw the faith of the friends of the paralysed man, he said to the paralysed man: 'Son, your sins are forgiven'

A man with a shrivelled (paralysed) hand (Mark 3$^{1-6}$)

- Jesus went into a synagogue and met a man with a shrivelled hand.
- Some people watched to see if he would heal on the Sabbath.
- Jesus asked if it was lawful to do good, or to do evil, on the Sabbath.
- He was distressed at their silent, stubborn reaction.
- He cured the man's hand.

The Pharisees left and plotted with the Herodians to kill Jesus.

Jairus' daughter (Mark 5$^{21-24, 35-43}$)

This miracle is a nature miracle as well as a healing miracle.

- Jairus, a synagogue ruler, pleaded with Jesus to cure his daughter, who was dying.
- Jesus went with Jairus. Some messengers met them and said the daughter had died.
- Jesus told Jairus not to be afraid, but only believe.
- Jesus took Peter, James and John – and only them – with him.
- They reached Jairus' house, where there were people weeping and wailing.
- Jesus said the girl was asleep, not dead. They laughed at him.

- He put them all out, except the girl's parents and his three disciples.
- He took her hand and said '*Talitha koum*'; it means 'little girl, get up'.
- She did. She was 12 years old.

Talitha koum is Aramaic, the language Jesus spoke. Mark wrote his gospel in Greek, but occasionally quotes Jesus' words in Aramaic.

A woman with a haemorrhage (Mark 5$^{25-34}$)

- A woman, who had experienced internal bleeding for 12 years – yet no doctor could cure it – was in a crowd pressing round Jesus; she touched his cloak.
- Immediately her bleeding stopped.
- Jesus turned round and asked who had touched his cloak.
- This question baffled Jesus' disciples, because there was a crowd shoving Jesus.
- The woman, trembling with fear, fell at his feet, and owned up.
- Jesus said it was her faith that had released her suffering.

A deaf and dumb man (Mark 7$^{31-37}$)

This miracle does not take place in Jewish territory.

- In the region of the Decapolis, some people asked Jesus to cure a deaf and dumb man.
- Jesus took the man away from the crowd, put his fingers in the man's ears, spat and touched the man's tongue.
- Jesus said '*Ephphatha*' – which is Aramaic for 'be opened' – and the man was cured.
- Jesus told them to tell no one. But they told everyone.

A blind man at Bethsaida (Mark 8$^{22-26}$)

- In Bethsaida, some people brought a blind man and asked Jesus to cure him.
- Jesus took the man by the hand, outside the village.
- Jesus spat on the man's eyes and put his hands on the man's head.
- The man saw people, but they looked like trees walking around.
- Jesus put his hands on the man's eyes again; and he saw everything clearly.

A blind man, Bartimaeus (Mark 10$^{46-52}$)

- Bartimaeus, a blind man, was sitting by the roadside as Jesus left Jericho.
- He shouted: 'Jesus, Son of David, have mercy on me!'

- People told him to shut up. But he shouted the same request even louder.
- Jesus stopped, and told his disciples to call the man.
- Bartimaeus jumped towards Jesus and said: 'Rabbi, I want to see.'
- He was healed. Jesus told him his faith had healed him.
- He followed Jesus along the road.

Nature miracles

The calming of the storm (Mark 4³⁵⁻⁴¹)

When Jesus calmed the storm, the disciples were terrified and asked each other: 'Who is this? Even the wind and the waves obey him.'

- Jesus and his disciples were crossing Lake Galilee in a boat.
- A furious storm broke and threatened to sink the boat.
- Jesus was asleep in the back of the boat. The disciples woke him, and asked if he cared that they would die.
- Jesus told the wind and waves to be quiet. It happened.
- He asked his disciples, 'Why are you so afraid? Do you still have no faith?
- They were terrified and wondered, 'Who is this? Even the wind and waves obey him!'

Jesus feeds 5000 people (Mark 6³⁰⁻⁴⁴)

- Jesus went with his disciples to a remote place to get some rest, but a large crowd found him.
- He was sorry for them, because they were like sheep without a shepherd; so he taught them.
- When it got late, the disciples told Jesus to send them away to buy something to eat.
- Jesus sat the people in groups of 50 and 100.
- He took the five loaves and two fish the disciples had,

said a prayer of thanks to God, broke the loaves, and got the disciples to share out the bread and fish.
- Everybody ate enough. The disciples collected 12 baskets of scraps.

Jesus walks on the water (Mark 6⁴⁵⁻⁵²)

- It was night. Jesus was on a hillside, alone, praying.
- He saw the disciples rowing across the lake, struggling against the wind.
- He went out to them, walking on the water, and was about to pass them.
- They thought he was a ghost; they shouted in terror.
- Jesus said, 'Take courage! It is I. Don't be afraid.'
- He climbed into the boat with them. The wind died down.
- They were amazed and did not understand.

Jesus feeds 4000 people (Mark 8¹⁻¹⁰)

- A large crowd was with Jesus at a remote place.
- He felt sorry for them because they had nothing to eat. He sat them down.
- He took the seven loaves the disciples had, said a prayer of thanks to God, broke the loaves, and got the disciples to share out the bread and some fish they had.
- Everybody ate enough. The disciples collected seven baskets of scraps.

Faith

Faith is important in many of the miracles. People who want Jesus to heal them can show faith (for instance, the woman with a haemorrhage, or the blind man Bartimaeus). A sick person's parents can have faith (for instance, Jairus, or the foreign woman at Tyre). A sick person's friends can have faith (for instance, the four who lowered their friend through a roof to Jesus).

Lack of faith is prominent in some miracles. For instance, the man whose son was possessed by an evil spirit. He asked Jesus to help his lack of faith. The disciples lacked faith when Jesus walked on the lake. The disciples lacked faith on another occasion, when Jesus calmed the storm.

There was one occasion when Jesus could not perform a miracle because people did not have faith. This was in his home town of Nazareth. The people there would not accept him as a prophet and a miracle worker. They knew his family and would think of Jesus only as an ordinary man.

The word 'faith' has different meanings in Mark's gospel. It can mean:

- a confidence that Jesus can cure people;
- trust in Jesus as the special messenger of God;
- trust in God and his power to do good through Jesus.

Conclusion

In Mark's gospel, there are 17 miracles: nine healing miracles, four exorcisms and four nature miracles. [Some people count the cursing of the fig tree (Mark 11$^{12-14,\ 20-25}$) as a miracle, but it is really an acted parable. See Chapter C12, *Mark's gospel – parables* for details.]

Thirteen of the miracles took place in Galilee. None of them took place in Jerusalem. Three of the miracles took place outside Jewish territory.

Fifteen miracles are in the first half of the gospel, before the incident at Caesarea Philippi; only two miracles occur in the second half of the gospel.

The main purpose of Jesus' miracles is to start the kingdom of God on earth, to show that God cares for us, to show that the power of God is at work and that it comes through Jesus.

A second purpose of some miracles, especially nature miracles, is to point out that Jesus is not just an ordinary person: he is different from the rest of us. In some miracles, Jesus does what only God can do. For example, he

- forgave people their sins;
- calmed a storm;
- fed many people with a few loaves and fish;
- walked on water.

Examination practice

1. What is the difference between a healing miracle, a nature miracle and an exorcism?

   (3 marks)

   Write about six lines.

2. Summarize the main points in these **two** miracles: Jairus' daughter; the paralysed man.
   What does each miracle reveal about Jesus?

   (10 marks)

   Write about one side of A4.

3. Jesus cured many people who were sick.
   What might a Christian learn from this?

   (6 marks)

   Write about half a side of A4.

4. 'According to Mark, Jesus did many miracles. But no man can do miracles such as raising a person from death. The gospel writer has exaggerated what Jesus did.'
   Do you agree? Give reasons to support your view.
   Show that you have considered the opposite view.

   (8 marks)

   Write about three-quarters of a side of A4.

MARK'S GOSPEL – PASSION AND RESURRECTION 14

Introduction

'Mark's gospel is about the death and resurrection of Jesus, with a long introduction.' This is often said about Mark's gospel. There are four reasons for saying this:

1. Much of Mark's gospel is about the last days of Jesus.
2. Mark's account of the last days of Jesus flows fluently, as though it was one continuous narrative; in contrast, Mark's account of Jesus' life before he went to Jerusalem is a series of unconnected incidents.
3. In Mark's gospel, Jesus talks increasingly about his death and resurrection.
4. According to Mark, Jesus did his healing and his preaching in Galilee. He went to Jerusalem (the chief city of the Jews) only for his death and resurrection.

The transfiguration
Mark 9$^{2-13}$

- Jesus took Peter, James and John to a high mountain.
- Jesus was transfigured: his clothes became dazzling white.
- Elijah and Moses appeared with Jesus, talking with him.
- Peter was frightened. He said, 'Rabbi, let us put up three shelters, one for each of the three of you.'
- A cloud covered them.
- A voice came from the cloud: 'This is my Son, whom I love. Listen to him!'
- Suddenly, the disciples saw no one except Jesus.
- As they came down from the mountain, Jesus told the three disciples not to tell anyone what they had seen until the Son of Man was risen from the dead.

Mountain, dazzling white, fear, shelter (tent), cloud, voice – these are symbols for God that the Old Testament uses.

Elijah represents the prophets. Moses represents the

Jewish law, since (according to Jewish and Christian belief) God gave the law to the Jews through Moses. So Elijah and Moses represent the Jewish religion.

The question about the resurrection
Mark 12¹⁸⁻²⁷

After he had reached Jerusalem, and before the Last Supper, the Sadducees asked Jesus about resurrection. The Sadducees were a Jewish group who did not believe in resurrection. They accepted only the first five books in the Jewish Bible as the certain revelation of God. In these five books, there is no belief in life after death.

- The Sadducees reminded Jesus of the Jewish law, that if a man's brother dies without children, he should marry the widow; the first son of this union would be the first husband's son.
- The Sadducees told Jesus about seven brothers. The first died without a son. So the second brother married the first brother's wife. He also died without a son. And the same happened with the other brothers.
- The Sadducees wanted to know who would be the woman's husband if there was a resurrection (implying that she could not have seven husbands simultaneously, so the belief in resurrection was absurd).
- Jesus said that when the dead rise, they do not marry.
- Jesus also said that (a) God was the God of Abraham, Isaac and Jacob; (b) God was the God of the living and not the God of the dead. (Jesus implied that there must be resurrection because Abraham, Isaac and Jacob had died long ago.)

Entry to Jerusalem
Mark 11¹⁻¹¹

- As Jesus and his disciples approached the Mount of Olives, he sent two of his disciples to the village ahead of them.
- As they entered the village, they would find a colt, tied, which no one had ever ridden.
- They should untie it and bring it to Jesus.
- If anyone asked them what they were doing, they should say that the Lord needed it and he would send it back shortly.
- They did as Jesus said. It happened as he said.
- When they brought the colt to Jesus, they threw their cloaks on it, and he sat on it.
- Many people spread their cloaks on the ground, and others spread branches they had cut.
- People shouted: 'Hosanna! Blessed is he who comes in the name of the Lord! Blessed is the coming kingdom of our father David!'
- Jesus entered Jerusalem and went to the temple. But it was late, so he left with the twelve for the village of Bethany.

The people of Jerusalem welcomed Jesus as their messiah (king). They said the great kingdom of their most successful king, David, was about to come again.

Sometimes when a Jew was anointed king, he would ride on a mule, or people would spread their cloaks on the ground.

Mark's account of Jesus entering Jerusalem uses part of a passage from Zechariah, an Old Testament book. According to Zechariah, God tells the Jews to rejoice, because he is sending them a king. This king would ride into Jerusalem on a colt.

The Last Supper
Mark 14¹²⁻³¹

- Jesus took a piece of bread, said a prayer of thanks, broke it, gave it to his disciples, and said,
- 'Take it; this is my body.'
- Jesus took a cup, said a prayer of thanks, gave it to his disciples; they drank. Jesus said:
- 'This is my blood of the covenant, which is poured out for many. . . . I will not drink again of the fruit of the vine until that day when I drink anew in the kingdom of God.'
- They sang a hymn, then went to the Mount of Olives.
- Jesus told the disciples they would desert him. Jesus said that, after he had risen, he would see them in Galilee.
- Peter protested that he would never desert Jesus. Jesus replied, 'Today – yes, tonight – before the cock crows twice you yourself will disown me three times.'

At the last supper Jesus had with his disciples, he took the bread and broke it, and gave it to his disciples, saying: 'Take it; this is my body'

Jesus prays in Gethsemane
Mark 14³²⁻⁵²

- Jesus went with his disciples to Gethsemane. He told them to pray.
- He took Peter, James and John with him. He told them he was deeply distressed. He told them to stay awake with him.
- He went off himself and prayed: 'Abba, Father,

everything is possible for you. Take this cup [of suffering] from me. Yet not what I will, but what you will.'

- He returned to the three disciples and found them asleep. He woke them and told them that the spirit was willing, but the flesh was weak.
- Twice more Jesus went off. He returned to find the disciples asleep.
- On the third occasion he said: 'The hour has come. Look, the Son of Man is betrayed into the hands of sinners. Rise! Let us go! Here comes my betrayer.'
- Judas, the Sanhedrin and soldiers arrived.
- Judas kissed Jesus and said, 'Rabbi'. The soldiers arrested Jesus.
- One of Jesus' disciples drew his sword. But Jesus would not let his disciples use violence.
- Then all of Jesus' disciples left him and ran away.

Jesus before the Jewish Council, the Sanhedrin
Mark 14⁵³⁻⁶⁵

- Jesus was taken to the high priest's house. Peter followed at a distance.
- The whole Council wanted to put Jesus to death.
- Some claimed Jesus had said he would tear down the temple. And that in three days he would replace it with one not made by men.
- The High Priest asked Jesus: 'Are you the Christ, the Son of the Blessed One?'
- Jesus replied: 'I am. And you will see the Son of Man seated on the right of the Mighty One, and coming on the clouds.'
- The Council sentenced Jesus to death. Some spat on him. They blindfolded him, hit him and said, 'Prophesy!'

Peter denies Jesus
Mark 14⁶⁶⁻⁷²

- Peter was in the courtyard.
- Three times someone said he was one of Jesus' disciples. Peter denied it each time.
- A cock crowed. Peter broke down and cried.

The Jewish Council was called the Sanhedrin. They condemned Jesus to death. Yet the Sanhedrin did not kill him. Instead they took him to Pilate, the Roman governor. It seems the Romans allowed the Sanhedrin to try Jews accused of breaking the Jewish law; and the Romans allowed the Sanhedrin to impose any penalty, except the death penalty. Hence the Sanhedrin took Jesus to the Roman governor, hoping that he would condemn Jesus to death.

The Roman trial
Mark 15¹⁻²⁰

- The Council brought Jesus to Pilate, the Roman governor.
- Pilate asked Jesus: 'Are you the king of the Jews?'
- 'Yes, it is as you say,' said Jesus. But Jesus refused to answer further questions from Pilate.
- Pilate released a prisoner every Passover festival. He tried to persuade the crowd it should be Jesus.
- The chief priests encouraged the crowd to ask Pilate to release Barabbas.
- The crowd demanded the crucifixion of Jesus.
- Pilate released Barabbas. Pilate had Jesus flogged, and handed him over to be crucified.
- The soldiers spat on Jesus, hit him, and mocked him.

Very early in the morning the Jewish High Council reached a decision. They bound Jesus, led him away and turned him over to Pilate.

The crucifixion
Mark 15²¹⁻⁴¹

- The soldiers took Jesus to Golgotha (which means 'place of the skull'), outside Jerusalem.
- They forced Simon, who came from Cyrene, to help Jesus carry the cross.
- They gave Jesus wine mixed with myrrh, which he did not take.
- They crucified him naked. It was nine in the morning.
- The notice on his cross was – the king of the Jews.

- They crucified two others with him.
- Passers-by insulted him. They challenged him to come down from the cross and save himself.
- The Council members mocked him. They said he could save others, but not himself. They told him to come down from the cross if he was the king.
- Those crucified with him also insulted him.
- From noon until three, the whole country was covered with darkness.
- Then Jesus cried out, '*Eloi, Eloi, lama sabachthani?*', which means 'My God, my God, why have you forsaken me?'
- Someone put a sponge soaked with wine vinegar on a stick and offered it to Jesus.
- The curtain of the temple was torn in two.
- The centurion said, 'Surely, this man was the Son of God.'
- Some women were watching from a distance. They had followed him in Galilee.

The burial
Mark 15⁴²⁻⁴⁷

- It was the day before the Sabbath.
- Joseph, a member of the Council, asked Pilate for the body of Jesus.
- Pilate was surprised that Jesus had died so soon. He checked Joseph's story, then gave the body to him.
- Joseph wrapped the body in a cloth. He put it in a tomb that was cut out of rock. He rolled a stone against the entrance of the tomb. Two women, both called Mary, watched him.

The empty tomb
Mark 16¹⁻⁸

- The two Marys and Salome came to the tomb on the Sunday morning. They had waited till the Sabbath was over. They wondered who would roll the stone away.
- But they found the stone rolled away. They went in and saw a young man dressed in white. They were afraid.
- The young man said: 'Jesus is risen; he is not here. Tell his disciples they will see him in Galilee.'

- The women fled from the tomb. They were terrified. They said nothing to anyone.

This is the original ending of Mark's gospel.

Resurrection appearances
Mark 16⁹⁻²⁰

Later writers have added these accounts to Mark's gospel. We know this because the earliest manuscripts of Mark's gospel do not include these appearances. The style of writing is also quite different from Mark's, as are the ideas and vocabulary.

- Jesus appeared to Mary Magdalene. She told the disciples Jesus was alive. They would not believe her.
- Jesus appeared to disciples while they were walking in the country. They told the other disciples, who would not believe them.
- Jesus appeared to the eleven, as they were eating. He told them to preach the good news and to baptize. After he spoke, Jesus was taken up into heaven.

Examination practice

1. Re-tell Mark's account of Jesus' trials before: the Jewish Council; the Roman governor.
   What are the similarities in the two accounts?
   (10 marks)
   Write about one side of A4.

2. What might a Christian learn about life after death from Mark's gospel?　　(8 marks)
   Write about three-quarters of a side of A4.

3. Jesus suffered and was crucified, even though he was innocent.
   What effect might this have on a Christian?
   (6 marks)
   Write about half a side of A4.

4. Do you believe in life after death?
   Give reasons for your view. Show that you have considered the opposite view.　　(8 marks)
   Write about three-quarters of a side of A4.

Introduction

We are not sure about the author of this gospel. According to Papias, who wrote in AD 125, it was someone called Mark.

Papias says that Mark obtained his information from Peter, a disciple of Jesus.

However, some modern writers suggest that Mark obtained his information not from Peter, but from the early Christian oral tradition. These writers point out that the first Christians passed on by word of mouth (orally) most of the things that Mark wrote about; and they suggest that Mark used these oral traditions when he wrote his gospel.

Whatever the source of Mark's information, he arranged his information about Jesus in his own way. He wanted to convince his readers that Jesus was the Christ, the suffering servant, and the Son of God.

Mark wrote the first gospel. Matthew and Luke used Mark's gospel. They copied parts of it, making small changes to the parts they copied. And they added information about Jesus that is not in Mark's gospel.

Mark wrote in Greek. This was the international language in his time, just as English is the international language today.

Mark wrote for people who were not Jews, which was the religion that Jesus was brought up in. And Mark wrote for people who lived outside Israel, which is the country that Jesus lived in. We know this because he sometimes explains Jewish customs: for example, he explains ceremonial washing (Mark 7$^{1-4}$).

Aramaic

Aramaic was the language that Jesus spoke. On a few occasions Mark quotes what Jesus said in Aramaic. Mark then translates these words into Greek. Why does Mark do this? Perhaps because when Mark wrote his gospel, this was how Christians living outside Palestine passed on these words of Jesus. Here are some examples of Mark quoting Jesus in Aramaic:

- When Jesus raised the daughter of Jairus, he said '*talitha koum*', which means 'little girl, I tell you to get up'.
- When Jesus cured a deaf and dumb man, he said, '*Ephphatha*', which means 'be opened'.
- When Jesus prayed to God in the garden of Gethsemane, he said, '*Abba*', which means 'father'.
- When he was hanging on the cross, Jesus cried out, '*Eloi, Eloi, lama sabachthani*', which means 'My God, my God, why have you forsaken me?'

Death and resurrection

It is often said that Mark's gospel is an account of the trials and death of Jesus, with a long introduction put in front of it. More than one third of Mark's gospel is about Jesus' last days in Jerusalem.

A young man dressed in a white robe told the three women who came to the tomb of Jesus: 'He has risen! He is not here. See the place where they laid him.'

According to Mark, Jesus went to Jerusalem once. He went there to be tried and crucified. Before this, Jesus spent all his time in Galilee – teaching, healing people and doing miracles. Yet it seems more likely, as John's gospel relates, that Jesus went to Jerusalem several times. Mark deliberately relates only one occasion when Jesus went to Jerusalem – the occasion of his death and resurrection – to highlight this most important event.

Mark interrupts his account of Jesus' life in Galilee to mention the death and resurrection of Jesus. He mentions, on three separate occasions, that Jesus spoke about his death and resurrection. For example:

> [Jesus] then began to teach them that the Son of Man must suffer many things and be rejected by the elders, chief priests and teachers of the law, and that he must be killed and after three days rise again. He spoke plainly about this. . .
>
> Mark 8$^{31-32}$

Each of these three occasions makes the reader aware of Jesus' final days, even while he was still teaching in Galilee.

After Jesus was dead and buried, some women visited the tomb. They found that his body was not there and that he was resurrected. They left the tomb and told no one about this because they were afraid. This is the end of Mark's gospel. He has no account of anybody meeting the risen Jesus.

A later writer has added resurrection appearances to Mark's gospel (16^{9-20}). These are taken from the other gospels. We know someone has added these to Mark's gospel because they are not in the earliest copies of Mark's gospel, and the style of writing is quite different from Mark's style of writing.

If the resurrection of Jesus is important to Mark, why has he no accounts of the risen Jesus meeting people? We can only guess the answer.

• Perhaps the real ending to Mark's gospel has been lost or destroyed.
• Perhaps Mark died before he finished his gospel.
• Perhaps Mark thought that the risen Jesus had not yet appeared, but that he would soon appear to the disciples in Galilee.
• Perhaps Mark was expecting the imminent end of the world, the return of Jesus in glory, and the start of a completely new life.
• Perhaps Mark believed that Jesus had risen, but that it was too difficult to describe what that was like.

Conflict

Mark says Jesus clashed with the Jewish religious leaders: the Pharisees, the teachers of the law, and the chief priests. The conflict was usually about keeping the Jewish law.

For example, one of the Jewish laws is that the Sabbath (Saturday) should be kept holy. For the Jews this meant that they should not work on that day. So the Pharisees criticized Jesus' disciples, because they picked corn one Sabbath as they went through a corn field with Jesus. Jesus replied:

> 'The Sabbath was made for man, not man for the Sabbath. So the Son of Man is Lord even of the Sabbath.'
> Mark 2^{27-28}

Some Pharisees, who were teachers of the law, also criticized Jesus for mixing with 'bad' people. Jesus was at a meal in the house of Levi the tax collector. There were many 'sinners' and tax collectors with him. The teachers of the law asked Jesus' disciples:

> 'Why does he eat with tax collectors and "sinners"'?
> Mark 2^{16}

On another occasion, the teachers of the law criticized Jesus for claiming to forgive the sins of a paralysed man. They thought to themselves:

> 'Why does this fellow talk like that? He's blaspheming! Who can forgive sins but God alone?'
> Mark 2^{7}

Some teachers of the law from Jerusalem recognized that Jesus had the power to heal. But they thought it was not the power of God. They suggested it was the power of the Devil. They said:

> 'He is possessed by Beelzebub! By the prince of demons he is driving out demons.'
> Mark 3^{22}

The criticisms were not one-sided. Jesus criticized the teachers of the law and the Pharisees. He called them hypocrites, and said:

> 'You have let go the commands of God and are holding on to the traditions of men.'
> Mark 7^{8}

Jesus also criticized the chief priests. He told them the parable of the tenants in the vineyard. (See Chapter C12, *Mark's gospel – parables*, for details.) They condemned him to death.

The secret of who Jesus is

Mark's gospel is like a suspense film, where the viewers know the identity of the main character, but the people in the story do not. In his opening sentence, Mark says Jesus is 'Christ, the Son of God', but the people in the gospel do not know this.

There are nine occasions in the gospel when Jesus tells someone to say nothing about him.

On four of these occasions, he has healed someone: the man who has leprosy; Jairus' daughter; the man who was deaf and dumb; the blind man at Bethsaida.

On three occasions, he tells evil spirits, who do recognize his true identity, to say nothing about him: the man with the evil spirit in the synagogue at Capernaum; later that day when he cured many people; and a subsequent occasion when he was teaching and healing a large crowd.

On the other two occasions, he tells the disciples not to say who he is: at Caesarea Philippi; and after the transfiguration.

Why is there this secrecy in Mark's gospel? We do not have an undisputed answer. Perhaps it was to remind the readers that they knew the real identity of Jesus. Perhaps it was because those who do not believe cannot see the real identity of Jesus.

Examination practice

1. Mark's gospel was written in Greek. Yet it has Aramaic phrases.
   Give some examples, and their meaning in English.
   (3 marks)
   Write about six lines.

2. Mark did not include in his gospel any appearances of the risen Jesus. This puzzles many people. Suggest why he did not include any appearances of the risen Jesus.
   (3 marks)
   Write about six lines.

3. Jesus clashed with the religious leaders of his day. What might a Christian today learn from this?

(8 marks)

Write about three-quarters of a side of A4.

4. 'It is not possible to rise from the dead.' What do you think? Give reasons for your view. Show that you have considered the opposite point of view.

(8 marks)

Write about three-quarters of a side of A4.

MARK'S GOSPEL – SPECIAL EMPHASES – II 16

Jesus, the Son of God

Mark was convinced that Jesus was more than just a man. He believed that Jesus was God in some way.

- Twice in the gospel (the baptism of Jesus and the transfiguration of Jesus), a voice from heaven addresses Jesus as Son. On the first of these occasions – the baptism – it is only Jesus who is aware of anything unusual. Mark says that, after John had baptized him, Jesus was coming up out of the water and he:

> saw heaven being torn open and the Spirit descending on him like a dove. And a voice came from heaven: 'You are my Son, whom I love; with you I am well pleased.'
>
> Mark 1$^{10-11}$

On the second occasion when a voice from heaven called Jesus Son, the disciples heard it.

> Then a cloud appeared and enveloped them, and a voice came from the cloud: 'This is my Son, whom I love. Listen to him!'
>
> Mark 9^7

- Jesus used the word 'dad' or 'father' when he talked to God. In his prayer in the garden of Gethsemane, just before the soldiers arrested him, he said:

> '*Abba*, Father, everything is possible for you. Take this cup from me. Yet not what I will, but what you will.'
>
> Mark 14^{36}

- Mark relates that Jesus did what only God can do. Jesus forgave the sins of a paralysed man; Jesus calmed a storm; Jesus walked on water; Jesus fed 5000 people with a few loaves and a couple of fish. No man can do these things.

Mark wants to emphasize his belief that Jesus is God in some way. So he states it at the beginning and at the end of his gospel. The opening statement in his gospel is:

> The beginning of the gospel about Jesus Christ, the Son of God.

At the end of Jesus' life, a centurion says:

> 'Surely this man was the Son of God!'

Jesus, the Son of Man

There are two curious features about the title Son of Man in Mark's gospel:

1. Jesus is the only person who uses it. No one else in Mark's gospel uses it.
2. Jesus uses it only for himself. He does not use this title to talk about anyone else.

There are 14 passages in Mark's gospel where Jesus used the title Son of Man. Let us look at three instances:

- In the healing of the paralysed man, Jesus said:

> 'Which is easier: to say to the paralytic, "Your sins are forgiven," or to say, "Get up, take your mat and walk?" But that you may know that the Son of Man has authority on earth to forgive sins' . . . he said to the paralytic, 'I tell you, get up, take your mat and go home.'
>
> Mark 2$^{1-12}$

- When James and John asked him if they could sit at his right and left side when he became a king, he said:

> '. . . The Son of Man did not come to be served, but to serve, and to give his life as a ransom for many.'
>
> Mark 10^{45}

- Three times Jesus predicted he would be rejected, suffer, and be crucified – but he would be resurrected. On each occasion he called himself Son of Man. On the second of these three occasions, at Caesarea Philippi, Mark says:

He then began to teach them that the Son of Man must suffer many things and be rejected by the elders, chief priests and teachers of the law, and that he must be killed and after three days rise again.

Mark 8[31]

So what does the title 'Son of Man' mean? There are different opinions. Here is one opinion. Jesus is talking about himself and he means that he:

- is a man, yet more than just a man;
- will have to suffer, be rejected and die;
- will rise to life again;
- and be in triumphant glory with God;
- will benefit other people, through his death and resurrection;
- will judge all of us when we die.

Jesus, the Christ (king)

'Christ' is a Greek word. It translates the Hebrew word 'Messiah'. This word, literally translated into English, means 'anointed one'. It really means 'king'.

'Messiah' was a word used by Jews for a Jewish king; but not just an ordinary king. They were hoping for an extraordinary king, such as their greatest king, David. They thought that this king would make the Jews a great nation again, as it had been in the days of David. So, they expected that the Messiah would expel the Romans, who had conquered their country, and he would re-establish Palestine as God's country.

Mark wrote his gospel in Greek, so he used the word 'Christ', not 'Messiah'. He started his gospel:

The beginning of the good news of Jesus Christ.

Then at the half-way stage in Marks's gospel, at Caesarea Philippi, Jesus asked his disciples what they thought about him. Peter answered on behalf of the disciples and said:

'You are the Christ.'

Mark 8[29]

Towards the end of Mark's gospel, the word 'Christ' is used more often. Shortly before Jesus entered Jerusalem, two disciples asked for the most important places in his coming kingdom (that is, the kingdom of the Christ.)

Then a blind man, Bartimaeus, called Jesus the 'Son of David', meaning 'Christ' or 'king'.

When Jesus entered Jerusalem, people welcomed him as their Christ: they spread cloaks and branches on the ground and shouted, 'Blessed is the coming kingdom of our father David'.

At the trial before the Jewish Council, the High Priest asked Jesus if he was the Christ (king).

The roman governor, Pilate, asked Jesus if he was the king (Christ) of the Jews; Pilate then asked the crowd if they wanted him to release the king of the Jews.

Before they crucified him, the soldiers mocked Jesus as a king. They put a purple robe on him and knelt before him.

The notice on Jesus' cross was – THE KING OF THE JEWS.

Finally, the chief priests and teachers of the law passed his cross and mocked him, saying:

'He saved others, but he can't save himself! Let this Christ, this King of Israel, come down now from the cross, that we may see and believe.'

Mark 15[31–32]

Jesus, a man of action

Although he says that Jesus did much teaching, Mark does not present many examples. Instead Mark concentrates on writing about the miracles of Jesus and his fight with evil spirits. See Chapter C13, *Mark's gospel – miracles*, for details.

Kingdom of God

Nowadays we use the expression 'God's family'. In Mark's gospel, Jesus talks about 'God's kingdom'. It is very important in his preaching.

- Jesus referred to it in his first and in his last speech in Mark's gospel.
    Jesus made his first speech when he came into Galilee after John was put in prison. He said:

    'The time has come. The kingdom of God is near. Repent and believe the good news.'

    Mark 1[15]

Jesus' final speech is at the last supper he had with his disciples. He took a cup and said he would never

drink this wine again until he drank new wine in the kingdom of God.

- There are three parables that explicitly mention the kingdom of God. (See Chapter 12, *Mark's gospel – parables*.)
- On one occasion people brought children to Jesus to touch them. The disciples told them off. But Jesus was indignant with the disciples. He told them:

    'The kingdom of God belongs to such as these. . . Anyone who does not receive the kingdom of God like a little child will never enter it.'

    Mark 10[14–15]

- Jesus mentioned the kingdom of God after a rich young man asked him about inheriting eternal life. At first, Jesus told the man to keep the commandments; then, Jesus told the man to sell his possessions, to give the money to the poor and to follow Jesus. The man walked away. Jesus said:

    'how hard it is to enter the kingdom of God. It is easier for a camel to go through the eye of a needle than for a rich man to enter the kingdom of God.'

    Mark 10[24–25]

- Jesus also mentioned the kingdom of God after a teacher of the law asked him about the most important commandment. Jesus told him to love God and to love his neighbour as himself. The teacher said this was a great answer. Jesus said:

  > 'You are not far from the kingdom of God.'
  >
  > Mark 12^{34}

Some writers emphasize that there are two aspects to the kingdom of God in Mark's gospel: it has started; and it is still to come.

Discipleship

The disciples are prominent in Mark's gospel. The word 'disciple' means 'learner'. The word 'apostle' means 'one sent out to do a task'. In Mark's gospel the followers of Jesus are called disciples when they listen to him; they are called apostles when Jesus sends them out to preach, to heal and to cast out evil spirits.

- Jesus' first action, after he started preaching, was to choose disciples. He saw Simon and his brother fishing. He told them to leave their nets and to follow him. He said:

  > 'I will make you fishers of men.'
  >
  > Mark 1^{17}

- Thereafter, disciples were constantly with Jesus on his travels. He chose 12 of them later on (Mark 3$^{13–19}$). He sent them out.

  > They went out and preached that people should repent. They drove out many demons and anointed many sick people with oil and healed them.
  >
  > Mark 6$^{12–13}$

- Jesus told his disciples that they would have to follow his style of life:

  > 'If anyone would come after me, he must deny himself and take up his cross and follow me. For whoever wants to save his life will lose it.'
  >
  > Mark 8$^{34–35}$

- Three of them (Peter, James and John) were with him on two occasions that intimated his resurrection: the raising of Jairus' daughter; and the transfiguration.

  Jesus praised the disciples for leaving everything to follow him.

  > 'No-one who has left home or brothers or sisters or mother or father or children or fields for me and the gospel will fail to receive a hundred times as much in this present age . . . and in the age to come, eternal life.'
  >
  > Mark 10$^{29–30}$

- On another occasion, in the Jerusalem temple, Jesus called his disciples to him, and praised a poor widow who put a couple of copper coins into the temple collection box. Jesus did not praise the rich people who put in large amounts. He said to his disciples:

  > 'They all gave out of their wealth; but she, out of her poverty, put in everything, all she had to live on.'
  >
  > Mark 12^{44}

- It was to his disciples, not to the crowd, that Jesus explained his teaching (for example, the parable of the sower).
- Jesus shared his last supper with his disciples and then, in the garden of Gethsemane, hoped they would be comforting companions to him. They failed him.
- There is a large section in Mark's gospel (8^{31}–10^{52}) where Jesus teaches the disciples and not the crowd. He explains to them what it means to be a disciple.
- Finally, in a passage that a later writer has added to Mark's gospel, the risen Jesus appears to the disciples and tells them to:

  > 'Go into all the world and preach the good news to all creation.'
  >
  > Mark 16^{15}

Importance of Peter

Peter is the disciple who gets special mention. His name occurs 25 times in Mark's gospel.

Peter was the first disciple that Jesus called.

Peter is also the last disciple that Mark mentions by name in his gospel. At the last supper, Jesus told his disciples that he would be killed and that they would all desert him. Peter protested that he wouldn't. When soldiers arrested Jesus in Gethsemane, all the disciples ran away, except Peter, who followed at a distance. Then, in the courtyard outside the high priest's house, Peter denied, three times, knowing Jesus (Mark 14$^{66–72}$).

Jesus changed Simon's name to Peter (which means 'rock').

When Mark gives a list of the disciples, he puts Peter's name first. And when one of the disciples speaks on behalf of the others, it is Peter (for instance, at Caesarea Philippi, when Jesus asks the disciples who they thought he was).

Examination practice

1. Peter is the most important disciple in Mark's gospel. Give some examples. (3 marks)
   Write about six lines.

2. Mark does not think that Jesus was an ordinary person. Explain what Mark does think about Jesus. (10 marks)
   Write about a side of A4.

3. What might a Christian today learn from the life of the first disciples? (6 marks)
   Write about half a side of A4.

Suffering

This is a prominent theme in Mark's gospel. It may explain why this gospel has never been the most popular of the four gospels, even though it is the shortest. There seems to be little joy in Mark's gospel. Luke, in his gospel, uses the word 'joy' frequently. Mark uses the word 'joy' once.

The focus of Mark's gospel is the death and resurrection of Jesus. It is the suffering of death, rather than the joy of resurrection, that is the dominant theme. According to Mark, Jesus said at his last supper that he suffered to benefit everyone. Jesus took the cup and said:

> 'This is my blood of the covenant, which is poured out for many.'
>
> Mark 14[24]

The disciples would also have to suffer. Jesus told them that they were no greater than their master, and that:

> 'If anyone would come after me, he must deny himself and take up his cross and follow me.'
>
> Mark 8[34]

Failure

This is an important theme in Mark's gospel.

At the start of Jesus' work, everybody was enthusiastic about Jesus – they were fascinated. The disciples left everything to follow Jesus. And crowds of people came to listen to him, and to be cured by him.

But after this came failures. The people failed to recognize Jesus. The religious leaders resented him and plotted to kill him. The disciples repeatedly failed to understand him. Last of all, Mark says that Jesus looked like a failure: on the cross he felt that God had forsaken him.

Many Christians have found it difficult to accept that failure is an important theme in Mark's gospel. This includes other gospel writers. When Matthew and Luke wrote their gospels they copied much of Mark's. Yet they omitted or changed passages about the disciples or Jesus failing.

For instance, Luke does not say that Jesus, on the cross, felt forsaken by God. Instead, Luke says that Jesus prayed to God to forgive those who crucified him.

Another example: Jesus walked across the lake to the disciples. Mark says that the disciples were completely amazed, and their hearts were hardened. Matthew says that the disciples worshipped Jesus and said he was truly the Son of God.

A last example – the ending of Mark's gospel. Mark says that some women came to Jesus' tomb. A messenger said that Jesus was risen; the messenger then told the women to tell the disciples and Peter. But the women left the tomb and said nothing to anyone, because they were afraid. Yet in Matthew's account of the empty tomb, the women left the tomb filled with joy and went to tell the disciples.

Let us look at who failed, according to Mark.

- The **ordinary people** failed Jesus. At the beginning of the gospel, the Galilean people enthusiastically sought him because he taught with authority and he healed people. Yet they failed to recognize who he really was. The people of Jerusalem welcomed Jesus into Jerusalem as their king, but within a short time they were yelling for Pilate to kill him.
- The **Jewish religious leaders** were antagonistic to Jesus throughout the gospel: first, the Pharisees and teachers of the Law in Galilee; then the high priests in Jerusalem. They failed to recognize the person that God had sent them.
- The **disciples** were initially enthusiastic and generous. The first four left all they possessed to follow Jesus, and the fifth one left his tax office to follow Jesus. But soon after this, Jesus told all his disciples that they had the wrong idea about the kingdom of God.

  But worse was to come. Judas, a disciple, betrayed Jesus to the high priests. The rest of the disciples ran away when soldiers arrested Jesus in the garden of Gethsemane. The soldiers led Jesus away and Peter followed, though at a safe distance. Yet when he was asked, three separate times, if he was a friend of Jesus, he strongly denied it each time. Mark tells us nothing more about the disciples after this. They did not witness the crucifixion, nor did they go to the empty tomb, nor did they meet Jesus after he rose from death.
- On one occasion **Jesus** struggled to accept God's will. In the garden of Gethsemane he did not want to go through any further suffering, and he asked God to take it away from him; but he ended by praying, 'yet not what I want, but what you want.' So this was an occasion when Jesus lost courage, yet he did not fail. However, soon after, he lost confidence in God. As he was hanging from the cross he cried, 'My God, my God, why have you forsaken me?' (Some commentators suggest that this is not a cry of despair; they point out that these are the first words of a prayer in the book of Psalms – Psalm 22. That psalm ends with the psalmist confident that God will help him.)

The theme of failure is like a crescendo. At the beginning of Mark's gospel, Jesus was very successful: he attracted large crowds by his teaching and his miracles. But then things started to go wrong. His family thought he had gone mad. The teachers of the law said he had the power of Satan, not God. The crowd did not understand his teaching. The people of Nazareth, his home town, thought there was nothing special about him. The disciples continuously failed to understand him; then they betrayed or deserted him. The Jewish Council condemned him to death. The Roman Governor sentenced him to death. Passers-by mocked him when he was on the cross; so did the Jewish leaders; so did those crucified with him. Finally, Jesus asked God: 'Why have you forsaken me?'

At this point in Mark's gospel, everyone seems to have failed. Yet there is more.

> Trembling and bewildered, the women went out and fled from the tomb. They said nothing to anyone, because they were afraid.
>
> Mark 16[8]

The women went to the tomb after the Sabbath. Jesus was not there. A messenger told them that Jesus was risen and that they should tell the disciples. They left and said nothing to anyone. These are the last words in the original version of Mark's gospel. Words of failure!

Good news

Despite Mark's emphasis on failure and suffering, he uses the expression 'good news'. He thinks that we can triumph over failure and suffering, sin and death. He uses the expression 'good news' to describe Jesus and his work. Mark starts his gospel with these words:

> The beginning of the good news about Jesus Christ, the Son of God.

Why is Jesus good news? There are several reasons. Here are the principal ones.

- **God sent Jesus**. At the baptism of Jesus a voice from heaven said: 'You are my Son whom I love.'
- **Jesus started the kingdom of God on earth**: a kingdom in which God overcomes suffering and evil. On the first occasion when he taught, Jesus said: 'The time

has come. The kingdom of God is near.'
- **Jesus showed that God forgives**. Some friends of a paralysed man made a hole in the roof of the house where Jesus was preaching. They lowered their friend to Jesus. Jesus healed the paralysed man. Jesus said that this showed: 'the Son of Man has authority on earth to forgive sins.'
- **Jesus died for us**. At the last supper, Jesus took the cup and said: 'This is my blood of the covenant, which is poured out for many.'
- **Jesus has made it possible for us to know God**. After Jesus died, Mark comments: 'The curtain of the temple was torn in two from top to bottom.'
- **God raised Jesus to life**. When the women went to the empty tomb, they met a young man dressed in a white robe. He said to them: 'You are looking for Jesus the Nazarene, who was crucified. He has risen!'

We usually say 'the gospel according to Mark', rather than 'the good news according to Mark'. This is simply because we use old English words instead of modern English words. *Godspel* is old English: *god* means 'good'; *spel* means 'news'. *Godspel* became shortened to *gospel*. There is no good reason why we still use old English words rather than modern English words.

Examination practice

1. Mark says his book is good news. Why does he believe this? (3 marks)
   Write about six lines.

2. Explain how the disciples failed Jesus. (10 marks)
   Write about one side of A4.

3. Suffering and failure are important themes in Mark's gospel.
   What might a Christian today learn from what Mark writes? (8 marks)
   Write about three-quarters of a side of A4.

4. 'Jesus was a loser.'
   Do you agree? Give reasons for your view. Show that that you have considered other views. (8 marks)
   Write about three-quarters of a side of A4.

John the Baptist

At the beginning of his ministry Jesus was baptized by John (Luke 3^{21-22}). The Holy Spirit came down on him in the form of a dove and a voice came from heaven, 'You are my Son, whom I love; with you I am well pleased'.

John had announced that the Christ was coming. He was put in prison by King Herod, because John denounced him for living in sin with his brother's wife.

While in prison John sent two of his own followers to ask Jesus, 'Are you the one who was to come, or should we expect someone else?' (Luke 7^{18-32}). Jesus kept them with him to see for themselves what he was doing and saying. Then he sent them back to John. 'Go back and report to John what you have seen and heard. The blind receive sight, the lame walk, those who have leprosy are cured, the deaf hear, the dead are raised, and the good news is preached to the poor.'

When John's followers had left, Jesus asked the crowd why they went into the desert to see John. It was not to see a reed blowing in the wind or a finely dressed man – whom they would have been more likely to see in a palace than a desert. It was because John was a prophet – and even more than that, he was the one sent to announce that the Christ was coming; there had never been a greater person than John the Baptist. Yet anyone who entered the kingdom of God would be greater than John.

The ordinary people were delighted to hear Jesus speak so highly of John. The Pharisees and others were less pleased, as they had not been baptized by John. Jesus told them they would find fault with anything. They were like children being awkward. Jesus said:

> 'They are like children sitting in the market-place and calling out to each other:
> "We played the flute for you,
> and you did not dance;
> we sang a dirge,
> and you did not cry." '
>
> Luke 7^{32}

(A dirge is a funeral-type song.)

The miracles of Jesus

Jesus performed many miracles. Luke, like the other gospel-writers, included some of the miracles in his gospel. Each selected miracle was chosen for a purpose.

Simon's mother-in-law (Luke 4^{38-39})

Jesus was asked to help her. He rebuked her fever and instantly she was cured – to the extent of waiting on them.

Jesus had healed one or two people on the Sabbath day (Luke 4^{40})

At sunset, when the Sabbath was over, crowds of people came to Jesus with sick loved ones – and he healed them all. The verse shows the power of Jesus – and the faith that made people come to him for healing.

The paralysed man (Luke 5^{17-26})

Some men brought a paralytic (paralysed man) on a mat. Because they could not get into the house where Jesus was teaching, they went onto the flat roof and lowered their friend in front of Jesus. Jesus saw their faith and told the man his sins were forgiven. This upset the Pharisees and teachers of the law. To them this was blasphemy. Only God could forgive sins; who did this fellow think he was? Knowing their thoughts, Jesus asked them, 'Which is easier; to say "Your sins are forgiven," or to say, "Get up and walk"?' (The point was, no ordinary human being could do either.) Jesus went on, 'That you may know that the Son of Man has authority on earth to forgive sins . . .' He said to the paralysed man, 'I tell you, get up, take your mat and go home.' The man did so. Everyone was amazed – and gave praise to God.

The centurion's servant (Luke 7^{1-10})

This incident gives an excellent example of a man's faith in Jesus. The centurion was an officer in the Roman army. So, he was not a Jew. He was good to the Jews of his area and they appreciated his generosity. But he did not share their religious belief. He did believe in Jesus. He didn't think he was good enough to have Jesus in his house. His faith was simple. He himself had authority. If he gave an order, it was obeyed. He believed Jesus had authority – authority over illness. If Jesus told a disease to go away, it would go. He had faith in Jesus – he did not doubt for a moment that his servant would be healed, even if Jesus did not come to his house. Jesus was impressed. 'I have not found such great faith even in Israel': even among the Jews, the people of Israel, he had not found faith like the centurion's.

The widow of Nain's son (Luke 7^{11-17})

This incident showed that Jesus had power even over life and death. No one had any doubt that the widow's son was really dead – he was on his way to be buried. Verses 16 and 17 show the effect that the news of this miracle had. Note also verse 13, showing the sympathy Jesus had for the woman.

Calming the storm (Luke 8²²⁻²⁶)

This incident showed the power of Jesus over the forces of nature.

Ten men with leprosy (Luke 17¹¹⁻¹⁹)

Leprosy is a disease that attacks the nerves (causing loss of feeling and making limbs waste away), or skin (causing a person to become disfigured). It was thought to be a highly infectious disease. At the time of Jesus, because of the risk of infection, a person who recovered from leprosy was not allowed back among other people until a priest had certified that the leprosy was cured. So, without healing them, Jesus told them to go to the priest. They had enough faith to go. As they went, they realized they were healed. Note also that one – only one – came back to thank Jesus. He was a Samaritan (remember that Samaritans were, traditionally, enemies of the Jews).

People who encountered Jesus
A sinful woman (Luke 7³⁶⁻⁵⁰)

Jesus was invited to a meal with a Pharisee called Simon. During the meal the woman came and wet Jesus feet with her tears, dried them with her hair, kissed them and anointed them with expensive perfume. Simon said to himself that if Jesus were a prophet he would realize that she was a sinner. Jesus told him of a man who had two debtors, one of whom owed him much more than the other. Neither could pay so he forgave them both. 'Which of them will love him more?' asked Jesus. 'The one who had the bigger debt cancelled', answered Simon. Jesus then pointed out that Simon had not welcomed him with the usual courtesies – he had not kissed him, he had not washed his feet, he had not anointed his head. What a contrast with this woman! How much love and repentance she had shown! Her sins were forgiven.

Mary and Martha (Luke 10³⁸⁻⁴²)

Martha was busy with the work of the house while Mary sat and listened to Jesus. Martha asked Jesus to tell Mary to help. Jesus told her that although she was bothered about lots of things that seemed important to her, only one thing really mattered – the word of God. Mary had chosen what was better.

Zacchaeus (Luke 19¹⁻¹⁰)

Zacchaeus was a tax collector. This made him a social outcast for two reasons.

1. He was working for the Romans – and that meant he was a traitor.
2. Tax collectors had a reputation for cheating people. Zacchaeus himself may have been admitting it when

he said to Jesus, 'If I have cheated anybody out of anything, I will pay back four times the amount.'

Zacchaeus had to climb a tree to see Jesus. Jesus saw him and clearly knew who and what he was. Some people criticized Jesus for visiting a man of bad reputation. To Jesus, Zacchaeus' change of heart meant that he had been saved.

Jesus was always concerned with the needs of individuals. He stressed the importance of individual human beings by saying that God cares for individual sparrows – and human beings are far more important than sparrows. God knows each individual person so well that he knows the number of hairs on each person's head (Luke 12⁴⁻⁷).

Key events in Jesus' ministry
The day Peter said that Jesus was the Christ (Luke 9¹⁸⁻²⁷)

Jesus asked the disciples who the crowds said he was. They told him – John the Baptist, or Elijah, or a prophet from long ago. 'What about you? Who do you say I am?' Peter answered, 'The Christ of God'. Jesus told them they must tell no one, because the Son of Man had to suffer many things, be killed and rise again. He added that anyone who wanted to follow him had to be ready to take up the cross and follow him – in other words, to be completely committed. If anyone was ashamed to be a follower of Jesus, Jesus himself would be ashamed of that person at the end of the world.

This event was a key moment, because for the first time one of Jesus' followers openly said that Jesus was the Christ – the Messiah.

The transfiguration (Luke 9²⁸⁻³⁶)

Eight days after Peter said that Jesus was the Christ, Jesus took Peter, James and John up a mountain to pray. While he was praying, he changed, and his clothes became dazzling white. Two men appeared with Jesus – Moses and Elijah; they talked with him about what Jesus would do in Jerusalem and what would happen to him there. The three disciples did not know what to make of this. Peter offered to make three shelters for them – but he did not really know what he was saying. Then a cloud came over them, and a voice was heard from the cloud: 'This is my Son, whom I have chosen; listen to him.' The three looked – and Jesus was alone.

The disciples would have realized the significance of some of what they saw. Their old religion was based on the law and the prophets. There was Jesus with Moses, giver of the law, and Elijah, perhaps the greatest of the prophets. It was as though the old religion was honouring Jesus. Even more, the cloud in the Old Testament could represent the presence of God – while the voice from heaven was the voice of God the Father. The whole event showed that Jesus had the power and authority of God.

Examination guidance

A Does it matter to Christians whether the miracles of Jesus actually happened?

B Do miracles happen today?

Both these are issues that the SEG Religious Studies A syllabus says candidates must have considered.

To answer the questions properly you must show what you understand by the word 'miracle'. A miracle is something outstandingly good which, in the ordinary course of events, cannot or does not happen. A miracle may go against the known laws of nature. It is something for which there is no natural explanation.

A Does it matter to Christians?

First, two questions need to be asked about the description of any miracle. Did it happen? Was it a miracle that it happened? Take, for instance, the calming of the storm (Luke 8$^{22-26}$). When Jesus told the storm to calm, did it happen? If so, was it a miracle or just plain chance? This is an open question, which means you may answer 'yes' or 'no'. What really matters is the way in which you offer your reasons for your opinion.

What this question is asking, of course, is not whether the miracles happened but whether it matters to Christians.

Some say, 'Yes, it does matter that the miracles really happened.'

- If we cannot believe what the gospel writers say about the miracles, how can we rely on the rest of what they write?
- If Jesus let people believe that he was healing people through miracles while really he was using some medical knowledge that others did not have at that time, he was deceiving them. That would mean saying the miracles were con tricks.
- The miracles are important because they are signs. They show that Jesus had much greater power than an ordinary human being could have. His power over the normal laws of nature is a sign that he is God the Son.

Others say, 'No, it does not matter whether the miracles really happened.'

- Christians believe in Jesus as the Son of God because of his teaching and because of his death on the cross and his resurrection. The miracles feel strange. One can believe in God and still not believe in miracles.
- Perhaps the miracles are parables. The writers did not expect them to be taken literally. They are to show the power of Jesus. For instance, Jesus has such great authority as Son of God that it is as if he could control the wind and the waves.

B Do miracles happen today?

If you answer 'yes', then clearly you must give examples. Such examples may be from your own knowledge rather than from textbooks. For instance, if you know of services of healing through the laying-on of hands, or if you know of people who have recovered after prayer when doctors had given up hope, by all means write about those cases. The examiner should give credit – up to full marks – for the way you present your response.

You could use an example of a miracle accepted by the Catholic Church. Such an example is the healing of John Fagan of Glasgow. In March 1967 he had been suffering for some time from cancer. Doctors had given up all hope of his recovery. He had not eaten for weeks. When he started to vomit up black lumpy matter the doctor assumed that his stomach was breaking up. People in his parish continued to pray to Blessed John Ogilvie for him. As his wife watched by his bed she tried to hear and feel his heartbeat but there was nothing. She thought he had died. Then she heard him say, 'Mary, I'm hungry'. Gradually his health built up and he was able to return to normal life. The Vatican carried out the most exhaustive tests and examination of medical records. No explanation could be found. The Pope declared the case a miracle – evidence for the canonization of John Ogilvy.

Do not lose sight of what you have said a miracle is. Make sure that any examples measure up to what you have said.

If you answer 'No', do still say what a miracle is and, if possible, give examples of what others claim to be miracles, such as those described above, and give your reasons for rejecting them. Give more general arguments as well. For instance, you may argue that if something happens that cannot be explained, it may well be that there is an explanation that nobody has spotted. Perhaps future scientific progress will show how the person was healed or why the unexplained event happened.

Examination practice

1. What happened when Jesus was transfigured? What did the event mean to the disciples who saw it?
   (6 marks)
   Write about half to three-quarters of a side of A4.

2. Describe Jesus' meeting with Zacchaeus. Why were some people surprised that Jesus visited Zacchaeus' house? (7 marks)
   Write about half to three-quarters of a side of A4.

3. Jesus told Martha, 'Mary has chosen what is better'. What had Mary chosen? Do you think it is possible for Christians to follow Mary's example rather than Martha's? (7 marks)
   Write about half to three-quarters of a side of A4.

Introduction

There are not many parables in the gospels of Mark or John. We find most of Jesus' parables in the gospels of Matthew and Luke. In this section we have included parables found only in Luke's gospel (apart from the parable of the lost sheep, which also comes in Matthew's gospel).

A parable is a story, usually quite short. The story has a meaning about God or his kingdom.

Some writers make a distinction between a **parable** and an **allegory**. What we call a parable, they call a story – the story can be either a parable or an allegory. How do they decide which is which? Take the story of the lost sheep (see the seventh parable below).

If it is a parable, it has a **simple** meaning; for example, that God is keen to forgive people.

If it is an allegory, it has a **detailed** meaning. For example:

- the shepherd is God,
- the lost sheep is a sinner,
- the 99 sheep are good people,
- the shepherd looking for the lost sheep is God looking for sinners who want to repent,
- the celebrating is the reaction in heaven when a sinner repents.

The parables

Two debtors (Luke 7$^{40–43}$)

We will find this parable easier to understand if we know its setting.

Jesus went to a Pharisee's house for dinner. A woman, who led a sinful life, came into the house and stood crying behind Jesus. Her tears wet his feet; she then dried his feet, kissed them and poured perfume on them. The Pharisee thought that if Jesus were really a prophet he would know what a sinful life this woman led.

Jesus then told the parable of the two debtors.

- Two men owed money to a money lender: one owed 500 silver coins and the other 50.
- Neither could repay the money, so the lender cancelled their debts.
- Which of the two would be more grateful?

Jesus explained the meaning of this parable. Those who have sinned much and have been forgiven for it show more gratitude than those who have been forgiven a little.

Good Samaritan (Luke 10$^{25–37}$)

- A man was attacked by robbers and left half dead.
- A priest walked past and took no notice.
- Another religious Jew (a Levite) did the same.
- But a Samaritan – an enemy of Jews – saw the injured Jew and had compassion; the Samaritan stopped and helped.
- He took the injured man to an inn and paid the innkeeper to tend him back to health.
- Jesus asked which of the three acted like a neighbour. He implied that the meaning of this parable is: do good to everyone, including our enemies.

Friend asking for help at midnight (Luke 11$^{5–8}$)

Jesus taught his disciples the Lord's prayer (which starts: 'Father, hallowed be your name'). He then told this parable, which is about how to pray. Jesus said to his disciples:

- One of you goes to a friend at midnight and asks to borrow three loaves, because of an unexpected visitor.
- The friend replies that he and his family are trying to sleep, and they want to be left alone.

Jesus commented that the friend might not give the bread because you are his friend; but he will eventually give it to you if you keep on asking him.

Jesus did not explain this parable. There is disagreement about the meaning of it. Some say it means that if we keep on praying, God will give us what we want. Others say it means that we should keep on praying, even though God does not give us what we want.

Rich fool (Luke 12$^{16–21}$)

- There was a rich farmer who had a marvellous crop one year.
- He knew he could not store the crop in his barns; so he resolved to built bigger ones.
- Then he would have enough wealth to take life easy for many years – he could enjoy himself.
- But God told the rich man he would die that night; someone else would inherit his wealth.

Jesus explained this parable: this is how it is with those who become wealthy, but do not do what God wants.

Unfruitful fig tree / Barren fig tree (Luke 13⁶⁻⁹)

- A man had a fig tree growing in his vineyard.
- He looked for figs, but found none.
- He told his gardener that there had been no figs for three years, so he should cut it down.
- The gardener recommended tending the tree for one more year.
- If there was fruit, then everything would be fine.
- If not, the master could chop down the tree.

Jesus did not explain this parable. Some people suggest the parable means: that Jesus had taught and worked with his fellow Jews, but they did not accept him as God's messenger. Consequently, God's message should be preached to non-Jews (Gentiles), who would believe it.

Tower builder and warring king (Luke 14²⁸⁻³²)

- If we decide to build a tower, we will first see if we can afford it.
- Otherwise, people will laugh at us because we have a half-completed building.
- If a king has 10 000 soldiers against an invading king who has 20 000 soldiers, he will carefully consider whether he can win.
- If he cannot, he will ask the invader for a peaceful settlement.

Jesus explained these parables: anyone who wants to follow him must realize what it involves – 'anyone who does not carry his cross and follow me cannot be my disciple . . . any of you who does not give up everything he has, cannot be my disciple.'

Lost sheep (Luke 15¹⁻⁷)

Jesus told this parable, and the following two parables, because the Pharisees and teachers of the law grumbled that he welcomed outcasts (rejects, people that nobody likes) and ate with them (a sign of friendship).

- Suppose one of us has 100 sheep and loses one of them.
- He leaves the 99 and looks for the lost sheep until he finds it.
- He is then so happy, he carries it home on his shoulders.
- He calls his friends and neighbours to celebrate with him.

Jesus explained this parable: God is more delighted by one sinner who repents (is sorry), than by 99 good people who do not need to be sorry.

Lost coin (Luke 15⁸⁻¹⁰)

- A woman has ten silver coins and loses one of them.

- She lights a lamp and sweeps everywhere in the house till she finds it.
- She is so happy to find it, she calls her friends to celebrate with her.

Jesus explained: God is so happy when one sinner repents.

Forgiving father / Lost son / Prodigal son (Luke 15¹¹⁻³²)

- A man had two sons.
- The younger one wanted his share of the property before his father died.
- The father agreed.
- The younger son sold his share of the property and went abroad with the money.
- He spent everything he had in reckless living.
- He ended up working on a pig farm.
- He was so hungry he decided to go home and seek a job with his father, telling his father he was not fit to be called his son – he had sinned against God and against his father.
- The father saw his son when he was a long way off, and he ran to his son to welcome him.
- The son said he was not fit to be called a son, but the father had a big celebration: he gave his son some expensive clothes and he killed the prize calf, 'for this son of mine was dead, but now he is alive'.
- Meanwhile, the elder son heard the celebrations.
- He became so angry when he learnt the reason for them, he would not go into the house.
- So the father came to the elder son and begged him to come in.

His father saw him and was filled with compassion for him: he ran to his son and threw his arms around him

- The elder son protested he had been a loyal worker for his father, that the younger son had been disloyal and wasted money, yet the father gave the younger son, not the elder son, a feast.
- The father answered, 'Everything I have is yours, and you are always with me. Your brother was dead, but now he is alive – so we had to celebrate.'

Jesus did not explain the meaning of this parable. You will notice that the parable can have many meanings. Make sure you include the following when you give an explanation. The father stands for God who is always waiting to forgive, as soon as someone is sorry. The younger son stands for people who are selfish, greedy and so on; they turn to God when they realize they need him. The elder son stands for those who refuse to forgive; they reject God when he forgives.

Shrewd manager / Unjust steward (Luke 16$^{1-8}$)

- An owner, a rich man, learnt that his manager was wasting money.
- So the owner called the manager, demanded an explanation, and threatened to sack him.
- The manager knew he would find it difficult to cope with other jobs, such as digging ditches or begging.
- So, to have friends after he lost his job, he called those who owed his master money or goods and told them to write a lesser amount on their account.
- The owner praised the manager for behaving shrewdly (cleverly).

Jesus did not explain the meaning of this parable. Nor is the meaning obvious. Here is one possible interpretation: prepare sensibly for the day when you will meet God.

Rich man and Lazarus (Luke 16$^{19-31}$)

- There was a rich man who lived in luxury every day.
- There was a very poor man, Lazarus, who hoped to eat the rich man's leftovers.
- The poor man died and went to heaven.
- The rich man died and went to hell, where he was in pain.
- He asked Abraham to send Lazarus with a drop of water to relieve the pain.
- Abraham told the rich man that he had his good time on earth, and that it was not possible to cross from heaven to hell.
- The rich man then wanted his five brothers warned about this place of pain.
- Abraham replied that they had Moses and the prophets to warn them.
- The rich man said that this was not enough; but he was sure that they would listen to someone who rose from the dead.
- Abraham said that if they would not listen to Moses and the prophets, they would not listen to someone who rose from the dead.

Jesus gave no explanation of this parable. It may mean: if the Jews at the time of Jesus would not take any notice of the teaching of Moses and the prophets, they would not listen to Jesus' teaching. In most parables you can clearly distinguish the story and its meaning. In this parable it is difficult to disentangle the story from its meaning.

Servant's duty / Servant's reward (Luke 17$^{7-10}$)

Jesus said to his disciples:

- Suppose one of us has a servant or slave, who comes home after his day's work, perhaps ploughing or looking after the sheep.
- Do you tell him to have his dinner, or to prepare dinner for you?
- The second, of course; the servant can have his meal after he has prepared yours.
- The servant does not deserve thanks for obeying orders.

Jesus explained that this parable was about his disciples: they should compare themselves with the servant in the story. When they have done everything they were told to do, they should say, 'We are unworthy servants; we have only done our duty.'

Widow and judge / Unjust judge (Luke 18$^{1-8}$)

- There was a judge who neither respected God nor cared about people.
- There was also a widow; she kept asking the judge to put right an injustice someone did to her.
- The judge kept refusing – he was not interested in her or her case – until he became exasperated by her continual pestering.
- He then heard her case and gave her justice.

Jesus told his disciples this parable to teach them that they should always pray and not give up.

Pharisee and tax collector (Luke 18$^{9-14}$)

- Two men went to the temple to pray.
- One was a Pharisee and the other was a tax collector.
- The Pharisee prayed: 'Thank you God that I am not like others, such as this tax collector, who are greedy, dishonest and commit adultery.
- 'I fast twice a week and I give one tenth of my earnings to the church.'
- The tax collector stood at a distance and bowed his head.
- He prayed: 'God, have mercy on me – I have done wrong.'

Jesus told this parable to those who were confident they were good people and who looked down on everybody else. He said that the second man pleased God, not the first.

Examination guidance

Re-tell the main points in the parable of the good Samaritan. (5 marks)

First answer

An old man had been assaulted and robbed in the street and he needed help. Various people started to walk by but nobody bothered even to look at him. Until one man, a foreigner, decided to help him out. The person didn't know the man who had been assalted he only helped him becasue he neded help. The meaning to this parable is if someone needs help even if you don't know them, help them out, don't leave it to the next person who walks by because the next person might not care.

This candidate has written a couple of the main points – that a man was robbed and assaulted; that a foreigner helped him.

The candidate's answer just merits two marks, but only just. The re-telling of the story is not very accurate, and there is waffle and repetition in the answer.

This candidate would have a poor mark for spelling, punctuation and grammar.
(Score: 2 marks out of 5)

Second answer

A man was lying on a road after being attacked by bandits. Some people (including a priest) walked past on the other side of the road and would not help even though the injured man was a Jew like them. A Samaritan, however, saw the man and decided to help. He dressed his wounds and took the man to an inn. He gave the innkeeper money for the man and said that he would make up the money if any extra was needed.

This candidate has included the main points in the story.

The candidate has not written every detail of the story, but that is not necessary, as the question asks for the main points in the story. This candidate is able to distinguish the main points from the detail in the story.
(Score: 5 marks out of 5)

Examination practice

1. What is a parable? How is it different from an allegory? (3 marks)
   Write about six lines of A4.

2. Re-tell: the parable of the rich man and Lazarus, and the parable of the Pharisee and tax collector. Explain how **one** of them illustrates an important theme in Luke's gospel. (10 marks)
   Write about one side of A4.

3. These two parables are about prayer: the parable of the widow and the judge; and the parable of friend asking for help at midnight.

   What might a Christian learn from them? (6 marks)
   Write about half a side of A4.

4. Choose **two** parables from Luke's gospel. Show how they might influence Christians to be less selfish. (6 marks)
   Write about half a side of A4.

5. 'The parable of the forgiving father (lost son) has little to teach an ordinary family.'
   Do you agree? Give reasons for your view. Show that you have considered the alternative view. (8 marks)
   Write about three-quarters of a side of A4.

LUKE'S GOSPEL – PASSION AND RESURRECTION 20

Introduction

Although Luke was not a Jew, his account of the suffering, death and resurrection states firmly that the Messiah had to suffer, die and rise again. The prophets in the Old Testament had foretold that all this would happen.

The suffering and death is not presented as a sad fate. Jesus is fulfilling his destiny, triumphantly completing what is necessary to gain forgiveness for the sins of all members of the human race.

The arrest of Jesus

Luke 22[35–53]: At the end of the last supper Jesus reminded the disciples that when he had sent them out to preach, without money or possessions, they found they were given everything they needed. Then he told them that at this time they would need a purse, a bag, even a sword. He was going to be arrested, as the prophets had said. 'Here are two swords,' they said. 'It is enough', replied Jesus.

It is not clear what Jesus meant when he told them that there might be a need for a sword. When the soldiers came to arrest him he stopped the disciple who tried to defend him. It was not his way to meet physical violence with physical violence. For instance, in the Sermon on the Mount he said 'If someone strikes you on the one cheek, turn to him the other also'.

Jesus went to pray on the Mount of Olives. He left the disciples to pray while he went apart from them. He prayed that he might not have to suffer – but if it was God's will, then he would accept it. 'Father, if you are willing. take this cup from me; yet not my will, but yours be done.' He went back and found the disciples were asleep.

Judas brought some men to trap Jesus. He kissed Jesus – a common greeting at that time and in that place. The kiss was the signal that Jesus was the one the crowd were looking for. Jesus knew it. He said, 'Judas, are you betraying the Son of Man with a kiss?'

One of Jesus' followers drew his sword and cut off the ear of the high priest's servant. This was a brave act; if the soldiers had attacked him for doing that, he would not have had a chance. Jesus checked the disciple and healed the servant.

Peter denied that he knew Jesus

Luke 22[54–62]: Jesus was taken into the house of the high priest. Peter followed at a distance and went into the courtyard. He was asked three times, by different people, if he was a follower of Jesus. (What gave him away was that people could tell he was from Galilee because he spoke with a Galilean accent.) Each time he said he was not. The third time he heard the cock crow. Peter remembered that Jesus had told him that before the cock crowed he would three times deny that he knew Jesus. He went out and wept.

Jesus tried by the Council

Luke 22[63–71]: At his trial the chief priests and teachers of the law asked Jesus directly if he was the Christ, the Son of God. When he made clear that he was, they condemned him. He had made himself equal to God. That meant he was guilty of blasphemy, for which the penalty was death.

The Roman trial

Luke 23[1–25]: The priests and teachers of the law brought Jesus to Pilate, the Roman governor. Pilate alone had the power to confirm a death sentence.

They told Pilate that Jesus had been stirring up rebellion. They said he was against paying taxes to Caesar and that he claimed to be the Christ – in other words, they said, he was claiming to be a king. All these charges – leading rebellion, telling people not to pay tax, saying he was a king – were treason against the Roman Emperor. If Jesus was guilty, Pilate would have to put him to death.

Pilate believed Jesus was innocent. He tried to get out of sentencing him.

When he realized Jesus was from Galilee, Pilate sent him to Herod, ruler of Galilee, who happened to be in Jerusalem at that time. Herod had wanted to see Jesus because he had heard about the miracles. Jesus would not answer Herod, so Herod and his soldiers made fun of him. They dressed him up as a king and sent him back to Pilate.

Pilate made the Jews an offer. As Jesus was innocent, Pilate would simply punish him and let him go. (A strange sort of justice, but Pilate wanted to satisfy the noisy crowd.) The crowd instead demanded the release of Barabbas, who was in prison for rebellion and murder. (We know from the other gospels that every year Pilate used to release one prisoner, chosen by the people.)

The crowd were so insistent that Pilate gave way and sent Jesus to be crucified.

The crucifixion

Luke 23[32–49]: He was crucified at the Place of the Skull, between two criminals. As he was nailed to the cross Jesus prayed for those who were crucifying him: 'Father, forgive them, for they do not know what they are doing.'

The onlookers and the soldiers mocked him. The onlookers said, 'If you are the Christ, save yourself.' The soldiers said, 'If you are the king of the Jews, save yourself.'

One of the criminals mocked Jesus and said, 'Aren't you the Christ? Save yourself and us!' The other told him to be quiet. They deserved to die. Jesus was innocent. He turned to Jesus. 'Jesus, remember me when you come into your kingdom.' Jesus promised him, 'Today you will be with me in paradise.'

Jesus' dying words were 'Father, into your hands I commit my spirit.' The centurion, the Roman officer in charge of the crucifixion, was moved to say, 'Surely this was a righteous man.'

The burial

Luke 23[50–56]:

- Joseph of Arimathea, a member of the Jewish Council, asked Pilate for Jesus' body so he could bury it.
- The body was wrapped in a linen cloth and placed in a tomb cut out of the rock.
- The women prepared spices and perfumes to complete the burial. As the next day was the Sabbath, they left the body as it was in the tomb, until the first day of the following week.

The empty tomb

Luke 24$^{1-12}$:

- After the Sabbath, on the first day of the week, the women came early to the tomb. They found the stone rolled away, but no body.
- Two men dressed in gleaming white said to them, 'Why do you look for the living among the dead? He is not here, he has risen!' The men reminded them that Jesus had said he would suffer, die and rise again.
- When the women told the 11 disciples what they had seen, the disciples did not believe them. Peter went to look for himself and came away wondering what had happened.

Resurrection appearances

Luke 24$^{13-53}$:

- On the evening of the day of the resurrection, Jesus appeared to two followers who were walking to Emmaus, a village about 7 miles from Jerusalem. They did not recognize him. He asked them why they were so sad.

    They told him, 'Jesus of Nazareth was a prophet. Our religious leaders crucified him. We had hoped he was the Messiah. Some women went to his grave this morning and it was empty. Some angels told them he was alive.'

    Jesus said, 'How foolish you are, and how slow of heart to believe all that the prophets have spoken!' He told them that the prophets had said the Messiah would suffer.

    They came to their home in Emmaus. They invited him to stay the night with them. He took bread, gave thanks, broke it and gave it to them. At once they recognized him. Instantly he disappeared.

- The two followers rushed back to Jerusalem. The others told them that Jesus had appeared to Simon.
- As they talked, Jesus appeared among them. He said, 'Peace be with you.' They thought he was a ghost. To reassure them, he showed them the wounds in his hands and side and ate a piece of fish.
- He told them that he had died and risen again because this is what the prophets had foretold; there would be forgiveness for those who repented.
- His disciples were the witnesses who had to tell people of all nations. They had to wait in Jerusalem until they received power from God.

    Jesus took the disciples to Bethany, just outside Jerusalem. There he ascended to heaven. Joyfully the disciples went back to Jerusalem.

Examination guidance

1. Describe the trial of Jesus by Pilate. Why did Pilate find it so difficult to decide what to do with Jesus? (12 marks)

2. Give an account of Jesus walking with two people to Emmaus. Pay particular attention to what was said. (8 marks)

1. Jesus was sent to Pilate by the priests, who told Pilate that he had to put Jesus to death. Pilate sent him to Herod but Herod simply sent him back again. Pilate told the people he would punish Jesus and release him. They shouted that they wanted Pilate to release Barabbas instead. Pilate asked what Jesus had done wrong. They didn't answer. They just shouted 'Crucify him.' Pilate was frightened of them so he did want they wanted.

Much more detail could be given here. Nothing is said about what the priests told Pilate about Jesus. The candidate does not explain that Pilate sent Jesus to Herod because Jesus was from Galilee and Herod was King of Galilee. Herod was in Jerusalem for the Passover, so Pilate could easily send Jesus to him.

Nothing is said here about the way Herod treated Jesus. A candidate could argue that when Jesus was with Herod he was not with Pilate and so there is no need to write about what happened when Jesus did visit Herod. However, a candidate who did explain why Herod made fun of Jesus would probably receive credit.

The candidate gives a brief account of the rest of the trial by Pilate, but does not say much about why things were said and done.

Why was it difficult for Pilate to know what to do?

- He knew in his heart that Jesus was innocent.
- If he let Jesus go free there might be trouble with the priests and others. His job was to avoid trouble.

(Score: 6 marks out of 12)

2. On the first Easter Sunday Jesus was walking to Emmaus, which is a village near Jerusalem, with two of his followers, who did not see who he was. He asked them why they were upset. They told him that Jesus of Nazareth had been a great teacher. They thought he was the Messiah. But the priests had turned against him and had him put to death. Then, that morning, some women said that some angels had said he was alive again. If he was, no one had seen him. Jesus told them that this is what they should expect because it is what the prophets said. They were amazed. When they got to Emmaus they asked him if he would like to stay with them. They gave him some bread to eat. When he broke it and said a prayer they recognized him but he vanished.

The candidate has covered the main points well. The answer could contain more details. For instance, the candidate does not describe how, when Jesus joined them, they were kept from recognising him. None the less, the main points are all given accurately.
(Score: 7 marks out of 8)

LUKE'S GOSPEL – SPECIAL EMPHASES 21

Who was Luke?

Luke was not a Jew. He did not see Jesus during his ministry. He was a doctor, who became a friend of Paul and sometimes travelled with him when Paul was going from place to place teaching people about Jesus Christ.

Why did he write his gospel? (Luke 1$^{1-4}$)

He tells us this in his first four verses – the opening verses of Chapter 1.

- Many others had written about the things that had happened – relying on eyewitnesses. Luke thought it right to write an account that was orderly and reliable.
- He addressed his gospel to 'Theophilus'. The word means 'lover of God' or 'beloved by God'. So Theophilus may have been an individual Christian, or the word may mean that the gospel is for any Christian, anyone beloved of God or who loves God.

Luke's gospel is one of the three **synoptic** gospels. The others are Matthew and Mark. They all have the same general pattern.

- Near the beginning they describe how John the Baptist was preparing for the coming of the Messiah and how he baptized Jesus.
- They describe his ministry, with the event at Caesarea Philippi as a turning point in the middle. Much of what Mark, the first of them to write, put in his gospel is also to be found in much the same words in Matthew and Luke.
- They give great detail in their descriptions of the events leading up to the death of Jesus. Here again the order of events and the words used are very similar in all three synoptic gospels – Matthew, Mark and Luke.
- They all describe what happened after the resurrection of Jesus. In Mark the account is shorter – he describes only the discovery of the empty tomb. In this part of the gospels the other writers, Matthew and Luke – and John as well, for that matter – all have a series of accounts of times when people really did see Jesus. It seems that for each it is important to say that Jesus really did rise from the dead. So, each describes eyewitness accounts, given by people who had seen Jesus for themselves. The fact that so many people saw Jesus is part of the proof that he truly rose from the dead.

So, what is special about Luke's gospel?

1. He stresses the importance of the Holy Spirit

- Note how often the Holy Spirit comes into the descriptions of the events concerning the births of John and Jesus (Luke 1–2). John was to be filled with the Holy Spirit from the time of his birth. The Holy Spirit caused Mary to conceive. Elizabeth, Zechariah and Simeon were all filled with the Holy Spirit.
- The Holy Spirit appeared when Jesus was baptized (3^{22}).
- The Holy Spirit is mentioned as being with Jesus on some occasions – such as when he was tempted (4^1) or when he preached at Nazareth (4$^{16-30}$ – see the comment below).

2.   The gospel is a **joyful** message

- The angel brought the shepherds 'good news of great joy' (2^{10}).
- When Christians are persecuted they should rejoice, because a reward in heaven awaits them (6^{23}).
- The 72 returned from their mission with joy (10^{17}). Jesus rejoiced with them (10^{21}).
- People rejoiced at the miracles of Jesus (13^{17}).
- There is joy in heaven when a sinner repents (15^{1-10}).
- The disciples responded with joy to the news that Jesus had risen (24^{41}) and ascended (24^{50}).

3.   He makes clear that Jesus came for everybody, of any nationality

Note how Luke chooses teachings and incidents that stress that Jesus came to save everyone. He presents them in a positive way. He does not try to criticize the Jewish people but to show that Jesus welcomed people of every race and nation.

- When Luke gives a list of the ancestors of Jesus he does not trace it back only to Abraham, as Matthew does. He traces it back to 'Adam, the son of God'.
- He describes the visit of Jesus to Nazareth (4^{16-30}) in a way that shows that Jesus was concerned with all nations. The people thought that they were God's chosen people and so the Messiah would come to them alone. Jesus made it clear to them that God cares for all nations.

   When Jesus, filled with the Holy Spirit, went to the synagogue in Nazareth, he was invited to read and to speak. He read from the scriptures and then said, 'Today the scripture is fulfilled in your hearing.' There was great excitement. But what he said next upset the people in the synagogue. He pointed out to them that two of the greatest prophets had helped Gentiles when they could have helped Jews. During a famine Elijah helped a widow in Sidon, not a Jewess. The leper whom Elisha healed was not a Jew but Naaman the Syrian. The people were furious. They took Jesus out of the town and were ready to throw him down the cliff; but he walked through the crowd and went away.
- When Jesus healed the centurion's servant (7^{1-10}) he was impressed by the centurion's faith. He said that he had not found so much faith, even in Israel. The centurion himself was not a Jew.
- One of the best known of Jesus' parables is the good Samaritan (10^{25-37}), in which the key person is the Samaritan, one of the traditional enemies of the Jews.
- Note how, in the healing of the ten lepers (17^{11-19}), the point is made that it was the foreigner who came back to thank Jesus.

Because Luke intended his gospel to be read by people of all nations, he made sure that anyone of any background could understand it. He didn't use words that only Jews would be likely to understand, such as 'rabbi' or 'scribe'.

Instead of 'rabbi' he wrote 'master' and instead of 'scribe' he wrote 'lawyer'.

4.   Luke shows his sympathy for poor people

- Jesus was placed in a manger when he was born. His first visitors were some ordinary working people, the shepherds (Luke 2^{1-20}).
- Luke does not hide the fact that Jesus was brought up in a poor family. The law of Moses stated that when a woman came to be purified after childbirth she was to bring as an offering 'a year-old lamb for a burnt offering and a young pigeon or a dove for a sin offering . . . If she cannot afford a lamb, she is to bring two doves or two young pigeons' (Leviticus $12^{6,8}$). Mary brought the cheaper offering – and Luke says so (Luke 2^{24}).
- In two places Jesus said that he had come to preach to the poor (Luke 4^{18}, 7^{22}).
- The parable of the great banquet stresses that people of every social background may enter heaven (Luke 14^{15-24}). In another parable it is the poor beggar Lazarus who, after death, goes to Abraham's side, not the rich man (Luke 16^{19-31}).

5.   Luke stresses that Jesus did not reject the social outcasts

- Jesus showed understanding and forgiveness to the sinful woman who washed and anointed his feet (Luke 7^{36-50}).
- Tax collectors were social outcasts – see what is said about the reasons for this in Chapter C18, *Luke's gospel – the ministry of Jesus*, regarding Zacchaeus. Yet Jesus accepted Zacchaeus (Luke 19^{1-10}). In the parable of the Pharisee and the tax collector (Luke 18^{9-14}) it is the tax collector who has Jesus' approval.
- When the criminal who was being crucified admitted his crimes and asked Jesus to remember him, Jesus replied, 'Today you will be with me in paradise' (23^{39-43}).

6.   Women are mentioned in Luke's gospel more than in the others

- Luke may well have learned from Mary about the events he describes in Chapters 1 and 2. Note how he describes her thoughts and feelings in Chapter 2, verses 19, 50, 51 – for example, 'Mary treasured up all these things and pondered them in her heart' (2^{19}).
- When Luke describes how Jesus raised to life the son of the widow at Nain, he makes a point of saying that Jesus' heart went out to her.
- Immediately after his account of Jesus' forgiving the sinful woman Luke mentions a group of women among his followers (7^{36}–8^3).
- Jesus had a special word for the women who wept as he was taken to be crucified (23^{26-31}).

- Jesus' attitude to women was in strong contrast with the attitude of most people at the time. In the family, in religious matters and in society as a whole they were regarded as inferior to men.

7. Luke mentions prayer in a number of ways

- In the first two chapters he includes four songs of praise, which are used by Christians in their worship (1^{46-55}, 1^{68-79}, 2^{14}, 2^{29-32}).
- He mentions a number of times when Jesus prayed – for example, at his baptism and before choosing the 12 disciples.
- The words of the Lord's Prayer are given in Luke's gospel (11^{1-4}). (The prayer is also to be found in Matthew, in the Sermon on the Mount.)
- Three parables about prayer are only to be found in

Luke – the friend at midnight (11^{5-13}), the persistent widow (18^{1-8}) and the Pharisee and the tax collector (18^{9-14}).

Examination practice

1. Choose a parable from Luke's gospel that teaches about prayer. Tell the parable in your own words and explain its meaning. (8 marks)
   Write about three-quarters of a side of A4.

2. Describe an occasion in Luke's gospel when Jesus met someone who was not a Jew. How does the incident show Jesus' attitude to people of other nations? (8 marks)

   Write about three-quarters of a side of A4.

THE ACTS OF THE APOSTLES – MAIN THEMES 22

Introduction

The book of Acts was written by Luke as a sequel to his gospel. It describes the early years of the Christian Church. It contains many decisive events from those early years.

The book is called The Acts of the Apostles because it describes how the first Christians, especially the apostles, spread the gospel. In a sense, it should be called The Acts of the Holy Spirit. So often in the book the writer says that something is said or done or guided by the Holy Spirit. See the last section of this chapter.

Note that the MEG syllabus is entitled 'Christianity through a study of Luke and Acts'. Throughout this section candidates preparing for the MEG examination should look for ways in which the texts are relevant to Christianity today.

- The festivals of Ascension and Pentecost/Whitsun should be studied along with the accounts in Acts 1 and 2; see Chapter A15, *Other festivals*.
- When studying the passages concerning the work of the Holy Spirit in the Church, reference should be made to Chapter C5, *God – the Holy Spirit*. The syllabus specifies a study of the Pentecostal movement in the

church; refer to Chapter D5, *The Church: Catholic, Orthodox, Protestant*, and Chapter A2, *Collective worship, non-liturgical*.
- When you study the section 'The first Jewish Christians and their community life' in this chapter you should ask, 'Could – or should – this system be used today?'
- MEG state: 'Candidates should know and understand the importance of the conversion of Paul and of his subsequent missionary work and should relate this to the evangelizing work of the church today'.

The ascension

Acts 1^{9-11}: Jesus was with the disciples on the Mount of Olives, overlooking the city of Jerusalem. As he spoke to them, he went up until a cloud hid him and they could not see him any longer. Two men in white appeared to them. They told the disciples that one day Jesus would return, just as he had gone from them into heaven.

The ascension was an important event in the lives of the disciples. It convinced them that Jesus was in glory in heaven. He was no longer on earth to lead them. From now on the future of the Church depended on them.

The Holy Spirit

Acts 2: Ten days after the ascension, the disciples were together in Jerusalem. Suddenly they were overwhelmed with power – power of the Holy Spirit. The power came dramatically. There was a great rushing wind, filling the place where they were. Tongues of fire appeared on the head of each. They were filled with the Holy Spirit. Out they went to preach and to convert.

At the time, Jerusalem was full of Jews who lived in all parts of the eastern Mediterranean area and beyond. It was the Feast of Pentecost, one of the great festivals for which people flocked to the ancient city. They heard the noise. They saw the commotion around 12 men preaching with great excitement and enthusiasm. They went to listen, wondering what it was all about. Some thought that, even so early in the morning, they were drunk.

Peter had this great opportunity to preach. He told them

- The Spirit of God is causing us to preach.
- Jesus was sent by God.
- You killed him.
- God has raised him from the dead.
- This is just what the prophets said would happen.
- We are witnesses of these things. We saw them and know they are true.
- Repent and be baptized.

Peter's words had a great impact. 3000 people were baptized. That is how the Christian Church began. From now on the 12 were no longer called disciples, which means 'learners'. They were called **apostles** – men sent out with a mission.

The power of the Spirit in the Church

Acts 3^{1-10}; 9^{32-43}: Inspired by the belief that the Holy Spirit was with them, the apostles preached and performed miracles, always in the name of Jesus.

- Peter and John went to the temple to pray. At the Beautiful Gate a lame man asked them for money. Peter healed with the words 'Silver or gold I do not have, but what I have I give you. In the name of Jesus Christ of Nazareth, walk.'
- Peter healed a paralytic called Aeneas, saying 'Jesus Christ heals you. Get up and tidy up your mat.'
- Peter was called to Joppa because a Christian woman called Tabitha or Dorcas had died. She had done a great deal to help the poor. Peter raised her to life with the words, 'Tabitha, get up'. Almost certainly he was echoing the words of Jesus when he raised the dead daughter of Jairus – '*Talitha, koum*' (Mark 5^{41}).

The first Jewish Christians and their community life

Acts 2^{42-47}, 4^{32-37}, 5^{1-11}, 6^{1-6}:

- The first Christians were a very close fellowship. They met regularly to hear the apostles' teaching and to pray.
- They also met for the breaking of bread. They broke bread together in two ways. They received bread and wine in Holy Communion as the body and blood of Christ. They also met for a fellowship meal. This meal they called the *agape*. *Agape* is a Greek word meaning 'love'.
- They shared their possessions. Those who owned land or houses sold them and put the money into a common fund. Barnabas is named as one who sold his field in this way. Ananias and Sapphira, who said they had done the same but had kept back part of the money, both died suddenly – it was said, as a punishment.

Sharing the possessions was a wonderful ideal, but it did lead to some unpleasantness. Those of a Greek background complained that the Hebrew widows were better treated than the widows in their own families when, each day, food was given out. The apostles found that distributing the food was likely to distract them from the more important work of preaching the Gospel. So seven men were chosen – among them Stephen – to be deacons (ministers), to be responsible for the distribution. They were chosen as men 'full of the Spirit and wisdom'.

Persecution

Acts 6^{8-15}, 7^{55-60}: Stephen preached fearlessly and powerfully. He was seen as a threat by some religious leaders. They tried to argue against him but failed. They brought charges against him. They said he was speaking against the Temple and the law, saying that Jesus had made both of them unnecessary. That meant that Stephen was going against God, which was blasphemy. The punishment was stoning to death.

Stephen in reply told them how, for centuries, from the time of Abraham on, God had been with the people of Israel. He had never needed a temple. Stephen quoted from Isaiah:

> Heaven is my throne,
> and the earth is my footstool.
> What kind of house will you build for me?

Then Stephen rounded on his critics. They had murdered Jesus Christ, God's promised Messiah, just as their ancestors had killed the prophets. They were the blasphemers! They were the ones going against God!

The accusers were furious. Yet Stephen remained untroubled and serene.

> Stephen, full of the Holy Spirit, looked up to heaven and saw the glory of God, and Jesus standing on the right hand of God. 'Look', he said, 'I see heaven open and the Son of Man standing at the right hand of God.'
>
> Acts 7^{54-56}

They dragged Stephen out of the city and stoned him to death, leaving their clothes at the feet of a young man called Saul. The words on his lips when he died – 'Lord

Jesus, receive my spirit. Lord do not hold this sin against them' – were echoes of words spoken by Jesus on the cross.

Saul becomes a Christian

Acts 9[1-19]: There was a fierce persecution of Christians in Jerusalem after the death of Stephen. Saul was one of the most active persecutors. Not content with hunting out Christians in Jerusalem, he went, with the authority of the high priest, to Damascus. He planned to seize Christians there and haul them back to Jerusalem.

On his way there he had a vision. He saw a great light and heard a voice saying, 'Saul, Saul, why are you persecuting me?'

'Who are you, Lord?' asked Saul.

'I am Jesus, whom you are persecuting.'

Saul was left sightless after the vision. As the voice had instructed him, he went into Damascus.

A Christian in Damascus, Ananias, was told by the Lord in a vision that he must go to Saul to restore his sight. Ananias protested that Saul was a danger to Christians in Damascus. The Lord told him to go, none the less. The Lord said that Saul would take the gospel to people of many nations.

Ananias went to Saul and healed him with the words, 'Brother Saul, the Lord – Jesus who appeared to you on the road as you were coming here – has sent me so that you may see again and be filled with the Holy Spirit.' Saul's sight returned as he was baptized.

Paul's teaching and missions

Acts 13, 14[23]; 20[38]: About 14 years after Saul became a Christian, he and some others were in Antioch (in Syria) fasting and praying. The Holy Spirit told them that he was calling Saul, who about this time became known as Paul, and Barnabas to a special task. They set out on a journey from place to place, preaching the word. They went to:

- Cyprus, where Paul blinded a sorcerer who opposed his teaching;
- Antioch (a different Antioch from the place from which they set out, in what is now Turkey). There Paul preached on one Sabbath to the Jewish community, stressing as always that Jesus was the long-awaited Messiah.

The impact of the teaching in Antioch was tremendous. Next Sabbath almost the whole city turned up to hear Paul. Paul preached again, this time to people who were not Jews as well as to the Jews themselves. The Church in Antioch and round about began to grow. However, opposition to the new teaching began to grow as well. Leading people in Antioch expelled Paul and Barnabas. As they went, the writer of Acts tells us, 'They were filled with joy and with the Holy Spirit.'

In Antioch, and in other places that Paul and others visited, Christian communities – local churches – began.

On this journey Paul and Barnabas chose leaders (elders) from among them, prayed for them and left them to grow in the faith and build up the Church. Paul kept in touch with the churches that he had founded – a number of his letters to the churches are to be found in the New Testament.

In some of the passages studied we see the beginnings of the organization of the church. The apostles were the first leaders of the church. They appointed deacons to assist them in the running of the church in Jerusalem and, as they took Christianity to other places, they appointed leaders for the congregations they established. In the MEG syllabus candidates are required to relate these beginnings of ministry to the organization and ministry of the church today. See Chapter D7, *The Church – authority and structures*.

The Holy Spirit in the book of Acts

Time after time the writer of the book of Acts refers to the work of the Holy Spirit.

- Just before the ascension, Jesus told the disciples that the Holy Spirit would come to them with power.
- The decisive event that brought the Christian Church into being was the powerful coming of the Holy Spirit to the apostles on the day of Pentecost.
- The first Christians saw their fellowship in worship and in everyday life as guided by the Holy Spirit.
- It was in the power of the Holy Spirit that Peter and others preached. Stephen, as he preached and as he faced death, was seen to be full of the Holy Spirit.
- Miracles performed by Peter and other Christians were seen as signs of the work of the Holy Spirit.
- When Saul was converted he was filled with the Holy Spirit. It was the Spirit who guided the Church at Antioch to send Paul and Barnabas on their journey of preaching. Even when they were expelled from a city, it was 'with joy and with the Holy Spirit' that they went on to the next.

Examination practice

1. Give an account of what happened when the Holy Spirit came to the disciples in Jerusalem on the day of Pentecost. Include in your account the main points in Peter's preaching. (10 marks)
   Write about one side of A4.

2. What does the book of Acts tell us about (a) the organization and (b) the worship of the first Christians? In what ways do Christians today follow their example? (10 marks)
   Write about one side of A4.

3. Do you think it would be possible or desirable for Christians today to share their possessions as some of the first Christians did? (5 marks)
   Write about half a side of A4.

PART D

The Church

Full courses: Part D

This chart tells you the chapters to study. Find your exam board. Then highlight your syllabuses (or syllabus). Study the chapters that are ticked.

Exam Board Syllabuses	NEAB Syllabus A: Christianity	NEAB Syllabus B: Christian tradition	Catholic Christian tradition	Christian life and Mark's gospel	Christian behaviour, attitudes and lifestyle	Catholic Christian behaviour, attitudes and lifestyle	MEG Syllabus C: Christian beliefs and practice (modular)	Christianity through Luke's gospel and Acts	Christian perspectives on personal, social issues	Christianity	EdExcel (London) Christianity	Catholic Christianity	Contemporary issues and Mark's gospel	SEG Syllabus A: Christian Church	Contemporary issues	Life of Jesus: synoptic gospels	Syllabus B: Inter-faith studies: Christianity	Syllabus C: Catholic Christian tradition
Chapter 1 Baptism	✓	✓			✓		✓	✓	✓	✓	✓	✓	✓	✓		✓	✓	✓
Chapter 2 Infant baptism	✓	✓		✓	✓		✓	✓	✓	✓	✓	✓	✓	✓		✓	✓	✓
Chapter 3 Believer's baptism	✓	✓		✓	✓		✓	✓	✓	✓	✓	✓	✓	✓		✓	✓	✓
Chapter 4 Confirmation	✓	✓			✓		✓	✓			✓	✓	✓	✓			✓	✓
Chapter 5 The Church: Orthodox, Catholic, Protestant	✓	✓	✓		✓		✓		✓	✓	✓			✓			✓	
Chapter 6 The Church – images	✓	✓	✓		✓		✓	✓		✓	✓			✓			✓	✓
Chapter 7 The Church – authority and structures	✓	✓	✓		✓		✓			✓	✓			✓			✓	✓
Chapter 8 The Church – missionary work	✓			✓	✓		✓		✓	✓			✓			✓		
Chapter 9 Church and State						✓	✓	✓										
Chapter 10 Ecumenism	✓						✓	✓	✓									
Chapter 11 Ministers	✓	✓	✓	✓	✓		✓	✓	✓	✓	✓			✓	✓	✓	✓	
Chapter 12 Bishops, priests, deacons	✓	✓	✓	✓	✓	✓	✓	✓	✓	✓	✓	✓	✓	✓	✓	✓	✓	✓
Chapter 13 Lay people	✓	✓	✓		✓		✓	✓	✓		✓			✓				
Chapter 14 Nuns, monks, sisters, brothers	✓	✓	✓		✓		✓		✓	✓	✓	✓		✓	✓			
Chapter 15 Mary, mother of Christ	✓				✓						✓							

Short courses: Part D

This chart tells you the chapters to study. Find your exam board.
Then highlight your syllabus.
Study the chapters that are ticked.

Exam Board	NEAB	NEAB	SEG	SEG	EdExcel (London) Syllabus A	EdExcel Syllabus B			MEG Syllabus A		MEG	MEG Syllabus B	
Syllabuses	Christianity	Christianity	Thinking about God and morality	Religious education	Religion and life	Christianity	Christianity: Catholicism	Christianity: Mark's gospel	Christianity through Luke and Acts	Christian perspectives on personal, social and world issues	Christianity	Christianity	
Chapter 1 Baptism	✓	✓				✓	✓		✓		✓		
Chapter 2 Infant baptism	✓	✓				✓	✓		✓		✓		
Chapter 3 Believer's baptism	✓	✓				✓	✓		✓		✓		
Chapter 4 Confirmation	✓				✓	✓	✓		✓				
Chapter 5 The Church: Orthodox, Catholic, Protestant	✓					✓	✓		✓		✓		
Chapter 6 The Church – images	✓					✓	✓				✓	✓	
Chapter 7 The Church – authority and structures	✓					✓	✓				✓	✓	
Chapter 8 The Church – missionary work	✓				✓	✓	✓		✓				
Chapter 9 Church and State							✓			✓	✓		
Chapter 10 Ecumenism	✓					✓	✓				✓		
Chapter 11 Ministers	✓					✓	✓		✓		✓		
Chapter 12 Bishops, priests, deacons	✓	✓	✓	✓	✓	✓	✓		✓		✓		
Chapter 13 Lay people				✓		✓	✓		✓				
Chapter 14 Nuns, monks, sisters, brothers	✓					✓	✓		✓		✓	✓	
Chapter 15 Mary, mother of Christ							✓		✓		✓		

BAPTISM

Introduction

Baptism is an **initiation** rite. That means, it is a ceremony by which a person is made a member of something. At baptism a person officially becomes a Christian.

For Catholics the first three sacraments – baptism, confirmation, communion – are sacraments of initiation. They are the foundation of Christian living. These sacraments enable someone to become part of God, receive the new life of Christ, become a full member of the Church, and become strengthened to follow Christ's example.

Baptism is:

- the sign of new life in Jesus – anyone who is baptized is said to be **born again**;
- the washing away of sin;
- the means of uniting the person baptized with other Christians, members of the Church;
- the means of sharing in the death and resurrection of Jesus;
- a sharing in life with God.

The New Testament

John the Baptist announced that he had come to 'prepare the way for the Lord' (Mark 1^3). He told people to prepare themselves for his coming. He told them to repent (be truly sorry for their sins and resolve to change their way of life). As a sign of their repentance they were baptized. God would forgive the sins of those who repented and were baptized.

Jesus was baptized by John (Matthew 3^{13-17}). When Jesus came to be baptized by John, John was reluctant to baptize him. Perhaps this was because Jesus had no sin and so did not need to be baptized. Jesus insisted – in this way he showed his approval of baptism.

When Jesus was baptized the Spirit of God was seen descending on him like a dove, and a voice was heard from heaven: 'This is my Son, whom I love; with him I am well pleased.'

After Jesus had risen from the dead, he told his disciples to '**go and make disciples of all nations, baptizing** them in the name of the Father and of the Son and of the Holy Spirit' (Matthew 28^{19}).

From the very start, Christians have been baptized. In Acts 2 the writer describes how, on the Day of Pentecost, the apostle Peter preached to a huge crowd in Jerusalem. 'Those who accepted his message were baptized, and about three thousand were added to their number that day' (Acts $2^{37-38,\,41}$).

At first, all those who were baptized were adults who said they believed in Jesus Christ. Later, those who had become Christians wanted their children to be baptized as well.

Baptism today

People are baptized in most Christian denominations. There are exceptions. The Salvation Army do not baptize, nor do the Quakers.

All Christians who do baptize agree that there are two important features in every baptism:

- What God does is important. He forgives the sins of those who are baptized. He receives them into his family, as his children. They are 'born again': that means, they have a new, spiritual life because Jesus died and rose again to save them. This new spiritual life into which they are born is one that does not end when they die; it continues after death as life with God for those who are followers of Jesus Christ.
- What human beings do is important. Those baptized must repent of their sins and accept Jesus Christ as Saviour and Lord. When a child is baptized, others make the promises and statements of belief for the child.

INFANT BAPTISM

2

Introduction

Infant baptism takes place in many Christian denominations, among them Orthodox, Catholic, Anglican, Methodist, and United Reformed Church.

Except in the Orthodox church, the baptism is normally by the pouring of water on the forehead, 'In the name of the Father, and of the Son, and of the Holy Spirit'. At an Orthodox infant baptism the child is totally immersed.

Remember: in all these denominations older children or adults may be baptized, if they were not baptized as babies.

- Those who are old enough to understand what baptism means will make their promises for themselves.
- Before the baptism they will have instruction about what Christians believe, how and why they worship, and the way in which a Christian should live in everyday life.
- They may go on to be confirmed soon after the baptism.

Why are infants baptized?

- **So that they may be God's children, members of his family, the Church**. If a child is born weak, so that there is a chance that he or she may die, the child may be baptized by a hospital chaplain or, if no official minister is present, by anyone else, such as a doctor or nurse. Children who are baptized in an emergency and live are normally brought to the church to be received and welcomed into the Church.
- **To cleanse from original sin.** How can a baby have sins? Clearly a baby cannot know the difference between right and wrong.

  Original sin is not something that a person does. It is a weakness with which a person is born. We all are born with some physical characteristics coming from our parents. Height, hair colour, skin colour, intelligence – all may be inherited. In the same way, human beings inherit a weakness that makes them sin. It is not a sin in itself – but it means that human beings are not perfect. If they are not perfect, they are not good enough to be with God.

  Baptism washes away all sin, including original sin. It is a fresh start for the person baptized.

Promises made at infant baptism

Remember that baptism involves **commitment on the human side**. Promises and statements of faith are made. The baby cannot make them. The baby cannot promise to be a Christian.

Whether the child does grow up a Christian or not will depend greatly on **the way the child is brought up**. A child from a Christian home is more likely to become a committed Christian than one who is given no Christian support or guidance at all.

Before the baptism, the parents choose some **godparents** (sometimes called sponsors). It is usual to choose godparents of about the same age as the parents – relatives or close friends. Such a choice is sensible, because the godparents are expected to share in the Christian upbringing of the child.

The responsibilities that the parents and godparents accept are

- to bring up the child as a member of the Church;
- to teach the child the Christian way of life, with Christian moral standards;
- to teach the child to worship;
- to teach the child to pray;
- to lead the child towards confirmation.

What can parents and godparents do to keep the promises they have made?

Parents have the greater responsibility by virtue of their position and their control of the child's upbringing.

Parents may well set out to teach the child to follow the two great commandments given by Jesus – love God and love your neighbour (Mark 12$^{28-34}$). That sets a very high standard. If you love a person you will do everything you can to please him or her.

Christian parents may teach their children to love God by teaching them to:

- pray and read the Bible;
- worship with others in church;
- take an active part in the activities of the local church.

Parents will bring the children to understand that 'love your neighbour' refers to anybody and everybody. It means much more than not harming or annoying others. It means caring, and letting that care show in the way one lives.

A parent will most effectively teach these things by encouragement and example.

A godparent's job is harder. However, many young people are greatly influenced by relatives and close friends of the family. A godparent may try to use a friendly influence to encourage a godchild to grow up a committed Christian.

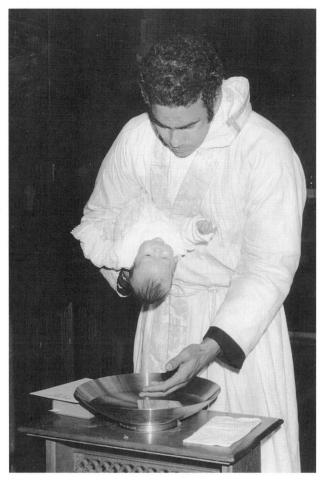

John, I baptize you in the name of the Father and of the Son and of the Holy Spirit

Infant baptism in three denominations

Anglican

The main features of the service are:

- The parents and godparents accept the duty of bringing the child up as a Christian.
- The child is signed with the sign of the cross.
- The water is blessed.
- The parents and godparents state their belief in God – Father, Son and Holy Spirit.
- The child is baptized by water being poured on the forehead three times, with the words 'N. I baptise you in the name of the Father, and of the Son, and of the Holy Spirit. Amen'.
- A lighted candle may be given to the parents and the child welcomed as a member of the Church.

Catholic

- A baptism should take place during a celebration of the eucharist (a sign, for example, that the local Christians welcome a new member).
- The priest meets the parents, godparents and child at the entrance to the church (a sign that he welcomes the child into the people of God). He asks the parents what they want for their child.
- The priest, parents and godparents make the sign of the cross on the child's forehead (a sign that the child belongs to Christ and has been saved by Christ).
- There are one or more readings, suitable for baptism, from the Bible: for example, Paul's letter to the Romans, where he explains that a baptized person enters into the death and resurrection of Christ.
- The priest then gives a homily, explaining the meaning of baptism.
- There are some prayers: for example, 'make the lives of his/her parents and godparents examples of faith to inspire this child.'
- The child is exorcized and anointed (as a sign that he or she will have the power to do good and avoid evil).
- The parents and godparents publicly state that they reject Satan, and that they believe – in God the Father, almighty and creator; in Jesus his son who was crucified, but rose from the dead; in the Holy Spirit; in the Catholic Church; in the forgiveness of sins; in the resurrection of the body; and in life everlasting. They say this on behalf of the child.
- The priest says: 'I baptize you in the name of the Father, the Son and the Holy Spirit.' Simultaneously he immerses the child or pours water three times on the child. (Water is a sign of many things: the two most important meanings in baptism are death and life – dying to original sin and rising with God's life.)
- The priest anoints the baptized child with chrism (a sign, for example, that the child is now a member of Christ's 'body', the Church, and so shares in the life of God).
- The priest puts a white garment on the child (a sign that the child is now 'clothed in Christ' and thus a person of dignity and importance).
- The priest lights a small candle from the paschal candle and gives it to one of the parents, saying, 'Receive the light of Christ' (a sign that the child has the guidance of Christ to believe and practise the Christian faith).
- Everyone says the Lord's Prayer and there is a final blessing.

Orthodox

Admission to membership of the Church is by baptism, followed immediately, on the same occasion, by **chrismation** (confirmation). The main elements of the service are

- Evil spirits are driven out.
- The godparent makes statements of turning from Satan and union with Christ.
- The oil and water are blessed.
- The sign of the cross is made with oil on the child's forehead and chest and between the shoulders.
- The child is baptized by being completely immersed in water three times.
- The child is dressed in a white robe.

Anglican infant baptisms often take place at a eucharist. Note, as an example, how the Anglican rite stresses the duties of parents and godparents. The service begins with a short statement about why children are baptized:

Priest: Children who are too young to profess the Christian faith are baptized on the understanding that they are brought up as Christians within the family of the Church.
            As they grow up, they need the help and encouragement of that family, so that they learn to be faithful in public worship and private prayer, to live by trust in God, and come to confirmation.
            Parents and godparents, the children whom you have brought to baptism depend chiefly on you for the help and encouragement they need. Are you willing to give it to them by your prayers, by your example and your teaching?
Answer: I am willing.

A little later parents and godparents state their belief in the Christian faith. They answer the questions put to them by the priest:

Priest: Those who bring children to be baptized must affirm their allegiance to Christ and their rejection of all that is evil.
            It is your duty to bring up these children to fight against evil and to follow Christ.
            Therefore I ask these questions which you must answer for yourselves and for these children. Do you turn to Christ?
Answer: I turn to Christ.
Priest: Do you repent of your sins?
Answer: I repent of my sins.
Priest: Do you renounce evil?
Answer: I renounce evil.
Priest: Do you believe and trust in God the Father, who made the world?
Answer: I believe and trust in him.
Priest: Do you believe and trust in his Son Jesus Christ, who redeemed mankind?
Answer: I believe and trust in him.
Priest: Do you believe and trust in his Holy Spirit, who gives life to the people of God?
Answer: I believe and trust in him.

Immediately after the child has been baptized in the name of the Father, the Son and the Holy Spirit, the priest hands a candle to a parent or godparent.

Priest: Receive this light. This is to show that you have passed from darkness to light.
All: Shine as a light in the world to the glory of God the Father.
Priest: God has received you by baptism into his Church.
All: We welcome you into the Lord's Family.
            We are members together of the body of Christ;
            we are children of the same heavenly Father;
            we are inheritors together of the kingdom of God.
            We welcome you.

Anglican Alternative Service Book

Note that the whole congregation join in these words of welcome. This is not just a family occasion. The child is now a member of the Church. All Church members join in the welcome.

Sometimes baptisms take place quietly, with few people present apart from the families of the babies. Sometimes the children are baptized during the eucharist on a Sunday. When the baptism is part of the main act of Sunday worship, the local church are there to welcome the new member.

Examination guidance

Baptism is a major subject, which must be well known. There are important differences between the denominations. You will be expected to know the difference between infant baptism and believers' baptism. If you are entered for a Catholic option make sure you know what is important in a Catholic baptism.

Examination practice

1. Choose any denomination and describe an infant baptism in that denomination.   (10 marks)
    Write at least a side of A4. Make sure you name the denomination; also, include the promises made by the parents and godparents and describe the way in which the child is baptized.

2. Explain why many Christians believe it is important that children should be baptized. Why do others believe it is right to wait until people are in their teens?   (10 marks)
    Write at least a side of A4, giving a full coverage of each side of the question.

BELIEVERS' BAPTISM

Introduction

Believers' baptism is the baptism of people who are old enough to understand what they are doing. Usually they have reached their late teens, though there is no hard and fast minimum age.

Believers' baptism is baptism by **total immersion**. The whole body of the person baptized is immersed in the water.

Believers' baptism is practised in the Baptist Church and in evangelical and Pentecostal churches.

- Those who are baptized must be able to understand, because they must **choose for themselves** to be Christians. When they make that choice they must commit themselves to Jesus Christ as Saviour. They must really love and serve him.
- Baptists believe that in the New Testament baptism was by total immersion. They point out that the Greek word βαπτιζω (*baptidzo*) originally meant 'to dip'. In particular, Jesus is believed to have been baptized in this way.
- Total immersion represents the believer identifying himself or herself with the death, burial and resurrection of Jesus. It is the response of the individual to the love of Jesus.

The first illustration shows a baptistry in a Baptist Church. It is a pool deep enough for a person to be completely covered in water when lowered into it. The second illustration shows a person being lowered into the water by the minister.

The plan on page 26 shows the layout of a Baptist Church. Notice how central the baptistry is. Everyone present can see and hear everything.

Before the candidates are baptized, each must state openly that baptism is a personal choice, based on a personal decision. Sometimes a candidate may be asked certain questions such as 'Do you accept Jesus Christ as your Lord and Saviour?' On other occasions those to be baptized give their testimony; they tell everyone present, in their own words, why they have chosen to be baptized.

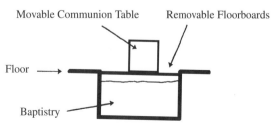

Movable Communion Table   Removable Floorboards

Floor →

Baptistry →

Side cross-section of a baptistry

Being **born again** is important to many Christians who practise believers' baptism. They believe that Jesus has come to them in a new, powerful way. Their new life is a wonderful experience of God being with them. They are not born again because they are baptized; they are baptized because they have been born again.

Dedication of children

Baptists and others who do not baptize children still believe that it is very important to bring up children within the Christian fellowship. There is a service of dedication in which the children are brought to the Church:

- The parents thank God for the birth of the child.
- The parents promise that the child will be brought up in the faith.
- The child is blessed; the scripture reading is of Jesus blessing the children who were brought to him.
- The congregation accept the responsibility of sharing in the child's instruction in the Lord.

Examination practice

1. Describe a believer's baptism.   (8 marks)
    Write about a side of A4. Use a drawing of a baptismal pool if you think it improves your answer – but be sure you let the examiner know how the drawing is relevant to your answer.

2. Why do Baptists believe in believers' baptism?
                                                        (6 marks)
    Write at least half a side of A4.

Development of confirmation

In the first years of the Christian religion, a bishop baptized all new Christians in his diocese, and he gave them first communion (eucharist). Later, in the fourth century, in Western Europe, an increasing number of people wanted to become Christians. There were too many people for a bishop to baptize. Consequently, bishops gave this task to local priests. However, bishops were reluctant to let priests do the last part of the ceremony of baptism – where the bishop laid his hands on the head of the newly baptized person. The bishops kept this part of the ceremony for themselves. This became the sacrament of **confirmation**. And when a bishop visited each local group of Christians, possibly once a year or once every two years, he confirmed new Christians.

In the Orthodox Church, confirmation has not been separated from baptism. When an Orthodox priest baptizes a baby, he also confirms the baby. Orthodox Christians usually call this sacrament **chrismation** rather than confirmation. It is called 'chrismation' because the priest anoints the baby with an oil named **chrism**. The priest traces the chrism in the shape of a cross on the baby's forehead, eyes, nostrils, mouth, ears, chest, hands and feet.

Age of confirmation

In the Orthodox Church, people are confirmed or chrismated when they are babies, straight after baptism.

In the Catholic Church in England, bishops confirm people at different ages. Some bishops confirm people when they are 16 years old, and mature enough to make up their own minds. Other bishops confirm people when they are about 11 years old, at the start of adolescence. Other bishops confirm people when they are 7 years old, just after first communion.

In the Anglican Church, confirmation may take place any time after 11 years of age; it is normally linked to admission to communion.

The United Reformed Church and some Methodists also practise confirmation.

Importance and meaning

The main importance of confirmation is that the person confirmed receives the Holy Spirit.

There are other reasons why confirmation is important; these will differ according to the age of confirmation.

For a person who is confirmed at about 7 years of age, confirmation is important as it is one of the three sacraments that bring a person into the Church. After receiving confirmation, a person is a full member of the Church. Parents make this choice for their child.

For those who receive confirmation at about 12 years of age, it is important in strengthening their faith as they move from being dependent on their parents, as a child, to becoming an adult, and independent of their parents. In the Anglican Church, it is the candidate who makes the decision about confirmation. In the Catholic Church, it is often the parents who make the decision for their child.

For those who receive confirmation when they are adolescents, it is important as their statement of what they believe. When they were baptized, their parents made that decision for them. Now, at confirmation, they make their own decision.

In the Catholic Church, confirmation is one of the three sacraments of initiation. These sacraments enable someone to become joined to God, to receive the new life of Christ, and to become a full member of the Church. Thus, the emphasis in these three sacraments is on sharing in God's life. These sacraments are the foundation of Christian living.

> [Straight after his baptism]
> the Spirit sent [Jesus] out
> into the desert . . . and he was in the desert for forty days, being tempted by Satan.
>
> Mark 1[12–13]

Preparation

For those who are confirmed after the age of 10, there are several ways they may prepare to receive the sacrament. For example:

- studying and discussing the meaning of confirmation;
- studying and discussing the life of Jesus;
- studying and discussing the life of the first disciples;
- studying the life of a Christian they admire;
- undertaking a special period of prayer or retreat;
- having a 'faith' partner with whom they can discuss spiritual growth;
- doing a special programme of community service in the parish;
- participating in a special service of enrolment, at the start of preparation for confirmation;
- receiving the sacrament of reconciliation;
- starting the habit of regular Bible reading;
- studying in detail the Church's worship.

Gifts of the Holy Spirit

The main purpose of confirmation is to receive the Holy Spirit. The Spirit of God is like the wind. We cannot see the wind. And yet we can recognize wind by its effects: the movement of leaves, pressure on our bodies, a whistling noise, and so on. In a similar way, we can recognize the Spirit of God by its effects. The effects of the Spirit are, for example:

1. **wisdom** to see things the way God does;
2. **understanding** to see things, habitually, from other people's point of view, as well as our own;
3. **right judgement** to decide, in stressful or difficult situations, what is the right thing to do;
4. **courage** to do what is right, when it is easier or more enjoyable to do what is wrong;
5. **knowledge** to see things as they are, without prejudice;
6. **reverence** to treat others with dignity;
7. **spirit of awe and wonder** to appreciate and respect the greatness of God.

These effects are often called the seven gifts of the Spirit.

> The Spirit helps us in our weakness. We do not know what we ought to pray for, but the Spirit himself intercedes for us with groans that words cannot express.
>
> Paul (Romans 8²⁶)

Ceremony in the Catholic Church

This sacrament, as any other sacrament, normally takes place during the eucharist.

- There are special readings from the Bible to do with the Holy Spirit (for example, the account of the coming of the Holy Spirit on the disciples, after the death of Jesus).
- Then those who are to be confirmed are called by name. The priest asks them to stand up, or to come to front of the church.
- The bishop talks to them about the meaning of confirmation. He may ask them questions to see if they understand the sacrament they are to receive.
- Those who are to be confirmed have to renew the promises made at their baptism. The bishop asks them:
  - Do you reject Satan and his evil ways?
  - Do you believe in God the Father, maker of heaven and earth?
  - Do you believe in Jesus Christ, his only Son, who was born of the virgin Mary, was crucified, died and was buried, rose from the dead, and is now seated at the right hand of the Father?
  - Do you believe in the Holy Spirit, the Lord, the giver of life, who came upon the apostles at Pentecost, and today is given to you sacramentally in confirmation?
  - Do you believe in the holy Catholic Church, the communion of saints, the forgiveness of sins, the

resurrection of the body, and life everlasting?
- The candidates reply: 'I do.'
- Then the bishop, first in silence, then in prayer, stretches out his arms and hands over the candidates. The bishop asks God to send the gifts of the Holy Spirit on the candidates (see the section above).
- Next, each candidate comes before the bishop with their sponsor. When the candidate kneels before the bishop, the sponsor stands, putting a hand on the candidate's shoulder – a sign of support.
- The bishop puts his right hand on the head of the candidate. At the same time, with the thumb of his right hand, he makes the sign of the cross, with oil of chrism, on the candidate's forehead.
- He says, 'Be sealed with the gift of the Holy Spirit.'
- Then he says, 'Peace be with you', and either shakes the hand of the candidate, or taps their cheek.
- After this, the bishop continues with the Mass.
- At the end of Mass, there is a special blessing. It includes the words: 'Jesus Christ the Son of God promised the Spirit of truth would be with his Church for ever: may he bless you and give you courage in professing the true faith.'

There are two important signs we see in the Catholic ceremony of this sacrament:

- First, the **'laying on of hands'**. The bishop does this twice: once, near the beginning of the ceremony, when he stretches out his arms and hands over all the candidates; later, at the actual moment of confirmation, when he puts his hand on the head of each candidate. This is an ancient sign, not a modern one. It means the giving of the Holy Spirit, his power and his courage.
- Second, the **anointing**. This is another ancient sign, not a modern one. Anointing can mean many things – such as cleaning, healing, soothing, giving joy, strengthening. Two other meanings, not very obvious, are that the confirmed person shares in the mission of Jesus, and the confirmed person receives the Spirit of God.

There is one important sign we hear in the Catholic ceremony: the words the bishop says as he anoints a candidate.

Ceremony in the Anglican Church

An Anglican confirmation often takes place during a eucharist, though it need not. The rite is as follows:

- Relevant prayers and readings.
- The Bishop speaks to the candidates about the meaning of confirmation.
- The candidates renew the vows made at their baptisms, using the same words as in the baptism service.

Priest:	Do you turn to Christ?
Answer:	I turn to Christ.
Priest:	Do you repent of your sins?
Answer:	I repent of my sins.
Priest:	Do you renounce evil?

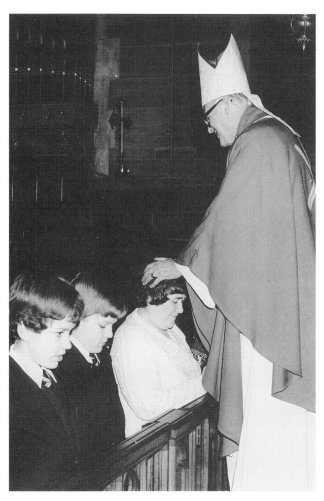

At an Anglican confirmation, the bishop lays his hands on the candidate's head and says: 'Confirm, O Lord, your servant with your Holy Spirit'

Answer:	I renounce evil.
Priest:	Do you believe and trust in God the Father, who made the world?
Answer:	I believe and trust in him.
Priest:	Do you believe and trust in his Son, Jesus Christ, who redeemed mankind?
Answer:	I believe and trust in him.
Priest:	Do you believe and trust in his Holy Spirit, who gives life to the people of God?
Answer:	I believe and trust in him.

Anglican Alternative Service Book

- The Bishop prays that the candidates may receive the sevenfold gifts of the Holy Spirit.
- Each candidate kneels before the Bishop, who lays his hand on the candidate's head and says, 'Confirm, O Lord, your servant *N* with your Holy Spirit.' This is an ancient sign, not a modern one. It means the giving of the Holy Spirit, his power and his courage.
- There follows either the eucharist or prayers for the newly confirmed.

Effects

We have seen that Christians believe that the main effect of this sacrament is the presence of the Holy Spirit. Other effects follow on this main effect. The person confirmed is:

- brought closer to God;
- made more like Christ;
- made a full member of the Church;
- emboldened to spread the good news about Christ;
- empowered to understand themself and others better;
- encouraged to follow the example and teaching of Christ;
- inspired to see things from God's point of view.

Examination guidance

'Be sealed with the gift of the Holy Spirit.' 'Confirm, O Lord, your servant with your Holy Spirit.'

1. In which sacrament do these words occur? (1 mark)

2. Select a Bible passage that could be used in this sacrament. Explain its relevance. (3 marks)

1. First answer
Ordination

Incorrect answer
(Score: 0 marks out of 1)

Second answer
Confirmation

Correct answer
(Score: 1 mark out of 1)

2. First answer
The coming of the Holy Spirit on the apostles.

The candidate has not explained why the named passage is relevant. An explanation is indispensable in an answer to this kind of question.
(Score: 0 marks out of 3)

Second answer
The coming of the Holy Spirit on the apostles. Because the person confirmed receives the Holy Spirit.

The candidate has given a simple explanation of why the named passage is relevant.
(Score: 1 mark out of 3)

Third answer

The coming of the Holy Spirit on the apostles. Because the persons confirmed receive the Holy Spirit, just like the first apostles. In both cases the Spirit gives people courage to practise and teach their Christian faith.

The candidate has given a developed explanation of why the named passage is relevant.
(Score: 3 marks out of 3)

Examination practice

1. List some of the ways in which people prepare for the sacrament of confirmation. (3 marks)
Write about six lines.

2. Christians believe that they receive the Holy Spirit in the sacrament of confirmation.
How might this change their lives? (8 marks)
Write about three-quarters of a side of A4.

3. State what happens and is said in the sacrament of confirmation. (8 marks)
Write about three-quarters of a side of A4.

4. 'Children should be confirmed about the age of seven, and not when they are teenagers.'
Do you agree? Give reasons for your view. Show that you have considered the opposite point of view.
(8 marks)
Write about three-quarters of a side of A4.

THE CHURCH: ORTHODOX, CATHOLIC, PROTESTANT 5

Introduction

Jesus founded one Church. In the creeds Christians state their belief in 'one holy catholic, apostolic Church'.

Over the centuries the Church has been divided. The main divisions of the Church are called **denominations**. The denominations are sometimes also referred to as Churches – the Methodist Church, the Anglican Church, the Catholic Church, the Orthodox Church and so on – as are their buildings.

Once there was great bitterness between different denominations. Where that bitterness is still to be seen, it is usually because of political issues. For instance, Christians from the different denominations in Northern Ireland have for a long time worked for peace and condemned the actions of terrorists on both sides.

Nowadays the greatest differences between the denominations are in the ways in which they worship and in their beliefs about the ministries of themselves and other Christians. There are differences in their attitudes to authority: see Chapter D7, *The Church – authority and structures*. There are some differences in attitudes to moral issues – for instance, the Quakers are pacifists, while other Christians take different attitudes to the issue of whether war is ever justified.

Christians accept each other and work together. See Chapter D10, *Ecumenism*.

Protestant

The word 'Protestant' comes from the sixteenth century, a time of great religious change or **Reformation**. Part of that change involved **protesting** against some of the teachings of the Roman Catholic Church of the time, against the authority of the Pope, and against abuses and corruption in the Church. That is why the name Protestant was used.

Nowadays the main characteristic of the Protestant movement is that these Christians regard the Bible as the supreme authority in all matters of faith. A number of Protestant groups do not believe there is any need for an ordained ministry.

In many of the denominations there is a dislike of hard-and-fast rules regarding how people should worship or how they should think of God. Indeed, religious freedom is for some a central part of their faith. For example, Baptists accept the Bible as the supreme authority in their search for truth. The local church is independent of any central authority, although it may form links with other congregations. Freedom to follow conscience is considered of the highest importance.

Beliefs Christians share

- There is one God, revealed as three persons – Father, Son, Holy Spirit. (See Chapter C2, *God: Trinity*.)

- God created everything. He loves all people.
- Jesus Christ, God the Son, was born as man, suffered, died and rose again. (See Chapter C7, *Jesus – his mission; sin and salvation.*) Through him Christians have hope of eternal life.
- Christians must respond to the love of God by the way they live.
- The Bible is the Word of God. (See Chapter C11, *The Bible.*)

Different Christian traditions

The **Orthodox Churches** are strongest in some countries in the east of Europe, among them Greece and Russia. They believe in the wonder of God, Father, Son and Holy Spirit. They believe in the Church as being a holy community, including Christians in both heaven and earth. They are very conscious of their oneness with those who have died and are now in the presence of God. The Liturgy (the eucharist) is their main act of worship.

The **Catholic Church** is by far the largest denomination throughout the world. The Pope, the Bishop of Rome, is the visible leader on earth. Catholic beliefs and practices are described in detail in many places in this book because of the needs of students entered for Catholic syllabuses. Catholics value the sacraments very highly. The eucharist is at the heart of their Church life.

The Roman Emperor Constantine became a Christian in AD 312. He also established a second capital for the Roman Empire – Constantinople (now called Istanbul). The two cities became the two most important centres of Christianity, and the two leaders, the Bishop of Rome (Pope) and the Patriarch of Constantinople, were recognized as having special authority.

The two strands of Christianity grew apart from each other in their forms of worship. There were also differences of belief – see what is said about the *filioque* clause in Chapter C5, *God – the Holy Spirit* – and differences over who had authority over whom. There was a split between the Pope and the Patriarch in AD 1054. The two churches have been separated ever since.

The **Anglican Church** is made up of churches in various countries worldwide – the Church of England, the Church of Wales, the Episcopal Church of Scotland and the Church of Ireland among them. Anglicans accept the authority of the Bible and the importance of the creeds, the sacraments of baptism and holy communion, and the apostolic succession (see Chapter D7, *The Church – authority and structures*). Anglicans also accept that there are matters in the Christian faith about which people hold different opinions. There are different ways of worshipping God, which appeal to different people. It is important to Anglicans that people can be guided by their own consciences, and worship in the way that helps them to know God – and yet remain part of the same denomination.

Anglicanism, as its name implies, has grown from the Church in England. Anglicans stress that their roots go back to the Church founded by Jesus Christ and that their traditions and ministry go back to the earliest days of the Christian Church. The Church was reformed in the sixteenth century; from that point on Anglicans ceased to accept the leadership of the Pope.

It is difficult to fit Anglicanism into the simple division of Orthodox, Catholic and Protestant. Some members stress the Catholic traditions of the Church; others regard themselves as in the Protestant tradition.

The Orthodox, Catholic and Anglican churches all have an apostolic ministry – see Chapter D12, *Bishops, priests, deacons: Orders.*

The **Baptist Movement** is a large number of individual churches, separate congregations, who share an acceptance of the Bible as the one authority for truth about God. They believe that the local church, active in its own area and community, is the church as God wants it to be. Some Baptist churches belong to the Baptist Union and similar groups; others remain quite independent of each other. They share a commitment to believers' baptism; in baptizing believers they see themselves as following the tradition of the New Testament Church. Baptists first emerged as a separate movement in the sixteenth century.

The **United Reformed Church** was formed in 1972 by the coming together of **Congregationalists** and **Presbyterians** in England. In other parts of the United Kingdom, and in other parts of the world, these two denominations remain separate, though similar in character. The Church of Scotland is Presbyterian. There are no firm rules with which all churches must comply. They share a strong emphasis on scripture and a congregation-based organization.

The **Methodist Movement** grew out of the Anglican Church in the eighteenth century and has developed into a movement of great variety. One of the main characteristics is the extensive use of local preachers and other lay leaders. There is an ordained ministry. Methodists have a strong sense of working for social justice. Methodists have a strong tradition of mission – one of the the founders of the Methodist movement, John Wesley, used to say 'The world is my parish.'

Pentecostalism stresses the outpouring of the Holy Spirit on the believers. This outpouring is a spiritual experience known as **baptism in the Spirit**. Their worship is charismatic, with ecstasy and excitement showing a great sense of the presence and activity of the Spirit. Speaking in tongues is a regular feature of their worship.

Quakers have few set beliefs, no ministers and no set forms of worship. They are committed to a search for God and his will for them. They are pacifists and work for peace. They join for **meetings** (they do not speak of services). These are times during which people wait in silence for the leading of the Spirit. If anyone is led by the

Spirit to do so, he or she does speak with a message for all present. The Quaker movement began in the seventeenth century.

The **Salvation Army** was founded by William Booth in the late nineteenth century. Salvationists use the language and the discipline of an army to stress the commitment in the battle to win souls for Christ. They regard themselves at war, not only against sin but also against poverty and suffering. They are greatly respected for their social work among the outcasts of society.

The Quakers and the Salvation Army do not have baptism or holy communion. The Salvation Army make the point that outward signs are in themselves nothing and so are unnecessary.

THE CHURCH – IMAGES TO EXPLAIN IT

6

Introduction

The word 'church' means a gathering of people.

- The Church is a group of Christians gathered to pray (particularly the eucharist).
- The Church is the local community of Christians.
- The Church is all the Christians in the world.

Christians believe that the Church is both visible and invisible. The human members of the Church are visible. The invisible aspect is the presence of God through the presence of the risen Jesus.

The Church is a **sacrament**. It is a sign of God's presence.

There are different ways of explaining the unity of the Church. Christians have found it useful to explain the Church using symbols or images, because a symbol or image can have many meanings. A number of images have been used, such as body of Christ or people of God. These images are explained in this chapter.

> The Church is not a club of saints; it is a hospital for sinners.
>
> George Stewart

One, holy, catholic and apostolic

Christians who accept the Nicene Creed (see Chapter C1, *Apostles' Creed and Nicene Creed*) say:

> 'We believe in one, holy, catholic and apostolic Church.'

This is what they understand this description to mean:

- **One** means undivided. The Church is one because the members of the Church are joined to Jesus, and so they are united with him. They are one with him and with each other. See Chapter D10, *Ecumenism*, for more information.
- **Holy** means 'belonging to God' or 'doing good to others, like God does'. The Church is holy in both these senses. It is holy because it is joined to God through Jesus; and it is holy because it does good to others, through the power of Jesus, its leader.
- **Catholic** means universal, worldwide. The Church is in different parts of the world, and includes different people. The Church is not for just one nation, nor for just one group of people, as the Church is catholic.
- **Apostolic** comes from the word 'apostle'. The Church is apostolic because the apostles were its first leaders after the death of Jesus; and it is apostolic because the bishops – the present-day leaders – are successors of the apostles. The bishops have the same tasks as the first apostles: to heal, to teach, and to govern the Church. See Chapter D12, *Bishops, priests, deacons: Orders*, for more information.

Body of Christ

This image starts with the last supper Jesus had with his disciples. He took bread and gave it to his disciples. He said: 'Take it; this is my body.' Christians do this at the eucharist. For most Christians, the eucharist is the most frequent and the most important act of worship. Through the eucharist, Christians believe they are united with Jesus. Christians today believe they have Jesus present with them, just as the disciples had Jesus with them 2000 years ago, but with a difference. It was the earthly Jesus who lived with the disciples 2000 years ago; it is the risen Jesus who lives with Christians today.

The apostle Paul used the image of a body to explain the unity of Christians with Jesus (1 Corinthians 12^{12-30}, Romans 12^{4-8}). He pointed out that there are many parts in a body, each of which does a different job. For instance, the hand does not do the same job as the leg; nor does the eye do the same job as the ear. Each part of the body is important, since the individual parts of the body rely on each other. For instance, the hand finds the eye very useful. Together, the parts make something more than just a collection of individual parts.

Thus the image of the body emphasizes the unity of Christians. They are united because they are all joined to Christ. Christians have different talents that they bring to their Church. Some may have an experience of the presence of Christ; others may be good at leading prayer; others may have a good understanding of their religion; and so on. Consequently, Christians may have different tasks in the Church. Some may be teachers, others may visit the sick, others may lead the worship, and so on. Nevertheless, each Christian is important. Paul said:

> Now you are the body of Christ, and each of you is a part of it. And in the church God has appointed first of all apostles, second prophets, third teachers, then workers of miracles, also those having gifts of healing, those able to help others, those with gifts of administration, and those speaking in different kinds of tongues.
>
> 1 Corinthians 12^{27-28}

The head is the most important part of the body. Hence Christ is the head. But the head must be united with the other parts to make a body. This image illustrates how Christians and Christ are united in the Church. This is the invisible or spiritual aspect of the Church. It is through baptism that Christians become united with Christ and become members of the Church. It is through unity with Christ that each Christian is united with other Christians.

The Church, as the body of Christ, is sometimes called the mystical body of Christ. This is simply to emphasize that the word 'body' is not used literally.

The bishops at the Second Vatican Council said:

> The head of this body is Christ. He is the image of the invisible God and in him all things came into being . . . He is the head of the body which is the Church. He is the beginning, the firstborn from the dead, that in all things he might hold the primacy. All members must be formed in his likeness, until Christ be formed in them.

People of God

This is a simple yet profound image of the Church. It was the favourite image of the Catholic bishops at the Second Vatican Council. (A council is a meeting of the bishops of the Church. The Second Vatican Council met in the 1960s at the Vatican in Rome.)

There is nothing common to the members of the Church, except that God has called them. They are people of

different nations, of different temperaments, of different colours, of different political views, of different customs, of different classes, and so on. But they all believe that Jesus has saved them through his death and resurrection. They are the people of God – so they belong to God.

These different people have become one people through baptism. They have been baptized into the death and resurrection of Jesus. They all belong to him. He is the head of the Church. Through him they all get to know the Father. This is what unites them. They also share in the work of Christ, who was priest, prophet and king.

Christ was a priest. In his life on earth he offered himself to God, a sort of sacrifice: he always did what God wanted him to do. Christians should follow his example.

Christ was a prophet. Since he knew God, he could speak about God with authority. And he had the courage to speak about God, even though this displeased the religious leaders. This cost him his life. Christians should be able to follow his example.

Christ was a king. He started the kingdom of God. He told his disciples to baptize others to enter the kingdom of God. Christians should bring others into the kingdom of God.

The people of God share the same freedom as Jesus. So, they have the power of God's Spirit to free themselves from addiction to selfishness, spite, deceit, and other evil inclinations.

> God has willed to make men holy, not as individuals without any bond or link between them, but rather to make them into a people.
>
> Second Vatican Council

Pilgrims

Pilgrims leave home for a while. They travel to another place, hoping to experience God or to obtain a special favour from him. They experience hard times as they journey through foreign and unknown countries. They do not know from day to day what will happen.

In a metaphorical sense, all Christians are pilgrims. Their life is like a pilgrimage. They are on a journey to God. Yet they are not alone. They have the prayer and support of other Christians. They have the help and comfort of Jesus. They have the power and strength of the Holy Spirit.

The image of the Church as pilgrims emphasizes that Christians are searching for a better understanding and experience of God. They do not have all the answers. They see life as a journey to God. At the start of this journey they have a limited knowledge of God. It is through the unknown events of life that they hope to come to a clearer awareness of God.

This image also emphasizes that Christians feel they need God's help. They experience failure as well as triumph in their lives. They look for God's help to cope with their darker moments and to overcome their shortcomings. Yet they are optimistic that they will reach their place of pilgrimage, God.

The bishops at the Second Vatican Council said this about the Church:

> On earth, still as pilgrims in a strange land, following in trial and in oppression the paths he [Jesus] trod, we are associated with his sufferings as the body with its head, suffering with him, that with him we may be glorified.

Family of God

This is a popular image because most of us easily understand it.

There is a strong bond in a family – a natural bond. In spite of arguments and disagreements, the members feel that they belong to one another: they defend each other; they help each other; and so on.

A family lives together. The members of the family have intimate relationships, and they come to know each other well. They share good times and bad times: they celebrate together if one of them does well; they suffer if one of them is in trouble; they grieve if one of them dies.

The Church is a group of people who are united, not naturally, but spiritually. They all have a second 'life' because they share in God's life. They receive this life when they are baptized. They are then joined to Jesus and, through him, to God. They are the family of God.

The local Church celebrates together, usually every Sunday, when most of its members celebrate the eucharist.

Each of the sacraments is a way in which the members of the Church come together, with God. They may rejoice or grieve. For example, the whole Church celebrates when two of its members marry. And there is pain in the whole Church when one of its members is seriously ill.

The image of family shows that Christians feel an intimate relationship with God. Jesus called God 'dad'. Christians do not use this rather personal and private – even unique – term for God. Yet they do use the term 'father' to express their close relationship with God. They are confident that God is close to them: he suffers when they suffer; he rejoices when they rejoice; he looks after them; he gives them sound advice; and so on.

In an age when there is gender equality, some Christians use the term 'mother', as well as the term 'father', to express their close relationship with God. However, other Christians are offended when they hear some Christians describe God as mother.

Temple of the Holy Spirit

A temple is the place where God is thought to live.

This image of the Church emphasizes that God is the centre of the Church. Christians are gathered round God. At baptism, they received the Spirit of God. This made them members of the Church.

We cannot see the Spirit of God. Still, the Spirit of God works in unseen ways. When Christians are patient, kind, courteous, forgiving, joyful, peaceful, self-controlled, considerate, and so on, then we know that the Spirit of God is there. However, when Christians are adulterous, selfish, jealous, hateful, over-ambitious, envious, quarrelsome, and so on, then we know that the Spirit of God is not there.

The Spirit of God encourages Christians to follow the example of Jesus: to care for those who are sick; to help those who are fragile; to forgive; to pray; to share; and so on.

The Spirit encourages a Christian to learn from mistakes. A Christian believes that one of the worst sins we can commit is pride – the conviction that we are perfect and cannot make any mistakes. The Spirit encourages Christians to accept that they have to grow and to develop. The Spirit encourages Christians to accept that they have faults and limitations. And the Spirit encourages Christians to accept God's help, so as to become like him.

Sacrament

A sacrament is a sign that God is present. And a sign that Jesus is present. (See Chapter A16, *Sacraments; liturgical worship*.)

The Church is a sacrament. The Church – the people of God – makes God present in this world. The Church also makes Jesus present in the world, in different ways:

- in its worship, especially when it celebrates one of the sacraments;
- in its work with the poor;
- in its preaching of the gospel;
- in its concern for those who suffer;
- in the care that its members show each other.

> The Church, in Christ, is in the nature of a sacrament – a sign and instrument, that is, of communion with God and of unity among all men.
> Catholic bishops at Second Vatican Council

Communion of saints

The word 'saint' means 'holy' or 'belonging to God'. The word 'communion' means 'sharing' or 'joining'.

In the Orthodox eucharist, after the priest consecrates the bread and wine, he holds them up, and says: 'God's holy gifts for God's holy people'. This illustrates that the communion of saints is:

- a **sharing in holy things**. Christians share the life of the risen Jesus, through baptism. Consequently, they are united with God. The other sacraments, but especially the eucharist, renew this sharing in the life of God. The eucharist is so important in helping Christians to share the live of God, it is called 'communion'.
- a **joining of holy people**. Baptism joins each Christian to Christ; so Christians are joined to each other, as well.

The Catholic Church teaches that there are three states of the Church: those on earth, those in heaven, and those who have died but are waiting to get into heaven. They all belong to the one Church with Jesus. Those on earth should pray for those who have died, to help them on their journey to heaven. Those in heaven do pray for everyone else.

- a **sharing in earthly goods**. The first Christians were particularly keen to share their goods with each other. They believed that God gave them these goods to use generously, to help each other.

Examination practice

1. Christians think that the Church is an important part of their lives.
   Explain why. (3 marks)
   Write about six lines of A4.

2. 'The Church is one, holy, catholic and apostolic.'
   Explain the meaning of **each** of these **four** descriptions. (6 marks)
   Write about half a side of A4.

3. Christians believe that Christ died for all people. How might this influence their understanding of the Church? (8 marks)
   Write about three-quarters of a side of A4.

4. Choose any three images of the Church. Show how they give different understandings of the Church. (10 marks)
   Write about one side of A4.

5. 'I can be a Christian without going to church.'
   Do you agree? Give reasons for your view. Show that you have considered the opposite view. (8 marks)
   Write about three-quarters of a side of A4.

THE CHURCH – AUTHORITY AND STRUCTURES 7

Introduction

- **What must a person believe** to be a Christian?
- **What must a person do** as a member of the Christian Church?
- **Who decides** what Christians must believe and do?

The same questions can be asked of each denomination – for example, what must a person believe to be an Anglican, a Methodist, or a Catholic?

In each denomination, there are rules and guidelines. There are also individuals or groups of people who have authority.

What sort of authority?

Christians regard the Church as a family – God's family. Authority is exercised as in a family.

- There are rules, which must be obeyed. If necessary, they must be enforced, with punishments in some cases.
- Most of the time there is no need for punishment. Members of a family love one another. They keep to the rules of the family not through fear of punishment but because of their love for the other members.

Authority in the Church is exercised and accepted in that spirit. Such authority is understood to be in the spirit of the teaching of Jesus.

> 'Love the Lord your God with all your heart and with all your soul and with all your mind and with all your strength . . . Love your neighbour as yourself.'
>
> Mark 12[30–31]

> 'A new commandment I give you: Love one another. As I have loved you, so you must love one another. By this all men will know that you are my disciples, if you love one another.'
>
> John 13[34–35]

The Bible

All Christians accept the authority of the Bible as the Word of God. They may have differing ideas as to what the phrase 'the Word of God' means or how it should be interpreted. See Chapter C11, *The Bible*.

All Christians accept Jesus as the Head of the Church.

All Christians accept that conscience must be taken seriously as a guide (though not an infallible guide) to right conduct. See Chapter E28, *Conscience*.

Catholic Church

The **Pope** is the visible leader on earth of the Catholic Church. He is the successor of Peter, whom Jesus named as the leader of the apostles:

> 'You are Peter, and on this rock I will build my church, and the gates of Hades will not overcome it. I will give you the keys of the kingdom of heaven; whatever you bind on earth will be bound in heaven, and whatever you loose on earth will be loosed in heaven.
>
> Matthew 16[18-20]

The Pope has the authority to pronounce infallibly on matters of faith and morals. ('Infallible' means completely free from error.) In practice, this authority is very rarely used. He is seen rather as the head of the college of bishops (meaning all the bishops of the Church).

When a Pope does give guidance on matters of faith or morals, he may do so through issuing an encyclical, a statement addressed to all Catholics. An encyclical is not regarded as infallible teaching, though it has a special authority. An example of an encyclical is *Humanae Vitae*, in which Paul VI stated the traditional Catholic teaching about birth control.

The Pope's titles include 'Bishop of Rome, Vicar of Jesus Christ, successor of the prince of the apostles, supreme pontiff of the universal Church, sovereign of the state of Vatican City, servant of the servants of God'

The Pope may call a **general council** of the church. All bishops are members of a general council. They are called very rarely – the last three were the Council of Trent (1545–1563), the First Vatican Council (1869–1870) and the Second Vatican Council (1962–1965). As the councils' decisions have the authority of the bishops they are treated as having the highest authority. Each individual bishop is a

successor of the apostles. If, all together, they pronounce something to be true, they can be infallible.

Bishops are the successors of the apostles. So when bishops in any part of the world meet in conference, their pronouncements carry very great authority. In such conferences they speak on matters of doctrine that are the concern of the whole Church. They also discuss and pronounce on things of local concern. They will interpret the rulings of the Church in the light of national or local circumstances. They will make sure that local customs and traditions are respected. For instance, in many countries black is a symbol of mourning. In Japan it is a symbol of celebration – and would certainly not be appropriate at a funeral.

There is a third source of infallible teaching in the Catholic Church, **the whole body of the faithful**; when they agree in matters of faith or morals, their belief is infallible.

The Catholic Church is composed of **dioceses**, which are grouped as provinces. The leader of the Church in each diocese is the Bishop and in each province is the Archbishop.

The Diocese is divided into **parishes** (which are grouped into deaneries). The parishes are the basic units of the Catholic church. Each is served by a priest or group of priests.

Anglican Church

The Anglican Communion, as it is called, is made up of churches all over the world – for example, the Episcopal Church in the USA, the Church of the Province of Central Africa, the Council of the Churches of East Asia. In the United Kingdom the Anglican churches are the Church of England, Church of Wales, Church of Ireland and Episcopal Church of Scotland. Each church is self-governing.

'Episcopal' means 'having bishops'. All Churches in the Anglican Communion are episcopal.

The representatives of churches from different countries meet every 10 years in England to discuss matters of common interest. These meetings are known as Lambeth Conferences – Lambeth Palace in London is the official residence of the Archbishop of Canterbury. Statements about the issues discussed are issued after each conference.

The Lambeth Conference of 1888 issued a statement known as the Lambeth Quadrilateral. It states that for Anglicans the essentials of the Christian Church are:

- the Bible;
- the Apostles' Creed and the Nicene Creed;
- the two sacraments given by Jesus himself – baptism and holy communion;
- the orders of bishops, priests and deacons.

Although the churches keep in close touch with each other, each may act independently of the others. For instance, the Bishop of Hong Kong ordained women as priests in the 1960s. The first women Anglican priests in

Ireland were ordained in 1992, in England and Scotland in 1994, and in Wales in 1997. Meanwhile, women have been consecrated as bishops in New Zealand and the USA.

The Archbishop of Canterbury is welcomed as a leading figure in the Anglican Communion – but he is in no way the equivalent of the Pope.

The organization of the Church of England

The Church of England is divided into two provinces and 43 dioceses. The leader of the Church in each province is the Archbishop and in each diocese is the Bishop. The diocese is divided into deaneries and parishes.

The government of the Church of England is based on a structure of **synods**. A synod is a group of representatives who debate and vote upon matters concerning the whole Church of England.

- The **General Synod** makes the decisions on the rules (called **canons**) that have to be followed by the Church. The members are bishops, clergy (priests or deacons) and lay people elected to represent each of the 43 dioceses.
- The **Diocesan Synods** make decisions that affect the running of each diocese. They also debate and vote on matters that will be decided by the General Synod – but the result of the vote is simply to allow the members to be consulted and to show what the members think. The results are not binding on anyone. The members are the bishops of the diocese along with clergy (priests or deacons) and lay people elected to represent each of the deaneries that make up the diocese.
- The **Deanery Synods** make decisions that affect the running of each deanery. They also debate and vote on matters that will be decided by the General Synod – but the result of the vote is simply to allow the members to be consulted and to show what the members think. The results are reported to the Diocesan Synod before that synod debates and votes. The members are clergy and lay people elected to represent each of the parishes that make up the deanery.
- The **Parochial Church Council** of each parish is responsible for the life of the parish – its worship, its mission and social work and activity. It is made up of people who worship at the church. It debates the key matters that will eventually be decided by the General Synod.

The United Reformed Church

If you are studying the NEAB Syllabus A, it is specified that you study the organization of the United Reformed tradition.

The URC finds the supreme authority for faith by the guidance of the Spirit in the Word of God in the Bible.

The basic unit of the URC is the **local church** or **congregation**. Each local church:

- welcomes people from any church background, or from no church at all, and aims to lead them to know Jesus;
- arranges its own worship;
- offers Christian service to the community;
- celebrates the sacraments of baptism and the Lord's Supper;
- works to build up links with other Christian churches in the area;
- has an elected body of ordained elders who share the leadership of the church with the minister.

The local churches are members of **District Councils**. Each District Council:

- arranges general oversight for the churches that belong to it;
- conducts ordinations of ministers;
- consults with every local church about its mission, on a regular basis.

The District Councils are each part of a **Provincial Synod**. Each Provincial Synod:

- discusses matters of faith and policy;
- is responsible for links with other denominations;
- gives practical help of a specialist nature – for example, in legal matters.

The central work of the whole URC is carried out by an annual council called the **General Assembly**, chaired by the Moderator. There are about 700 delegates, about half ministers and half lay people, mostly chosen by District Councils. They make decisions on the general policy of the church.

For the ministry of the URC, see Chapter D11, *Ministries*.

The Baptists

For Baptists the only source of authority is the Bible.

The local church is independent of outside authority. Members are chosen to be deacons, responsible for the running of the church. They choose and appoint the pastor.

It may be that the local church chooses to be a member of a wider association such as the Baptist Union. The Union carries out tasks that would be impossible for each small local church. The Union organizes such things as missionary work and the training of pastors. It helps in setting up new churches. It supports the publishing and distribution of the Bible and other religious literature.

Membership of the Union does not take away the independence of the local congregation. That is why the denomination is called the **Baptist Union** and not the Baptist Church. The term 'Baptist church' is used to describe a local congregation. Some Baptist churches do not belong to any sort of wider union.

It follows that a church must be independent of the state. Baptists have always insisted that no outside authority has any right to tell a person what to believe.

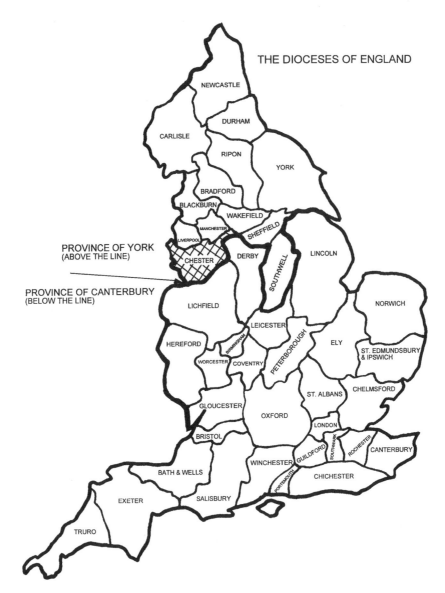

THE DIOCESES OF ENGLAND

The Church of England has the country divided into 43 dioceses (including the Isle of Man)

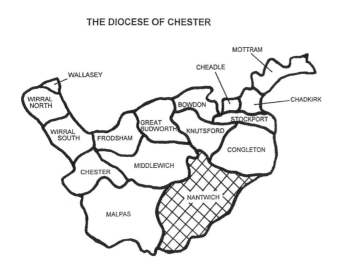

THE DIOCESE OF CHESTER

Each diocese is divided into deaneries

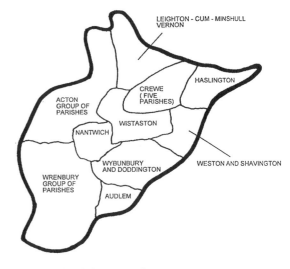

THE DEANERY OF NANTWICH

Each deanery is divided into parishes

> A magistrate is not by virtue of his office to meddle with religion or matters of conscience, to force or compel men to this or that form of religion or doctrine, but to leave Christian religion free to every man's conscience.
>
> John Smyth

Freedom of conscience does not mean that members of a Baptist church can believe anything they wish and still remain members. The authority of the Bible still comes first. If people believe that infants should be baptized or that the Bible is not true, they should not be punished – but they cannot call themselves Baptists.

Authority – the position of the Baptist Union

That our Lord and Saviour Jesus Christ, God manifest in the flesh, is the sole and absolute authority in all matters pertaining to faith and practice, as revealed in the Holy Scriptures, and that each church has liberty, under the guidance of the Holy Spirit, to interpret and administer his laws.

Examination practice

1. Why do Baptists speak of the Baptist Union rather than the Baptist Church? (6 marks)
   Write about three-quarters of a side of A4, making clear the importance of the local congregation and its links, if any, with other congregations.

2. Where might Catholics look for authoritative guidance as to what they should believe? (8 marks)
   Write about a side of A4, covering the various sources of authority. Do not forget those bases of belief that are common to all Christians, such as the Bible, as well as those important to Catholics in particular.

THE CHURCH – MISSIONARY WORK 8

Jesus had a mission

His mission was to preach the kingdom of God. In each of the three synoptic gospels, immediately after the Temptation, the writer describes the beginning of Jesus' ministry:

- Mark 1[14–15]: Jesus went into Galilee, proclaiming the good news of God. 'The time has come,' he said. 'The kingdom of God is near. Repent and believe the good news!'
- Luke 4[14–15]: Jesus returned to Galilee in the power of the Spirit, and news about him spread through the whole countryside. He taught in their synagogues, and everyone praised him.
- Matthew 4[17]: From that time on Jesus began to preach, 'Repent, for the kingdom of heaven is near.'

He taught his followers to tell others about the kingdom

- He called his 12 disciples 'that they might be with him and that he might send them out to preach' (Mark 3[14]).
- He sent his disciples out in twos to preach (Mark 6[7–13]).

After the resurrection Jesus gave the disciples a mission:

- 'Go and make disciples of all nations, baptizing them in the name of the Father and of the Son and of the Holy Spirit, and teaching them to obey everything I have commanded you. And surely I am with you always, to the very end of the age' (Matthew 28[19–20]).
- 'Go into all the world and preach the good news to all creation' (Mark 16[15]).
- 'Repentance and forgiveness of sins will be preached in his name to all nations, beginning at Jerusalem. You are witnesses of these things' (Luke 24[47–48]).

After Jesus' ministry, the disciples became **apostles** (which means 'sent out'). See Chapter C22, *The Acts of the*

Apostles – main themes. Note in particular the missionary activity of Peter and Paul.

> Mission began nearly 2000 years ago.
> For the call to be on mission means attempting to practice what Jesus presented as mission when in his hometown of Nazareth he quoted the prophet Isaiah.
>
> 'The Spirit of the Lord is on me;
> because he has anointed me
> to preach good news to the poor.
> He has sent me to proclaim freedom to the prisoners
> and recovery of sight to the blind,
> to release the oppressed,
> to proclaim the year of the Lord's coming.'
>
> Fr Ed O'Connell, Columban Mission Priest

Every Christian has a mission

Christians believe that every Christian has a duty to bring others to know God and to accept Jesus as Saviour. For most Christians, this means living a Christian life at work, at school, at home, in the neighbourhood or wherever they happen to be. They should be ready to say what they believe and why.

Some Christians are called by God to devote themselves full time to mission. They are known as **Church workers**, and minister to others in the name of Jesus Christ.

Christian missionary work today

Christians going from one country to another must be able to offer a skill that is needed. The skills are of a wide variety:

- **Training local hospital and other health service staff in new skills**. Advances in knowledge can benefit those who suffer from disease or who need surgery. As in Europe and North America, so in less advanced parts of the world doctors and nurses need training to take advantage of progress.

  An important part of health work is the provision of clinics in areas where there is a lack of basic health care and education.
- **Advising and helping those involved in food production**. Agriculturalists and engineers with the right skills are welcomed. The help given must be suitable for the situation of the people being helped. Farm machinery needing skilled maintenance and access to supplies of spare parts is useless hundreds of miles from the nearest town. Ability to locate water, drill wells and create a reliable water supply is valuable.
- **Teaching**. For instance, an Anglican missionary society called USPG (United Society for the Propagation of the Gospel) has supported the sending of English language teachers to China.

On the face of it, these are not religious matters. All these things could be done by anyone, regardless of their religious belief. The missionary side comes from the missionary's motive – the work is done in the name of Christ, to show the love of God.

Albert Schweitzer, who worked as a missionary doctor in French Equatorial Africa (now known as Gabon), used to go to see patients on whom he had performed operations. They would say to him, with great joy, 'I'm cured, Doctor, I'm cured!' Then he would tell them that the reason he had come to Africa, the reason he was in the hospital performing operations, was because he wanted to show people the love of Jesus Christ.

Much missionary work is done through Christian agencies. See Chapter E17, *Christian relief agencies*.

Other missionary work is more obviously Christian:

- **Training priests and other ministers**. Much of the training is done by leaders of the local churches. Sometimes they need help with particular subjects or skills.
- **Translation**. There are thousands of languages and dialects throughout the world. The scriptures have to be translated before people can read them. Missionaries go and live among people to learn their language. They must learn it very thoroughly to be able to translate into words that keep the real meaning of the Bible and yet are understandable.

  For instance, one translator found himself working among people who had never heard of sheep. He had to translate Psalm 23 – 'The Lord is my shepherd'. What he wrote meant, in the language of the country, 'The Lord is my gooseminder'. That made more sense to the local people.

How the role of the missionary has changed

Ed O'Connell is a member of a Catholic order, the Columban Mission Priests. The Columban Mission Priests

Father Ed O'Connell, a Christian missionary, who has worked in the shanty towns of Lima, Peru

often work among people of different cultures and different religions. He has worked in the shanty towns of Lima, Peru, and knows the position of Christians in Lahore, Pakistan, where they are in a minority compared with other faiths.

Fr O'Connell has seen a change in the way which Christians understand what mission is. He describes the changing roles in this way:

- **Building up local churches**. 'We used to see our role as one of going out to the countries of Asia and Latin America to help people build up their own local Church. We did this mainly by providing catechetical (teaching) classes and through the celebration of the sacraments.'
- **Living alongside people**. 'From the 1960s onwards Columbans have done their best to share the struggles for the basics of life of those who live in poverty. We shared times of repression and imprisonment, of martyrdom and expulsion.'
- **Linking Christians in different communities**. 'It is crucial that today's missionary should be a link person between local churches, helping them to share their experiences of faith and struggle for the reign of God with others around the world.'

> Mission is more about being with and amongst people as all struggle to live as children of God, as sisters and brothers of each other. This presence with and amongst people, a sense of solidarity, is central to mission.
>
> Fr Ed O'Connell

Examination practice

1. Why did Jesus have a group of disciples with him? What instructions did he give them after the resurrection? (8 marks)
   Write about three-quarters of a side of A4. Make sure you have given a full coverage of both parts of the question.

2. Give two examples of work done by Christian missionaries nowadays. Why do they think this work is important? (8 marks)
   Write about three-quarters of a side of A4. Choose contrasting examples – e.g. nursing, and translating the scriptures.

3. Why might people decide to offer themselves for missionary work? (4 marks)
   Write about half a side of A4. Make sure you include the idea of vocation: see the relevant section in Chapter E20, Work and leisure.

CHURCH AND STATE

Biblical teaching

A 'Then give to Caesar what is Caesar's, and to God what is God's.'

Luke 20$^{20-26}$

Some religious leaders wanted to catch Jesus with a trick question: 'Is it right for us to pay taxes to Caesar or not?' The thinking behind the question was that either way Jesus would be caught out. If he answered 'No', he would be in trouble with the Romans. If he answered 'Yes', people would think he was on the side of the Romans; he would not be the great Jewish leader, the Messiah. Jesus asked for

a denarius, a Roman coin. He asked them, 'Whose portrait and inscription is this?' 'Caesar's', they replied. He said, 'Then give to Caesar what is Caesar's, and to God what is God's.'

Jesus was not just getting out of a tricky situation. He was saying that the state, the government, has rights, and that Christians have a duty towards the government – for instance, to obey the law and pay taxes. Their duty to God, which is the first great commandment, must be honoured as well.

B The authorities that exist have been established by God.

Romans 13$^{1-7}$

Paul teaches that state authority is necessary. People should live together in communities and there must be government. Paul writes that all authority is from God. To rebel against the state is to challenge what is God's will. The authorities have a right to tax and to demand respect.

> Rulers hold no terror for those who do right, but for those who do wrong. Do you want to be free from fear of the one in authority? Then do what is right and he will commend you.'
>
> Romans 13[3]

What if the state is unjust?

Note that Jesus himself was killed, unjustly, by the established authorities. Paul was also executed for his beliefs. Many Christians in the first century died because they were Christians.

Sometimes laws are passed that Christians regard as immoral. The campaign against apartheid in South Africa was justified by Christians on the grounds that it is immoral to discriminate against people because of the colour of their skin.

Other laws prevent Christians from exercising their duty to spread the Christian faith. Many have suffered for insisting on telling others about Jesus Christ, even when it meant breaking the law.

Church and state – the beginnings

For the first three to four hundred years after Christ, Christians were a minority in the Roman empire, often persecuted. From time to time, Roman emperors decided to kill or persecute people who were Christians. Then, in the fourth century, the emperor Constantine favoured Christians. He encouraged people to become Christians.

After him, the emperor Theodosius made the Christian religion the official religion of the Roman empire. Thus began the idea that society should be Christian, that Church and state should be united, that the laws of the state should be Christian laws, that the bishops should support the king or government. The Christian Church became firmly wedded to the state.

Kings and governments have often believed it helped them if there was just one religion in their country. It meant that their people were more likely to live in peace with each other, and unite behind the king or government. Consequently, many kings and governments allowed only one religion in their country.

An established church

An established church is one that has an official link with the state.

The Church of England and the Church of Scotland are established Churches. The Church of Wales used to be established until early in the twentieth century.

To take the example of the Church of England, establishment means:

- There is a link between Church and state.
- Everyone in the country has a legal right to the ministry of the Church. For instance, anyone can be baptized or married in their parish church. The funeral of any person can be held in the parish church.
- The Church is represented in Parliament by the senior bishops having seats in the House of Lords. Obviously, they have not the time to be in Parliament more than a few days each year. Their influence is strongest when they speak on moral matters, especially as they do not have to vote according to party politics but are genuinely independent.

  Some people think it wrong that Church leaders should have a place in Parliament, even if it is in the House of Lords. Others think it is an excellent thing that there should be this official Christian influence in Parliament. They think it should be extended to include other religious leaders as well.
- The Queen is the Supreme Governor of the Church. In theory she appoints the bishops and archbishops. In fact, a small committee of clergy and lay people from a diocese put forward to the Queen, through the Prime Minister, a first and second choice. As those choices are confidential, we cannot know how the final decision is made. Many people feel that neither the Queen nor the Prime Minister should have any say in the appointment.

The Orthodox view

The Orthodox have always believed that Christ redeemed every aspect of human life, including the spirit and organization of society. So they believed that Christian beliefs should influence everything that happens in a country. They encouraged Christians to see the king or government as the representatives of God. Thus Christians should obey the king or government as they should obey God.

This often seemed to work, until the twentieth century. Then the largest Orthodox country, the USSR, had a Communist government that did not believe in God, or in the value of religion. The Communist government persecuted Christians. It closed the seminaries where men studied to become priests. It closed many churches, turning some of them into museums. And it tried to get Communists appointed as bishops. The government discriminated against people who were religious: it was difficult for them to get jobs or flats. Sometimes the government persecuted people who were religious; at other times it tried to persuade people that religion was a waste of time.

In Russia today the government does not treat the Church in such an oppressive way. Yet the Orthodox Church is not quite sure if it should be separate from, or joined to, the government.

The Catholic view

The attitude of the Catholic Church has varied. At times, it has wanted to be joined to the government: it has backed the government and expected the king or government to favour the Catholic religion. At other times, it has emphasized that the state and the Church are separate; that the Church can criticize a king or government that behaves unjustly.

At times, the leader of the Catholic Church, the Pope, has himself been the leader of a state as well as the leader of the Church. A hundred and fifty years ago, the Pope ruled a large part of Italy. He ruled it as any king ruled his territory. However, he lost this territory to Italian patriots.

Since then, the Catholic Church has been a Church and not a state – though the Pope today still rules one square mile of land in Rome, called the Vatican. The Church does not want to go back to the days when the Pope was a king as well as a religious leader. In our time, the Catholic Church sees itself as independent of the state.

The Church used to teach that it was the one and only true religion, and consequently a government should not allow any other religion in its country: because, if a government allowed other religions, then it tolerated what was false; yet only the truth had the right to be taught. So the Catholic Church did not believe anybody had the right to believe or teach any religion other than the Catholic one. And the Church expected the state to enforce this view. In return, the Church taught that Christians had a duty to obey their rulers.

Nowadays, the Catholic Church believes that it is individuals who have rights, not abstract ideas such as 'truth'. So the Church teaches that everyone has the right to practise their religious beliefs. The state should respect this right. The bishops at the Second Vatican Council said:

> The Vatican Council declares that the human person has a right to religious freedom . . . The Council further declares that the right to religious freedom is based on the very dignity of the human person as known through the revealed word of God and by reason itself.

The teaching of the Catholic Church about religious freedom has changed. It is a good example of how a long-established Christian tradition can be changed. For hundreds of years the Church taught that the state should not allow any other religion to be taught. Then the bishops at a Council changed this teaching. They said that every individual has the right to teach and practise their religious beliefs.

The Catholic Church now believes that it should not be the only religion favoured by the state. The Catholic Church also believes it has the right to criticize a government that makes unjust laws.

At the Second Vatican Council, the Catholic bishops said:

> The Church . . . is not identified with any political community nor bound by any ties to any political system. It is at once the sign and safeguard of the transcendental dimension of the human person.

The Baptist view

Baptists believe that there should be no link between the Church and the state.

Baptists have always believed that everyone should be free to follow whatever their consciences told them. That is not to say that a Christian can believe absolutely anything and still be called a Christian. Anyone who does not believe in Jesus as Saviour cannot be a Baptist.

But Baptists do not believe that it would be right for the state to force a person to hold certain religious beliefs. If people believe what is wrong, then convert them – but by argument and by prayer, not by brute force.

Examination practice

1. 'Then give to Caesar what is Caesar's, and to God what is God's.' Outline the conversation that led up to Jesus saying that. What did he mean and why did he say it? (6 marks)
   Write about three-quarters of a side of A4.

2. Give and comment on an example of a situation where a Christian might think it right to go against the law. (6 marks)
   Write at least half a side of A4.

3. Do you think it good that Christian leaders should have places in the House of Lords?
   How could they best use the opportunities their membership of the House of Lords gives them? (8 marks)
   Write at least half a side of A4 on each of the two parts of the question.

What does it mean?

Ecumenism is to seek the unity between Christians that Jesus longed for when he prayed 'that they may be one'.

Why is ecumenism considered important?

- On the night before he was crucified Jesus prayed for his followers. He prayed to God the Father 'that they may be one as we are one: I in them and you in me. May they be brought to complete unity to let the world know that you sent me and have loved them even as you have loved me' (John 17$^{22-23}$).
- The two great commandments are 'Love God' and 'Love your neighbour' (Mark 12$^{28-34}$). If Christians did love as Jesus taught them, there would be no divisions.
- Paul wrote that Christians are the Church. The Church is one body, the body of Christ. Individual Christians are different parts of the same body – but there is still only one body.

> There is one body and one Spirit – just as you were called to one hope when you were called – one Lord, one faith, one baptism; one God and Father of all, who is over all and through all and in all.
>
> Ephesians 4$^{4-5}$

How is that unity expressed?

Churches do not try to hide their differences and pretend they are all the same. They accept that there are things in every tradition that are well worth keeping. What is more, different people find they can best worship God in different ways. The mystic atmosphere of the Orthodox Church is very different from the lively worship of the Salvation Army. The beauty of the singing in an Anglican Cathedral is far removed from the free expression of the Pentecostalists or the silence of the Quakers.

Many Christians believe that unity should allow the different traditions in Christianity to continue as they are. However, any restrictions about joining in communion with other or welcoming members of other churches should disappear.

Many positive steps towards unity have been taken.

- Every year the week 18–25 January is kept as Christian Unity Week.
- One week in the middle of May each year is Christian Aid Week, when Christians from many different churches join to support work for underprivileged people in many countries.
- The World Council of Churches (WCC) has been established, to help Christians work more closely together and to make it possible for Christians to speak together on moral and social issues. Churches representing 400 million Christians are members of the WCC. The Catholic Church does not belong to the WCC but cooperates closely with it.
- At the Second Vatican Council of the Catholic Church, other Christian Churches were invited to send observers.
- The Anglican–Catholic International Commission (ARCIC) meets to to discuss points of difference between Catholics and Anglicans.
- Some Churches have actually joined together. In England the Presbyterians and Congregationalists have joined to form the United Reformed Church. In India the Free Churches and Anglicans joined to make a large united Church. A number of unity schemes have been completed in the USA.
- In some places different denominations use the same building for worship.

Local covenants

A local covenant is a commitment by the Churches in a particular area to work together more closely. The Churches resolve to join regularly in worship, in study, in witness and in showing their Christian faith in practical ways.

The Nantwich Covenant

Nantwich is a small town in Cheshire, population about 12 000. The covenant, which was made in 1989, was signed by Methodists, Anglicans, Catholics, Pentecostalists, Baptists and the United Reformed Church.

The different congregations meet separately and worship in their own way as they always have done. They also work closely together as Christians in that community, the town of Nantwich.

They commit themselves to

- **pray and study together** – The clergy meet regularly to pray together for the Church's work in Nantwich and elsewhere. They discuss matters of the Christian faith, sharing what they agree and learning to understand the things on which they differ.
- **worship together** – On certain occasions, such as Bible Sunday or Christian Unity Week, they join for their Sunday evening worship. In Christian Unity Week three

or four members of one congregation go to another church, to preach, read the scriptures and lead some of the prayers.
- **work together in mission** – The churches run holiday clubs for children. On Holy Saturday morning they join for a presentation of music, drama, readings, singing and preaching, to bring home to people the message of Easter.
- **serve the community** – A team of church members, drawn from a number of congregations, regularly visit sick people in the town. They also together provide hospitality at Christmas for those who need it.
- **develop a sense of fellowship** – During Christian Aid Week and on other occasions they share in the work of raising money for a Christian agency that helps deprived people in other countries. They also enjoy shared social events.

Corrymeela

The Corrymeela Centre at Ballycastle, Co Antrim, is a place dedicated to reconciliation among the people of Ireland. The community based there is a group of Christians of different denominations who are committed to breaking down the barriers in Northern Ireland society.

People from all walks of life and from all over the world come to Corrymeela. They spend their time in worship, discussion and fellowship. Others, particularly those caught up in the tensions of Northern Ireland during the troubles, are simply there for a holiday. At different times different groups will be there:

- a group of single mothers, including both Protestants and Catholics, there with their children, relaxing in friendship together;
- a group of young people working on a Third World project;

Opening of Christ the Cornerstone Church, Milton Keynes, Britain's first purpose-built city centre ecumenical church

- a support group for the families of prisoners;
- a group of people from different churches in the same area, getting to know and understand each other.

Examination practice

1. Describe **three** ways in which Christians of different denominations join together. (9 marks)
   Write a few lines for each example.

2. Why do many Christians think it is important to work closely together? (6 marks)
   Write about half a side of A4.

3. Jesus prayed for his followers 'that they may be one'. Do you think it matters if there are differences between the Christian churches? Give reasons for your answer. (5 marks)
   Write about half a side of A4.

MINISTERS 11

Ordained ministry

In Chapter D12 there is an account of the ministry of bishops, priests and deacons. This is the ordained ministry of the Catholic, Anglican and Orthodox Churches.

Other Churches have people working full time in their ministry. The ministers are not ordained into the apostolic ministry, but they are chosen by their denominations and are ordained or set aside in some way for their particular

role in the life of the Church. Examples are Methodist, United Reformed Church and Baptist ministers. Their role is much the same as that of Catholic, Anglican and Orthodox priests in their parishes, though without the daily celebrations of the eucharist or the liturgy that are part of the lives of many priests:

- They give time to regular prayer and Bible reading.
- They prepare for the conduct of the services. In

particular, they prepare by reading and by planning how they will preach God's Word.

- By visiting and through contact with members of church organizations, they get to know the members of the Church community.
- They lead Church members in outreach (mission) among those living in the area served by the local church.
- They give instruction to particular people in the Church, such as those preparing for full membership or those in positions of leadership.
- They lead or support Church members in work for the benefit of people in need, either locally or through national and international Church organizations and charities.
- They visit people who have personal or spiritual problems.
- They keep in touch with those who are ill, visiting them and praying with them.
- They are responsible for a certain amount of administrative work.

In these Churches some people do hold senior positions. For instance, in the United Reformed Church, England, Scotland and Wales are divided into a number of provinces, each with a provincial moderator. Each year a moderator is appointed for the annual General Assembly of the United Reformed Church. Moderators are not regarded as different from other ministers, even though they hold senior positions. They are 'first among equals'. In the same way, Methodists have superintendent ministers with wider responsibilities.

There are many ordained ministers who are not paid by the Church. They include many who teach in schools and universities, though there is no rule to say what occupations they may or may not follow. They are sometimes called **non-stipendiary**. (The money paid to a minister is often called a stipend rather than a salary; it is seen as money to cover living expenses rather than a payment reflecting the true cash value of the ministry.) In many cases they are people who have been trained for the ministry in the same way as those in the paid ministry. Some people move from the stipendiary ministry to the non-stipendiary; for instance, someone may leave a post as a minister of a local congregation to teach in a school. Equally, of course, some people move the other way, from the non-stipendiary ministry to the stipendiary.

In the United Reformed Church some people are ordained as locally authorized ministers. They are ministers in the same way as others, but minister only to the local church to which they were ordained.

Ordained priests and ministers are called **clergy**. Those who are not ordained are called **lay people** or **laity**.

Lay ministry

A number of denominations choose and authorize certain lay people to exercise a preaching ministry.

- Methodists have relied on **lay preachers** for a long time. Methodist churches are organized into **circuits**. A typical circuit in the country may include 12 or more churches. There may be only three ordained ministers. On a Sunday the ministers will lead the worship at some of the churches, while lay preachers do so at the others.
- Similarly, the United Reformed Church has a large number of lay people who are recognized as **preachers**.
- The Anglican Church has **readers** who are trained and licensed to preach. They assist the clergy in the parishes to which they are licensed. They may assist in the distribution of the bread and wine. They may not celebrate Holy Communion, conduct a marriage or give a blessing.
- Some Baptist churches are led by **lay pastors**. They may lead the worship at all services, including the communion, in the same way as any other Baptist minister.

Examination practice

1. What is the role of an ordained minister in a local church? (10 marks)
   Write at least a side of A4, covering a range of points.

2. Do you think that there are any occupations that would be unsuitable for a non-stipendiary minister? Give reasons for your answer. (6 marks)
   Write at least half a side of A4, discussing particular occupations and making such general comments as you think necessary.

Introduction

Most Protestant Christians have ministers, not priests. See Chapter D11, *Ministers*.

Anglican, Orthodox and Catholic Christians have deacons, priests and bishops. When someone becomes a deacon, a priest or a bishop, they receive the **sacrament of orders**. They are ordained.

Thus, there are three degrees of 'orders'. The first two – bishop and priest – are counted as priestly. The third – deacons – are not counted as priests.

Only a bishop has power to ordain. And only someone who is a priest can be ordained a bishop.

Jesus, a priest?

The Jewish religion had priests in the time of Jesus. Their task was to:

- be a mediator (go-between) between people and God;
- offer animal sacrifices, on behalf of people, to God – so he would forgive their sins, and so he would give them a long and happy life.

Jesus did not use the word 'priest' to describe his work. Neither did the gospel writers use the idea of priest to explain the work of Jesus. Nor did Paul use the word 'priest' to explain the work of Jesus.

But the writer of a letter to the Hebrews did use the word 'priest' to explain the work of Jesus. The writer said (Hebrews 4^{14}–5^{10}) that Jesus achieved what priestly sacrifices never achieved:

- Jesus saved us from sin and death. He did this by being obedient to God's will; and by his death and resurrection.
- Jesus is now with God and continues to intercede with God for us.

Consequently, the writer of the letter to the Hebrews concluded that the work of priests was of no use to anyone. The priests' sacrifices did not save people from their sins, nor from death. But Jesus did. And Jesus is now with God, and continues to intercede with God on our behalf. This is much more effective than animal sacrifices in saving us from sin and death.

In spite of all this, about 200 years later, it became quite common to describe Jesus as a priest who sacrificed himself to God. Christians commemorated this sacrifice when they celebrated the eucharist.

Development of the priesthood

From the earliest years of the Christian Church, there were bishops, presbyters (also called elders) and deacons.

After about 200 years, it was common to describe bishops as priests. They still used the title 'bishop'. But they also described themselves as priests, since they offered the sacrifice of Jesus in the eucharist, on behalf of the people, to God.

Later, presbyters were also described as priests. The bishops had given them authority to lead the celebration of the eucharist in their area (parish). So, they also offered the sacrifice of Jesus in the eucharist, on behalf of the people, as a sacrifice to God.

Later still, Christians stopped using the title 'presbyter'. Instead, they used the title 'priest'.

Choosing priests

In the early Christian Churches, it was customary for all local Christians to have a voice in choosing bishops, presbyters and deacons.

In the Catholic, Anglican and Orthodox Churches today, it is the bishops that decide whom to ordain as a deacon, a priest or a bishop.

Priesthood today

Many Protestant Christians do not use the term 'priest' because the first Christians did not use the word; nor, they say, did Jesus offer a sacrifice to God.

Orthodox, Anglican and Catholic Christians have priests. The Catholic and Anglican Churches believe in two forms of priesthood:

- the common priesthood of all Christians. Because they have been baptized, they share in the life and work of Christ. This includes his priesthood;
- the ministerial priesthood of those who have been ordained (priests and bishops).

Apostolic succession

Bishops claim they have received their authority from the apostles: they claim to be the successors of the apostles.

Jesus sent out – this is what the word 'apostle' means – 12 of his disciples. He sent them to preach, to heal the sick, and to cast out evil spirits:

> They went out and preached that people should repent. They drove out many demons and anointed many sick people with oil and healed them.
>
> Mark 6$^{12-13}$

After Jesus had risen from the dead, he sent the Holy Spirit to the apostles. The Spirit gave them power and courage, to preach and to heal the sick. The apostles later appointed other people to carry on these tasks. There is a line of succession from these people to the present bishops.

A bishop cannot personally help everyone in his diocese; so he ordains priests to help him. They share in the priesthood of the bishop. But it is only the bishops who have the fullness of the sacrament of orders.

The visible head of each particular Church is the bishop. He should sanctify, teach and rule in his own Church. Together, the bishops have care for the whole Church. The Catholic bishops at the Second Vatican Council said:

> Individual bishops, in so far as they are set over particular Churches, exercise their pastoral office over the portion of the People of God assigned to them, not over other Churches nor over the Church universal . . . [yet] all the bishops have the obligation of fostering and safeguarding the unity of the faith and of upholding the discipline which is common to the whole Church.

The bishop of Rome (the Pope) is the successor of Peter, who was the first bishop of Rome. The Pope claims to be the leader of the bishops, just as Peter was the leader of the disciples. In the gospels, Peter is more prominent than the other disciples. For instance, when Jesus asked the disciples who they thought he was, Peter replied on their behalf:

> 'But what about you?' [Jesus] asked [his disciples].
> 'Who do you say I am?'
>   Peter answered, 'You are the Christ.'
>
> Mark 8[29]

See Chapter C16 *Mark's gospel – special emphases – II* for further details of the special place that Peter had among the disciples.

Catholic ceremony of ordination of a priest

In the Catholic Church, about a year before ordination, a candidate for ordination has to promise to remain unmarried and celibate for the rest of his life.

The ordination ceremony takes place within a celebration of the eucharist.

- It starts with the candidate sitting with the people. A priest, who knows the candidate well, recommends him to the bishop for ordination.
- The bishop calls the candidate to come forward, saying: 'We chose this man for priesthood in the presbyteral order'.
- The bishop gives a homily. He tells everyone what is the task of a priest. He may say: 'This man is called to preach the gospel, sustain God's people, and celebrate the liturgy, above all, the Lord's sacrifice.'
- The candidate then states: first, his intention to cooperate with the bishop; second, his resolve to celebrate the sacraments; third, his determination to preach the

A moment in the Catholic ceremony of ordination. The priests at the ceremony welcome a new priest (the person with his back to us) just after he has been ordained by the bishop.

gospel; lastly, his willingness to unite himself more closely to Christ.
- The candidate places his hands between the hands of the bishop and promises obedience to the bishop and his successors.
- The candidate lays prostrate on the floor, a sign that he needs the help of God to do his work. The congregation prays to God to help the candidate.
- Next come the two most important signs:
- In silence, as the candidate kneels before him, the bishop lays his hands on the candidate. Other priests do the same. This is a sign that they give the power of the Spirit of God to the candidate.
- Then the bishop says the prayer of consecration. '. . . Almighty Father, grant to this servant of yours the dignity of the priesthood. Renew within him the Spirit of holiness . . .'
- The candidate is now a priest.
- The stole is now arranged in the way a priest wears it; round the back of the neck, and both sides draped down the front of the body. The congregation sings: 'Come, Holy Spirit . . .'
- The bishop anoints the priest, on the hands, as a sign that he is consecrated to do the work of Christ.
- The newly ordained priest receives a chalice and paten. He joins the bishop in continuing the celebration of the eucharist.
- Before the eucharist continues, the bishop and the other priests congratulate and welcome the new priest.

Tasks of ordained men in the Catholic Church

Bishops

A bishop's tasks are similar to those of priests, except that he will spend more time in administration and less time in helping the sick, the broken-hearted and the dying. He will spend more time in caring for the priests in his diocese.

The bishop also has the unique tasks to:

- administer the sacraments of ordination and confirmation;
- ensure that the correct Christian beliefs are taught in his diocese;
- resolve any disputes in his diocese;
- join with other bishops in looking after the whole Catholic church.

The bishops at the Second Vatican Council said about a bishop:

> The bishops, as vicars and legates of Christ, govern the particular Churches assigned to them . . . Sent as he is by the Father to govern his family, a bishop should keep before his eyes the example of the Good Shepherd, who came not to be waited upon but to serve and to lay down his life for his sheep. Taken from among men and oppressed by the weakness that surrounds him, he can have compassion for those who are ignorant and erring.

A bishop often wears a distinctively shaped hat called a **mitre**. It is shaped like a pointed arch. A mitre symbolizes that the person who wears it is a bishop.

A bishop also has a tall stick that is hooked at the top. It is called a **crozier** or **crook**, and is a copy of a shepherd's crook. It symbolizes that a bishop should imitate Jesus, the good shepherd (pastor). Jesus cares for people as a shepherd (pastor) looks after his sheep.

Priests

They are expected to:

- assist the bishop in his work;
- follow the example of Christ;
- abstain from some normal activities – for example, marriage and politics. So a priest will not have a wife, nor any children. Nor will he stand as a member of parliament;
- preach about Jesus and God;
- administer four of the seven sacraments frequently, especially the eucharist. The other three are baptism, reconciliation, and anointing of the sick;
- visit the sick, to comfort them;
- pray privately, each day;
- teach people how to pray;
- continue their studies, and increase their understanding of the Bible and of theology;
- care for the dying and console those who grieve;
- listen to those who are agitated and distraught;
- understand and help those who are broken in spirit;
- live a simple life (even though they do not take a vow of poverty).

The bishops at the Second Vatican Council said about priests:

> Priests, while being taken from amongst men and appointed for men in the things that appertain to God, that they offer gifts and sacrifices for sins, live with the rest of men as with brothers . . . In the pursuit of this aim priests will be helped by cultivating those virtues which are rightly held in high esteem in human relations. Such qualities are goodness of heart, sincerity, strength and constancy of mind, careful attention to justice, courtesy . . .

A priest often wears a **stole**. This is like a rigid narrow scarf. The stole symbolizes that the person wearing it is a priest.

Permanent deacons

They are expected to:

- assist the priests and bishops in the celebration of the sacraments (for example, by baptizing, by preaching at the eucharist, by presiding at funerals). Deacons cannot lead the celebration of the eucharist, nor can they give the sacrament of the anointing of the sick, nor can they give the sacrament of reconciliation.
- engage in works of charity.

Most permanent deacons are married and have full time jobs. Their work as a deacon is part-time.

The bishops at the Second Vatican Council said about a deacon:

> The deacon is at the disposal of the bishop in order that he may serve the whole people of God and take care of the sick and the poor; he is correctly and rightly called 'one who shows love for orphans, for the devout and for the widowed' . . . Furthermore, he is entrusted with the mission of taking holy eucharist to the sick confined to their homes, of conferring baptism, and of attending to preaching the Word of God in accordance with the express will of the bishop.

Male and female

Protestant churches have women ministers. Some Churches in the Anglican Communion now accept the ordination of women as priests. The Orthodox and Catholic churches accept only men as candidates for the priesthood. They do not accept women. Why? They say:

- The 12 apostles were all men. Jesus had some women disciples, but he did not include any of them among the 12 apostles.
- Jesus was a man.
- In 2000 years of the Catholic and Orthodox Churches, no woman has been ordained a priest. It is tradition to ordain only men.

The arguments to ordain women as priests are :

- God created both women and men in his likeness, not just men.

In the Church of England women who are ordained priests have authority to celebrate the eucharist

Unmarried and married

In the early years of the Christian Church, there was no rule that bishops and other leaders had to be celibate. Today, in the

- Protestant Churches, ministers may marry or be celibate;
- Anglican Church, priests and bishops may marry or be celibate;
- Catholic Church, a man has to make a vow of celibacy to become a priest or bishop;
- Orthodox Church, both married and unmarried men may become priests; but an unmarried priest may not marry. And only an unmarried priest may become a bishop.

Some arguments for married priests and ministers are:

- It is the will of God that people should marry and have children.
- They can understand the problems of married people.
- It is unnatural to be celibate – perhaps impossible.
- Jesus did not tell the first apostles they had to be unmarried.
- Among Anglicans, the priest's wife has an important role in the parish – the vast majority of Anglican parishes prefer to have a married priest.
- At least one of the apostles, Peter, was married.

Some arguments for celibate clergy are:

- Jesus suggested that some people would be celibate for the kingdom of God.
- Jesus was unmarried. Priests take him as their model:
- they can give their undivided attention to people in their parish;
- they dedicate themselves undividedly to Christ and God;
- they are a sign of life in the kingdom of God, after death (when there is no marriage);
- it is less expensive to support unmarried priests;
- bishops can more easily move unmarried priests to another place in the diocese.

- There is no reason to suppose that only men have the qualities appropriate in a priest.
- That Jesus chose only men as apostles simply reflected the custom in his time, when women did not undertake apostolic tasks. If the Churches today closely followed everything Jesus did, they would ordain only Jews and Palestinians as priests. Yet the Churches do not do this.
- Men dominate the Catholic and Orthodox Churches; these men are reluctant to accept equality between men and women. They are prejudiced.

Examination guidance

'Almighty Father, grant to this servant of yours the dignity of the priesthood.'
(from the Catholic ordination service)

1. What does the bishop do just before he says this prayer? (1 mark)

2. During the ceremony of Ordination, the bishop preaches a homily (sermon). What sort of things might he say? (3 marks)

3. Some people argue that there should be women priests. Do you agree? Give reasons to support your view. (3 marks)

1. **First answer**
Blesses the man who will be a priest

An incorrect answer.
(Score: 0 marks out of 1)

Second answer
The bishop lays his hands in silence over the candidate.

A correct answer.
(Score: 1 mark out of 1)

2. **First answer**

    He tells the man to be ordained that he should follow the example of Christ. He tells him all the sorts of things he ought to do. He tells him how to behave as a priest and what his duties are, how he should do the sort of things that Christ did and help other people.

    The candidate has made one substantial point, that a priest should follow the example of Christ. The rest of the answer is either waffle or is expressed ambiguously: it is not clear whether the 'he' refers to the candidate for ordination, the bishop or Christ.

    The examiner will only award marks if you express yourself clearly and unambiguously. So when you use a word like 'he', make sure the examiner knows who you are writing about.

    (Score: 1 mark out of 3)

    Second answer

    The bishop tells the candidate that he must devote his life to the people of God, just as Christ did; that a priest must help the weak, the poor, the broken-hearted and the sick.

    A priest should administer the sacraments, especially the eucharist, which is the central sacrament of the Church.

    A priest should lead people to God through prayer: through the public prayer of the Church and through his private prayer; he should also teach people how to pray, just as Jesus taught his disciples how to pray.

    The candidate has given a relevant account of what a bishop may say. There are many other points a bishop might make, but the candidate is not required to write them – only five lines were given for the answer.

    There is sufficient detail to merit the three marks for this question.

    (Score: 3 marks out of 3)

3. **First answer**

    No, I do not think there should be women priests. Jesus chose twelve men to be priests; it has always been the tradition of the Church to have male priests.

    The candidate has presented two relevant and valid arguments.

    (Score: 2 marks out of 3)

    Second answer

    Yes, I think there should be women priests. God made men and women equal, so there is no reason to think he gave one sex the qualities required of a priest. In our age of gender equality, the Church is male dominated and reluctant to change traditions that are outdated.

    Jesus chose twelve male apostles as priests, but this does not mean that women cannot be priests. If we followed Jesus' example exactly, only Palestinian Jews should be priests.

    A substantial answer that easily merits full marks.

    (Score: 3 marks out of 3)

Examination practice

1. List **two** arguments for ordaining women as priests. List **two** arguments against ordaining women as priests. (3 marks)

    Write about six lines of A4.

2. Do you think there should be married priests? Give reasons for your opinion. Show that you have understood the opposite point of view. (8 marks)

    Write about three-quarters of a side of A4.

3. Christians believe a priest has to follow the example of Jesus. Jesus said that any man who wants to follow him will have to take up his 'cross'. What might a priest learn from this? (6 marks)

    Write about half a side of A4.

4. What happens and what is said at the ordination of a priest? (10 marks)

    Write about one side of A4.

Introduction

Most members of the Church are lay people. A lay person is someone who is neither ordained (such as a priest, bishop, deacon), nor a member of a religious congregation (such as a sister, nun, brother, or monk).

Until the Second Vatican Council, the Catholic Church had little to say about the specific tasks of lay people. The Second Vatican Council was a meeting of the bishops of the Catholic Church in the mid-1960s. The bishops spent much time talking about the Church; and for the first time in the history of the Church they talked about the role of lay people.

Before the Second Vatican Council, bishops had often spoken about the tasks of ordained people and the tasks of members of religious congregations, but not about the tasks of lay people. The implied view was that the clergy and the religious were the really important people in the Church. They accomplished all the tasks of the Church. Lay people did not contribute much to the work of the Church; they benefited from the work of clergy and from the work of members of religious institutes.

The bishops at the Second Vatican Council changed this. They said that lay people had a task – to show the love of God in the everyday world. Ordained people and religious withdraw from the world, to occupy themselves with sacred matters. Lay people live in the world. They have the task of making it holy.

Common task of all Catholics

All Catholics share the same task because of their baptism. The bishops at the Second Vatican Council emphasized this. A baptized person becomes a member of the Church. Every member of the Church is baptized into the risen life of Jesus. Thus they receive the life of God himself. All members of the Church should follow the example of Jesus. They all share in the priestly, prophetic and kingly office of Christ. They should love their neighbour and love God. Yet clergy, religious and lay people do this in different 'states'.

> It belongs to the laity to seek the kingdom of God by engaging in temporal affairs.
> Catholic bishops at the Second Vatican Council

Lay tasks in worship

The main task of lay people in church worship is to join in the celebration of the sacraments, especially the celebration of the eucharist. It is traditional for Christians to meet and share the eucharist every Sunday, to celebrate the resurrection of Jesus, to develop unity with other members of the Church, and so on. (See Chapter A1, *Eucharist (Holy Communion, Mass)*.)

Lay people can be readers or eucharistic ministers (acolytes). Most lay people do not wish to do either of these two tasks.

Readers, obviously, read: they can read the first or second reading at the eucharist (only a priest or deacon can do the last reading, which is from the gospel). Eucharistic ministers can assist the priest to distribute the consecrated bread at communion time. They can also take communion to those who are too sick to come to church to join in the celebration of the eucharist.

Lay tasks at home

This is a task for all lay people: to show the love of Christ in the way they treat their spouse and children – to be tolerant, forgiving, kind, patient, understanding, generous, encouraging, appreciative, self-controlled, and so on. If they can manage this, they show the love that Christ has for his Church.

But they will need the Spirit of God to behave like this: hence the importance of prayer. A lay person's home should be a place of prayer, both private prayer and regular family prayer. They will then have the Spirit of God encouraging and guiding them to imitate God. In this way they make God present in their family life. They bring the kingdom of God.

Paul said:

> For the sinful nature desires what is contrary to the Spirit . . . The acts of the sinful nature are obvious: sexual immorality . . . idolatry and witchcraft; hatred, discord, jealousy, fits of rage, selfish ambition . . . drunkenness, orgies and the like . . . But the fruit of the Spirit is love, joy, peace, patience, kindness, goodness . . . and self-control.
>
> Galatians 5[16–26]

Lay tasks at work and at leisure

This is another task for all lay people, similar to their task in the home, although this time they have to demonstrate the same qualities with people they may not know or may not like. The world of work is competitive. This can encourage us to be selfish, to manipulate other people, to be unscrupulous, to be inconsiderate towards other people, and so on. A Christian's task is to show the qualities of Christ. Instead of naked ambition, there should be understanding of others. Instead of sheer greed, there should be generosity. Instead of control and power over other people, there should be service. Instead of envy and resentment, there should be recognition of other people's talents. And so on. In these ways a Christian spreads the love of Christ and establishes the kingdom of God.

In the story of the good Samaritan, Jesus taught that it is important to help those we do not like. In the story a Jew is attacked and robbed. He is left half-dead. A Jewish priest, and then another religious Jew, see the badly wounded Jew, but ignore him. A Samaritan (Jews and Samaritans were enemies) sees the half-dead Jew, bandages his wounds, takes him to the nearest inn and pays the innkeeper to take care of the wounded man.

> 'Look after him', he said, 'and when I return, I will reimburse you for any extra expense you may have.'
>
> Luke 10$^{25-37}$

The commandment – you must love your neighbour as yourself – works both ways because you must love yourself as you love others. In fact if you don't love yourself you will never be able to love your neighbour properly.

Seraphim of Sarov

Lay tasks in politics

This is another task for all lay people.
- For instance, if they live in a rich country, they should seek to influence the government's policy on aiding very poor countries, so that rich countries can develop a more just attitude towards poorer countries.
- They should argue for a just distribution of wealth in their own country.
- They should pressure the government to care for the environment.
- They should encourage the government to pass just laws.
- They should campaign for the rights of minority groups, such as unborn children threatened by abortion.
- They should support interest in helping the sick and frail.

In these ways they present God's love for the neglected and weak. They work to establish God's kingdom on earth.

In the parable of the sheep and the goats, Jesus taught that, when we meet God after death, he will want to know if we helped the sick, the homeless, the hungry, strangers and those in prison, because 'whatever you did for one of the least of these brothers of mine, you did for me' (Matthew 25$^{31-46}$).

Examination guidance

Catholics believe the following groups in the Church have important tasks:

   Ordained people (bishops, priests, deacons)
   Members of religious institutes (nuns, sisters, monks, brothers)
   Lay people

Explain what the tasks of these groups are.

(8 marks)

First answer

The bishop, priest, deacons are people who tell you about God and what happened in his life.

The members of religious institutes are the followers of God.

The lay people are us people that listen to them and spread the word of God. They help other people

A couple of correct points. The candidate's answer barely merits 2 marks.

Some of the statements, such as the second sentence and the last sentence, are too vague; the candidate should express these ideas more precisely and specifically.

(Score: 2 marks out of 8)

Second answer

Ordained people say the Mass, give the sacraments, help people in need, preach the word of God, try to bring more people together as Christians.

Members of religious institutes pray to God and help in third world countries, eg Mother Teresa. They look after the dying and pray for the sick and dying. They dedicate their lives to God.

Lay people help the parish priest. They take communion to sick people.

This candidate's answer is correct. There are accurate statements about all three groups.

The answer is terse. Yet it is to the point and it does not waste words. To gain a higher mark, the candidate should improve the answer in two ways: first, give more information about the specific tasks of each of the three groups; second, give an account of the common tasks of all three groups.

(Score: 4 marks out of 8)

Third answer

All three groups of people are baptized Christians. They share in the life of the risen Christ and God. Thus they all have the task to model their lives on the life of Christ: to pray, to get to know God, to help the sick and broken-hearted, to accept God's will, to 'take up their cross', to share their possessions with the poor, and so on. Their common task is to love God and to love their neighbour.

Yet they fulfil these common tasks in distinctive ways.

Ordained people have three tasks: to teach, lead the worship of God and govern the Church.

They spend much of their time doing the second task. Ordained priests lead the celebration of the eucharist and consecrate the bread and wine. They hear confessions in the church and administer the sacrament of the sick to people who are ill at home. They have to help prepare people for the sacraments. Priests also have to organize things in the parish, like collections for charity, the parish accounts and parish organizations. They also have to counsel people who are struggling with marriages, struggling with pregnancies.

Members of religious congregations follow Christ in a special way because they take three vows: to be poor, to be celibate, to do as their superior tells them. Some of them live in isolated places and do not like to mix with people outside their convent. They pray a lot as well as work and study. Others pray for people, but also work in the community. They teach, help the sick, or work in the parish. Many of them go abroad to developing countries to preach about Jesus and help the poor.

Lay people can help the priest in the church or the parish. They may be ministers of communion or read at the Eucharist. But their main task is to live a 'normal' life'. They teach other people about the importance of Jesus and God through the way they live their lives at home, in their job, at leisure, and in their social and political activities.

Thus people in each of the three groups have distinctive tasks, even though they share a common purpose.

An answer that deserves full marks. The candidate has written about the common tasks of the three groups and about the specific tasks of each group. There is good scope to the answer. It includes general points as well as detailed points.
(Score: 8 marks out of 8)

Examination practice

1. Lay people may be readers and eucharistic ministers. What are the tasks of readers and eucharistic ministers? (3 marks)
    Write about six lines.

2. Catholics believe that lay people should follow the teaching and example of Christ.

    They should do this at home, at work and at leisure. Explain how they might do this. (10 marks)
    Write about one side of A4.

3. 'Priests and nuns and brothers are more important than lay people in the Catholic Church.'
    Do you agree? Give reasons for your view. Show that you have considered the opposite view. (8 marks)
    Write about three-quarters of a side of A4.

NUNS, MONKS, SISTERS, BROTHERS: RELIGIOUS INSTITUTES

Introduction

There are three 'states' in the Catholic Church:

- laity
- clergy
- religious.

Lay people are what most of us would call the ordinary members of the Church.

Clergy are those who have received the sacrament of orders: deacons, priests, bishops.

'**Religious**' is a technical term for people who have vowed to be poor, celibate and obedient. They are often called sisters, nuns, monks or brothers. They belong to a religious institute or society. There are many religious institutes and societies (sometimes called **congregations**). Each has its own name.

For example, Ed O'Connell (Chapter D8) and Mary Clune (see Chapter A10, *Pilgrimage*) are members of the Society of Saint Columban. John Daley (later in this chapter) is a member of the Institute of Charity. The anonymous writer of the 'statement by a member of a monastic institute' (later in this chapter) is a member of the Benedictine community at Turvey.

There is a difference between an institute and a society, though we have not explained it, as you do not need to know this for your exam. We include both under the word 'institute'.

Common task of all Christians

It is through baptism that a person becomes a member of the Church. All members of the Church have the same tasks:

- to deepen their understanding of God;
- to become more open to receive the love of God;
- to learn to love God;
- to proclaim and share their love of God;
- to learn to love others as they love themselves.

Christians believe they can fulfil these tasks through Christ. He is the way to God, and he is the way to love other people. He is also the most important way in which God makes himself known to us.

However, the Catholic Church teaches that its members fulfil these tasks in different ways and in different circumstances.

The clergy deal with 'sacred' things, especially the administration of the sacraments, such as the sacrament of the eucharist, the sacrament of reconciliation, and sacrament of the anointing of the sick.

Lay people live in the world, so they have 'normal' jobs and they usually have families. It is through their work and through their family life that they bring Christ to the world.

Religious have a way of life that is distinctly different from that of clergy and of lay people (although some religious are also priests).

The monks at Mount St Bernard Abbey celebrate the eucharist. This is one of several times each day that they pray together.

Special purpose of religious life

The bishops of the Catholic Church, at the Second Vatican Council, said that those who lead a religious life should:

- **follow Jesus in all aspects of his life**. He was poor and he was unmarried. Accordingly, religious take one vow to be poor and another vow to be celibate.

  Religious feel they have received a personal call from Jesus to follow very closely his style of life. They feel they are like a rich young man who came to Jesus and asked what he should do to inherit eternal life. Jesus told him to keep the commandments. The rich man replied that he had always kept them. Jesus advised him there was one thing he lacked:

  > 'Go, [said Jesus] sell everything you have and give to the poor, and you will have treasure in heaven. Then come, follow me.'
  >
  > Mark 10[17-22]

So religious give up everything they own. They give it away. And they remain poor, for the rest of their lives. They deliberately decide to follow the example of Jesus, and to share the life of those who are poor.

They also remain unmarried, like Jesus. Therefore they can be totally committed to Jesus and to God. Religious decline to have an intimate sexual relationship with another person, so they can give all their time to the work of Jesus, so they can give all their energy to helping others, so they can be a sign of the kingdom of God.

- **be a sign that the kingdom of God transcends this world** – that is, that there is more in the kingdom of God than eating and drinking, marrying and having a family, working and spending money, enjoying the pleasures of this world, and so on. The way of life of religious is a sign of this. They dedicate their lives to God in a special way. They are 'married' to Jesus or God. They give up everything for the sake of the kingdom of God. They take a vow of obedience: they vow to do certain tasks, or to go to another place, if their superior tells them. They are totally dedicated to doing the will of God.

Religious admire the way the first disciples responded to Jesus. Jesus was walking by the Sea of Galilee. He saw Simon and Andrew fishing.

> 'Come, follow me,' Jesus said, 'and I will make you fishers of men.' At once they left their nets and followed him.
>
> Mark 1[17–18]

Religious feel they have received a similar call from Jesus, to follow him, and to be fishers of people.

- **be a sign that this world is transient** (lasts but a short while). We can be sure of one thing – we shall die. So religious withdraw from this world. They live as though they were not part of this world. They avoid the pleasures of this world. Instead, they seek God in prayer, in work, in helping those in need, and in study.

This is a sign that our immediate interests – in getting a good job, in getting sexual gratification, in getting prestige, in getting money, in feeling important, and so on, do not bring us lasting satisfaction. These things, though immediately appealing, fade. They can leave us yearning for something more – God.

Three vows

These are the distinguishing marks of a religious – the vows of poverty, of celibacy and of obedience. These are taken for life. These vows are sometimes called **evangelical counsels**.

Some religious take additional vows. Benedictine monks, for instance, take a vow of stability: that is, they vow to stay in a monastery for the rest of their lives. Others, such as the Jesuits, take a vow of obedience to the Pope: they vow to do whatever he tells them to do.

Apostolic institutes

Some religious institutes are called **apostolic**. Their members usually call each other 'brother' or 'sister'. They have withdrawn from the world, but they usually work in the world. Some of them are missionaries. (See the statement by Ed O'Connell at the end of this chapter and Chapter D8, *The Church – missionary work*). Many of them have jobs as teachers, nurses or parish workers.

If they have a paid job, they do not keep any of the money they earn, since they have taken a vow of poverty. The money they earn goes to their religious institute.

They have taken a vow of celibacy, so they do not marry or have families. Instead, they live with other members of their institute. This is not always easy, as they have to live amicably with people they may not naturally like.

They pray regularly, to know God better, and to become more like Jesus. They pray together, as well as privately, each day.

If their superior tells them to move to another house of the institute, then they will go because they have taken a vow of obedience. However, before the superior makes a decision, both the superior and the member will pray to discern God's will. And it is usual for members to have a say in decisions the superior makes about where they live.

Contemplative institutes

Some religious institutes are called **contemplative**. Their members are monks or nuns. They live in a monastery or abbey. They withdraw completely from the world.

If we went to a monastery, one of the monks or nuns

A monk's day			
Mount Saint Bernard Abbey, near Leicester			
3.15 am	Rise		
3.30 am	Community prayer	12.15 pm	Community prayer
	Breakfast any time	12.30 pm	Dinner and washing up
	between 4.15 and 6.00	2.15 pm	Community prayer
	Time for private prayer	2.30 pm	Afternoon work
	and reading	4.30 pm	End of afternoon work
7.00 am	Community prayer	5.30 pm	Community prayer
	Reading	6.00 pm	Private prayer
8.00 am	Community mass		Supper
9.15 am	Morning work	7.30 pm	Community prayer
12.00 noon	End of morning work	8.00 pm	Bed

would greet us at the door. They would welcome us, but they would not invite us into the monastery, because they want to insulate themselves from all distractions. Silence is important to them – they do not even talk at meal times. As we can see from the timetable at Mount Saint Bernard Abbey, contemplatives spend most of their day praying and working; they also do some reading or study.

> Language has created the word loneliness to express the pain of being alone, and the word solitude to express the glory of being alone.
>
> Paul Tillich

Statement by a member of a contemplative institute

I am often asked why I gave up a successful career, house, car, and busy social life to live in a monastery! My answer is quite simple: although I found my life interesting, enjoyable and very full, I felt unfulfilled. I wanted something more, but it was quite a long time before I realized that I was actually seeking God.

And so I came to a monastery: it was quite a change, a world away from what I had been used to! It took a long time to get used to the new lifestyle. The silence was quite a shock: I had been surrounded by sound stimuli; traffic noise, people moving around, voices, radio, images, advertising, newspapers, noticeboards, all demanding my attention. The silence of my new environment made me aware of the noise and confusion in my mind. Gradually the silence gave me space for reflection and prayer.

Remaining in one place all the time with the same set of people was and is a real challenge. I can no longer jump into the car and go to visit a friend if I feel lonely or bored, or walk away at the end of a trying day, go home and close the door on irritating people. Instead, I have to sweat my way through forgiveness and reconciliation, as I meet with them in the chapel, and in recreation, before the sun goes down!

We meet in the chapel five times a day to worship God. To this worship we each bring our gifts – art, poetry, music, dance, silence – all used to give glory to God. We also have periods of private prayer during the day. Prayer is our main 'work' and affects every aspect of our lives, putting all our work, relationships, joys and sorrows into context, leading us into God's life and peace. Many people come to us to share in our prayer and to find help in their search for peace and wholeness. Our art and embroidery are also means by which we reach out to others.

We work in the monastery to earn our living by producing religious art, mosaics, calligraphy, icons, wall-hangings and vestments, running a programme of retreats and editing an ecumenical periodical. We also have a large garden where we grow most of our own vegetables. Our small goat herd provides us with milk, cheese and yoghurt and a lot of fun!

One lifetime is not long enough to experience all the good things open to us: we have to make choices. I have decided against a continuing intimate relationship with one other person, against marriage and children, and instead have chosen to live as a celibate in a monastic community, dedicated to God. Over the years that decision is challenged and requires a new and conscious re-commitment, but deep down I know that this way of life, searching for God, living among, and loving, many people is the way for me.

A nun of the Benedictine Communities, Turvey

Statement by a member of an apostolic institute

To enter religious life is to discover that the great vocation is to be a Christian, a follower of Christ worthy of the name. Whatever high ideals of service and sacrifice may have brought someone to the idea of a religious vocation, the sheer simplicity of the gospel and its call to love God and one's neighbour is what is offered by every religious order and congregation.

So we learn that we have chosen this way to be a Christian. No need to make comparisons – single life, married life, priesthood, religious life – the joy is the discovery, anew, of being another Christ, his follower, a sharing in the mystery of belonging to his kingdom.

The Rosminian shares this understanding and develops it by study of the rule that Antonio Rosmini drew up in the early part of the nineteenth century for his Institute of Charity. He learns that his first call is to union with God in love and prayer. He is guided and encouraged in various forms of prayer – the liturgy, above all the Eucharist, the scriptures, traditional prayer down through the ages, personal prayer leading to meditation and contemplation.

Then, out of that love for God he must be prepared to work within the Church at whatever he is asked: to love and serve his neighbour. Many religious institutes were founded for specific good works: education, medicine, social work, apostolic work, etc., but Antonio Rosmini had no such particular vision. His ideal was to trust in the providence of God to guide to work in ways that best suited the talents and abilities of the men who come to this Institute. Effectively he was saying: 'Come, to love and serve God. Live with a community of like-minded men. Then be prepared, when we are asked to help others, to do so to the utmost of your ability and according to the talents that God has given you.'

Thus you will find Rosminians who are priests in parishes, retreat directors, seminary professors, schoolteachers, specialists in working for the blind, or mentally infirm, or with deprived families; who are gardeners, cooks, maintenance men in our larger community houses or out in the missions in Africa or South America. There are specialists in canon law, leaders in charismatic prayer groups, the editor of a national Catholic newspaper. 'You name them, we've got them' laconically summarized one of our brethren, and he wasn't being entirely complimentary. He was referring to the truth that we are very human, have our faults and foibles, and can be difficult to live with and get on with.

We share such limitations with all religious institutes, and with the Church. But we share the ideals, too, that Christ has asked us to follow him.

John Daley, Institute of Charity

Statement by a member of a missionary society

I belong to a society of secular priests. Our primary charism is to be on mission in a cross-cultural and often inter-faith situation, especially among those who are poor and powerless. I have lived in the shantytowns of Lima, Peru. I also know first hand the situation of the Christian minority in Lahore, Pakistan.

The Columban story of mission has had many phases. It all began nearly 2000 years ago. For the call to be on mission means attempting to practise what Jesus presented as mission. In his hometown of Nazareth, he quoted the prophet Isaiah: The Spirit of the Sovereign Lord is on me, because the Lord has anointed me to preach good news to the poor. He has sent me to bind up the broken-hearted, to proclaim freedom for the captives and release for the prisoners, to proclaim the year of the Lord's favour (Isaiah 61^{1-2}).

Mission, we have discovered over the years, is about being with and amongst people as we all struggle to live as children of God, as sisters and brothers of each other. This presence with and amongst people, of solidarity with them, is essential to mission.

The role played by ordained, religious and lay Columbans has changed periodically in response to the needs of the people we serve. Our society started in Ireland in 1918. For the first 50 years we went out to the countries of Asia and Latin America, to help people build up their own local Church. We did this mainly by providing catechetical programmes [discussing with people our belief in Jesus and the Church] and by celebrating the sacraments.

From the 1960s onwards, Columbans have done their best to share the life of poor people who struggle to earn a living. We have shared the lives of poor people when governments have repressed them. Some of our members have been imprisoned; some have been martyred; and some have been expelled. The cost has been high from the early days right up until present times.

Now, in the 1990s, a new type of response is required of us. It is crucial that today's missionary be a link person between local Churches – to help them to share, with others around the world, their experiences of faith and their struggle for the reign of God. Hopefully a new missionary era will strengthen the friendships between Christian communities of the Universal Church. And strengthen the friendships between Christian communities and communities of people of other faiths.

Two recent developments in the Columban family will help us to meet this challenge. Firstly, we are becoming more international in our priest and sister members, as Fijians, Filipinos, Koreans, Chileans and Peruvians join our ranks. Secondly, our lay missionary programme (of men and women from Latin America and Asia, as well as Ireland and Britain) has taken off with 47 lay missionaries on overseas mission.

We are convinced that the missionary work of tomorrow will be about working with people of other religions, on issues relevant to the needs of the poor. This blending of two approaches, the option for the poor and inter-faith dialogue, has developed out of many years of missionary work with people in different countries.

Our lives are full and the work is demanding. But we always insist – the people we join in the search for life have enriched us. This enrichment has always been greater than anything we have given.

Ed O'Connell, Columban Missionary Priest

Examination guidance

Do you think that the way of life of members of religious institutes (congregations) is worthwhile? Give reasons for your answer. Show that you have considered the opposite point of view. (5 marks)

First answer

I agree to a certain extent but not fully. Their way of life is accepted. If they lived any other way they could easily be tempted to do things they should not. But I think the rules should be relaxed about what how they live, what type of car they can have, etc. They should not be so poor. Everybody needs some comfort and not many of them watch much television. The way of life of religious should not be conserved as it is now.

This is a marginally relevant answer. It is too vague and imprecise. Candidates have to state more clearly and specifically what is in their mind. Besides, they must answer the actual question.

Some candidates waffle when they are not sure what the answer to the question is. They rarely gain any marks.

(Score: 1 mark out of 5)

Second answer

I personally do not think it is worthwhile. God created male and female so they could go together. Why should religious have to be celibate? God intended men to love women. Members of religious institutes have a job to do, but I think they should relax and have fun sometimes. Their jobs are very demanding but can be quite tedious. I could not enjoy it. But it is not up to me to say how religious are to live their lives. Their way of live has been going on for a long time, so I suppose it will probably survive.

The candidate has developed a relevant and clear view.

To gain further marks, you should do two things.

First, consider one or more reasons for the opposite point of view, and even say why these reasons are not convincing.

Second, present further reasons and arguments to support your point of view.

(Score: 3 marks out of 5)

Third answer

Yes, I do think that their lives are worthwhile. Everyone in the world has a special task to do. This is theirs.

These people pray for all the people in the world who don't have time to pray for themselves. Also they give a lot to the community and many people in need are helped by them. They do not marry and so they have time to care for all those people who are neglected.

In a way I think their lives are not worthwhile as they miss out on things like having families of their own and being able to go out with friends on their own to have fun.

I understand the argument that the lives of contemplative religious are not worthwhile because they do not do much for other people. Jesus did say in the parable of the sheep and the goats that whatever you do to others you do to me. And these people do hide away. Yet I think they help us with their prayers.

Basically it depends upon what you feel a worthwhile life is. If you think of it as lots of money, children and material possessions, it is not worthwhile. If you think being able to get closer to God and help many people is worthwhile, then yes.

This is a notable answer: the candidate has presented a clear opinion and has proposed several reasons to justify that opinion.

Moreover, the candidate has carefully considered and commented on the opposite point of view.

Notice, first, the scope of the answer, and second, the development in the answer.

The answer has scope because the candidate has made more than three distinct, relevant points; and there is development in the answer because the candidate has explained the points in some detail.

(Score: 5 marks out of 5)

Examination practice

1. What is the difference between a lay person and a 'religious' person in the Catholic Church? (3 marks)
   Write about 6 lines.

2. 'Religious' (monks, nuns, sisters, brothers) lead an unusual life.
   Explain what kind of life they lead. (10 marks)
   Write about one side of A4.

3. Many people are inspired to follow the life of Jesus. Explain why. (8 marks)
   Write about three-quarters of a side of A4.

4. Would you consider becoming a 'religious'?
   Give reasons for your answer. Show that you have considered the opposite point of view. (8 marks)
   Write about three-quarters of a side of A4.

Model for Christians

Catholics and Orthodox emphasize that they do not worship Mary. They do not believe she is God. She was a human person, but one who set an example of how a Christian should live. So they greatly admire and respect her.

Orthodox Christians frequently call Mary 'all holy', because she cooperated fully with what God wanted. According to Luke's account of the birth of Jesus, Gabriel told Mary she would become the mother of Jesus. She freely accepted. All Christians should follow her example and cooperate with God.

Although Catholics and Orthodox do not worship Mary, they do pray to her. They ask her to join them in their prayers, to worship God, to ask for his help, to seek his forgiveness, and so on.

> Mary, mother of Jesus, woman of deep faith, first priest of the New Testament, pray for us.
> Missionaries of St Columban

Virgin

Many Christians (including Catholics and Orthodox) believe that Mary was a virgin, even though she gave birth to Jesus. They say that this belief is in two of the gospels, Matthew's and Luke's. These two gospels tell about the birth of Jesus. Both gospel writers say that Mary was a virgin, as she did not conceive Jesus through intercourse with Joseph: rather, the power of the Spirit of God caused her to conceive.

Some Christians do not believe that Mary conceived Jesus without intercourse with Joseph. They point out that the gospel of John and the gospel of Mark say nothing about Mary as a virgin; these gospels also say nothing about the conception and birth of Jesus.

Some Christians believe that Mary was a virgin after she gave birth to Jesus: she had no sexual intercourse with Joseph. But other Christians doubt this tradition. They point out that the gospels mention the brothers and sisters of Jesus (for example, Matthew 13[55-56]).

Mother of God

This seems a bizarre title. Christians believe that God is uncreated. So how can there be a mother of God? Besides, Mary was the mother of Jesus, a woman, betrothed to Joseph. So how can she be a sort of goddess?

The New Testament does not describe Mary as the mother of God. This title was first used when Christians were discussing whether Jesus was God. Some Christians used the title to defend the view that Jesus was truly God as well as a man. They said he was one being, not two different beings existing side by side. If he was one being, and Mary was his mother, then Mary was the mother of God.

The Catholic and Orthodox Churches accept this title. Most Protestant Churches do not accept it.

Catholics also call Mary the 'mother of the Church', because she gave birth to Jesus, who is the founder and leader of the Church.

> Mary has by grace been exalted above all angels and men to a place second only to her Son, as the most holy mother of God who was involved in the mysteries of Christ.
> Catholic bishops at Second Vatican Council

Assumption

This is the belief that when Mary died, her body did not rot and disintegrate. Instead, God raised her to life and took her to heaven. A recent pope, Pius XII in 1950, formally declared that this belief was a dogma (certain belief) of the Catholic Church. The Pope also said that when God took Mary to heaven, immediately after her death, she became 'Queen of heaven'. He wrote:

> We . . . do pronounce, declare, and define as a divinely revealed dogma: the immaculate Mother of God, Mary ever virgin, after her life on earth, was assumed, body and soul, to the glory of heaven.

The Orthodox Church also firmly believes Mary was assumed into heaven when she died, though a Council has not formally stated this belief.

Most Protestant Christians do not talk about the assumption of Mary. And they do not believe God assumed Mary into heaven when she died.

The feast of the Assumption is 15 August. Orthodox Christians call it the feast of Dormition (falling asleep).

Immaculate conception

By the time of the Middle Ages, Christians had come to believe that Mary had lived a good life, without committing any sin.

Some Christians thought that she was conceived with original sin, but did not commit any sin. Thus, as with any normal human, Mary was tempted to do wrong. Yet she did not do anything wrong. (See Chapter C9, *Human nature*, for an explanation of original sin.)

Other Christians believed in the immaculate conception. They thought Mary was conceived without original sin. Thus Mary was never tempted to do wrong in the way that a normal human is tempted to do wrong. Consequently, Mary did not commit any sin.

Just over 100 years ago, in 1854, Pope Pius IX supported the second of these two views. He declared that the immaculate conception of Mary was a dogma (certain belief) of the Catholic Church. He declared that:

> the doctrine which holds that the Blessed Virgin Mary, at the first instant of her conception (by a singular privilege and grace of the omnipotent God, in consideration of the merits of Jesus Christ the Saviour of mankind) was preserved free from all stain of original sin, has been revealed by God.

The Orthodox Church believes that Mary did not commit any sin, but it is undecided about the immaculate conception.

Most Protestant Christians do not believe in the immaculate conception of Mary. Nor do they believe that Mary did not sin. They believe that Mary did sin, as all humans do.

Many people confuse the immaculate conception with the virginal conception. The immaculate conception means that, when Mary was conceived in her mother's womb, she did not have original sin. The virginal conception (or virgin birth) means that when Mary conceived Jesus, she did not have sexual intercourse with Joseph, or any other person.

Different views about Mary

'Mary is a member of the Church.' This may seem an insignificant statement to make. Yet the Catholic bishops at the Second Vatican Council thought it was an important statement to make. They thought that some Catholics were over-emphasizing the significance of Mary, the mother of Jesus. So the bishops did not write a separate document on Mary. Instead, they wrote about her in their document on the Church. They wrote about her importance in the Church and they affirmed traditional statements about her. They called her mother of God, mother of the Church, virgin, model for Christians. They also affirmed the two dogmas that popes in the last 150 years have made: the assumption and the immaculate conception.

Orthodox Christians have the same beliefs as Catholics about Mary, except that they are not sure about the immaculate conception.

Most Catholic and Orthodox beliefs about Mary are not in the New Testament. The Church developed these beliefs after they had decided the books of the New Testament.

The Protestant Churches do not say much about Mary. Most Protestants:

- think the traditional teaching about Mary is an unhelpful development of Christian belief;
- claim that the Bible is the only source of Christian belief – they point out that the Bible says little about Mary;
- emphasize the Christian belief that God sent Jesus to die for all of us, and that Jesus is the only way to get to God.

Some Protestants:

- feel that Catholics have made Mary to be just as important as Jesus in helping us to get to God, which they say is a bad mistake;
- allege that Catholics have made Mary equal to God, for instance by calling her mother of God. They say that this is blasphemy and an insult to God.

Examination practice

1. What is the difference between immaculate conception and virginal conception? (3 marks)
    Write about six lines.

2. Explain what the Catholic Church teaches about Mary. (8 marks)
    Write about three-quarters of a side of A4.

3. Protestants do not share Catholic and Orthodox beliefs about Mary.
    Explain why not. (6 marks)
    Write about half a side of A4.

PART E

Moral Behaviour

Full courses: Part E

This chart tells you the chapters to study. Find your exam board. Then highlight your syllabuses (or syllabus). Study the chapters that are ticked.

SEG Syllabus C: Catholic Christian tradition	SEG Syllabus B: Inter-faith studies: Christianity	SEG: Life of Jesus: synoptic gospels	SEG: Contemporary issues	SEG Syllabus A: Christian Church	EdExcel: Contemporary issues and Mark's gospel	EdExcel: Catholic Christianity	EdExcel (London): Christianity	EdExcel: Christianity	MEG: Christian perspectives on personal, social issues	MEG: Christianity through Luke's gospel and Acts	MEG Syllabus C: Christian beliefs and practice (modular)	NEAB: Catholic Christian behaviour, attitudes and lifestyle	NEAB: Christian behaviour, attitudes and lifestyle	NEAB: Christian life and Mark's gospel	NEAB: Catholic Christian tradition	NEAB Syllabus B: Christian tradition	NEAB Syllabus A: Christianity	Chapter
✓	✓		✓	✓	✓	✓	✓	✓	✓		✓	✓	✓				✓	Chapter 1 How Christians decide right and wrong
✓	✓		✓	✓	✓	✓	✓	✓	✓		✓	✓	✓				✓	Chapter 2 Absolute and relative morality
✓	✓		✓	✓	✓	✓	✓	✓	✓		✓	✓	✓				✓	Chapter 3 Marriage, love, sex, children, birth control
✓	✓		✓	✓	✓	✓	✓	✓	✓		✓	✓	✓				✓	Chapter 4 Marriage; sex; celibacy
✓	✓		✓	✓	✓	✓	✓	✓	✓		✓	✓	✓			✓	✓	Chapter 5 Marriage ceremony
✓			✓	✓	✓	✓	✓	✓	✓		✓	✓	✓	✓			✓	Chapter 6 Parenthood; religious education
✓			✓		✓	✓	✓	✓	✓		✓	✓	✓				✓	Chapter 7 Abortion
✓			✓	✓	✓	✓	✓	✓	✓		✓		✓				✓	Chapter 8 Childlessness; eugenics
✓	✓		✓	✓	✓	✓	✓	✓	✓		✓	✓	✓				✓	Chapter 9 Divorce; annulment; separation
✓			✓	✓	✓	✓	✓	✓	✓		✓	✓	✓				✓	Chapter 10 Euthanasia
✓			✓		✓	✓		✓	✓		✓	✓	✓				✓	Chapter 11 Prejudice and discrimination
✓			✓	✓	✓	✓	✓	✓			✓	✓	✓					Chapter 12 Sin, crime and punishment
✓			✓	✓	✓				✓		✓	✓	✓					Chapter 13 War and peace
✓			✓	✓	✓	✓	✓	✓	✓	✓	✓	✓	✓				✓	Chapter 14 Injustice; protest; conflict
✓				✓				✓	✓	✓	✓	✓	✓				✓	Chapter 15 Poverty; wealth

Full courses: Part E

This chart tells you the chapters to study. Find your exam board.
Then highlight your syllabuses (or syllabus).
Study the chapters that are ticked.

Exam Board	Syllabuses	Description	Ch 16 Wealth; money; materialism	Ch 17 Christian relief agencies	Ch 18 Liberation theology	Ch 19 Hospices; care of the elderly	Ch 20 Work and leisure	Ch 21 Drugs; alcohol	Ch 22 Environmental pollution; conservation	Ch 23 Christian discipleship	Ch 24 Christian discipleship – special texts	Ch 25 Love: two great commandments	Ch 26 Situation ethics	Ch 27 Sermon on the Mount	Ch 28 Conscience	Ch 29 The Ten Commandments	Ch 30 Natural law: reasoning
NEAB	Syllabus A	Christianity	✓	✓	✓	✓		✓	✓	✓	✓	✓	✓	✓	✓	✓	✓
	Syllabus B	Christian tradition														✓	
		Catholic Christian tradition			✓	✓											
		Christian life and Mark's gospel														✓	
		Christian behaviour, attitudes and lifestyle							✓	✓							
		Catholic Christian behaviour, attitudes and lifestyle			✓	✓				✓							
	Syllabus C	Christian beliefs and practice (modular)	✓	✓	✓	✓	✓	✓	✓	✓	✓	✓	✓	✓	✓	✓	✓
		Christianity through Luke's gospel and Acts	✓	✓	✓	✓			✓	✓	✓	✓	✓	✓	✓	✓	✓
		Christian perspectives on personal, social issues	✓	✓	✓	✓			✓	✓	✓	✓	✓	✓	✓	✓	✓
MEG		Christianity	✓	✓	✓	✓				✓	✓	✓	✓	✓	✓	✓	✓
		Catholic Christianity		✓	✓				✓	✓	✓	✓	✓		✓	✓	✓
		Contemporary issues and Mark's gospel										✓	✓	✓	✓	✓	✓
ExExcel (London)		Christianity	✓	✓	✓	✓	✓	✓	✓	✓	✓	✓	✓	✓	✓	✓	✓
SEG	Syllabus A	Contemporary issues	✓	✓	✓	✓	✓	✓	✓	✓	✓	✓	✓	✓	✓	✓	✓
		Christian Church								✓	✓	✓	✓		✓	✓	✓
		Life of Jesus: synoptic gospels			✓					✓	✓						
	Syllabus B	Inter-faith studies: Christianity														✓	✓
	Syllabus C	Catholic Christian tradition	✓	✓		✓		✓	✓	✓	✓	✓	✓	✓	✓	✓	✓

Short courses: Part E

This chart tells you the chapters to study. Find your exam board. Then highlight your syllabus. Study the chapters that are ticked.

Chapter	MEG Syllabus B: Christianity	MEG: Christian perspectives on personal, social and world issues	MEG Syllabus A: Christianity through Luke and Acts	MEG: Christianity: Mark's gospel	MEG: Christianity: Catholicism	EdExcel (London) Syllabus B: Christianity	EdExcel (London) Syllabus A: Religion and life	SEG: Religious education	NEAB: Thinking about God and morality	NEAB: Christianity
Chapter 1 How Christians decide right and wrong	✓		✓	✓		✓	✓	✓	✓	✓
Chapter 2 Absolute and relative morality	✓		✓	✓		✓	✓	✓	✓	✓
Chapter 3 Marriage, love, sex, children, birth control	✓	✓		✓		✓	✓	✓	✓	✓
Chapter 4 Marriage; sex; celibacy	✓	✓		✓		✓		✓	✓	✓
Chapter 5 Marriage ceremony	✓	✓		✓		✓		✓	✓	✓
Chapter 6 Parenthood; religious education	✓	✓		✓		✓	✓	✓	✓	✓
Chapter 7 Abortion	✓			✓				✓	✓	✓
Chapter 8 Childlessness; eugenics	✓	✓		✓				✓	✓	✓
Chapter 9 Divorce; annulment; separation	✓	✓		✓		✓		✓	✓	✓
Chapter 10 Euthanasia	✓		✓	✓		✓	✓	✓	✓	✓
Chapter 11 Prejudice and discrimination	✓	✓	✓	✓				✓		✓
Chapter 12 Sin, crime and punishment	✓	✓	✓							
Chapter 13 War and peace	✓	✓	✓				✓		✓	✓
Chapter 14 Injustice; protest; conflict	✓	✓	✓	✓	✓	✓	✓	✓	✓	✓
Chapter 15 Poverty; wealth	✓			✓		✓	✓	✓	✓	✓
Chapter 16 Wealth; money; materialism	✓	✓		✓		✓	✓	✓	✓	✓
Chapter 17 Christian relief agencies	✓	✓	✓	✓	✓	✓	✓	✓	✓	✓
Chapter 18 Liberation theology	✓	✓		✓	✓	✓	✓	✓	✓	✓
Chapter 19 Hospices; care of the elderly	✓			✓			✓	✓	✓	✓
Chapter 20 Work and leisure	✓									✓
Chapter 21 Drugs; alcohol		✓								
Chapter 22 Environmental pollution; conservation	✓		✓		✓	✓	✓	✓	✓	✓
Chapter 23 Christian discipleship	✓			✓	✓	✓	✓	✓	✓	✓
Chapter 24 Christian discipleship – special texts	✓	✓	✓	✓	✓	✓	✓	✓	✓	✓
Chapter 25 Love: two great commandments	✓	✓	✓	✓	✓	✓	✓	✓	✓	✓
Chapter 26 Situation ethics	✓	✓	✓	✓	✓	✓	✓	✓	✓	✓
Chapter 27 Sermon on the Mount	✓	✓	✓		✓	✓	✓	✓	✓	✓
Chapter 28 Conscience	✓		✓		✓	✓	✓	✓	✓	✓
Chapter 29 The Ten Commandments	✓	✓	✓	✓		✓		✓	✓	✓
Chapter 30 Natural law: reasoning	✓							✓	✓	✓

A common opinion

If we want to know what is right or wrong, then let us listen to what God says. All Christians agree on this.

But they have different opinions about how to find out what God wants us to do.

Different opinions

Most Protestant Christians say that there is one essential way to find out what God wants – **read the Bible**. For example, the Baptist Union states:

> ... our Lord and Saviour Jesus Christ ... is the sole and absolute authority in all matters pertaining to faith and practice [including moral behaviour], as revealed in the Holy Scriptures [Bible].

Catholic, Orthodox and Anglican Christians agree that reading the Bible is a way to discover what is right or wrong. They say that the Church leaders – the bishops – decided what books to include in the Bible and what books to exclude from it; they did this after judging that some writers were inspired by God and others were not. And if God inspired these writers, then we can find out what is right and what is wrong by reading their books.

Nevertheless, Catholics, Orthodox and most Anglicans think that the Bible is not the only way to find out what God wants. They believe that there are two other important ways: first, the **traditions of the Church**, and second, the **teachings of the Church leaders** – the bishops. Catholics put special emphasis on the teachings of the bishops of Rome. They use the title 'pope' for a bishop of Rome. See Chapter D12, *Bishops, priests, deacons: Orders*, for more information.

Alongside these three ways, Catholics and some Anglicans use a fourth way. They use reasoning to discover what God wants us to do. The Catholic Church usually calls this **natural law** rather than reasoning.

Finally, all Christians say that they rely on the **Holy Spirit** to guide them.

Two ways or five ways?

So Christians use five ways to discover what is right and what is wrong:

1. what the Bible says, especially about the teaching and the example of Jesus;
2. what the bishops teach, particularly what the councils of bishops teach, and (for Catholics) what the bishops of Rome solemnly teach (Catholics accept the teachings of 21 councils of bishops, the latest of which was the Second Vatican Council, which met at Rome from 1962 to 1965. Orthodox accept the teachings of the first seven councils of bishops, the last of which met at Nicaea in 787. Some Anglicans accept the teachings of some councils of bishops);
3. Christian traditions;
4. natural law (reasoning);
5. the Holy Spirit.

Most Protestant Christians use only two of these ways – the first one and the last one – to discover what is right and what is wrong. For example, the United Reformed Church says, in its ordination ceremony:

> The United Reformed Church acknowledges the Word of God in the Old and New Testaments, discerned under the guidance of the Holy Spirit, as the supreme authority for the faith and conduct of all God's people.

Catholic Christians use all five of these ways to discover what is right and what is wrong. For example, Pope John Paul II mentions four of them when speaking about euthanasia:

> I confirm that euthanasia is a grave violation of the law of God, since it is the deliberate and morally unacceptable killing of a human person. This doctrine is based upon the natural law and upon the written word of God, is transmitted by the Church's Tradition and taught by the ordinary and universal Magisterium.

Teachings of Jesus

Christians say that God made himself known in the life and teachings of Jesus. Christians also say that God has told us, through the example and teachings of Jesus, what he wants us to do. The life and teachings of Jesus are written in the second part of the Bible – the New Testament. So Christians believe that we can use the New Testament to find out if something is right or wrong.

For example, Jesus taught that we should love God and we should love our neighbour. Thus it is right to love others; and it is wrong to hate others or to be indifferent to them. Jesus also taught that we should forgive. Thus it is right to forgive and it is wrong to bear a grudge. A third example is that Jesus taught that divorce was wrong. Thus a marriage should last until death breaks it.

Yet, though the New Testament does teach that divorce is wrong, it does not say much about marriage, and it says even less about parenthood. It says nothing about abortion,

How Christians decide whether something is right or wrong

Christians believe we discover what is right and what is wrong by finding out what God thinks is right and wrong.
And how do we find out what God thinks is right and wrong?
Christians give diverging answers.

Protestant Christians say — **Catholic Christians say**

this way, and only this way | this way, yet not only this way | this way, as well | this way, as well | this way, as well | this way, as well

by considering the example and teaching of Jesus. Christians believe that, in the life of Jesus, God clearly revealed himself and what he thinks. So if we consider what Jesus did and said, we can discover what God thinks.

and also by the influence of God's Holy Spirit, who guides us to understand correctly Jesus and the Bible.

and by reading the Bible, particularly the New Testament (the second half of the Bible), and especially the gospels, which are about Jesus. Christians believe that God inspired the authors of the Bible to write accurately about him and what he thinks.

by **thinking** about ourselves and the world. Christians believe that God made us in his image and likeness. Catholics believe that we are partly like God because we can reason. Catholics also believe that, by **reasoning** about ourselves and the world, we can work out how God wants things to be. We thus discover what he thinks. Catholics call this natural law.

by listening to the teachings of the **bishops.** Catholic and Orthodox Christians believe that the bishops are the successors to the twelve disciples of Jesus. Jesus gave these twelve disciples authority to teach about God and what he thinks. As successors to the disciples, the bishops have the same authority to teach about God and what he thinks.

by paying attention to the **traditions** of the Church. These traditions were started by early Christians and maintained by later Christians. So these traditions are the collective wisdom of Christians for the last two thousand years. Hence they are a respected source for deciding what God thinks.

by the influence of the God's **Holy Spirit.** Catholics believe that the Holy Spirit not only guides us to understand correctly Jesus and the Bible, but also guides us to think and reason objectively about ourselves and the world, guides us to listen discerningly to what the bishops teach, and guides us to examine respectfully the traditions of the Church.

---

nothing about contraception, and nothing about helping infertile couples to have children. It says nothing about euthanasia. It says nothing about pollution. It says something about religious discrimination, but nothing about racial discrimination. The New Testament says frequently that it is right to forgive, but it says little about war. It occasionally mentions wine, but it says nothing about the right use of alcohol or drugs.

So the New Testament has little specific teaching on most moral issues.

Worse still, the New Testament approves of slavery; it also approves of sex discrimination. Yet Christians today believe that neither of these is right. As a result, Christians disregard the New Testament teaching on slavery and sex discrimination.

Does this mean that Christians cannot use the New Testament to decide what is right and wrong?

Some Christians believe that, though the New Testament does not say whether actions such as going to war or having an abortion are right or wrong, we can use the New Testament to discover the principle of right and wrong. And the New Testament teaches that this principle is to love others as we love ourselves. We have to work out for ourselves what this entails in any situation. See Chapter E26, *Situation ethics*, for details and examples.

However, if we use this way to discover right and wrong, we use the Bible to find just the basic principle. We still have to work out what is the loving thing to do in any situation. We use reasoning to do this. Thus reasoning is just as important as the Bible to discover what is right and wrong.

Example of Jesus

Christians believe that the example of Jesus is just as important as the teaching of Jesus. As a result, Christians look at Jesus' style of life to find out how they should live their lives. For example, Jesus cared for disabled people, such as the blind man Bartimaeus. Consequently, Christians believe that it is right to care for disabled people. Jesus made friends with those who were despised, such as the tax collector Zacchaeus. Hence Christians believe that it is right to respect and to mix with outcasts. Jesus forgave those who hurt him. Consequently, Christians believe that it is right to forgive those who hurt us; and they believe that it is wrong to bear a grudge.

Yet Christians do not copy every aspect of Jesus' life. Jesus was poor; he was a wandering preacher; he was celibate. Most Christians do not think that this means they have to be poor, wandering preachers, or celibate – though there are a few Christians who feel that God wants them to follow this style of life. (See Chapter D14, *Nuns, monks, sisters, brothers: religious institutes.*)

Again, if we decide which aspects of Jesus' life we should copy, and which aspects we should not copy, then we are not using the Bible to decide what is right and wrong. We are using reasoning, or something else, to decide what is right and what is wrong.

Not just the New Testament

Christians believe that the New Testament is an important source for discovering what is right and wrong because:

- They believe that God inspired the writers of the New Testament.
- They believe that God sent Jesus to teach what is right and wrong.
- They believe that Jesus was the perfect person: he did nothing wrong.

Yet we have seen in the previous two sections that, by itself, the New Testament is not enough. Consequently, most Christians also use other ways to discover what God thinks is right and wrong.

Church leaders

All Christians believe that Jesus is the head of the Church.

Catholics, Orthodox and Anglicans believe that the visible leaders of the Church are the bishops: they are the successors of the apostles. Jesus taught the apostles about God and about himself. (See Chapter C16, *Mark's gospel – special emphases – II.* See also Chapter C12, *Mark's gospel – parables.*) Consequently, the bishops have the authority to teach about God and about Jesus.

When the bishops meet, there is a council.

The Orthodox accept the teachings of the first seven councils (that is, the councils up to AD 787) as authoritative guides.

Catholics accept the teachings of 21 councils as authoritative guides. The latest was the Second Vatican Council, which met in the 1960s. The teachings of the councils and the solemn teachings (called *ex cathedra*) of the bishops of Rome are authoritative guides for Catholics. They call these teachings the **solemn magisterium**.

For example, the bishops at the Second Vatican Council taught that we should not use nuclear weapons. Such weapons kill many people, including innocent people; the weapons also devastate large areas of land. The bishops said that it is wrong to use weapons that cause widespread and indiscriminate destruction. So Catholics believe that it is wrong to use nuclear weapons.

Another example is marriage. The bishops at the Second Vatican Council taught that there are two purposes in marriage: that the couple should love and cherish each other, and that they should be open to having children. So Catholics believe that it is right to marry, to love their spouse, and to have children.

Tradition

Most Christians take notice of established, traditional ways of behaving. They think that what Christians have invariably practised and believed is a good guide to what is right or wrong.

Catholics sometimes call this the **ordinary magisterium** of the Church.

For example, Christians have always collected and given money to help people who are poor. So a Christian says that it is right to go without some luxuries, to help hungry people in other countries. It is right to be generous. It is wrong to refuse to share.

Another example is male priests. There have been only male priests in the Catholic and Orthodox Churches since the start of the Christian religion. Thus some Christians argue that it is wrong to have female priests.

A third example concerns sex. Christians have always believed that only a sexual relationship between a man and a woman can be right, and that a sexual relationship between two people of the same sex is wrong. Thus some Christians argue that this belief must still be right today.

However, many Christians are wary of quoting tradition. They feel that there can be bad traditions as well as good traditions. They also know that the Church has changed some traditions. For instance, for a long time Christians thought that slavery was quite acceptable. But eventually this tradition was changed: so nowadays Christians do not believe that slavery is right.

Another example is usury (lending money at interest). For a long time Christians thought that this was wrong. But Christians today do not accept this tradition. They believe that it is acceptable to lend money and to charge interest on a loan.

Natural law

Some, but not all, Christians believe that natural law is a way to discover what God wants. See Chapter E30, *Natural law: reasoning* for a more detailed explanation of natural law.

Natural law:

- uses reasons and arguments, to decide right or wrong;
- looks at what is fitting to human nature, to decide what is right or wrong.

For example, I might say that a man who commits adultery breaks the marriage vows he made: he betrays the trust his wife put in him; he shatters a unique relationship between the two; and he shows lack of consideration and thought for his wife. For all these reasons, I would conclude that adultery is wrong.

Another example is telling the truth and telling lies. I might say that if we look carefully at what happens when we tell lies, we shall see that we do not trust each other, that we are suspicious of each other, that we spend our time wondering what other people are up to, and so on – there is little harmony and goodwill between people. On the other hand, when we tell the truth, we notice that we tend to respect each other, that we know where we stand, that we relax, that we are not suspicious of each other, that we do not have to spend our time worrying what other people are up to, and so on. There is a much more peaceful and constructive atmosphere. So we can conclude that telling the truth is right, and telling lies is wrong.

> We profess two wisdoms in Christ:
> the uncreated wisdom of God,
> and the created wisdom of man.
>
> St Thomas Aquinas

Inspiration of the Holy Spirit

Some Christians feel that the Holy Spirit inspires them to know what they should do. So they pray to God when they want to know what is right in a situation. They trust that his Spirit will put the answer into their minds.

For Quakers, this is the most important way to decide right and wrong. However, they also believe that we can deceive ourselves: we may believe that God inspires us when it is our own desires that inspire us.

Many Christians decide what is right or wrong by asking the Holy Spirit to help them, and by using one or more of the methods noted above. For instance, they may pray to the Holy Spirit and use natural law. Some seek the guidance of the Holy Spirit and look carefully at a tradition of the Church. Others ask the Holy Spirit to guide them when they read the Bible.

For instance, the Baptist Union says:

> . . . each [local group of Baptists] has liberty, under the guidance of the Holy Spirit, to interpret and administer [Jesus'] laws.

And, according to the Catholic bishops at the Second Vatican Council:

> . . . in the supremely wise arrangement of God, sacred Tradition, sacred Scripture and the Magisterium of the Church are so connected and associated that one of them

cannot stand without the others. Working together, each in its own way under the action of the one Spirit, they all contribute effectively to the salvation of souls.

If Christians use the guidance of the Holy Spirit to decide what is right and wrong, they cannot present evidence to support a decision, as it is subjective. But if Christians use any of their other ways to decide right and wrong, they can present evidence. For instance, if they use natural law to decide what is right and wrong, they can explain the reasons for a decision. Or if they use the Bible to decide right and wrong, they can quote passages from the Bible to support a decision.

See Chapter C5, *God – the Holy Spirit*, for more information.

Examination practice

1. Christians use the Bible to help them to decide what is right and wrong. (3 marks)
   Explain why.
   Write about six lines.

2. Christians use the Bible to decide what is right and wrong.
   Why do some Christians think that this is not sufficient? (8 marks)
   Write about three-quarters of a side of A4.

3. Christians have different ways to decide what is right and what is wrong.
   What are they? (10 marks)
   Write about one side of A4.

4. Christians do not always agree on how to decide what is right and what is wrong.
   What effect does this have on their decisions? (8 marks)
   Write about three-quarters of a side of A4.

5. Suppose someone asked you to spy on a pupil in your class. How might you decide whether it was right or wrong?
   Give reasons for your view. Show that you have considered other views. (6 marks)
   Write about half a side of A4.

Introduction

Suppose we think that it is always wrong to abort a foetus; this is an example of **absolute morality**. And suppose we think that it is always right to share our possessions with others; this is also an example of absolute morality.

But suppose we think that abortion is sometimes right and sometimes wrong; this is an example of **relative morality**. And suppose we think it is sometimes right and sometimes wrong to share our possessions with others. This is another example of relative morality.

Absolute morality

Some Christians have an absolute view on some moral issues. The Catholic Church, for instance, teaches that some actions are always wrong – for example, that:

- to abort a child is always wrong;
- to divorce is always wrong;
- to commit euthanasia is always wrong;
- to be prejudiced is always wrong;
- to have sex outside marriage is always wrong;
- for rich countries not to share their wealth with poor countries is always wrong;
- to destroy indiscriminately (as in nuclear war) is always wrong.

The Catholic Church also teaches that some actions are always right – for example, that:

- to forgive is always right;
- to love is always right;
- to be self-controlled is always right;
- to care for the sick is always right;
- to help starving people is always right.

However, the Catholic Church does not have an absolute view on all moral issues. It has a relative view on some moral issues. For example, it teaches that:

- contraception can be right when using natural methods; yet contraception is wrong when using artificial methods, such as the condom or the pill;
- war can be right, when people defend themselves from an unjust attacker; yet war is wrong when people attack another country, just to conquer the other country and to gain natural resources;
- capital punishment can sometimes be right, for instance when someone has murdered and may murder again; yet capital punishment is wrong for less serious crimes.

Relative morality

Some Christians have a relative view on all moral issues, not just some moral issues. They believe that an action is never always right or wrong. It depends on the circumstances. So they believe that we cannot say that abortion is always right, nor can we say that it is always wrong, as we have first to look at the circumstances before we can decide. Aborting a foetus (or baby) is not right or wrong in itself. It is the situation that makes an abortion right or wrong.

Likewise, we cannot say that euthanasia is always right or always wrong. Nor can we say that caring for sick people is always right or always wrong. Nor can we say that forgiving others is always right or always wrong. And so on. It all depends on the situation. People who hold this belief are usually called **situationists**.

However, situationists do believe in one absolute principle. They believe that it is always right to love other people (that is, to do good to them). They say that we should decide whether an action is right in any situation by asking: 'If I did this action, would I be loving the other person?' If I answer 'yes', then my action would be right in this situation; but I cannot infer that this action would be right in another situation.

See Chapter E26, *Situation ethics*, for more information.

Do our beliefs influence our behaviour?

Some Christians in the Protestant tradition answer: 'Hardly, as we are innately inclined to be selfish and to do evil. We do not have free will – that is, we do not decide what we do. Rather, God has predestined us to be good or bad.' These Christians follow the teachings of Calvin, a leader of the Protestant Reformation. They emphasize what Paul said in his letter to the Christians at Rome:

> I have the desire to do what is good, but I cannot carry it out. For what I do is not the good I want to do; no, the evil I do not want to do – this I keep on doing. Now if I do what I do not want to do, it is no longer I who do it, but it is sin living in me that does it.
>
> Romans 7[18–20]

These Christians believe that we can do good only when we have been personally baptized and redeemed by Jesus. We then have the power of Jesus in us to do good. Yet it is not our beliefs that influence our behaviour; it is the power of God working in us.

Most Christians answer: 'Sometimes, but not always'. Or they answer: 'Partly, but not wholly'. These Christians believe that we have free will, so our beliefs can influence what we do and what we say. They also believe that when we die, God will judge us according to our moral behaviour. This implies that we are responsible for our behaviour.

For example the Catholic bishops at the Second Vatican Council said:

> Man's dignity requires him to act out of conscious and free choice, as moved and drawn in a personal way from within, and not by blind impulses in himself or by mere external constraint . . . Before the judgement seat of God an account of his own life will be rendered to each one according as he has done either good or evil.

Yet the bishops at the Second Vatican Council also said:

> Since human freedom has been weakened by sin it is only by the help of God's grace that man can [manage to do good].

So most Christians believe that our beliefs do not always influence our behaviour. Instead, our selfish instincts often influence our behaviour. Christians call this **original sin**. (See Chapter C9, *Human nature*, for details.) They agree with Paul that we often do wrong, even though we know it is wrong. So we need the help of God to do good.

Conclusion

It was bitterly cold. Four men were trudging through a snow blizzard, on their way back from the South Pole. They had hoped to be the first people ever to reach the South Pole, but when they arrived they found that a group led by Amundsen had been at the Pole a few days before them. One of the four, Lawrence Oates, had frostbitten toes. This made him walk very slowly. Yet he knew they must move more quickly to reach their base camp, to eat and to warm themselves. That night, when they had pitched their tent, he told the other three he was going outside for a short while. He walked out of the tent and kept walking to his death.

Was his action right or wrong?

Examination practice

1. What is the difference between absolute and relative morality? (3 marks)
   Write about six lines.

2. Does the Catholic Church believe in absolute or relative morality? (6 marks)
   Write about half a side of A4.

3. Do Christians think that our beliefs influence our behaviour? (8 marks)
   Write about three-quarters of a side of A4.

4. 'Lawrence Oates committed suicide. He did it for a good reason. But it was still wrong, because suicide is wrong.'
   Do you agree? Give reasons for your opinion. Show that you have considered the opposite point of view. (6 marks)

   Write about half a side of A4.

MARRIAGE, LOVE, SEX, CHILDREN, BIRTH CONTROL 3

Purpose of marriage

Many Christians believe that there are two purposes of marriage. For instance, the Catholic bishops, at the Second Vatican Council, said that the purpose of marriage is:

- to love another person, in a distinct and unique way, and to develop your love for that person;
- to create children.

The bishops at the Council said that love naturally leads to the creation of children.

> Marriage and married love are by nature ordered to the procreation and education of children.
> Catholic bishops at Second Vatican Council

Other Christians, however, believe that a couple who never have any intention of having children, and who use artificial means to prevent their birth, are still married in the eyes of God.

Marriage in the Old Testament

In the first book in the Bible, Genesis, there are two stories of creation. Each one has something important to say about marriage.

The first story relates that God made the world in six days. On the sixth day he made humans: male and female. They were equal. They were to have children and to rule the earth:

> So God created man
>   in his own image,
> in the image of God
>   he created him;
> male and female
>   he created them.
>   God blessed them and said to them, 'Be fruitful and increase in number; fill the earth and subdue it.'
>
> Genesis 1[27–28]

The second story tells about a garden in Eden. It emphasizes that male and female are made for companionship. They are equal and that is why they can be companions:

> The Lord God said, 'It is not good for the man to be alone. I will make a helper suitable for him.'
>   Now the Lord God formed out of the ground all the beasts of the field . . . He brought them to the man . . . But for Adam [man] no suitable helper was found. So the Lord God caused the man to fall into a deep sleep; and while he was sleeping, he took one of the man's ribs . . . made a woman from the rib . . . and brought her to the man.
>   The man said:
> 'This is now bone of my bones and flesh of my flesh.'
>   For this reason a man will leave his father and mother and be united to his wife, and they will become one flesh.
>
> Genesis 2[18–24]

Marriage in the New Testament

There are two important passages about marriage in the New Testament:

* Mark 10[1–12], where Jesus answers a question about divorce, and so talks about marriage. He says that God created man and woman to be united in marriage. They join to each other in marriage, in a way that no one should separate. Any person who separates the two, undoes what God has joined:

> A man will leave his father and mother and be united with his wife, and the two will become one flesh. So, they are no longer two, but one. Therefore what God has joined together, let man not separate.

* Paul's letter to the Christians at Ephesus (Ephesians 5[21–33]), in which he compares the love of a husband and wife to the love of Christ for his people (Church). Paul says that husbands should love their wives as Christ loves the Church and gave his life for it; husbands should love their wives as they love themselves. He says wives should submit themselves to their husbands, just as the Church does to Christ:

> Wives, submit to your husbands as to the Lord. For the husband is the head of the wife as Christ is the head of the Church . . . Now as the Church submits to Christ, so also wives should submit to their husbands in everything.
>   Husbands, love your wives, just as Christ loved the Church and gave himself up for her . . .

Marriage, a sacrament

Some Christians – such as Baptists and Methodists – believe that there are two sacraments.

Catholics, Orthodox and many Anglicans believe that there are seven sacraments. Marriage is one of them.

A sacrament is a sign – something that you can see or hear – that the risen Jesus and God are present. Thus a sacrament brings us closer to God; it helps us to follow his example; and it binds us closer to other people in the Church. Yet marriage is different from the other sacraments. The main aim in the other sacraments is to bring a person closer to Christ and God. The main aim in the sacrament of marriage is to bring one person closer to another.

Christians who believe that marriage is a sacrament believe that it includes more than two people: it includes God. This means that God is there to help married people, to grow in love, especially if their marriage is going through hard times.

As marriage is a sacrament, it also means that the risen Jesus is present. Thus Jesus' love for the Church is an example to the couple of what their love for each other

At the Anglican marriage ceremony the husband and wife exchange rings, saying: 'I give you this ring as a sign of our marriage'

should be like. And their love for each other is a sign of Jesus' love for the Church.

In the Catholic Church marriage is the only sacrament that a priest cannot give. The couple give the sacrament to each other. The priest is a witness to the marriage, on behalf of the Church. In the Orthodox Church, it is the priest who gives the sacrament.

Freedom and marriage

The Catholic and Orthodox Churches believe that there is no marriage unless the two freely and willingly agree to marry each other. Take, for example, an arranged marriage. If the parents decide whom their son or daughter should marry, and one of the couple does not want to marry the other person, then this is not a valid marriage. The two have not validly married, even though they had a marriage ceremony in a church.

The Catholic Church believes that freedom of choice is just one condition for a valid marriage: see the subheading 'annulment' for other conditions.

> 'What is wedlock forced but a hell,
> An age of discord and continual strife?
> Whereas the contrary bringeth bliss
> And is a pattern of celestial bliss.'
>
> Shakespeare

Sex in marriage (common life)

Christians believe that sex is an important part of marriage. For instance, the Catholic Church states that, despite a marriage ceremony, until the couple consummate their marriage (that means, have sex) there is no valid marriage. The Catholic Church also believes that sexual enjoyment is one of the two purposes of marriage. This means that sex between the husband and wife should express:

- a special love – the two regard each other in a unique manner: the spouse is more important than anybody else;
- a sole love – the two belong to each other in a way that they do not belong to anyone else;
- a development of love – the two, through sex, develop a bond with each other;
- an enjoyment – the two bring delight and satisfaction to each other, through sexual gratification;
- encouragement – the two reassure each other that they are wanted and that they belong to someone;
- forgiveness – the two forgive each other for any hurt they may have caused each other. The sexual relationship is a healing relationship.

In the Anglican marriage service, it is said that:

> Marriage is given . . . that with delight and tenderness they may know each other in love, and, through the joy of their bodily union, may strengthen the union of their hearts and lives.
>
> *Anglican Alternative Service Book*

Faithfulness (fidelity) in marriage

Christians believe that marriage is an exclusive relationship between a man and a woman.

All Christians believe that fidelity between a married couple is important. They think that marriage is a special relationship. It is a bond between two people. An essential part of this bond is the sexual relationship that the two enjoy. The two people join to each other in a special way. So if one of them has a sexual affair with another person, this badly damages the special relationship of marriage; it breaks the trust between the two married people.

Christians believe that sexual loyalty is an important part of marriage. If husbands or wives do not find their partner alluring after several years of marriage, or if they do not obtain much sexual satisfaction in their marriage, is it acceptable to have an affair? The Christian answer is 'No'. Love means that you stay loyal to your husband or wife, even if this means that you do not have full emotional or sexual satisfaction in the marriage. Christians believe that it is a false dream to think that someone can obtain full contentment and gratification in marriage. They believe that you can achieve full happiness only in God – and not in this life, but in life after death.

Sex outside marriage: fornication and adultery

As Christians believe that marriage is the appropriate relationship for sex, they think that sex outside marriage is harmful. It cannot build the special relationship that marriage can. Nor can it provide a secure situation for a child born outside marriage.

Christians think that adultery (sex outside marriage) is more harmful than fornication (sex before marriage) because it damages, even destroys, the special relationship between the spouses. The two feel that they belong to each other in a unique way through their sexual relationship; if a husband or wife commits adultery, their spouse feels cheated, betrayed, bitter, devastated, and so on.

Paul says (in 1 Corinthians 6$^{18-19}$):

> Flee from sexual immorality. All other sins a man commits are outside his body, but he who sins sexually sins against his own body. Do you not know that your body is a temple of the Holy Spirit?

If the initial enthusiasm in marriage wanes, courage and self-control become important. Otherwise, one of the partners easily wanders into adultery. As marriage is a sacrament, the presence and help of God may also assist the couple to remain faithful. This help from God is especially valuable when there is unusual stress in a married relationship.

> 'A man will leave his mother and father
> and be united to his wife,
> and the two will become one flesh.'
>
> Jesus (Mark 10$^{7-8}$)

Children

Most Christians believe that one main purpose of marriage is to have children. The Catholic Church even believes that a marriage is not valid unless the two are willing to have children. The Catholic Church does not that say the couple *must* have children. One of them may be sterile and incapable of having children. And this does not make their marriage invalid. But they should be open to having children.

Other Christians believe that there is one main purpose of marriage: to love another person. These Christians believe that a couple who never have any intention of having children, and who use artificial means to prevent their birth, are still married in the eyes of God.

Most Christians believe that children are an essential part of marriage

Christians believe that it is the primary responsibility of parents to bring up their children, to look after them, to protect them, to teach them about God, and so on. The education of children is not primarily the responsibility of a government. For example, the bishops at the Second Vatican Council said:

> As it is the parents who have given life to their children, on them lies the gravest obligation of educating their family.

Family planning

Family planning is a deliberate decision by a married couple about:

- when they will have children;
- how many children they will have.

Christians approve of family planning.

Most Christians approve of both natural and artificial methods of contraception, though not of abortion as a method of contraception. They think that God created the sexual instinct, so that married people could love each other and create a child. Yet the two do not always go together. There are many times when a couple wish to love each other, without having a child. Consequently, most Christians believe that it is good for a married couple to use contraceptive methods when they wish to express their love for each other, without this resulting in a child.

However, popes in the Catholic Church have approved only natural methods of contraception. They have condemned artificial methods of contraception. The popes have argued that artificial contraception is against the natural law – meaning that it is wrong to interfere in the God-made natural process that leads to conception. In other words, God created people with sexual instinct. This may result in a pregnancy. It is wrong to stop the pregnancy.

Examination practice

1. 'Marriage is a sacrament.'
   What does this mean?   (3 marks)
   Write about six lines of A4.

2. Explain the similarities and differences between a Christian's and an atheist's view of marriage.
                                           (8 marks)
   Write about three-quarters of a side of A4.

3. Most Christians marry. Why?   (8 marks)
   Write about three-quarters of a side of A4.

4. What is the Christian view of sex (in marriage and outside marriage)?   (10 marks)
   Write about one side of A4.

5. 'Sex is for enjoyment.'
   Do you agree? Give reasons for your view. Show that you have considered more than one view. (8 marks)
   Write about three-quarters of a side of A4.

Heterosexuality and homosexuality

Most Christians believe that heterosexual acts (sex between a man and a woman) can be right, and that homosexual acts are wrong. The Catholic Church is definite about this. There are two main reasons for this view.

First, in the Bible, heterosexuality is recommended and homosexual acts are repudiated. Christians regard the Bible as the voice of God.

Second, male–female sexual intercourse has a biological purpose – the conception of a child. Homosexual acts have no biological purpose. Consequently, heterosexual acts are natural, and homosexual acts are unnatural. God is the creator of the natural world. Therefore, what is natural must reflect how God wants us to behave. What is natural will also lead, in the long term, to making us happy.

Fulfilment or self-denial?

A good number of Christians do achieve real happiness and fulfilment in a strong marriage. They feel joyful and contented. They love someone and are loved by someone. Their love grows and changes over the years. They emphasize that God's purpose in marriage is to make people happy.

Some suggest that a happy marriage is the nearest we can come in this life to understanding God, as a good marriage has some of God's qualities, such as compassion, self-sacrifice, joy, peace, generosity, patience, and love. They also point out that the best way to understand the love between Christ and his Church is to notice the love between a husband and wife.

Nevertheless, there is an increase in the number of marriages that break up, including marriages of Christians. And in many unbroken marriages, children notice arguments between their parents. Or the children notice that their parents are unhappy, distant, and do not talk to each other much.

Does this mean that it is better to divorce, or even not to marry, because marriage makes some people dissatisfied and unhappy?

One answer is that marriage should help people to fulfil all their desires and aspirations: so that if we do not continually get what we want from our present husband or wife, then we should divorce and look for another husband or wife to fulfil our desires. Or we should seek some other way to satisfy our sexual and emotional desires. This view is often taught, at least implicitly, in the newspapers and on television. It is not a Christian view.

Another answer is that two people have enjoyment, excitement and happiness in the early years of marriage. This helps them to grow personally and spiritually. But it is unrealistic to expect total and continuous happiness in marriage. Christians say that we cannot obtain total happiness in this life. This is earth, not heaven. We can gain complete happiness only when we meet God after death.

Once a couple have one or more children, then the husband and wife can no longer enjoy each other's undivided attention. The children often become the centre of attention. It is at this stage that the couple have to learn self-sacrifice and self-denial. They can no longer satisfy their sexual and personal desires as they did in the first years of marriage. In the early stage of their marriage, love meant a romantic attachment. In the later years, it means staying faithful to their spouse, especially if the couple do not get the sexual or emotional satisfaction that they enjoyed before they had children.

The parents have to learn that some self-denial is an important way to personal and spiritual growth. They have to understand that Jesus did not teach that we can reach full happiness in this life – instead, he taught that self-sacrifice was important. It helps if we understand that spoilt people always want their own way. They do not achieve happiness. They often go from one unhappy marriage to another unhappy marriage.

Marriage or living together?

Some people believe that living together is better than marriage, because, for example:

- You can find out what the other person is really like.
- You can leave the other person more easily if you fall out of love.
- You want to enjoy yourself, with some commitment to the other person, but not a permanent commitment.

Christians think that marriage is better than living together, because:

- You have to make a permanent commitment to the other person; this assures them of your enduring love, and your loyalty.
- It is better for children who are born to the couple.
- It is the teaching of Jesus.
- It is the condition of your own personal growth.

It is worth noting that statistics show that couples who have lived together before marriage are more likely to have their marriages break down.

'Till death us do part'

The couple say these words to each other in the wedding ceremony. Christians do not believe that marriage is for eternity – there is no marriage after death, at the resurrection – but they believe that a marriage should last until one of the partners dies.

Some Christian Churches, such as the Orthodox Church, allow separated or divorced people to remarry in a church, if one of the partners has committed adultery. They quote the words of Jesus in Matthew's gospel. Jesus says divorce is wrong, except in the case of adultery:

> 'I tell you that anyone who divorces his wife, except for marital unfaithfulness, and marries another woman commits adultery.'
>
> Matthew 19⁹

Some Christian Churches allow separated or divorced people to remarry in church, if there is no prospect of reconciliation. They say that 'till death do us part' is the ideal, which not everybody can keep.

However, the Catholic Church is quite strict. It will not allow a Catholic to re-marry in church if their partner is alive; nor will it allow a divorced and re-married Catholic to receive communion. The Catholic Church quotes the words of Jesus in Mark's gospel:

> 'A man will leave his father and mother and be united to his wife, and the two will become one flesh. So they are no longer two, but one. Therefore what God has joined together, let man not separate . . . Anyone who divorces his wife and marries another woman commits adultery against her.'
>
> Mark 10⁷⁻¹¹

Mixed marriages

A mixed marriage is:

- either a marriage between two people of different Christian denominations (for example, one is Methodist and the other is Catholic);
- or a marriage between a person who is a Christian and someone who is not a Christian: the latter may be a member of another religion (for example, Jewish or Muslim), or may not be a member of any religion.

There are advantages in a mixed marriage. Because the couple bring different religious beliefs and practices to their marriage, they can learn from each other how to become more like God, and they can learn to understand themselves better, if they are open minded, as no religion has the whole truth about God and the world.

There can also be disadvantages in a mixed marriage. Most religious leaders are cautious about a mixed marriage, especially the second kind of mixed marriage. They fear that a member of their Church may abandon their religion when married to someone from another religious group, or married to someone who does not belong to any religious group.

And it is often asked if people in mixed marriages face more stresses than people who marry within their religion. For instance, the couple may not agree about where to marry – in this church, that church, or the registrar's office? And what if one is keen to read the Bible every night and the other thinks this is ridiculous? What if the couple disagree about whether to baptize their children? What if one of them believes that family prayer is important and the other believes prayer is for deluded people? Suppose the couple cannot agree whether they should send their children to a Christian school or to the local county school? And suppose one wants to go to church on Sundays and the other wants to go shopping instead? Will differences such as these, arising from divergent religious beliefs, create a tension in the marriage and disunite the couple?

Church weddings

In the Orthodox Church it is the priest who marries a couple, and so it is customary for weddings to take place in a church. In the Catholic Church, it is the couple who marry each other, but they have to do this in front of a priest, who is the Church's official witness to a marriage; and so a wedding normally takes place in a church.

There are other reasons why Christians wed in a church. For instance:

- They may want other members of their local church to be present at their wedding: to witness their wedding, to celebrate their wedding, and to pray for a happy marriage. The natural place to do all this would be at the local church building.
- They may want God's blessing on their marriage, given by a minister or priest.
- They may want their wedding to be part of a religious service, to remind them how important God should be in their married lives.
- They may be used to celebrating sacraments in a church. They may have been baptized in a church and confirmed in a church. They may also have celebrated regularly the sacraments of the eucharist and reconciliation in a church. Consequently, if they believe that marriage is a sacrament, they will want to marry in a church.

However, some Christians criticize church weddings.

- They may say that many church weddings are between people who rarely go to church to worship, and that such people should marry in a registrar's office, as church weddings should be for people who attend a church regularly.
- They may also criticize extravagant weddings: weddings in which the couple spend excessively on romantic things such as flowers, dresses, music, decorative cars or horse-drawn carriages, and so on. They criticize such weddings because they think it is more useful to spend money on more practical things, such as a house, or furniture for a house.

Annulment

The Catholic Church does not allow divorce, but it permits annulment. This is a statement that, at the time of marriage, one of the couple did not agree to one of the necessary conditions for marriage. They regard the following as necessary conditions for marriage:

- the intention to remain faithful to the partner;
- the intention to be willing to have a child;
- the intention to have a sexual relationship;
- the intention to remain wedded until the other one dies;
- maturity, and an understanding of the demands of marriage.

Preparation for marriage

Marriage is possibly the most important decision that anyone has to make. Christians think that it is important to avoid an impulsive, immature or half-hearted decision. So they think it important to prepare for marriage. For instance, the Catholic Church insists that an engaged couple must agree to a series of talks before they can marry each other in a church. They must demonstrate, for instance, that they understand:

- the purpose of marriage;
- the teaching of the Church on marriage;
- that they are undertaking a life-long commitment of fidelity and love;
- and that they are willing to have children.

Celibacy: voluntary

A celibate is someone who does not marry and does not have sexual intercourse.

Most Protestant Christians reject celibacy as unnatural.

But there is a long tradition in some Christian groups, notably the Catholic and Orthodox Churches, that values celibacy. Some Catholics and Orthodox deliberately choose to be celibate. They usually join religious congregations; they sometimes become priests.

Why do these Christian celibates deliberately choose to have no children, no married partner to share their life, and no sex? They have different reasons:

- Jesus was celibate (even though this was not the Jewish tradition), and Christian celibates want to model their lives on his life.
- Jesus taught (Mark 12^{18-27}) that there is no marriage when we rise from the dead into the kingdom of God. Christian celibates want to be a sign of this life in the kingdom of God, even though celibacy is not the normal way of life in this world.
- Christian celibates dedicate their lives and work totally and exclusively to God, or Jesus, or both. If they married, they would have to divide their attention between members of their family and God. So they choose to remain celibate.

> The essence of chastity is not the suppression of lust, but the total orientation of one's life towards a goal.
> Dietrich Bonhoeffer

Celibacy: involuntary

Some Christians do not want to lead a celibate life, yet they do.

One reason, in the Catholic Church, is that all priests must be celibate. Any man that applies to be a priest in the Catholic Church must first consider if he can be celibate. Some men feel so strongly that God is calling them to be a priest that they are willing to be celibate, even though they do not feel this is right for them.

Other Christians are involuntarily celibate because they have not yet found the 'right' person to marry. They hold the Christian belief that sex is part of marriage: so they refrain from sexual intercourse until they marry.

Examination guidance

'A sexual relationship outside marriage can never be right.' Do you agree?
Show that you have thought of more than one point of view.

(5 marks)

First answer

If you have sex outside marriage, you will get to know someone before you marry them.

This is a relevant point. But there is no development of this point.

There are no other arguments.

There is no consideration of the opposite point of view.
(Score: 1 mark out of 5)

Second answer

It is wrong because you have to think of the child you might have and they want a proper mother and father.

This is a relevant point. But there is no development of this point.

There are no other arguments.

There is no consideration of the opposite point of view.
(Score: 1 mark out of 5)

Third answer

I agree. The Church has always taught that sex outside marriage is wrong, and the Church has the inspiration of the Holy Spirit to guide it. The Church teaches that one of the main purposes of marriage is to have children and educate them, and that this is best done within marriage.

This candidate has presented a valid argument, and has then gone on to develop that argument. This merits 3 of the 5 marks. The candidate would have to present a variety of argument to obtain higher marks.

There is no consideration of the alternative point of view.
(Score: 3 marks out of 5)

Fourth answer

I disagree. A sexual relationship outside marriage is the only way to get to know someone properly. Sex is such an important part of marriage. You can find out if you are really suited before you marry. That way, you can part easily if you are sexually incompatible, rather than go through the trauma of divorce.

This candidate has presented a valid argument, and has then gone on to develop that argument. This merits 3 of the 5 marks.

The candidate would have to present a variety of argument to obtain higher marks.

There is no consideration of the alternative point of view.
(Score: 3 marks out of 5)

Fifth answer

This is wrong. People today are liberated to enjoy sex. They are not forced by any church or government to be limited to one partner. Artificial contraceptives can be used to prevent unwanted children, and this has helped liberate people.

Most people do not get married until they are in their twenties, and you cannot expect them to be celibate for that long. In any case, they want to enjoy themselves. This is the purpose of the sexual instinct, until you get married.

I think you should be faithful in marriage, but you must sleep with someone to find out if they are the right person to marry.

I know that Christians say that sex is for one person and that you have a special relationship through sex, but I see no reason to accept that Jesus or the Church has God on their side. You get much more enjoyment from having sex with different people.

This candidate has presented a variety of arguments to oppose the view that a sexual relationship outside marriage is wrong.

There is progression and development in the answer.

The candidate has also considered the alternative point of view and explained why it is not convincing.

These are the important characteristics of an answer that deserves full marks.
(Score: 5 marks out of 5)

Sixth answer

This is right. Sex is special. You cannot have sex with someone and expect your relationship not to be different. This shows that sex is not simply for enjoyment. It is part of a relationship. It should make a deep and unique relationship; it should also be a demonstration of such a relationship.

People regard themselves as belonging to each other in a very special way through sex. The anger and bitterness caused by adultery illustrates this.

One possible result of a sexual relationship is a child. The best environment for the education of a child is a stable relationship between two people. So this is a good argument for not having sex outside marriage.

Some people say sex is simply for fun, and so sex outside marriage is all right. I know you can try and have sex simply for fun, but I don't think this is possible for many people. If you can have it simply for fun, there is something wrong in the way you treat other people.

This is another very good answer.

The question tests a candidate's ability to justify a personal opinion.

This answer illustrates the skills you will have to demonstrate to obtain full marks:

- relevant argument;
- diversity and variety of argument;
- development and progression of argument;
- consideration of the alternative point of view.

(Score: 5 marks out of 5)

Examination practice

1. Most Christians disapprove of homosexual sex. Why?
   (3 marks)
   Write about six lines of A4.

2. What are the arguments for and against celibacy?
   (8 marks)
   Write about three-quarters of a side of A4.

3. Expain the advantages and disadvantages of a mixed marriage. (6 marks)
   Write about half a side of A4.

4. Explain why most Christians marry at a church.
   (8 marks)
   Write about three-quarters of a side of A4.

5. After many years of marriage, a couple may find their relationship becomes strained.
   How might religious beliefs help a Christian to deal with this? (10 marks)
   Write about one side of A4.

6. Getting married, or living together without getting married; which of the two do you think is better? Give reasons for your view. Show that you have considered more than one view. (8 marks)
   Write about three-quarters of a side of A4.

 # MARRIAGE CEREMONY  5

Introduction

See Chapters E3 and E4 for an explanation of the Christian understanding of marriage.

> May you always bear witness to the love of God in this world so that the afflicted and the needy will find in you generous friends, and welcome you into the joys of heaven.
>
> Catholic Marriage ceremony

Ceremony in the Catholic Church

The marriage ceremony usually takes place during the celebration of the eucharist. The priest leads the celebration of the eucharist and, on behalf of the Church, he is a witness to the marriage. He does not give the sacrament of marriage. The husband and wife give the sacrament to each other.

In a prayer near the beginning of the eucharist, the priest mentions that God has made marriage a mystery, a symbol of Christ's love for his Church.

There are readings from the Bible, as there are in every sacrament, because Christians believe that God inspired the authors of this book. Christians believe the Bible is a credible source for finding out what God is like, for finding out how we should live, and for finding out how we should treat other people.

One suitable reading would be the passage in John's gospel about the wedding celebration that Jesus went to. It was at Cana (John 2^{1-11}).

Another suitable passage would be Paul's explanation of love – that it outlasts faith and hope; that it means being patient, and kind, not envious, not boastful, not selfish, never rude, nor easily angered, nor holding grudges, and always loving the truth (1 Corinthians 13^{1-13}).

Then the marriage ceremony starts. The priest asks some questions:

- Are you ready freely and without reservation to give yourselves to each other in marriage?
- Are you ready to love and honour each other as man and wife for the rest of your life?
- Are you ready to accept children lovingly from God and bring them up according to the law of Christ and his Church?

The couple have to say that they do not know of any reason why they should not marry (thus, for instance, declaring they are not already married).

Then the couple declare that they freely want to marry each other (meaning that no one has forced them into it, as in an arranged marriage).

The couple exchange vows. They join hands and say:

- I call upon these persons here present to witness that I ... do take thee ...

- to be my lawful wedded husband/wife;
- to have and to hold from this day forward;
- for better for worse, for richer for poorer, in sickness and in health;
- to love and to cherish;
- till death do us part.

The husband and wife exchange rings, saying: 'Take this ring as a sign of my love and fidelity. In the name of the Father, and of the Son, and of the Holy Spirit.'

The priest concludes the marriage ceremony. He leads some prayers, for the married couple and everyone else involved. The married couple then sign the civil register.

Later in the eucharist, just before everyone says the Lord's Prayer, there is a special blessing that the priest says on the married couple. He may pray, '. . . Father, keep them always true to your commandments. Keep them faithful in marriage and let them be living examples of Christian life . . .'

Finally, after communion, there is a concluding prayer by the priest. He might say, 'May you always bear witness to the love of God in this world so that the afflicted and the needy will find in you generous friends, and welcome you into the joys of heaven.'

Ceremony in the Anglican Church

There are two forms of the marriage service, the traditional and the modern. What follows is a summary of the modern service. Some couples prefer the traditional service.

The main emphasis of the ceremony is love. The prayer with which the ceremony begins sets the tone of the service:

God our Father,
you have taught us through your Son
that love is the fulfilling of the law.
Grant to your servants
that, loving one another,
they may continue in your love until their lives' end;
through Jesus Christ our Lord. Amen.
Anglican Alternative Service Book

There is a reading from the Bible, such as 1 Corinthians 13, Ephesians 3^{14-end} or I John 4$^{7-11}$. A sermon on the meaning of marriage is preached.

The priest reads a statement about the meaning of the ceremony.

- The congregation have come together in the presence of God, to witness the marriage of *N* and *N*, to ask his blessing upon them and to share in their joy.
- Husband and wife are to be united in love as Christ is united with his Church.
- Marriage is given that husband and wife may comfort and help each other, living faithfully together in need and in plenty, in sorrow and in joy.
- They are to enjoy the physical union of intercourse – 'with delight and tenderness they may know each other

in love and, through the joy of their bodily union, may strengthen the union of their hearts and lives.'
- They are to have children and accept the responsibility of caring for them and bringing them up as Christians.
- They are about to begin a new life together in the community.

The couple, and all present, are challenged to say if there is any reason why they should not marry.

The couple exchange vows. They join hands and say –

I, *N*, take you, *N*,
to be my husband/wife,
to have and to hold
from this day forward;
for better, for worse,
for richer, for poorer,
in sickness and in health,
to love and to cherish,
till death us do part,
according to God's holy law;
and this is my solemn vow.

The husband and wife exchange rings, saying:

I give you this ring,
as a sign of our marriage.
With my body I honour you,
all that I am I give to you,
and all that I have I share with you,
within the love of God,
Father, Son, and Holy Spirit.
Anglican Alternative Service Book

The priest binds their hands together with his stole. He pronounces them husband and wife.

There may be a eucharist, though this is not usual.

The service ends with prayers and blessings for the couple in their married life.

Ceremony in the Orthodox Church

Orthodox Christians call marriage **the crowning**. The priest or bishop gives the sacrament of marriage, after the couple have expressed their consent to marry. There is a slightly different ceremony for someone marrying for the second or third time; some of the joyful prayers in the ceremony are left out. The Orthodox Church allows its members to marry a second, even a third time, but not a fourth time. See Chapter E9, *Divorce; annulment; separation* for details.

The marriage service is in two parts: the betrothal and the crowning.

The betrothal

- This usually takes place at the entrance to the church.
- At the betrothal, the couple pledge to love each other and to remain faithful to each other.
- There is a blessing of the rings, which the couple then exchange. The rings are a sign of fidelity and love; a

sign also that the two freely decide to marry. (Unless the two freely decide to marry, there is no valid marriage.)

The crowning

- This usually takes place at a table in the centre of the church.
- There is a procession of the priest and couple from the entrance of the church, where the betrothal took place. The couple hold lighted candles. Everyone sings a hymn about going into God's holy place. The priest puts the gospel book on the table.
- There are some preliminary prayers.
- Then the priest chants the three great prayers of marriage. In the prayers the priest says that: God created man to be king of all creation; that the couple should have children and, together, they should care for the earth; that the marriage is a sign of the unity between Christ and his Church; that the family will be a small church of its own.
- Then comes the coronation: the priest places crowns on the heads of the bride and groom. The crowns are made of leaves and flowers, or silver and gold. This is the most important sign in the ceremony: it signifies that the two are married. The priest says:

> 'The servant of God, [name], is crowned unto the handmaiden of God, [name], in the name of the Father, and of the Son, and of the Holy Spirit.'

They receive the power of the Spirit of God to help them love each other and their children. The crowns signify both joy and sacrifice. The couple have a loving,

emotional attachment when they marry. They will need sacrifice and self-discipline to make their marriage work.

- There are two readings from the Bible. The first one is Paul's description of love (1 Corinthians 13); the second is about Jesus at a wedding feast in Cana (John 2^{1-11}).
- At the conclusion, after the Lord's Prayer, the two drink wine three times from the same cup, to symbolize that they now share a common life.
- Finally the priest joins the right hands of the couple and leads them three times in procession around the table, while the congregation sings hymns.

Ceremony in a Quaker building

At a Quaker (Society of Friends) wedding, the whole congregation witnesses the wedding.

- The meeting begins in silent prayer and with worship. The couple arrive, simply dressed, and join in the silent prayer.

- About 15 minutes later, the couple stand and make their promises. They hold each other by the hand and say:

> 'Friends, I take this Friend [name] to be my wife/husband, promising through divine assistance, to be unto her a loving and faithful husband/wife, so long as we both on earth shall live.'

- The couple sign the register. So does everyone else.
- The meeting for worship continues, as usual. At the end, people shake hands.

Examination guidance

There is usually a Bible reading at the celebration of a sacrament. Why do Christians think that the Bible is important?

(2 marks)

First answer
Because they read it at all their sacraments.

There is nothing here that is not already in the wording of the question. Repeating what is in the wording of the question does not gain any marks.
(Score: 0 marks out of 2)

Second answer
It is important because each time the priest tells us a different part of Jesus' life we can try to understand it.

This answer does not merit any marks because it is vague and indistinct. The candidate may have a valid point; but the candidate has to express it clearly to gain a mark.
(Score: 0 marks out of 2)

Third answer
Because it has the teachings of Jesus in them.

This candidate has a made relevant point. However, there are two marks for this answer. So the candidate should write a fuller explanation to gain more than 1 mark.
(Score: 1 mark out of 2)

Fourth answer
Because it gives information on how to conduct our lives correctly in the eyes of the Church.

This candidate has also a made relevant point, though different from the last candidate's. But there are two marks for this answer. So the candidate must write a more detailed explanation to gain more than 1 mark.
(Score: 1 mark out of 2)

Fifth answer
The Bible is important because we learn the teachings of God and how to become a better person and also God's word and his rules.

This is a good answer: the candidate has made more than one relevant point, and thus deserves 2 marks. But you will notice that the candidate presents each point concisely, and writes only one sentence, with little punctuation. It would be wiser to use punctuation to separate the different points, so the examiner easily notices the distinctive points in the answer. For instance, the candidate could have written:
The Bible is important because we learn the teachings of God; in particular, we learn his rules, and how to become a better person.
(Score: 2 marks out of 2)

Examination practice

1. Choose a Christian marriage ceremony.
   State what happens and what is said in the ceremony.
   (10 marks)
   Write about one side of A4.

2. In what ways might the marriage ceremony influence the way a couple live their lives?
   (8 marks)
   Write about three-quarters of a side of A4.

3. 'Only practising Christians should be allowed to marry in a church.'
   Do you agree? Give reasons for your view. Show that you have considered the opposite point of view.
   (8 marks)
   Write about three-quarters of a side of A4.

PARENTHOOD; RELIGIOUS EDUCATION 6

Parenthood

Marriage, according to most Christians, has two purposes: to express and develop a unique love between two people; and to give birth to children. But conceiving a child is only the start of this second purpose of marriage. The parents brought a child into the world, so they have the responsibility to care for and educate their child. This is a 'natural' task for parents. They have a sort of instinct to look after their own children – they feel a bond with, and responsibility for, their children, and so they want to do something about bringing them up. They usually have high hopes and aspirations for their children. They want their children to do better than other children. They look after their children's interests, and they stand up for them.

Parents see their children as a reflection of themselves. This helps parents to take a pride in their children's progress and education. Yet there is also a danger – parents may try to make their children a clone of themselves, thus forgetting that their children have their own identities. Parents risk promoting their own ambitions in their children. So they must consciously remind themselves to respect their children's aspirations. Parents must let their children make their own decisions when they are grown up.

> The child is not likely to find a father in God unless he finds something of God in his father.
> Ingersoll

Purpose of education

How we educate a child depends on what we think the purpose of life is. Christians have a definite view about life. They believe that:

- God made us and the world we live in.
- God made the things in this world, partly for our enjoyment, but nothing will give us lasting happiness, except knowing God.
- God sent his Son to be a human being – Jesus.
- Jesus, in the way he treated people and in what he said to them, showed what God is like.
- Jesus taught that God wants us to love him and to love each other.
- Jesus, through his death and resurrection, enabled all of us to get to know God.
- We can get to know God, though only partly, in this life. We can know him more clearly when God raises us after death.

This view of life affects a Christian's view of education.

Baptism

The Catholic ceremony of baptism starts at the door of the church. The priest or deacon asks the parents what they want of God's Church. The parents reply, 'baptism'. The celebrant then says:

> You have asked to have your child baptized. In doing so you are accepting the responsibility of training him (her) in the practice of the faith. It will be your duty to bring him (her) up to keep God's commandments as Christ taught us, by loving God and our neighbour. Do you understand what you are undertaking?

This is a succinct summary of the Christian view of the role of parents as religious educators. Some parents want a religious education for their children, but they want someone else to provide it; they expect the local priest and the Christian school to provide it. The Christian view is that parents are the prime educators of their children. If parents neglect this task, then neither the local priest nor the school can replace them. The role of a priest and a school in the education of children is different from that of parents. The Christian view is that the example and influence of parents are far more powerful than those of anybody else.

Parents as religious educators

Are children naturally religious? Some people argue that all children are born with a sense of God. If they lose this sense of God, it is because adults stifle it.

Others believe that children are natural agnostics (not sure that there is a God – God might exist, but he might not exist). Many children come to believe in God. So it must be their education and upbringing that cause them to believe in God. If parents show they believe in God, and if they show that they love him, then their children will probably be theists (people who believe in God). If parents never pray, never mention God, never go to church, and so on, then their children will probably be atheists (people who do not believe in God) or agnostics.

It is not clear whether children are naturally religious or naturally agnostic.

But there is no doubt that the example of parents influences the religious disposition of their children. Consequently, Christians believe that parents should:

- pray at home with their children;
- go to church regularly with their children;
- be kind to other people, especially those they dislike, despise or resent;
- show self-discipline in their lives, and in their reactions to frustrating situations;
- listen: be open to their children, other people, and events in their lives;
- forgive their children when they do wrong;
- show their concern for those who are poor and underprivileged;
- care for those who are sick – visit them, comfort them, listen to them;
- value creation – demonstrate that they appreciate the natural world, wonder at it, embrace it, enjoy it;
- show their children tenderness and affection – something that is natural to most parents, but difficult for some parents;
- demonstrate disinterested service – can they help other people without expecting a reward or something in return?
- recognize their own failings – accept that they are not always right, and not always considerate;
- exemplify self-sacrifice. This is the crunch issue. Can parents forgo their own interests for the sake of their child?

We may think that all this is an impossible ideal for any parent. Agreed. Still, it is the Christian ideal of a parent. It is founded on the example of Jesus. He is the model. Some Christians count marriage as a sacrament. Consequently, they believe that married people have the assistance of God to help them attempt the ideal. He will forgive them when they fail, and he will encourage them to try again.

> As it is the parents who have given life to their children, on them lies the gravest obligation of educating their family . . . It is the duty of parents to create a family atmosphere inspired by love and devotion to God and their fellow-men.
> Catholic bishops at Second Vatican Council

Parish

The Christian view is that the parish has a subsidiary role in the education of children. Parents have the main role.

The parish is the local group of Christians. They should

come together regularly (usually on a Sunday) to worship. Thus the educational task of Christians in the parish is to welcome people and to worship sincerely. They show, by example, how to worship.

Christian (Church) school

Children spend more of their waking day at school than at home. However, this does not make the school the main educator. It has an ancillary role in the education of children.

The Christian school is for baptized Christians, though it may admit some students who are not baptized. A Christian school usually appoints teachers who are Christians. The school aims to assist Christian parents in the education of their children, so that there is continuity between the religious education given at home, at church and at school.

A Christian school aims to:

- **Integrate Christian faith and culture**. Education is about culture – the development of the intellectual, aesthetic, manual, affective, moral, spiritual and social talents of young people. Truth is a key word in education. God is the source of truth; the devil is the father of lies.

  So education should develop knowledge of, and enquiry about, the world in which we live – not just the natural world and human artefacts, but the supernatural world as well. Therefore, subjects such as science, technology and religious education are all important.

- **Integrate Christian faith with life**. Education is learning to practise what we believe and teach. Most people in a Christian school are baptized Christians. They believe that Christ is the model human. They have to 'put on' Christ: that is, adopt his attitude to God and to others. Hence the way people listen to and speak with God is important in a Christian school, as is the way people listen to and speak with each other. Thus religious education encourages pupils to integrate faith with life. It encourages pupils to practise what they believe.

  Religious education also aims to develop pupils' knowledge and understanding of the Christian faith, and to develop pupils' knowledge and appreciation of other faiths. The teachers would assume Christian belief to be true, though there would a critical approach to it, and respect for other beliefs.

Thus the Christian school encourages young people to be open to the world, to be open to other people, and to be open to God.

Secular school

In a country such as England, most schools are secular schools: that is, they do not assume belief in God. The schools are equally open to students with no religious faith as well as to students with religious beliefs. Religious belief is not used to decide whether to admit a person to secular schools.

Consequently, the school does not presume that Christian belief about God and man determines its work (even though, in English law, schools must have a Christian act of worship). The school does not teach any particular religious beliefs as true. It should be neutral.

Although most schools agree that spiritual qualities are important, they do not agree that religion is important. In most schools, religion is not important.

There is no agreed view about the purpose of education in secular schools. There are different, often conflicting, views. Some people think that the main purpose of schools is to produce good citizens, who respect the government's laws. Others believe that the main purpose of schools is to educate people to be critical of society, and to want to change society. Some people want schools simply to produce enterprising and enthusiastic workers who will make the country wealthier. Others emphasize that schools should encourage people to be more humane and less interested in making wealth.

A Christian might agree with any of these, but would find none of them sufficient. Most Christians believe that the fundamental purpose of education is to teach people to love God and to love their neighbour. Any education that omits this is defective.

Religious education in a secular school is a critical examination of different religious beliefs, without supporting any one of them as true, perhaps suggesting that they are all equal.

Examination practice

1. Some Christians think it is important to send their children to a Christian school.
   Explain **two** reasons why they might think this.
   (3 marks)
   Write about six lines.

2. Christians believe that God made people to know and love him.
   How might this belief affect their view of education?
   (8 marks)
   Write about three-quarters of a side of A4.

3. The Catholic Church teaches that parents are the prime educators of their children.
   Suggest how parents might teach their children about God and the Church. (10 marks)
   Write about one side of A4.

4. 'Religious education is indoctrination. It is not genuine education.'
   Do you agree? Give reasons for your view. Show that you have considered the opposite point of view.
   (8 marks)
   Write about three-quarters of a side of A4.

ABORTION

Introduction

This is an emotive subject. Hardly surprising. We may be talking about human life, and there is nothing more precious than life. We value life more than anything else. We may also be talking about babies. Babies are defenceless and vulnerable. Everyone has a soft spot for babies, even brothers and sisters who resent a new-born baby that is the centre of their parents' attention.

In England there are about 180 000 abortions each year; that is, one abortion every 3 minutes.

The official reasons for abortion in England, in 1989, were:

In an emergency to save the mother's life	2
To prevent grave permanent injury to the mother's life	3
Because of risk to the mother's life	357
Because the child may be handicapped	1695
Because of risk to the health of existing children in the family	18 246*
Because of risk to the mental or physical health of the mother	180 604*

*These reasons can be combined with other reasons

Development of the foetus/human being

Conception	Development starts at conception. From this moment all inherited characteristics are fixed: such as colour of eyes, body shape, height, colour of hair, sex.
3 weeks	The heart begins to beat.
3–4 weeks	The nervous system, lungs and stomach start to form. The mother may not be certain that she is pregnant.
6 weeks	Brain waves are detectable. Fingers and toes are forming. The embryo can probably feel pain.
8 weeks	The embryo is complete. From now on it is a matter of growth, not development.
39–40 weeks	The time when a child normally comes out of the womb.

When does human life begin?

This is an important issue. Those against abortion argue that it is the murder of a human being. Those in favour usually argue that abortion is removing an unwanted part of a woman's body.

There are at least five views about when human life starts:

- **At conception**. This is the moment when there is something new, living and different. The baby starts to grow and develop from this moment. The baby's genetic features are fixed.
- **After 15 days**, when the fertilized egg implants itself in the womb. More than 50% of fertilized eggs do not implant in the womb, suggesting that this is the test of when human life starts.
- **At about eight weeks**, when the foetus looks like a human being. Although it is tiny, the foetus now has the features of a grown person – head, hands, toes, and so on. Before this time it is unrecognizable as a human being. At the moment of conception, it was a growing cell and did not have any recognizable human features.
- **When the foetus can survive outside the womb**. This stage may be reached after about 23 weeks, though intensive nursing will be needed to help a child born so prematurely.
- **At the moment of birth**. At this moment the baby becomes independent, physically, of its mother. Before this moment, it is still part of its mother.

Some people argue that it is not possible to identify the moment when human life starts. They say that life starts at conception, but it is not possible to say when it becomes human life, because there is continual growth or change. A fertilized egg may later split and become twins, thus demonstrating that fertilization is not the start of a human life. Or two eggs may later fuse to become one.

Main argument for abortion

It is a woman's right to do with her body what she wants. Nobody else has the right to tell her what to do with her body.

It is not clear whether all those in favour of abortion have a distinct view about whether the foetus is human. Some people in favour of abortion accept that they are removing a human being, but they argue that they have a good reason to do so. Many of those in favour of abortion argue that the foetus is not human. It is simply a growth in a woman's body.

Nobody is morally required to make large sacrifices, of health, of all other interests and concerns, of all other duties and commitments, for nine years, or even nine months.

J. Thomson

Other arguments for abortion

- It is expensive to look after mentally and physically handicapped children. It is better to abort such children before they are born.
- Mentally and physically handicapped children cannot have a life that is worth living. It is better to abort them before birth. They will then avoid the difficult and painful life of a disabled person.
- The foetus, human or not, does not have a right to embed itself in a woman's womb and live off her for nine months. It is draining her life and causing her discomfort. The pregnant woman has the right to rid herself of it.
- In the early days of pregnancy, the foetus is pre-human. It is not recognizable as human.
- A woman who is made pregnant by a rapist should not have to go through a traumatic nine months, carrying the baby of the man who raped her. In any case she will hate the child, and this would be no good for the child.
- A pregnant schoolgirl needs to continue her education; she can't if she has to look after a baby. She is too young, anyway, to be a mother. And it is wrong to punish her by forcing her to have a child she does not want.
- Similarly, a more mature woman has her career to think of. If she becomes pregnant by mistake, she does not want to ruin her job and her career.
- A mother who already has a child or children should not be made to have another child just because she becomes pregnant. An extra child in the family might cause her to have a mental breakdown. An extra child might also cause her to neglect her other children.
- If a woman's life is in danger because she is pregnant, it is better to abort the foetus than let the mother die.
- If parents do not want a child, and the wife is pregnant, it is better to abort the foetus than coerce the mother to have the child. Otherwise that child will grow up unhappy and feel rejected. Better that it was never born.

Main argument against abortion

It is murder. It is the murder of a human being who has done nothing wrong – an innocent human being. Even worse, it is the murder of a human being who cannot defend him or herself.

> I am sure that deep down in your heart you know that the unborn child is a human being loved by God like you and me. If a mother can kill her own child what is there to stop you and me from killing each other?
>
> Mother Teresa

Other arguments against abortion

- Jesus did not talk specifically about abortion. However, we can look at his actions and draw some conclusions about abortion. He cared for those who were unwanted (such as the lepers). He cared for the sick who thought they had little hope of recovering (such as the woman with a haemorrhage). He cared for children (such as Jairus' daughter). Jesus is the example of how a Christian should behave. Thus Christians should care for people, not destroy them.
- Jesus taught that we should love our neighbours.
- Every person is sacred. God made us, more than any other creature, in his image and likeness. It is wrong to destroy something that is like God.
- It says in the Bible that it is wrong to murder. This is one of the ten commandments, in the Old Testament. The Old Testament accepts that killing can be right, but not murder.
- It is a traditional Christian belief that abortion is wrong. An early Christian document, the Didache, written about the time of the New Testament, says: 'You shall not kill the foetus in its mother's womb.' This has been the traditional Christian teaching since that time.
- The bishops of the Catholic Church teach that abortion is wrong. At the Second Vatican Council, they said:

> God, the Lord of life, has entrusted to men the noble mission of safeguarding life . . . Life must be protected with the utmost care from the moment of conception: abortion and infanticide are abominable crimes.

Pope John Paul II said:

> I confirm that the direct and voluntary killing of an innocent human being is always gravely immoral. This doctrine, based upon that unwritten law which man, in the light of reason, finds in his own heart, is reaffirmed by Sacred Scripture, transmitted by the Tradition of the Church and taught by the ordinary and universal Magisterium.

- If we accept the murder of innocent babies, then there will be declining respect for other people in society. A society in which we have declining respect for each other is becoming uncivilized.
- If we accept the abortion of unborn babies that may have handicaps, we shall soon accept the murder of handicapped people who are already born.
- A healthy person does not have the right to decide that disabled people do not have lives worth living. Consequently, healthy people should not abort unborn children that have a disability. Let disabled people decide themselves if they have lives worth living.
- Disabled people would rather not be disabled, but this does not mean they would rather be dead.
- Most people who have an abortion do so because the child would be an inconvenience to them. This is a

selfish and unacceptable reason to abort a child.

- There are no unwanted babies. Some natural parents may not want their unborn child, but there are many infertile couples who desperately long to love a child. They are keen to adopt a child. They would love that child as if it was their own. Before the abortion law in 1967 these couples happily adopted unwanted children. Since the abortion law, unwanted children are aborted, and infertile couples are left wanting a child they cannot have.

- Abortion harms the mother. She may, eventually, feel disturbed and anxious about it. She may feel guilty that she has destroyed her own child. She may be haunted by it. She may suffocate her emotions and become depressed.

- An abortion may damage a woman's chance of having a successful pregnancy when she wants a child. She may have repeated miscarriages or become infertile.

Examination practice

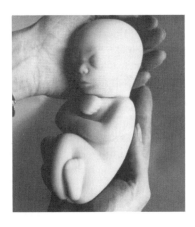

1. Do you think this picture would convince people who support abortion that they are mistaken?
   Write about six lines. (3 marks)

2. Write a discussion between someone in favour of abortion and someone opposed to abortion.
   Show that you know the arguments on both sides.
   (10 marks)
   Write about one side of A4.

3. Jesus told us to love our neighbours.
   What might a Christian conclude from this about abortion? (6 marks)
   Write about half a side of A4.

4. There are different views about when human life starts. What are they? (8 marks)
   Write about three-quarters of a side of A4.

CHILDLESSNESS; EUGENICS (GENETIC ENGINEERING) 8

Introduction

One reason why people marry is to have one or more children. There is a sort of instinct in most women to want a child. It is therefore distressing and frustrating for a woman if she cannot conceive a child because she, or her husband, is sterile. Couples in such a situation used to adopt a child. Unfortunately for them, since 1967, there has been a law in England that permits abortion. Consequently, unwanted babies are usually aborted before they are born, and there are few babies available for adoption today. This has caused distress for the 12% of couples who are infertile: they want to love a child as their own, yet they cannot.

However, in recent years, there have been unbelievable advances in reproductive technology – that is, in our ability to control the conception of a child. In particular, we can fertilize a human egg outside the womb, in a laboratory. This is good news for couples who want a child, but who have been unsuccessful in conceiving a child in the normal way.

Nevertheless, there are doubts about some uses of this new knowledge.

Some doubts

- Is it right for a 20-year-old career woman to choose a sperm donor, have one of her eggs fertilized (in a laboratory) with his sperm, have the resulting embryo frozen for 25 years, and at the age of 45, have the embryo implanted in her womb, after she has retired from her career?
- Is it right for a woman who is past child-bearing age, to have an embryo implanted in her womb? If she is 50 years of age when she is pregnant, she will be 65 when her child is 15. Is this a suitable age for a teenager's mother?
- Is it right to take the eggs from an aborted embryo, and implant them in a woman who is infertile? Might we then have a child who, when grown up, seeks out its natural grandmother to ask: 'Why did you kill my mother, your daughter?'
  [NB. Eggs are formed in the ovaries of the foetus before birth.]
- Is it right to use someone else's eggs or sperm?
- Is it right for a man or woman deliberately to beget ten children, and not know any one of them? And not be responsible for any one of them?
- Is it right for doctors to make extra embryos, in case an implanted embryo does not survive, or in case a couple might want to have another child later? The doctors will freeze the extra embryos and store them in a laboratory. Sometimes the laboratory loses contact with the parents; or the parents might divorce and not want the embryos any more. Orphaned embryos?
- Is it right to conceive a child after the father's death? Perhaps a year, even ten years, after the father's death? If a husband gave sperm before he died, and it has been frozen, his wife can use it when she wants to. Eggs are taken from her ovary, fertilized (in the laboratory) with her husband's sperm, and implanted in her womb.

In all these instances, people are eager for a child. Some yearn desperately for a child.

Yet there is a distinction between what we want and what is right. We may want something. This does not make it right. We have to ask: is what we want right or wrong?

Deciding right and wrong

Jesus did not speak about assisted conception.

The Churches have no traditional judgements about methods of assisting conception, because they are recent inventions.

That leaves Christians two ways of deciding what is right and what is wrong about ways of assisting conception:

1. judgements by present Church leaders;
2. reasoning (natural law).

In some Churches, contemporary leaders have made preliminary judgements about methods of assisting conception, but most Church leaders hesitate to make final judgements. Methods of assisting conception are recent. The first test tube baby was in 1978. The first frozen embryo was in 1985. There will be many other advances in reproductive technology in our time. So most Church leaders are not sure what is right and what is wrong. No one wants to make hasty judgements that may later seem to be rash or premature. Hence Church leaders prefer not to make final judgements.

Some Catholic bishops have said that artificial conception is wrong. They justify this judgement using reasoning (natural law). In particular, they consider the act of conception. They say that marriage is the proper place for sexual intercourse. And they say that a child should be born from human intercourse. Artificial conception separates the conception of a child from human intercourse. Therefore it is wrong.

Pope John Paul II said that techniques of artificial conception are:

> morally unacceptable, since they separate procreation from the fully human context of the conjugal act.

He added that artificial conception could also be wrong because:

> the number of embryos produced is often greater than that needed for implantation in the woman's womb, and these so-called 'spare embryos' are then destroyed or used for research which, under the pretext of scientific or medical progress, in fact reduces human life to the level of simple 'biological material' to be freely disposed of.

Christians who defend artificial ways of assisting conception also decide whether these ways are right or wrong by using natural law (reasoning) – though they tend to consider the consequences of artificial conception and the motives for artificial conception, rather than the act of conception.

For instance, they argue that it is right to donate sperm, eggs or embryos – because the consequence is that this helps a sterile mother to have a child.

They also argue that when people donate sperm or eggs for money, they do wrong – because their motive is bad. Though when people donate sperm or eggs because they want to help someone, then they do right – because their motive is good.

See Chapter E30, *Natural law: reasoning*, for a more detailed explanation of natural law.

Techniques to assist conception

There are several ways of assisting conception. Here are the most important ones.

AIH (artificial insemination, husband)

A husband's sperm is put into his wife's womb using a syringe. A married couple can use this method if they have difficulty conceiving through sexual intercourse.

AID (artificial insemination, donor)

A woman has sperm put into her womb, using a syringe. It is not her husband's sperm. A married woman can use this method to conceive if her husband is infertile. A single woman, or a lesbian couple, can use this method to conceive without having sexual intercourse with a man.

IVF (*in vitro* fertilization) – sometimes called test tube babies

In vitro is Latin: it means 'in glass'. A woman normally produces one egg every month. To make her ovaries produce several eggs, she has special treatment. These eggs are removed from her ovaries. Each egg is placed in a glass dish or in a test-tube, and mixed with some sperm. Two days after conception, three of the fertilized eggs will be put into the woman's womb. The successful pregnancy rate is about 10%.

In most cases of IVF, the man and woman who provide the sperm and eggs are husband and wife.

However, there can be more complex situations. For instance, a husband and wife may want a child; yet they cannot conceive using the normal method, and the wife is not able to carry a child in her womb for nine months. So they use the sperm of another man and the egg of another woman. The sperm and egg are mixed in a laboratory. The fertilized egg is then placed in the womb of a third woman. When the child is born, it is given to the couple. In this situation, we might say the child has five parents.

Surrogate mothers (womb leasing)

A couple want a child, but they cannot conceive in the normal way because the woman is infertile. So the husband's sperm is put into the womb of another woman, using a syringe. This woman carries the child for nine months. When the child is born, it is given to the couple.

Arguments for assisting conception

Many of the arguments are similar to the arguments about abortion. See Chapter E7, *Abortion*.

- God created us with a natural inclination to want a child. Hence it is natural for a woman to feel unfulfilled if she does not have a child. So if we can use our intelligence to assist infertile people to have a child, we are supporting the way God created us – we are working in harmony with God.
- Jesus said we should love our neighbour as we love ourselves. It is a disturbing and distressing experience to be infertile. If anything can be done to remove the pain of being infertile, then it must be a good act.
- Everyone has a right to a child.
- It is an individual's right to choose what to do with their body. No one has the right to tell someone else what to do with their own body. It is a private matter, not a moral issue. It is certainly not an issue on which the government should pass laws.
- Those who oppose methods of artificial conception are only against them because these methods are new. Some people always oppose anything new or strange: they are comfortable with what they know, but change disturbs them. So they reject new methods of assisting conception. Yet instead of saying they are not comfortable with these new methods of conception, they say the new methods are wrong.
- There is a 'yuk' factor. Those who are against artificial conception play on our emotions, and emphasize aspects of artificial conception that we feel are 'yukky'. They fail to consider the benefits of artificial conception.

Arguments against some forms of assisting conception

Many of the arguments are similar to the arguments about abortion. See Chapter E7, *Abortion*.

- A man or woman may donate sperm or eggs. They deliberately beget many children. Yet they are quite unaware that their children exist: they take no responsibility for being the natural parents of such children. This is wrong.
- Marriage is the right place for begetting children.
- All children have the right to know their natural parents. A child who cannot find out about its natural parents may have identity problems. It is wrong to deprive a child of the right to know its natural parents.
- No one has a right to a child. There are fundamental human rights, such as the right to life, the right to dignity, and so on. However, having a child is not one of these fundamental human rights.
- A child is not just a possession, such as a car or a house. A couple that make a child from other people's sperm and eggs are treating that child as a sort of possession. This is wrong. Every child should be treated as a human being, not a possession.
- Married couples have primal feelings of belonging and of jealousy. A couple that want a child may ignore these feelings when they use someone else's sperm or egg. Yet these feelings will not disappear. These feelings will threaten the relationship between the couple, and their relationship with the child. The family may break up.

- Marriage is the right place for sexual activity. Sexual activity outside marriage is wrong. The relationship between a husband and wife is unique: it includes sexual activity that they do not share with anyone else. This sexual relationship includes using their own eggs and sperm. Consequently, using someone else's sperm or eggs goes against this special sexual relationship.

English law – 1990 – on the use of eggs, sperm and embryos

The 1990 English law says:

- A man who donates sperm, and a woman who donates eggs, should be anonymous: children born from donated sperm or eggs will not be able to find out who their natural father or mother is.
- A couple who donate an embryo should be anonymous: a child who develops from such an embryo will not know their natural mother and father.
- A woman may contribute eggs that result in the birth of up to ten children. A man may contribute sperm that result in the birth of up to ten children.
- A man who contributes sperm, and a woman who contributes eggs, have no rights over any child that may result from their sperm or eggs.
- Frozen embryos may be stored for up to ten years. During that time the natural parents have the right to decide who may have the embryo. They also have the right to decide whether to dispose of the embryo. After ten years, the laboratory that has a frozen embryo can decide what to do with it.
- It is permissible to experiment on a human embryo for 14 days after conception. After 14 days, it must not be kept alive.
- It is an offence to put an embryo that researchers have experimented on, into a woman's womb.

What do Christians think about the law on the use of eggs, sperm and embryos?

Some Christians think that this is a bad law, an immoral law. They say it permits things that are wrong.

They argue that human life starts at conception. They argue that it is wrong to experiment on human beings without their consent. They argue that it is wrong for a man or woman deliberately to father or mother a child that they do not intend to love and educate. They argue that it is wrong deliberately to eliminate unborn children that are handicapped.

(Most Christians believe they do not have to obey a bad law. Pope John XXIII, for instance, taught:

Authority ... derives from God. Consequently, laws ... in contravention of the moral order, and hence of the divine will, can have no binding force in conscience ... indeed the passing of such laws undermines the very nature of authority and results in shameful abuse.)

Other Christians think that the law on the use of eggs, sperm and embryos is a good law. It is a morally acceptable law.

They argue that it helps couples to have a child when they cannot do so unaided. They argue that it may give information that will prevent the birth of handicapped people. They argue that a fertilized egg is not yet a human being.

Experimenting on embryos

We are in the dark about scientists' experiments on human embryos. Scientists experimenting on the human embryo are somewhat secretive about what they are doing. In English law, scientists can experiment on a human embryo for 14 days after conception. After the fourteenth day, according to English law, the scientist should destroy the human embryo.

One purpose of experimentation on the human embryo is to search for genes that cause specific illnesses, such as cancer.

Another purpose of embryo experimentation is to be able to detect hereditary illness in an embryo. A mother could then decide whether to have an abortion.

There must be other reasons for experimenting on the human embryo.

Arguments about experimenting on embryos

The main issue is: when does human life start? See Chapter E7, *Abortion*, for different answers.

If human life starts at conception, then most of us would agree that it is wrong to experiment on an embryo, because every human person has rights – including the right not to be treated as an object by experimenters who want to discover more about the human body; and the right not to be destroyed when the experimenters have finished their work.

If human life starts some time after conception, then there is no serious objection to experimenting on young embryos. Rather, we can justify such experiments, particularly by the knowledge that may be gained about causes of illnesses. With such knowledge, experimenters may find ways of dealing with illnesses, such as cancer, that cannot be cured at present.

Examination practice

1. State **one** thing that English law says about the use of embryos.

   Explain why you agree or disagree with this.

   (3 marks)

   Write about six lines of A4.

2. Compare the arguments for and against assisted conception. (10 marks)

   Write about one side of A4.

3. Christians believe that God created everyone in his image and likeness.

   How might this affect what they think about methods of artificial conception (such as AIH, AID and IVF)? (8 marks)

   Write about three-quarters of a side of A4.

4. 'It is a woman's right to chose a sperm donor if she wants to conceive.'

   Do you agree? Give reasons for your view. Show that you have considered the opposite point of view. (8 marks)

   Write about three-quarters of a side of A4.

DIVORCE; ANNULMENT; SEPARATION 9

Christian views of divorce

Christians do not agree about divorce.

Most Protestant Churches consider that divorce is acceptable if the marriage has broken down.

The Catholic Church considers that divorce between two baptized persons is wrong; it has no exceptions to this rule. The Catholic Church is against divorce. It uses the teaching of Jesus to justify its view. In Mark's gospel, Jesus says:

> '. . . a man will leave his father and mother and be united with his wife, and the two will become one flesh . . . what God has joined together, let man not separate . . . Anyone who divorces his wife and marries another woman commits adultery against her.'
>
> Mark 10[7-11]

The Catholic Church will not allow divorced and re-married people to receive the sacraments of the eucharist or reconciliation. It says that such people are living in adultery: they must stop living in adultery if they wish to receive a sacrament.

The Orthodox Church considers that divorce is not ideal, but allows it if a marriage cannot be repaired. The Orthodox Church thinks that a lifelong marriage is the ideal. However, it recognizes that this is not always possible, because we are weak and commit sins. The Orthodox Church follows the teaching in Matthew's gospel, where Jesus says:

> 'anyone who divorces his wife, except for marital unfaithfulness . . . causes her to commit adultery.'
>
> Matthew 19[9]

So, in theory, the Orthodox Church permits divorce, but only in the case of adultery. Yet in practice it often permits divorce for any reason, if the marriage seems beyond repair.

> Nobody's family can hang out the sign:
> **nothing the matter here**
>
> Chinese proverb

Christian view of separation

All Christians accept that separation might be the best way to resolve a never-ending marriage difficulty or conflict. The separation could be temporary. It is better to try a temporary separation than rush into a divorce; the former is not as conclusive as the latter. The separation could be permanent. The Catholic Church, in particular, recommends permanent separation, rather than divorce, in cases such as continual abuse or repeated adultery, if the innocent partner cannot tolerate the situation.

However, the Catholic Church teaches that the separated couple are still married to each other. So they should be celibate if they separate. The Orthodox and Protestant Churches permit divorce if one partner has irretrievably shattered the marriage. In cases such as continual abuse or repeated adultery, they are more likely to accept divorce than to recommend permanent separation.

Annulment

The Catholic Church does not permit divorce. It allows annulment. This is a statement that a couple did not validly marry, even though they made the marriage vows at a wedding ceremony. Consequently, they are free to marry.

There are several reasons why someone can ask for a marriage annulment in the Catholic Church. The applicant must show that these reasons applied before the marriage service. The reasons will not count if they occurred after the marriage service. Here are some examples. One of the couple did not:

- intend to remain faithful;
- intend to have children;
- intend to make the marriage a lifelong union;
- have the maturity to understand what marriage involved;
- freely agree to marry.

> I read about divorce, and I can't see why the two people can't get along together in harmony, and I see two people and I can't see how either of them can live with the other.
>
> F. Adams

Arguments in favour of divorce

- It is unrealistic to expect two unhappily married people to be tied to each other for the rest of their life. It is like demanding a life prison sentence if the marriage is not successful.
- People change over the years, so it is impractical to expect that all marriages will last a lifetime. A person may not like the changes in their partner. Their partner may turn out to be quite different from the person they married.
- It is better for the children that their parents divorce if the couple are always arguing. All children need a calm and pleasant atmosphere at home.
- A married couple can end up hating each other if they decide to stay together when their marriage is not working. It is better to part good friends, before bitterness and hatred sour their relationship.
- People fall out of love. They were once in love, but this does not mean that their love will last. It is more sensible, if they fall out of love, to divorce and then to marry someone they *do* love. There cannot be a profound marriage without love.
- The sex bond is the most intimate part of the married relationship; to 'cheat' on a partner is to break the marriage relationship. If a husband or wife commits adultery, he or she effectively dissolves the marriage.
- If a partner turns out to be a drunkard, a spouse-beater, or insane, then it is foolish to remain with that person.
- If the husband or wife abuses the children, physically or sexually, it is better for the children that the parents divorce.
- A major purpose of marriage is to provide for the children. If only one of the parents is working, and he or she does not provide enough money to feed and clothe the children, then there is no point in continuing with the marriage.
- Some people do not want the same partner for the rest of their life. They feel that a variety of partners are more satisfying than just one partner.

- To forbid divorce is to take away a person's freedom. The right to be free is a fundamental human right.
- If a husband or wife leaves home, they have effectively broken the marriage. The remaining person is entitled to a divorce so he or she can re-marry. It is not much different when a husband or wife is rarely at home (because they have a greater interest in their job or leisure activity). An absentee husband or wife effectively breaks the marriage through neglect.

Arguments against divorce

- When they married, the couple promised to love each other, 'for better or for worse, in sickness and in health, for richer or for poorer,' till one of them died. They should keep their promises.
- Jesus taught that divorce was wrong.
- Most children suffer badly when their parents divorce. The children want both their parents, and they want their parents to stay together. Children feel guilty and responsible when their parents divorce. They suffer in other ways:
  - Children often do not do well at school when their parents divorce: they find it difficult to concentrate, because they are preoccupied with family matters.
  - Some children become delinquents when their parents' marriage breaks up – the children feel that their parents do not love them any more; the children feel angry with everyone; and they feel a general hatred.
  - Many children find it difficult to accept a stepmother or a stepfather as a substitute for their natural mother or father.
  - Many children find it difficult to trust people if their parents have divorced, so they will be reluctant to believe that marriage should be for life, and they will be hesitant to commit themselves fully to marriage.
  - Many children are spoilt – and this is not good education – when their parents divorce. There can be a competition between the parents to please the children; each parent wants the children's support against the other parent. So each may spoil the children.
- Marriage makes most people happy. But some people are unrealistic and believe they can gain lasting happiness in marriage. So, when they experience difficulties in their marriage, they divorce and re-marry, hoping to gain perfect happiness – an impossible dream.
- If divorce is easy to obtain, then people will not deal with arguments, disagreements and disappointments when they occur in their marriage. They will look for the quick solution that divorce provides.
- Divorced people usually find they have the same problems, in their second marriage, that they had in their first marriage.
- Marriage is both a fulfilment and a sacrifice. It gives both sensual delight and suffering. It results in tender understanding and a strained relationship. Those who

rush into divorce want the first without the second, but this is not possible. A wise person realizes this.

- Marriage is the opportunity to love: this means that we are concerned about the other person as much, if not more, than ourselves.
- Marriage is the opportunity to grow – spiritually, morally and emotionally. People who always get their own way do not develop as people. They are spoilt. Because marriage is such a close relationship, it gives a unique opportunity to people to learn to give themselves to another person and to learn not to have their own way. This is hard, but it is the price of personal growth. Married people have the opportunity to put the interests of their spouse and children before their own interests.

Re-marriage in church

The Orthodox permit divorce. They also permit re-marriage in a church. Yet their service for a second marriage is different from their service for a first marriage: it omits several of the joyful parts of the ceremony, thus showing that they do not think a second marriage is the same as the first one.

Anglicans accept divorce. Some priests do re-marry divorced people in a church. Yet most Anglican bishops are reluctant to allow people to re-marry in a church. It may not be long, however, before most Anglican bishops do permit a divorced person to re-marry in church.

Most Protestants, such as Methodists, accept both divorce and re-marriage in a church. They believe that a person's mistakes should not be counted against them. If

their first marriage failed, they should have the opportunity to start again. So they allow divorced people to re-marry in a church.

The Catholic Church does not accept divorce. Nor does it permit re-marriage in a church. It believes that no one can re-marry if their first partner is alive. It will allow someone to re-marry if their first partner has died. In this case, the ceremony is the same.

Examination practice

1. What is the Catholic Church's attitude to divorce?
   (3 marks)
   Write about six lines of A4.

2. Why do some marriages end in divorce? Why do some marriages last? (10 marks)
   Write about one side of A4.

3. Christians believe that God loves them; and that he forgives them.
   How might this help Christians in their marriage?
   (8 marks)
   Write about three-quarters of a side of A4.

4. Do you think divorce should be allowed?
   Give reasons for your view. Show that you have considered the opposite point of view.
   (8 marks)
   Write about three-quarters of a side of A4.

EUTHANASIA 10

What is euthanasia?

Euthanasia is from the Greek word for 'good death' or 'dying well'. It means 'ending a person's life painlessly, as an act of kindness, especially in a case of incurable and painful illness'.

Why do some Christians support euthanasia?

Because a person has reached a point where his or her life is no longer worth living. This applies to people such as:

- people whose minds have so deteriorated that they are helpless and unable to live with any dignity at all;
- people who are brainstem dead – who have no hope of recovering consciousness but whose bodies are still, technically, alive.

How could legalized euthanasia work?

It would be morally wrong if people could have their lives taken away against their will – this would be hard to disguish from execution. Therefore, the choice should first be made by those who might be affected. A possible procedure could be:

- A person could decide at any time in their life that, if the stage were reached when their life was no longer worth living, they would wish to receive euthanasia. They would sign a statement making their wishes clear. They could change their mind at any time.
- The decision that the time for euthanasia had come would be made by someone medically qualified to do so.
- Once the medical decision had been made, it would be up to the patient (if they were able) or their close family to decide whether or not to go ahead.

What teaching in the Bible could be used to support euthanasia?

Euthanasia itself is never mentioned in the Bible. Supporters would quote some of Jesus' basic teachings.

- For instance, the Golden Rule: 'Do to others what you would have them do to you'. Also, the second great commandment: 'You shall love your neighbour as yourself'. If you love a person who is enduring excruciating pain, the argument goes, you would wish to end that person's suffering.
- Those in favour of euthanasia would also say that when committed Christians die they go to be with Jesus Christ. Death is not to be feared but is a positive blessing, far better than a life of suffering.

> Thou shalt not kill, but needst not strive
> Officiously to keep alive.
>
> A.L. Clough

Why do other Christians oppose euthanasia?

- They believe that all human life is sacred and that it is wrong to kill another person. (A belief that all human life is sacred may also affect their views on the morality of war or on capital punishment.)
- Many doctors feel strongly against euthanasia. Their

mission in life is to give health or ease pain, not to end life. They may well give a drug to ease pain knowing that it will probably shorten a person's life – but that is not the same as killing.
- They feel that the system is open to abuse. A person might feel obliged to sign a statement even though they do not really want to. A very sick person is not in a state to make a rational decision in choosing between life and death. If the sick person cannot make the choice, the decison might be taken by relatives who stand to benefit from that person's death. It is claimed by some people that unofficial euthanasia already happens, when a person's life is deliberately shortened by a deliberate use of painkillers, more than needed to deaden the pain.
- Some people have shown great courage and faith in the way in which they have coped with pain. They have been an inspiration to others. They are following the example of Christ.
- The way in which people accept suffering may have spiritual value for their own souls.
- Jesus always cared for the sick. He never suggested or even hinted at euthanasia as an option.
- Hospice doctors say there is no need for euthanasia.

Examination guidance

In discussing euthanasia, remember that if you are asked for your opinion you should say what you think and give your reasons. Show that you are aware of views with which you do not agree and say why you do not agree with them.

If you are asked what a Christian's view might be, present both points of view and give reasons for each.

Examination practice

1. What is euthanasia? In what circumstances might Christians think it right to allow euthanasia?

   (10 marks)

   *Write about a side of A4. Make sure you give a **very clear** definition of what euthanasia is.*

2. Many Christians are opposed to euthanasia. Why is this so? (8 marks)

   Write about a side of A4, giving as wide a range of reasons as you can.

Types and examples of prejudice

There are many types of prejudice, but the following are quite common.

- **Age**. 'Young people do not appreciate the things they have.' 'Old people cannot understand young people.'
- **Social class**. 'We can recognize snobs by their accent.' 'Working class people are less generous than middle class people.'
- **Colour**. 'White people are colour prejudiced.' 'Black people are less intelligent than white people.'
- **Nationality**. 'Italians are cowards.' 'Irish people are violent.'
- **Religion**. 'Christians are arrogant.' 'Muslims are fanatics.'
- **Gender/sex**. 'Women have greater inner strength than men.' 'A woman's place is in the home.'
- **Appearance**. 'All boys who wear earrings are gay.' 'People who wear suits are important.'

Definition

Prejudice describes the way we think about other people.

Discrimination describes the way we treat other people.

Prejudice is an unfounded opinion that we have about people. We prejudge them. We have a firm opinion for which we have no evidence. Indeed there is usually clear evidence that the prejudice is wrong, but we are blind to such evidence – we either ignore the evidence, or we argue that it is wrong.

Prejudice is often an unjust general judgement we make about a group of people: for example, 'Christians are arrogant'. We may make this judgement because we have met some Christians who are arrogant; but we have wrongly concluded that all Christians are arrogant.

Discrimination is when we treat people differently and unfairly because of a prejudice we have about them. For example, I may not speak with someone who is a Christian, because I think they are arrogant. Or I may not give a job to an Irish person, because I think they are violent.

> A great many people think they are thinking when they are merely rearranging their prejudices.
> William James

Origins of prejudice and discrimination

- **Parents**. Young children uncritically accept their parents' views and opinions. Teenagers often think that their ideas and interests conflict with those of their parents, but if they are close to their parents, they have absorbed their parents' crucial beliefs, including prejudiced opinions. It is usually difficult to get rid of them later in life.
- **Ignorance**. This is rarely the origin of prejudices. Yet it is an important reason why we easily accept a prejudice. It is also an important reason why prejudices, which we have inherited from our parents, continue to influence our behaviour. Once we come to know those against whom we are prejudiced, we often recognize that we have a prejudice against them.
- **Pride**. I like to think I am more important than other people. Consequently, I want to believe that the groups I identify with are more important than the groups other people belong to. People in my group think as I do: we think that those in other groups are inferior to us. We become prejudiced against them.

> No one can eliminate prejudices – just recognize them.
> Ed Morrow

Consequences of prejudice and discrimination

Prejudice and discrimination often have chronic, harmful effects on harmony in a society, and on the way people think of themselves. If some people are prejudiced against us and discriminate against us, we may feel:

- **Anger and revenge**. We may be puzzled why they should treat us differently. We will be keenly aware that they have no good reason to treat us with disdain. Consequently, we will feel resentful and spiteful. We become prejudiced ourselves: we want to retaliate against all those who belong to the group of the person who discriminated against us.
- **Inferiority and antagonism**. We may feel small and subordinate. We may think we are less important and less intelligent than those who have discriminated against us. Yet, deep down, we do not accept this, and we will harbour a grudge, which we may not immediately recognize.

- **Alienation and ostracism**. If the person or persons who discriminate against us belong to the majority group in the nation, we may feel we are no longer a member of that nation. Or we may feel ambivalent: we were born in this country and so we know we belong to this country; yet some people make us feel a foreigner. Hence we feel no attachment to the country.

Christian view of prejudice and discrimination

> The Church reproves, as foreign to the mind of Christ, any discrimination against people . . . on the basis of their race, colour, condition in life or religion.
>
> Catholic bishops at Second Vatican Council

God created all humans, according to Christians. We are equal in the sight of God. Thus it is wrong to treat another person as inferior, which is what happens when we are prejudiced.

Christians also believe that there is a serious defect in our nature. God made us, but something has gone wrong – we do not always think objectively or dispassionately about other people; and we often tend to treat other people to suit our own selfish interests. Christians call this human defect **original sin**. Prejudice and discrimination are clear examples of original sin. Christians believe that we are unable to overcome original sin by ourselves. We can try to be good by our own effort, but we shall not succeed. It is only when we have the power of God that we will manage to treat other people with dignity. This power of God is available through the death and resurrection of Jesus Christ.

Christians believe that we should follow the example of Jesus. According to the Bible, Jesus rejected the prejudices of his day. He welcomed, without discrimination, all who came to him. The first Christians followed his example.

Jesus – prejudice based on nationality

Jesus helped a Roman army officer who sent some Jewish elders to him. The officer sent the elders because he was a foreigner and a Gentile, and he thought Jesus would not help him. So the elders made the officer's request for him – would Jesus cure his servant, who was close to death? The elders told Jesus that the centurion 'loves our nation and has built our synagogue'. Jesus went with them. The centurion sent friends to say:

> 'Lord, don't trouble yourself, for I do not deserve to have you come under my roof . . . But say the word, and my servant will be healed. For I myself am a man under authority, with soldiers under me. I tell this one, "Go", and he goes; and that one, "Come", and he comes . . .'

Jesus was impressed by the man's faith. He told the crowd:

> 'I have not found such great faith even in Israel' [meaning his fellow Jews].

The men who had been sent returned and found the servant well (Luke 7^{1-10}).

Jesus – religious prejudice

- Jesus helped a man in Gerasa. This man was not a Jew. He was possessed by many evil spirits who screamed at Jesus to leave them alone. Jesus sent the evil spirits out of the man, who then came to his right mind. The evil spirits went into some pigs, which stampeded into the sea and drowned (Mark 5^{1-20}).
- Jesus told a story of a good Samaritan. He helped a Jew. Samaritans and Jews had different religions and were enemies (Luke 10^{30-37} – See Chapter C19, *Luke's gospel – parables*, for details).
- The first apostles were slow to understand that they had to preach, not just to Jews, but to anybody of any religion. They were slow to realize that anybody of any nationality could please God, not just the Jews. They criticized Peter for eating with non-Jews. Peter explained a vision he had seen:

> 'I saw something like a large sheet being let down from heaven by its four corners, and it came down to where I was. I looked into it and saw four-footed animals of the earth, wild beasts, reptiles and birds of the air [animals that Jews were forbidden by their religion to eat]. Then I heard a voice telling me, "Get up, Peter. Kill and eat."'

Peter understood from this vision that God welcomed people of all nations, not just the Jews (Acts 11^{1-18}).

Jesus – sexism

- Jesus helped people irrespective of their sex. He did not discriminate against women. For example, a woman in Tyre asked him to cure her daughter. At first he refused to help (it was unusual for a woman to approach a male teacher in Jesus' time); but when she persisted, he cured her daughter. He told her that her faith had made the girl well (Mark 7^{24-30}).
- On another occasion, while Jesus was at Bethany, a woman came with a jar of very expensive perfume. She poured the perfume over his head. Some of those present thought this was a waste: it could have been sold and the money given to the poor. Jesus said:

> 'She has done a beautiful thing to me. The poor you will always have with you, and you can help them any time you want. But you will not always have me . . . She poured perfume on my body beforehand to prepare for my burial . . . wherever the gospel is preached throughout the world, what she has done will also be told.'
>
> Mark 14^{3-9}

Jesus – prejudice based on poverty

Jesus did not discriminate against poor people and in favour of rich people. For instance, he helped a woman who was penniless. She had a haemorrhage, and had spent all her money on doctors, but they had not cured her. Jesus cured her (Mark 5$^{25-34}$).

Jesus – prejudice based on appearance

A leper came to Jesus and begged for a cure. The man would have appeared repulsive. People were terrified that they would catch disease from lepers, so they avoided them. Jesus touched the man and cured him (Mark 1$^{40-45}$).

Jesus – colour prejudice

There are no examples in the gospels of Jesus contesting colour prejudice. He was a Palestinian Jew, with a tanned complexion, and as far as we know there were no people with a black or white complexion in Palestine in his time. Nor are there examples of Jesus avoiding age or social class discrimination. These may not have been prejudices in his time; or perhaps the gospel writers may not considered including such examples.

Examination guidance

'We Christians are the only good people in this world.'
Explain why this statement shows prejudice.

(3 marks)

1. **First answer**

    It shows prejudice because prejudice is the thoughts in your mind about a certain group of people. Here, the person is saying Christians are the only good people here.

    This answer is quite irrelevant to the question. The first sentence does not answer the question and the second sentence repeats the question.
    (Score: 0 marks out of 3)

    Second answer

    The first statement shows prejudice because all races and religions have 'good' people. For example, Ghandi was assassinated because he stood up for the rights of all the people, but he wasn't Christian. So the person saying this has a high opinion of himself and does not have an objective opinion of other people.

    An excellent answer because it tackles the question and does not waffle. The candidate clearly explains why the statement is prejudiced.
    (Score: 3 marks out of 3)

    Third answer

    It is prejudiced because he cannot give any evidence to support his statement. People of any religion can be good – not just Christians. I know some non-Christians who are much better people than some Christians I know.

    The speaker must also know that all Christians are not good people, but he ignores the fact; this also shows that his comment is prejudiced.

    Another excellent answer because it clearly explains why the statement is prejudiced
    (Score: 3 marks out of 3)

Why do Christians believe that prejudice is wrong?

(3 marks)

2. **First answer**

    Christians think that prejudice is wrong because prejudice is the thought of judgement.

    Christians believe that only God can judge – no man on earth has the authority to judge others.

    This answer is quite irrelevant to the question. The first sentence is confused and does not make much sense; the second sentence is clear, but it is not a correct answer to the question.
    (Score: 0 marks out of 3)

    Second answer

    Prejudice is when you have an unreasonable attitude to someone. Christians think this is wrong as Jesus taught that you should love your neighbour. Prejudice does not follow this rule.

    This is a clear and correct answer. The candidate has made a relevant point and developed that point. This is worth 2 of the 3 marks. The candidate should write an answer with more scope to earn all 3 marks
    (Score: 2 marks out of 3)

Third answer

Christians believe prejudice is wrong because as all life comes from God we are all part of the same family; so to treat one group of people wrong would be harming our family.

Also Jesus wasn't prejudiced as he mixed with all kinds of 'social outcasts'; we should follow his example.

An answer that merits full marks. It is clear and correct. There is as much breadth or scope in the answer as can be expected in an answer limited to five or six lines. *(Score: 3 marks out of 3)*

Examination practice

1. Explain the difference between prejudice and discrimination. (3 marks)
   Write about six lines of A4.

2. Christians believe prejudice and discrimination are wrong.
   Why? Give a full account. (10 marks)
   Write about one side of A4.

3. The gospels have examples of Jesus helping foreigners and outcasts.

   How might this affect the way Christians think about other people? (8 marks)
   Write about three-quarters of a side of A4.

4. 'Colour prejudice is far worse than religious or gender prejudice'.
   Do you agree with this view? Give reasons for your view. Show that you have considered the opposite point of view. (8 marks)
   Write about three-quarters of a side of A4.

SIN, CRIME AND PUNISHMENT 12

Sin

Sin is anything against the will of God. It can be thought, word or deed – something evil that a person thinks, or says, or does.

Christians believe there is something called **original sin**. Every person has original sin. It is something in human nature that makes a person open to temptation. It is not something people do – it is a weakness that is part of each person.

Every child is born with this weakness. It is inherited from the parents. Just as children can have their parents' characteristics, such as height, hair colour, general appearance, so they have their weakness – their original sin.

Sin and crime

A crime is something said or done that is against the law of the land.

- Most crimes are either crimes against a person (such as murder, rape, or assault) or crimes against property (such as theft or vandalism).
- It is not a crime to **think** something wrong. If the

thought leads to someone saying, or writing, or doing something against the law, then that person may be punished. It will be for their words or actions that offenders will be punished, not for thoughts.
- Obviously, something that is a sin may not be a crime. It may be a sin to refuse to do your share of the washing up or selfishly to insist on watching a programme on TV when others want to watch something else, but it is not likely to bring a policeman to the door.
- It is harder to think of a crime that is not a sin. Some Christians would say that it is not a sin to break a bad law or to break a law in the cause of justice or freedom. Other examples would be refusing to join the army when there is an unjust war or refusing to give evidence in court on something that you promised to keep confidential.

Dietrich Bonhoeffer was a German pastor who became involved in the plot to assassinate Hitler in 1944. Undoubtedly he committed a crime. Could it be said that his action was not a sin, because it would have saved many lives and would have been for the general good of the human race?

Punishment

Punishment is a means by which people are made to suffer for what they have done. The suffering involves, for instance, physical pain, taking away privileges or property, or humiliation.

The main reasons for inflicting punishment are:

- **Retribution** – The punishment must be seen to be a fair way of paying for the offence.
- **Deterrence** – The punishment must stop the offender from offending again – and also convince others that they should not offend.
- **Protection** – People in society must be protected.
- **Reform** – Ideally, the punishment will change the offender's attitude to life so that in future there is no desire or temptation to offend.
- **Compensation** – The victim has a right to receive something to make up for what has been suffered.

What would be an appropriate punishment for

- a young boy who has stolen and crashed a car?
- a mother of two small children who was guilty of drug dealing?
- a lorry driver who has caused the deaths of two children through drunken driving?
- a wife who kills her husband because he treats her violently?
- someone who stabs and kills a burglar who is attacking him/her?

Now look at each of your chosen punishments and ask yourself

- Does the punishment fit the crime? Is it a fair **retribution**?
- Is the punishment likely to frighten those who might think of committing the offence? Is it an effective **deterrent**?
- Will it make people safer? Does it give **protection**?
- What effect will it have on the offender? Will it help him or her to **reform**?
- What about the victim? Can he or she be **compensated** in any way?

How far do your punishments meet the requirements of retribution, deterrence, protection, compensation and reform? Do they meet all the requirements equally?

Does it matter if punishments do not meet the requirements of retribution, deterrence, protection, compensation and reform?

Capital punishment

Capital punishment occurs when someone is punished by being sentenced to death in a court of law and then is put to death under the rule of law.

Throughout history the death penalty was regularly used for serious offences (and sometimes for less serious crimes as well). Nowadays capital punishment has been abolished in the United Kingdom and in many other countries. It is legal in some states of the USA and in many countries in Asia and Africa.

Arguments for capital punishment:

- It is seen as being a proper retribution for the most serious crimes, especially murder. There is an apparent natural justice in 'a life for a life'.
- Putting a person to death obviously protects the public from that particular murderer.
- It is claimed that the death penalty is a great deterrent.

Arguments against capital punishment:

- There is the dreadful possibility of a mistake. In recent years a number of people who had been found guilty of murder have been pardoned and released many years later, long after they would have been executed. In the past there were cases of people being executed and later being found to have been innocent.
- The death penalty is brutal and uncivilized. Society should not use so violent and brutal a punishment.
- There is very little evidence that the death penalty is a deterrent.
- What about the effect on the person who has to carry out the execution?

Biblical teaching

In the Sermon on the Mount Jesus considered the Old Testament law, 'an eye for an eye, a tooth for a tooth' (Matthew 5$^{38-48}$). The law is known as the *lex talionis* and is based on a principle of retribution that is seen to be fair. The full law from Exodus 21$^{23-25}$ is 'But if there is serious injury, you are to take life for life, eye for eye, tooth for tooth, hand for hand, foot for foot, burn for burn, wound for wound, bruise for bruise.'

Jesus told his followers that they should not look for revenge in this way. He taught that they should turn the other cheek, go the second mile and love their enemies. (See Chapter E27, *The Sermon on the Mount; the Beatitudes*.)

A woman caught in the act of adultery was brought to Jesus (John 8$^{1-11}$). Those who brought her, teachers of the law and Pharisees, said (correctly) that the law said that she should be stoned to death. They asked Jesus what he thought should be done to her. Jesus said that any of them who had never sinned should throw the first stone. Nobody did; one by one they went away.

Jesus said to the woman, 'Woman, where are they? Has no one condemned you?' 'No one, sir', she replied. Jesus answered, 'Then neither do I condemn you. Go now and leave your life of sin.'

These passages both emphasize the importance of **forgiveness**.

Forgiveness of sin

Forgiveness is a central theme of Christianity.

- Jesus died so that sins might be forgiven.
- His actions showed a spirit of forgiveness. Note his treatment of the woman caught committing adultery (John 8[1–11] – see above) and his words to the criminal being crucified with him (Luke 23[39–43]).
- For sin to be forgiven there must be repentance. People must genuinely turn from their sins and turn to God.
- Jesus taught that God forgives sin – and that we should be ready to forgive those who sin against us.

Jesus' teaching about forgiveness

God is always ready to forgive someone who is penitent.

This is the theme of the parables in Luke 15 – the lost sheep, the lost coin and the lost son. In each parable, there is **joy** – when the sheep and the coin are found and when the son returns. The message is not just that God forgives – he wants to forgive, and is full of joy when a sinner repents.

Christians should be ready to forgive. Note the teaching in the Sermon on the Mount (Matthew 5[38–48] – see above).

The Lord's Prayer contains the words 'Forgive us our sins as we forgive those who sin against us'. Jesus adds the warning, ' If you forgive men when they sin against you, your heavenly Father will also forgive you. But if you do not forgive men their sins, your Father will not forgive your sins' (Matthew 6[14–15]).

Peter asked Jesus, 'Lord, how many times shall I forgive my brother when he sins against me? Up to seven times?' Jesus answers, 'I tell you, not seven times but seventy-seven times.' (Some versions say 'seventy times seven'). Jesus then told the parable of the unforgiving servant to show what the kingdom of heaven is like (Matthew 18[21–35]):

- A king decided to collect the debts his servants owed him.
- One servant owed him an impossibly big sum – 10 000 talents (millions of pounds). He could not pay: so his master ordered him and his family to be sold into slavery.
- The servant begged, 'Be patient with me and I will pay back everything.' His master took pity on him and cancelled the debt.
- The servant went to another who owed him 100 denarii (a few pounds). He grabbed him, beginning to choke him, and demanded payment in full. The other servant begged, 'Be patient with me and I will pay you back.' The first servant refused; he had him thrown into prison until the debt was paid.
- The other servants were upset. They reported the matter to their master.
- The master told the servant that he should have had pity on his fellow-servant, just as he himself had been shown mercy. He had the servant thrown into prison and tortured until the debt was paid.

Jesus finished by saying, 'This is how my heavenly Father will treat each of you unless you forgive your brother from your heart.'

Paul's teaching about revenge

In Romans 12[17–21], Paul wrote that Christians should not take revenge, repay evil with evil. It was for God to take revenge. He continued:

> If your enemy is hungry, feed him;
> if he is thirsty, give him something to drink.
> In doing this you will heap burning coals on his head.
> Do not be overcome by evil, but overcome evil with good.

Philemon

Paul wrote a letter to Philemon, a wealthy man who had become a Christian. Before Philemon had been converted, one of his slaves, Onesimus, had run away. For this the penalty could be death.

Onesimus too had become a Christian. He was with Paul. He had become very dear to Paul. Paul wrote to ask Philemon to receive him back – 'no longer as a slave, but better than a slave, as a dear brother.' If Onesimus owed him anything, Paul would repay it – though he felt that Philemon owed him his very life, as Paul had brought him to know Jesus; Paul had in this way brought Philemon to eternal life.

Examination practice

1. What is capital punishment? What arguments are put forward both for and against the use of capital punishment? (10 marks)
    Write at least a side of A4.

2. Jesus taught that people should be ready to forgive.
    (a) Describe an event in the life of Jesus in which he showed forgiveness.
    (b) Tell in your own words a parable in which Jesus taught about forgiveness. (10 marks)
    How much you write depends on the event you choose. Make sure your account is as detailed as you can make it.

3. What did Jesus say about forgiveness in the Sermon on the Mount? Do you think a Christian could follow this teaching in everyday life? (10 marks)
    Write at least a side of A4.

4. 'Forgive us our sins as we forgive those who sin against us.'
    Do you think that these words should influence Christians in their attitude to hardened criminals? Give reasons for your answer. (10 marks)
    Write at least a side of A4.

WAR AND PEACE

Introduction

'There always have been wars. There always will be wars.'

This is a common view, even though we desire peace. There have been two 'world wars' in the twentieth century, and numberless local wars. More people have died in wars in the twentieth century than in any previous century: quite astounding!

> Peace is better than war, because in peace the sons bury their fathers, but in war fathers bury their sons.
>
> Croesus

Causes of war

There is rarely a single reason why wars start. There is usually a group of reasons, which could include any of the following:

- **Power**. A government or king wants to control more territory and more people.
- **Resources**. A government or the people want some resources that another government or people control: for instance, oil, or fertile land, or important minerals such as silver or bauxite.
- **Pride**. The government of a country feels that it has to go to war, otherwise it may look foolish in the eyes of other people, or in the eyes of its own people.
- **Status**. The leader of a government wants to win a war so that he or she can appear successful, strong and important.
- **Diversion**. A government is in difficulty with its own people, so it wants to divert their attention to something else and to give the nation a sense of unity. A war against another nation can achieve this.
- **Defence**. A nation is attacked and it determines to repel the invader.
- **Helping others**. One country sees another country attacked and invaded unjustly by a third country. It goes to war to help the invaded country to regain its independence.
- **Vengeance**. A leader or a country feels that another nation has snubbed, insulted or humiliated them. Thus, they retaliate – perhaps with considerable violence – to get their own back.
- **Oppression**. When people are oppressed, they will eventually turn against their oppressor. They will be violent. They will kill their oppressors and destroy their property.

Peace

Christians esteem peace.

Peace is the absence of war or conflict.

More positively, it indicates that we have the right relationship with God and with other people. Peace is a sign of what Jesus called the **kingdom of God**. It means that we are forgiving rather than vengeful; we are merciful rather than punishing; we are peacemakers rather than stirrers; we love our enemies, rather than hate them; we give blessings rather than curses; we seek to understand our enemies rather than react vindictively to their nasty behaviour. It means we are like God. In his kingdom there is peace – perfect peace. Martin Luther King was an example of a Christian who worked for peace in the twentieth century. There is more information about him in Chapter E14, *Injustice; protest; conflict.*

> 'Blessed are the peacemakers,
> for they will be called sons of God.'
>
> Jesus (Matthew 5[9])

Christians believe that peace is a gift that God gives through Jesus. Jesus told his disciples, just before he left them:

> 'Peace I leave with you; my peace I give you. I do not give to you as the world gives. Do not let your hearts be troubled and do not be afraid.'
> (John 14[27])

Peace gives us the opportunity to relax, to enjoy God's creation, to care for our families. Only when there is peace can we properly follow God's commandment to look after and develop his world (Genesis 1[28–30]).

At the heart of peace is forgiveness. Unfortunately, we are unable to live with other people without hurting them. Unless we forgive each other, there is no peace.

Jesus taught that God forgives us, whatever we have done, even the worst possible behaviour. (See the parable of the forgiving father in Chapter C19, *Luke's gospel – parables.*)

Jesus forgave. For instance, some people brought to him a woman caught in adultery. They said that according to the Jewish law she should be stoned to death. Did he agree?

> Jesus bent down and started to write on the ground with his finger. When they kept on questioning him, he straightened up and said to them, 'If any one of you is

without sin, let him be the first to throw a stone at her.'
Again he stooped down and wrote on the ground.

At this, those who heard began to go away one at a
time, the older ones first, until only Jesus was left, with
the woman still standing there. Jesus straightened up and
asked her, 'Woman, where are they now? Has no-one
condemned you?'

'No-one, sir,' she said.

'Then neither do I condemn you,' Jesus declared. 'Go
now and leave your life of sin.'

John 8$^{1-11}$

Holy war

A holy war is one fought in support of a religious cause.
There is no Christian tradition of a holy war, though there
have been instances of holy wars fought by Christians, and
there is a tradition of holy war in the first part of the Bible,
the Old Testament.

In the Old Testament, the writers picture God in many
ways. One of them is 'warrior'. For instance, when he freed
the Jewish people from slavery in Egypt, the Jews sang this
song:

I will sing to the Lord, . . .
The Lord is a warrior; . . .
Pharaoh's chariots and his army
    he has hurled into the sea.
The best of Pharaoh's officers
    are drowned in the Red Sea.

Exodus 15$^{1-4}$

God then told these freed people that he had chosen
them, out of all the peoples on earth, to be his people. God
ordered them to go to Canaan (Palestine) and to conquer it.
He said he was giving this country as his gift to them. God
taught them to fight. He also fought with them. This was
holy war. The enemies of the Jews were the enemies of
God.

When the Lord your God brings you into the land . . .
and when the Lord your God has delivered them [the
people of that land] over to you and you have defeated
them, then you must destroy them totally. Make no treaty
with them, and show them no mercy. Do not intermarry
with them . . . Break down their altars, smash their sacred
stones . . . and burn their idols in the fire.

Deuteronomy 7$^{1-5}$

Once the Jews had conquered Palestine, according to the
Old Testament, they had the right to defend the land, as it
was God's gift to them alone. Such wars of defence were
holy wars.

Holy war since the New Testament

There is no mention of a holy war in the second part of the
Bible, the New Testament.

In the New Testament the enemies of the Jews are not
seen as the enemies of God, as Jesus taught that God loves
everyone, not just the Jews; and God wants everyone, not
just the Jews, to know and to worship him.

The first Christians also thought that Jesus did not
believe in violence. So they were pacifists – they thought
that killing and wars were wrong. Thus they did not believe
in a holy war.

Then, 1000 years later, the idea of a holy war appeared in
Christian belief. In 1095 Pope Urban II started the first
crusade. He promised forgiveness of all sins (and a place in
heaven) to any man who joined a holy war to recapture
Palestine from the Muslims who had invaded it. This first
crusade captured Galilee and Jerusalem, which the
crusaders thought were holy places, as it was here that
Christ taught, died and rose to life. But the Muslims
regained control of Jerusalem in 1144. From then until
1261 a series of armies went from western Europe on
crusade to Palestine to try and recapture the holy places.
They were called holy wars.

Some Christians at that time did not agree that these wars
were holy wars. They thought that a war to defend humans
might be justifiable; but they thought that a war for God
was incompatible with the Christian belief in a God who
loves and forgives. And after 150 years of crusades, which
included much treachery, bloodshed and cruelty, there were
few Christians who still believed in a holy war. Since then
the idea of a holy war has disappeared from Christian
belief.

Christian tradition

There is a contradictory Christian tradition about war.
Some Christians believe in a just war. Others are pacifists.
These contrasting views have existed for centuries.

In the first two centuries after Christ, Christians would
not join the army. They thought it was wrong to kill. This
worked as long as non-Christians joined the army and
defended everyone, including Christians.

In the third century Christianity became the official, and
perhaps most widespread, religion in the Roman empire.
Christians now had to think about defending their country,
as there was no one else to do it for them. From this time
there is a belief that a war may be justified. But not all
Christians have accepted this belief. In every century some
Christians have been convinced pacifists.

There are pacifists, as well as just war advocates, among
Catholics, Orthodox and Protestants.

However, some Protestant groups such as Baptists and
Quakers tend to be pacifists, though Baptists and Quakers
have no official teaching about pacifism.

Many Catholics are ardent pacifists, but the predominant
tradition in the Catholic Church is that there *can* be a just
war. The bishops at the Second Vatican Council said:

As long as the danger of war persists and there is no
international authority with the necessary competence
and power, governments cannot be denied the right of
lawful self-defence, once all peace efforts have failed.

Just war

Some Christians believe in just wars. They quote Jesus' commandment that we should love others as we love ourselves. This commandment implies that we have a duty to defend our lives. We should do this without harming the aggressor. Yet if the death of the aggressor is the only way to defend life, then this is justifiable.

The belief in a just war is also derived from natural law: on the rights we all have, and on what is fitting for our human nature. The view starts with the 'instinct' in every human to survive and to avoid death. God has placed this 'instinct' in us; it demonstrates his law that human life is important.

This means that we all have the right to life, and that murder is wrong. Thus we all have the right to defend our lives. We can use violence to defend our lives if all other means of defence have not deterred the attacker.

Those who unjustly attack others and kill them, lose their right to life.

Christians believe that God created life, and that he created us in his image and likeness (Genesis 1^{26-27}). It is wrong for another human to take such a valuable gift. Therefore, we have the right to defend our lives if someone unjustly attacks us.

Most liberation theologians agree that we may use violence to change an unjust situation, if other action has failed. They start with the example of Jesus. He helped the poor and oppressed. He taught us to love our neighbours. However – argue some liberation theologians – we cannot love a neighbour if we allow a dictator to oppress and abuse them. We cannot excuse ourselves by saying it is against the teaching of Jesus to use violence. If we are to love our oppressed neighbour, then we may have to use violence to liberate them, if peaceful protest has failed.

Some Christians believe that we must support our government if it declares war. They quote Paul's advice to the Christians at Rome, that they should obey the government, because God has given authority to the government:

> Everyone must submit to the governing authorities . . . The authorities that exist have been established by God. Consequently, he who rebels against the authority is rebelling against what God has instituted . . . Therefore, it is necessary to submit to the authorities, not only because of possible punishment but also because of conscience.
>
> Romans 13^{1-5}

Some Christians also point out that Jesus behaved violently on one occasion. Consequently, it must be permissible for Christians to use violence if they have a just reason.

> On reaching Jerusalem, Jesus entered the temple area and began driving out those who were buying and selling there. He overturned the tables of the money changers and the benches of those selling doves, and would not allow anyone to carry merchandise through the temple courts.
>
> Mark 11^{15-16}

Conditions for a just war

Those who support the idea of a just war do not think that all wars are just. Some are unjust. Thus they propose conditions, such as the following, to judge whether a war is just. A just war must:

- not harm innocent people: the war must not kill people who are not involved in the war (including children of the enemy), nor destroy their property;
- have a reasonable prospect of success – otherwise the killing and destruction is pointless;
- have a just cause, such as to defend a country against an unjustified attack;
- have the right motives – vengeance is a wrong motive; defending the lives of innocent people is a good motive;
- be declared by a legitimate government;
- be proportionate to the original cause. It is not a just cause to devastate another country because it has imprisoned, even unjustly, someone from our country. Our action would be out of proportion to the original offence.

Nuclear war

Some Christians argue that – within the just war conditions – a country may legitimately possess nuclear weapons, provided it uses the weapons to deter a potential invader, or to attack military targets. It would be wrong to use nuclear weapons to attack cities.

Other Christians believe that it is wrong to use nuclear weapons. No reason can justify their use. Nuclear weapons devastate indiscriminately. Such devastation cannot be proportionate to any cause, however noble the cause.

The Catholic bishops at the Second Vatican Council said:

> Every act of war directed to the indiscriminate destruction of whole cities or vast areas with their inhabitants is a crime against God and man.

Pacifism

Some Christians are pacifists. They believe that all wars are wrong. They might argue that:

- Jesus was a pacifist. He never once killed anyone or used violence against anyone. When the soldiers arrested him in the garden of Gethsemane, one of his disciples attacked the soldiers with his sword, cutting off the ear of one of them. Jesus said:

> 'Put your sword back in its place . . . for all who draw the sword will die by the sword. Do you not think I cannot call on my Father, and he will at once put at my disposal more than twelve legions of angels?'
>
> Matthew 26^{52-53}

- Jesus forgave those who crucified him:

> 'Father, forgive them, for they do not know what they are doing.'
>
> Luke 23^{34}

- Jesus taught that we should always forgive, no matter how many times. Peter asked Jesus how many times he should forgive someone, perhaps as many as seven? Jesus replied: 'Not seven, but seventy-seven times.' Peter must have been gobsmacked! Jesus went on to tell a story about a master and two servants. One servant owed his master an enormous amount of money. The master was going to put the servant in jail, but the servant begged for time to repay the money. The master simply cancelled the whole debt. This servant then met a fellow servant who owed him a very small amount of money. As the latter was unable to repay the debt, the first servant had him put in prison. The story suggests that if God forgives us, we should forgive others (Matthew 18^{21-35}).
- Jesus taught that God always forgives. He never returns an evil act for an evil act. He loves his enemies. He expects his followers to be as perfect as he is: to love those who hate them; to pray for those who persecute them. It is easy to love a friend. A follower of Jesus has to love an enemy as well (Matthew 5^{38-48}).

    The story of the forgiving father (see Chapter C19, *Luke's gospel – parables*) also teaches that God forgives.
- God made all humans in his image and likeness. Therefore, all killing is wrong.
- An evil action never justifies an evil retaliation. It is evil to kill, whatever the cause.
- Wars never solve any problems. The problems are still there 20 years later. In every war are the seeds of the next war.
- Killing just leads to more killing, and to destruction of property and land, and to hatred. It is the psychotic's dream come true.

Examination guidance

2 700 000 Americans served in Vietnam.

The war in Vietnam cost the American government 1 000 000 000 dollars (one thousand million dollars).

The Americans dropped ten million tons of bombs and shells on Vietnam.

They killed 900 000 Vietnamese.

The Americans still lost the war.

1. Look at these facts about the Vietnam war.. What can you learn about war from them? (3 marks)

2. Explain why Christians believe that peace is better than war. (7 marks)

1. **First answer**

    You can learn that Christians think that war is wrong and that it should not happen. You can learn that war is expensive and governments should really spend their money on better things, like helping the poor.

    There is one relevant point in this answer. The candidate cannot deduce the first sentence from the stimulus, nor the second point in the second sentence.

    The one inference the candidate can justifiably make is: you can learn that war is expensive.
    (Score: 1 mark out of 3)

    Second answer

    You learn that in war there can be a dreadful loss of live (900 000 Vietnamese, and an undisclosed number of Americans). You learn that you can spend a fortune on war (the Americans spent one thousand million dollars) and still not win it. You learn that in a war there can be enormous destruction of property (damage from ten million tons of explosives).

    The candidate has made three relevant points. Each point can be clearly deduced from the stimulus. To avoid any doubts about this, the candidate has quoted evidence from the stimulus to support the deductions.
    (Score: 3 marks out of 3)

2. **First answer**

    Christians believe that loving your enemies is better than fighting them. For example if everyone didn't get along then there would always be war. Because of a disagreement there is a war on in Bosnia that I believe would be a world war unless a peaceful agreement can be found beforehand.

    If people can learn to love and forgive their enemies then the world will be peaceful and a better place to live in.

    There are some correct and relevant points in this candidate's answer.

    However, the candidate repeats and meanders in the answer. There are no extra marks for repeating the same thing in different words, nor for writing 50 words when the same idea could be easily expressed in 20 words.

    There are a limited number of relevant points in the answer. To obtain a higher mark, the candidate should extend the scope of the answer by making further relevant points.

Christians believe that peace is better than war because if war breaks out lives will be lost and that can be prevented by a peaceful resolution which is to learn to love and forgive your enemies.

Second answer

In war there is often the unjust killing of innocent human beings. Christians believe that there are peaceful means of approach before a war is inevitable. All true Christians believe human life is sacred and God is the only author of all life – so why do we have the right to take a person's life? The answer is we definitely don't, so it should not happen. War also begins with people who have greed for power or a love of doing harm. We Christians believe this is a wrong way to behave; so we disagree with war.

The Church has always taught that war is evil and destroys God's creation. Peace gives people the opportunity to enjoy God's creation and live in joy and peace. These are gifts of the Holy Spirit.

Christians also strive in following the teachings of Jesus on, for example, discipleship, and this shows us we must be peaceful in all we do and not retaliate at any sign of disagreement. Jesus taught us to love our neighbour, forgive and be reconciled with those who do us wrong. He told us to imitate God who is kind to those who like Him and those who do not like Him.

There is no reference to the teaching and example of Jesus, nor the traditions of the Church. Both of these are important sources for what a Christian believes about peace and war.
(Score: 3 marks out of 7)

Here is an answer with a variety of relevant ideas. This is what obtains maximum marks for a candidate.

However, some examiners may give six, not seven marks for this answer, as the candidate could improve the organization of the answer.

Most of us realize it is difficult to organize information and ideas coherently if we are writing as we are thinking.

Consequently, it is always better to pause before you start to write an answer to a question. You should spend a few moments searching your mind for relevant ideas, and sorting these ideas into some order. You can even jot them down on the exam paper (and cross them out when you have written the answer).

If you do this, rather than rush into writing an answer, you will find that you think of several relevant ideas, and you will express them coherently.
(Score: 7 marks out of 7)

Examination practice

1. Why do most Christians believe that nuclear war is wrong? (3 marks)
   Write about six lines.

2. What causes wars? (6 marks)
   Write about half a side of A4.

3. What is said about holy war in the Bible?
   (6 marks)
   Write about half a side of A4.

4. Christians think that peace is better than war. What reasons do they give for this attitude?
   (6 marks)
   Write about half a side of A4.

5. Explain the just war theory. (8 marks)
   Write about three-quarters of a side of A4.

6. 'All Christians should be pacifists.'
   Do you agree? Give reasons for your view. Show that you have considered the opposite view. (10 marks)
   Write about one side of A4.

Protest

All Christians should oppose injustice. Some believe that it is legitimate to use violence, though they believe there are limits to the use of violence.

Others, pacifists, will not use violence. Yet they do not accept injustice. They oppose it, but non-violently. **Martin Luther King**, a Baptist minister, was a prominent example of a Christian in the twentieth century who protested against injustice. He was an eloquent spokesman for those who protested against prejudice and discrimination, because of colour or race, in the USA in the twentieth century. They boycotted buses or cafes that practised racial discrimination. They protested outside places that practised racial discrimination. They held rallies and they marched, in thousands, to protest against injustice. When they were attacked violently, they did not retaliate. They remembered Jesus' teaching that they should turn the other cheek. They triumphed; they changed the laws that permitted racial discrimination. Racial discrimination became illegal. Yet there was a price; Martin Luther King was assassinated.

Martin Luther King, a Baptist minister. He followed the example of Jesus and, without using violence, protested against injustice.

Martin Luther King followed the example of Jesus, who protested against injustice. Jesus protested to the Jewish religious leaders about the unnecessary burdens they imposed on people. He quoted from the prophet Isaiah:

> These people honour me with their lips,
>   but their hearts are far from me.
> They worship me in vain;
>   their teachings are but rules taught by men.
>
> Mark 7 ^{6–7}

Consequently, it is the timid Christian who meekly acquiesces, and accepts unjust situations. It is the spirited Christian who follows the example of Jesus, encouraged by the Spirit, and protests. Such Christians risk the fate of Jesus – rejection and death.

See Chapter E18, *Liberation theology and the developing world*, for additional information.

Another non-violent protest

Oscar Romero was another Christian who was killed for protesting against injustice. A gunman shot and killed Archbishop Romero as he was standing at the altar celebrating the eucharist with some of his parishioners in the town's cathedral. Romero was Archbishop of San Salvador in Central America, and he lived in the second half of the twentieth century. He believed that a Christian had to protest against injustice; but he also believed that the protest should not be violent.

San Salvador is a farming country of a few rich people and many poor people. The rich people own the land and make much money from it. They live in large houses and have the normal luxuries of rich people. Most poor people live in shacks; they have few possessions. The rich people employ the poor people to work on the land, and pay the poor people a very low wage.

Government ministers usually come from the rich class. The government supports the rich people. It makes laws to help rich people stay rich and to ensure that poor people stay poor.

San Salvador is also a mainly Catholic country. The bishops have generally supported the rich people and the government. When Oscar Romero was appointed Archbishop of San Salvador, most people assumed that he would continue the Catholic bishops' habit of supporting the government and the rich people. But a short while after he became Archbishop, Romero started preaching that it was wrong for the landowners to make so much money from owning the land, while the workers got so little money from working on the land.

The rich people tried to get the bishops to persuade Romero to preach about other things. But Romero kept on preaching against injustice. And, because he was the chief bishop in the country, his preaching was encouraging poor people to believe they should have a better standard of life. They wanted a just wage for their work. They wanted a fairer share of the country's wealth. The government became worried. It tried to get the Pope to stop Romero preaching about injustice. Romero kept preaching that it was wrong for the rich people to have so much money when other people in their country had barely enough to live on. In the end, those who were incensed by this preaching had only one way left to silence Romero. So they had him killed.

See Chapter E18, *Liberation theology and the developing world*, for additional information, especially about violent protest against injustice.

Should Christians obey unjust laws?

In an earlier section we explained how Martin Luther King refused to obey laws that were unjust: he would not obey laws that discriminated against black people. And some Christian leaders have taught that it is right not to obey unjust laws. For instance, Pope John XXIII taught:

> Authority. . . derives from God. Consequently, laws. . . in contravention of the moral order, and hence of the divine will, can have no binding force in conscience . . . indeed the passing of such laws undermines the very nature of authority and results in shameful abuse.

Yet some Christians believe that Christians should keep all the laws of their country, out of obedience to their government, even though they think that some of the laws are bad. See the first part of Chapter D9, *Church and state*, for an account of the passages from the Bible that could be used to support either opinion.

In England and the USA there are no longer laws allowing racial discrimination. So what are examples of current laws that some Christians might consider unjust, and so refuse to obey?

• the law allowing abortion;
• the law prohibiting euthanasia;
• the law allowing experiments on human embryos;
• the law restricting immigration;
• the law allowing divorce.

Human rights

It is claimed that we all have the right:

• to own personal possessions, such as clothes, a car, a house, land, and so on (private property);
• to speak and write freely about whatever we believe in, or to speak and write about what other people have done (freedom of speech);
• to move (migrate) freely from one country to another, or within a country;
• to marry, to have children, or both or these;
• to join a trade union whose members may strike as a method of getting a better wage or better working conditions;
• to a job;
• to life – and so the right to enough clothes, food, and housing to live;
• to keep private anything about our lives that we do not want other people to know about (privacy);
• to defend any of our rights, with violence if we have to.

These are all examples of human rights. Christians say that they are God-given human rights. But not all people agree that these are human rights. For instance, do you think that everyone has the right to strike, or the right to have children? And do we all have the right to defend our rights with violence?

The concept of human rights is recent. There is nothing in the Bible about human rights.

A Christian who believes in human rights might say: 'They are obvious, self-evident. There is no need to give evidence why we should accept them.' Another Christian might say: 'Some human rights are obvious, but some human rights are not obvious; we have to give reasons for the latter.' In both cases, Christians are using human thinking to justify their belief in human rights. They do not quote from the Bible. See Chapter E30, *Natural law: reasoning* for more information about how some Christians use reasoning to decide right and wrong.

Prisoners of conscience

Prisoners of conscience are people who have not used violence, but have been put in prison – perhaps because they have criticized the government, or perhaps because their beliefs are different from the government's. Sometimes government ministers and officials do not like people who criticize them, nor do they like people who have different beliefs. And so they want these people out of the way. Government ministers such as these take away from people their right to freedom of speech.

Orson Santoyo is a Pentecostal minister in Cuba (West Indies). In 1995 local government officials told him to shut down his church, even though the law in Cuba allows Pentecostal churches. Santoyo refused. The police arrested Santoyo, confiscated his church equipment, and charged him with 'disobedience'. The judge sentenced Santoyo to 18 months in prison. Santoyo became a prisoner of conscience.

To cope with their suffering and with the injustice done to them, Christians who are prisoners of conscience may think of Christ: he was flogged, humiliated and sentenced to an agonizing death, though he had done nothing wrong. They may ask Christ to be with them in their loneliness, anger and fear. They may ask Christ to have compassion on their imprisoners, and to change the government ministers and officials into people who have a sense of justice. They may ask Christ to make everyone an instrument of his peace.

Terrorism

We use the word 'terrorist' to describe those who kill innocent people as part of their attempt to defeat a government. They may plant a bomb in a crowded shopping centre; the bomb will kill and maim those who just happen to be there when it explodes. Or terrorists may hijack a plane and kill passengers whom the terrorists do not know. This does not matter to them. The purpose of terrorism is to pressure a government into giving freedom to the group of people that the terrorists support.

Of course, if we are on the side of the terrorists, we shall call them freedom fighters, not terrorists.

State 'terrorism' is quite widespread. Some governments do not like people who criticize or oppose them. They imprison, torture, or kill people who criticize and oppose them. There is no trial. People disappear in the middle of the night. We do not read much in the newspapers about state terrorism. When the newspapers write about terrorists, they usually mean groups that endeavour to overthrow a government, or they mean groups that want freedom for their nation. If you want more details about state terrorism, then write to Amnesty International.

Any terrorism accepts the principle that 'the end justifies the means': that is, if our purpose is good – for example to free our nation from foreign rule – then any action we take to achieve our purpose must be right. But most Christians have never accepted this principle. There are some exceptions; see Chapter E26, *Situation ethics*.

Most Christians say that it is wrong to do something evil, even if our purpose is good. It is wrong to torture or murder innocent people to get freedom for our nation. It is wrong to torture or murder people because they criticize us. This is not the spirit of Jesus.

Some people think that, in war, atrocities will inevitably happen. They are right. Yet Christians do not accept that this makes murder and torture of innocent people right or acceptable. Such acts are degrading – for the people who are mistreated, and for the people who mistreat them. This is evil. The Spirit of God is absent.

Examination practice

1. What does 'human rights' mean? Give **three** examples of human rights. (3 marks)
    Write about six lines of A4.

2. What is a prisoner of conscience? Give **one** example of a Christian prisoner of conscience.
    How might Christian beliefs have helped that person to cope with imprisonment? (6 marks)
    Write about half a side of A4.

3. Name a Christian who has struggled against injustice. Explain what that Christian did. (6 marks)
    Write about half a side of A4.

4. 'Terrorism can sometime be right.'
    Do you agree? Give reasons for your answer. Show that you have considered the opposite point of view.
    (8 marks)
    Write about three-quarters of a side of A4.

5. Jesus taught and practised forgiveness.
    How might this modify a Christian's desire for vengeance? (8 marks)
    Write about three-quarters of a side of A4.

6. Do you think there will be a time when there is no more violence?
    Give reasons for your view. Show that you have considered the opposite view. (8 marks)
    Write about three-quarters of a side of A4.

POVERTY; WEALTH 15

Introduction

Suppose I won a large amount of money on the lottery. How would I spend it? On myself? Or partly on myself and partly on others? I may find it difficult to make up my mind. Perhaps I dither because I would like to spend some of it on others, but I want to spend it on myself – greed!

Most of us are like this. We have a deep 'instinct' to want to be affluent. We want to have more money and possessions than other people. We fear poverty.

Yet Jesus taught that it was better to be poor than to be rich.

> Poverty goes hand in hand with hunger . . . no one can state the exact numbers who experience hunger and malnutrition, but all estimates count them hundreds of millions.
>
> Brandt Report

How we describe and draw our world

Any map that we use will be distorted in one way or another. The map used in this pack is called the "Peters Projection" map. Developed in 1983, this map presents countries of the world according to the area they take up in the world.

Try comparing this map with other maps you may use in History and Geography.

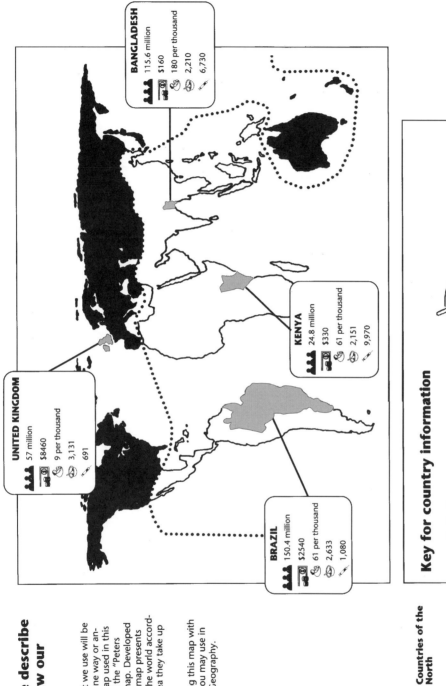

BANGLADESH
115.6 million
$160
180 per thousand
2,210
6,730

UNITED KINGDOM
57 million
$8460
9 per thousand
3,131
691

KENYA
24.8 million
$330
61 per thousand
2,151
9,970

BRAZIL
150.4 million
$2540
61 per thousand
2,633
1,080

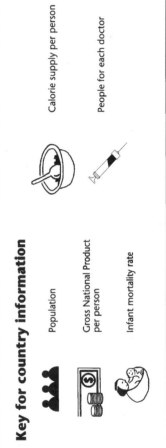

Key for country information

Population

Gross National Product per person

Infant mortality rate

Calorie supply per person

People for each doctor

Countries of the North

Countries of the South

Source: CAFOD

Distribution of world's resources

The map opposite shows the poorer countries and the richer countries. The poorer countries are often called the **third world**. These countries are also called **developing countries**, because they are trying to improve their standard of living; they are also sometimes called **the South**, as most poor countries are in the southern hemisphere.

Less than 20% of the world's population lives in the richer countries called **first world** countries, yet these countries have most of the world's wealth. These countries have important industries, the source of much of their wealth.

Over 75 per cent of the world's population live in third world countries. They have a small proportion of the world's wealth: about 30 per cent of the world's food grains; about 8 per cent of the world's industries. Many people in these countries are undernourished and have poor health. The adults did not have the chance to go to school. Their children may have some schooling, but not much. Famines occur in these countries.

All the poor countries have some people who are rich. In these countries, there are notable differences between the lifestyle of the majority – who are poor – and the lifestyle of the few who are very rich.

> God destined the earth and all it contains for all peoples . . . Therefore every man has the right to possess a sufficient amount of the earth's goods for himself and his family . . . When a person is in extreme necessity he has the right to supply himself with what he needs out of the riches of others.
>
> Catholic bishops at the Second Vatican Council

Causes of poverty

It is difficult to be certain about the causes of poverty. Here are some suggestions.

- **Inability to recover from natural disaster**. A flood, an earthquake or a drought can devastate an area. It can take many years to recover the land and to rebuild houses.
- **Cycle of debt**. People in the poorer countries want to improve their standard of living. And the governments and banks of the richer countries are willing to lend money to the governments of the poorer countries, who use this money to build a major project, such as a dam. The third world government expects to repay the interest and the loan without difficulty. However, the project is often more expensive than first thought. Or there is a natural disaster in the third world country, resulting in the government raising less money in taxes. Or the bank raises the interest rate on the loan. For any of these

reasons, the third world government has to borrow more money, which it finds difficult to pay back. Consequently, in many instances where a third world country borrows money, it has an increasing debt to the bank or government of the first world country.

- **Disease**. Diseases cause early death, especially of children. Now children are an important asset to a family – they work and thus help to raise the family's standard of living. Thus the death of children affects the family's standard of living. Diseases also weaken and maim people, who are then unable to work effectively.
- **Malnutrition**. If we are undernourished, we have little energy to work. Our ability to think is also hindered: we find it difficult to plan and improve our standard of living.
- **Population explosion**. Most people in third world countries want to have as many children as they can, because the children can work, to help the family improve its standard of living. Thus the birth rate is high. A few years ago, many children died very young. But the standard of health care has improved in these countries, so fewer children now die young. Consequently, there is a population explosion. More food is needed, which the country may find hard to provide.
- **Unjust trading conditions**. Western countries sell their goods, especially manufactured goods such as weapons, to third world countries at high prices. Yet third world countries sell their goods, usually agricultural products, at low prices to Western countries. A further handicap for the third world countries is that the price of agricultural products can change enormously from one year to the next.
- **Ignorance and illiteracy**. If we can read and write, and if we have been to school, we can tackle poverty more effectively. Poor people cannot afford to send their children to school. Even if school is free, poor people find it difficult to send their children to school, because the children still need books they cannot afford. In any case, very poor people need their children to earn some money to relieve the family's poverty.
- **War**. Wars are expensive – very expensive. An enormous amount of money is spent on weapons. This money would have been useful in raising people's standard of living. War also causes enormous damage – crops are destroyed; homes are destroyed; roads and tools are destroyed. This makes poor people even poorer. Wars also create refugees, who have no home or income of their own. Most of them take refuge in other poor countries. Poor people in these countries have to share the little they have with refugees, who have nothing.

Jesus and poverty

> 'Blessed are you who are poor, for yours is the kingdom of God.'
>
> Jesus (Luke 6[20])

Jesus was a wandering preacher, with few possessions. He did not live an affluent lifestyle. When he died, his only possessions seem to have been the clothes he wore. He taught a carefree attitude to money and possessions. He said:

> 'I tell you, do not worry about your life, what you will eat; or about your body, what you will wear. Life is more than food, and the body more than clothes. Consider the ravens: they do not sow or reap, they have no storeroom or barn; yet God feeds them. And how much more valuable you are than birds!
>
> Consider how the lilies grow. They do not labour or spin. Yet I tell you, not even Solomon [a very wealthy king] in all his splendour was dressed like one of these. If that is how God clothes the grass of the field . . . how much more will he clothe you.'
>
> Luke 12$^{22-28}$

Jesus praised poverty. He said that it would be difficult for rich people to get into the kingdom of God: it would be easier for a camel to go through the eye of a needle than for a rich man to get into the kingdom of God. He said this to a wealthy man who had asked him what he should do to inherit eternal life. Jesus told him to keep the commandments, such as not committing adultery, not murdering, not giving false testimony. When the wealthy man said he had always kept these commandments, Jesus said:

> 'You still lack one thing. Sell everything you have and give to the poor, and you will have treasure in heaven. Then come, follow me.'
>
> Luke 18^{22}

Jesus told a story to illustrate his view that it was not worth becoming rich. He said there was a rich farmer who had a bumper crop one year. The farmer decided to pull down his barns and build new, bigger ones to store his bumper crop. Then he could take life easy: eat, drink and be merry.

> 'But God said to him, "You fool! This very night your life will be demanded from you. Then who will get what you have prepared for yourself?"'
>
> Luke 12^{20}

Jesus told another story to illustrate his point that it is the poor, not the rich, who get into God's kingdom. He said there was a wealthy man who dressed in purple and fine linen and who lived in luxury every day. At his door there was a beggar named Lazarus, covered with sores and longing to eat what fell from the rich man's table. Even the dogs came and licked his sores. The poor man died and went to heaven; the rich man died and went to the underworld, from where he envied the good life of Lazarus (Luke 16$^{19-31}$).

First Christians

The first Christians accepted the teaching of Jesus, that wealth was worthless. James, for instance, said:

> 'Now listen, you rich people, weep and wail because of the misery that is coming to you. Your wealth has rotted, and moths have eaten your clothes. Your gold and silver are corroded.'
>
> James 5$^{1-3}$

The first Christians also followed the teaching of Jesus. They shared what they had.

> There were no needy persons among them. For from time to time those who owned lands or houses sold them, brought the money from the sales and put it at the apostles' feet, and it was distributed to anyone as he had need.
>
> Acts 4$^{34-35}$

> I used to think that Christ might have been exaggerating when he warned about the dangers of wealth.
>
> Today I know better. Money has a dangerous way of freezing people's hands, eyes, lips, and hearts.
>
> Helder Camara

Francis of Assisi

Francis was a famous Christian, who emphasized the poverty of Jesus. Francis believed there were considerable benefits if we chose to be poor.

He was born in 1182, in the town of Assisi in northern Italy. His father was wealthy, so Francis had an easy, light-hearted life. He enjoyed expensive clothes, parties and having a good time. He did not need to find a job, as his father gave him all the money he wanted.

When he was 20, there was a war between his town of Assisi and the nearby town of Perugia. Francis was captured and imprisoned for a year. This must have shocked him. However, when he returned to Assisi, he re-started his light-hearted life.

Then a second shock hit him. He became seriously ill. This made him think carefully about his way of life.

A year later, he joined the army of Assisi for another war. One night, a strange dream unsettled him, and he returned home straight away. Back at Assisi, he no longer enjoyed the parties; he preferred solitude. He was uncertain and unsettled. He started to rebuild a broken church. He sold many of his possessions, which irritated and angered his father. Then one morning, he listened to the gospel passage about Jesus sending out his disciples. Jesus said:

> 'Take nothing for the journey except a staff – no bread, no bag, no money in your belts. Wear sandals but not an extra tunic.'
>
> Mark 6$^{8-9}$

Francis resolutely decided to renounce his wealth, which infuriated his father, who wanted Francis to inherit his wealth. Francis resolved to be poor. He even handed back his clothes to his father. Francis wore a coarse tunic, and travelled from town to town preaching good news about Jesus. Francis was 26. Eighteen years later, he died prematurely, worn out.

Curiously, there were hundreds who joined him. They sold their possessions, gave the money to poor people, and followed Francis' lifestyle. They prayed with God. They helped sick people. They encouraged people to settle their quarrels. And they preached about Jesus.

There are still many people today who follow Francis' style of life. They call themselves Franciscans.

> May the Lord bless you and keep you,
> Show you his face, and be merciful to you,
> Turn upon you the light of his face, and give you peace.
>
> Francis of Assisi

Relief of poverty

See Chapter E17, *Christian relief agencies*. See also Chapter E18, *Liberation theology and the developing world*.

Examination practice

1. Select a passage from the New Testament about poverty.
   Explain what it says. (3 marks)
   Write about five lines of A4.

2. What are the causes of poverty? (8 marks)
   Write about one side of A4.

3. Jesus was poor.
   How might this influence a Christian's outlook and actions? (8 marks)
   Write about three-quarters of a side of A4.

4. 'Poverty is a curse, not a blessing.'
   What would you say? Show that you have considered more than one answer. (8 marks)
   Write about three-quarters of a side of A4.

WEALTH; MONEY; MATERIALISM 16

Biblical teaching

Both work and leisure are part of God's design for the human race. One of the commandments is 'Six days you shall labour and do all your work, but the seventh day is a Sabbath to the Lord your God. On it you shall not do any work' (Exodus 20$^{8-11}$). Jesus said, 'The Sabbath was made for man, not man for the Sabbath' (Mark 2^{27}).

'The love of money is a root of all kinds of evil'. Note exactly what Paul *does* write here. He does not write 'Money is the root of all evil' – it is the **love of money** he condemns. He also writes 'We brought nothing into the world, and we can take nothing out of it. But if we have food and clothing, we will be content with that. People who want to get rich fall into temptation and a trap and into many foolish and harmful desires that plunge men into ruin and destruction' (1 Timothy 6$^{6-10}$). Remember the words of the commandment – 'You shalt not covet' (Exodus 20^{17}).

'How hard it is for the rich to enter the kingdom of God.' The rich young man who came to Jesus was obviously quite genuine. He asked what he must do to inherit eternal life. Jesus told him to obey the commandments – that is, the Ten Commandments. The young man said he had done so since he was a boy.

> Jesus looked at him and loved him. 'One thing you lack,' he said. 'Go, sell everything you have and give to the poor, and you will have treasure in heaven. Then come, follow me.'
>
> Mark 10$^{17-31}$

The young man went away sorrowful. He wanted to follow Jesus, but the price was too great.

The disciples were amazed when Jesus said 'How hard it is for the rich to enter the kingdom of God.' Jesus told them that it is easier for a camel to go through the eye of a needle than for a rich man to enter the kingdom of God – in other words, all but impossible. (Incidentally, there is no evidence at all for the theory you may find in some books that there was a gate to Jerusalem nicknamed 'the eye of a needle'; guides showing people round Jerusalem know the theory, but even they do not take it seriously.)

Again, the disciples were amazed and asked who could be saved, if rich people could not. Jesus replied, 'With man this is impossible, but not with God; all things are possible with God' (Mark 10^{27}).

Acts 2$^{42-45}$ describes how the first Christians shared all their possessions and all were given according to what they needed. This might seem the ideal, unselfish way. Acts 4$^{36-37}$ describes how Barnabas sold his field and gave the whole price to be shared. However, Acts 5$^{1-11}$ tells how Ananias and Sapphira kept back some of the money when they sold some property but lied to the apostles by saying they had given the whole price. In Acts 6^1 we read that a dispute had arisen about the way the food was distributed. So even those Christians could not ignore the attraction of money; jealousy broke out.

James 2$^{1-7}$ describes how some Christians might treat a rich man who came to worship better than they might treat a poor man, giving the rich man a good seat and telling the poor man to stand or sit on the floor. James tells them this is not the way Christians should treat others.

Poverty

Money is very unevenly distributed among the people of the world. It is estimated that 1 billion people in the world live in absolute poverty – meaning that they do not have enough to provide themselves and their families with enough to eat or with the basic necessities of clothing and housing. The average income in Zaire and Ethiopia is less than 2 per cent of average income in the USA. See Chapter E15, *Poverty; wealth*, for more detail here. A Christian attitude to money must recognize a responsibility to help the poor.

Christian attitudes to money and materialism

- Money and possessions in themselves are not evil. They are God's gifts to the human race. Without money or possessions people suffer hunger, poverty, homelessness. Many Christian charities work to make sure that people *do* have money, food, home, possessions.
- People work better when they have something to work for. The whole of society is likely to benefit if everyone sees the point in working because there is a reward for their work.
- But money and possessions can *cause* evil. They may lead people into crime. They can make people work to gain at the expense of others. Money may become so important to some people that they neglect their families.
- It is the **love of money** that is the root of all evil, as it says in 1 Timothy 6^{10}.
- All human beings are equally precious in God's sight. Rich people are not better than poor people.
- Christians have a duty to God to use their money and possessions properly. The word often used to describe this duty is **stewardship**. A steward is someone who

looks after something for someone else. Everything belongs to God. Everyone has possessions that are, as it were, loaned to them by God while they are alive. Everyone will be judged by God on the use they make of their possessions.
- Because of that duty, that stewardship, people who have money and possessions have a responsibility to help those who are in need.

Gambling

Some Christians object to gambling because it is based on coveting – which is against the tenth commandment. People gamble because they want a lot of money for no effort.

The reason why a few Christians have spoken against the National Lottery is that huge sums of money can be won. The jackpot can be so large that it could ruin a person's life. Those who have won millions of pounds might move away to a big house and find that they lose touch with friends and neighbours. They may even be the victims of threats and blackmail.

Many Christian people see nothing wrong in gambling – so long as it is in moderation. Often it is little more than innocent amusement. Some churches have raffles or draws to raise money, and people buy the tickets to support the church as much as to win a prize. In the same way, people may bet on the Derby or the Grand National just because other people do, to join in a social activity. They get pleasure from talking about their good – or bad – luck.

Gambling is wrong when it is on a scale that a person cannot afford. Sometimes a man with a young family gambles and loses money that is needed to clothe and feed the family properly. That is obviously wrong. It is wrong if someone inherits the family business and gambles so much that it is lost and the next generation does not have a business or a home. Gambling can also lead to crime.

Examination practice

1. Describe an occasion when Jesus met a rich man. What did Jesus say to him and how did he react? (7 marks)
   Write half to three-quarters of a side of A4, depending on whom you choose.

2. How did the first Christians share their property and possessions? Do you think such a system could work today? Give reasons for your answer. (8 marks)
   In describing how the first Christians used to share, do show that you are aware of the problems that cropped up. This answer might well run over a side of A4.

3. Do you think gambling is against the Christian faith? Give reasons for your answer. (5 marks)
   *Probably an answer will take up to a side of A4. Remember to quote teaching from the Bible or other Christian teaching. You are not simply being asked if **you** think gambling is right or wrong.*

CHRISTIAN RELIEF AGENCIES

Introduction

Cafod, Christian Aid, Tear Fund and Trócaire are relief and development agencies in England, Ireland, Wales and Scotland. They are Christian relief agencies. They all have the same aim: to help very poor people overseas. They help people in third world countries regardless of their religion, race or colour. Though they are Christian groups, Cafod, Christian Aid, Tear Fund and Trócaire aim to help Hindus, Muslims, Buddhists, and people with no religion, as well as Christians.

They have three objectives:

* to enable people in southern countries to help themselves, so they are no longer poor;
* to educate people in Britain and Ireland about the causes of poverty and injustice;
* to provide emergency relief when there is sudden disaster.

The richer countries in the world are mainly North American and Western European countries. The poorer countries are mainly Asian, African and Latin American countries. The poorer countries have most of the world's population, but not much of the world's wealth, as the barchart below shows.

See Chapter E15, *Poverty; wealth* for more detailed information about poverty.

Raising money

The Christian development agencies have various ways of collecting money: family fast days; 24-hour fasts; Lenten campaigns; Friday groups; appeals in churches; individual contributions; covenants; legacies; groups in parishes and

schools who arrange coffee mornings, hunger lunches, sponsored events, and so on.

Cafod, Christian Aid, Tear Fund and Trócaire also receive grants from the governments in Britain and Ireland.

Spending money

In 1992–3, Tear Fund spent over nineteen million pounds (£19 000 000). The barchart on the next page shows how it spent the money.

Long-term aid (development projects)

> Give a starving man a fish, and he will be hungry tomorrow. Teach a starving man how to fish, and he will never be hungry again.
>
> Proverb

The Christian development agencies help poor people in southern countries to be self-reliant, so they do not have to depend on further help from richer people in northern countries. The agencies give money to projects that aim to:

* assist leaders to develop the skills to lead protests against unjust situations;
* help local people learn specific vocational skills, to improve their standard of living;
* increase agriculture and food production, to prevent people from going hungry;
* teach illiterate people to read and write, so they can help themselves;

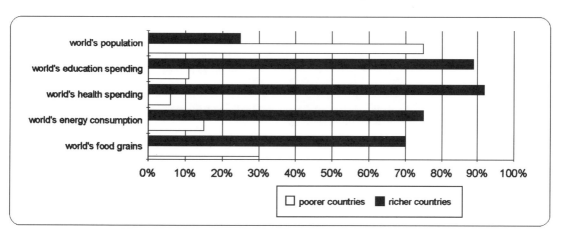

This barchart shows some differences between richer and poorer countries. Source: CAFOD

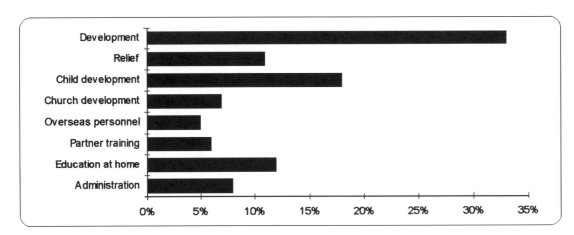

This barchart shows the ways in which Tear Fund uses its money. Source: Tear Fund

- improve health care, so people do not die at an early age;
- supply clean water, so people can enjoy life;
- encourage community education, especially education that makes people aware of their human rights.

Tear Fund and Trócaire send personnel to developing countries to decide suitable projects. Cafod and Christian Aid do not have full-time personnel abroad who plan projects. Instead, they work through local Christians, and they will give money to a group of people who take the initiative in helping themselves, and who can involve all their members in the project. The project must tackle the causes of poverty, to help local people to become independent. The illustration opposite shows how a typical project benefits people.

The Christian agencies believe that it is degrading for very poor people repeatedly to receive short-term aid. Such aid might encourage the people who give it to feel that they are doing a good deed; it may also make them feel important and superior. It does not help poor people to feel dignified and to have self-respect. Dignity and self-respect come when they can support themselves and earn their own living, without depending on others.

Thus the Christian agencies support projects that allow people in third world countries to become economically independent and to have a pride in themselves.

Short-term aid (emergency aid)

> The Council asks individuals and governments to remember the saying of the Fathers:
> 'Feed the man dying of hunger, because if you do not feed him you are killing him.'
> Catholic bishops at Second Vatican Council

Natural disasters such as floods, earthquakes and droughts are inevitable. They destroy people's homes and leave them without food and clothing. Wars cause the same difficulties. To help the victims of such disasters, Christian relief agencies provide emergency assistance: they give blankets, clothing, tents and food. The purpose of such help is to stop people from dying. It enables them to survive until they can restore their normal way of life.

Education

The development and relief agencies use books, posters, factsheets, videos and regular newsletters to publicize their work. They use these in Britain and Ireland to

- help people to understand the causes of poverty (see Chapter E15, *Poverty; wealth*, for details);
- encourage people to consider what they should do to eliminate poverty.

People in our country are more likely to help if they feel and appreciate what hungry and very poor people suffer. They are more likely to take action if they become aware of what they can do to remove the causes of poverty.

One Church leader, Pope Paul VI, asked people to ask themselves:

- Am I really doing all I can to help the poor and hungry?
- Am I prepared to pay more taxes so the government can do more for development?
- Am I prepared to pay more in the shops for goods imported from abroad so that people who produced these goods are paid a decent wage?
- Am I prepared to leave my country to help the younger nations?

Motivation

> The human race as far as brain power is concerned, shows that it truly shares in God's creative power, yet when it comes to will-power, we're still no better than monkeys. We're unable to overcome our own selfishness.
> Helder Camara

On the outskirts of a wealthy Latin American city lies one of the world's many favelas (shanty towns). A few years ago, the people felt annoyed and frustrated by the conditions in which they were living. The biggest problem was water, which was not provided by the authorities and had to be carried long distances.

Often the water was dirty but there was no choice but to use it. As a result, many children died at a very early age. Their relatives buried them in coffins made of cardboard. Instead of getting better, things seemed to be getting worse. Everyone's future was very uncertain.

Eventually, it was decided to call a meeting of the local people. they discussed their problems and decided what action to take. It was agreed that the most important thing was to build a good water system which would bring clean water to the whole district all year round.

Having made the decisions about who was to dig the channels, where the standpipes would go, who would benefit first and so on, they came up against one problem; lack of money with which to buy the pipes. CAFOD was able to help by making available a small amount of money. Everyone set to work with great enthusiasm.

After a lot of hard work and a tremendous community effort, the water system was built. Now there would be enough water for everyone. For cooking, washing and drinking. No more mystery illnesses. A real success story.

This was only the beginning. Having seen what is possible when everyone works together, the people of this favela are improving the life of their community in a spirit of cooperation.

Here is an example of a development project
Source: CAFOD

Christians believe that it is not enough to help poor people and those suffering injustice in their own country. They think that national boundaries are unimportant. God made all people and loves all people. Nationality is not important to him. Hence Christians believe they should help poor people in other countries. As Pope Paul VI said:

> Normally, a country's population should be the first to benefit from all it can produce. But nowadays, no country can keep its wealth just for itself alone. All nations should produce more goods, and better goods, for the benefit of all mankind.

Perhaps an even more important Christian belief is that God made the world for everyone: people have the right to what they need to live. The world belongs to God, not to a few human beings. Thus those who have an unfair amount of the world's wealth are 'stealing' from those who do not have enough to live humanely.

The example of Jesus is important for Christians. He showed what God is like. He was also the perfect human. So, he is the model of how we should behave. Jesus spent most of his time helping poor people, such as the leper who wanted to be healed, or the Gerasene man who lived in a graveyard and was possessed by demons.

Jesus commended poor people, such as the widow who put more – proportionately – than the rich people, into the temple box. He told his disciples:

> 'This poor widow has put more into the treasury than all the others. They all gave out of their wealth; but she, out of her poverty, put in everything – all she had to live on.'
> Mark 12$^{43-44}$

Jesus did not mix much with rich people. He spent his time with the poor. Jesus told some messengers to tell John the Baptist:

> 'Go back and report to John what you have seen and heard: the blind receive sight, the lame walk, those who have leprosy are cured, the deaf hear, the dead are raised, and the good news is preached to the poor.'
> Luke 7^{22}

Poverty and justice

See Chapter E18, *Liberation theology and the developing world* for information about poverty and justice.

Sharing

There are many passages in the New Testament about sharing. Here are four examples:

- Jesus told a parable about sheep and goats (see Chapter E24, *Christian discipleship – special texts*). The main point of this parable is that there is a judgement after death. Jesus will reward those who helped the poor, the starving, the naked and the homeless. He will reject those who did not help the poor, the starving, the naked and the homeless (Matthew 25$^{31-46}$).
- Jesus told a parable of a rich fool. This man was a farmer. He had an exceptional crop one year. So he built new barns to store it all. He then decided to take life easy: to eat, drink and be merry. But that night God told him he would die. What good would his wealth be to him then? The main point of this parable is that those

who are selfish and self-indulgent will find, when they die, that God is not pleased with them (Luke 12$^{13-21}$).

- The first Christians were generous with their possessions. No one claimed what they owned as theirs. There were no needy persons among them. From time to time, those who owned land or houses, sold them. They gave the money to the disciples, who distributed it among those who needed it (Acts 4$^{32-35}$).
- An early Christian writer, James, said that faith was no good if the believer did not help other people. James said that if a Christian saw other Christians without clothes or food and wished them well, but did nothing to help them, then this person's faith was dead.

> What good is it, my brothers, if a man claims to have faith but has no deeds? Can such faith save him? Suppose a brother or sister [fellow Christian] is without clothes and daily food. If one of you says to him, 'Go, I wish you well; keep warm and well fed,' but does nothing about his physical needs, what good is it? In the same way, faith by itself, if it is not accomanied by action, is dead.
> James 2$^{14-17}$

Government aid

Christians believe that they should help the poor overseas. Yet they also believe that governments have a responsibility to help the poor, both in their own country, and overseas. For example, Pope Paul VI said:

> Men must be brothers; so must peoples. The Council [Second Vatican Council of bishops] said, 'Developed nations have an urgent duty to help the developing ones' . . . It should be normal, now, for all developed nations to help the under-developed with some agreed percentage of their national income . . . Again we say: the surplus riches of wealthy countries must help those countries still in need . . . If help does not arrive, God's judgement, and the anger of the poor, will both rise up against the rich man's sin of greed. Civilizations die when they turn in on themselves.

Examination guidance

FOOD PRODUCTION   ADULT EDUCATION   HEALTH CARE   CLEAN WATER   TECHNICAL SKILLS   COMMUNITY DEVELOPMENT

Source: CAFOD

1. Cafod, Christian Aid, Tear Fund and Trócaire support projects among very poor people. Describe one type of project. Explain how it helps people. (6 marks)

2. Christians believe they should share what they have with those who have little. Why do they believe this? (3 marks)

1. First answer

They build dams so that people can get their own water. This means that people can have access to water all year round and they are not solely dependent on the rain that falls in the rainy season.

There is a simple statement about a type of project that a Christian agency supports: providing water. But there are no details of how the project starts and finishes.

There is a relevant statement – but no elaboration – about the benefits of this type of project.

A candidate has to present a more developed answer on both these points to gain higher marks.
(Score: 2 marks out of 6)

Second answer

The production of clean water is one type of project, for instance the digging of a well just outside a village. The village community must have a clear idea of what they want to do, and must show that everyone in the community will benefit from the project. They must also show that this is a self-help project to which most of the villagers will contribute in some way. The aid agencies will then grant money. But they will want to be sure that there will be long-term benefits to the village and that there will be a permanent improvement in the villagers' standard of living. There must be some continuous benefit, such as the reliable cultivation of crops, because they can guarantee a reliable supply of water.

This candidate has given accurate details of one type of project, the improvement of water supply. The candidate has also clearly elaborated the purpose of the project, particularly the long-term benefits.

The candidate has therefore satisfactorily answered the question, and gained full marks.
(Score: 6 marks out of 6)

2. First answer

Christians believe they should share with others because this is the right thing do. It is the Christian thing to do. How would you like it if someone did not help you when you were in trouble?

This candidate has not made a relevant response to the question. The first two sentences of the answer simply repeat what is in the question. There are no marks for doing this.

The last sentence would have gained a mark if the candidate had phrased it as a statement of what Christians believe. Unfortunately the candidate has expressed an opinion, instead of stating what Christians believe.

Candidates should appreciate that if a question asks for information, then they should give information. If a question asks for an opinion, then they should express their opinion, supported by relevant argument and appropriate information.
(Score: 0 marks out of 3)

Second answer

Christians believe they should follow the example and teaching of Jesus; he was the model of how a person should behave in the eyes of God. He shared with his disciples all the money they had; he shared with his disciples his ability to heal. Christians also believe Jesus taught how God wants us to behave. He praised the example of the poor widow who put more, relative to her wealth, than the rich people, into the temple treasury.

This is a full answer. The candidate has written relevant information on why Christians believe they should share. There is also sufficient detail to merit the three marks for this question.
(Score: 3 marks out of 3)

Third answer

The first Christians practised and taught the importance of sharing. If any one of them was in need, then their fellow Christians provided for them; they sold their possessions so that every one of them had enough to live on.

This is a quite different answer from the previous one. Yet it also merits full marks. It is a relevant answer to the question and it presents sufficient detail to gain all three of the available marks.

James also pointed out to his fellow Christians that they should not discriminate between the rich and the poor. He taught that it is not possible to have faith in Jesus without helping the poor.

You should learn from this that there is often – but not always – more than one way to gain full marks. The important feature of any good answer is to answer the actual question!

If a question tests your knowledge, then you should give relevant information.

If the question tests understanding, then show you have grasped the subject of the question.

If the question tests your ability to give an opinion, then you should present relevant ideas and arguments, and show you have appreciated the opposite point of view.

(Score: 3 marks out of 3)

Examination practice

1. What are the main purposes of Cafod, Tear Fund, Trócaire or Christian Aid? (3 marks)
    Write about six lines of A4.

2. Explain why a Christian should support an organization like Cafod, Tear Fund, Trócaire or Christian Aid. (8 marks)
    Write about three-quarters of a side of A4.

3. Christians believe that God made the world for everyone.

    How might this moderate the instinctive greed of Christians in Western countries? (8 marks)
    Write about three-quarters of a side of A4.

4. 'People are poor because they are inadequate. Let them help themselves.'
    Do you agree? Give reasons to support your view. Show that you have considered the opposite point of view. (8 marks)
    Write about three-quarters of a side of A4.

LIBERATION THEOLOGY AND THE DEVELOPING WORLD 18

The poor and oppressed

The Christian Church today favours rich people – so say liberation theologians. They believe that Christians in the wealthy countries have lost some important Christian beliefs, and so have wealthy Christians in the poorer countries – they have forgotten that Christ's mission was to poor people.

Liberation theology focuses on people who are poor and oppressed. It says that:

*   Jesus spent his time with poor people, not with rich people.
*   Christians today should, likewise, concern themselves with poor people.
*   However, the Church has tended to side with unjust governments, which oppress poor people and support rich people.

*   And Christians in the West have become satisfied with their wealthy life. They enjoy it. As a result, they have altered the Christian religion to suit their interests, though they may not have done this deliberately. They have made religion into a private relationship with God. They have forgotten Jesus' demands about justice; they have forgotten his emphasis on human rights; and they have forgotten his insistence on a fair distribution of God's earth and its wealth among all people. Thus liberation theologians think that Christians in the first world (that is, richer countries) have missed some important points – these Christians need to go back to the gospels to rediscover the values of Jesus.

Liberation theologians constantly emphasize the example and teaching of Jesus. His example is the model for how Christians should behave; his teaching is the guide for how Christians should behave.

> Inequality in the sharing of wealth is not the only scandal crying out for justice.
>
> Now, increasingly, the scandal is inequality in the sharing-out of power. In many lands a few rich people dominate the rest.
>
> Pope Paul VI

Kingdom of God

Jesus preached that the kingdom of God was coming. He went into the synagogue at Nazareth and read the following passage from the Bible (Luke 4[18–19]):

> 'The Spirit of the Lord is on me,
>   because he has anointed me
>   to preach good news to the poor.
> He has sent me to proclaim freedom for the prisoners
>   and recovery of sight for the blind,
>   to release the oppressed,
>   to proclaim the year of the Lord's favour.'

After reading this passage, Jesus told the people in the synagogue that the passage had come true that day.

Luke reports that, after this incident, Jesus spent his life helping those who were poor and destitute. In this way he started the kingdom of God on earth.

Hence liberation theologians stress that the kingdom of God is on earth; or, at least, it must start here. Miranda, a liberation theologian from Central America, says:

> because tradition has taught for centuries that the kingdom is in the other world only demonstrates that tradition betrayed Jesus and founded another religion completely different.

Images of Jesus

Liberation theology stresses the following aspects of Jesus' life.

- The gospel writers report ferocious conflict between Jesus and the Jewish leaders. For example, Jesus fiercely criticized the Pharisees and teachers of the Law. He said that they were hypocrites. He also said they put their laws in place of God's laws (Mark 7[1–13]).

    Another example occurred when the Jewish chief priests tried Jesus: they condemned him to death. They then took him to Pilate, and they encouraged the people to pressurize Pilate to crucify Jesus. They succeeded.
- The Roman governor, Pilate, crucified Jesus, despite knowing that Jesus was innocent. Pilate knew that the chief priests wanted Jesus dead because they were jealous of him. Yet Pilate gave in to their demands, and he crucified Jesus.
- Jesus lived in poverty. He did not seek wealth. When he died, he possessed only the clothes he was wearing.
- Jesus mixed with poor people, and with outcasts. He did not mix much with wealthy people. Nor did he mix much with the political leaders.
- Jesus criticized people who had wealth. He said it was harder for a camel to go through the eye of a needle than for a rich man to get into God's kingdom (Mark 10[25]).

> We must learn to regard people less in the sight of what they do or do not do,
> and more in the sight of what they suffer.
>
> Dietrich Bonhoeffer

Privatization of religion

Liberation theologians criticize those Christians who have made religion a private matter. Liberation theologians agree that it is important to pray to God; they agree that religion is a private, personal relationship between us and God. However, they say that religion is not just that. Nor is religion simply preparing for life after death. Nor is religion simply about people saving themselves.

Liberation theologians say that religion is more than these. They point to the escape of the Jews from Egypt. God freed the Jews from slavery. He showed that he cared for them. This is religion. It is about:

- peoples' political and human rights;
- freeing people who are oppressed;
- everyone sharing in the earth and its wealth. God made the world. It belongs to him. He wants everyone to enjoy it and benefit from it. So, it is wrong for some people to take the earth's wealth and keep it to themselves, since God has given everyone the right to live from his earth.

Thus liberation theologians point to the economic and political aspects of religion. They say these are just as important as the spiritual and moral aspects of religion. Liberation theologians criticize those Christians who have made religion simply a private matter.

Liberation

This is the key term. Liberation theologians say that the most important event in the Old Testament was when God liberated the Jews. They were slaves of the Egyptians. God set them free. He sent Moses to lead them to a country of their own, Palestine, where they would be free people.

Liberation theologians also emphasize a basic Christian belief: that the most important event in the New Testament was the liberation of Jesus. God liberated Jesus from death. God raised Jesus to life.

Liberation theologians point out that Jesus liberated people. Just as God sent Moses to liberate people, so he sent Jesus to liberate people. Jesus liberated people in several ways.

Liberation theologians understand liberation to include:

A series of 14 posters depicting the stations of the cross on the theme of suffering in South America
Source: Way of the Cross from Latin America by Adolfo Pérez Esquivel, 1992, Misereor Medienproduktion und Vertriebsgellschaft mbH, Aachen, Germany

- liberation from **death** – so that we can experience God, and eternal happiness, after death;
- liberation from **sin** – so that we can follow the example of God, and love other people in this life;
- liberation from **dependence on others** – so that we can think for ourselves, and stand up for our rights in this life;
- liberation from **exploitation by other people** in this life – so that we can develop our own lives, and not be poor;
- liberation from **unjust governments**, which use violence to ensure that rich people stay rich and poor people stay poor – so that poor people can have some dignity and happiness in this life.

Christianity and Marxism

Liberation theologians combine ideas from the gospel with ideas from Karl Marx.

Marx said that there have always been two opposing groups in society: the smaller group that exploits, and the larger group that is exploited. This leads to conflict between the two groups. The exploiting group want to hold on to their privileged and dominant position, and so they refuse to allow the exploited group to share their wealth; and the exploited group want to change things, so that they can have a fairer share of wealth. In the end, there has to be a violent revolution. This is the only way the exploited group can change the situation.

Marx believed there was no God. The exploiting class invented God to help them maintain their dominant position. And the exploited class was willing to believe in God and his love. It helped them. They could put up with misery and exploitation in this life, if they believed that, after death, they would enjoy happiness in heaven, and the exploiters would go to hell and suffer.

> Religion is the opium of the people.
>
> Karl Marx

Marx said that God does not exist. Liberation theologians do not agree. But they think Marx was quite right about class conflict. They think this is inevitable, since rich people will not share. Liberation theologians believe that Christ liberated all people when he started God's kingdom. God's kingdom on earth includes the right to a decent living, as well as the duty to care for other people. We cannot have the second without the first. Yet the rich will not share; nor will the poor accept their poverty for ever. Violence is inevitable.

Achieving liberation in this world

Some liberation theologians support just revolutions. They say it is right to use violence to overthrow an unjust and dictatorial government.

They point out that Jesus commanded us to love one another. And if we know other people are exploited – and we do nothing about it – we do not love them. It is no good saying, 'I have tried peaceful means of persuading the government to stop rich owners from exploiting their employees. I should not use violence, as Jesus forbade this.' This is no excuse. It shows no love for the people who are still exploited. Jesus commanded love, which means we may have to use violence, if all other means fail, to help exploited people. We have to stop the exploitation.

These liberation theologians observe that the Catholic Church has never been pacifist. It has always supported the use of violence to overthrow an unjust government, if all other means to change an unjust situation have failed. They quote Church leaders, such as Pope Paul VI who said:

> Some human situations cry to heaven for justice. Revolution may well seem justified when whole nations are deprived of basic human rights.
>
> But, unless the tyranny defied persistently attacks the fundamental rights of man and so endangers grievously the good of all, a revolution, as a rule, brings only greater evil in its wake.
>
> A wrong cannot be righted at the price of something else.

One priest, Camilo Torres, in the South American country of Colombia, gave up practising as a Catholic priest. He became a guerrilla fighter. He thought this was the only way to change a corrupt and tyrannical government.

Other liberation theologians reject violence. They support active, non-violent campaigning against an unjust government. They say this is the most suitable way for Christians to change unjust governments (governments that support the rich and exploit the poor).

They argue that Jesus was a pacifist. He never tolerated violence, even for a good cause. For example, he would not allow his disciples to use violence to defend him when soldiers arrested him in the garden of Gethsemane. Nevertheless, they argue that Christians should actively oppose unjust governments – but without resorting to violence, as this would mean fighting evil with evil.

A personal statement

Before I went to work as a missionary sister in the shanty towns of Lima, Peru, I had read and studied liberation theology. But it was only when I found myself among the poor and marginated that I really understood the need for a liberation theology. The theory of Gustavo Gutierrez – the great liberation theologian – came alive. (I might add he was totally against violence.)

My work was with women. I saw families hungry, children dying, mothers toil-worn and emaciated, struggling to support the family when the husband earned only one third of what was considered a living wage. And all because most of the country's revenue went to pay the national debt.

I began my work by reading the scriptures with small groups, helping them to relate incidents in their lives to the gospels and to the words of Jesus. They began to see their dignity as God's children and to understand his love for them. They were just as important as the Pope or the President.

As I encouraged them to recognize their gifts and see how they might use them, they responded in a marvellous way. The result was the forming of a knitting cooperative, and in time the quality of their work was fit for the overseas market. But how could a small group like ours compete with big business? The struggle goes on and will go on until it is universally recognized that we are *all* God's children with a right to a fair share of good things God has given to our world.

Mary Clune, a Missionary sister of the Society of Saint Columban

Examination practice

1. 'Some liberation theologians support violence. Others reject violence.'
   Explain this difference.   (3 marks)
   Write about six lines.

2. What are the main beliefs in liberation theology?
                                                (10 marks)
   Write about one side of A4.

3. Jesus taught that the rich should share with the poor. How might this affect some rich Christians? Why might it not affect others?   (8 marks)
   Write about three-quarters of a side of A4.

4. 'Religion is about an individual's relation with God. It is not about the poor sharing the wealth of the rich.' Do you agree? Give reasons for your view. Show that you have considered the opposite view.   (8 marks)
   Write about three-quarters of a side of A4.

HOSPICES; CARE OF THE ELDERLY

19

Introduction

Death is a taboo subject for many people. They do not like to talk or even think of it. If a person is dying, they try to hide the fact from the person concerned.

Yet many people know when they are dying. They recognize in themselves signs and symptoms that they have seen in others. They realize what is happening as the illness progresses.

Many Christians believe it is important that a person should be helped to die with dignity.

Mother Teresa (see Chapter E23, *Christian discipleship*) was distressed when she saw sick and dying people on the streets of Calcutta. She said, 'We cannot let a child of God die like an animal in the gutter.' She opened a home for dying people who had no home and no one to care for them. She called it Nirmal Hriday – Place of the Pure Heart.

The hospice movement

Cicely Saunders founded the modern hospice movement. She opened the first hospice, St Christopher's Hospice in

Sydenham, London, in 1967. Since then many other hospices have been opened throughout Britain. They provide a place for dying people who need special, professional care 24 hours a day.

- The first consideration is the relief of pain.
- Patients must have a warm, happy atmosphere in which they will receive loving care.
- The patients, with their relatives and friends, must be helped to cope with the fact of death and with the natural feelings of grief.

A hospice is a bright, happy place. It is made to be more like a home than a hospital. Visitors, including children, are welcome. The staff make sure they have time to talk to patients as well as see to the things they need.

How the hospice movement began

It was a close friend of Cicely Saunders, **David Tasma**, who inspired her in her care for the dying. He was a patient

A hospice is a cheerful, welcoming place

in a hospital where she was on the staff. Although he was only 40 he was dying of a painful cancer. Until she befriended him he was very lonely – he had no one to share his thoughts and fears. Her friendship with him convinced her that God was calling her to care for people who were dying.

When Cicely told David that she planned to build a special hospital for the care of people who were terminally ill (suffering from an illness that was sure to lead to death), David was thrilled. He made a will in which he left her £500. She went to medical school, where she was years older than any other student. When she had qualified as a doctor she spent some time studying the treatment of pain for those who had incurable diseases. Then she set about raising the money and planning St Christopher's.

Examination guidance

1. Describe a typical hospice for people who are terminally ill. (9 marks)

2. 'It would be better to spend money on people who have a chance of living a long time than on people who have no hope.' What do you think of this judgment on the hospice movement? Give reasons for your opinions. (6 marks)

1. There is a hospice near where I live. It is called St Luke's. It is named after Luke, who was a doctor in the Bible.

We went to visit it from our school. The first thing I noticed was how bright and cheerful the place looked. There were pictures on the wall and some lovely vases of flowers. The nurses seemed to be such happy people.

A few patients were sitting out in the garden. Some of them had visitors with them. I saw one boy who was about eight years old. He had come to see his grandad. He told me, 'My grandad is ever so happy here. He used to be upset at home because he couldn't get up and down the stairs easily. He can manage here. We come to see him as often as we can, two or three times a week.'

I know that the people there are very ill and they are likely to die quite soon. They are helped by the nurses, who give them injections and tablets to help them with the pain.

The candidate has given a good account, which shows knowledge of what a hospice is and an understanding of what it is for. There is no indication that patients and families are helped to come to terms with death; though this is hardly a high-profile feature of a hospice, it is one of the aims.
(Score: 7 marks out of 9)

2. I can understand why some people say this sort of thing. They think about starving and homeless people in other parts of the world. There are people who are ill who could get better as well. People in hospices are going to die anyway.

I still think it is right to help people in the hospices. For a start, they are not people without any hope. The people I saw are happy and enjoying life, even though they have no pain. They don't look as though they think everything is hopeless. In any case, they need to be able to end their lives in peace and dignity.

The candidate has considered both sides of the argument. A very good point is made in the words 'they are not people without any hope'.
(Score: 5 marks out of 6)

Examination practice

1. In what ways do Christians offer help to those who are terminally ill? (8 marks)
Write about three-quarters of a side of A4.

2. Do you think Christians who are terminally ill should be told that they are dying? Give reasons for your answer. (6 marks)
Write about half a side of A4.

Biblical teaching about work

- 'Go to the ant, you sluggard'. The ant instinctively knows there is a need to work; without any compulsion it harvests and stores food during the summer. The sluggard (a sluggard is a lazy person) will suffer poverty – through his own fault (Proverbs 6[6]).
- 'If a man will not work, he shall not eat'. Paul told the Thessalonians that everyone should earn his or her own living. Paul himself had set them an example: 'We were not idle when we were with you, nor did we eat anyone's food without paying for it. On the contrary, we worked night and day, labouring and toiling so that we would not be a burden to any of you' (2 Thessalonians 3[6–15]).

Christian attitudes to work

- Work is a necessary part of everyday life.
- All people have a right to a fair share of God's earth. They have a right to provide for themselves and their families. They should be given the means to earn a living; they should not need to rely on charity.
- People are made in the image of God, the Creator. Work can allow them to be creative and to use their God-given talents.
- Work can be a way of pleasing God by supplying human wants and needs.
- Work can be more than a way of providing for yourself and your family. It can be a way of serving the community.
- Each person has a part to play in the community. (In 1 Corinthians 12 Paul teaches that different people have different gifts to offer to the Church. In the same way, people have different gifts to offer to the community.)
- It would be good for all to have worthwhile jobs – jobs that are useful to society as a whole.

Paul's words quoted above – 'If a man will not work, he shall not eat' – are not to be applied to those who are unemployed through no fault of their own. They suffer need through not being able to earn. They may lose some of their self-respect. They are to be regarded with compassion.

The Protestant work ethic

Some writers have come up with the idea that there is a link between capitalism (the idea that individuals should be able to work for their own profit) and the beliefs of some Protestants. The theory is that these Protestants believe that hard work and discipline are good. It is a person's religious duty to use the talents given by God. Another good characteristic is thrift, not being wasteful but using money well or saving it.

Workers' rights

This section is important if you are studying the NEAB Catholic syllabus. It summarizes what Catholics call the social teachings of their Church.

Industry was more important than farming in northern Europe by the end of the nineteenth century. The owners of the new industries exploited their workers. They paid their workers low wages, made them work long hours with little rest time, and gave them few holidays. The dark, damp conditions in many factories undermined the health of those who worked there. As the workers could not afford to buy their own property, they rented houses that were overcrowded and had poor sanitation.

Many people, including Church leaders and other Christians, started to protest that workers had rights. As a result of the protests, much was done to improve working conditions. Since that time, Church leaders have continued to argue for workers' rights, such as:

- **The right to receive a just wage**, so that workers and their families can live with dignity. For instance, Pope John XXIII said that it is unjust for employers to pay low wages, because low wages do not match what workers give to the community; because low wages do not match what workers contribute to the profit of the company they work for; and because low wages do not match what workers add to a country's wealth.
- **The right to rest time and leisure time**, particularly on Sundays and holidays. This includes the right not to work excessive hours.

  The bishops at the Second Vatican Council said that workers have this right for two broad reasons.

  First, so that workers can cultivate their family, cultural, social and religious life. By this they meant: time to spend with their family; time to listen to music, to watch television, to read, and so on; time to mix with friends and other people; time to pray, to read the Bible, to go to church to worship, and so on.

  Second, so that workers can enjoy and develop interests that are not part of their job.
- **The right to work in suitable conditions**. Pope Pius XI said that workers have this right so that their health is not damaged. He said that suitable conditions have to take into account the sex or age of the individual workers. Pope John Paul II added that suitable

conditions should also take into account the disability of any workers.

- **The right to join a trade union**. Pope Leo XIII said that unions are indispensable to defend workers' rights. When workers cooperate, they have more influence on their employer, and this is good, as workers should help each other to obtain their common rights.

- **The right to strike**. The bishops at the Second Vatican Council said that when there is a dispute between workers and employers, both sides should settle it peacefully. They should do this through genuine discussion. The bishops said that if this does not succeed, workers have the right to strike, though this should be the last resort. And the bishops said the workers should re-start both negotiations and a working relationship with their employers as soon as possible.

  However, we know that some strikes harm not only the employers of the strikers, but also other people in the country. They can even paralyse the social and economic life of a country. Pope John Paul II has said that such strikes are wrong, as they harm everyone.

- **The opportunity to find employment**. Pope John Paul II said that workers have this right so that they can look after themselves and their families, and so that they can have self-respect. He said the State should provide this opportunity.

- **The right to migrate to another country**, to find better paid work. Pope John Paul II has said that workers have not only this right, but also the right to be treated fairly even though they are migrants (whether permanent or seasonal) and new to a country. He has also said that immigrant workers should not be given different wages because of their race or religion, as every worker has the right to a just wage.

- **The right to own private property**. Pope Leo XIII said (in 1891) that wages should be enough to enable workers to buy and own property, including land. This is because every one has the right to ownership. Pope Leo XIII also said that widespread ownership has important benefits for the state. It gives working people an incentive to work harder, thus increasing the wealth of the country. And it gives every working person a share in the wealth of the country, thus increasing their loyalty to the State.

Vocation

A vocation is a special call from God – a mission in life.

- Some people feel that God has a special task for them. Jesus called Peter and Andrew and the other disciples because he had chosen them to carry on his work of preaching the gospel. In the same way, some people today are convinced that they have been called by God.

- Some occupations are called vocations. People are called to serve God as priests or nuns. A doctor, nurse or teacher may be said to have a vocation – a call to serve the community. However, there is a danger in saying that only these occupations are vocations. The suggestion is that these people are serving God – and that people in other occupations, such as shopkeepers or mechanics, are not.

The word 'vocation' is often understood as a call to share in the mission of the church. The vocation can lead a person to take an active part in the life of the Church community. Another person's vocation can show itself in a Christian life at home and at work. Each of these people is taking a part in the mission of the Church.

> Whatever you do, work at it with all your heart, as working for the Lord, not for men.
> Colossians 3[23]

Leisure

People need time to relax and to enjoy themselves. There are a few Christians who believe that rest comes in the next life; in this life we are to give all our energies to doing God's work. Generally speaking, though, Christians regard leisure time as a precious part of life, something for which they should thank God. We are told that Jesus at times wanted to get away from the crowds and be alone with his friends and close companions. Leisure is to be enjoyed for its own sake.

> Because so many people were coming and going that they did not even have a chance to eat, [Jesus] said to [his disciples], 'Come with me by yourselves to a quiet place and get some rest.'
> Mark 6[31]

Some leisure activities are in themselves creative or educational. People may enjoy painting or reading. Other leisure activities, such as listening to music, may be purely for pleasure.

All Christians have a duty to serve others. One way of serving is to use a part of your leisure time for other people. Youth club leaders are using their leisure time for the good of others.

Leisure, like everything else, must be morally right. Some leisure activities are thought to be wrong in themselves. For instance, sports such as foxhunting are judged by many to be cruel. Drunkenness and drug addiction are against Christian teaching.

Examination guidance

1. What did Paul say about people who would not work? (5 marks)

2. What is a vocation? Give an example of someone who has a vocation. (10 marks)

3. Do you think it matters how Christians use their leisure time? Give reasons for your answer. (5 marks)

1. Paul said that anyone who did not work should not eat. He said that he used to do ordinary work when he visited one of the churches because he wanted to pay his way and not be a burden. He wanted to set a good example to all the other Christians. He criticized the ones who were lazy. He told them they should work, just as he did.

The candidate has covered the main points well.
(Score: 5 marks out of 5)

2. A vocation is when God calls you to do something. You feel something inside you telling you that you ought to give your life to help other people in some way. Usually a person is called to be a priest or a nurse or a nun, but it doesn't have to be like that. It can be anything if God calls you.

The person I have chosen is someone I know. She is called Mrs Mary Scott. She is the crossing lady at the junior school. She is always very kind. Whenever there is something wrong she is always ready to help. She goes to the church every Sunday and sometimes on other days too. My gran was ill once and I was very upset. I couldn't stop crying on the way to school. Mrs Scott asked me, 'Why are you crying?' I said, 'My gran's ill.' She said, 'We'll pray for her in church.' My gran got better. I'm sure Mrs Scott and the others did pray for her.

The candidate has given a good description of what a vocation is, though there is no reference to the mission of the church.

The example is quite a good one. Note that the question does not say that the candidate has to choose a well-known Christian. The candidate does not say that Mrs Scott has been called by God. The problem is that, unless people say they believe they have been called by God, you cannot tell! None the less, the example comes across as someone who is motivated as a Christian and who serves God in her work by serving others. The answer would be improved by a reference to the teaching and example of Jesus – for example, by relating her life to the parable of the good Samaritan or the sheep and the goats.
(Score: 7 marks out of 10)

3. No, I don't think it matters how a Christian uses their free time. It is their own time, to do what they like. If they want to enjoy themselves, or if they want to do nothing at all, it is up to them.

I do think that what they do must be all right to start with. It is obviously wrong to steal or commit a crime. It is wrong to upset other people by playing your music so loudly that the neighbours are upset.

I think that you should use some of your time to help other people. Perhaps help your mum in the house or help raise money for children or old people in need. I don't think you should be too selfish with your time.

The candidate has given a simple, sensible answer. Three different approaches are used, with examples. A better answer would consider whether people should try to improve themselves during their leisure time or whether it is important to use leisure to prepare for work.
(Score: 3 marks out of 5)

Examination practice

1. Why might a Christian think it important to have a job? (6 marks)

   Write at least half a side of A4.

2. There are some occupations that might be considered unsuitable for a Christian. Choose **two** such occupations and, giving your reasons, say if you think a Christian should avoid them. (10 marks)

   Write at least three-quarters of a side of A4.

Introduction

Christians do not believe that all alcohol and all drugs are evil. Alcohol drunk in moderation is enjoyed by many people. Many drugs are used for medical purposes.

This section deals with alcohol abuse and with illegal drugs, which have bad effects on users and which lead people to become addicts.

Drugs

Different drugs have different effects on people's feelings.

Some drugs, such as amphetamine and ecstasy, are taken to stimulate a person's nervous system. They make a person feel less tired, more alert and more confident. They make people feel they can, for example, dance all night. Others, such as heroin, have a relaxing effect.

Still other drugs cause hallucinations. In extreme cases those under the influence of the drug can, for example, imagine that they are driving at only 30 m.p.h. when they are actually driving at 80 m.p.h.

The after-effects of the drugs can produce sharp and distressing reactions. After a stimulant drug a person can be utterly drained of energy and become very depressed. After a depressant the addict can become hypersensitive, unable to relax or escape from unbearable tension.

It is difficult to assess just what effects particular drugs can have on addicts. Those who sell the drugs illegally may add other substances to them. The extra substances can have unpredictable, harmful effects. Injection is one of the most dangerous methods of taking drugs, leading to possible HIV, gangrene or thrombosis.

All drugs can be addictive. When a person is addicted to drugs their problems can be horrific. They become desperate for drugs.

Drug-taking can have a devastating effect on the personalities of addicts:

- They can have very violent mood swings.
- They can become unusually aggressive and dangerous to live with.
- They lose interest in home, family, friends, school, work and so on.
- They suffer loss of appetite.
- They lie and steal, often to obtain more drugs.

Apart from the harmful nature of drugs, note that over a quarter of all crime (some surveys say half of all crime or even more) is drugs-related. Such crime includes the actual trafficking in drugs. It also includes theft by drug addicts – often to raise money for the purchase of drugs. Crimes and other antisocial actions may occur when a person under the influence of drugs is acting abnormally, with their standards of morality lowered.

Some argue that soft drugs such as cannabis should be made legal. Making cannabis legal would bring the price down. This would reduce the amount of crime that is drug-related. Cannabis users would be able to afford the drug and would not need to steal to get the money.

Others say that cannabis can be as addictive as any other drug. True, it is not as harmful in itself, but it can lead people to more harmful drugs. Once they find that they don't get the right buzz from cannabis, they will move on to hard drugs. In any case, to legalize cannabis might give the signal that drugs are really not so harmful after all.

Alcohol

Some Christians believe that it is wrong to drink alcohol. They see the evils caused by alcoholism and drunkenness. They become **total abstainers** or **teetotallers**.

Most Christians do not see anything wrong in drinking alcohol. They do appreciate the dangers of drinking too much. They are also aware of the effect that regular heavy drinking can have on a person's way of life.

Christian attitude to drugs and alcohol

- 1 Corinthians 6^{19-20}:

  > Do you not know that your body is a temple of the Holy Spirit, who is in you, whom you have received from God? You are not your own; you were bought at a price. Therefore honour God with your body.

  For the Jews of that day, the temple was the holiest spot on earth, because God was actually present there. Paul is saying that because God the Holy Spirit comes to every Christian and is in every Christian, each Christian's body is a temple. A temple is holy. It must not be used in an unholy way.

- In the Sermon on the Mount Jesus said:

  > 'Let your light shine before men, that they may see your good deeds and praise your Father in heaven.'
  > Matthew 5^{16}

  If people suffer the effects of drug and alcohol abuse, other people are not going to look at them and see their lives as showing the goodness of God.

USE AND MISUSE OF ALCOHOL

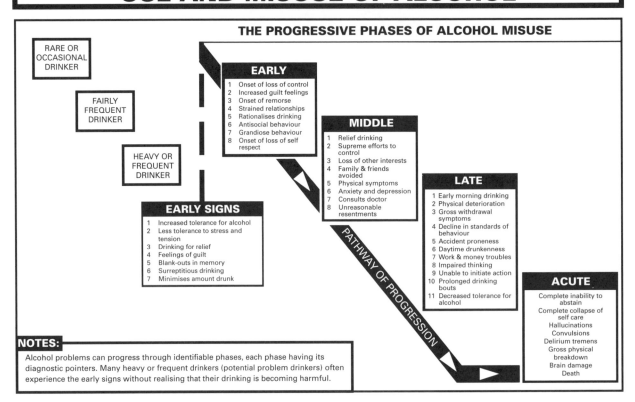

THE PROGRESSIVE PHASES OF ALCOHOL MISUSE

RARE OR OCCASIONAL DRINKER

FAIRLY FREQUENT DRINKER

HEAVY OR FREQUENT DRINKER

EARLY
1. Onset of loss of control
2. Increased guilt feelings
3. Onset of remorse
4. Strained relationships
5. Rationalises drinking
6. Antisocial behaviour
7. Grandiose behaviour
8. Onset of loss of self respect

MIDDLE
1. Relief drinking
2. Supreme efforts to control
3. Loss of other interests
4. Family & friends avoided
5. Physical symptoms
6. Anxiety and depression
7. Consults doctor
8. Unreasonable resentments

EARLY SIGNS
1. Increased tolerance for alcohol
2. Less tolerance to stress and tension
3. Drinking for relief
4. Feelings of guilt
5. Blank-outs in memory
6. Surreptitious drinking
7. Minimises amount drunk

LATE
1. Early morning drinking
2. Physical deterioration
3. Gross withdrawal symptoms
4. Decline in standards of behaviour
5. Accident proneness
6. Daytime drunkenness
7. Work & money troubles
8. Impaired thinking
9. Unable to initiate action
10. Prolonged drinking bouts
11. Decreased tolerance for alcohol

PATHWAY OF PROGRESSION

ACUTE
Complete inability to abstain
Complete collapse of self care
Hallucinations
Convulsions
Delirium tremens
Gross physical breakdown
Brain damage
Death

NOTES:
Alcohol problems can progress through identifiable phases, each phase having its diagnostic pointers. Many heavy or frequent drinkers (potential problem drinkers) often experience the early signs without realising that their drinking is becoming harmful.

Drug and alcohol abuse harm both the body and the personality. A Christian must reject both forms of abuse.

- Humans are made in the image and likeness of God (Genesis 1). One important way in which they are like God is in their ability to think and reason. But heavy use of alcohol and drugs diminishes and then removes this ability. So drugs and alcohol not only diminish people's humanity; they also spoil their likeness to God.

- Excessive use of drugs and alcohol usually results in people becoming 'locked into their own world' – they are aware of themselves and their problems, but nothing else. But Christians believe that God wants people to be open to other people, the natural world and God himself. Drugs and alcohol can inhibit this.

An alcohol-free bar

The **British National Temperance League** campaigns to encourage young people to adopt a lifestyle free of alcohol and harmful drugs. One of their strategies is to run an alcohol-free bar. The atmosphere in the bar is relaxed. The sort of games that are often enjoyed in pubs are there and so is the music. The League wants the young to realize that they can enjoy themselves without alcohol having to be part of the background. The enjoyment comes from the atmosphere and the company, not the drink.

Helping drug addicts back into society

Chatterton Hey is a large house in the country a quarter of a mile from the village of Edenfield in Lancashire. It is run by the Langley House Trust. The Langley House Trust was founded by **John Dodd** to help men being released from prison (see Chapter C11, *The Bible*). Chatterton Hey is a house for drug addicts, most of whom have been in prison. It is a rehabilitation centre: that is, a place that gives them the chance to break the habit and to prepare themselves for life in the community.

The house has a small farming area with a donkey, a sheep, some hens, some geese – and one pigeon! There is a vegetable garden and a lawn surrounded by flower beds.

During a stay at Chatterton Hey, a resident passes through three stages. The first stage, lasting 16 weeks, is a time of strict discipline. Residents are not allowed to leave the house or grounds without a member of staff. Accompanied by staff, they are able to go to Bury Sports Centre or to go shopping.

- The men may well have come straight from prison. Life in prison is harsh. Prisoners have to to be tough, aggressive, even violent, in order to survive among the other inmates. One or two may have been involved in prison riots. The atmosphere at Chatterton Hey is totally different. They need time to adjust.

- They may still be facing the problems of withdrawal from drugs.
- They have to learn to accept the strict discipline. They have lost the ability to discipline themselves.
- They are not allowed to drink alcohol. No alcohol is allowed on the premises.

After the 16 weeks, residents are assessed by staff. If it is felt, by the staff and by the resident, that he is ready to cope with some freedom, then he proceeds to the next stage. During this period residents take positive steps towards adapting to society.

- They are encouraged to take an active role in running the house – gardening, caring for the animals and poultry, painting and decorating, small building works. One – under careful supervision – may be put in charge of the kitchen.
- They are given the option of doing voluntary work (such as helping people with learning difficulties) or taking a college course with a view to obtaining a qualification.
- They are allowed to go to the paper shop in the village or to a nearby town at the weekend.
- After 20 weeks' residence they may be taken for a drink in a pub. This will be under the supervision of a member of the staff. They are allowed a maximum of three pints or the equivalent, not more than once a week. Local pubs are out of bounds, under an agreement with the local community.
- They are allowed to go home for the odd day. It is important to be aware that this probably means going back to the area where the drug problem began.

By the time residents have been at Chatterton Hey for 8–9 months, they may be able to cope with greater freedom.

- They may be able to accept responsibility for looking after another, newer, resident on some occasions – for example, accompanying him to the hospital, the dentist, or even to court.
- They may be able to cope with up to a week at home.
- They may, with the help of the staff, begin to look for accommodation and jobs, ready for the time when they go to face life in the community.

Up to 14 men are resident at Chatterton Hey at any one time. There is one bedroom for four residents; this is used for those who have recently come to the house. Most of the other rooms are doubles. When a resident leaves, his roommate is consulted about who should come to share the room with him. Usually he will choose one of the four in the large room – someone with whom he thinks he can get on.

One of the hardest things for residents to cope with is the firm routine.

- They get up at 7.45 a.m. and go to bed at 11 p.m.

- Smoking is allowed only in certain places. It is forbidden in their own bedrooms.
- The amount of money they may have is carefully controlled.
- They have to take their share in the chores of the house. Their rooms have to be kept tidy. They take turns in doing some of the cleaning jobs or in washing up.

No drugs are allowed on the premises. Anyone found with drugs has to leave immediately. Similarly, anyone committing a criminal offence cannot remain at Chatterton Hey.

Twice a week there are group therapy discussions. The residents talk about their problems and experiences, often with startling honesty. They all receive one-to-one counselling on a regular basis.

There are weekly visits – which are compulsory – to Bury Sports Centre for activities such as volleyball and swimming.

Chatterton Hey is a Christian house. The staff meet for prayer from 10.15 to 10.30 every morning – the same time as the staff members of the Langley House Trust houses in other parts of the country. Residents are always welcome to join them – but it is not compulsory. All the staff are Christians. Here and there on the walls are plaques with simple texts.

Team leader Sue Heaton sees her work at the house as a vocation. 'This is God's work,' she says. 'The glory must be his'.

Visiting Chatterton Hey, one is struck by the happy, caring, relaxed air about the place. Of course there are times when tension is high and tempers flare – the men are together all the time and have little chance to get any privacy. But by and large, the residents are deeply appreciative of what is done for them.

For most of these men, the problem is not drug addiction. The problem is the insecure background that caused them to turn to drugs. Some come from strong loving homes, where there is enough money to support them and their needs – but that is not usually the case. The majority come from backgrounds where there was no security. Some had to cope with drunken parents. Some were abused as children or were simply neglected. What they never had was a sense of belonging. They did not know real caring love.

In the name of Christ, at Chatterton Hey these men experience an atmosphere of Christian care they have never known before. A few – very few – cannot accept it and have to leave. Some go through the year's residence and, after a time, lapse into the old ways. Many are able to take their places in the community again – often moving to a place where they are not known, to make a fresh start. They return to Chatterton Hey only to see old friends, staff and residents alike, and to show their appreciation for what has been done for them.

Examination practice

1. Describe **three** of the dangerous consequences of either drug addiction or alcoholism.

    (6 marks)

    Write two or three lines on each.

2. Choose **two** passages from the Bible that are relevant to the problems of drug addiction and alcoholism. In each case, outline the teaching of the passage and say why it is relevant.

    (6 marks)

    Write four or five lines on each.

3. Describe the work of a Christian organization dedicated to helping people with a problem of drug addiction or alcoholism.   (8 marks)

    Write about a side of A4.

ENVIRONMENTAL POLLUTION; CONSERVATION

22

What is pollution?

Pollution is any damage done to the environment that is caused by any disposal of waste and which lowers the quality of life. The damage may be short term, such as the mess caused by dumping scrap metal and rubbish. Something can be done to put things right if the damage is short term; in the case given, the rubbish can be cleared away. There can be long-term damage, which it is difficult or impossible to correct; an example would be the destruction of a rainforest.

Until fairly recent times pollution was a local problem – for instance, lack of proper sanitation or a polluted local water supply. Changes in modern ways of living have created new, much greater threats to the ecology of the world as a whole. An example is the way in which emissions of certain gases have led to damage to the ozone layer.

Conservation

The environment is under threat from various forms of pollution. Every effort must be made to protect – to conserve – the environment, and to use the earth's resources in a way that best serves the needs of the human race and other species, both in the present and in the future.

*   Non-renewable resources, such as fossil fuels (e.g. coal, oil) and metals should be used carefully, and should be recycled whenever possible.
*   Renewable resources should be used in such a way that they are not depleted. For instance, forests should be managed to preserve not only the long-term supply of trees but also the wildlife whose habitat the forest is.

*   Every attempt should be made to use such resources as the power of the sun, the wind and the sea.
*   The growth in the world's population should be controlled, so that there is not too much demand upon the world's limited resources.

Most of the steps that can be taken to conserve the earth's resources are the responsibility of governments rather than individuals. For example:

*   setting up green belt areas and preserving forests, especially the tropical rainforests;
*   enforcing strict anti-pollution laws;
*   supporting international agreements to conserve wildlife, especially those creatures that migrate;
*   encouraging control of the growth in population;
*   sharing in the task of protecting water supplies, especially with regard to international rivers such as the Amazon and the Nile.

Nations are working together for conservation. The Earth Summit that took place in Rio de Janeiro in 1992 was the largest gathering of world leaders there has ever been. They accepted that, though economic growth in the present was vital, particularly for the poorest nations, it was also vital to take strong action to conserve resources.

Individuals have ways in which they can contribute to conservation by

*   buying and using products that, even in the smallest ways, make less use of non-renewable resources, or which avoid pollution (so-called **green** products);
*   returning for recycling reusable materials such as glass, metal and plastic;
*   supporting charities that are committed to responsible use of resources;
*   writing letters to politicians, leaders of key industries and others with influence.

Common areas of pollution

Most usual causes	Danger
Water	
Untreated and partially treated sewage. Solid objects thrown into water.	To human life and health. To plant and animal life.
Oil pollution.	
Chemicals washed into rivers from fields. Water used in huge quantities for cooling and discharged into nearby waterways at temperatures up to 20 °C.	To all forms of life in the affected waterways – in particular, by making the heated water less able to retain dissolved oxygen.
Land	
Exploitation of minerals and other non-renewable resources. Poor agricultural methods, leading to topsoil erosion or reduced quality of soil. Unsanitary and excessive waste disposal. Use of pesticides and other chemicals. Disposal of nuclear waste	Exhausting resources. Damage to landscape, environment and ecology. Land becomes much less productive. Breeding grounds for pests; good land lost for other purposes. Chemicals are retained by organisms and become part of the biologic food chain. Possibility of radiation.
Air/atmosphere	
Discharge of dangerous substances – e.g. hydrocarbons and carbon monoxide. Damaging emissions – e.g. of nitrogen oxides from supersonic aircraft and chlorofluorocarbons from aerosols and fridges. Upsetting the balance of nature by, for instance, the destruction of the rainforests.	Smog, reducing visibility and affecting the respiratory system. Damage to ozone level. An increase of carbon dioxide in the atmosphere.

Biblical teaching

Christians believe that God created the universe and gave the human race special powers and special responsibilities:

> Then God said, 'Let us make man in our image, in our likeness, and let them rule over the fish of the sea and the birds of the air, over the livestock, over all the earth, and over all the creatures that move along the ground.'
>
> Genesis 1[26]

Many passages from the Bible stress the wonder of creation. Note in particular Psalm 19[1–10] (MEG) and Job 38–39.

Christian view of conservation

Christians take what would appear the commonsense view – that the world and its resources must be used in a responsible way. Their view is based on their belief that they are responsible to God for the use they make of the universe.

> When I consider your heavens,
>   the work of your fingers,
> the moon and the stars,
>   which you have set in place,
> what is man that you are mindful of him,
>   the son of man that you care for him?
> You made him ruler over the works of your hands;
>   you put everything under his feet.
>
> Psalm 83,4,6

The world – indeed, the whole universe – is God's. God not only made everything; he is at all times concerned with the universe and every living creature in it, great or small.

The earth is entrusted to each generation in turn. Each generation has authority from God to use the earth – but not to abuse it. They have a responsibility to other species and to future generations.

Christians are stewards. They believe they have been given their possessions to use for the good of themselves, their families and the whole community, present and future.

Examination guidance

Remember that you are taking a religious studies examination. The Bible does not contain teaching about modern pollution issues. It does contain teaching about God as creator and of the universe belonging to him. Also, you may wish to introduce the idea of natural law into your argument and say that it is obviously right to conserve the environment, for its own sake and for the good of all living creatures.

This section has concentrated on the problems and the steps that can be taken to counteract them. Use some of the information in your answers. Read the questions carefully and, whenever you can, give teaching from the Bible and state the Christian attitude to the problems.

Where you are asked to give examples of pollution or of conservation, choose your examples in ways that allow you to say plenty about them. For instance, let us say you thought of writing about pollution of the atmosphere through emissions from car exhausts. Choose pollution of the atmosphere in general, not just pollution from car exhausts. Then write about car exhausts, giving plenty of information if you can and if it is relevant. Give other examples of atmospheric pollution as well. That way you are giving the examiner every opportunity to give you full credit.

Examination practice

1. Give **three** examples of pollution problems.

    (12 marks)

    Write a few lines on each – enough to describe each of the chosen problems with the cause and the overall effect.

2. What can be done about these problems by
    (a) individuals;
    (b) governments?   (8 marks)

    Write enough to make sure you have discussed what individuals and governments can do about each problem. It is not possible to say how much you should write on each part. In some cases you may be saying that there is nothing an individual can do. Even then, give a reason for saying so.

3. Do you think Christians should be more concerned than others about pollution issues? Give reasons for your answer.   (5 marks)

    Write about three-quarters of a side of A4. Discuss the reasons for being concerned about pollution and how far these reasons are anything to do with religious belief.

CHRISTIAN DISCIPLESHIP

What is a disciple?

A disciple is one who follows a teacher and learns from him. The disciple then continues the work of the teacher.

Jesus called the disciples

At the beginning of his ministry Jesus called certain men to be his disciples.

Peter, Andrew, James, John

Mark 1[16–20]: Jesus called the fishermen Simon (Peter) with his brother Andrew and James with his brother John. He called them to be **fishers of men**. They left everything and followed him without hesitation.

Luke 5[1–11]: This is another account of Jesus calling the same men. This account tells of a miracle that Jesus

performed, as a result of which Simon caught a large number of fish:

> When Simon Peter saw this, he fell at Jesus' knees and said, 'Go away from me Lord; I am a sinful man!' For he and all his companions were astonished at the catch of fish they had taken, and so were James and John, the sons of Zebedee, Simon's partners.
>
> Then Jesus said to Simon, 'Don't be afraid; from now on you will catch men.' So they pulled their boats up on shore, left everything and followed him.

Levi

Luke 5[27–31]: Levi the tax collector was sitting collecting taxes. Jesus called him, and Levi immediately left everything to follow him. Jesus went to Levi's house for a meal; many tax collectors and others who were regarded as sinners were there as well. The Pharisees and their supporters complained to the disciples because they mixed with such people. Jesus replied, 'It is not the healthy who need a doctor, but the sick. I have not come to call the righteous, but sinners to repentance.'

What does discipleship mean?

Being ready to learn

The word 'disciple' means learner – so, the disciples were learners. Jesus called the 12 disciples to be with him and to learn from him. As he got nearer to the time of the crucifixion he spent more and more time with the disciples, preparing them for the time when they would take over his work of preaching and teaching.

Being ready to suffer

Mark 8^{34-38}: The passage follows Peter's confession of Jesus as the Christ. When Peter said 'You are the Christ', Jesus told the disciples not to tell anyone. He said that the Son of Man must suffer, be rejected by the religious leaders, be killed and rise again. Peter tried quietly to stop him talking like that. Jesus turned on Peter.

'Get behind me, Satan!' he said. 'You do not have in mind the things of God, but the things of men.'

He told his disciples that anyone who followed him must be prepared to suffer. If anyone disowned him, he would disown them at the Second Coming. Note Jesus' actual words:

'If anyone would come after me, he must deny himself and take up his cross and follow me. For whoever wants to save his life will lose it, but whoever loses his life for me and for the gospel will save it. What good is it for a man to gain the whole world, yet forfeit his soul? If anyone is ashamed of me and my words in this adulterous and sinful generation, the Son of Man will be ashamed of him when he comes in his Father's glory with the holy angels.'

Being ready to give up possessions

Mark 10^{17-31}: A rich young man came to Jesus and asked him, 'Good teacher, what must I do to inherit eternal life?' Jesus replied, 'You know the commandments: do not murder, do not commit adultery, do not steal, do not give false testimony, do not defraud, honour your father and mother.' The young man replied that he had kept all these commandments ever since he was a boy. Jesus looked at him and loved him, but told him there was one more thing he had to do: 'Go, sell everything you have and give to the poor, and you will have treasure in heaven. Then come,

follow me.' This was something the young man could not do. He went sadly away.

Jesus taught that being in the kingdom of God was all-important for his followers. Being in the kingdom of God means accepting God as king and obeying him. Jesus taught that people had to enter the kingdom. He told the disciples that it was hard for a rich man to enter the kingdom of God. It was easier for a camel to go through the eye of a needle – in other words, just about impossible. The disciples were amazed. They thought rich men deserved respect. If they could not enter the kingdom of God, who could?

Then Jesus spoke of some of the rewards of discipleship. Those who had left their homes, families and possessions for him would be rewarded. They would receive other homes, families and possessions through being part of God's family; other people would welcome them into their homes and give them whatever they needed. There would still be persecution to be faced. But then, after death, they would have eternal life.

Real giving

Mark 12^{41-44}: Jesus saw a poor widow put a small amount of money into the Temple treasury. Other people were putting far more into the treasury than she was. Jesus said that because she had given all she had, she was the one who had put most into the treasury.

What Jesus taught about discipleship

- **Commitment**. Jesus expected his disciples to be completely committed to him. When he called them, they followed him right away. Anyone who was ashamed to say he followed Jesus would be rejected by Jesus himself.
- **Nothing else must get in the way**. The rich young man was told to give his wealth away. Because he would not, he could not be a disciple. Jesus praised the widow because she was prepared to give so much. Disciples might have to give up their possessions, homes – even their families.
- **Ready to suffer**. A disciple has to be ready to suffer – to take up his cross.
- **Eternal life**. For those who do follow Jesus, the reward is eternal life.

Christian discipleship in the modern world

Mother Teresa of Calcutta is seen as a wonderful example of Christian discipleship.

Mother Teresa has dedicated her life to helping the poor, first in Calcutta, then in other places as well. She was born in 1910 in Skopje, in Serbia. She first went out to India to teach in the pleasant hill settlement of Darjeeling, among the tea plantations in the foothills of the Himalayas. It was when she moved to teach in Calcutta that she realized what great suffering and poverty there was in that huge city. She pleaded to be allowed to leave the teaching order of nuns to which she belonged. She trained at a mission hospital so that she could help the poor in a practical way.

She founded the Missionaries of Charity to work among the suffering and poor. Like other nuns, they made vows of poverty, chastity and obedience. They made an extra vow – to give whole-hearted and free service to the poorest of the poor.

The Missionaries of Charity make regular prayer and receiving of the Blessed Sacrament their first priority.

Mother Teresa has opened a home for homeless children. They are children who have been found abandoned on the streets, outside homes or offices. She has asked in the city hospitals of Calcutta that all unwanted children are handed on to her. In her own words, 'I am fighting abortion with adoption.'

She started clinics to treat lepers. Mobile clinics are sent to certain places at the same times each week so that lepers may come for treatment. She makes it clear that they are not social outcasts, even though they have what can be a dangerously infectious disease.

She set up a home for people who are dying and who have no one to care for them. The home is called Nirmal Hriday – Place of the Pure Heart. Those who are left in the street to die can be taken there to die in peace and dignity.

Mother Teresa shows many of the characteristics of Christian discipleship. She has turned away from being wealthy – her father was a prosperous merchant. Money for herself is unimportant, for she simply trusts God to provide what she needs. She is ready to suffer – almost *too* ready.

When she was studying medicine the staff of the training hospital had to insist that she ate proper meals rather than fast. She works with complete faith in Jesus Christ. She shows her love for Jesus by her care and love for all.

All Christians are disciples

Christians believe that they are all called to be disciples. But Christian discipleship is not the same for everyone. Jesus told the rich young man to sell all his possessions and give to the poor. He did not tell everyone to do the same. If everyone did give all their possessions away and leave home and family, human society would collapse.

Christians believe that God has a special calling for certain people. They are said to have a **vocation**. (See Chapter E20, *Work and leisure*.) They know in their hearts that God is calling them in this way. When they follow their vocation they feel a sense of fulfilment, knowing they are doing God's work. For some it may mean leaving home and family, though not necessarily completely.

Sue is a nurse. She was engaged to marry Mark. She felt a call from God to work for a time in a mission hospital in Zambia. She and Mark prayed together about her vocation. For a year she worked in Zambia, her expenses partly paid by Christians in England, in congregations where she was known. At the end of the year she returned home and married Mark.

Annie is a farmer's wife in her eighties. She lives near Sue's parents. She heard what Sue was doing. She thought Sue would be homesick. She decided to encourage her. She sent her some boiled sweets and some packets of soup and sauce, which she knew Sue could not get in a remote part of Zambia. Sue was thrilled to receive these simple, thoughtful gifts from a stranger.

Sue and Annie are both examples of Christian discipleship. So are all who are trying to work out what God wants them to do – whoever and whatever they are.

Examination guidance

- When answering questions on discipleship, make sure you know the main points of Jesus' teaching.
- If your syllabus includes accounts from the gospels of the call of some disciples or of Jesus meeting the rich young man, the examiner may well ask you to describe what happened. Make sure you are prepared, paying special attention to what was said.
- Have ready examples such as Mother Teresa – but know some facts about them! You won't get much credit for 'Mother Teresa goes round the world helping people'!

Examination practice

1. 'Good teacher, what must I do to inherit eternal life?' Give an account of the meeting of Jesus and the person

who asked him this question. What did Jesus say to his followers when that person had left him?   (10 marks)
Write at least one side of A4 so that your answer may have enough detail.

2.   Give an example of someone living in this century who tries to live as a disciple of Jesus.

(6 marks)

Write at least half a side of A4. Make sure your answer relates to the teaching of Jesus.

CHRISTIAN DISCIPLESHIP – SPECIAL TEXTS

24

Introduction

You must know these passages if you are studying an NEAB syllabus about the Catholic tradition – Paper 2B. These passages are in the syllabus under the section on Christian discipleship. The examiner will use them in your exam.

If you are studying Christian discipleship on a different syllabus or with a different exam board, then select some of these passages and learn them. You will find them useful in answering a question about Christian behaviour today.

As you read these passages, you must ask yourself: what does this passage teach about being a disciple of Jesus? At the end of this chapter, there are some suggestions.

> There are two words used a great deal in the gospels: one is **come** and the other is **go**. It's no use coming unless you go, and it's no use going unless you come.
> Missionaries of St Columban

Passages

1. The commission

Matthew 28[18–20]: Jesus told his disciples that all authority had been given to him.

- He told them to make disciples in all nations,
- and baptize them in the name of the Father, the Son and the Holy Spirit,
- and teach the new disciples to obey everything he had commanded.

2. Parable of the good Samaritan

Luke 10[25–37]: See Chapter C19, *Luke's gospel – parables.*

3. Parable of the sower

Matthew 13[1–23], Mark 4[1–20]: See Chapter C12, *Mark's gospel – parables.*

4. Parable of the weeds

Matthew 13[24–30]:

- A man sowed good wheat seed in his field, but, secretly, an enemy sowed weeds among the wheat.
- When the servants saw the weeds growing, they asked if they should pull them out.
- The owner said they should leave the weeds and wheat until the harvest.
- Then the harvesters would collect the weeds and burn them, and then collect the wheat and put it in the barn.

Jesus explained the parable to his disciples:

- The sower is the Son of Man, and the field is the world.
- The enemy who sowed the weed is the devil.
- The good seeds are those who belong in God's kingdom, and the weeds are those who belong to the evil one.
- The harvest is the end of the age.
- The Son of Man will send those who do evil into the fiery furnace.
- The good people will then be happy in the Father's kingdom.

5. Parable of the mustard seed

Matthew 13[31–32], Mark 4[30–32]: See Chapter C11, *Mark's gospel – parables.*

6. Parable of the yeast

Matthew 13[33]: A woman mixed yeast into a large amount of flour, which made all the dough rise.

7. Parable of the hidden treasure

Matthew 13[44]:

- A man found hidden treasure in a field.
- He hid it again.
- Then he sold all he owned, to buy the field.

8. Parable of the pearl

Matthew 13[45–46]:

- A man, looking for fine pearls, found one of great value.
- He sold all he had, to buy the pearl.

9. Parable of the net

Matthew 13[47–50]:

- Some fishermen caught all kinds of fish in their net. They pulled it ashore.
- They put the good fish into their baskets; they threw the worthless ones away.

Jesus explained this parable:

- It will be like this at the end of the age.
- God's messengers will throw evil people into the fiery furnace.

10. Status of discipleship

Matthew 20[24–28]: The mother of James and John asked Jesus a favour: when Jesus became king, could her sons have the most important places in his kingdom?

The other disciples were angry when they heard about this.

Jesus told all of them:

- Leaders and rulers have power over their subjects;
- but if you want to be great, then become a servant or slave –
- just like the Son of Man,
- who came to serve and not to be served,
- and to give his life as a ransom for many.

11. Parable of the forgiving father

Luke 15[11–32]: See Chapter C19, *Luke's gospel – parables*.

12. Respect for all people

James 2[1–9]: James wrote to a group of Christians, somewhere (we do not know where):

- Do not show favouritism.
- Do not give a rich man the best seat in church, and tell a poor man to sit on the floor.
- Isn't it poor people who believe in Jesus?

- Isn't it rich people who exploit you? They do not believe in Jesus.
- If you keep the law, 'Love your neighbour as yourself', you will not show favouritism.

13. Parable of the talents or the three servants

Matthew 25[14–30]: A talent was a Jewish coin, worth 3000 shekels – a lot of money! We do not have a banknote that is worth such a large amount of money.

- A rich man went on a journey.
- He entrusted his money to three servants, according to their ability: five talents to one, two talents to another, and three talents to the third one.
- The first two servants doubled the money entrusted to them.
- The third servant buried his money in the ground.
- After a long time, the master returned.
- He congratulated the first servant, and put him in charge of many things, a happy man.
- He congratulated the second servant, and put him in charge of many things, a happy man.
- The third servant returned the talent, and explained he was afraid to do anything with it.
- The master called him a wicked and lazy servant, because he could have invested the money.
- The master threw the servant into the darkness, a place of weeping and fear.

> It is easy enough to tell the poor to accept their poverty as God's will . . . But if you want them to believe you – try to share some of their poverty and see if you accept it as God's will yourself.
>
> Thomas Merton

14. The sheep and the goats

Matthew 25[31–46]: Jesus said that when the Son of Man returns in glory, he will separate people as a shepherd separates the sheep from the goats. He will say to the 'sheep':

- Come into my kingdom, for –
- I was hungry and you fed me,
- I was thirsty and you gave me a drink,
- I was a stranger and you invited me in,
- I was without clothes and you clothed me,
- I was sick and you took care of me,
- I was in prison and you visited me.

The 'sheep' will say:

- When did we see you hungry and feed you,
- thirsty and give you a drink, . . . (and so on)

The king will reply:

- Whatever you did for the least of my brothers, you did for me.

Then the king will say to the 'goats':

- Go to the eternal fire prepared for the devil and his angels, for –
- I was hungry and you gave me nothing to eat,
- I was thirsty and you gave me nothing to drink,
- I was a stranger and you did not invite me in,
- I was without clothes and you did not clothe me,
- I was sick and you did not take care of me,
- I was in prison and you did not visit me.

The 'goats' will say:

- When did we see you hungry and feed you, . . . (and so on)

The king will reply:

- Whatever you did for the least of my brothers, you did for me.

15. Sickness and healing

James 5^{13-15}: James wrote to a group of Christians, somewhere (we do not know where):

- Is anyone in trouble? He should pray.
- Is anyone happy? He should sing.
- Is anyone sick? He should call the elders of the church; they will pray for him and rub oil on him.
- Their prayer made in faith has two effects: the sick person is healed and his sins are forgiven.

16. Parable of the unmerciful servant

Matthew 18^{23-35}: Peter asked Jesus: how many times should I forgive someone? As much as seven times?

Jesus said: seventy seven times. Then he told this parable:

- A king had a servant who owed him 10 000 talents (a fortune).
- The king ordered that the servant and his family should be sold to pay the debt.
- The servant pleaded for time.
- The king cancelled the debt and let him go.
- As he left, the servant saw a fellow-servant who owed him 100 denarii (a small sum of money).
- He had the man thrown into prison until the debt was paid.
- The other servants told the king.
- The king angrily reprimanded the first servant for not showing mercy.
- The king put this servant in jail.

Jesus said that is how his Father would act if a disciple would not forgive.

Implications

Here are some suggestions about what each passage teaches about Christian discipleship (the numbers in this list correspond to the numbering of the passages).
A disciple should:

1. • Teach about Jesus and God, in other countries as well as at home.
   • Teach everything that Jesus taught, not just the parts that appeal to the disciples.
   • Baptize new disciples.
2. • Help anybody in trouble, including those they dislike or hate.
3. • Listen attentively to what Jesus has to say.
   • Believe in Jesus and his teachings.
   • Put their belief into practice.
4. • Accept that there is evil in the world; and in the Church; and there always will be.
   • But accept that there is also good in the world, and in the Church; and there always will be.
5. • Let their faith grow.
   • Become more like Christ.
6. • Influence other people for the better.
   • Spread the kingdom of God.
7. • Believe in Jesus, because it is worth it.
   • Behave like Jesus – it costs, but it is worth it.
8. • Believe in Jesus, because it is worth it.
   • Behave like Jesus – it costs, but it is worth it.
9. • Accept that there is evil in the world; and in the Church; and there always will be.
   • But accept that there is also good in the world, and in the Church; and there always will be.
10. • Check that they have correctly understood the teaching of Jesus, as it is easy for disciples to mislead themselves into thinking that their ideas are Jesus' ideas.
    • Accept that it is natural for people to want others to serve them – but a disciple should serve other people. Jesus taught by example that a disciple should serve. And a disciple cannot be greater than the master.
    • Accept that suffering is an inevitable part of being a disciple.
11. • Ask God to forgive them, no matter what they have done, and God will forgive.
    • Forgive others. The worst sin is to refuse to forgive.
    • Not be resentful that God forgives others, no matter what they have done.
12. • Not be a snob. They should always treat other people, no matter how poor or rich, with dignity and respect.
    • Know that poor people are nearer to God than rich people are.
13. • Help other people, rather than pray at home all day.
    • Know they will be judged, one day, on how faithful a disciple they have been.
14. • Realize that Jesus will judge them one day. His main question will be: did they help people in third

world countries whom they thought were unimportant?
- Not expect to have marvellous experiences of Jesus. Rather, their religious duty is to help those who suffer, and to help those who are deprived.

15.
- Not neglect prayer; it can have powerful consequences.

- Take care of the sick.
- Call the church leaders when someone is ill.

16.
- Understand that God forgives them; and that they should be grateful for this.
- Imitate God: he forgives those who offend him.

Examination guidance

Re-tell the main points in the parable of the forgiving father. (5 marks)

First answer

A man has some sons, one of them run away for a long time, he spent all of his riches on parties. One day he went home and his father took him in his arms. Some people said that the man should not took his son back but the man was overjoyed to see his son. He said that any man would go looking for his lost sheeps until he found them.

This candidate has written only a couple of the main points – the son leaving home and leading a dissolute life; and the father welcoming the son home. There is a partly relevant statement about people objecting to the man welcoming his son back.

The examiner would not give a mark for the statement about the man and his sheep; it is not part of the story.

This candidate would have a poor mark for spelling, punctuation and grammar.
(Score: 2 marks out of 5)

Second answer

A man has two sons and he divides his property between them. One of them goes away and spends all his money on wine, women and enjoying himself. He had lots of friends because of his money. But one day his money had to run out and his friends left. He did not even have any money to buy food and none of his friends helped him. So he went home to his father because he knew his family would welcome him home. His father had a feast for him and celebrated his return. They killed the fatted calf and the son had a special robe and ring and sandals. He was happy that he had returned home at last. His father was happy as well.

This candidate has some of the main points in the story. But there are important points missing. In particular, there is nothing about the elder son. Any reasonable re-telling of this story must include something about each of the three people in it. There is also no mention of the younger son asking his father's forgiveness; of the father waiting for the son; of the father telling the elder son that the younger son was lost and was found. The candidate concentrates on giving detail about some parts of the story and neglects other important parts of the story. The question requires the candidate to re-tell the main points.
(Score: 3 marks out of 5)

Third answer

A father divided his property into two between his sons. One son gathered up his share and took off to spend it and he threw it all away. When he realized what he'd done he decided to get a job but soon realized that his own father's servants were better treated than he was. So he resolved to return home and ask for a job from his father. When his father saw him from a distance he was very happy and rushed to him. The son said he was not worthy to be his son. The father told him that was nonsense and he held a big feast for him. The other son was not pleased at this. He was angry and resentful. But the father explained that his son was lost and was now found.

This candidate has included the main points in the story.

The candidate has not written everything that there is in the story; but that is not necessary. The question asks for the main points in the story. This candidate is able to distinguish the main points from the detail in the story.
(Score: 5 marks out of 5)

Examination practice

1. What is the meaning of the parable of the talents (the three servants)? (3 marks)
   Write up to six lines.

2. Re-tell one of the following parables:
   the parable of the sheep and the goats
   the parable of the weeds.
   Explain the meaning of the parable you have retold. (8 marks)
   Write about three-quarters of a side of A4.

3. Christians believe that Jesus' teachings are still important.
   What might a contemporary Christian learn from them? (6 marks)
   You should write about half a side of A4.

4. Do you think that Jesus expects too much of his disciples?
   Give reasons for your point of view. Show that you have understood the opposite point of view. (8 marks)
   Write about three-quarters of a side of A4.

LOVE: THE TWO GREAT COMMANDMENTS 25

What Jesus taught

When Jesus was asked what the greatest commandment was, he replied by giving two commandments. The ones he chose were both from the Jewish law of the Old Testament, but neither was from the Ten Commandments given by Moses:

> 'Hear, O Israel, the Lord our God, the Lord is one. Love the Lord your God with all your heart and with all your soul and with all your mind and with all your strength.' The second is this: 'Love your neighbour as yourself.'
> Mark 12²⁸⁻³⁴

Notice here the positive emphasis on **love**. Time and again in the New Testament love is stressed as the greatest Christian virtue.

Jesus was not speaking of the sort of love one feels for one's family or friends. He was speaking of the sort of love a person could show for anyone, even a complete stranger. From the way he spoke it is clear that he meant such love to be real and deep. To love another person, perhaps one you do not even know, as you love yourself is very demanding indeed.

Jesus taught that Christians should love not only those close to them. They should even love those they do not like:

> 'I tell you: love your enemies and pray for those who persecute you . . .
> If you love those who love you, what reward will you get? Are not even the tax collectors doing that? And if you greet only your brothers, what are you doing more than others? Do not even pagans do that?'
> Matthew 5⁴⁴, ⁴⁶⁻⁴⁷

In the parable, the good Samaritan sees the injured man and feels compassion for him – and that is why he helps him (Luke 10²⁵⁻³⁷).

How did Jesus show love?

- When he saw people in need, he felt compassion – a deep-feeling sympathy – for them. He fed the 4000 people because he felt compassion for them (Mark 8¹⁻¹⁰). He healed the widow of Nain's son because he felt compassion for her (Luke 7¹¹⁻¹⁷).
- Jesus felt love for a person (the rich man in Mark 10¹⁷⁻³¹) and yet still asked him to do something that was beyond him – and did not change his mind when the man turned sadly away.

> Jesus looked at him and loved him. 'One thing you lack,' he said. 'Go, sell everything you have and give to the poor, and you will have treasure in heaven. Then come, follow me.'
> Mark 10²¹

- Above all, Christians believe that Jesus showed love by dying on the cross to save the world from sin:

> 'God so loved the world that he gave his one and only Son, that whoever believes in him shall not perish but have eternal life.'
> John 3¹⁶

Paul: love is the greatest Christian virtue

In 1 Corinthians 13, the word Paul uses for love is *agape* (pronounced ag-ap-ay). The word is used in the Bible to describe the highest, purest love. It is used for the love of God for the human race and the love of Christians for each other.

Verses 1–3: Without love everything else is meaningless:

- being a wonderful speaker – without love this talent is like a gong – mindless and empty;
- being able to prophesy;
- having enough faith to move mountains;

- giving everything away to the poor;
- going through dreadful pain and torture.

All these things are worth nothing unless they are done in a spirit of love.

Verses 4–7: some of the ways real love is shown:

- Love is patient and kind.
- Love is not envious; love is not boastful or proud; love is not rude.
- Love is not self-centred; love is not quick-tempered.
- Love does not keep score of wrongs – that is, does not bear a grudge.
- Love does not take pleasure in evil but in what is true.
- Love always protects; always trusts, hopes and perseveres.

Verses 8–12: Love is unending – even though other precious things, such as prophecy and knowledge will end.

Just as a child becomes an adult and sees things more clearly, with more understanding, so, as Christians grow in Christian love they know and understand God more fully.

Verse 13: Three things endure: faith – hope – love. The greatest of these is love.

God is love (MEG Paper 2)

In 1 John 4$^{7–21}$, John describes the love of God, and the way Christians should respond to it, in these words:

- God is love.
- This is how God showed his love among us: he sent his

one and only Son into the world that we might live through him. He sent his Son as an atoning sacrifice for our sins.

- Since God so loved us, we also ought to love one another.
- Whoever lives in love, lives in God and God in him.
- There is no fear in love; perfect love drives out fear.
- If anyone says, 'I love God', yet hates his brother, he is a liar. For anyone who does not love his brother, whom he has seen, cannot love God, whom he has not seen.

Christian love

> Love God and do what you like.
>
> Saint Augustine

Christians believe that, properly obeyed, the two great commandments are all that are needed. They are, however, extremely demanding. They are very difficult to obey properly. If you really love a person, you will want to do everything you can for that person. If Christians really love God, they will keep all the other commandments. They will keep them, not because they have to but because they want to. If Christians love their neighbours, it will not be enough to avoid hurting or upsetting them. Christians should want to do what they can for others.

That is the point of what Augustine said: 'Love God and do what you like.' If you love God, you will want to do what pleases him.

Examination guidance

1. What did Paul write about Christian love in 1 Corinthians 13? (6 marks)

2. Give an example of a Christian who showed Christian love. (6 marks)

3. Give an example of a way in which a young person might show the sort of love about which Jesus spoke when he said, 'Love your neighbour as yourself' (3 marks)

1. Paul said that without love everything is worthless. Even being a wonderful preacher, or being wonderfully wise, or having tremendous faith or even giving everything away is not worth anything if there is no love.

Paul said that love is patient, kind, unselfish and caring. Love doesn't enjoy seeing other people in trouble. Love does not take offence easily and doesn't bear grudges against people.

Love will last for ever. The three greatest things are faith, hope and love, and love is the best of them all.

This is an example of a good answer. There are other points that could have been made, but the candidate is not expected to know every detail by heart. What is written is accurate and relevant.
(Score: 6 marks out of 6)

2. The example I have chosen is Father Maximilian Kolbe. He was a Polish priest who founded a movement called the Knights of the Immaculata, who were very devoted to the Virgin Mary. This society had very many members in Poland and in other countries. He was a prisoner in the extermination camp of Auschwitz during the Second

The candidate has made a good choice. Fr Kolbe's self-sacrifice is described clearly. His love for others is shown by the way he gave his life for a man whom he hardly knew, and by the way in which he supported the other nine who were dying with him. The last paragraph does not just say that Fr Kolbe is a good example of obeying Jesus'

World War. One day one of the prisoners in Cell Block 14 escaped. The other prisoners in that cell block were told that as a punishment for the one who had escaped ten prisoners would be taken to starve to death. One of those chosen began to weep, sobbing for his wife and children. Fr Kolbe stepped forward and offered to take his place. They were taken to cells in the basement of one of the bunkers, stripped and left in the cells without furniture or blankets. Kolbe led them in prayers and hymns as they died one by one. After sixteen days he and the other three who were still alive were given injections to kill them. Now the place in Auschwitz where he died is a place of pilgrimage and a light burns there to mark the spot.

I think Maximilian Kolbe is a very good example of someone who showed Christian love. Jesus said 'A man cannot show greater love than by dying for his friends.'

teaching. The candidate quotes a relevant teaching of Jesus. The verse quoted might not be in the syllabus the candidate was studying, but would still receive credit.
(Score: 6 marks out of 6)

3. One way in which a person could show this sort of love would be by spending some time digging the garden for an old person who was keen on gardening but could not dig any more. It might be at a time when he wanted to go to a football match or be with his mates but if the grass needed cutting because it was too long he would do it. It would be a way of showing love becase what the other person wanted would count for as much as what he wanted himself.

The candidate has chosen a good example and described it clearly. He has related it to the question well.
(Score: 3 marks out of 3)

Examination practice

1. What did Jesus say were the two great commandments? Tell in your own words a parable that Jesus told to show the meaning of the second of the Great Commandments.

    (10 marks)
    Write about half to three-quarters of a side of A4.

2. Why do Christians think the first great commandment is important? (3 marks)
    Write about a third of a side of A4.

3. Give an example of a Christian whose life shows that he or she does keep these two commandments.
    (7 marks)
    Write about half to three-quarters of a side of A4.

SITUATION ETHICS 26

Introduction

Situation ethics is a way of making the right decision. It is a way of making a moral decision. When we have to decide to do something that can be right or wrong, it is a moral decision we have to make.

One case

We are in a ship that sinks in the Atlantic. Fortunately, we manage to reach a lifeboat. There are 70 people in the lifeboat. One of the survivors is a ship's officer. He tells us that the lifeboat has rations for 20 people for ten days, and that 20 people could row the lifeboat to the nearest land in ten days. He says it is impossible to row the lifeboat to land with 70 people in it. He adds that the ship was miles off course when it sank and that it failed to send out an SOS. Everyone realizes that we would certainly starve or freeze to death if we stayed put. No search plane would know where to find us.

What should we do? Put overboard the 50 eldest or frailest people, so that 20 healthy people can row to the nearest land and live? Or should we do nothing, knowing that this will lead to the death of all 70?

Wrong principles

According to those who use situation ethics, there are two wrong ways to make moral decisions.

- **Use a set of moral rules**, such as: do not kill; do not steal; do not commit adultery; do not make false accusations against someone; do not act out of jealousy; be forgiving; be patient; be kind; be good mannered; and so on. We decide whether an action is right or wrong by seeing if it keeps or breaks one of these moral rules. Situationists suggest that most Christians use this way of making moral decisions.
- **Use no rules**. Decide spontaneously what is right or wrong. Alternatively, trust that the Spirit of God will tell us what to do.

Right principle

According to those who use situation ethics, there is one right way to make moral decisions. We apply the moral rule, 'Love our neighbour as ourselves.' We apply this rule in any situation to discover what is the right thing to do. Take, for instance, the lifeboat situation in the example above. We decide what we should do by asking: what should I do to love my neighbour in this situation?

Why do situationists say that 'Love your neighbour' is the only moral rule? Because, say Christian situationists, this is the only moral rule that Jesus taught. They argue that Jesus did not teach a set of moral rules – just this rule.

> 'Love the Lord your God. . . . Love your neighbour as yourself.'
>
> Jesus (Mark 12[30–31])

See Chapter E25, on *Love: the two great commandments*, for the meaning of love.

Another case

A house is on fire. I am standing outside it. Inside the blazing building there are two people: my father and a skilled surgeon. I have the chance to dash into the house and rescue one of the two people, but I do not have time to rescue both of them. Which one should I rescue? Notice the question! It does not ask, which one do I feel I want to rescue? It asks, which one should I rescue?

Guidelines

According to situationists we should decide which would be the most loving thing to do in any situation. We should not act on impulse, but think carefully about the right thing to do. We should make our decision using rational calculation, not sentimental feelings.

In the two cases outlined above, it would be loving to rescue all the people shipwrecked, and both of the people in the building. However, it is not possible to do this. So we must decide which of the people we will help. Fletcher, a leading situationist, argues that in a situation such as this we should use the following principles to decide what to do.

- Help the person whose need is greater.
- Do the action that helps the greatest number of people.
- Help the person who is more valuable.

Let us consider these principles. It seems that in the case of the lifeboat, the second principle could apply. Thus the right thing would be to jettison 50 people so that 20 can survive. This would help 20 people. Otherwise everyone would die and we would have helped nobody.

In the case of the burning building, the third principle could apply. So, the loving thing would be to rescue the surgeon, because she would be able to save many more lives than my father.

A third case

A hundred years ago a group of migrants were making their way across America to settle in the West. They spotted some local Indians, so they hid in some bushes. They knew that the Indians would kill settlers. The group of Indians came very close to where the settlers were hiding in the bushes. One of the settlers had a baby who had been asleep when they first hid. But the baby was now wakening and was about to cry. The mother put her hand over the baby's mouth. If the baby made a noise the Indians would quickly discover the settlers and kill them. The mother saw that she was suffocating her baby. She had a difficult decision to make. If she kept her hand over her baby's mouth, she would kill her child. If she took her hand away, the baby would cry and the Indians would kill the settlers. What should she do?

What do you think a situationist would say? Remember that a situationist thinks that only one thing is right: to love other people. Nothing else is right or wrong. Fletcher says that 'everything is permitted' – killing, jealousy, generosity, stealing, and so on. None of these is right or wrong. Any of them becomes right if it is a loving action. It becomes wrong if it is done out of hatred or indifference.

Objections

Many Christians reject the situationist method of making moral decisions, for different reasons. Here are some of the criticisms that they have made about situation ethics.

- It is not possible to make a separate moral decision in every situation. We could not live a normal life if we had to do this. We need moral rules to help us make quick and consistent decisions.
- Most people recognize that certain types of action are wrong: for example, making false accusations against other people, lying, murdering, stealing, torturing, cheating, and so on. There may be occasions when such actions are right, but that would be exceptional. The assumption should be that these actions are wrong unless, in a particular instance, there are good reasons to think they are right. Thus it is not acceptable to say that making false accusations is not right or wrong in itself.
- Situationists use extreme situations to illustrate their point that there is only one moral rule. Such situations are not typical of what most of us face every day.

Exceptional situations may involve exceptions to moral rules. Exceptional situations do not demonstrate that there are no moral rules. If situationists used everyday situations to illustrate their view, then their argument would not be convincing. Consequently, they use extraordinary situations to make their view appear convincing.

- Situation ethics assumes – an unwritten assumption – that the most important task is to preserve human lives on earth. Consequently, it accepts that any action that preserves human life must be right. However, Christians believe that there is a life after death, and so death is not the final tragedy. Thus the preservation of life on earth cannot be used to justify any action, including evil actions.

Examination practice

1. Some people think that situation ethics is not a valid way to decide what is right and wrong.
   Explain one reason they might have to support their view. (3 marks)
   Write about five lines of A4.

2. What is situation ethics?
   Use examples to show how situationists make moral decisions. (10 marks)
   Write about one side of A4.

3. Christians believe that Jesus showed God's love. How might this belief influence the way they treat other people? (8 marks)
   Write about three-quarters of a side of A4.

4. 'It's obvious what is right and what is wrong. You do not have to work it out.'
   Do you agree? Show that you have considered more than one answer. (8 marks)
   Write about three-quarters of a side of A4.

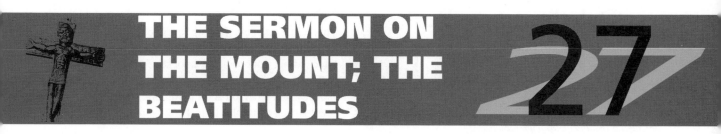

THE SERMON ON THE MOUNT; THE BEATITUDES 27

Introduction

The Sermon on the Mount is found in Matthew's gospel, Chapters 5, 6 and 7.

The Beatitudes

Matthew 5³⁻¹²: These are a series of blessings on those who show the qualities of true Christians. They are listed in the box on the next page.

Christian influence

Matthew 5¹³⁻¹⁶: A Christian must be:

- the salt of the earth – people who show the real purpose and meaning of life;
- the light of the world – people who, through the way they live, make others turn and give glory to God.

The Old Testament law

Matthew 5¹⁷⁻⁴⁸: The Jews believe that the first five books of the Old Testament, known as the **Torah**, the law, were

The Beatitudes

Blessed are . . .	For . . .
the poor in spirit	theirs is the kingdom of heaven
those who mourn	they will be comforted
the meek	they will inherit the earth
those who hunger and thirst for righteousness	they will be filled
the merciful	they will be shown mercy
the pure in heart	they will see God
the peacemakers	they will be called sons of God
those who are persecuted because of righteousness	theirs is the kingdom of heaven

given by God. Therefore they have a unique authority. They should not be changed or altered in any way.

Jesus agreed. He said that the law should not be altered, not even a letter or a part of a letter. What was important is not the letter but the spirit of the law.

He went on to give examples of Old Testament laws and the way in which they should be obeyed. Jesus is concerned with motives. Human law cannot deal with thoughts, only with words and actions. Jesus taught that his followers should discipline their minds. In doing so he went beyond the old law and, in places, did in effect change it.

Some, though not all, of the laws about which Jesus spoke are among the Ten Commandments or the two great commandments. See Chapters E25 and E29.

Daleth   Resh

ד   ר

'. . . not the smallest letter, not the least stroke of a pen, will by any means disappear from the Law . . .'

The Hebrew letters daleth *and* resh *are very similar – they differ by a tiny stroke of a pen. Jesus said the Law of God is so holy that not even a part of a letter should be ommitted.*

Do not murder (verses 21–26)

Jesus said that anger is wrong. He meant uncontrolled, bitter, unforgiving anger; he himself showed righteous anger when confronted with something wrong.

* A person who was about to make an offering to God should first make peace with his brother, then offer the gift.
* Better to agree with someone rather than, full of anger, take them to court.

Do not commit adultery (verses 27–30)

Jesus said, 'Whoever looks at a woman lustfully has already committed adultery with her in his heart.'

Jesus did not mean that it is wrong to be attracted by someone of the opposite sex! He was talking about an attitude of mind that is obsessed with thoughts of immoral sexual acts.

Anyone who divorces his wife must give her a certificate of divorce (verses 31–32)

Jesus taught that divorce is wrong. Anyone who marries a divorced person commits adultery.

The one concession he makes is in the words, 'Anyone who divorces his wife, except for marital unfaithfulness, causes her to become an adulteress.'

Keep the oaths that you have sworn to the Lord (verses 33–37)

The law said that oaths sworn – promises made – by the name of God should be kept.

Jesus said there was no need to swear by anything. 'Simply let your "Yes" be "Yes" and your "No", "No".' If a person said something, that should be good enough, without any oath to back his word up.

Eye for eye and tooth for tooth (verses 38–42)

This was a just law, limiting revenge to what was just. Uncontrolled revenge might want to repay a person who knocked out your tooth by knocking out half a dozen of his!

Jesus said a person should not look for revenge. He gave some strong examples to make the point:

* If someone strikes you on the right cheek, turn to him the other also.
* If someone wants to sue you and take your tunic, let him have your cloak as well.
* If someone forces you to go one mile, go with him two miles.

Love your neighbour and hate your enemy (verses 43–48)

Jesus said, 'Love your enemies and pray for those who persecute you.' Those who love those who love them and greet those close to them are not doing anything especially good.

Spiritual matters

Matthew 6^{1-18}:

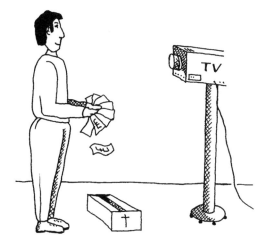

Do not announce it with trumpets

Do not let your left hand know what your right hand is doing

Giving to the needy (verses 1–4)

Jesus did not discuss whether or not people should give to those in need. He clearly took it for granted that they should. The question is how it is done.

The giving is a matter between the person and God. 'Do not announce it with trumpets' said Jesus – meaning, 'Do not make a great fuss and let everyone know.' Those who do make a fuss have a reward already, because people will praise them. 'Do not let your left hand know what your right hand is doing' – meaning, 'Do it really secretly.'

Prayer (verses 5–15)

Jesus said that prayer, like giving to the needy, should be a private matter, between the individual and God. A person should not show off when praying. Also, prayer should be simple and clear.

Jesus gave the people the **Lord's Prayer** – see Chapter A3.

Fasting (verses 16–18)

Again, this is a private matter between the believer and God. You should not look as though you are fasting.

Treasures in heaven

Matthew 6^{19-34}: Jesus said that money and wealth on earth are not important – both can be stolen or be destroyed. Treasure in heaven, life after death with God, is far more important. 'Where your treasure is, there your heart will be as well.'

'The eye is the lamp of the body.' If a person looks on life in a good way, that person's whole life will be good. If he looks in a jaundiced or cynical way, that too will affect his whole way of life. One cannot be on the side of God and on the side of money at the same time.

Do not be like the hypocrites for they love to pray on street corners announcing it with trumpets

Go into your room, close the door and pray to your father who is unseen

Jesus urged his followers not just to worry about money and possessions, even for ordinary things. God cares for birds and for the lilies. Human beings are far more important to him.

> 'So do not worry, saying, "What shall we eat?" or "What shall we drink?" or "What shall we wear?" . . . your heavenly Father knows that you need [these things]. Seek first his kingdom and his righteousness, and all these things will be given to you as well.'

Judging others

Matthew 7$^{1-6}$: Jesus warned against judging others. In particular, he warned against finding others guilty of a fault when you are much more guilty yourself. He made his point in a striking, comical way, talking about a speck of dust in someone's eye – and a plank in the eye of the person offering to remove the speck of dust.

Ask, seek, knock

Matthew 7$^{7-12}$: Jesus told his followers to trust God, as a father. When in need they had only to turn to God. As Jesus put it, they had only to ask, seek or knock – in other words, to pray. If a child asks a human father for something he or she needs, the father will give it to them. He will not give his child something useless or even harmful. How much more will a heavenly Father give good gifts!

Jesus gave what is often known as the golden rule:

> Do to others what you would have them do to you. Everything in all the teaching in the law and the prophets can be summed up in those few words.

It is hard to be a good Christian

Matthew 7$^{13-27}$: Jesus used a number of examples to make his followers realize how demanding the Christian life is:

- The way to heaven is like a difficult narrow path, not a wide, easy one.
- There will be people trying to lead others away from the truth. Jesus called them 'wolves in sheep's clothing'.
- Just as a tree is judged by the quality of the fruit, so people are judged by the quality of their lives, their actions. Just calling Jesus 'Lord' (just saying prayers to him) will not be enough.
- Someone who follows Jesus is like a person who builds a house on a foundation of rock. Someone who does not follow Jesus is like a person who builds a house on a foundation of sand.

Examination guidance

You need to show that you know and understand the teaching of Jesus in the Sermon on the Mount.

You may be given a choice of laws on which to comment. If so, you may find it better to choose a teaching that is controversial, such as the teaching about divorce.

- If you are asked for the relevance of the teaching to the present day, it is your ability to evaluate that is being tested. Make your own opinions clear. You will receive credit if what you write is relevant and sensible, regardless of whether or not the examiner agrees with you.
- However, if you are asked how a Christian might try to follow these teachings, you are being tested for your understanding of Christian beliefs, not your own opinions.

1. In the Sermon on the Mount, Jesus took a number of laws and said how they should be obeyed. Give **one** example of a law and Jesus' teaching regarding it. (6 marks)

2. How far is Jesus' teaching relevant today? (14 marks)

1. I am choosing the law 'Don't have a divorce'. Jesus said that divorce is wrong. Getting divorced and remarried is as bad as adultery. If your husband goes off with another woman, then it is alright to divorce.

The choice of a law is sensibly made though, strictly speaking, the candidate has got it wrong. The law is, 'Anyone who divorces his wife must give her a certificate of divorce', not 'Don't have a divorce'.

The main points in Jesus' response are there in recognizable form. Jesus did not actually say divorce is wrong, but that is clearly implied in what he did say. Credit is given for knowledge that is known and relevantly selected, though clumsily expressed in places.
(Score: 3 marks out of 6)

2. I think that teaching is too hard for nowadays. Lots of people get married and then are very unhappy together. They quarrel a lot and the children get upset. Then I think they should be allowed to divorce.

The candidate expresses a clear view. Some arguments are given to support the view. Two good points in the response are:

After all, Jesus said you should forgive people who sin. Once some people found a woman who had committed adultery and they wanted to crucify her. Jesus said she should be forgiven. I think people who get divorced should be forgiven.

I know why Jesus said divorce is wrong. It's because he thought families are important. He was probably thinking of the children. He said that God joins them together so they shouldn't separate. But I still think divorce is alright.

- An attempt is made to put both sides of the argument, even though the candidate's views are clear.
- The arguments are backed by the teachings of Jesus.

On the other hand, there are mistakes.

- The woman who was caught committing adultery would by the law have been stoned, not crucified.
- Those accusing her brought her to Jesus to try to catch him out. Jesus did not intervene to stop them.
- The key words used by Jesus – 'Go now and leave your life of sin' – are left out.

(Score: 8 marks out of 14)

Examination practice

1. What did Jesus say about prayer in the Sermon on the Mount? (8 marks)
   Write about half a side of A4. Don't forget Chapter 7^{7-11} as well as Chapter 6^{5-15}.

2. What did Jesus say in the Sermon on the Mount about the birds and the lilies? What did he mean by these teachings? (8 marks)

Write about three-quarters of a side of A4. Make sure you cover both what Jesus said and what he meant by it.

3. Do you think it would be difficult for a Christian today to live by the teachings in the Sermon on the Mount? Give reasons for your answer. (6 marks)
   Write about three-quarters of a side of A4. Refer clearly to two or three different teachings – do not simply ramble on vaguely.

CONSCIENCE

Introduction

Conscience is the inner sense by which we judge what is right and what is wrong.

How reliable is conscience?

'Dear friends, if our hearts do not condemn us, we have confidence before God' (1 John 3^{21}). In other words, if our consciences are clear then we can feel we are right with God.

But there are problems. How can people be sure that their consciences are telling them the right thing? They may do what is wrong even though they are trying to do what is right:

- When they have to decide what to do, they may not know the whole truth about the situation.
- Even if they do know the whole truth, they may simply make mistakes.

Some people's consciences tell them that something is wrong while others, also guided by conscience, believe it to be right. For example:

- A **conscientious objector** is someone who objects to war in any circumstance as evil. Another person may hate the very idea of war, but believe, as a matter of conscience, that it is his duty to join the army and fight, even kill another person, in defence of his country and people because their cause is just.
- **Vegetarians** believe, as a matter of conscience, that it is wrong to eat meat. They believe that they should not take the God-given lives of other creatures. Others eat meat in good conscience, believing that it is right and necessary for good health. God gave the human race meat and fish as part of their natural diet; Jesus ate both meat and fish.
- **Jehovah's Witnesses** will not accept blood transfusions. They believe it is against the teaching of the Old Testament. Most people regard blood transfusions as an

important way of saving a person's life or building up their strength.

Conscience and belief

Many Christians hold that all have a right to believe whatever their consciences tell them is true – in other words, everyone has **liberty of conscience**:

> It is contrary to the right of Christian government to force faith upon the world with the sword and other violent compulsion . . . evil should be resisted alone with the mighty Word of God and the person erring in faith should not be knocked down suddenly but should be tolerated in all Christian love as a harmless person.
>
> Memmingen Resolutions (Baptist) 1531

However, tolerance does not mean saying that people may believe whatever they wish and still be called Christians.

In some cases people's consciences tell them to accept some other authority and to follow that authority's judgement. For instance, when there is a pronouncement on a moral issue by the Church, that pronouncement is based on the experience and judgement of a number of members of the Church. Other Church members may well accept the authority of the Church. Therefore they may be guided by their consciences to accept the Church's teaching.

Biblical teaching

The word 'conscience' is not found at all in the Old Testament or in the gospels. It is obvious that the prophets took it for granted that people did have consciences and knew the difference between right and wrong.

Jesus also assumed that people understood what conscience is. For example, his parable of the Pharisee and the tax collector (Luke 18^{9-14}) does not mention conscience but is obviously based on the idea. The two men are praying. The Pharisee is telling God how proud he is that he is better than other people. The tax collector is asking God to forgive his sins. The tax collector's conscience is telling him that he is a sinner.

In Romans 14, Paul wrote about the need for everyone to be true to their conscience. Even if people disagree over what is right and wrong, they must respect the other person's conscience. Some Christians believed it was all right to eat anything they wished; others thought it was wrong to eat certain things.

> As one who is in the Lord Jesus, I am fully convinced that no food is unclean in itself. But if anyone regards something as unclean, then for him it is unclean. If your brother is distressed because of what you eat, you are no longer acting in love. Do not by your eating destroy your brother for whom Christ died.
>
> Romans 14^{14-15}

The closer people are to God and the more they know of what he wants, the better. People who are filled with the Holy Spirit will have their consciences guided by the Spirit.

> The man without the Spirit does not accept the things that come from the Spirit of God. . . The spiritual man makes judgments about all things. . . We have the mind of Christ.
>
> 1 Corinthians 2^{14-16}

Examination practice

1. Choose and tell in your own words **one** of Jesus' parables that shows a person obeying his or her conscience. What is the teaching of that parable?

   (8 marks)

   Write about a side of A4 – depending, of course, on the length of the parable you have chosen.

2. What does Paul say about respecting other people's consciences? How relevant is his teaching today?

   (7 marks)

   Write about a side of A4. Paul takes the example of a person's feelings over what should or should not be eaten. Discuss that and then go on to other examples such as conscientious objectors, or Jehovah's Witnesses refusing blood transfusions.

Introduction

Exodus 20 records that the Ten Commandments were given to Moses on Mount Sinai. The commandments were part of the Old Covenant. (A covenant is a binding agreement between God and members of the human race. For the New Covenant, see Chapter A1, *Eucharist*.)

Note that the commandments begin with God saying that he has kept his part of the covenant by rescuing them when they were slaves in Egypt. Now the people must keep their part of the covenant.

> Some syllabuses include the passage containing the Ten Commandments, Exodus 20 $^{1-17}$, as a set text. This means that questions may be asked, and sometimes are asked, on the words of any of the commandments.
>
> 1. I am the Lord your God, who brought you out of Egypt, out of the land of slavery. You shall have no other gods before me.
> 2. You shall not make for yourself an idol in the form of anything in heaven above or on the earth beneath or in the waters below. You shall not bow down to them or worship them; for I, the Lord your God, am a jealous God, punishing the children for the sin of the fathers to the third and fourth generation of those who hate me, but showing love to a thousand generations of those who love me and keep my commandments.
> 3. You shall not misuse the name of the Lord your God, for the Lord will not hold anyone guiltless who misuses his name.
> 4. Remember the Sabbath day by keeping it holy. Six days you shall labour and do all your work, but the seventh day is a Sabbath to the Lord your God. On it you shall not do any work, neither you, nor your son or daughter, nor your manservant or maidservant, nor your animals, nor the alien within your gates. For in six days the Lord made the heavens and the earth, the sea and all that is in them, but he rested on the seventh day. Therefore the Lord blessed the seventh day and made it holy.
> 5. Honour your father and your mother, so that you may live long in the land the Lord your God is giving you.
> 6. You shall not murder.
> 7. You shall not commit adultery.
> 8. You shall not steal.

> 9. You shall not give false testimony against your neighbour.
> 10. You shall not covet your neighbour's house. You shall not covet your neighbour's wife, or his manservant or maidservant, or his ox or donkey, or anything that belongs to your neighbour.

> In many older Anglican churches the words of the commandments are written on the wall, so that people would read and learn them. Before people were confirmed they were expected to learn the Ten Commandments in full by heart.

The meaning of the commandments

1 You shall have no other gods before me

2 You shall not make for yourself an idol

Originally the first commandment would be taken to mean that one should not worship other gods such as Baal or Jupiter. The second commandment said that it was wrong to make something out of wood, metal or stone and pray to it.

Nowadays the two commandments are both taken to mean that a Christian should be loyal to God and place him first. There should be nothing taking the place of God. Not only would it be wrong for a Christian to worship another God; it would be wrong to treat, say, a pop star or money as more important than God.

3 You shall not misuse the name of the Lord your God

Some people would recognize this commandment better in the older version 'Thou shalt not take the name of the Lord thy God in vain'.

The commandment can be understood in two ways:

- *You shall not use the name of God as a swearword.* In discussing this idea note how common such swearing is and how little the words God and Christ mean to those who use them as swearwords. Also remember that to many Christians the name of God is holy and to be treated with great reverence; they are genuinely hurt and offended when the name is used so disrespectfully.

- *When you swear by Almighty God that you will keep a promise, you must keep it.* Note here what Jesus said in the Sermon on the Mount (Matthew 5[33–37]) (see Chapter E27, *The Sermon on the Mount; the Beatitudes*): if you make a promise you should keep it, whether or not you have sworn by Almighty God or anything else.

4 Remember the Sabbath day by keeping it holy

It is important to know what the commandment actually says. It says that there are six days in the week for work but the seventh day is the Sabbath, a day of rest. The reason given is that God created the world in six days. He rested on the seventh and set it apart as a holy day.

(There is an older version of the commandment in Deuteronomy 5, which gives a different reason for having a day of rest each week. There the reason given is simply that servants and animals need a weekly day of rest.)

Christians keep Sunday, not Saturday, as their holy day because Jesus rose from the dead on a Sunday. So, above all, Sunday is a weekly celebration of the resurrection. None the less, many Christians do assume that the fourth commandment, the Sabbath law, applies to Sunday.

Any discussion on the Christian attitude to Sunday should start from the idea that Sunday is a day when Christians meet for worship. You should also consider whether it is right that people should work on a Sunday and whether shops or places of entertainment should be open.

5 Honour your father and your mother

The commandment originally was concerned with a duty to care for one's elderly parents – so that in time you may be cared for and enjoy long life.

The natural way to understand the commandment is, of course, in terms of young people and the way they should treat their parents. What does 'honour' mean? Does it mean 'obey'?

6 You shall not murder

In Hebrew there are three words that mean 'kill'. Each has a different shade of meaning. One means 'kill in battle'. One means 'execute'. The third, the one used here, means 'murder'.

Discussion of the meaning of this commandment can cover many issues:

- Is killing in battle morally the same as murder? Or is there such a thing as a **just war**, which makes killing in battle acceptable?
- Is capital punishment acceptable, or it it another form of murder?

- What about such issues as abortion, euthanasia, or killing in self-defence? Do they go against the commandment? Are they justified?

Suicide is an important issue here. Note that:

- It is thought by some that people have the right to end their lives as and when they wish.
- Christians generally oppose suicide. They believe:
  - Life is given by God to be used in the service of God and of other people.
  - Suicide is a rejection of God's gift – a rejection of his love and authority.
  - Suicide is an offence against other people, especially those who love you or depend on you.
- Most suicides are done in desperation or despair – or simply irrationally, with no one ever knowing why. Christians may think it the fault of society that people feel driven to take their own lives. Many Christians are active in the Samaritan movement, which is dedicated to helping people who are desperate and lonely, needing someone to whom they can talk.

Suicide is not the same as **self-sacrifice**. On Captain Robert Scott's Antarctic expedition in 1912 Captain Lawrence Oates was suffering from frostbite and general physical weakness. He was afraid that he was delaying his companions as they headed north towards safety. So he walked out into the freezing wastes to die rather than be a burden to his companions; he wanted to give them every chance to reach safety before the weather grew worse and their strength gave way. That was self-sacrifice, not suicide. (See page 216)

7 You shall not commit adultery

Christians see this commandment in a very positive way. They believe that God created human beings in such a way that men and women would fall in love and express their love through sexual intercourse. Within marriage that is God's will. When married couples have children there is a basis for strong family life.

Intercourse should be part of the unique relationship between husband and wife. The teaching found in the Bible is that not only adultery (intercourse with someone else's husband or wife) but fornication (intercourse between two unmarried persons) weakens family life because it threatens the uniqueness of the married relationship.

There are controversial matters here, which should be discussed in any consideration of this commandment.

8 You shall not steal

Christians believe that everyone has a right to own and keep what is rightfully theirs. It is wrong to ignore that right and to steal. It is not only that a person's property is taken. People lose their sense of security and no longer feel safe in their own homes.

9 You shall not give false testimony against your neighbour

The basic idea behind this commandment is that it is wrong to lie. In particular, it is wrong to lie in such a way as will harm another person.

Whether there are times when it is permissible to lie is something worth discussing in an exam essay. For instance, does loyalty to friend or family ever justify a lie? What about times when it seems kinder to conceal the truth?

10 You shall not covet

'Covet' means 'desire something excessively or wrongfully'.

Coveting can lead a person to commit a sin – jealousy, theft or even murder. The commandment says that coveting does not just cause a person to do wrong – it is wrong in itself.

Examination guidance

1. Remember (observe) the Sabbath Day by keeping it holy.
  (a)   What is said in the rest of the commandment? (4 marks)
  (b)   In what ways do Christians believe the commandment should be followed in the present day? (6 marks)

2. What did Jesus say are the two great commandments? (4 marks)

3. Do you think it is harder for young people to live by the commandments than it is for older people? Give reasons for your answer. (6 marks)

1 (a) You have six days in which to work but the seventh day is a day of rest dedicated to me. You shall pray to me on that day.

The candidate has correctly said that the commandment says that one should work on six days and rest on the seventh. There is no reference to God creating the world in six days and resting on the seventh.

The points mentioned above are the main things to be recorded; if they were clearly and fully made the candidate would be awarded full marks. If these points were not made clearly enough to receive full credit, some credit might be given instead for other detail from the commandment – such as reference to the whole household, or to the words 'The Lord blessed the Sabbath day and made it holy'.

No credit would be gained for the words 'You shall pray to me on that day.' While it is true that Christians and Jews do worship on their day of rest, that is not what the commandment actually says.
(Score: 2 marks out of 4)

(b) Christians have Sunday, not Saturday, as their holy day. This is because Jesus rose from the dead on a Sunday.

Some Christians believe that no one should work on a Sunday. People should celebrate with their families and worship. They say that shops shouldn't open on Sundays. Why shouldn't people be able to shop if they want to? It's up to them.

The candidate has correctly distinguished between the Jewish Sabbath and the Christian Sunday. The reason for the distinction is correctly given – 'Jesus rose from the dead on a Sunday'. Clearly this is an important part of the Christian attitude to the Sabbath commandment.

The rest of the answer is far too short. The idea of worshipping together should be developed. The special atmosphere of a Sunday should be mentioned, including the chance for families to be together. Candidates would receive credit for saying that not all Christians agree that Sunday laws should be enforced. They may say that if Christians give some time to worship, the rest of the day may be used as the person wishes. For instance, it may be argued that having shops open allows families to enjoy shopping together.

Note that the question asks 'In what ways do Christians believe. . .?' Not necessarily *all* Christians but *any reasonably typical* Christians.

The candidate here has not made this point. No credit would be given for 'Why shouldn't people be able to shop if they want to? It's up to them' because it does not say what Christians believe but simply asks a question.
(Score: 3 marks out of 6)

2. Jesus said that the two great commandments are to love God and to have no other God but him and to love your neighbour as yourself.

The candidate has correctly given the two basic commandments – Love God and love your neighbour.

The second commandment is completely correct – Love your neighbour as yourself. The first of the two great commandments given by Jesus has been confused with the first of the Ten Commandments. The correct answer would have been Love the Lord your God with all your heart and with all your soul and with all your mind and with all your strength.
(Score: 3 marks out of 4)

3. I think that it is harder for young people to live by the commandments than it is for old people because young people are more naive and are easily led e.g. their friends might persuade them to steal from a shop and then they would have broken a commandment. Young people may not honour their parents because their parents may not let them do something and the young person might think that their parents are unreasonable. Older people are more strong willed and sensible.

The candidate has taken a firm line – it is harder for young people to live by the commandments than it is for old people. Actually, the question asks about older people, not old people – and the two are not necessarily the same.

Two sensible general reasons are given. Young people are more naive and are easily led. A better candidate would use and explain the phrase 'peer pressure'.

Two examples of commandments are given, both relevantly. We are told why a young person might be tempted to steal or disobey a parent. This would be sufficient; a candidate could not discuss all ten commandments. Those chosen are relevant to young people; the candidate would not have received so much credit had the essay concentrated on 'You shall not murder' as very few people of any age are murderers. Far more young people either steal or disobey their parents.

The essay lacks detail and depth. For instance, a discussion on what honouring a parent means would improve it. The candidate simply assumes that to honour is to obey automatically; it would have been better to discuss the meaning.
(Score: 4 marks out of 6)

NATURAL LAW: REASONING

Introduction

Suppose we work out for ourselves that something is right, or that something is wrong, and we can give a reason. This is natural law. However, our reason must be in the interest of people.

For example, suppose a headteacher suspended a pupil from school. We might argue that the headteacher made the right decision: first, because the pupil was continually disrupting lessons, and thus taking away other pupils' rights to an education: second, because the pupil was constantly offensive to other people, and thus ignored their right to be treated with dignity. This is using natural law to decide right and wrong.

Natural law is also about principles of right and wrong. And so we are using natural law if we say it is obvious (self-evident) that people have the right to free speech; or if we say that people have the right to govern themselves; or if we say or that people have the right to defend themselves. We have not reasoned out that these are right. But we have intuitively understood that they are right.

This method of deciding right and wrong is called natural law, as reasoning is natural to us. Reasoning is a distinctive characteristic of humans. It is an ability that God gave us. It is one way in which we are like God.

> So God created man
>   in his own image,
> in the image of God
>   he created him;
> male and female
>   he created them.
>
> Genesis 1[27]

Motive, act and consequences

Is it wrong to hit someone? It depends. Suppose I hit someone who was hysterical, and my motive was to make them calm, then it could be right. But if I hit someone because I did not like the colour of their hair, then it would be wrong. In these instances, we judge whether an action is right or wrong by considering the **motive** of the action.

Is it wrong to torture someone? Yes. Is it wrong to rape someone? Yes. In these instances, we judge whether an action is right or wrong by considering the **action** itself. The motive for the action may be good, but this does not make the action right.

In some instances, we judge whether an action is right or wrong by considering the **consequences** of the action. Is it wrong to lie? Well, suppose I see a friend steal money at school. The teacher asks me if I saw anyone taking the money. I lie: I omit to say I saw my friend steal the money; instead I name someone I do not like and say I saw him near the place where the money was stolen. Consequently, this person, who is innocent, gets unjustly blamed for the theft. The consequences of my action make my action wrong.

Now suppose someone comes into school holding a knife. He is angry and wild-eyed. He asks us where Bill Yatix is. Bill is in the classroom with us, but we lie and tell the intruder that Bill is in a classroom at the other side of the school. We have probably saved Bill from being knifed. Our action was good because of its **consequence**.

Thus, when we use natural law, we can reflect on the **motive**, the **action itself**, or the **consequences** of the action, to decide whether an action is right or wrong.

Catholic view of natural law

For many Christians, natural law is an important way of deciding right and wrong. For example, the Catholic and Anglican view of natural law says:

- The purpose of God's laws is to help us to be happy. Thus it is important to know what God's laws are.
- God made all humans in his image. One way in which we are like him is that we can think, reason and understand. We can use this God-given ability to find out what is right and wrong. We can thus discover God's laws.
- All people – including atheists, agnostics, Jews, Muslims, Hindus, Christians – can know what is right and what is wrong.
- The Ten Commandments are examples of natural law. We can all recognize that actions such as stealing, adultery, false accusations, killing, rejecting parents, and so on are wrong. We can reason this out for ourselves.
- Yet not everyone clearly perceives these natural laws. For instance, some people do not have a guilty conscience about making false accusations or about stealing. This is because their desires and emotions override their sense of right and wrong. They fail to pay attention to what their dispassionate reason would tell them.

According to the Catholic Catechism:

> Man participates in the wisdom and goodness of the Creator who gives him mastery over his acts . . . The natural law expresses the original moral sense which enables man to discern the good and the evil, the truth and the lie.

Aquinas' version of natural law

Some theologians have suggested more systematic and precise accounts of natural law: for instance, **Thomas Aquinas**. He is an important Christian theologian who lived in the thirteenth century. He argued that we all intuitively know the fundamental rule – that we should do good and avoid evil. We do not need any reasons to believe this. We find it obvious.

Besides this fundamental law, he suggested that there are three basic rules that we can recognize:

- Do not kill.
- Love, marry, and take care of our children.
- Do not lie.

We can recognize these rules when we think about our natural inclinations. What are our basic natural inclinations? Aquinas reckoned that our basic inclinations are:

- to preserve our lives;
- to have a sexual relationship, to have children, and to protect and educate them;
- to find out the truth, about anything.

Aquinas argued that we are all aware of the these basic inclinations. So we must all be aware of the rules derived from them. No one can genuinely doubt them. They are obvious.

- From the natural inclination to preserve our lives, we can derive the rule that it is wrong to kill.
- From the natural inclination to have sex and want children, we can derive the rule that it is right to marry, to have children and to care for them.
- From the natural inclination to want to know the truth, we can derive the rule that it is wrong to tell lies.

Aquinas said that if we want to find out other rules, we have to reason from these fundamental rules.

For instance, we might start with the rule that it is right to marry and to have children. We might then argue that monogamy, rather than polygamy, is the better form of marriage. We might reason that monogamy provides a more tranquil and harmonious atmosphere than does polygamy, because wives are not competing with each other for the attention of the husband. This is a better atmosphere in which to educate children.

Aquinas said that, although we should all reach the same conclusion about the fundamental rules. we may reach different conclusions about further moral laws. For instance, some people may reason that monogamy is better than polygamy. Yet other people may reason that polygamy is better than monogamy.

There are two reasons why people disagree about the further rules. First, some people may genuinely find the arguments for monogamy more convincing than the arguments for polygamy, and other people may genuinely disagree. Second, some people may have a vested interest in arguing for monogamy or polygamy. This can distort their reasoning.

Objections to natural law

Some people judge that the idea of a natural law is not convincing, because:

- People have different ideas of what is right and what is wrong. For instance, some people firmly believe that divorce is wrong; but other people consider it right. Or take sex before marriage. Some people believe that it is good to have sex before we marry. Other people think it is quite wrong and unhelpful to have sex before we marry.
- Human reasoning is inaccurate and untrustworthy. There is no guarantee that our reasoning reliably reflects the way God thinks. The only reliable way to discover God's thoughts is to read the Bible. Its author is God. He cannot be wrong.

Advantages of natural law

There are arguments to support the value of natural law.

- The Bible says nothing specific about many important moral issues: abortion, euthanasia, slavery, prejudice, war, euthanasia, assisted conception, pollution, capitalism — the list is endless. These are the issues that perplex people today. We need some way of finding out God's view on these matters. That way is reasoning.
- God made humans – all humans, not just Christians – in his likeness. God has given us the ability to think and reason, to find the truth. So presumably he wants us to use this power of reasoning to find out what is right and wrong.
- Natural law means that people of any religion (not just Christians) and people with no religion can know right and wrong.

> All [religious] sects differ, because they come from men; morality is everywhere the same, because it comes from God.
>
> Voltaire

Examination practice

1. Some Christians use natural law to decide what is right and what is wrong.

Give **one** argument to support this way of making moral decisions. (3 marks)
Write about six lines.

2. Explain what 'natural law' means. (10 marks)
Write about one side of A4.

3. Suppose a wealthy western country like the USA invaded a poor country.

How might a Christian use natural law to decide whether it was right or wrong? (6 marks)
Write about half a side of A4.

4. What do you think is the best way to decide what is right and what is wrong?
Give reasons for your view. Show that you have considered other views. (8 marks)
Write about three-quarters of a side of A4.

PART F
Exams

HOW TO WRITE ESSAYS

1. Think before you write anything.

   Make a short list of the points that you think should be in your answer.

   If you do this, your answer will usually include several important points, rather than just one or two. You will also carefully order your answer. Thus your answer will be two levels higher than if you had rushed into writing your answer without stopping to think about it.

   If you start writing your answer as soon as you have read the question, you will forget to include some important points. You will also order your answer poorly. It will be one or two levels below what you could have obtained.

2. Make sure you have not misread the question because you are in a hurry. Take your time. Understand the question correctly, because you will get no marks for answering the wrong question.

3. Make your first paragraph a short summary of what your answer to the question is going to be. This impresses examiners. They think you have a clear mind.

   But do not be dogmatic: do not give examiners the impression you can see only one point of view.

   And do not write at length about what you are going to say. Just say it.

4. Make sure that each of your paragraphs is not too long. This will make it easy for the examiner to read and to understand your answer.

5. Indent each of your paragraphs clearly, so you do not lose the benefits of using paragraphs. If you indent a paragraph clearly, you make it obvious to the examiner that you are making a separate point.

   This may seem trivial to you. Nevertheless, you should know that the exam boards pay examiners a small fee for marking your papers. Examiners will not spend a lot of time trying to work out what you mean if you have not presented your work clearly.

   One very important way you can do this is to indent each paragraph clearly. An examiner, reading a page of poorly indented paragraphs, will not read carefully what you write. You will not get the mark you deserve. Knowing this may make you mad. You may feel it is pathetic and unjust. Yet, if you want to get the best grade, you must realize how important it is to indent clearly!

6. Express yourself precisely and simply. It is worth hesitating before you write, to articulate your ideas; otherwise you may write your information or opinion in a way that does not make immediate sense to the person reading your answer. Examiners have only a short time to read your answer. They will not try to disentangle what you mean, if you do not present your ideas exactly.

7. Write simple and short sentences. Avoid long, complicated sentences.

8. Pay attention to punctuation and grammar. They are necessary if your essay is to make sense.

9. Spell correctly. You will lose marks for poor spelling.

10. You may find a question difficult: you think you cannot present a satisfactory answer to the actual question. You will then be tempted to write an answer to a slightly different question. You hope that the examiner believes you have misunderstood the question, and that the examiner will give you marks for your answer.

    You will not gain any marks, even if it is an excellent answer!

    The examiner will only award marks for an answer that is relevant to the question. So try and answer the actual question. It is better to get some marks for a poor answer than to get no marks for an irrelevant answer.

Think before you write anything

11. Do not waffle or repeat yourself. You will not gain a higher mark.

12. Write legibly. Your writing does not have to be impressively neat; but if it is not clear, the examiner cannot award any marks.

    Do not write in very small letters or very large letters. Large or small writing, usually very neat, is very difficult for examiners to read.

13. If you have to answer a question that you find hard, do not leave it unanswered. Think carefully and calmly. You will often find some appropriate information in your mind.

Now read the following question and then examine the start of two answers to the question. Can you see ways in which the answers are impressive or incomplete?

Question: What do Christians believe about euthanasia?

First answer

Christians are divided: some believe euthanasia can be right; others think it is always wrong. All use the argument that Jesus taught people to love their neighbour.

The view that euthanasia is always wrong is usually based on the example of Jesus and on the commandment against murder.

Christians say that Jesus spent much of his time helping people who were sick or in need of help. Some of these people had little hope. An example of such a person is the woman with a haemorrhage who had spent twelve years searching in vain for a cure. Another example would be the man who suffered from a dreadful skin disease and begged Jesus for help.

In the many instances of Jesus meeting people in such unhappy circumstances, he always offered help; he never suggested to the sick person or anyone else that euthanasia was the answer. Jesus claimed to bring God's care and relief in this life to those who knew they needed it.

Christians believe that Jesus was the best example of how humans should act because his behaviour always mirrored what God is like. They believe that what he did as well as what he said should be the basis for how Christians

behave. He always helped sick people to recover, not to die. So most Christians think that euthanasia is wrong.

One of the commandments given by God through Moses was: 'Do not murder'. Euthanasia is murder because it is killing a person who has done nothing wrong . . .

Second answer

Euthanasia is wrong, because you are taking the life of a person and God said you shall not kill and so euthanasia is wrong. A human life is sacred to God because he made him and no one has the write to take his life because it is murder and god said murder is not write. In any case you do not now if the person how is ill is going get better soon because the doctors have not got the right cures and might have them tomorrow.

Another reason why it is wrong is that you can to easily persuade someone who is ill to die because they are a nuisance and not wanted and do not have a life worth living because they are no use to anyone and themselves. And this is wrong because you might do it because you are selfish and do not want to help someone who is in the way or has got money that you want to get.

Another thing is how do you know if that person is going to change there mind tomorrow. They mite be fed up today and want to die but tomorrow they mite change there mind and want to live and you now when you are ill you can be low and depressed. And all sick people will be scared of doctors when they can kill them and call it euthanasia . . .

You may see several ways in which you can improve the second answer. Rewrite this second answer so that it will attain a much higher mark. You should use the points the writer has made, but express them in a way that makes them easier to understand.

Make sure you:

- express each separate idea as a separate sentence or phrase;
- use a new paragraph when you start a new idea;
- indent each paragraph properly;
- spell correctly, and use capital letters as appropriate;
- use punctuation (commas, full stops, and so on) to indicate mental pauses.

Mark schemes

Suppose 50 000 students sit the same exams in religious studies as you. The principal examiner (that's the person, such as either author of this book, who writes the exam papers) cannot mark all the papers. He or she would have a team of about 125 examiners to mark the papers.

The Exam Board knows that you want to be confident you will receive an accurate result, no matter who marks your papers. So the Exam Board gets the principal examiner to write a mark scheme. All examiners will use this when they mark a paper, to ensure they mark accurately. The mark scheme tells examiners how to mark each question.

The principal examiner has a meeting with the examiners to show them how to use the mark scheme. At this meeting the examiners have to take a test to see if they can use the mark scheme correctly. Only if they pass this test can they mark your papers. This should ensure you get the same mark, no matter who marks your exam paper.

You can see a full copy of mark schemes for last year's exam papers, if you wish. They are available from your Exam Board. Ask your teacher to contact the Exam Board and request a copy.

Here are four sets of sample questions. See how well you can answer them. The mark schemes, which come later in this chapter, tell you how to mark your answers.

The following questions are all taken from NEAB papers.

Sample 1 questions

> Sacraments
> (Catholic and Orthodox traditions)
>
> Baptism
> Confirmation
> Eucharist (Mass)
> Penance
> . . .
> . . .
> Anointing of the Sick

1. Which two sacraments are missing from the list? (2 marks)

2. Name one sacrament that may be received only once. (1 mark)

3. What is another name for the sacrament of Penance? (1 mark)

4. What does the word 'sacrament' mean? (3 marks)

Sample 2 questions

1. Some Christians believe that abortion is wrong. Choose a statement in the illustration (opposite) they might use to support this view. Explain why the statement supports this view. (3 marks)

2. Choose a statement in the illustration that shows prejudice.
Explain why it shows prejudice. (3 marks)

Sample 3 questions

1. The gospel writers describe occasions when Jesus appeared to people after his resurrection. Summarise one of these occasions. (3 marks)

2. Death and resurrection are important themes in the eucharist. Explain why. (3 marks)

3. How might attending the eucharist influence a Christian in this country to do something to help very poor people overseas? (3 marks)

4. How might a Christian understanding of the crucifixion of Jesus help those who are sick or in need of healing? (3 marks)

Sample 4 questions

1. (a) What happens and what is said in the story of the forgiving father (prodigal son)? (10 marks)
   (b) Explain how this story might help
   – someone who has been badly treated by someone else
   – someone who has done something seriously wrong. (8 marks)

2. 'All Christians should be pacifists.'
Do you agree with this statement?
Give reasons for your answer. Show that you have considered the opposite view. (5 marks)

Sample 1 mark scheme

1. 1 mark each correct answer
    ✓ Marriage : Ordination

2. 1 mark for a correct answer

    ✓ E.g. Baptism / Confirmation / Ordination

3. 1 mark for a correct answer

    ✓ E.g. Reconciliation / Confession / Forgiveness

4.

	Nothing relevant	0
L1	Partially relevant	1
L2	Relevant and accurate	2
L3	Relevant and accurate + some scope or development	3

An answer of scope would include some reference to three of the following elements:

✓ A sign that can be seen or heard – started by Jesus Christ – symbolizing God – and making God present in the sacrament – and making the risen Jesus present in the sacrament – bringing their help to believers in this life.

Sample 2 mark scheme

1.

	Nothing relevant	0
L1	Glimmer of understanding	1
L2	Clear understanding	2
L3	Clear understanding + some scope	3

Award marks for the explanation why the chosen statement is supportive.

✓ For example, in support of the belief that 'God is the Father of all people', a candidate might make any of the following points – God is the Originator of all human life. It belongs to him; therefore no one has the right to take life unjustifiably. Instead, all humans should respect the gift that God has given to other humans. Humans share in some of the divine qualities; therefore human life is more precious that any other form of life.

2. 1 mark for identification of a statement that is subsequently justified
    ✓ E.g. 'We Christians are the only good people in this world'

    Plus up to two marks for a relevant explanation

	Nothing relevant	0
L1	Glimmer of understanding	1
L2	Clear understanding	2

✓ E.g. Prejudice is an attitude or opinion. It is not supported by any evidence, experience or reason. So, it is an unsubstantiated attitude or opinion. It is believed even though there is often evidence that it is wrong.

A candidate who can clearly present an explanation like this attains L2.

Sample 3 mark scheme

1.

	Nothing relevant	0
L1	Partially accurate	1
L2	Accurate, but insufficient scope	2
L3	Accurate, extensive summary	3

An example of Level 3 is:

In Luke's gospel, two disciples were walking to Emmaus, soon after Jesus was crucified. They were talking about the death of Jesus, trying to make sense of it, especially as some women had said he was now alive. As they were walking, someone joined them. It was Jesus, but they did not recognise him.

Jesus explained to them that the Messiah had to suffer before entering his glory.

When the two disciples came to Emmaus, they persuaded the third man to join them for a meal. They recognised him as Jesus when he took some bread, said the blessing, broke it and gave it to them.

2.

	Nothing relevant	0
L1	Partially relevant	1
L2	Relevant and accurate	2
L3	Relevant and accurate + some scope or development	3

Candidates might make any of the following points:

- The eucharist commemorates the death and resurrection of Jesus.
- Jesus commanded this at the last supper he had with his disciples.
- The risen Jesus is made present under the appearance of bread and wine.
- The communion is a sharing of the life of the risen Jesus;
- through it the communicants may die to their sin and rise to a holier life.

An answer of scope would have at least three substantial points.

3.

	Nothing relevant	0
L1	Glimmer of understanding	1
L2	Clear understanding	2
L3	Clear understanding + some scope	3

Candidates may make points such as the following. Note that these are only examples of acceptable points.

- Communicants may be grateful to God for the gift of Jesus in the eucharist. This may inspire them to be generous to very poor people.
- The readings may state or imply that the world belongs to God and to everyone, not just to some people. This may encourage communicants to share some of their wealth with very poor people.
- There may be prayers that ask for a spirit of generosity. This might influence the communicants to be generous.
- In the homily, the priest or deacon may exhort members of the congregation to follow the example of Christ, who helped people in need.

An answer of scope would have at least three substantial points.

4.

	Nothing relevant	0
L1	Glimmer of understanding	1
L2	Clear understanding	2
L3	Clear understanding + some scope	3

Candidates might include any of the following suggestions. Note that these are simply some relevant answers, not the only ones.

- Christians may feel that God is not distant from their suffering.
- They may think that, because of his own suffering, God understands their situation.
- They may believe that God voluntarily involved himself in suffering to demonstrate his care for people.
- They may understand that human suffering has a useful contribution to make to human growth and to the development of the kingdom of God on earth.

An answer of scope would have at least three substantial points.

Sample 4 mark scheme

1(a)

	Nothing relevant	0
L1	Slight relevant information	1–2
L2	Some relevant information limited in detail and scope	3–4
L3	Some relevant information with some detail, but limited in scope	5–6
L4	Relevant information of suitably broad scope and tersely presented	7–8
L5	Relevant information of suitable broad scope and some detailed elaboration	9–10

The parable of the forgiving father (prodigal son) has the following points:

- The younger son wanted his share of the property.
- The father divided the property between his two sons.
- The younger son squandered his wealth in a far country.
- He was reduced to dire circumstances.
- He resolved to return to his father and ask to be accepted as a servant, as he was no longer worthy to be called a son.
- His father saw him when he was a long way off.
- He ran to his son and threw his arms round him.
- The son said he had sinned against God and against his father.
- The father arranged a great feast.
- His son was dead but now he was alive.
- The elder son was angry about the feast.
- He refused to go in.
- The father pleaded.
- The elder son compared his goodness with the younger son's selfishness.
- The father's reply.

Candidates who reach level 4/5 will mention most of these points.

1(b)

	Nothing relevant	0
L1	A gleam of understanding but no evidence of insight	1–2
L2	Some understanding showing insight but very limited scope and development	3–4
L3	Understanding showing insight with some scope or development	5–6
L4	Understanding showing insight with development and scope	7–8

Candidates might make points such as the following:

- Someone who has been badly treated might learn from this story that the father is not only ready, but also willing, to forgive an action that must have hurt him badly.
- The father in the story stands for God, who provides an example for everyone. So the story might be an inspiration and an example to someone who has been badly treated. At least, if that person cannot bring themselves to forgive, the story may provide an ideal of a long-term goal.
- The story also shows the elder son's reaction, which is the usual reaction of someone badly treated: self-pity and resentment. The reader can glimpse the self-pity that does not lead to positive action or a generous attitude. It is small minded and selfish.
- Another lesson, which anyone can learn, is that we have all offended others at some time. We have also all been offended by others. If we want to receive God's forgiveness and the forgiveness of those we have offended, we may realize we have to forgive those who have offended us.
- Someone who has done something seriously wrong may understand that God wants to forgive, no matter

what the offence; that God is only waiting for the offender to repent; that God does not punish or retaliate. Such a realization may encourage repentance and healing.
- What the offender may also realize is that those offended may be resentful and unwilling to forgive; that just because the offender repents, this does not necessarily entail forgiveness by those who have been wronged, or by those who witnessed the wrong-doing. The story suggests that God does not condemn people who are unforgiving. It is an attitude that the offender may learn to share.

2.

	Nothing relevant	0
L1	Marginally relevant response	1
L2	Relevant response but with little progression of argument and no diversity of argument	2
L3	Relevant response with progression of argument or diversity of argument	3
NB	*some consideration of the alternative perspective raises each of the above criteria by one level.*	
L4	Relevant response with progression of argument and diversity of argument	4
L5	Relevant response with progression of argument and diversity of argument and some consideration of the alternative perspective	5

Candidates might make points such as the following:

✓ Yes, because:

- Jesus Christ taught us to love and forgive, not to kill.
- For example, in the Sermon on the Mount, he said we should love our enemies.
- When he was crucified, he asked God to forgive those who crucified him.
- Christians should follow the example of Jesus, who was a pacifist; he never used violence against anyone.
- The first Christians were pacifists: they did not join the army.
- The 'just war' theory was introduced into the Christian religion after about the third century.
- All war degrades and destroys. Wars never solve problems.
- Wars simply increase hatred.

✓ No, because:

- Jesus said love your neighbour. That means defending the weak when they are oppressed by a stronger person, using violence if necessary.

- Letting tyrants have their way is allowing evil to go unchallenged.
- According to the just war theory, everyone has a right to defend life in certain circumstances.

- God created life. No one else has the right to take it unjustifiably.

PART G Coursework

Introduction

Coursework is an important part of your GCSE course. 20 per cent of the marks will depend on coursework. The mark could make a real difference to your final grade.

There is much more to coursework than collecting lots of facts and copying them down. The person who marks your coursework will be looking for certain things:

1. What you know and what you understand about the things that are central to the Christian faith – such things as
    *   what Christians believe – and why;
    *   what Christians do in their worship – and why;
2. What you know and what you understand about the way in which their Christian beliefs affect the way in which people live – such things as
    *   what actions they believe to be right or wrong;
    *   how they treat other people;
    *   what their attitudes are likely to be to important moral issues.
3. How you express your own opinions. The person marking your work will be less concerned with which side of an argument you take than with the quality of the reasons you give.
4. In addition, 5 per cent of the marks are awarded for spelling, punctuation and grammar.

An assignment may not test all three of these requirements.

For instance, in the NEAB Syllabus B candidates must produce two assignments, one on each of the two sections of the syllabus. The assignment for section 1 tests requirements 1 and 3 above, that for section 2 tests requirements 2 and 3.

On the other hand, MEG test all three requirements in each piece of coursework.

Make sure you know which of the requirements your assignment must meet. Your teacher should have set it in such a way that you are guided to meet those requirements.

Who will assess your coursework?

*   First of all, your teachers. They will assess the work according to the requirements listed above.
*   After your teachers, some pieces of coursework may be seen by the moderator for your centre. The moderators have the responsibility to make sure that the coursework has been fairly assessed, in line with other centres. Once they have received the coursework marks, the

moderators choose certain names at random, including some of the best, the worst and some in between.

The moderators will judge, from the work they see, whether the teachers have marked to the correct standard, too harshly or too leniently. They will adjust the marks for the whole centre on the basis of the work they see. So, as long as your teachers have marked consistently, you will receive the right final mark.

Approaching an assignment

It is vital that you understand from the start exactly what is being demanded of you. Think out what the assignment is asking. Look carefully at the list above of things that are being tested and, as far as the assignment goes, make sure you are showing the knowledge and understanding required.

(You will not necessarily be tested on all the points in every assignment. Together, the assignments should cover all the points, but you may not be tested on every point in each one.)

Let us say that one part of an assignment is

1. Select and explain a parable in which Jesus taught about the way in which a Christian should live.
2. Choose one Christian whose life is an example of the way in which, in that parable, Jesus said a person should live.

You will, of course avoid the obvious error of writing about two or three different parables or about two or three different people. They may all be excellent examples, but that is not required.

So, you choose the parable of the sheep and the goats. Then you pick Albert Schweitzer – a first-class example. So far, so good. But then you pick up a little book all about him. The book tells you all about his childhood, about what a brilliant young man he was, his life until he was 30, his training to work in Africa and his travelling to Lambarene. You describe how he built the hospital in about 1913. You then tell how he was awarded the Nobel Peace Prize in 1952 and of other honours heaped upon him at the end of his long life.

You will hardly score any marks at all! For one thing, you have relied on one source of information. Copying from one book does not score any marks at all. You have said virtually nothing about the years in which he actually cared for those in need at the hospital at Lambarene – and caring for those in need is the main point of the parable of the sheep and the goats.

You might think it was not your fault. After all, you can

only use the information available to you. The book is your main source of information about Albert Schweitzer. If the book misses out the important information about Schweitzer, what can you do about it?

The answer is simple. You look to see what is being tested. In this case you are being tested for your understanding of the parable. You are being tested for your ability to select relevant information – the question is not 'Write 2000 words about anything to do with Albert Schweitzer'. You see that the information in the book about him does not answer the question.

So – **you choose someone about whom you have the right sort of information**. And you make sure, before you start the assignment, that you have made a sensible choice! One candidate, faced with the topic 'Choose one example of Christian work for those in need in Britain', began with the words 'I have chosen Mother Teresa and her work in Calcutta because she is a wonderful Christian and I don't think it matters that Calcutta is not in Britain.' You can probably guess how many marks that part of the assignment was given!

Gathering information

- **Books** will probably be your main source of information. It is important that you select the material properly.
- Make sure you have more than one source of information – more than one book, tape, video or other resource.
- Make sure the sources are relevant to the subject.
- Be sure that you can understand the sources.
- Choose the material carefully, making sure it is relevant.

Interviews are an excellent way of gaining information. It is important to prepare for the interview carefully. Make sure you know why you are interviewing the person concerned and what you want to gain from the interview.

For instance, imagine that your assignment involves a study of the local Baptist church, and that you are interviewing the minister. He may not understand why you want to interview him. He may have plenty to tell you about how old the building is and about the people who presented some of the furnishings. What you want to know is what is special about the building and what happens there.

- Ask him factual questions about what you can see. Why is the pulpit there in the centre? Why do you have a baptismal pool and not a font? When do you have Holy Communion? Who can receive Holy Communion here?
- Ask some other, less obvious questions. Why do people sit and not kneel when they pray? Would you let people have cups of tea in here after a service – and why? (or, Why not?)

- Ask questions that will help you with your evaluation. What is special about the church building? Is it important to have a place set aside for worship?

What you can **find out for yourself** is vital. If your assignment involves something local, go and look for yourself. Make careful notes of what you see and hear.

You may wish to carry out a **survey**. That is fine – as long as you plan it properly.

- Choose carefully the people you will question. Generally speaking, the more you interview, the better. The more varied they are, the better. For instance, if you are in an all-girls school and you interview the whole of your class, you have the opinions of 25–30 people who are very like each other in many ways – age, gender, education. If you interview friends, family and neighbours, all ages and both male and female, you have a much better survey.
- Plan the questions carefully. Give people a chance to say what they really think. For instance, if you are working on an assignment concerning war and peace, do not simply ask 'Do you think war is wrong?' The great majority of people will not wish to answer with a direct 'Yes' or 'No'. A question such as 'In what circumstances, if any, could it be right to fight a war?' allows people to say what they believe.
- Note their opinions as they give them. Listen to what a person has to say in answer to the question. Don't just rush straight to the next question.
- Don't just list the answers you have received. Try to evaluate them – to point out what they show. Do older people, by and large, have different opinions from younger people? Do males have views that are different from those of females? Can you explain any of the differences?
- Show that you realize that your sample may be too small to be accurate. A majority of 40 people may believe that all war is wrong. That does not mean that a majority of 400 or 4000 would believe the same.
- Where possible, use a diagram, graph or chart to show what the figures say.

When you have your material

- Check the question again.
- Make sure you really understand everything you have to do. If there is anything you do not understand, ask someone to explain it.
- Make sure that the information you have is relevant. If some of what you have gathered is not relevant, scrap it. However interesting it is, however much work you put into it, it will gain you no credit.
- Make sure you have covered all parts of the question. If there is any part that you have not researched or thought through, give it your full attention.

WRITING

Remind yourself again – what is the moderator looking for?

1. What you know and what you understand about the things which are central to the Christian faith – such things as
    *   what Christians believe – and why;
    *   what Christians do in their worship – and why;
2. What you know and what you understand about the way in which their Christian beliefs affect the way in which people live – such things as
    *   what actions they believe to be right or wrong;
    *   how they treat other people;
    *   what their attitudes are likely to be to important moral issues.
3. How you express your own opinions. The person marking your work will be less concerned with which side of an argument you take than with the quality of the reasons you give.

The exam syllabus will say what length your piece of work should be. For instance, you may be told that it should be between 1500 and 2000 words. It is unlikely that anyone will count the words! None the less, it is good to stay roughly within the limits.

*   If you use much less than 1500 words, you are risking not covering the subject sufficiently thoroughly.
*   If you go well over 2000 words you may include material that is irrelevant. That will show that you have not selected the material well enough. Also, the person assessing would be entitled to ignore anything after 2000 words. You would not suffer for using, say 2100! If you went up to, say, 3000 or more you could not complain if you were penalized.

    Remember that you are not being tested on how much material you can find and how many words you write. You are being tested on your ability to know and understand what is relevant to the assignment.

Writing

Start each section of your assignment on a new piece of paper! Later you may want to rewrite some sections. You don't want to have to rewrite the whole assignment when only one page needs to be altered.

If each section is on a separate piece of paper, it does not matter which part you write first. Once you feel confident to tackle a section, do so. You may well need to rewrite it later, but better that than leave all the writing till the last minute.

Make sure that you are using your own words. Don't copy straight from a book. If you don't understand what you read in a book, find out what it means by asking someone or looking in a dictionary. Otherwise:

1. Read the material you have collected from books and elsewhere.
2. Write in your own words.
3. Read again the material you have collected and make any alterations that are necessary.
    *   Make sure that you correct mistakes or add anything that is omitted.
    *   Do not change things just to use the same words as the book you were using. Using your own words is better.

There may be times when you think it right to quote the exact words of a book. If you do, then put the words you quote in inverted commas. Say who wrote the words and where they are to be found. (You can put the name of the writer, the book and the page number in brackets or in a footnote at the bottom of the page.) You should also let the reader know why you have quoted them. And don't do it too often!

Be careful about your writing, spelling and punctuation. Work that is full of errors makes the moderator think from the start that the assignment is not going to be very good. What is more, 5 per cent of your marks will be for spelling, punctuation and grammar.

All the time, keep an eye on the question. Check that what you are writing is really relevant.

Evaluation

Part of your assignment will be testing your own judgement. You will be asked your own opinion on something relevant to the assignment.

*   Give your own views – but think them over carefully first.
*   Give reasons for your views. The way you present your reasons is what will most influence the moderator.
*   Make sure you are not being prejudiced.
*   Show that you know what other people think. State, accurately and fairly, ideas with which you do not agree. Then say why you think they are wrong. To deserve credit here it is important to present those other opinions fairly.

Illustrations

By all means use pictures and diagrams in your coursework – but, as you use them, remember that you are being tested on the skills listed above, not on how pretty the work looks. Each picture or diagram must have a caption that makes clear why it is relevant.

For instance, assume part of your topic is 'Describe a church building that you have visited.' Your dad is a keen photographer and he takes a number of pictures of the inside of the church. That's fine. It is perfectly all right to use them. Let us say he has taken three photos, from slightly different angles. You would not gain credit for placing them together in the middle of your assignment. You will not get a single mark extra because your dad is a good photographer. What you should do is

- Choose the picture that shows best the things you want to write about – whether it is Dad's favourite picture or not!
- Give it clear captions. For example: 'Note that the altar is the focal point of the church.' 'The font is by the door to show that at baptism we enter the Church of God.' 'The church is decorated with flowers because the picture was taken at Easter, which is a joyful time when Christians celebrate the resurrection of Jesus.'
- Refer to it in the main part of the assignment.

Other points to bear in mind

- You will have to complete a cover sheet. Make sure you do it accurately. Use a photocopy to practise first.
- Acknowledge any help you have been given. If you have consulted people who know about the subject, or have chosen sensible books and other resources, that is to your credit.

Finally

Read the assignment. Check that you have covered everything. Hand it in – and wait for the good news.

INDEX –
BIBLICAL REFERENCES

INDEX – TOPICS

When you are looking for a word, look not only in this index but also at the contents list, which is at the front of the book. Most words in the contents list are not repeated in this index.

Macmillan Work Out Series

For GCSE examinations
Accounting
Biology
Business Studies
Chemistry
Computer Studies
English Key Stage 4
French (cassette and pack available)
Geography
German (cassette and pack available)
Modern World History
Human Biology
Core Maths Key Stage 4
Revise Mathematics to further level
Physics
Religious Studies
Science
Social and Economic History
Spanish (cassette and pack available)
Statistics

For A Level examinations
Accounting
Biology
Business Studies
Chemistry
Economics
English
French (cassette and pack available)
Mathematics
Physics
Phychology
Sociology
Statistics